Frommer's®
Boston

My Boston

by Marie Morris

SO YOU'RE THINKING OF VISITING BOSTON. GOOD THINKING.
You could hardly have picked a better time. The highway project that plagued downtown for the better part of the past decade (the world-famous "Big Dig") is substantially complete. Boston Harbor is cleaner than it's been in at least a generation. Art museums are moving and expanding, the restaurant scene is gaining a national reputation for quality and variety, and the local sports teams are collecting world championships like, well, baseball cards.

Some Boston destinations are so beautiful that I just have to point them out. Others are so interesting, mostly because of their historical associations, that I want you to know a little something about them. My favorites are both. They range from a family of adorable waterfowl to a legendary patriot whose first name is not "Listen, my children, and you shall hear."

I'm not a Boston native—I live here because I love it. In the pages that follow, I'll try to show you why.

© Rick Friedman/Corbis

No less an expert than Hall of Fame pitcher Tom Seaver called **FENWAY PARK** (left) "the essence of baseball." It's old and cramped, Red Sox tickets are expensive, the players are overpaid, the fans won't shut up about the team's 2004 World Series title, and none of that matters. Mere words can't capture the thrill of seeing the field for the first time. Just go. You'll never forget it.

If **BEACON HILL** (above) didn't exist, someone—probably a postcard photographer—would have to invent it. Narrow cobblestone streets, elegant Federal-style architecture, and flowering window boxes make "the Hill" the iconic Boston neighborhood. It's one of my favorite places to go walking. Just don't tackle the uneven streets in good shoes (you only make that mistake once).

Snow begins to fly, and a hush falls over the city. Step away from traffic—into a building courtyard, a college quad, or a park—and the calm is almost magical. The prettiest park in town, the **PUBLIC GARDEN** (above), looks even better under a fresh coating of white flakes. Enjoy it while you can. Before long, the scratchy hum of snowplows will fill the air, and the spell will be broken.

The cutest thing in Boston—even cuter than all those buff college students—is **MAKE WAY FOR DUCKLINGS** (right). The Mallard family from Robert McCloskey's beloved children's book waddles eternally across the Public Garden, heading toward the lagoon. I don't know how they'll ever get there with all those little kids climbing on them.

COPLEY SQUARE (below) is the architectural equivalent of a movie with an
all-star cast—you hardly know where
to look first. I like to start with Trinity
Church, executed in Richardsonian
Romanesque style (named for the
architect, the legendary H. H.
Richardson). Its blue-mirrored backdrop is I. M. Pei's distinctive John
Hancock Tower.

Say hello to **PAUL REVERE (left)**, 18th-century mensch. That's the Old North Church over his shoulder. As a kid, he helped ring the church bells; as an adult, he got an important message ("one if by land, two if by sea") through lanterns in the steeple. His nearby house, where the "midnight ride" started, is one of my favorite Boston attractions: It helps visitors get to know a historic figure as a real person.

BOSTON HARBOR (above) is a perfect destination on sultry, sticky summer days when you can't remember what was so bad about winter. (Oh, right—subzero temperatures, howling winds, and waist-high snowdrifts.) The waterfront abounds with places to catch a breeze, take a break, and recharge. My favorite retreat is at the end of Long Wharf, not far from the New England Aquarium.

I've been to the **JOHN F. KENNEDY LIBRARY AND MUSEUM (left)** more times than I can count, but I always jump at the chance to accompany out-of-town-ers. You might think it appeals most to people who remember Camelot (which I don't), but visitors of all ages find it fascinating. The museum, in a gorgeous building designed by I. M. Pei, regularly schedules special exhibitions to complement the permanent collection.

The **MCKIM BUILDING OF THE BOSTON PUBLIC LIBRARY (below)** is a showpiece of 19th-century art. The magnificent murals, sculptures, and architecture make it a fascinating place to explore, on your own or on a free guided tour. The perfect complement to this building is Trinity Church, which stands across Copley Square in all its polychrome (art lingo for "multicolored") glory.

The delightfully eccentric **ISABELLA STEWART GARDNER MUSEUM (above)** centers on a soaring courtyard filled with sculpture and changing displays of flowers and greenery. Horticulture is such an important element that the museum has its own greenhouses and even a "curator of landscape." If you harbor even a passing fondness for art or gardening, it's a wonderful refuge.

THE MINUTE MAN STATUE (right) in Concord unites two of New England's big names: sculptor Daniel Chester French and philosopher-poet Ralph Waldo Emerson. (When did people with three names stop being celebrated artists and start being assassins and serial killers?) The musket-wielding revolutionary hasn't forgotten that he's a farmer: His other hand grips a plow. The inscription on the pedestal recalls the events of April 19, 1775, in a verse that includes the lines, "Here once the embattled farmers stood / And fired the shot heard round the world."

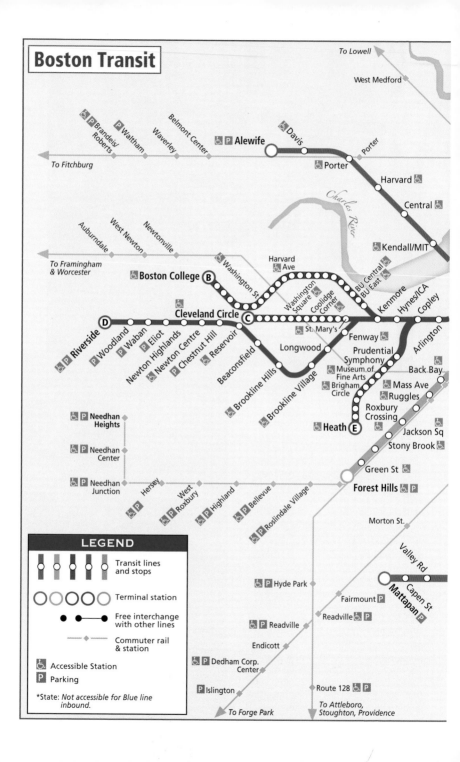

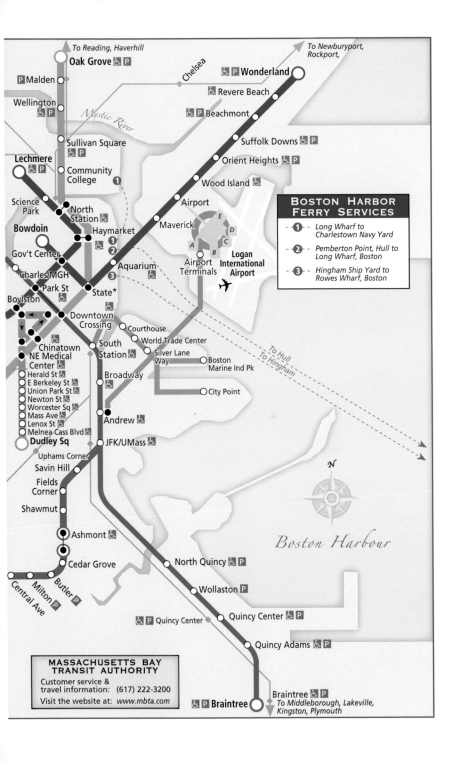

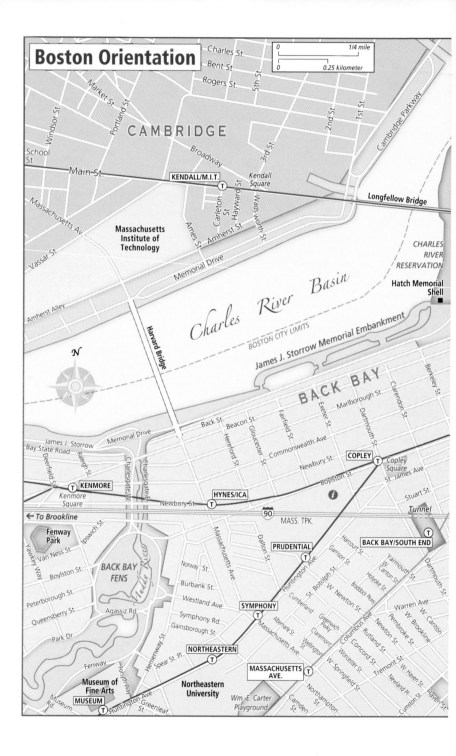

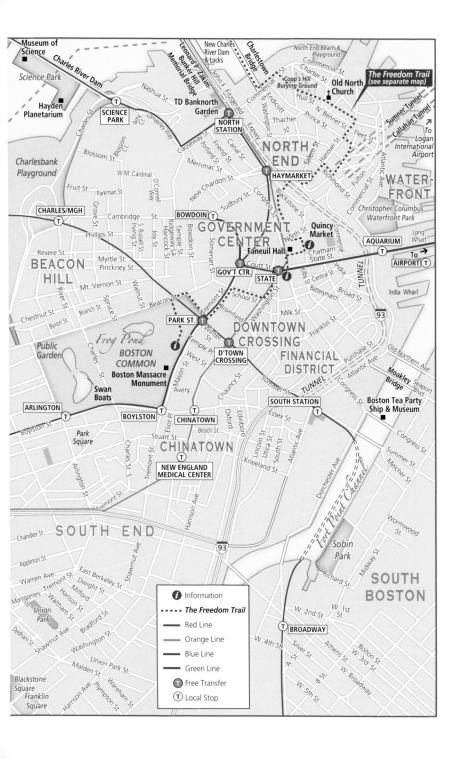

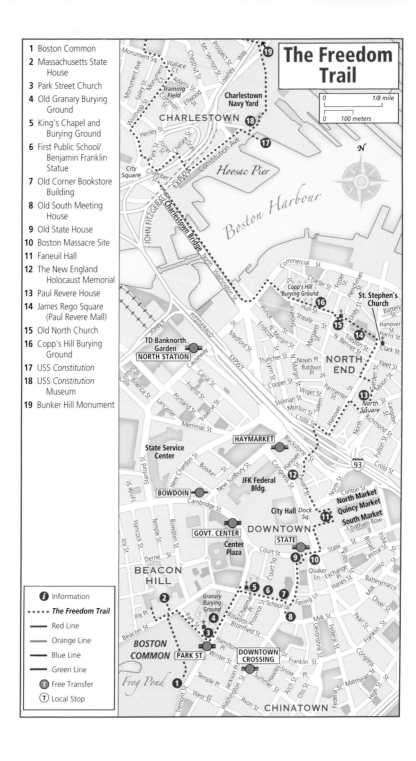

The Freedom Trail

1 Boston Common
2 Massachusetts State House
3 Park Street Church
4 Old Granary Burying Ground
5 King's Chapel and Burying Ground
6 First Public School/ Benjamin Franklin Statue
7 Old Corner Bookstore Building
8 Old South Meeting House
9 Old State House
10 Boston Massacre Site
11 Faneuil Hall
12 The New England Holocaust Memorial
13 Paul Revere House
14 James Rego Square (Paul Revere Mall)
15 Old North Church
16 Copp's Hill Burying Ground
17 USS Constitution
18 USS Constitution Museum
19 Bunker Hill Monument

0   1/8 mile
0   100 meters

i Information
••••• The Freedom Trail
—— Red Line
—— Orange Line
—— Blue Line
—— Green Line
Ⓣ Free Transfer
Ⓣ Local Stop

CHARLESTOWN
Training Field
Charlestown Navy Yard
City Square
Hoosac Pier
Boston Harbour
Copp's Hill Burying Ground
St. Stephen's Church
NORTH END
North Square
TD Banknorth Garden
NORTH STATION
HAYMARKET
93
State Service Center
BOWDOIN
JFK Federal Bldg.
North Market
Quincy Market
South Market
City Hall
GOVT. CENTER
DOWNTOWN
STATE
Center Plaza
BEACON HILL
Granary Burying Ground
BOSTON COMMON
PARK ST.
DOWNTOWN CROSSING
Frog Pond
CHINATOWN

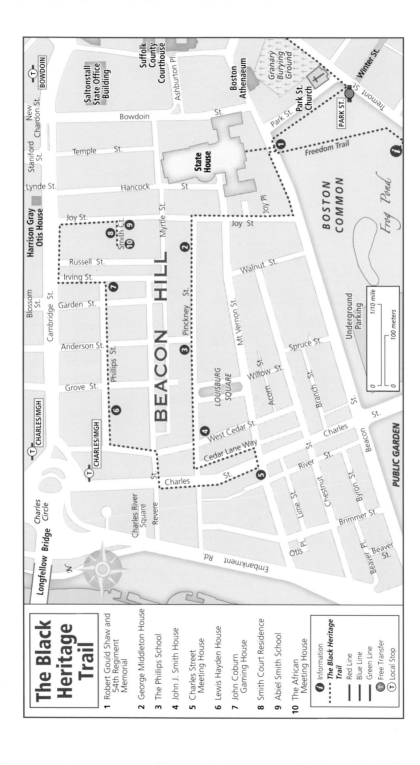

The Black Heritage Trail

1 Robert Gould Shaw and 54th Regiment Memorial
2 George Middleton House
3 The Phillips School
4 John J. Smith House
5 Charles Street Meeting House
6 Lewis Hayden House
7 John Coburn Gaming House
8 Smith Court Residence
9 Abiel Smith School
10 The African Meeting House

ℹ Information
•••••• *The Black Heritage Trail*
━━ Red Line
━━ Blue Line
━━ Green Line
Ⓣ Free Transfer
Ⓣ Local Stop

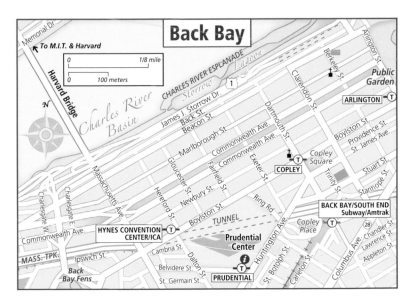

Back Bay

To M.I.T. & Harvard

0 — 1/8 mile
0 — 100 meters

Memorial Dr.

Harvard Bridge

Charles River Basin

CHARLES RIVER ESPLANADE

CHARLES RIVER ESPLANADE

Storrow Lagoon

James J. Storrow Dr.

Back St.

Beacon St.

Marlborough St.

Commonwealth Ave.

Commonwealth Ave.

Newbury St.

Boylston St.

TUNNEL

Massachusetts Ave.

Charlesgate W.

Charlesgate E.

Commonwealth Ave.

MASS.-TPK.

Ipswich St.

Back Bay Fens

Gloucester St.

Hereford St.

Fairfield St.

Exeter St.

Dartmouth Ave.

Berkeley St.

Clarendon St.

Arlington St.

Public Garden

ARLINGTON

COPLEY

Copley Square

Trinity St.

Boylston St.

Providence St.

St. James Ave.

Stuart St.

Stanhope St.

BACK BAY/SOUTH END
Subway/Amtrak

Ring Rd

HYNES CONVENTION
CENTER/ICA

Cambria St.

Belvidere St.

St. Germain St.

Dalton St.

Prudential Center

PRUDENTIAL

Copley Place

Huntington Ave.

St. Botolph St.

Carleton St.

Columbus Ave.

Chandler St.

Lawrence St.

Appleton St.

28

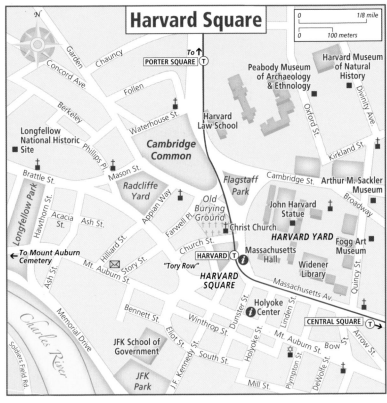

Harvard Square

0 — 1/8 mile
0 — 100 meters

Garden

Chauncy

Concord Ave.

Follen

Berkeley

Longfellow
National Historic
Site

Phillips Pl.

Brattle St.

Mason St.

Waterhouse St.

Cambridge
Common

Radcliffe
Yard

Appian Way

Farwell Pl.

Old
Burying
Ground

Hawthorn St.

Acacia
St.

Ash St.

Hilliard St.

Story St.

Mt. Auburn St.

Longfellow Park

To Mount Auburn
Cemetery

Ash St.

"Tory Row"

HARVARD
SQUARE

Memorial Drive

Soldiers Field Rd.

Charles River

JFK School of
Government

JFK
Park

Bennett St.

Eliot St.

Winthrop St.

South St.

J.F.K. St.

Mill St.

To Porter Square
PORTER SQUARE

Harvard
Law School

Peabody Museum
of Archaeology
& Ethnology

Harvard Museum
of Natural
History

Oxford St.

Divinity Ave.

Kirkland St.

Flagstaff
Park

Cambridge St.

Arthur M. Sackler
Museum

Broadway

John Harvard
Statue

Christ Church

Church St.

HARVARD

Massachusetts
Hall

HARVARD YARD

Fogg Art
Museum

Widener
Library

Quincy St.

Massachusetts Av.

CENTRAL SQUARE

Holyoke
Center

Dunster St.

Holyoke St.

Linden St.

Mt. Auburn St.

Plympton St.

Bow St.

DeWolfe St.

Arrow St.

Frommer's®

Boston

2009

by Marie Morris

Here's what the critics say about Frommer's:

"Amazingly easy to use. Very portable, very complete."

—*Booklist*

"Detailed, accurate, and easy-to-read information for all price ranges."
—*Glamour Magazine*

"Hotel information is close to encyclopedic."

—*Des Moines Sunday Register*

"Frommer's Guides have a way of giving you a real feel for a place."
—*Knight Ridder Newspapers*

WILEY

Wiley Publishing, Inc.

About the Author

Marie Morris grew up in New York and graduated from Harvard, where she studied history. She has worked for the *Boston Herald, Boston* magazine, and the *New York Times.* She's the author of *Frommer's Boston Day by Day* and *Boston For Dummies,* and she covers Boston for *Frommer's New England.* She lives in Boston, not far from Paul Revere.

Published by:

Wiley Publishing, Inc.

111 River St.
Hoboken, NJ 07030-5774

ISBN 978-0-470-28552-7

Editors: Erica Rex and Matthew Brown
Production Editor: Jana M. Stefanciosa
Cartographer: Andy Dolan
Photo Editor: Richard Fox
Production by Wiley Indianapolis Composition Services

Front cover photo: Fans gathering outside of Fenway Park before a double header between the Boston Red Sox and the Detroit Tigers
Back cover photo: Cambridge, Harvard University and Charles River, elevated view: Lowell House

For information on our other products and services or to obtain technical support, please contact our Customer Care Department within the U.S. at 800/762-2974, outside the U.S. at 317/572-3993 or fax 317/572-4002.

Wiley also publishes its books in a variety of electronic formats. Some content that appears in print may not be available in electronic formats.

Manufactured in the United States of America

5 4 3 2 1

Contents

List of Maps   vi

What's New in Boston   1

1   The Best of Boston   4

1 The Most Unforgettable Travel
Experiences 4

2 The Best Splurge Hotels 5

3 The Best Moderately Priced Hotels . . .5

4 The Most Unforgettable Dining
Experiences 5

5 The Best Free (Or Almost Free)
Things to Do .6

6 The Best Outdoor Activities 7

7 The Best Museums 7

8 The Best Activities for Families 7

2   Boston in Depth   9

1 Boston Today 9

2 Looking Back at Boston 11

3 Boston in Popular Culture:
Books, Films, TV & Music 16

4 Eating & Drinking in Boston 19

3   Planning Your Trip to Boston   21

1 Visitor Information 21

2 Entry Requirements 24

3 When to Go 25

   Boston Calendar of Events 26

   Let's Make a Deal 31

4 Getting There & Getting Around 32

5 Money & Costs 43

   What Things Cost in Boston 43

6 Health 44

7 Safety 45

8 Specialized Travel Resources 45

   It's Easy Being Green 48

9 Sustainable Tourism 49

   *Frommers.com: The Complete
Travel Resource* 50

10 Packages for the Independent
Traveler 50

11 Escorted General-Interest Tours 51

12 Special-Interest Trips 51

13 Staying Connected 52

4   Suggested Boston Itineraries   55

1 The Neighborhoods in Brief 55

2 The Best of Boston in 1 Day 60

3 The Best of Boston in 2 Days 61

   Suggested Evening Itineraries 65

4 The Best of Boston in 3 Days 65

5 Where to Stay 67

1 Saving on Your Hotel Room 68
2 Best Hotel Bets 70
3 Downtown 71
4 Beacon Hill/North Station/
  North End 78
5 Charlestown 80
6 South Boston Waterfront
  (Seaport District) 80
7 Chinatown/Theater District 81
8 The South End 83
9 The Back Bay 83
  Family-Friendly Hotels 87
10 Outskirts & Brookline 92
11 Cambridge 94
12 At & Near the Airport 99

6 Where to Dine 102

1 Best Restaurant Bets 102
2 Restaurants by Cuisine 104
3 The Waterfront 106
4 The North End 107
  Breakfast & Sunday Brunch 114
5 Faneuil Hall Marketplace &
  the Financial District 114
6 Downtown Crossing 117
7 Beacon Hill 118
8 Chinatown/Theater District 118
  Yum, Yum, Dim Sum 120
9 The South End 121
10 The Back Bay 123
  Family-Friendly Restaurants 124
  Quick Bites & Picnic
  Provisions...................126
11 Kenmore Square to Brookline 128
  The Great Outdoors:
  Alfresco Dining 129
12 Cambridge 130

7 What to See & Do in Boston 139

1 The Top Attractions 139
  Let's Make a Deal 142
  On Top of the World 146
2 The Freedom Trail 148
3 More Museums & Attractions 159
4 Historic Houses 161
5 African-American History 162
  Focus on Women's History 162
6 Parks & Gardens 163
7 Cambridge 164
  Celebrity Cemetery 166
8 Boston Neighborhoods
  to Explore 168
  Welcome to the North End 169
9 Especially for Kids 171
10 Organized Tours 173
  Missing This Would Be a Crime ...179
11 Outdoor Pursuits 180
  A Vacation in the Islands 183
12 Spectator Sports 184

8 Boston Strolls 189

Walking Tour 1: The Back Bay 189
Walking Tour 2: Harvard Square ...193

(9) Shopping   201

1 The Shopping Scene 201   **2** Shopping A to Z 202

(10) Boston After Dark   220

1 Getting Tickets 220   **4** The Bar Scene 235
2 The Performing Arts 220   **5** More Entertainment Options 240
3 The Club & Music Scene 229   **6** Late-Night Bites 242

(11) Side Trips from Boston   243

1 Lexington & Concord 243   *North Shore Beaches* 272
2 The North Shore & Cape Ann 253   **3** Plymouth .277
A Whale of an Adventure 265   *A Presidential History Twofer* 278

Appendix: Fast Facts, Toll-Free Numbers & Websites   284

1 Fast Facts: Boston 284   **2** Toll-Free Numbers & Websites 292

Index   295

General Index 295   Restaurant Index 306
Accommodations Index 306

List of Maps

Boston & Surrounding Areas   23

Boston Transit   39

Boston Orientation   56

The Best of Boston in
   1, 2 & 3 Days   62

Where to Stay in Boston   72

Where to Stay in Cambridge   95

Where to Dine in Boston   108

Where to Dine in the North End   111

Where to Dine in Cambridge   131

Boston Attractions   140

The Freedom Trail   149

Harvard Square Attractions   165

Walking Tour 1: The Back Bay   191

Walking Tour 2: Harvard Square   195

Back Bay Shopping   203

Boston After Dark   222

Lexington   245

Concord   247

Marblehead   255

Salem   259

Gloucester   267

Rockport   275

Plymouth   279

An Invitation to the Reader

In researching this book, we discovered many wonderful places—hotels, restaurants, shops, and more. We're sure you'll find others. Please tell us about them, so we can share the information with your fellow travelers in upcoming editions. If you were disappointed with a recommendation, we'd love to know that, too. Please write to:

Frommer's Boston 2009
Wiley Publishing, Inc. • 111 River St. • Hoboken, NJ 07030-5774

An Additional Note

Please be advised that travel information is subject to change at any time—and this is especially true of prices. We therefore suggest that you write or call ahead for confirmation when making your travel plans. The authors, editors, and publisher cannot be held responsible for the experiences of readers while traveling. Your safety is important to us, however, so we encourage you to stay alert and be aware of your surroundings. Keep a close eye on cameras, purses, and wallets, all favorite targets of thieves and pickpockets.

Other Great Guides for Your Trip:

Boston For Dummies
Frommer's New England
Frommer's Nantucket, Cape Cod & Martha's Vineyard
Frommer's Portable Boston

Frommer's Star Ratings, Icons & Abbreviations

Every hotel, restaurant, and attraction listing in this guide has been ranked for quality, value, service, amenities, and special features using a **star-rating system.** In country, state, and regional guides, we also rate towns and regions to help you narrow down your choices and budget your time accordingly. Hotels and restaurants are rated on a scale of zero (recommended) to three stars (exceptional). Attractions, shopping, nightlife, towns, and regions are rated according to the following scale: zero stars (recommended), one star (highly recommended), two stars (very highly recommended), and three stars (must-see).

In addition to the star-rating system, we also use **seven feature icons** that point you to the great deals, in-the-know advice, and unique experiences that separate travelers from tourists. Throughout the book, look for:

Finds	Special finds—those places only insiders know about
Fun Fact	Fun facts—details that make travelers more informed and their trips more fun
Kids	Best bets for kids and advice for the whole family
Moments	Special moments—those experiences that memories are made of
Overrated	Places or experiences not worth your time or money
Tips	Insider tips—great ways to save time and money
Value	Great values—where to get the best deals

The following **abbreviations** are used for credit cards:

AE	American Express	DISC	Discover	V	Visa
DC	Diners Club	MC	MasterCard		

Frommers.com

Now that you have this guidebook to help you plan a great trip, visit our website at **www.frommers.com** for additional travel information on more than 4,000 destinations. We update features regularly to give you instant access to the most current trip-planning information available. At Frommers.com, you'll find scoops on the best airfares, lodging rates, and car rental bargains. You can even book your travel online through our reliable travel booking partners. Other popular features include:

- Online updates of our most popular guidebooks
- Vacation sweepstakes and contest giveaways
- Newsletters highlighting the hottest travel trends
- Podcasts, interactive maps, and up-to-the-minute events listings
- Opinionated blog entries by Arthur Frommer himself
- Online travel message boards with featured travel discussions

What's New in Boston

The U.S. dollar is weak, and the destination reputed to be the most European of American cities is more tempting than ever to international travelers. With dollars not worth much abroad, Americans are planning domestic trips. Boston, with its new parks, new visibility in multiple movies, new NBA championship trophy (from 2008), and longstanding reputation as a manageable destination, is practically full. Hotel prices and occupancy rates are up, and the sidewalks are packed. "Hot" has no real formula, but you don't have to be a Supreme Court justice to know it when you see it. Boston is hot. Stroll along the emerging Rose Kennedy Greenway or the easily accessible waterfront, and you'll quickly see why.

BOSTON IN DEPTH A change in the state tax code (asleep yet?) has turned Massachusetts into a red-hot center of film production (*now* I have your attention). As the number of movie sets clogging traffic and enthralling civilians multiplies exponentially, the odds that you'll get a peek behind the scenes improve—constantly. See chapter 2.

PLANNING YOUR TRIP TO BOSTON The **MBTA** (© **800/392-6100** or 617/222-3200; www.mbta.com) plans to implement its new fare-collection system on **ferries and commuter trains** sometime in 2008. Check ahead for details if you plan to rely on public transportation.

International travel to the United States, never simple, is more complicated than ever. Be ready to pose for a photograph, have all 10 fingers printed, and answer a lot of questions.

See chapter 3.

ACCOMMODATIONS Luxury and high-end business hotel operators continue to flood the Boston market with plush, pricey accommodations. In 2008, openings included the tech-happy **Renaissance Boston Waterfront Hotel,** 606 Congress St., in South Boston near the convention center (© **800/HOTELS-1;** www.marriott.com); and the over-the-top **Mandarin Oriental, Boston,** on Boylston Street next to the Prudential Center (© **866/526-6567;** www.mandarinoriental.com).

For information about the luxury property at Battery Wharf on Commercial Street in the North End, a 150-room hotel with high-end dining options and a sprawling spa, visit www.batterywharf.com (management was in search of a new operator for the property at press time).

Properties in all price categories are renovating, redecorating, and boosting their "green" quotient. The **Chandler Inn Hotel,** 26 Chandler St. (© **800/842-3450;** www.chandlerinn.com); the **Colonnade Hotel Boston,** 120 Huntington Ave. (© **800/962-3030;** www.colonnadehotel.com); the **Copley Square Hotel,** 47 Huntington Ave. (© **800/225-7062;** www.copleysquarehotel.com); the **MidTown Hotel,** 220 Huntington Ave. (**800/343-1177;** www.midtownhotel.com); the

Millennium Bostonian Hotel, 26 North St. (© **866/866-8086;** www.millennium hotels.com); and the **Omni Parker House** (© **800/THE-OMNI;** www.omniparker house.com) should have emerged from their construction cocoons by the time you visit.

Finally, the Sheraton chain has joined the Westin and Marriott chains in going completely smoke-free, a policy many smaller properties were already following. See chapter 5.

DINING   Boston Restaurant Week added a week, bringing the total to 4 per year—but it's not Restaurant Month: It's 2 weeks in August and 2 in March. I prefer the seasonal raw materials available to chefs in the summer, but the offer ($20.08 or $20.09 for lunch, $10 or so more for dinner) is a great deal at any time. The Greater Boston Convention & Visitors Bureau lists participating establishments on its website (www.bostonusa.com).

La Voile, 261 Newbury St. (© **617/ 587-4200;** www.lavoileboston.net), may look familiar to travelers who have spent a lot of time in Cannes. The owners of the promising French/Mediterranean newcomer created it by shipping an existing restaurant across the Atlantic, lock, stock, and metal-topped bar.

The beloved **L'Espalier** (© **617/262-3023;** www.lespalier.com) closed its Gloucester Street home in 2008. Its clientele of diners celebrating special occasions with astonishingly good New England cuisine followed a bit reluctantly to the new Mandarin Oriental complex on Boylston Street next to the Prudential Center.

In a cats-and-dogs-living-together moment, 82-year-old **Pizzeria Regina,** 11½ Thacher St. (© **617/227-0765**) accepted its first credit card in 2008.

Spire, in the Nine Zero Hotel, has closed, and the Milk Street Café no longer runs the kiosk in Post Office Square Park. Two longstanding family restaurants—Garden of Eden, in Boston, and Cambridge's La Groceria—closed in 2008.

Nashoba Brook Bakery & Cafe has closed its branch in Boston's South End; the original location, in Concord (see chapter 11), continues to thrive. Also in the South End, Bob's Southern Bistro, a landmark for a half-century, closed in 2007. See chapter 6.

WHAT TO SEE & DO   You may find the **Boston Common Visitor Information Center** closed during your visit as it undergoes badly needed renovation. The staff at your hotel and the nearby National Park Service center at 15 State St. can fill in.

Two of the three **Harvard Art Museums** closed in 2008 for renovations that are expected to take 5 years. Starting in the fall of 2008, the **Arthur M. Sackler Museum** (© **617/495-9400;** www.art museums.harvard.edu) will showcase the highlights of its own collections and those of the Fogg Museum and the Busch-Reisinger Museum.

Park Street Church, 1 Park St. (© **617/ 523-3383;** www.parkstreet200.org), will celebrate its bicentennial in 2009; check ahead for information about special events.

The **New England Aquarium,** Central Wharf (© **617/973-5200;** www. newenglandaquarium.org), which will celebrate its 40th anniversary in 2009, has discontinued its Harbor Discovery Cruises.

The **Boston Tea Party Ship & Museum** (© **617/269-7150;** www.boston teapartyship.com), which closed indefinitely after a fire in 2001, is now scheduled to reopen in 2009. See chapter 7.

SHOPPING   This news is spreading inexplicably slowly: The original **Filene's Basement,** at Downtown Crossing, is temporarily closed for construction.

Bargain shoppers can hit the Back Bay location at 497 Boylston St. (© **800/843-8474**; www.filenesbasement.com), but it doesn't offer the automatic-markdown policy that makes the century-old original catnip for thrifty fashionistas.

The denim-intensive boutique Jean Therapy spun off a little sibling that carries business attire: **Therapy,** 152 Brookline Ave. (© **617/266-6501**).

Another spin-off is **WardMaps.com,** 12 Bow St., Cambridge (© **617/497-0737**; www.wardmaps.com)—it started as a website and evolved into a 3-D store.

The South End Open Market has changed its name to the **SoWa Open Market,** 540 Harrison Ave. (© **617/481-2257**; www.southendopenmarket.com); here's hoping it gets around to changing its web address too. In 2008, after a half-century in the North End, Dairy Fresh Candies closed. See chapter 9.

BOSTON AFTER DARK   Boston Ballet (© **617/695-6955**; www.bostonballet.org) ended its latest lease-renewal negotiations by (almost literally) walking out. The 2008–09 season will be the company's last on its current home stage, the Citi Wang Theatre, before it moves all of its productions, not just *The Nutcracker,* to the Opera House.

The **Isabella Stewart Gardner Museum,** 280 The Fenway (© **617/566-1401**; www.gardnermuseum.org), has followed the lead of the Museum of Fine Arts and started scheduling one evening a month of after-work drinking and music in the galleries.

Boston's nightlife backbone, **Lansdowne Street,** was in transition at press time and may not have settled down by the time you read this. Avalon and Axis, stalwarts of the lively strip across from Fenway Park, closed in late 2007, roiling the straight and gay club scenes. In an everything-old-is-new-again twist (the original link in the chain was in Cambridge), the **House of Blues** is expected to replace the popular nightclubs in early 2009. Visit **www.hob.com** or ask at your hotel before heading out for live music, Southern food, or the famed Sunday gospel brunch.

The space that was once the Big Easy nightclub opened in 2007 as **The Estate,** 1 Boylston Place (© **617/351-7000**; www.theestateboston.com). It's still cleverly laid out and acoustically pleasing, with a more stylish crowd.

Jimmy Tingle's Off Broadway Theater in Somerville closed permanently in 2008. The owner/comedian/actor/social critic has better things to do—he says he's running for president.

See chapter 10.

SIDE TRIPS FROM BOSTON   Visitors in 2008 will find the **Hancock–Clarke House,** 36 Hancock St. (© **978/862-1703**; www.lexingtonhistory.org), one of Lexington's best-known historic attractions, closed for restoration. It reopens in 2009.

The Cape Ann Historical Museum, not so long ago the Cape Ann Historical Association, is now the **Cape Ann Museum,** 27 Pleasant St. (© **978/283-0455**; www.capeannmuseum.org).

And Maddie's Sail Loft, a landmark Marblehead tavern, closed in 2008 just shy of its 62nd birthday.

See chapter 11.

1

The Best of Boston

For the past 25 years, downtown Boston has changed in some significant way almost daily. A gargantuan construction project with a cute name (the Big Dig) proceeded slowly but unstoppably, making a mile-long strip of prime real estate look like a scene from a post-apocalyptic movie before it finally looked better. Today, the elevated highway that once sliced across the city like a green scar is a distant memory, and the green we see everywhere is the color of trees, plants, and flowers.

A subterranean highway carries traffic through the new Boston, a modern metropolis that's also a relentlessly historic destination, with buildings of all ages and styles, from colonial-era to Frank Gehry's latest brainstorm. From the South Boston waterfront, once a wasteland of parking lots and fish carcasses, to the Back Bay, Boston's architecture is newer, taller, and more dramatic than before. Walking around downtown provides a good reminder: The building boom may overshadow the city's famous 18th- and 19th-century architecture, but even rampant development can't change central Boston's colonial character.

It's not perfect, of course. Nightmarish traffic, daredevil drivers, and grating accents don't help any city's reputation. Although Boston is the biggest college town in the world, it doesn't have much of a late-night scene. And far from gone is the inferiority complex epitomized by the description "like New York, but smaller." Still, as it has since 1630, Boston offers cosmopolitan sophistication on a comfortable scale, balancing celebration of the past with pursuit of the future.

Here's hoping your experience is memorable and delightful.

1 The Most Unforgettable Travel Experiences

- **A Sky Full of Fireworks:** The Fourth of July fireworks flash over the Charles River; Boston's New Year is hailed by the First Night show flaring above the Inner Harbor. See "Boston Calendar of Events," in chapter 2.

- **A Ride on a Duck:** Board a reconditioned amphibious World War II landing craft (on Huntington Ave. near the Prudential Center, or at the Museum of Science) for a sightseeing ride that includes a dip in the river—for the Duck boat, not you. See p. 174.

- **An Afternoon Red Sox Game:** Since 1912, baseball fans have made pilgrimages to Fenway Park, the "lyric little bandbox of a ball park" (in John Updike's words) off Kenmore Square. Soak up the atmosphere and bask in the sun. See p. 185.

- **A Walk Around the North End:** Boston's Little Italy (but don't call it that!) has an old-world flavor you won't want to miss. Explore the shops on Salem Street, and be sure to stop for coffee and a pastry at a Hanover Street *caffè*. See "Welcome to the North End," on p. 169.

2 The Best Splurge Hotels

- **Charles Hotel,** 1 Bennett St., Cambridge (✆ **800/882-1818**). Steps from the hubbub of Harvard Square, the unfailingly elegant Charles is a sanctuary of contemporary design and traditional pampering. See p. 94.
- **Eliot Hotel,** 370 Commonwealth Ave., Back Bay (✆ **800/44-ELIOT**). Location and layout give the Eliot the feel of a luxury apartment building. Business amenities and elegant traditional furnishings contribute to its seamless blend of commerce and comfort. See p. 86.
- **Four Seasons Hotel,** 200 Boylston St., Back Bay (✆ **800/819-5053**). The best hotel in New England has everything—and what it doesn't have on the premises, the incredible staff will track down. Superb service, plush accommodations, and lavish amenities make a stay here unforgettable. See p. 83.
- **Boston Harbor Hotel,** Rowes Wharf, Waterfront (✆ **800/752-7077**). Dazzling architecture, a great location, and maniacal attention to detail—the latest guest-room renovation added curved trim that echoes the hotel complex's signature arch—add up to pampering on a suitably dramatic scale. See p. 71.

3 The Best Moderately Priced Hotels

- **Charlesmark Hotel,** 655 Boylston St. (✆ **617/247-1212**). The Charlesmark's thoughtful features—plush bedding, free local phone calls, friendly service, custom-designed everything—more than make up for the modest size of the rooms. Bonus: Units at the front of the building overlook the Boston Marathon finish line. See p. 90.
- **Doubletree Guest Suites,** 400 Soldiers Field Rd., Brighton (✆ **800/222-TREE**). Every unit here is a spacious two-room suite. The location, straddling Boston and Cambridge, is especially good if you're driving. See p. 92.
- **Harborside Inn,** 185 State St., downtown (✆ **888/723-7565**). Hardwood floors and exposed-brick walls give this updated 19th-century warehouse its character. Close to downtown attractions, it's convenient to the nearby Financial District. See p. 75.
- **MidTown Hotel,** 220 Huntington Ave., Back Bay (✆ **800/343-1177**). A unique combination of comfortable, no-frills rooms and a handy location make this hotel the most motel-like lodging in central Boston. And the cheapest guest parking in the Back Bay can save you as much as $25 per day. See p. 91.
- **Newbury Guest House,** 261 Newbury St., Back Bay (✆ **800/437-7668**). This place would be a bargain even if it weren't ideally situated in the heart of Boston's best shopping. Room prices even include continental breakfast. See p. 91.

4 The Most Unforgettable Dining Experiences

- **Durgin-Park,** 340 Faneuil Hall Marketplace (✆ **617/227-2038**). This Boston institution has packed 'em in since 1827. It serves classic New England fare in abundant portions at communal tables, delighting everyone from local tycoons to visiting toddlers. Well, almost everyone: The famously crotchety staff is so much a part of the legend that some people are disappointed when—quite often—the waitresses are courteous and pleasant. See p. 115.

- **Legal Sea Foods,** 255 State St. (*©* **617/227-3115**), and other locations. Like the culinary equivalent of a medical specialist, Legal's does one thing and does it exceptionally well. It's a chain for a great reason: People can't get enough of the freshest seafood around. See p. 106.

- **Mr. Bartley's Burger Cottage,** 1246 Massachusetts Ave., Cambridge (*©* **617/354-6559**). Trends in food and fashion come and go, and this neighborhood sees them all. Luckily, Harvard Square has a place that puts the "comfort" in comfort food. Bartley's is famous for its juicy burgers,

incredible onion rings, and a down-to-earth atmosphere that's increasingly rare in these parts. See p. 133.

- **Pizzeria Regina,** 11½ Thacher St. (*©* **617/227-0765**). With its red-and-white-checked tablecloths and fiery oven, Regina's does look like Hollywood's idea of a pizza joint. After one bite of that slightly smoky crust, you'll be sending Martin Scorsese to the back of the line. See p. 114.

- **Ye Olde Union Oyster House,** 41 Union St. (*©* **617/227-2750**). Wise guys sneer about all the tourists, but the Union Oyster House is a local favorite for a reason—the unbeatable combination of historic atmosphere and traditional food that's drawn crowds since 1826. See p. 115.

5 The Best Free (Or Almost Free) Things to Do

- **Picnic by the Water:** Head for the harbor or river, relax on a park bench or patch of grass, put away your watch, and enjoy the spectacular scene. Whether it's sailboats or ocean liners, seagulls or scullers, there's always something worth watching. My favorite spot is Sargent's Wharf, on the edge of the North End, but it's just one of thousands of pleasant spots. See chapter 7.

- **Visit a Museum:** Schedule your visit to take advantage of free or reduced admission at certain times. The **USS Constitution Museum** is free all the time; the **Museum of Fine Arts** is free after 4pm Wednesday; the **Institute of Contemporary Art** is free after 5pm Thursday; and the **Children's Museum** costs just $1 after 5pm on Friday. See chapter 7.

- **Take a Ranger-Led Tour:** The National Park Service is such a good use of tax money. Free and cheap tours of historic attractions all over eastern Massachusetts elevate a visit

to a park, a house, a neighborhood, or even a government installation (the Charlestown Navy Yard) from good to great. See chapters 7 and 11.

- **Relish a Vicarious Thrill:** Without so much as lacing up a sneaker, you can participate in the world-famous Boston Marathon. Stretch a little. Drink plenty of fluids. Claim a piece of sidewalk with a front-row view of the course. Cheer as the runners thunder past. Then put your feet up—you must be exhausted. See p. 187.

- **Prowl Newbury Street:** From the genteel Arlington Street end to the cutting-edge Mass Ave. end, Newbury Street—Boston's legendary shopping destination—is 8 blocks of pure temptation: galleries, boutiques, jewelry and gift shops, and more. Fortunately, window-shopping is free. See chapter 9.

- **Check Out a College Concert or Show:** Countless student groups just want an attentive audience, and the free or minimal admission can pay off in the long run. Imagine the credit card commercial: "Ability to say you recognized the talent of [insert name of big star] in a student production? Priceless." See chapter 10.

6 The Best Outdoor Activities

- **A Ride across the Harbor:** The ferry that connects Long Wharf and the Charlestown Navy Yard is a treasure hidden in plain sight. You might notice the boat traffic on the Inner Harbor as you make your way around downtown; for just $1.70, you can be part of it. See chapter 4.
- **An Interlude at a Cafe:** When it comes to good ideas, outdoor seating in a place with great people-watching is right up there with fire and the wheel. A passing parade of shoppers and students (on Newbury St. and in Harvard Sq.) is more interesting than suits and ties (downtown and the rest of the Back Bay), but if the breeze and the iced cappuccino are cool, what's not to like? See chapter 8.

- **A Free Concert:** The Boston area's cultural scene has no real off season. During the summer, many musicians and musical groups take their acts outside—to parks, plazas, and even a barge (behind the Boston Harbor Hotel). Plan well and you can enjoy music alfresco almost every night. See chapter 10.
- **A Stroll (or Jog) along the River:** The bike path that hugs both shores of the Charles accommodates pedestrians, runners, and rollerbladers, as well as cyclists. The Esplanade (adjacent to the Back Bay) offers both people-watching and gorgeous trees and shrubs; the Cambridge side has abundant seating and fabulous views of the Boston skyline. See chapter 7.

7 The Best Museums

- **Concord Museum:** Always informative, never overwhelming, it shows and tells visitors enough about the town's history to help them make the most of a visit here. See p. 249.
- **The Isabella Stewart Gardner Museum:** The Gardner is a magnificent repository of art and nature in a building that's as impressive as anything hanging on the walls. See p. 144.
- **The John F. Kennedy Presidential Library and Museum:** This library captures the personality of its charismatic namesake as well as the spirit that continues to make the Camelot era so compelling, all these years later. See p. 144.
- **The Museum of Fine Arts:** The MFA truly is world-class—and all over the place, you'll stumble on masterpieces so familiar that seeing them is like running into an old friend on the street. See p. 145.

8 The Best Activities for Families

- **A Visit to Faneuil Hall Marketplace:** Street performers, crowds from the world over, the food court, restaurants, bars, and shops make Faneuil Hall Marketplace (you'll also hear it called Quincy Market) Boston's most popular destination. It's conveniently located across the street from the harbor, where a stroll along the water can help your crew decompress. See p. 142.
- **An Exploration of the Museum of Science:** Your kids will revel in the displays and exhibits that cram every

branch of science and inquiry into this enormous and child-accessible institution. See p. 146.

- **An Excursion to the Public Garden:** A perfect retreat during or after a busy day of sightseeing. Ride a Swan Boat, visit with the Mallard family of *Make Way for Ducklings* fame, admire the real birds, and marvel as the whole family starts to chill out. See p. 163.
- **A Trip to the Children's Museum:** The hands-on exhibits, noisy galleries, and overall air of discovery and excitement make this excursion catnip for the elementary-school set. See p. 172.
- **A Thrill "Ride":** The Mugar Omni Theater (at the Museum of Science) and the 3-D Simons IMAX Theatre (at the New England Aquarium) offer intrepid visitors hair-raising experiences in the safety of a comfortable auditorium. Most of the large-format films concentrate on the natural world. See p. 147 for the Mugar Omni Theater and p. 148 for the Simons IMAX Theatre.

2

Boston in Depth

Boston embodies contrasts and contradictions—blueblood and blue collar, Yankee and Irish, Brahmin banker and budget-conscious graduate student. It's home to the country's first public school and to a problematic educational system. A onetime hotbed of abolitionism, it retains an intractable reputation for racism. It's a proud seaport that faces a harbor just recently reclaimed from crippling pollution. Boston is a famously parochial, insular city whose traditional obsessions are "sports, politics, and revenge," but it's also a magnet for students and intellectuals from all over the world, and the capital of the only U.S. state where same-sex marriage is legal.

Compact in size yet boasting a virtually inexhaustible supply of interesting activities and diversions, Boston is a magnet for history buffs, art lovers, sports fans, shoppers, families, and convention-goers. Whether you fit into one or more or none of those categories, you're still in for an enjoyable time. The interests that draw you here can monopolize your schedule, but you'll have a better experience if you make some room for serendipity—on your schedule and in your attitude.

The fact that you're reading this means that you have the chance to become one of the countless visitors who arrive in Boston planning to concentrate on one thing and wind up dipping into something completely unexpected that becomes a highlight of their visit. They come for a convention and linger at the Museum of Fine Arts, come for a college tour and can't get enough of the fresh seafood, come for the Revolutionary history and detour for the great shopping. They walk the narrow streets and stately avenues, soak up the local and international accents, marvel at the natural and manmade scenery, and lament the fact that they can't spend even more time exploring.

Boston is a living landmark that bears many marks of its colonial heritage, but where it's theoretically possible (this is an observation, not a suggestion) to spend days without going near anything built before 1960, or even going outdoors. Pick out a suitcase that has room for your walking shoes and get ready for your own adventure.

1 Boston Today

Over the past few years, a mysterious combination of factors has turned Boston into a hot destination. It's like a math problem: a new convention center plus hundreds of new hotel rooms plus multiple Red Sox and Patriots championships plus a weak dollar plus a huge college-age population plus widespread development equals scads of travelers. Underlying all of this—literally—is a new interstate, which has helped transform downtown.

Boston greeted the new century by wrapping up a gargantuan highway-construction project and presenting a new face to the world. An evolving ribbon of parkland known as the Rose Fitzgerald Kennedy Greenway winds through downtown, reuniting neighborhoods that had

Moments Written in Stone

All over central Boston, you'll see plaques commemorating some long-gone people, event, or even place ("On this site stood . . ."). Each one tells a little story, not just in its text but also in its context. A plaque commemorating the first Catholic Mass in Boston (on School St. near Borders, across the street from the Freedom Trail) doesn't seem like a big deal now, but in a Puritan city, toleration of "popery" couldn't have come easily. On Commercial Street near Hull Street, a marker describes the Molasses Flood of 1919, during which 2 million gallons of raw molasses spilled out of a ruptured storage tank into the streets, killing 21 people. The story recalls the days when manufacturing and industry dominated the area that's now the residential North End and scenic waterfront. Look around as you walk around—history is everywhere, just waiting for you to discover it.

been separated for half a century by an ugly elevated highway and connecting downtown directly with increasingly beautiful Boston Harbor. The Greenway is one of the most eye-catching products of the "Big Dig," which cost $14.6 billion before formally wrapping up at the end of 2007. The boom in development and construction it helped launch is still going on, fairly impervious to the ups and downs of the economy.

Today you'll find a metropolis of nearly 600,000 at the heart of the Greater Boston area, which encompasses 83 cities and towns and some 4 million people. The hospitals and medical centers are among the best in the world, and health care was a hot topic long before the state took a leading role in the country's ongoing debate over universal coverage. Education and tourism are pillars of the local economy, which has mirrored national trends (positive and negative) in unemployment statistics. Though hardly recession-proof, the banking, financial services, insurance, and high-tech industries are vital components as well. The ongoing real-estate downturn has put a damper on the red-hot Boston market, but the city remains one of the most expensive places in the country to live (and to visit, if you don't budget carefully).

As they have for more than a century, immigrants flock to the Boston area, where Irish, eastern European Jewish, Italian, Portuguese, African American, Latino, West Indian, and, most recently, Asian arrivals have settled. Between 1990 and 2000, the city's Asian population nearly doubled, and the Latino population grew by more than one-third.

Because of "white flight," Boston is what urban planners call a "doughnut city." It has a relatively large black population (23.8% of Boston residents are black, compared with 11% of the U.S. population) surrounded by many lily-white suburbs. The 2000 Census showed that Boston had become a "majority minority" city, with whites making up less than 50% of the population for the first time. One of the only neighborhoods that gained white residents in the 1990s is the South End, where gentrification is sweeping through, homogenizing an area long known for its economic and ethnic diversity.

Whatever their origins, Bostonians share at least a passing interest in sports. ("How about those Red Sox?" is a favorite conversational gambit all over town.) The New England Patriots, who play in a distant suburb, triumphed in the Super Bowl in 2002, 2004, and 2005—only to find that their third title was virtually a footnote. Three months earlier, in October 2004, the Red Sox won the World Series for the first time since 1918. Many Sox fans believe that victory ended a curse, and they point to the Sox' 2007 Series crown as evidence. Meanwhile, many Pats fans are wondering whether their previously undefeated team's loss in the 2008 Super Bowl signals another run of mystical bad luck.

Pro sports are only part of the story, though: In a region with an enormous student population, college athletics are a big deal, too. You may have heard that Boston is a college town, but you may not realize just how true that is until you're out and about, tripping over chattering post-adolescents nearly everywhere—even downtown (where Suffolk University and Emerson College are expanding their footprints). They infuse their youthful energy into every facet of life in the Boston area.

To get a sense of what present-day Boston is (and is not) like, hit the streets. The puritanical Bostonian is virtually extinct, but you can still uncover traces of the groups, institutions, and events that shaped Boston's history and created the complex city you see today.

2 Looking Back at Boston

Permanently settled in 1630 by representatives of the Massachusetts Bay Company, Boston was named for the hometown of some of the Puritans who left England to seek religious freedom in the New World. They met with little of the usual strife with the natives, members of the small, Algonquian-speaking Massachuset tribe that roamed the area. The natives might have used the peninsula they called Shawmut (possibly derived from "Mushau-womuk," or "unclaimed land") as a burial place. They grew corn on some harbor islands but made their permanent homes farther inland.

In 1632, the little peninsula became the capital of the Massachusetts Bay Colony, and the population soon increased rapidly because of the great Puritan migration. Thanks to its excellent location on a deep, sheltered harbor, Boston quickly became a center of shipbuilding, fishing, and trading.

The only thing more important than commerce was religion, and the Puritans exerted such a strong influence that their

---

We're Number 1!

Boston's list of firsts is a long one. Here are some highlights:

- America's first public school (Boston Latin School, 1635)
- America's first printing press (in Cambridge, 1638)
- America's first post office (1639)
- America's first regularly published newspaper, the *Boston News Letter* (1704)
- America's first chocolate factory (1765)
- First operation under general anesthesia (removal of a jaw tumor, at Massachusetts General Hospital, 1846)
- America's first subway (1897)
- First successful human-to-human organ transplant (of a kidney, at Peter Bent Brigham Hospital, 1954)
- First successful reattachment of a human limb (a 12-year-old boy's right arm, at Mass. General, 1962)

Impressions

Tonight I appear for the first time before a Boston audience—4,000 critics.

—Mark Twain, 1869

legacy survives to this day. A concrete reminder is Harvard College's original (1636) mission: preparing young men to be ministers. In 1659, the town fathers officially banned Christmas (the town children apparently had second thoughts—records show that the holiday was back in favor by the 1680s). Another early example of Puritanical stuffiness was recorded in 1673. One Captain Kemble was sentenced to confinement in the stocks for 2 hours because he kissed his wife on their front steps—on a Sunday. He had been away for 3 years.

THE ROAD TO REVOLUTION

The Crown began exerting tighter control over the colonies as early as the 1680s. Over the years, laws increasing taxes and restricting trading activities led to trouble. The situation came to a head after the French and Indian War (known in Europe as the Seven Years' War) ended in 1763.

Having helped fight for the British, the independent-minded colonists were outraged when the Crown expected them to help pay off the war debt. The Sugar Act of 1764 imposed tariffs on sugar, wine, and coffee, mostly affecting those engaged in trade; the 1765 Stamp Act taxed everything printed, from legal documents to playing cards, affecting virtually everyone. Boycotts, demonstrations, and riots ensued. The repeal of the Stamp Act in 1766 was too little, too late—the revolutionary slogan "No taxation without representation" had already helped rouse the colonists to action.

The Townshend Acts of 1767 imposed taxes on paper, glass, and tea, sparking more unrest. The following year, British troops occupied Boston. Perhaps inevitably, tension led to violence. In the Boston Massacre of 1770, five colonists were killed in a scuffle with the redcoats. The first to die was a former slave named Crispus Attucks; another was 17-year-old Samuel Maverick. The site, represented by a circle of cobblestones, sits on what is now State Street, and the colonists' graves are nearby, in the Old Granary Burying Ground on Tremont Street.

HELP YOURSELVES TO TEA

Parliament repealed the Townshend Acts but kept the tea tax and, in 1773, granted the nearly bankrupt East India Company a monopoly on the tea trade with the colonies. The idea was to undercut the price of smuggled tea, but the colonists weren't swayed. In December, three British ships sat at anchor in Boston Harbor (roughly where present-day Atlantic Avenue meets the Evelyn Moakley Bridge), waiting for their cargo of tea to be unloaded. Before that could happen, the rabble-rousing Sons of Liberty, stirred up after a spirited public meeting at the Old South Meeting House, boarded the ships and dumped 342 chests of tea into the harbor. The "Boston Tea Party" became a rallying point for both sides, and the meeting house stages a re-creation of the inflammatory rally every December.

The British responded by closing the port until the tea was paid for and forcing Bostonians to house the soldiers who began to flood the community. They soon numbered 4,000 in a town of 16,000. Mutual distrust ran high—Paul Revere wrote of helping form "a committee for the purpose of watching the movements of the British troops." When the royal commander in Boston, General

Gage, learned that the patriots were accumulating arms and ammunition, he dispatched men to destroy the stockpiles. They departed from what's now Charles Street South, between Boston Common and the Public Garden, to cross the Charles River. A lantern signal soon illuminated the steeple of the Old North Church, alerting Revere to their route—the "two if by sea" made famous nearly a century later by Cambridge resident Henry Wadsworth Longfellow.

A NEW WORLD ORDER

Troops marched from Boston toward Lexington and Concord late on April 18, 1775. On their "midnight ride," William Dawes and Revere alerted the colonists to the British advance. Just north of Harvard Square, horseshoes embedded in the sidewalk show part of Dawes' route. The riders sounded the warning to mobilize the local militia companies, or Minutemen. The next day, some 700 British soldiers under Major John Pitcairn emerged victorious from a skirmish in Lexington. The troops and Minutemen clashed on the town common, a public area that's still known as the "Battle Green." Later that day, they were routed at Concord near the site of what's now a replica of the North Bridge, and forced to retreat to Charlestown.

It took the redcoats almost an entire day to make the trip, along the route now marked "Battle Road." You can cover it in a car in about half an hour. Thanks in no small part to Longfellow's 1861 poem "Paul Revere's Ride" ("Listen my children and you shall hear / Of the midnight ride of Paul Revere"), Lexington and Concord are closely associated with the beginning of the Revolution. In the early stages, military activity left its mark all over eastern Massachusetts, particularly in Cambridge. Royalist sympathizers, or Tories, were concentrated so heavily along one stretch of Brattle Street that it was called "Tory Row." When the tide began to turn, George Washington made his headquarters on the same street (in the same house later occupied by Longfellow, which is now a National Park Service site). On nearby Cambridge Common is the spot where Washington took command of the Continental Army on July 3, 1775.

The British won the Battle of Bunker Hill in Charlestown on June 17, 1775, but at the cost of half their forces. (Win a trivia contest by knowing that the battle actually took place on Breed's Hill.) The redcoats abandoned Boston the following March 17—still a legal holiday, Evacuation Day, in Suffolk County. On July 4, 1776, the Continental Congress adopted the Declaration of Independence. Although many Bostonians fought in the 6-year war that followed, Boston itself saw no more battles.

COMMERCE & CULTURE

After the war, Boston again became a center of business. Fishing, whaling, and trade with the Far East dominated the economy. Exotic spices and fruits, textiles, and porcelain were familiar luxuries in Boston and nearby Salem. The influential merchant families who became known as Boston Brahmins spearheaded a cultural renaissance that flourished even after the War of 1812 ravaged international shipping, toppling Boston from its commercial pedestal. As banking and

---

Impressions

For we must consider that we shall be as a city upon a hill. The eyes of all people are upon us. . . .

—John Winthrop, sermon, "A Model of Christian Charity" (1630)

Welcome to "the Hub"

Boston State-house is the hub of the solar system. You couldn't pry that out of a Boston man if you had the tire of all creation straightened out for a crow-bar.

—Oliver Wendell Holmes, Sr., *The Autocrat of the Breakfast-Table* (1858)

manufacturing rose in importance, Boston took a back seat to New York and Philadelphia in size and influence. But the "Athens of America" became known for fine art and architecture, including the luxurious homes you see today on Beacon Hill, and a burgeoning intellectual community.

In 1822, Boston became a city. From 1824 to 1826, Mayor Josiah Quincy oversaw the landfill project that moved the waterfront away from Faneuil Hall. The market building constructed at that time, which still stands, was named in his honor. The undertaking was one of many, all over the city, in which hilltops were lopped off and deposited in the water, transforming the coastline and skyline. For example, the filling of the Mill Pond, now the area around North Station, began in 1807 and in 25 years consumed the summits of Copp's and Beacon hills.

In the 19th century, landfill work tripled the city's area, creating badly needed space. The largest of the projects, started in 1835 and completed in 1882, was the filling of the Back Bay, the body of mud flats and marshes that gave its name to the present-day neighborhood. Beginning in 1857, much of the fill came by railroad from suburban Needham.

By the mid-1800s, Ralph Waldo Emerson, Oliver Wendell Holmes, Henry Wadsworth Longfellow, Nathaniel Hawthorne, Bronson Alcott, Louisa May Alcott, John Greenleaf Whittier, Walt Whitman, Henry David Thoreau, and even Charles Dickens (briefly) and Mark Twain (more briefly) had appeared on the local literary scene. William Lloyd Garrison published the weekly *Liberator*

newspaper, a powerful voice in the anti-slavery and social reform movements. Boston became an important stop on the Underground Railroad, the secret network the abolitionists developed to smuggle runaway slaves into Canada.

LOCAL GLORY

During the Civil War (1861–65), abolitionist sentiment was the order of the day in Boston—to such a degree that only names of members of the Union Army appear on the rolls listing the war dead in Harvard's Memorial Hall, which is open to the public. Massachusetts' contributions to the war effort included enormous quantities of firearms, shoes, blankets, tents, and men.

Black abolitionist Frederick Douglass, a former member of the Massachusetts Anti-Slavery Society, helped recruit the 54th and 55th Massachusetts Colored Regiments. The movie *Glory* tells the story of the 54th, the first army unit made up of free black soldiers, and its white commander, Colonel Robert Gould Shaw. The regiment's memorial, a gorgeous bas-relief by Augustus Saint-Gaudens, stands on Boston Common opposite the State House.

A CAPITAL CITY

The railroad boom of the 1820s and 1830s and the flood of immigration that began soon after had made New England an industrial center. Then as now, Boston was the region's unofficial capital. Thousands of immigrants from Ireland settled in the city, the first ethnic group to do so in great numbers since the French Huguenots in the early 18th century.

Signs reading NO IRISH NEED APPLY became scarce as the new arrivals gained political power, and the first Irish mayor was elected in 1885.

By this time, Boston's class split was a chasm, with the influx of immigrants adding to the social tension. The Irish led the way and were followed by Italian, Portuguese, and eastern European Jewish immigrants. Each group had its own neighborhoods, churches, schools, newspapers, and livelihoods that intersected only occasionally with "proper" society. A small but concrete example: The birthplace of Rose Fitzgerald—later Rose Kennedy, matriarch of the political dynasty—is in the North End, an Irish stronghold at her birth in 1890 that has been a predominantly Italian neighborhood for over half a century.

Even as the upper crust was sowing cultural seeds that would wind up enriching everyone—the Boston Symphony, the Boston Public Library, and the Museum of Fine Arts were established in the second half of the 19th century—its prudish behavior gained Boston a reputation for making snobbery an art form. In 1878 the censorious Watch and Ward Society was founded (as the New England Society for the Suppression of Vice), and the phrase "banned in Boston" soon made its way into the American vocabulary. In 1889, the private St. Botolph Club removed John Singer Sargent's portrait of Isabella Stewart Gardner from public view (it's now at the museum that bears her name) because her dress was too tight.

The Boston Brahmins could keep their new neighbors out of many areas of their lives, but not politics. The forebears of the Kennedy clan had appeared on the scene—John F. "Honey Fitz" Fitzgerald, Rose's father, was elected mayor in 1910—and the city slowly transformed yet again as WASPs and Catholics struck an uneasy truce.

World War II bolstered Boston's Depression-ravaged industrial economy, and the war's end touched off an economic transformation. Shipping declined, along with New England's textile, shoe, and glass industries, at the same time that students on the G. I. Bill poured into area colleges and universities. The rise of the local high-technology industry led to new construction, changing the look of the city. The 1960s saw the beginning of a building boom that has continued, save during the occasional economic slowdown, to this day.

THE TURN OF THE CENTURY

Still reeling from the international social upheaval of the 1960s, Boston was the center of a school-busing crisis in the mid-1970s. Sparked by a court-ordered school desegregation plan enacted in 1974, it touched off riots, violence, and a white boycott (that age group includes a fair number of prominent Bostonians who have GEDs rather than high school diplomas because their parents pulled them out of school). In the years since, the city has battled its reputation for racism with varying degrees of success.

Impressions

The Bostonians are really, as a race, far inferior in point of anything beyond mere intellect to any other set upon the continent of North America. They are decidedly the most servile imitators of the English it is possible to conceive.
—Boston native Edgar Allan Poe, 1849

We are Boston, Glasgow is Cleveland.
—John McKay, Lord Provost of Edinburgh, 1985

You Can't Spell "Boston" Without "Snob"

I come from good old Boston,
The home of the bean and the cod,
Where the Lowells talk to the Cabots,
And the Cabots talk only to God.
     —attributed to John Collins Bossidy and Samuel C. Bushnell, ca. 1905

And the accent! ... When a real Boston man used to approach me uttering
sounds like those of a brick-throated bullfrog it used to occur to me that if
the Cabots really had the ear of the Almighty, He must bitterly have regret-
ted that He ever invented the vocal organs of humanity.
     —Ford Madox Ford, *Return to Yesterday* (1932)

As a family, the Bradlees had been around for close to three hundred years,
but well down the totem pole from the Lowells and the Cabots.
     —Former *Washington Post* executive editor Ben Bradlee, *A Good Life* (1995)

The school system has yet to fully recover from the traumatic experience of busing, but every year it sends thousands of students on to the institutions of higher learning that continue to be Boston's greatest claim to fame.

Those schools are also magnets for international students, just one element of the city's profound transformation in the late 20th and early 21st centuries. Boston has largely shed its reputation for insularity and become known as one of the "most European" American cities. High-tech businesses helped create a worthy rival for Silicon Valley, and the gentrification that emerged as early as the 1960s continues at high speed—the rapidly changing definition of what's a "good" area of the South End is just one indicator of the trend.

It's not all good restaurants and great shopping, of course—for instance, the Catholic Church's sex-abuse scandal came to light in the Boston Archdiocese, a major presence in this predominantly Catholic area. But social divisions are fading. In 2003, the Massachusetts Supreme Judicial Court ruled that not allowing same-sex couples to marry violated the state constitution, institutionalizing an attitude that had already taken hold outside the courtroom. The typical reaction to legal gay marriage was, more or less, "What's the big deal?" The election of Deval Patrick, who in 2006 became the second African American since Reconstruction (after Virginia's Douglas Wilder) elected governor, inspired similar sentiments.

Thanks in no small part to the college students who clog rapid transit and drive property values out of sight—and who stick around, keeping the cutting edge nice and sharp—Boston continues to grow and change. A time traveler from the 18th or even 17th century would still recognize small parts of the physical city. Its attitude and spirit might be unfamiliar to a visitor from as recently as 20 years ago.

3 Boston in Popular Culture: Books, Films, TV, & Music

A list of authors, screenwriters, and musicians with ties to Boston could fill a book of its own and only scratch the surface. To get in the mood before visiting, let the impulse that inspired you to make the trip guide you. Here are some suggestions:

BOOKS
FOR CHILDREN

The timeless classic *Make Way for Ducklings,* by Robert McCloskey, tells the story of Mrs. Mallard and her babies on the loose in the Back Bay. After your kids fall for this book (and they will), you can thrill them with a trip to the Public Garden, where bronze statues of the family occupy a place of honor.

Slightly older kids might know the Public Garden as the setting of part of *The Trumpet of the Swan,* by E. B. White. After reading it, a turn around the lagoon on a Swan Boat is mandatory.

An excellent historical title is *Johnny Tremain,* by Esther Forbes, a fictional boy's-eye-view account of the Revolutionary War era. The book vividly describes scenes from the American Revolution, many of which take place along the Freedom Trail.

We're Off to Harvard Square, by Sage Stossel, is a delight, written in sprightly verse and beautifully illustrated. It's intended for 9- to 12-year-olds, but younger kids and adults will like it, too.

FOR ADULTS

My favorite introduction to the city's early history is *Paul Revere and the World He Lived In,* Forbes's look at Boston before, during, and after the Revolution. *Common Ground: A Turbulent Decade in the Lives of Three American Families,* by J. Anthony Lukas, is the definitive account of the busing crisis of the 1970s and the attendant social upheaval. Both won the Pulitzer Prize for nonfiction. A Pulitzer winner for fiction (though not for this book), Edwin O'Connor captured Boston machine politics in a book many have challenged but none has surpassed, *The Last Hurrah.*

The Proper Bostonians, an entertaining, perceptive nonfiction look at a bygone era that helped earn Boston its longstanding reputation for stuffiness, is an early work by well-known animal-rights activist Cleveland Amory. *The Friends of Eddie Coyle,* by George V. Higgins, is a crime novel famed for its realistic dialogue and unvarnished take on Boston hoods. *Black Mass,* by Dick Lehr and Gerard O'Neill, updates the story of local organized crime with a non-fiction take on the rise of fugitive mobster James "Whitey" Bulger.

Architecture buffs will enjoy *Cityscapes of Boston,* by Robert Campbell and Peter Vanderwarker, and *Lost Boston,* by Jane Holtz Kay. If trivia's your thing, check out the treasury of "did you know" items in *Boston A to Z,* by historian Thomas H. O'Connor.

"Paul Revere's Ride," Henry Wadsworth Longfellow's classic but historically inaccurate poem about the events of April 18 and 19, 1775, is collected in many anthologies. It's a must if you plan to walk the Freedom Trail or visit Lexington and Concord.

If you're venturing to Gloucester (or even if you're not), Sebastian Junger's *The Perfect Storm* makes an excellent introduction. The story of a fishing boat caught in historically bad weather, it will change the way you look at fish on a menu for a long time after you finish reading—or watching. The movie version, though heavy on the special effects, is a better-than-average effort.

FILM

Boston is hardly Hollywood on the Charles, but it's getting there. Don't be surprised to run across a film crew or hear about a location shoot while you're in town. The best-known recent film that used Boston as a backdrop was *The Departed* (2006), better known as the picture that finally won Martin Scorsese his Best Director Academy Award (and captured Best Picture). *The Departed* filmed all over town, in alleys and warehouses as well as easily recognizable locations like

---

Tips Summer Lovin'

The axiom that you should order **oysters** only in months with an "R" in them originates in biology. Summer is breeding season, when the energy that usually goes into bulking up (and making lots of juicy meat) gets diverted to reproduction. To experience the best the oyster has to offer, wait till the weather turns colder.

Long Wharf, and it stars Matt Damon, who grew up in Cambridge. In 2007, Boston was part of the scenery of *Gone Baby Gone,* local boy Ben Affleck's directorial debut; Denzel Washington's second effort behind the camera, *The Great Debaters* (which filmed scenes on the Harvard campus); and family comedy *The Game Plan* (hey, The Rock needs work too). And by the time you read this, you'll probably know whether you want to spend 10 bucks to see *21* (2008), a based-on-a-true-story caper about card-counting MIT students who won millions at Las Vegas casinos.

One huge potential stumbling block for movies set (not just filmed) in Boston is the nearly impossible feat of rendering local accents accurately. With one big exception, the cast of *Good Will Hunting* hardly trips up. This is the Boston movie to see if you have time for just one. It makes Boston and Cambridge look sensational and perceptively explores the town-gown divide, Robin Williams' unfortunate brogue notwithstanding. Coauthors and costars Affleck and Damon are boyhood friends, and Damon is a couple of semesters short of his Harvard degree.

Good Will Hunting, The Perfect Storm, and *Mystic River* are among the best movies with Boston-area backdrops, and they have an awful lot of bad company. Pictures worth checking out for more than just the locations include *A Civil Action, The Spanish Prisoner, Next Stop Wonderland* (all Boston),

State and Main (Manchester-by-the-Sea), and *The Love Letter* (Rockport).

If you have a high tolerance for sports and sentiment, rent *Fever Pitch,* a 103-minute video valentine to Boston and the Red Sox. Many scenes were filmed at Fenway Park, and the ending had to be reshot after the Sox won the World Series in 2004 for the first time in 86 years. The script is sappy but captures the maniacal-fan persona with alarming accuracy, and the soundtrack is excellent.

Some older movies are worth setting the DVR for. They include *Blown Away* (especially the scenes when the action first shifts to Boston), *The Verdict* (Boston), *Glory* (a stylish re-creation of 19th-century Beacon Hill), *The Witches of Eastwick* (Cohasset), and the sentimental favorite, *Love Story* (Cambridge).

Numerous projects are in the pipeline, including *Pink Panther 2,* in which Steve Martin plays Inspector Clouseau and Boston plays Paris; romantic comedies *Ghosts of Girlfriends Past* (Jennifer Garner and Matthew McConaughey), *The Proposal* (Sandra Bullock and Ryan Reynolds), *Bachelor Number 2* (Kate Hudson and Dane Cook), and *Ashecliffe,* which is based on *Shutter Island,* by Dennis Lehane (who also wrote the novels *Mystic River* and *Gone, Baby, Gone),* and will be directed by Scorsese.

TELEVISION

Most TV shows set in Boston use an occasional exterior location shot but otherwise don't get anywhere near the city.

They include *Boston Legal, The Practice, St. Elsewhere,* and *Spenser: For Hire* (if you can find it). But that's not why you're wondering whether everybody knows your name, is it? *Cheers* was based on a local pub called the Bull & Finch, and the show became so popular that the original bar changed its name and a spin-off opened in Faneuil Hall Marketplace. See p. 235.

MUSIC

Highbrow associations abound: The first American performance of Handel's *Messiah* was in Boston, the city is home to one of the best orchestras in the world, and the Boston Symphony even commissioned a recent Pulitzer Prize winner (George Walker's "Lilacs"). The jukebox or mp3 player is where the recent action is. The 1970s and '80s were the heyday of local rock, with Boston (the band), the Cars, and the J. Geils Band leading the pack. But the piece of music perhaps most closely associated with the city is the Standells' "Dirty Water." Released in 1966,

it was written by the band's producer after he was mugged on the Mass. Ave. bridge, which connects Boston and Cambridge "down by the banks of the river Charles."

The movie soundtrack to seek out is *Fever Pitch* (see above), a superb collection of recent songs associated with Boston. It includes "Dirty Water," which plays after Red Sox (and Bruins) victories, as well as Neil Diamond's "Sweet Caroline"—a random selection that caught on out of superstition—which booms through Fenway Park in the bottom of the eighth inning.

Download the Dropkick Murphys' "Tessie" and Augustana's "Boston," dig through your grandparents' LPs to find the Kingston Trio's "Charlie on the MTA," learn the words to "Where Everybody Knows Your name" (The *Cheers* theme song), and you'll be well on your way to passing for a local, or at least a local college student.

4 Eating & Drinking in Boston

The days when restaurant snobs sniffed that they had to go to New York to get a decent meal are long gone. Especially in warm weather, when excellent local produce appears on menus in every price range, the Boston area holds its own with any other market in the country. Celebrity chefs and rising stars spice up a dynamic restaurant scene, and traditional favorites occupy an important niche. The huge student population seeks out value, which it often finds at ethnic restaurants.

Seafood is a specialty in Boston, and you'll find it on the menu at almost every restaurant—trendy or classic, expensive or cheap, American (whatever that is) or ethnic. Some pointers: **Scrod** or **schrod** is a generic term for fresh white-fleshed fish, usually served in filets. **Local shellfish** includes Ipswich and Essex clams,

Atlantic lobsters, Wellfleet oysters, scallops, mussels, and shrimp.

Lobster was once so abundant that the Indians showed the Pilgrims how to use the ugly crustaceans as fertilizer, and prisoners rioted when it turned up on the menu too often. Order lobster boiled or steamed and you'll get a plastic bib, drawn butter (for dipping), a nutcracker (for the claws and tail), and a pick (for the legs). Restaurants price lobsters by the pound; you'll typically pay at least $15 to $20 for a "chicken" (1- to 1¼-lb.) lobster, and more for the bigger specimens. If you want someone else to do the work, lobster is available in a "roll" (lobster-salad sandwich), stuffed and baked or broiled, in or over pasta, in a "pie" (casserole), in salad, and in bisque.

Well-made **New England clam chowder** is studded with fresh clams and thickened with cream. Recipes vary, but they *never* include tomatoes. (Tomatoes go in Manhattan clam chowder.) If you want clams but not soup, many places serve **steamers,** or soft-shell clams cooked in the shell, as an appetizer or main dish. More common are hard-shell clams—**littlenecks** (small) or **cherrystones** (medium-size)—served raw, like oysters.

Traditional **Boston baked beans,** which date from colonial days, when cooking on the Sabbath was forbidden, earned Boston the nickname "Beantown." House-made baked beans can be hard to find (Durgin-Park does an excellent rendition), but where you do, you'll probably also find good cornbread and **brown bread**—more like a steamed pudding of whole wheat and rye flour, cornmeal, molasses, buttermilk, and usually raisins.

Finally, **Boston cream pie** is golden layer cake sandwiched around custard and topped with chocolate glaze—no cream, no pie.

3

Planning Your Trip to Boston

A visit to Boston requires as much or as little forethought as you want, taking into account one important general rule: The later you plan, the more you'll pay. That isn't strictly true in the depths of winter, but for the other 46 or so weeks of the year, you'll most likely find yourself balancing spontaneity against thriftiness.

This chapter addresses practical issues such as transportation to and around Boston, timing your visit, and finding more information before you leave home and after you arrive. Getting your bearings is famously difficult, thanks mostly to the baffling street pattern (urban legend says it originated as a network of cow paths, but the layout owes more to 17th-century London and to Boston's original shoreline); this chapter will help you start getting acclimated. Here I'll also fill you in on the unpredictable climate and the events, festivals, and parades that can help make your trip even more memorable.

For additional help in planning your trip and for more on-the-ground resources in Boston, please turn to the "Fast Facts, Toll-Free Numbers & Websites" appendix on p. 284.

1 Visitor Information

BEFORE YOU LEAVE HOME

The **Greater Boston Convention & Visitors Bureau,** 2 Copley Place, Suite 105, Boston, MA 02116-6501 (© **888/SEE-BOSTON** or 617/536-4100, 0171/431-3434 in the U.K.; www.bostonusa.com), offers a comprehensive visitor information kit ($10) that includes a travel planner, a guidebook, a map, pamphlets, and coupons for shopping, dining, attractions, and nightlife discounts. The bureau also publishes a *Kids Love Boston* guide ($5) and free smaller guides to specific seasons and special events.

For information about Cambridge, contact the **Cambridge Office for Tourism,** 4 Brattle St., Suite 208, Cambridge, MA 02138 (© **800/862-5678** or 617/441-2884; fax 617/441-7736; www.cambridge-usa.org).

The **Massachusetts Office of Travel and Tourism,** 10 Park Plaza, Suite 4510, Boston, MA 02116 (© **800/227-MASS** or 617/973-8500; fax 617/973-8525; www.massvacation.com), distributes information about the whole state. Its free *Getaway Guide* magazine includes information about attractions and lodgings, a map, and a calendar.

AFTER YOU ARRIVE

Head to a **visitor information center** to pick up free maps, brochures, listings of special exhibits and events, and other materials.

National Park Service rangers staff the **Boston National Historical Park Visitor Center,** 15 State St. (© **617/242-5642;** www.nps.gov/bost; T: Blue or Orange Line to State St.), across the street from the Old State House, and lead seasonal free tours of the Freedom Trail. The center is open daily from 9am to 5pm. The ranger-staffed center at the

Charlestown Navy Yard (© 617/242-5601) keeps the same hours.

The **Freedom Trail** (p. 148), a line of red paint or painted brick on or in the sidewalk, begins at the **Boston Common Information Center,** 148 Tremont St., on the Common. The center is open Monday through Saturday from 8:30am to 5pm, Sunday from 9am to 5pm. The **Prudential Information Center,** on the main level of the Prudential Center, 800 Boylston St., is open Monday through Friday from 8:30am to 6pm, Saturday and Sunday from 10am to 6pm. The **Greater Boston Convention & Visitors Bureau** (© **888/SEE-BOSTON** or 617/536-4100; www.bostonusa.com) operates both centers.

There's a small information booth at **Faneuil Hall Marketplace** between Quincy Market and the South Market Building. It's outdoors and staffed in the spring, summer, and fall Monday through Saturday from 10am to 6pm, Sunday from noon to 6pm.

In Cambridge, an information kiosk (© **800/862-5678** or 617/497-1630) sits in the heart of **Harvard Square,** near the T entrance at the intersection of Massachusetts Avenue, John F. Kennedy Street, and Brattle Street. It's open Monday through Saturday from 9am to 5pm, Sunday from 1 to 5pm.

USEFUL WEBSITES

- **Boston.com** (www.boston.com): The comprehensive online home of the *Boston Globe;* also check out the affiliated website **Explore New England** (www.explorenewengland.com).
- **Citysearch** (http://boston.citysearch.com): Exhaustive listings, including restaurants and clubs, accompanied by professional and hit-or-miss amateur reviews.
- **National Park Service** (www.nps.gov): An endlessly helpful resource

for visitors to Boston and its history-rich suburbs.

- **MBTA** (www.mbta.com): The go-to site for subway, trolley, bus, ferry, and commuter-rail schedules and route maps, plus fare and pass information and an interactive route planner.
- **Hopstop** (www.hopstop.com/?city=boston): This interactive site makes a decent backup to the MBTA route planner, which generally does a better job of accommodating local quirks.
- **Gridskipper** (www.gridskipper.com/travel/boston): Gawker Media's irreverent travel blog; check the homepage for coverage of eclectic general-interest topics.
- **Bostonist** (www.bostonist.com): A lively blog; features include original and rehashed news coverage and enjoyably random event listings.
- **Boston-to-English Dictionary** (www.boston-online.com/glossary.html): Hilarious yet useful lingo and slang.

MAPS

To supplement the maps provided with this guide, pick up free maps of downtown Boston and the subway lines at visitor information centers around the city, from hotel concierge desks and pamphlet racks, and from most trolley operators (ask the ticket seller). **National Park Service** maps, available from the visitor centers at 15 State St. and the Charlestown Navy Yard, are especially useful. *Where* magazine, available free at most hotels, contains maps of central Boston and the T.

Streetwise Boston ($6.95) and *Artwise Boston* ($7.95) are sturdy, laminated maps available at most bookstores. Less detailed and a bit unwieldy but more fun is *MapEasy's GuideMap to Boston* ($5.50), a hand-drawn map of central areas and major attractions.

Boston & Surrounding Areas

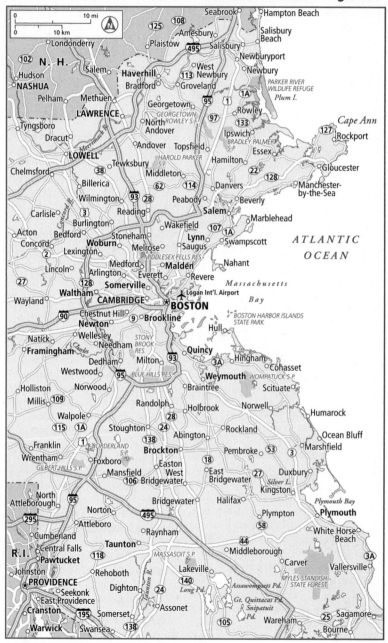

2 Entry Requirements

PASSPORTS

With a few exceptions, the United States requires international travelers to carry a passport; most visitors must also have a visa.

Department of Homeland Security regulations require virtually every air traveler entering the U.S. to show a passport. As of January 23, 2007, all persons, including U.S. citizens, traveling by air between the United States and Canada, Mexico, Central and South America, the Caribbean, and Bermuda are required to present a valid passport. As of January 31, 2008, U.S. and Canadian citizens entering the U. S. at land and sea ports of entry from within the western hemisphere will need to present government-issued proof of citizenship, such as a birth certificate, along with a government-issued photo ID, such as a driver's license. A passport is not required for U.S. or Canadian citizens entering by land or sea, but carrying one is highly encouraged.

For information on how to obtain a passport, go to "**Passports**" in the "**Fast Facts**" appendix (p. 290).

VISAS

The U.S. State Department has a **Visa Waiver Program (VWP)** allowing citizens of the following countries to enter the United States without a visa for stays of up to 90 days: Andorra, Australia, Austria, Belgium, Brunei, Denmark, Finland, France, Germany, Iceland, Ireland, Italy, Japan, Liechtenstein, Luxembourg, Monaco, the Netherlands, New Zealand, Norway, Portugal, San Marino, Singapore, Slovenia, Spain, Sweden, Switzerland, and the United Kingdom. (*Note:* This list was accurate at press time; for the most up-to-date list of countries in the VWP, consult www.travel.state.gov/visa.) Canadian citizens may enter the United States without visas; they will need to show passports (if traveling by

air) and proof of residence, however. *Note:* Any passport issued on or after October 26, 2006, by a VWP country must be an **e-Passport** for VWP travelers to be eligible to enter the U.S. without a visa. Citizens of these nations also need to present a round-trip air or cruise ticket upon arrival. E-Passports contain computer chips capable of storing biometric information, such as the required digital photograph of the holder. (You can identify an e-Passport by the symbol on the bottom center cover of your passport.) If your passport doesn't have this feature, you can still travel without a visa if it is a valid passport issued before October 26, 2005, and includes a machine-readable zone, or between October 26, 2005, and October 25, 2006, and includes a digital photograph. For more information, go to **www.travel.state.gov/visa**.

Citizens of all other countries must have (1) a valid passport that expires at least 6 months later than the scheduled end of their visit to the U.S., and (2) a tourist visa, which may be obtained without charge from any U.S. consulate.

With some exceptions, international visitors traveling on visas to the United States will be photographed and fingerprinted on arrival at Customs in airports and on cruise ships under a Department of Homeland Security program called **US-VISIT.** Exempt from the extra scrutiny are visitors entering by land or those (mostly in Europe; see above) who don't require a visa for short-term visits. For more information, go to the Homeland Security website at **www.dhs.gov** and click "Travel Security & Procedures."

For specifics on how to get a visa, go to "**Visas**" in the "**Fast Facts**" appendix (p. 292).

MEDICAL REQUIREMENTS

Unless you're arriving from an area known to be suffering from an epidemic (particularly cholera or yellow fever), inoculations or vaccinations are not required for entry into the United States.

CUSTOMS
WHAT YOU CAN BRING INTO THE U.S.

Every visitor over 21 years of age may bring in, free of duty, the following: (1) 1 liter of wine or hard liquor; (2) 200 cigarettes, 100 cigars (but not from Cuba), or 3 pounds of smoking tobacco; and (3) $100 worth of gifts. These exemptions are offered to travelers who spend at least 72 hours in the United States and who have not claimed them within the preceding 6 months. It is forbidden to bring into the country almost any meat products (including canned, fresh, and dried meat products such as bouillon, soup mixes, and the like). Generally, condiments including vinegars, oils, spices, coffee, tea, and some cheeses and baked goods are permitted. Avoid products made from rice, which can often harbor insects. Bringing fruits and vegetables is not advised, though not prohibited. Customs will allow produce depending on where you got it and where you're going after you arrive in the U.S. International tourists may carry in or out up to $10,000 in U.S. or foreign currency with no formalities; larger sums must be declared to U.S. Customs on entering or leaving, which includes filing form CM 4790. For details regarding U.S. Customs and Border Protection, consult your nearest U.S. embassy or consulate, or **U.S. Customs** (www.customs.ustreas.gov).

WHAT YOU CAN TAKE HOME FROM BOSTON

Canadian Citizens: For a clear summary of Canadian rules, write for the booklet *I Declare,* issued by the **Canada Border Services Agency** (© 800/461-9999 in Canada, or 204/983-3500; www.cbsa-asfc.gc.ca).

U.K. Citizens: For information, contact **HM Customs & Excise** (© 0845/ 010-9000, or 020/8929-0152 from outside the U.K.; www.hmce.gov.uk).

Australian Citizens: A helpful brochure available from Australian consulates or Customs offices is *Know Before You Go.* For more information, consult the **Australian Customs Service** (© 1300/ 363-263; www.customs.gov.au).

New Zealand Citizens: Most questions are answered in a free pamphlet available at New Zealand consulates and Customs offices: *New Zealand Customs Guide for Travellers, Notice no. 4.* For more information, contact **New Zealand Customs,** The Customhouse, 17–21 Whitmore St., Box 2218, Wellington (© 04/473-6099 or 0800/428-786; www.customs.govt.nz).

Boston's Average Temperatures & Rainfall

	Jan	Feb	Mar	Apr	May	June	July	Aug	Sept	Oct	Nov	Dec
Temp. (°F)	30	31	38	49	59	68	74	72	65	55	45	34
Temp. (°C)	−1	−1	3	9	15	20	23	22	18	13	7	1
Rainfall (in.)	3.8	3.5	4.0	3.7	3.4	3.0	2.8	3.6	3.3	3.3	4.4	4.2

3 When to Go

Boston attracts throngs of visitors year-round. Between April and November, the city sees hardly any slow times. Make reservations as early as possible if you plan to visit during traditionally busy periods.

The periods around college graduation (May and early June) and major citywide events (see "Boston Calendar of Events" below) are especially busy. Spring and fall are popular times for conventions.

Fun Fact Poetry 101 (Degrees)

In Boston, you can check the weather forecast by looking up at the short column of lights on top of the old John Hancock building in the Back Bay. (The new Hancock building is the 60-story glass tower next door.) It has its own poem: *Steady blue, clear view; flashing blue, clouds due; steady red, rain ahead; flashing red, snow instead.* During the summer, flashing red means that the Red Sox game is canceled.

Families pour into the area in July and August, creating long lines at many attractions. Summer isn't the most expensive time to visit, though: Foliage season, from mid-September to early November, when many leaf-peepers stay in the Boston area or pass through on the way to other New England destinations, is a huge draw. December is less busy but still a convention time—look out for weekend bargains.

The "slow" season is January through March, when many hotels offer great deals, especially on weekends. However, this is when unpredictable weather plagues the Northeast (often affecting travel schedules) and when some suburban attractions close for the winter.

WEATHER

You've probably heard the saying about New England weather: "If you don't like it, wait 10 minutes." Variations from day to day (if not minute to minute) can be enormous. You can roast in March and freeze in June, shiver in July and sweat in November. Dressing in layers is always a good idea.

Spring and fall are the best bets for moderate temperatures, but spring (also known as mud season) is brief. It doesn't usually settle in until early May, and snow sometimes falls in April. Summers are hot, especially in July and August, and can be uncomfortably humid. Fall is when you're most likely to catch a comfortable run of dry, sunny days and cool nights. Winters are cold and usually snowy—bring a warm coat and sturdy boots.

BOSTON CALENDAR OF EVENTS

The **Greater Boston Convention & Visitors Bureau** (© 888/SEE-BOSTON or 617/536-4100; www.bostonusa.com) operates a regularly updated hot line that describes ongoing and upcoming events. The **Mayor's Office of Arts, Tourism & Special Events** (© 617/635-3911; www.cityofboston.gov/arts) can provide information about specific happenings. If you're planning at the last minute, the arts sections of the daily *Boston Globe* and *Boston Herald* are always packed with ideas.

For an exhaustive list of events beyond those listed here, check http://events.frommers.com, where you'll find a searchable, up-to-the-minute roster of what's happening in cities all over the world.

January

Martin Luther King, Jr., Birthday Celebration, various locations. Events include musical tributes, gospel concerts, museum displays and programs, readings, speeches, and panel discussions. Check special listings in the *Globe* for specifics. Third Monday in January.

Boston Wine Festival, Boston Harbor Hotel and other locations. Tastings, classes, lectures, receptions, and meals provide a lively liquid diversion throughout winter. Look for 20th-anniversary events in 2009. Call the festival reservation line (© **888/660-WINE** or 617/330-9355;

www.bostonwinefestival.net) for details. January to early April.

Chinese New Year, Chinatown. The dragon parade (which draws a big crowd no matter how cold it is), fireworks, and raucous festivals are part of the celebration. Special programs take place at the **Children's Museum** (© 617/ 426-8855; www.bostonkids.org). For more details, visit **www.chinatown mainstreet.org**. Depending on the Chinese lunar calendar, the holiday falls between January 21 and February 19. In 2009, it's January 26.

February

African-American History Month, various locations. Programs include special museum exhibits, children's activities, concerts, films, lectures, discussions, readings, and tours of the Black Heritage Trail led by National Park Service rangers (© 617/742-5415; www.nps.gov/boaf). All month.

School Vacation Week, various locations. The slate of activities includes special exhibitions and programs, plays, concerts, and tours. Contact individual attractions or check the *Globe* for information on programs and extended hours. Third week of February.

March

New England Spring Flower Show, Bayside Expo Center, Dorchester. This annual harbinger of spring, presented by the **Massachusetts Horticultural Society** (© 617/933-4900; www.mass hort.org), draws huge crowds starved for a glimpse of green. Plan to take public transit. Second or third week of March.

St. Patrick's Day Celebrations, various locations. Concerts, talks, special restaurant menus, and other offerings celebrate the heritage of one of the most Irish American cities. Note that the parade, along Broadway in South Boston, is not a city-sponsored event; the organization that runs it is private and therefore free to bar any group it wants to from marching. That includes gays and, at least once in recent years, antiwar veterans. March 17; parade is on the closest Sunday.

College Sports Extravaganza. In 2009, Boston plays host to the semifinals and finals of the **Men's Hockey East Tournament,** to an **NCAA Men's Basketball East Regional,** both at the TD Banknorth Garden (© 617/624-1000; www.tdbanknorthgarden.com), and to the **NCAA Women's Frozen Four** (hockey), at Boston University's Agganis Arena (© 617/358-7000; www.bu.edu/agganis). Expect giddy crowds, sold-out hotels, and packed sports bars. Hockey East (www.hockey east.com), late March; Frozen Four (www.ncaa.com), March 20–22; East Regional, March 26–28 (www.ncaa. com).

April

Big Apple Circus (www.bigapple circus.org), City Hall Plaza, Government Center. The New York–based "one-ring wonder" performs in a heated tent with all seating less than 50 feet from the ring. Proceeds support the Children's Museum. Visit the museum box office or contact Ticketmaster (© 617/931-ARTS; www.ticket master.com). Late March to early May.

Red Sox Opening Day, Fenway Park. Even if your concierge is a magician, this is an extremely tough ticket. Check ahead (© 877/REDSOX-9; www.redsox.com) when tickets for the season go on sale in December. If you can't get tickets to Opening Day, try to see the 10am game on **Patriots Day,** the third Monday in April. It begins so early to allow spectators to watch the Boston Marathon afterward. Early and mid-April.

Swan Boats Return to the Public Garden. Since their introduction in 1877, the Swan Boats (✆ 617/522-1966; www.swanboats.com) have been a symbol of Boston. Like real swans, they go away for the winter. Saturday before Patriots Day (in 2009, April 18).

Patriots Day, North End, Lexington, and Concord. Festivities commemorate and reenact the events of April 18 and 19, 1775. Lanterns glow in the steeple of the **Old North Church** (✆ 617/523-6676; www.oldnorth. com). Participants dressed as Paul Revere and William Dawes ride from the **Paul Revere House** (✆ 617/523-2338; www.paulreverehouse.org) in the North End to Lexington and Concord to warn the Minutemen that "the regulars are out" (not that "the British are coming"—most colonists considered themselves British). Musket fire rings out on the Battle Green in Lexington and then at the North Bridge in Concord. Contact the **Lexington Chamber of Commerce Visitor Center** (✆ 781/862-1450; www.lexington chamber.org), or the **Concord Chamber of Commerce** (✆ 978/369-3120; concordchamberofcommerce.org), for information on battle reenactments. See chapter 11 for information on visiting both towns. Third Monday of April (in 2009, April 20).

Boston Marathon, Hopkinton, Massachusetts, to Boston. International stars and local amateurs join in the world's oldest and most famous marathon (www.bostonmarathon.org). The first wave of competitors begins at 9:25am. Cheering fans are welcome until the last weekend warriors stagger across the Boylston Street finish line in the late afternoon. Third Monday of the month (in 2009, April 20).

Freedom Trail Week, various locations in Boston, Cambridge, Lexington, and Concord. This is another school vacation week, with plenty of crowds and diversions. Family-friendly events include tours, concerts, talks, and other programs related to Patriots Day, the Freedom Trail, and the American Revolution. Third week of April.

Independent Film Festival of Boston, various locations. Features, shorts, and documentaries by international filmmakers make up the schedule for this increasingly buzz-worthy event. Check ahead (✆ 617/697-8511; www.iff boston.org) for the schedule. Late April.

May

Museum-Goers' Month, various locations. Contact individual museums or surf ahead for details and schedules of special exhibits, lectures, and events. See chapter 7. All month.

Volvo Ocean Race 2008–2009, Boston Harbor and various waterfront locations. The biggest deal in professional yacht racing makes the only North American stop on its round-the-world route. An in-port competition on or near the harbor takes place the day before the pro-am race, which uses a course designed to make the boats easily visible from the shore. Visit **www. volvooceanrace.org** for more info. Two weeks leading up to the competitors' departure for Galway on May 16.

Lilac Sunday, Arnold Arboretum, Jamaica Plain. This is the only day of the year that the arboretum (✆ 617/524-1717; www.arboretum.harvard. edu) allows picnicking. From sunrise to sunset, wander the grounds and enjoy the sensational spring flowers, including more than 400 varieties of lilacs in bloom. Mid-May.

Street Performers Festival, Faneuil Hall Marketplace. Everyone but the pigeons gets into the act as musicians, magicians, jugglers, sword swallowers, and artists strut their stuff. Late May.

June

Boston Pride March, Back Bay to Beacon Hill (© **617/262-9405;** www. bostonpride.org). The largest gay pride parade in New England is the highlight of a weeklong celebration of diversity. The parade, on the second Sunday of the month, starts at Copley Square and ends on Boston Common. Early June.

Dragon Boat Festival, Charles River near Harvard Square, Cambridge (www. bostondragonboat.org). Teams of paddlers synchronized by a drummer propel boats with dragon heads and tails as they race 500m (1,640 ft.). The winners go to the national championships; the spectators go to a celebration of Chinese culture and food on the shore. Second or third Sunday of June.

Central Square World's Fair, Cambridge (© **617/868-3247;** www. cambridgema.gov). This celebration of unity and diversity features the usual food, crafts, and kids' activities—and a twist that elevates the event far above the usual street festival: local and national rock, jazz, and blues musicians. Early or mid-June.

Cambridge River Festival (© **617/ 349-4380;** www.cambridgeartscouncil. org), Memorial Drive from John F. Kennedy Street to Western Avenue. A salute to the arts, the festival incorporates live music, dancing, children's activities, crafts and art exhibits, and international food on the banks of the Charles. Mid-June.

July

Boston Harborfest, downtown, the waterfront, and the Harbor Islands. The city puts on its Sunday best for the Fourth of July, a gigantic weeklong celebration of Boston's maritime history. Events surrounding Boston Harborfest (© **617/227-1528;** www.boston harborfest.com) include concerts, children's activities, cruises, fireworks, the

Boston Chowderfest, guided tours, talks, and USS *Constitution's* turnaround cruise. Beginning of the month (June 30–July 5, 2009).

Boston Pops Concert and Fireworks Display, Hatch Shell, on the Esplanade. Spectators start showing up at dawn (overnight camping is not permitted) to stake out a good spot on the lawn and spend all day waiting for the sky to get dark enough for fireworks. Others show up at the last minute—the Cambridge side of the river, near Kendall Square, and the Longfellow Bridge are good spots to watch the spectacular aerial show. The program includes the *1812 Overture,* with real cannon fire and church bells. For details, check the website (www.july4th.org). July 4.

Sail Boston 2009, Boston Harbor and the Inner Harbor waterfront. The Tall Ships—magnificent sailing vessels from around the world—parade majestically into the heart of the harbor, berth at piers that are open to the public, and leave town in another stately procession. Festivals, fireworks, and tours of the ships await the millions of visitors who flood eastern Massachusetts for this uniquely enjoyable event. Make reservations as early as possible. For more info, visit **www.sailboston.com**. July 8–13.

Puerto Rican Festival and Parade, Franklin Park. This 5-day event, instituted in 1967, is part street fair, part cultural celebration, with plenty of live music and traditional food. The festival ends with a gala carnival. For details, contact **Festival Puertorriqueño de Massachusetts** (© **866/481-0695;** www.prfestma.org). Late July.

August

Italian-American Feasts, North End. These weekend street fairs begin in July and end in late August with the two biggest: the Fisherman's Feast and the Feast of St. Anthony. The sublime (fresh seafood prepared while you wait, live music, dancing in the street) mingles with the ridiculous (carnival games, tacky T-shirts, fried-dough stands) to leave a lasting impression of fun and indigestion. Visit www.fisher mansfeast.com or www.saintanthonys feast.com for a preview. Weekends throughout August.

August Moon Festival, Chinatown. A celebration of the harvest and the coming of autumn, the festival includes dragon and lion dances during the parade through the crowded streets, and demonstrations of crafts and martial arts. It's also an excuse to stuff yourself with tasty mooncakes. For details, visit **www.chinatownmain street.org**. Mid-August.

September

Boston Film Festival (℃ 617/523-8388; www.bostonfilmfestival.org), various locations. Independent films continue on the festival circuit or make their premieres, sometimes following a lecture by an actor or filmmaker. Most screenings are open to the public without advance tickets. Mid-September.

October

Salem Haunted Happenings, various locations. Parades, parties, a special commuter-rail ride from Boston, fortune-telling, cruises, and tours lead up to a ceremony on Halloween. Contact **Destination Salem** (℃ 877/SALEM-MA) or check the website (www. hauntedhappenings.org) for specifics. All month.

An Evening with Champions, Bright Athletic Center, Allston. World-class ice skaters and promising local students stage three performances to benefit the Jimmy Fund, the children's fundraising arm of the Dana-Farber Cancer Institute. Sponsored by Harvard's **Eliot House** (℃ 617/493-8172; www.hcs.

harvard.edu/~ewc). Early or mid-October (tickets on sale in August).

Oktoberfest, Harvard Square, Cambridge. This immense street fair is a magnet for college students, families, street performers, musicians, and crafts vendors. Sponsored by the Harvard Square Business Association (℃ 617/ 491-3434; www.harvardsquare.com). Second Sunday of October.

Ringling Brothers and Barnum & Bailey Circus, TD Banknorth Garden (℃ 617/624-1000 events line, 617/ 931-2000 Ticketmaster; www.tdbank northgarden.com). The Greatest Show on Earth makes its annual 2-week visit. Mid-October.

Head of the Charles Regatta, Boston and Cambridge. High school, college, and postcollegiate rowing teams and individuals—some 4,000 in all—race in front of tens of thousands of fans along the banks of the Charles River and on the bridges spanning it. The Head of the Charles (℃ 617/868-6200; www.hocr.org) has an uncanny tendency to coincide with a crisp, picturesque weekend. Late October.

November

Thanksgiving Celebration, Plymouth (℃ 800/USA-1620; www.visit-plymouth.com). Plymouth observes the holiday with a "stroll through the ages," showcasing 17th- and 19th-century Thanksgiving preparations in historic homes. Menus at **Plimoth Plantation,** which re-creates the colony's first years, include a Victorian Thanksgiving feast. Reservations (℃ 800/262-9356 or 508/746-1622; www.plimoth.org) are accepted beginning in June. Thanksgiving Day.

December

The Nutcracker, Opera House, Boston. Boston Ballet's annual holiday extravaganza is one of the country's biggest and best. This is *the* traditional

Value **Let's Make a Deal**

Southwest (© 800/435-9792; www.southwest.com) doesn't serve Boston, but it has helped redefine "Boston-area airport," creating two magnets for budget-conscious travelers. They're not nearly as convenient as Logan, but fares to either of these airports—on Southwest and other national carriers—can be considerably cheaper than those to Logan.

If you're not renting a car, try to fly into Manchester, New Hampshire. **Manchester–Boston Regional Airport** (© 603/624-6556; www.flymanchester.com; airport code MHT) is in southern New Hampshire, about 51 miles north of Boston. Under a pilot program, the airport offers free **Manchester Shuttle** van service to and from Boston (the Sullivan Square Orange Line T stop) and suburban Woburn, Mass.; check the website for details. In addition, **Vermont Transit** (© 800/552-8737; www.vermonttransit.com) runs buses to Boston's South Station eight times a day; three continue to Logan Airport. The trip takes 60 to 90 minutes; the fare is $20 one-way, $39 round-trip.

T. F. Green Airport (© 888/268-7222; www.pvdairport.com; airport code PVD) is in the Providence suburb of Warwick, Rhode Island, about 60 miles south of Boston. **Peter Pan Bonanza** (© 888/751-8800; www.peterpanbus.com) buses run to and from Boston; the fare is $20 one-way, $37 round-trip. If necessary, you can also take a cab or the local bus (© 401/781-9400; www.ripta.com) to downtown Providence and transfer to either the **MBTA** commuter rail (© 800/392-6100 or 617/222-3200; www.mbta.com) or **Amtrak** (© 800/USA-RAIL; www.amtrak.com). Allow at least 2 hours, and pack light.

way to expose young Bostonians (and visitors) to culture, and the spectacular sets make it practically painless. Visit the website (www.bostonballet.org) for more info. For tickets, call **Tele-charge** (© 800/447-7400 or TTY 888/889-8587; www.telecharge.com) as soon as you plan your trip, ask whether your hotel offers a *Nutcracker* package, or cross your fingers and visit the box office when you arrive. Thanksgiving weekend through late December.

Boston Tea Party Reenactment, Old South Meeting House (© 617/482-6439; www.oldsouthmeetinghouse.org) and Tea Party Ship and Museum, Congress Street Bridge (© 617/338-1773; www.bostonteapartyship.com).

Chafing under British rule, American colonists rose up on December 16, 1773, to strike a blow where it would cause real pain—in the pocketbook. A re-creation of the pre-party rally at the meeting house is a lively all-ages audience-participation event; call ahead to see whether the ship has reopened during your visit. Mid-December.

Black Nativity, Converse Hall, Tremont Temple Baptist Church, 88 Tremont St. (© 617/723-3486; www.blacknativity.org). Poet Langston Hughes wrote the "gospel opera," and a cast of more than 100 brings it to life. Check ahead for 40th-anniversary events in 2009. Most weekends in December.

Christmas Revels, Sanders Theatre, Cambridge. This multicultural celebration of the winter solstice features the holiday customs of a different culture each year. Themes have included the Balkans, Victorian England, and Romany Gypsies. Be ready to sing along. For information, contact the **Revels** (*C* **617/972-8300;** www.revels. org); for tickets, call the **box office** (*C* **617/496-2222**). Last 2 weeks of the month.

First Night, Back Bay and the waterfront. This is the original arts-oriented, no-alcohol, citywide New Year's Eve celebration. It begins in the early afternoon and includes a parade, ice sculptures, art exhibitions, theatrical performances, and indoor and outdoor entertainment. Some attractions require tickets, but for most you just need a First Night button, available for $15 or so at visitor centers and stores around the city. Fireworks light up the sky above Boston Common at 7pm and over Boston Harbor at midnight. For details, contact **First Night** (*C* **617/ 542-1399;** www.firstnight.org) or check the newspapers when you arrive. December 31.

4 Getting There & Getting Around

GETTING TO BOSTON
BY PLANE

Most major U.S. carriers serve Boston's **Logan International Airport,** which the locals usually just call "Logan" (airport code BOS).

Boston is an increasingly popular direct destination for international travelers, although many itineraries from overseas still go through another American or European city. Because of fluctuating demand, international routes and schedules are subject to change; double-check details (especially if you're traveling in the winter) well in advance.

Logan is in East Boston at the end of the Sumner, Callahan, and Ted Williams tunnels, 3 miles across the harbor from downtown. For a preview and real-time flight arrival and departure information, visit the website (www.massport.com/ logan).

The airport has four terminals—A, B, C, and E (there's no D)—each with ATMs, Internet kiosks, pay phones with dataports, fax machines, and an information booth (near baggage claim). Wireless Internet access is available all over the airport for $8 a day through **Logan WiFi** (*C* **617/561-9434;** www.loganwifi.com). Terminals C and E have bank branches that handle currency exchange. Terminals A and C have children's play spaces.

See the "Let's Make a Deal" box below for information on flying into Providence, Rhode Island, and Manchester, New Hampshire.

Arriving at the Airport
IMMIGRATION & CUSTOMS CLEARANCE International visitors arriving by air, no matter what the port of entry, should cultivate patience and resignation before setting foot on U.S. soil. U.S. airports have considerably beefed up security clearances in the years since the terrorist attacks of September 11, and clearing Customs and Immigration can take as long as 2 hours.

Getting into Town from the Airport

The Massachusetts Port Authority, or **MassPort** (*C* **800/23-LOGAN;** www. massport.com), coordinates airport transportation. The toll-free line provides information about getting to the city and to many nearby suburbs. It's available 24 hours a day and is staffed weekdays from 8am to 7pm.

The ride into town takes 10 to 45 minutes, depending on traffic, your destination, and the time of day. Except at off hours, such as early on weekend mornings, driving is the slowest way to get into central Boston. If you must travel during rush hours or on Sunday afternoon, allow plenty of extra time or plan to take the subway or water taxi (and pack accordingly).

You can get into town by bus, subway, cab, van, or boat. If you're taking the Silver Line bus or the subway, look for MBTA fare kiosks tucked into corners near the exits closest to the public transit pick-up area in each terminal.

The Silver Line **bus** stops at each airport terminal and runs directly to South Station, where you can connect to the Red Line subway and the commuter rail to the southern suburbs. It takes about 20 minutes, not including waiting time, and costs just $1.70 (with a pass or CharlieCard) or $2 (with a CharlieTicket or cash)—a great deal if your final destination is near South Station or in Cambridge.

The **subway (the T)** takes just 10 minutes to reach downtown, but first you have to reach the subway. Free **shuttle buses** run from each terminal to the Airport station on the Blue Line of the T from 5:30am to 1am every day, year-round. The Blue Line stops at Aquarium, State Street, and Government Center, downtown points where you can exit or transfer to the other lines. The fare is $1.70 (with a pass or CharlieCard) or $2 (with a CharlieTicket or cash).

Just getting into a **cab** at the airport costs an appalling $9.75 ($7.50 in fees plus the initial $2.25 fare). The total fare to downtown or the Back Bay usually runs $20 to $35, and may be as high as $45 in bad traffic. Depending on traffic, the driver might use the Ted Williams Tunnel for destinations outside downtown, such as the Back Bay. On a map, this doesn't look like the fastest route, but often it is.

The Logan Airport website (www. massport.com/logan) lists numerous companies that operate **shuttle-van service** to local hotels. One-way prices start at $14 per person and are subject to fuel surcharges as gas prices fluctuate.

The trip to the downtown waterfront in a weather-protected **boat** takes about 7 minutes and costs $10 one-way. Service is available from early morning through early evening, with reduced schedules on weekends; at press time, all four providers operate year-round. The free no. 66 shuttle bus connects the airport terminals to the Logan ferry dock. Leaving the airport, ask the shuttle driver to radio ahead for water-taxi pickup; on the way back, call ahead for service.

Three on-call water-taxi services serve the downtown waterfront and other points around Boston Harbor: **City Water Taxi** (© 617/422-0392; www.citywatertaxi.com), **Rowes Wharf Water Transport** (© 617/406-8584; www.roweswharfwatertransport.com), and **Boston Harbor Water Taxi** (© 617/593-9168; www.bostonharborwatertaxi.com). The MBTA (© 800/392-6100 or 617/222-3200; www.mbta.com) contracts out scheduled ferry service to **Harbor Express,** which runs to Long Wharf, behind the Marriott Long Wharf hotel.

Some hotels have their own **shuttles** or **limousines;** ask about them when you make your reservation. To arrange private limo service, call ahead for a reservation, especially at busy times. Your hotel can recommend a company, or try **Boston Coach** (© 800/672-7676; www.bostoncoach.com), **Carey Limousine Boston** (© 800/336-4646 or 617/623-8700; www.carey.com), or **Commonwealth Limousine Service** (© 800/558-LIMO or 617/787-1110; www.commonwealthlimo.com).

Unless you need it right away, seriously consider waiting to pick up your **rental car** until you're starting a day trip or other excursion. You'll avoid airport fees, tunnel tolls, hotel parking charges, and, most important, Boston traffic.

BY CAR

Renting a car for a long trip will almost certainly be more expensive and less convenient than any other means of reaching Boston, and I can't recommend it. It's not that driving to Boston is difficult. But parking is scarce and wildly expensive, gasoline gets pricier by the day, traffic is terrible, and the drivers are famously reckless. If you're thinking of driving to Boston only because you want to use the car to get around town, think again.

If you have to drive, try to book a hotel or a special package that offers free parking (see chapter 5). If you pay for parking, expect it to cost at least $25 a day downtown, and build that into your budget.

Three major highways converge in Boston. **I-90,** also known as the Massachusetts Turnpike ("Mass. Pike" to the locals), is an east–west toll road that originates at Logan Airport and links up with the New York State Thruway. **I-93/U.S. 1** extends north to Canada. **I-93/Route 3,** the Southeast Expressway, connects Boston with the south, including Cape Cod. To avoid driving downtown, exit the Mass. Pike at Cambridge/Allston or at the Prudential Center in the Back Bay. **I-95** (Massachusetts Rte. 128) is a beltway about 11 miles from downtown that connects Boston to highways in Rhode Island, Connecticut, and New York to the south, and New Hampshire and Maine to the north.

Note: The Mass. Pike's **FastLane** program is compatible with New York's **EZPass;** your regular transponder will work in designated lanes in all states that use these systems, including New Hampshire and Maine. If you have a prepaid device from another highway system, check before you leave home to see whether you too can zip (at the speed limit, 15 mph) through the special lanes.

The approach to Cambridge is **Storrow Drive** or **Memorial Drive,** which run along either side of the Charles River. Storrow Drive has a Harvard Square exit that leads across the Anderson Bridge to John F. Kennedy Street and into the square. Memorial Drive intersects with Kennedy Street; turn away from the bridge to reach the square.

Boston is 218 miles from New York City; driving time is about 4½ hours. The 992-mile drive from Chicago to Boston should take around 21 hours; from Washington, D.C., it takes 8 to 9 hours to cover the 468 miles.

In an emergency, you can call the **State Police** on a cellphone by dialing ✆ *911. The **American Automobile Association (AAA;** ✆ **800/AAA-HELP;** www.aaa.com) provides members with maps, itineraries, and other travel information, and arranges free towing if you break down. The Mass. Pike is a privately operated road that arranges its own towing. If you break down there, ask the AAA operator for advice.

It's impossible to say this often enough: **When you reach your hotel, leave your car in the garage** and walk or use public transportation. Use the car for day trips, and before you set out, ask at the front desk for a route that avoids construction (it's everywhere).

For listings of the major car rental agencies in Boston, please see the Toll-Free Numbers & Websites appendix (p. 284).

BY TRAIN

Boston has three rail centers: **South Station,** 700 Atlantic Ave. (at Summer St.), near the Waterfront and the Financial District; **Back Bay Station,** 145 Dartmouth St. (between Huntington and Columbus aves.), across from the Copley Place mall; and **North Station,** on Causeway Street under the TD Banknorth Garden. **Amtrak** (✆ **800/USA-RAIL** or 617/482-3660; www.amtrak.com) serves

Tips High- & Low-End New York Bus Options

Many travelers find standard interstate bus service inadequate; for others, it's too swanky. Both have options on the New York–Boston route.

Business-oriented **LimoLiner** (© 888/546-5469; www.limoliner.com) service connects the Back Bay Hilton, 40 Dalton St., to the Hilton New York, 1335 Ave. of the Americas (with an on-request stop in Framingham, Mass.). The luxury coach seats 28 and has Internet access, work tables, leather seats, and an on-board attendant. The one-way fare is $89.

At the other end of the spectrum is the so-called **Chinatown bus,** the generic term for service between Boston and New York's Chinatown. I've seen too many news reports and heard too many anecdotal accounts of poor maintenance and unsatisfactory service to give this option an unqualified recommendation, but it's madly popular with students and other bargain-hunters. The one-way fare is about $15. The largest operator is **Fung Wah** (© 212/925-8889 or 617/345-8000; www.fungwahbus.com), which connects Boston's South Station and Canal Street in Manhattan. Two recent entrants to this cutthroat competition are **BoltBus** (no phone; www.boltbus.com), which offers on-board WiFi service, and MegaBus (© 877/GO2-MEGA; www.megabus.com). Boston–New York fares start at $1 and top out around $20, subject to fuel-price adjustments.

---

all train stations, and each one is also a stop on the MBTA **subway.** At South Station you can take the Red Line to Cambridge or to Park Street, the system's hub, where you can make connections to the Green, Blue, and Orange lines. The Orange Line connects Back Bay Station with Downtown Crossing, where there's a walkway to Park Street station. North Station is a Green and Orange Line stop.

Amtrak runs to South Station from New York and points south and in between, with stops at Route 128 and Back Bay. Its Downeaster service (www. thedowneaster.com) connects North Station to Portland, Maine, with several stops en route. At press time, continued funding for this route was uncertain; check long before you plan to travel to be sure it's still operating. The MBTA **commuter rail** runs to Ipswich, Rockport, and Fitchburg from North Station and to points south of Boston, including Plymouth, from South Station.

Bear in mind that the train might not be cheaper than flying, especially for long trips. Like the airlines, Amtrak adjusts fares depending on demand, so plan as far ahead as possible to get the lowest fares. Discounts are never available Friday or Sunday afternoon. Always remember to ask for the discounted rate.

Standard service from New York takes 4½ to just under 6 hours. High-speed Acela Express service is scheduled to take just over 3 hours. From Washington, D.C., count on a grueling 7½ to 8½ hours for the slowest service, 6 hours for Acela service.

BY BUS

The bus is the only way out of many small New England towns. If you're coming from almost anywhere else, consider long-distance bus travel a last resort. The exception is the **New York** route, which is so desirable that Greyhound and Peter Pan have upgraded service. It's frequent and relatively fast (4–4½ hr.), and the price is about half the regular train fare. If you can catch an express bus, which makes only one stop, it's worth the extra $5 or so.

Tips The T's Fare-Collection System

Boston has come a long way since the Kingston Trio sang about "Charlie on the MTA"—the transit authority even has a different name—but some things don't change: "Charlie" is the face of the T's automated fare-collection system. Passengers store prepaid fares on two different reloadable passes: The **Charlie-Ticket** is heavy paper with a magnetic strip, and the **CharlieCard** is a plastic "smart card" with an embedded chip. What's the difference? (1) The Charlie-Ticket goes into the front of the turnstile and pops out of the top, while the CharlieCard registers when you hold it in front of the rectangular reader on the front of the turnstile; and (2) fares are lower if you pay with a CharlieCard than if you use a CharlieTicket. CharlieCards are not available from the self-service kiosks that stand at the entrance to each subway station and in each terminal at the airport. In addition to dispensing CharlieTickets, kiosks allow you to add value onto CharlieTickets and CharlieCards, using cash or a credit or debit card. To get a CharlieCard, ask a T employee, order one in advance, or visit a retail location (check the website for a list of convenience stores, newsstands, and other outlets). Consider ordering CharlieCards or CharlieTickets online before you leave home; at press time, shipping is free, and you won't have to buy one immediately upon arriving.

The bus terminal, formally the **South Station Transportation Center,** is on Atlantic Avenue next to the train station. The major lines are **Greyhound** (© 800/231-2222 or 617/526-1800; www.greyhound.com) and **Peter Pan** (© 800/343-9999; www.peterpanbus. com). Other operators include **American Eagle** (© 800/453-5040 or 508/993-5040), Peter Pan affiliate **Bonanza** (© 888/751-8800; www.bonanzabus. com), **Brush Hill Tours** (© 800/343-1328 or 781/986-6100; www.brushhill tours.com), **Concord Trailways** (© 800/639-3317; www.concordtrailways.com), **Plymouth & Brockton** (© 508/746-0378; www.p-b.com), and **Vermont Transit** (© 800/552-8737; www.vermont transit.com).

GETTING AROUND
ON FOOT
If you can manage a fair amount of walking, this is the way to go. You can best appreciate Boston at street level, and walking the narrow, picturesque streets takes you past many gridlocked cars.

Even more than in a typical large city, be alert. Look both ways before crossing, even on one-way streets, where many bicyclists and some drivers blithely go against the flow. The "walk" cycle of many downtown traffic signals lasts only 7 seconds, and a small but significant part of the driving population considers red lights optional anyway. Keep a close eye on the kids, especially in crosswalks. And you're all wearing comfortable shoes, right?

BY PUBLIC TRANSPORTATION
The **Massachusetts Bay Transportation Authority,** or MBTA (© **800/392-6100** or 617/222-3200; www.mbta.com), is known as the "T," and its logo is the letter in a circle. It runs subways, trolleys, buses, and ferries in and around Boston and many suburbs, as well as the commuter rail, which extends as far as Providence, Rhode Island. The automated fare-collection system is a bit involved, but getting the hang of it is easy, and T employees who man every station can answer questions.

For information on services and discounts for seniors and travelers with disabilities, see p. 45.

By Subway & Trolley

Subways and trolleys take you around Boston faster than any other mode of transportation except walking. The oldest system in the country, the T dates to 1897, and recent and ongoing improvements have made it generally reliable. The trolleys on the ancient Green Line are the most unpredictable—leave extra time and carry cab fare if you're on the way to a vital appointment, because you may need to bail out and jump into a taxi. The system is generally safe, but always watch out for pickpockets, especially during the holiday shopping season. And remember, downtown stops are so close together that it's often faster to walk.

The subways are color-coded: the Red, Green, Blue, and Orange lines. The commuter rail to the suburbs is purple on system maps and is sometimes called the Purple Line. The Silver Line is a fancy name for a bus line; the Waterfront branch runs from South Station to the airport via the South Boston waterfront, including the convention center and the World Trade Center. The fare on the subway and the Waterfront Silver Line is **$1.70** if you use a CharlieCard (transfers to local buses are free), **$2** with a CharlieTicket. Children under 12 ride free with a paying adult. Route and fare information and timetables are available through the website (www.mbta.com) and at centrally located stations.

Service begins at around 5:15am and ends around 12:30am. (The exception is New Year's Eve, or First Night, when closing time is 2am and service is free after 8pm.) A sign in every station gives the time of the last train in either direction; if you're planning to be out late and don't see a sign, ask the attendant in the booth near the entrance.

By Bus

The MBTA runs buses and "trackless trolleys" (buses with electric antennae) that provide service around town and to and around the suburbs. The local routes that you'll most likely need are **no. 1,** along Mass. Ave. from Dudley Square in Roxbury through the Back Bay and Cambridge to Harvard Square; **no. 92** and **no. 93,** which connect Haymarket and

---

Value Ride & Save (Maybe)

The MBTA's 1-day and 7-day **LinkPasses** (© **877/927-7277** or 617/222-4545; **www.mbta.com**) can be a great deal—but only if you plan to use public transit enough. Passes cover unlimited travel on the subway and local buses, in commuter rail zone 1A, and on the Inner Harbor ferry. The cost is $9 for 24 hours, which translates to an awful lot of riding before you start to save money. But the longer pass, which costs $15 for 7 consecutive days, is a bargain. At press time, passes must be loaded onto CharlieTickets. Check ahead to see whether you can put yours on a CharlieCard; that should be possible after the commuter rail and water transportation fare-collection systems are converted sometime in 2008. You can order passes—long-term visitors may find one of the numerous commuter passes a better deal than a visitor-oriented LinkPass—in advance over the phone or the Web (minimum six; at press time, shipping is free), or buy them when you arrive at any kiosk or retailer that sells CharlieTickets and CharlieCards.

Charlestown; and **no. 77,** along Mass. Ave. north of Harvard Square to Porter Square, North Cambridge, and Arlington. The Washington Street branch of the **Silver Line,** which runs from Temple Place, near Downtown Crossing, to the South End and Roxbury, is considered a bus line.

The fare on the local bus and Washington Street Silver Line is **$1.25** with a CharlieCard (transferring to the subway costs 45¢), **$1.50** with a CharlieTicket or cash. Children under 12 ride free with a paying adult. If you're paying cash, exact change is required.

By Ferry

The MBTA Inner Harbor ferry connects **Long Wharf** (near the New England Aquarium) with the **Charlestown Navy Yard**—it's a good way to get back downtown from "Old Ironsides" and the Bunker Hill Monument. The fare is $1.70, or show your LinkPass. Call ✆ **617/ 227-4321** for more information.

BY TAXI

Taxis are expensive and not always easy to find—seek out a cab stand or call a dispatcher. Always ask for a receipt in case you have a complaint or lose something and need to call the company.

Cabs usually queue up near hotels. There are also busy cab stands at Faneuil Hall Marketplace (on North St. and in front of 60 State St.), South Station, and Back Bay Station, and on either side of Mass. Ave. in Harvard Square, near the Harvard Coop bookstore and Au Bon Pain.

To call ahead for a cab, try the **Independent Taxi Operators Association,** or ITOA (✆ 617/426-8700; www.itoataxi. com); **Boston Cab** (✆ 617/536-5010 or 617/262-2227); **Town Taxi** (✆ 617/ 536-5000; www.towntaxiboston.com); **City Cab** (✆ 617/536-5100); or **Metro Cab** (✆ 617/782-5500; www.boston-cab. com). In Cambridge, call **Ambassador**

Brattle (✆ 617/492-1100) or **Yellow Cab** (✆ 617/547-3000). Boston Cab will dispatch a wheelchair-accessible vehicle upon request; advance notice is recommended.

The fare structure: The first ¼ mile (when the flag drops) costs $2.25, and each additional ⅛ mile is 30¢. Wait time is extra, and the passenger pays all tolls, as well as a total of $7.50 in fees, which includes the tunnel toll on trips leaving Logan Airport. Charging a flat rate is not allowed within the city; the police department publishes a list (available on the airport website, www.massport.com/logan) of flat rates for trips to the suburbs. If you want to report a problem or have lost something in a cab, call the police department's **Hackney Unit** (✆ 617/343- 4475; www.cityofboston.gov/police; click "Taxi Issues" for the complaint form).

BY WATER TAXI

Three companies serve various stops around the waterfront, including the airport, in covered boats. They operate daily year-round, from 7am until at least 7pm (later in the summer). One-way fares start at $10. Reservations are recommended but not required; you can call from the dock for pick-up. The companies are **City Water Taxi** (✆ 617/422-0392; www.city watertaxi.com), **Rowes Wharf Water Taxi** (✆ 617/406-8584; www.roweswharf watertransport.com), and **Boston Harbor Water Taxi** (✆ 617/593-9168; www. bostonharborwatertaxi.com).

BY WATER SHUTTLE

Seaport Express (✆ 617/939-4802; www.seaporttma.org) is a weekday-only scheduled service operated by Rowes Wharf Water Transport (see above). It connects Rowes Wharf, behind the Boston Harbor Hotel; the Seaport World Trade Center on the South Boston waterfront; and Central Wharf, behind the New England Aquarium. It's a commuter

Boston Transit

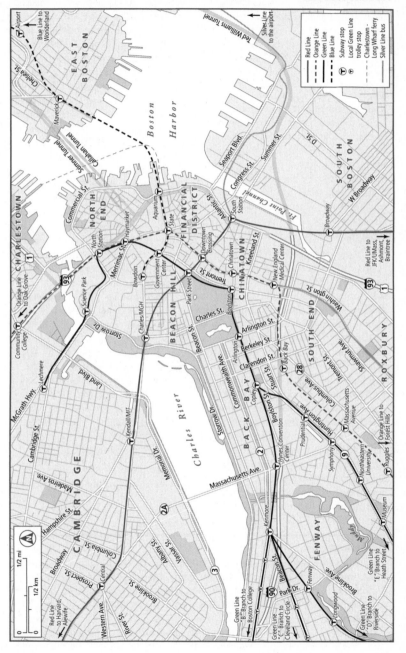

service that doesn't operate on weekends or holidays. The one-way fare is $2; visit the website for the schedule.

BY CAR

If you plan to visit only Boston and Cambridge, there's absolutely no reason to have a car. With its pricey parking and narrow, one-way streets, not to mention abundant construction, Boston in particular is a motorist's nightmare. If you arrive by car, park at the hotel and use the car for day trips. Drive to Cambridge only if you're feeling flush—you'll pay to park there, too. If you're not motoring and you decide to take a day trip (see chapter 11), you'll probably want to rent a car. Here's the scoop:

Rentals

The major car-rental firms have offices at Logan Airport and in Boston, and most have other area branches. Seriously consider waiting to pick up the car until you need it, to save yourself the hassle of driving and parking. Rentals that originate in Boston carry a **$10 convention center surcharge**—you can get around it by picking up your car in Cambridge, Brookline, or another suburb. Note that the Enterprise and Thrifty airport locations are nearby but not on the grounds, and allow time for the shuttle-bus ride.

When making a reservation, it's important to remember that in general, Boston doesn't conform to the pattern of a big city that empties out on weekends, when business travelers leave town and rental-car rates plummet. The parts of downtown Boston that aren't densely populated residential neighborhoods are near them, and at busy times—especially on summer weekends and during foliage season—you'll want to reserve a car well in advance or risk getting shut out.

Some logistics: Most companies set aside cars for nonsmokers, but you have to ask. To rent from the major national chains, you must be at least 25 years old and have a valid driver's license and credit card. Some companies allow drivers aged 21 to 24 to rent, subject to a steep daily fee. And some chains enforce a maximum age; if you're over 70, check ahead to avoid an unpleasant surprise.

If you're visiting from abroad and plan to rent a car in the United States, keep in mind that foreign driver's licenses are usually recognized in the U.S., but you should get an international one if your home license is not in English.

Money-saving tips: If you belong to **Zipcar** or another car-sharing service at home, check ahead to see whether your membership is good in the Boston area. And if you don't mind taking a short T ride to (potentially) save a bundle, check rates at **Enterprise's** neighborhood locations and call ahead to request pick-up at the station closest to the office you choose.

See "Getting to Boston: By Car," above, for information about driving (or not) to eastern Massachusetts.

Insurance

If you hold a private auto insurance policy, it probably covers you in the U.S. for

---

Impressions

Boston's freeway system was insane. It was clearly designed by a person who had spent his childhood crashing toy trains. Every few hundred yards I would find my lane vanishing beneath me and other lanes merging with it from the right or left, or sometimes both. This wasn't a road system, it was mobile hysteria.

—Bill Bryson, *The Lost Continent* (1989, but it's still true)

Tips Boston Drivers: Beware

The incredibly sappy movie *Love Story* includes one hilarious observation: "This is Boston—everybody drives like a maniac." And that was before cellphones. Boston drivers absolutely deserve their notoriety, and even though the truly reckless are a tiny minority, it pays to be careful. Never assume that another driver will behave as you might expect, especially when it comes to the rarely used turn signal. Watch out for cars that leave the curb and change lanes without signaling, double- and triple-park in the most inconvenient places imaginable, and travel the wrong way down one-way streets. And remember that most pedestrians and bicyclists are just drivers without their protective covering.

loss of or damage to the rental car, and for liability in case a passenger is injured. The credit card you use to rent the car may also provide some coverage, but don't assume—check before you leave home.

Car-rental insurance typically does not cover liability if you caused the accident. Check your own auto insurance policy, the rental company policy, and your credit card coverage for the extent of coverage: Is your destination covered? Are other drivers covered? How much liability is covered if a passenger is injured? If you rely on your credit card for coverage, you may want to bring a second credit card with you, because damages may be charged to your card and you may find yourself stranded with no money.

Car rental insurance costs about $20 a day.

Package Deals

Many packages include airfare, accommodations, and a rental car with unlimited mileage. Compare these prices with the cost of booking airline tickets and renting a car separately. Don't saddle yourself with a car for a long period if you won't be using it, though. And don't forget to add the price of parking, which can quickly wipe out any savings a package might represent.

Booking Online

For booking rental cars online, the best deals are usually on rental-car company websites, although all the major online travel booking engines also offer rental-car reservations services.

Check out **Breezenet.com**, which offers domestic car-rental discounts with some of the most competitive rates around. Also worth visiting are Orbitz.com, Hotwire.com, Travelocity.com, and Priceline.com, all of which offer competitive online car-rental rates. For additional car rental agencies, see the "Toll-Free Numbers & Websites" appendix, p. 294.

Parking

It's difficult to find your way around Boston and practically impossible to find parking in some areas. Most spaces on the street are metered (and patrolled until at least 6pm Mon–Sat) and are open to nonresidents for 2 hours or less between 8am and 6pm. The penalty is a $45 ticket—the same as a full day at the most expensive garage. Read the sign or meter carefully. Some areas allow parking only at certain hours. Rates vary in different sections of the city (usually $1/hr. downtown); bring plenty of quarters. Time limits range from 15 minutes to 2 hours.

If you blunder into a tow-away zone, retrieving the car will cost well over $100 and a lot of running around. The city tow lot (© 617/635-3900) is at 200 Frontage Rd. in South Boston. Take a taxi, or ride the Red Line to Andrew and flag a cab.

It's best to leave the car in a garage or lot and walk, but be aware that Boston's parking is the second most expensive in the country (after Manhattan's). A full day at most garages costs no more than $30, but some downtown facilities charge as much as $45, and hourly rates can be exorbitant. Many lots charge a lower flat rate if you enter and exit before certain times or if you park in the evening. Some restaurants offer reduced rates at nearby garages; ask when you call for reservations. Regardless of where you park, visit the attendant's booth as you exit on foot to ask whether any local businesses offer discounted parking with a purchase and validation; you may get lucky.

The city-run garage under **Boston Common** (℡ 617/954-2096) accepts vehicles less than 6 feet, 3 inches tall. Enter from Charles Street between Boylston and Beacon streets. Enter the garage in the state **Transportation Building,** 10 Park Plaza (℡ 617/973-7054), from Charles Street South. The **Prudential Center** garage (℡ 617/236-3060) has entrances on Boylston Street, Huntington Avenue, and Exeter Street, and at the Sheraton Boston Hotel. Parking is discounted if you buy something at the Shops at Prudential Center and have your ticket validated. The garage at **Copley Place** (℡ 617/375-4488), off Huntington Avenue, offers a similar deal. Many businesses in Faneuil Hall Marketplace validate parking at the **75 State St. Garage** (℡ 617/742-7275).

Good-size garages downtown are at **Government Center** off Congress Street (℡ 617/227-0385), **Sudbury Street** off Congress Street (℡ 617/973-6954), the **New England Aquarium** (℡ 617/367-3847), and **Zero Post Office Square** in the Financial District (℡ 617/423-1500). In the Back Bay, there's a large facility near the Hynes Convention Center on **Dalton Street** (℡ 617/421-9484). The lots off **Northern Avenue** in the Seaport District are among the cheapest in town, but downtown proper is some distance away. Allow time for the walk or Silver Line bus ride.

Driving Rules

When traffic permits, drivers may turn right at a red light after stopping, unless a sign is posted saying otherwise (as it often is downtown). The speed limit on most city streets is 30mph.

Seat belts are mandatory for adults and children, children under 12 may not ride in the front seat, and infants and children under 5 must be strapped into car seats in the back seat. You can't be stopped just for having an unbelted adult in the car, but a youngster on the loose is reason enough to pull you over.

Legislation pending at press time would outlaw operating a vehicle while talking on a hand-held cellphone. Visit **www.iihs.org/laws/cellphonelaws.aspx** for an update.

And be aware of two state laws, if only because drivers break them so frequently it'll take your breath away: Pedestrians in the crosswalk have the right of way (most suburbs actually enforce this one), and vehicles already in a rotary (traffic circle or roundabout) have the right of way.

BY BICYCLE

This is not a good option unless you're a real pro or plan to visit Cambridge, which has bike lanes. The streets of Boston proper, with their bloodthirsty drivers and oblivious pedestrians, are notoriously inhospitable to two-wheelers.

For information about renting a bike and about recreational biking, see "Biking" on p. 181. If you bring or rent a bike, be sure to lock it securely when leaving it unattended, even for a short time.

5 Money & Costs

Like other large American cities, Boston can be an expensive destination. At the high end, it's nearly as costly as New York. The average hotel room rate is lower, but still nearly $200—and that average includes deep off-season discounts. At the thrifty end, an abundance of reasonably priced establishments cater to the area's large student population. Dining options, from hole-in-the-wall noodle joints to internationally acclaimed special-occasion restaurants, are particularly diverse.

If you're visiting Boston from overseas, exchange enough petty cash to cover airport incidentals, tipping, and transportation to your hotel before you leave home, or withdraw money upon arrival at an airport ATM. My favorite international travelers swear by the universal currency converter at **www.xe.com/ucc**.

ATMs

Don't worry about being caught without cash in the Boston area: ATMs (also known as "cash machines" or "cashpoints") are everywhere, even in some subway stations. Throughout eastern

Massachusetts, even the smallest towns usually have at least one ATM. The **Cirrus** (© 800/424-7787; www.mastercard.com) and **PLUS** (© 800/843-7587; www.visa.com) networks span the globe. The **NYCE** network (www.nyce.net) operates primarily in the eastern United States. NYCE administers the **SUM** network (www.sum-atm.com), which waives fees for customers of member banks using most ATMs belonging to other members. Look at the back of your bank card to see which network you're on, then call or check online for ATM locations in the Boston area.

Be sure you know your personal identification number (PIN) and your daily withdrawal limit before you depart. If you have a 5- or 6-digit PIN, ask whether it will work; you may need to change it to a 4-digit number. Also keep in mind that most banks impose a fee every time you use your card at a different bank's ATM. Domestic fees are climbing—some institutions charge $3—and an international transaction may cost you $5 or more. On top of that, the bank from which you

What Things Cost in Boston	$	£
Taxi from airport to downtown or Back Bay	20.00–45.00	10.00–22.50
Water shuttle from airport to downtown	10.00	5.00
MBTA subway fare	1.70–2.00	0.85–1.00
Double at moderately priced hotel	159.00–259.00	80.00–130.00
Lunch for one at inexpensive restaurant	7.00–13.00	3.50–6.50
Three-course dinner for one, without wine, at moderately priced restaurant	17.00–26.00	8.50–13.00
Glass of beer	3.00–7.00	1.50–3.50
Cup of coffee	1.50 and up	0.75 and up
Adult admission to the Museum of Fine Arts	17.00	8.50
Child (under 18) admission to the Museum of Fine Arts	free	free

withdraw cash may charge its own fee. As a rule, ATMs in convenience stores, which cater to middle-of-the-night impulse buyers, charge the steepest fees. At Massachusetts ATMs, a message should appear— onscreen or on a sticker near the keypad—to warn you that you're about to be charged. To compare banks' ATM fees within the U.S., use www.bankrate.com. Visitors from outside the U.S. should also find out whether their bank assesses a 1% to 3% fee on charges incurred abroad.

CREDIT CARDS & DEBIT CARDS

Credit cards are the most widely used form of payment in the United States: **Visa** (Barclaycard in Britain), **Master-Card** (EuroCard in Europe, Access in Britain, Chargex in Canada), **American Express, Diners Club,** and **Discover.** Visa and MasterCard are the most widely accepted, Diners Club the least. You can withdraw cash advances from your credit cards at banks or ATMs (provided you know your PIN), but high fees make this a pricey way to get cash.

Traveling with at least one major credit card is highly recommended, but I'd suggest you carry at least one emergency back-up. You must have a credit card to rent a car, and hotels and airlines usually require an imprint as a deposit against expenses.

Debit cards look like credit cards, complete with Visa or MasterCard logo, but they draw money directly from your checking account. Stores and restaurants that accept credit cards generally accept debit cards, and some stores and most U.S. post offices enable you to receive "cash back" on your debit-card purchases

as well. If you don't keep a large checking balance, be aware that most banks "freeze" a portion of your account when you initiate a purchase without a definite total, such as a car rental or tank of gas.

TRAVELER'S CHECKS

Credit cards and debit cards are more often used, but traveler's checks are widely accepted in the U.S. In tourist-friendly Boston, you won't have much trouble using traveler's checks at any business. International visitors should make sure that they're denominated in U.S. dollars; foreign-currency checks are often difficult to exchange.

You can buy traveler's checks at most banks. Be sure to keep a copy of their serial numbers separate from the checks in the event that they are stolen or lost. You'll get a refund faster if you know the numbers.

Prepaid traveler's check cards, such as the American Express Travelers Cheque Card, are reloadable cards that work much like debit cards but aren't linked to your checking account.

AMERICAN CURRENCY

The most common bills are the $1 (a "buck"), $5, $10, and $20 denominations. There are also $2 bills (seldom encountered), $50 bills, and $100 bills (the last two are usually not welcome as payment for small purchases).

Coins come in seven denominations: 1¢ (1 cent, or a penny); 5¢ (5 cents, or a nickel); 10¢ (10 cents, or a dime); 25¢ (25 cents, or a quarter); 50¢ (50 cents, or a half dollar); the gold-colored Sacagawea coin, worth $1; and the rare silver dollar.

6 Health

STAYING HEALTHY

Here's hoping you won't need to evaluate Boston's reputation for excellent medical care. The greatest threat to your health is the same as in most other North American

cities: overexposure to the summer sun. Be sure to pack sunscreen, sunglasses, and a hat, and don't forget to keep yourself hydrated.

WHAT TO DO IF YOU GET SICK AWAY FROM HOME

Medical care in the Boston area is among the best in the world. For U.S. travelers, most reliable health-care plans provide coverage if you get sick away from home. International visitors will probably have to pay on the spot and request reimbursement later.

The closest hospitals to downtown are **Massachusetts General Hospital,** 55 Fruit St. (© **617/726-2000;** www.mass general.org), and **Tufts Medical Center,** 800 Washington St. (© **617/636-5000;** www.tufts-nemc.org). In Cambridge, equidistant from Harvard Square, are

Mount Auburn Hospital, 330 Mount Auburn St. (© **617/492-3500;** www.mountauburn.caregroup.org), and **Cambridge Hospital,** 1493 Cambridge St. (© **617/655-1000;** www.challiance.org/cambridge/index.shtml).

In January 2008, the state approved the opening of nonemergency Minute-Clinics at some Boston-area branches of **CVS** (© **800/746-7287;** Mon–Fri 8:30am–8pm; www.cvs.com). They deal with ear infections, strep throat, and such, but not with dire emergencies.

We list **additional emergency numbers** in the "Fast Facts" appendix, p. 286.

7 Safety

Boston and Cambridge are generally safe, especially in the areas you're likely to visit. Nevertheless, you should take the same precautions you would in any other large North American city. Stash wallets and billfolds in your least accessible pocket, don't wave your expensive camera or biggest map around in a dicey-looking neighborhood, and take off your headphones (or at least turn the volume way down) when you're wandering around alone. In general, trust your instincts—a dark, deserted street is probably deserted for a reason.

As in any city, stay out of parks (including Boston Common, the Public Garden, and the Esplanade) at night unless you're in a crowd. Specific areas to avoid at night include Boylston Street between Tremont and Washington streets, and Tremont Street from Stuart to Boylston streets. Try not to walk alone late at night in the Theater District or on the side streets around North Station. Public transportation in the areas you're likely to visit is busy and safe, but service stops between 12:30 and 1am.

8 Specialized Travel Resources

TRAVELERS WITH DISABILITIES

Boston, like all other U.S. cities, has taken the required steps to provide access for people with disabilities. Hotels must provide accessible rooms, and museums and street curbs have ramps for wheelchairs. Some smaller accommodations, including most B&Bs, have not been retrofitted. In older neighborhoods (notably Beacon Hill and the North End), you'll find many narrow streets, cobbled thoroughfares, and brick sidewalks that can make getting

around difficult. In the construction areas that dot the entire metropolitan area, especially in downtown Boston, you may have to negotiate uneven road surfaces and pedestrian detours.

Newer stations on the Red, Blue, and Orange lines of the **subway** are wheelchair accessible; the transit authority is converting the Green Line (which uses trolleys). Contact the **Massachusetts Bay Transportation Authority** (© **800/392-6100** or 617/222-3200; www.mbta.com)

to see if the stations you need are accessible. All MBTA **buses** have lifts or kneelers; call ℭ **800/LIFT-BUS** for more information. Some bus routes are wheelchair accessible at all times, but others may require a reservation as much as a day in advance. To learn more, contact the **Office for Transportation Access,** Back Bay Station, 145 Dartmouth St., Boston, MA 02116 (ℭ **800/543-8287** or 617/222-5976, or TTY 617/222-5854).

One taxi company with wheelchair-accessible vehicles is **Boston Cab** (ℭ **617/536-5010**); advance notice is recommended. In addition, an **Airport Accessible Van** (ℭ **617/561-1769**) operates within Logan Airport.

An excellent resource is **VSA Arts Massachusetts,** 2 Boylston St., Boston, MA 02116 (ℭ **617/350-7713**, TTY 617/350-6836; www.vsamass.org). The organization's **Access Expressed** network maintains a website with a searchable directory of cultural venues (www.access expressed.net; click "Directory).

The **America the Beautiful—National Park and Federal Recreational Lands Pass—Access Pass,** administered by a cooperative agreement between several federal agencies, including the National Park Service, the Bureau of Land Management, the Bureau of Reclamation, the Fish and Wildlife Service, and the U.S. Department of Agriculture Forest Service, gives visually impaired or permanently disabled persons (regardless of age) free lifetime entrance to federal recreation sites. Pass holders can visit national parks, monuments, historic sites, recreation areas, and national wildlife refuges without paying entrance fees.

The America the Beautiful Access Pass can only be obtained in person at any federally administered recreational facility that charges an entrance fee. You need to show proof of a medically determined disability. Besides free entry, the pass also offers a 50% discount on some federal-use fees charged for such facilities as camping, swimming, parking, boat launching, and tours. The United States Geological Survey (ℭ **888/275-8747;** http://store. usgs.gov/pass/general.html) offers more information about the interagency pass program.

For more on organizations that offer resources to disabled travelers, go to www. frommers.com.

GAY & LESBIAN TRAVELERS

The capital of the only state in which same-sex marriage is legal, Boston is overall a gay- and lesbian-friendly destination, with a live-and-let-live attitude that long ago replaced the city's legendary Puritanism.

Two free weeklies cover New England's GLBT community and feature extensive entertainment listings: *Bay Windows* (ℭ **617/266-6670;** www.baywindows. com) and the *New England Blade* (formerly *In Newsweekly;* ℭ **426-8246;** www.newenglandblade.com). The alternative weekly *Boston Phoenix* publishes cultural and nightlife listings (www. bostonphoenix.com).

An excellent guide to local gay- and lesbian-owned and -friendly businesses is the *Pink Pages* (www.pinkweb.com/ boston.index.html). Other useful resources include the **Gay, Lesbian, Bisexual and Transgender Helpline** (ℭ **888/340-4528** or 617/267-9001) and the **Peer Listening Line,** for people under 26 (ℭ **800/399-PEER** or 617/267-2535), both operated by Fenway Community Health (www.fenwayhealth.org); the **Boston Alliance of Gay and Lesbian Youth** (ℭ **617/227-4313;** www.bagly. org), which holds a general meeting every Wednesday at 8pm; and the **Bisexual Resource Center** (ℭ **617/424-9595;** www.biresource.org).

For more gay and lesbian travel resources, visit www.frommers.com.

SENIOR TRAVEL

Mention that you're a senior citizen when you make your travel reservations. Boston-area businesses offer many discounts to seniors with identification (a driver's license, passport, or other document that shows your date of birth). The cut-off age is usually 65, sometimes 62. Restaurants, museums, and movie theaters may offer special deals. Restaurants and theaters usually offer discounts only at off-peak times, but museums and other attractions offer reduced rates—usually the equivalent of the student price—at all times.

With a special photo ID card, seniors can ride the **MBTA** subways, local and express buses, commuter rail, and Inner Harbor ferries for at least half off the regular fare. The Senior Pass is available in person only from 8:30am to 5pm weekdays at the Downtown Crossing station and at the Office for Transportation Access, Back Bay Station, 145 Dartmouth St., Boston, MA 02116 (© **617/222-5976** or TTY 617/222-5854; www.mbta.com; under "Riding the T," click "Accessible Services").

The Interagency Pass Program, created by the Federal Lands Recreation Enhancement Act of 2004, offers an America the Beautiful—National Parks and Federal Recreational Lands Pass—Senior Pass which gives seniors 62 years or older lifetime entrance to all properties administered by federal agencies including national parks, national monuments, historic sites, recreation areas, the national forests and national wildlife refuges, for a one-time processing fee of $10. The pass must be purchased in person at any federal recreational facility that charges an entrance fee. Besides free entry, the America the Beautiful Senior Pass offers a 50% discount on some federal-use fees charged for such facilities as camping, swimming, parking, boat launching, and tours. The United States Geological Survey (© **888/275-8747;** http://store. usgs.gov/pass/general.html) offers more information about the interagency pass program. Frommers' website (www.frommers.com) offers more information and resources on travel for seniors.

FAMILY TRAVEL

Boston is a top-notch family destination, with tons of activities that appeal to children and relatively few that don't. All hotels and most restaurants in the area have extensive experience meeting kids' needs.

The **Greater Boston Convention & Visitors Bureau** (© **888/SEE-BOSTON;** www.bostonusa.com) sells a *Kids Love Boston* guide ($5) filled with travel information for families.

Throughout this book, the "Kids" icon flags destinations that are especially welcoming and interesting to youngsters. Also consult the boxes on "Family-Friendly Hotels" (p. 87) and "Family-Friendly Restaurants" (p. 124), and the section "Especially for Kids" (p. 171).

To locate particularly kid-friendly accommodations, restaurants, and attractions, refer to the "Kids" icon throughout this guide and to *Frommer's 500 Places to Take Your Kids Before They Grow Up* (Wiley, 2006). For a list of more family-friendly travel resources, turn to the experts at www.frommers.com.

STUDENT TRAVEL

Students don't actually rule Boston—it just feels that way sometimes. Many museums, theaters, concert halls, and other establishments offer discounts for college and high school students with valid identification. Some restaurants near college campuses offer student discounts or other deals. Visiting students can check campus bulletin boards for information about events and activities, many of which are open to them. The weekly *Boston Phoenix* also lists activities for students.

Check out the **International Student Travel Confederation** (**ISTC;** www.istc.org) website for comprehensive travel

Tips It's Easy Being Green

Here are a few simple ways you can help conserve fuel and energy when you travel:

- Before traveling to Boston, visit the website of the **Greater Boston Convention & Visitors Bureau** (www.bostonusa.com), click "Press," and search for "Green News" to get the latest info about the bureau's Green Visitors Program.
- Each time you take a flight or drive a car, greenhouse gases release into the atmosphere. You can help neutralize this danger to the planet through "carbon offsetting"—paying someone to invest your money in programs that reduce your greenhouse gas emissions by the same amount you've added. Before buying carbon-offset credits, make sure you're using a reputable company with a proven program that invests in renewable energy. Reliable carbon-offset companies include **Carbonfund** (www.carbonfund.org), **TerraPass** (www.terrapass.org), and **Carbon Neutral** (www.carbonneutral.org).
- Whenever possible, choose nonstop flights; they generally require less fuel than indirect flights that stop and take off again. Try to fly during the day—some scientists estimate that nighttime flights are twice as harmful to the environment. And pack light—each 15 pounds of luggage on a 5,000-mile flight adds up to 50 pounds of carbon dioxide emitted.
- Where you stay during your travels can have a major environmental impact. To determine the green credentials of a property, ask about trash disposal and recycling, water conservation, and energy use; also question if sustainable materials were used in the construction of the property. The

services information and details on how to get an **International Student Identity Card (ISIC),** which qualifies students for substantial savings on rail passes, plane tickets, entrance fees, and more. It also provides students with basic health and life insurance and a 24-hour helpline. The card is valid for a maximum of 18 months. You can apply for the card online or in person at **STA Travel** (© 800/781-4040 in North America; © 132 782 in Australia; © 0871 2 300 040 in the U.K.; www.statravel.com), the biggest student travel agency in the world; check out the website to locate STA Travel offices worldwide. If you're no longer a student but are under 26, you can get an **International Youth Travel Card (IYTC)** from the same people, which entitles you to some discounts. **Travel CUTS** (© 800/592-2887; www.travelcuts.com) offers similar services for both Canadians and U.S. residents. Irish students may prefer to turn to **USIT** (© 01/602-1904; www.usit.ie), an Ireland-based specialist in student, youth, and independent travel.

website **www.greenhotels.com** recommends green-rated member hotels around the world that fulfill the company's stringent environmental requirements. Also consult **www.environmentallyfriendlyhotels.com** for more green accommodation ratings.

- At hotels, request that your sheets and towels not be changed daily. (Many hotels already offer this option.) Turn off the lights and the air conditioning or heat when you leave your room.
- Use public transport where possible—trains, buses and even taxis are more energy-efficient forms of transport than driving. Even better is to walk or cycle; you'll produce zero emissions and stay fit and healthy on your travels.
- If renting a car is necessary, ask the rental agent for a hybrid or rent the most fuel-efficient car available. You'll use less gas and save money.
- Eat at locally owned and operated restaurants that use produce grown in the area. This contributes to the local economy and cuts down on greenhouse gas emissions by supporting restaurants that minimize the use of ingredients transported across long distances. **Chefs Collaborative** (© 617/236-5200; www.chefscollaborative.org) is a Boston-based nonprofit dedicated to promoting "sustainable food service businesses"; its website has a search function that locates member restaurants. Visit **Sustain Lane** (www.sustainlane.org) to find sustainable eating and drinking choices around the U.S.; also check out **www.eatwellguide.org** for tips on eating sustainably in the U.S. and Canada.

9 Sustainable Tourism

Sustainable tourism is conscientious travel. It means being careful with the environments you explore and respecting the communities you visit. Two overlapping components of sustainable travel are **ecotourism** and **ethical tourism.** The **International Ecotourism Society** (TIES) defines ecotourism as responsible travel to natural areas that conserves the environment and improves the well-being of local people. TIES suggests that ecotourists follow these principles:

- Minimize environmental impact.
- Build environmental and cultural awareness and respect.
- Provide positive experiences for both visitors and hosts.

- Provide direct financial benefits for conservation and for local people.
- Raise sensitivity to host countries' political, environmental, and social climates.
- Support international human rights and labor agreements.

You can find some ecofriendly travel tips and statistics, as well as touring companies and associations—listed by destination under "Travel Choice"—at the **TIES** website, www.ecotourism.org. Also check out **Ecotravel.com**, which lets you search for sustainable touring companies in several categories (water-based, land-based, spiritually oriented, and so on).

Frommers.com: The Complete Travel Resource

Planning a trip or just returned? Head to **Frommers.com**, voted Best Travel Site by *PC Magazine*. We think you'll find our site indispensable before, during, and after your travels—with expert advice and tips; independent reviews of hotels, restaurants, attractions, and preferred shopping and nightlife venues; vacation giveaways; and an online booking tool. We publish the complete contents of over 135 travel guides in our **Destinations** section, covering over 4,000 places worldwide. Each weekday, we publish original articles that report on **Deals and News** via our free **Frommers.com Newsletters**. What's more, **Arthur Frommer** himself blogs 5 days a week, with cutting opinions about the state of travel in the modern world. We're betting you'll find our **Events** listings an invaluable resource; it's an up-to-the-minute roster of what's happening in cities everywhere—including concerts, festivals, lectures, and more. We've also added weekly **podcasts, interactive maps,** and hundreds of new images across the site. Finally, don't forget to visit our **Message Boards,** where you can join in conversations with thousands of fellow Frommer's travelers and post your trip report once you return.

While much of the focus of ecotourism is about reducing impact on the natural environment, ethical tourism concentrates on ways to preserve and enhance local economies and communities, regardless of location. You can embrace ethical tourism by staying at a locally owned hotel or shopping at a store that employs local workers and sells locally produced goods.

Responsible Travel (www.responsible travel.com) is a great source of sustainable travel ideas; the site is run by a spokesperson for ethical tourism in the travel indus-try. **Sustainable Travel International** (www.sustainabletravelinternational.org) promotes ethical tourism practices, and manages an extensive directory of sustainable properties and tour operators around the world.

In the U.K., **Tourism Concern** (www.tourismconcern.org.uk) works to reduce social and environmental problems connected to tourism. The **Association of Independent Tour Operators** (AITO; www.aito.co.uk) is a group of specialist operators leading the field in making holidays sustainable.

10 Packages for the Independent Traveler

Good sources of package deals that let you set your own itinerary are the airlines themselves. Major carriers that offer air-land packages to Boston include **American Airlines Vacations** (✆ 800/321-2121; www.aavacations.com), **Midwest Airlines Vacations** (✆ 888/235-9693; www.midwestairlinesvacations.com), **United Vacations** (✆ 888/854-3899; www.united vacations.com), **US Airways Vacations** (✆ 800/455-0123; www.usairways vacations.com), and **Virgin Holidays** (✆ 0871/222-5825; www.virginholidays.co.uk). Flights with **Southwest Airlines Vacations** (✆ 800/243-8372; www.southwestvacations.com) serve Manchester, New Hampshire, and Providence, Rhode Island (see box, "Let's Make a

Deal," p. 142). Several big **online travel agencies**—Expedia.com, Travelocity, Orbitz, and Lastminute.com—also do a brisk business in packages.

Trolley tour companies (see "Organized Tours" in chapter 7) play a prominent role in Boston tourism. The sightseeing portion of a package is often a free or discounted 1-day trolley tour.

Brush Hill Tours (© 800/343-1328 or 781/986-6100; fax 781/986-0167; www.brushhilltours.com) is Gray Line's New England incarnation. Its 3-night "Boston City Package" includes lodging, airport or train station transfers, and a tour on Beantown Trolley (which it owns). Prices start at about $375 per person, based on double occupancy. Brush

Hill also offers a variety of half- and full-day escorted tours to destinations such as Plymouth, Salem, Cape Cod, and Newport, Rhode Island.

One often-overlooked option, if you live close enough to take advantage of it, is **Amtrak Vacations** (© **800/AMTRAK-2** or 978/867-1208; www.amtrakvacations. com). Prices are competitive and can undercut air-land packages from many destinations. The train definitely isn't for everyone, though. Sleepers are available on long routes, but if you're paying extra for a berth, an air package might be cheaper and certainly will take less time.

For more information on package tours and for tips on booking your trip, see www.frommers.com.

11 Escorted General-Interest Tours

Hundreds of companies offer escorted tours that stop in Boston, especially during foliage season, when 5- to 10-day tours of New England are wildly popular with travelers from around the world. Few spend more than 2 days in Boston, however, meaning that you'll be rushing around trying to cram maximum action into minimum time, or skipping sights and activities you were looking forward to. If you plan to focus on Boston, most escorted tours won't meet your needs; you'll almost always be better off with a package tour (see the previous section).

If a quick stop is all you can manage, most major tour operators can accommodate you. They include **Liberty** **Travel** (© 888/271-1584; www.liberty travel.com), **Collette Vacations** (© 800/340-5158; www.collettevacations.com), **Globus and Cosmos** (© 866/821-2752; www.globusandcosmos.com), **Insight Vacations** (© 888/680-1241; www.insightvacations.com), **Maupintour** (© 800/255-4266; www.maupintour. com), **Tauck World Discovery** (© 800/788-7885; www.tauck.com), and **Trafalgar Tours** (© 866/544-4434; www.trafalgar.com).

For more information on escorted general-interest tours, including questions to ask before booking your trip, see www.frommers.com.

12 Special-Interest Trips

ACADEMIC TRIPS

Enormous college town that it is, Boston abounds with educational opportunities. Two nonprofit organizations offer itineraries that are notable for giving participants a good sense of their destination rather than trying to cram in as many attractions as possible.

Travel-study programs with **Road Scholar** (© **800/466-7762;** www.road scholar.org) incorporate scheduled activities led by local experts and free time for you to explore on your own. The trips are for groups no larger than 24, and they're open to anyone 21 or over.

Road Scholar is a spin-off of the venerable **Elderhostel** (© **800/454-5768;** www.elderhostel.org), which offers an enormous variety of programs to travelers 55 and over (a younger companion is permitted on many tours). Its "learning adventures" include everything from sessions with college instructors to behind-the-scenes experiences at cultural events.

ADVENTURE TRIPS
The **Massachusetts Audubon Society** (© **800/AUDUBON** or 781/259-9500; www.massaudubon.org), the largest conservation organization in New England, owns and operates wildlife sanctuaries across the state and offers programs that help people of all ages connect with nature. Classes, workshops, programs, and special events of all types, many designed specifically for children and families, take place throughout the year. Memberships start at $44 per year.

A good introduction to New England's diverse terrain is an excursion with the **Appalachian Mountain Club** (© **617/ 523-0655;** ww.outdoors.org). The recreation and conservation organization is perhaps best known for its indispensable trail guides and maps, but it coordinates volunteer-led activities that range from walking dogs on a beach to multiple-day backpacking tours. Though closely associated with the White Mountains, the AMC has chapters all over the Northeast and offers many activities in the Boston suburbs. First-time membership costs $40 for an individual, $60 for a family, or $25 if you're under 30 or over 69.

VOLUNTEER & WORKING TRIPS
The Greater Boston chapter of **Habitat for Humanity** (© **617/423-2223;** www. habitatboston.org) welcomes individual volunteers as well as groups to help construct and renovate affordable housing for low-income families. Be prepared and dress appropriately for 7 hours of construction work, which can be strenuous. Volunteers are responsible for their own transportation and should bring lunch, drinks, and work gloves. The minimum age is 16 years old, and 16- and 17-year-olds must have an adult with them. There is no maximum age. Note that you must complete a 1-hour orientation before you can start work, and those sessions fill up quickly.

The **Massachusetts Audubon Society** and the **Appalachian Mountain Club** (see "Adventure Trips," above) rely heavily on volunteers. Most Mass Audubon activities are long-term commitments, but some are one-shot deals suitable for out-of-town visitors. AMC opportunities range from a day of trail-clearing to leading a longer-term program.

13 Staying Connected

TELEPHONES
For calls within the United States and to Canada, dial 1 followed by the area code and the seven-digit number. In eastern Massachusetts, you can leave off the 1 but must dial all 10 digits. **For other international calls,** dial 011 followed by the country code, city code, and the number you are calling. To place **international calls to the United States,** dial your country's international code plus the country code (1), the area code, and the local number.

Most long-distance and international calls can be dialed directly from any phone. Many convenience groceries and packaging services sell **prepaid calling cards** in denominations up to $50; for international visitors, these can be the least expensive way to call home.

Generally, hotel surcharges on both local and long-distance calls are astronomical, so you're better off using your **cellphone** or a **public pay phone. Local calls** made from pay phones in most locales cost either 25¢ or 35¢ (no pennies, please). Many pay phones at airports accept American Express, MasterCard, and Visa credit cards.

For **local directory assistance** ("information"), dial 411; for long-distance information, dial 1, then the appropriate area code and 555-1212.

For **reversed-charge or collect calls,** and for person-to-person calls, dial the number 0, then the area code and number; an operator will come on the line, and you should specify whether you are calling collect, person-to-person, or both. If your operator-assisted call is international, ask for the overseas operator.

Calls to area codes **800, 888, 877,** and **866** are toll-free. However, calls to area codes **700** and **900** (chat lines, bulletin boards, "dating" services, and so on) can be very expensive—usually a charge of 95¢ to $3 or more per minute, and they sometimes have minimum charges that can run as high as $15 or more.

CELLPHONES

The major North American service providers all cover Boston; in the suburbs, you'll occasionally encounter dead spots.

If you're not from the U.S., you'll be appalled at the poor reach of the **GSM (Global System for Mobile Communications) wireless network,** which is used by much of the rest of the world. Your phone will probably work in most major U.S. cities; it definitely won't work in many rural areas. To see where GSM phones work in the U.S., check out www.t-mobile.com/coverage. And you may or may not be able to send SMS (text messaging) home.

If you prefer to **rent** a phone, you can have it shipped to you before you leave from **InTouch Global** (© 800/872-7626

or 703/222-7161; www.intouchglobal. com), which charges 89¢ a minute or more for airtime.

If you want a phone just for emergencies and don't have to know your number ahead of time, I'd suggest heading straight to one of the Boston area's ubiquitous freestanding cellphone stores or to **Radio Shack** (© 800/THE-SHACK; www. radioshack.com) and buying a prepaid phone to use during your visit. Ask a lot of questions: Make sure you're choosing a provider that allows you to activate international calling immediately (try making an international call while you're still in the store), and be sure you understand all fees and per-minute charges and have enough money loaded onto the phone to cover the calls you're likely to make and receive.

VOICE-OVER INTERNET PROTOCOL (VOIP)

If you have web access while traveling, consider a broadband-based telephone service (in technical terms, **Voice over Internet protocol,** or **VoIP**) such as Skype (www.skype.com) or Vonage (www. vonage.com), which allow you to make free international calls from your laptop or in a cybercafe. Neither service requires the people you're calling to have the same service (though there are fees if they do not). Check the websites for details.

INTERNET & E-MAIL
WITH YOUR OWN COMPUTER

Internet access is widely available in Boston, where a wireless connection is often easier to come by than a wired one. Most hotels and many businesses offer Wi-Fi access, and it's often free. (Paradoxically, high-end hotels tend to charge guests by the day for Web access, while many cheaper lodgings include Wi-Fi in their room rates.) The city of Boston provides free Wi-Fi in and around the Quincy Market rotunda at Faneuil Hall Marketplace and at Christopher Columbus

Waterfront Park. The best way to find public Wi-Fi hotspots is by searching **www.jiwire.com**, which has the world's largest directory of public wireless hotspots, both free and paid.

WITHOUT YOUR OWN COMPUTER

Boston's Logan and most other major airports have **Internet kiosks** that provide basic Web access for a per-minute fee that's usually higher than cybercafe prices. Check out copy shops like **FedEx Kinko's,** which offers computer stations with fully loaded software (as well as Wi-Fi).

For help locating cybercafes and other establishments that offer Internet access, please see "Internet Access" in the "**Fast Facts**" appendix (p. 288).

4

Suggested Boston Itineraries

Living near the Freedom Trail, I meet my beloved *Frommer's Boston* readers all the time. After I assure them that I'm not trying to pick their pockets or enlist them in a cult (why so suspicious, readers?), they usually make one of two comments. They want to know where they can find a public bathroom, or they want to praise the book's suggested itineraries.

Read on for strategies that can help you organize your time. These itineraries include sightseeing destinations, snack and meal suggestions, and shopping pointers.

Two tips: **Wear comfortable shoes,** and don't ignore the **breaks** built into each itinerary, which can help you feel more like a relaxed insider and less like a crazed participant in a scavenger hunt.

Unless otherwise indicated, turn to chapter 7 for descriptions of the recommended attractions and activities. For an introduction to Boston's **neighborhoods,** flip to p. 168. And see "Fast Facts: Boston," p. 284, for pointers on finding a public toilet.

1 The Neighborhoods in Brief

These are the areas visitors are most likely to frequent. When Bostonians say **"downtown,"** they usually mean the first six neighborhoods defined here; there's no "midtown" or "uptown." The numerous neighborhoods outside central Boston include the Fenway, South Boston, Dorchester, Roxbury, West Roxbury, and Jamaica Plain. With a couple of exceptions (noted here), Boston is generally safe, but you should still take the precautions you would in any large city, especially at night. *Note:* I include some compass points here to help you read your map, but that's not how the locals will give you directions: They typically just point you on your way.

The Waterfront This narrow area runs along the Inner Harbor, on **Atlantic Avenue** and **Commercial Street** from the Charlestown bridge (on North Washington St.) to South Station. Once filled with wharves and warehouses, today it abounds with luxury condos, marinas, restaurants, offices, and hotels. Also here are the New England Aquarium and embarkation points for harbor cruises and whale-watching expeditions.

The North End Crossing the Rose Kennedy Greenway as you head east toward the Inner Harbor brings you to one of the city's oldest neighborhoods. Home to waves of immigrants in the course of its history, it was predominantly Italian for most of the 20th century. It's now less than half Italian American; many newcomers are young professionals who walk to work in the Financial District. Nevertheless, you'll hear Italian spoken in the streets and find a wealth of Italian restaurants, *caffes,* and shops. The main street is **Hanover Street.**

North Station Technically part of the North End but just as close to Beacon Hill, this area around **Causeway Street**

Boston Orientation

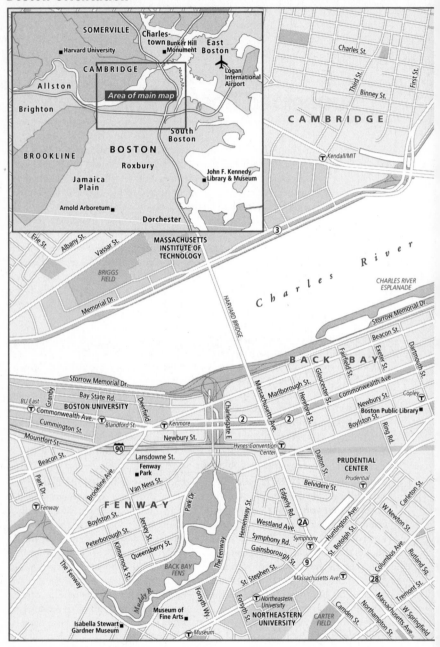

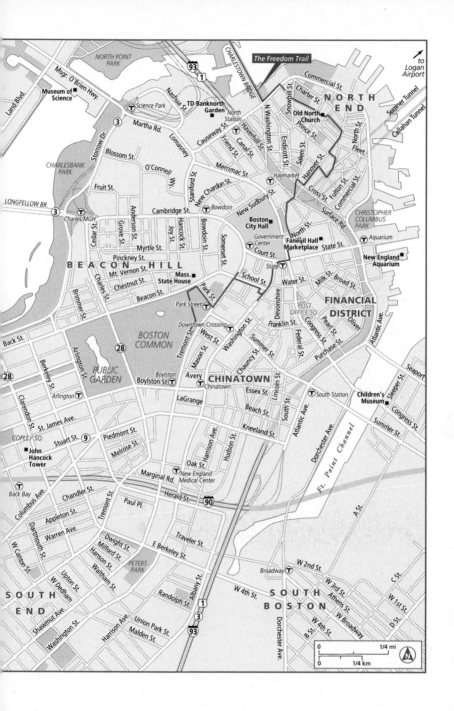

is home to the **TD Banknorth Garden** (sports and performance arena), **North Station,** and many nightspots and restaurants. The neighborhood gets safer by the day, but wandering alone late at night (especially on the side streets away from the Garden) is not a good idea.

Faneuil Hall Marketplace Employees aside, Boston residents tend to be scarce at Faneuil Hall Marketplace (also called Quincy Market, after its central building). An irresistible draw for out-of-towners and suburbanites, this cluster of restored market buildings—bounded by the Waterfront, the North End, Government Center, and **State Street**—is the city's most popular attraction. You'll find restaurants, bars, a food court, specialty shops, and Faneuil Hall itself. **Haymarket,** off I-93 on **Blackstone Street,** is home to an open-air produce market on Fridays and Saturdays.

Government Center Love it or hate it, Government Center's modern design breaks up Boston's traditionally staid architecture. Flanked by Beacon Hill, Downtown Crossing, and Faneuil Hall Marketplace, it's home to state and federal offices, City Hall, and a major T stop. Government Center's major feature, the red-brick wasteland of City Hall Plaza, lies between **Congress** and **Cambridge streets.**

The Financial District Bounded loosely by Downtown Crossing, **Summer Street, Atlantic Avenue,** and **State Street,** the Financial District is the banking, insurance, and legal center of the city. Aside from some popular after-work spots, it's generally quiet at night.

Downtown Crossing The intersection that gives Downtown Crossing its name is at **Washington Street** where **Winter Street** becomes **Summer Street.** The Freedom Trail runs along one edge of this shopping and business district between Boston Common, Chinatown, the Financial District, and Government Center. Most of the neighborhood hops during the day and slows down in the evening.

Beacon Hill Narrow tree-lined streets, brick and cobblestone alleyways, and architectural showpieces, mostly in Federal style, make up this largely residential area in the shadow of the State House. Two of the loveliest and most exclusive spots in Boston are here: Mount Vernon Street and Louisburg Square (pronounced "Lewisburg," and home to John and Teresa Heinz Kerry). Bounded by Government Center, Boston Common, the Back Bay, and the river, this is where you'll find Massachusetts General Hospital. **Charles Street,** which divides the Common from the Public Garden, is the main street of Beacon Hill. Other important thoroughfares are **Beacon Street,** on the north side of the Common, and **Cambridge Street.**

Charlestown One of the oldest areas of Boston is where you'll see the Bunker Hill Monument and USS *Constitution* ("Old Ironsides"). Yuppification has brought some diversity to what was once an almost entirely white residential neighborhood, but pockets remain that have earned their reputation for insularity.

South Boston Waterfront/Seaport District Across the Fort Point Channel from the Waterfront neighborhood, this area is home to the convention center, the World Trade Center, the Institute of Contemporary Art, three large hotels, the Fish Pier, a federal courthouse, Museum Wharf, one end of the Ted Williams Tunnel, and a lot of construction. A scattering of restaurants makes this area far more inviting than it was as recently as 2 years ago, but it's still not quite a destination. **Seaport Boulevard** and **Northern Avenue** are the main drags.

Chinatown The fourth-largest Chinese community in the country is a small area jammed with Asian restaurants, groceries, and gift shops. Chinatown takes up the area between Downtown Crossing and the Mass. Pike extension. The main streets are **Washington Street, Kneeland Street,** and **Beach Street.** The tiny **Theater District** extends about 1½ blocks in each direction from the intersection of Tremont and Stuart streets; be careful there at night after the crowds thin out.

The South End Cross **Stuart Street** or **Huntington Avenue** heading south from the Back Bay, and you'll find yourself in a landmark district packed with Victorian row houses and little parks. The South End has a large gay community and some of the city's best restaurants. With the gentrification of the 1980s and '90s, **Tremont Street** (particularly the end closest to downtown) gained a cachet that it hadn't known for almost a century. **Washington Street** and, to a lesser extent, **Harrison Avenue** are up-and-coming destinations for diners and shoppers. Long known for its ethnic, economic, and cultural diversity, the neighborhood is now thoroughly yuppified nearly all the way to Mass. Ave. *Note:* Don't confuse the South End with South Boston, a residential neighborhood on the other side of I-93.

The Back Bay Fashionable since its creation out of landfill more than a century ago, the Back Bay overflows with gorgeous architecture and chic shops. It lies between the Public Garden, the river, Kenmore Square, and either **Huntington Avenue** or **St. Botolph Street,** depending on who's describing it. Students dominate the area near **Mass. Ave.** but grow scarce as property values soar near the Public Garden. This is one of the best neighborhoods in Boston for aimless wandering. Major thoroughfares include **Boylston Street,** which starts at Boston Common and runs into the Fenway; largely residential **Beacon Street** and **Commonwealth Avenue** (colloquially referred to as Comm. Ave.); and boutique central, **Newbury Street.**

Huntington Avenue The honorary "Avenue of the Arts" (or, with a Boston accent, "Otts"), though not a formal neighborhood, is where you'll find the Christian Science Center, Symphony Hall (at the corner of Mass. Ave.), Northeastern University, and the Museum of Fine Arts. It begins at Copley Square and touches on the Back Bay, the Fenway, and the Longwood Medical Area before heading into the suburbs. Parts of Huntington can be a little risky, so if you're leaving the museum at night, stick to a cab or the Green Line, and try to travel in a group.

Kenmore Square The white-and-red CITGO sign that dominates the skyline above the intersection of **Comm. Ave., Beacon Street,** and **Brookline Avenue** tells you that you're approaching Kenmore Square. Its shops, bars, restaurants, and clubs attract students from adjacent Boston University, and the Hotel Commonwealth and its high-end retail outlets lend a touch of class. The college-town atmosphere goes out the window when the Red Sox are in town and baseball fans pour into the area on the way to historic Fenway Park, 3 blocks away.

Cambridge Boston's neighbor across the Charles River is a separate city. The areas you're likely to visit lie along the MBTA Red Line. **Harvard Square** is a magnet for students, sightseers, and well-heeled shoppers. It's an easy walk along Mass. Ave. southeast to **Central Square,** a gentrifying area dotted with ethnic restaurants and clubs; a short walk away is boho **Inman Square,** a stronghold of independent businesses. North along shop-lined Mass. Ave.

from Harvard Square is **Porter Square,** a mostly residential neighborhood with quirky retail outlets of the sort that once characterized Harvard Square. Around **Kendall Square** you'll find MIT and many technology-oriented businesses.

2 The Best of Boston in 1 Day

A single day affords the opportunity to sample some experiences unique to Boston. You won't have time for full immersion, but you can touch on several singular attractions and destinations. Your focus will be the downtown area, home to the city's oldest and most historic neighborhoods. *Start: Boston Common (Red or Green Line to Park Street), 15 State St. (Green or Blue Line to State), or Faneuil Hall (Green or Blue Line to Government Center).*

❶ The Freedom Trail ✸✸✸

Boston's signature attraction is a 2½-mile line of red paint or brick laid out at the suggestion of a local journalist in 1958. Following the whole Freedom Trail (p. 148) can consume the better part of a day, but several options that concentrate on the downtown part of the walk take 2 hours or so. Your goal is to cover—at whatever pace suits you, as carefully or as casually as you like—the first two-thirds of the trail, from **Boston Common** through **Faneuil Hall.** Start at the Boston Common Visitor Information Center with a pamphlet describing the self-guided tour or with the audio tour available for rental from the Freedom Trail Foundation. If you prefer a guided tour, check the schedule of tours with **National Park Service rangers, Boston By Foot,** and the **Freedom Trail Foundation.**

❷ Retail Therapy ✸

The legendary Filene's Basement will likely be closed during your visit (for building construction not slated to end until 2009), but **Downtown Crossing** is still worth checking out; see chapter 9 for pointers. Your next stop, **Faneuil Hall Marketplace,** offers more shopping

options. You can give your wallet a workout before, after, or even (this can be our little secret) during your sightseeing.

> ### ❸ FANEUIL HALL MARKETPLACE ✸✸
> Giving new meaning to the term "one-stop shopping," Faneuil Hall Marketplace (✆ 617/523-1300), bordered by North, Congress, and State streets and Atlantic Avenue, encompasses a Freedom Trail stop (the original Faneuil Hall; p. 154), retail outlets galore, numerous restaurants and bars, and tons of picnic possibilities. The main level of Quincy Market is a gigantic food court. You can eat at the marketplace, but I suggest crossing Atlantic Avenue and enjoying your snack or lunch with a glorious view. Stake out a seat overlooking the marina next to **Christopher Columbus Waterfront Park** (next to the Marriott, on the side opposite the New England Aquarium). If you'd rather eat indoors, head to **Durgin-Park** ✸✸✸, 340 Faneuil Hall Marketplace (✆ 617/227-2038; p. 115), or across the street to **Ye Olde Union Oyster House** ✸, 41 Union St. (✆ 617/227-2750; p. 115).

❹ Paul Revere House ✸✸✸

My favorite Freedom Trail stop is a little 17th-century home overlooking a picturesque cobblestone square. See p. 155.

Tips **One Singular Sensation**

On a 1-day visit, consider concentrating on just **one or two things** you're most excited about, plus a good meal or two. If what really gets you going is the Museum of Fine Arts, the Museum of Science, Newbury Street's art galleries and boutiques, or even a day trip (see chapter 11), you have a good excuse for not doing more—and for a return trip to Boston!

❺ **The North End** ★★★

The Freedom Trail continues here with another famous Paul Revere hangout, the fascinating **Old North Church** ★. But there's more to this historic neighborhood than just history. The city's "Little Italy" (locals don't actually call it that) is a great place for wandering around. See p. 156.

❻ **HANOVER STREET**

Coffee outlets throughout the city valiantly attempt to serve good espresso and cappuccino; the shops here always succeed— and if they don't, they don't stay in business very long. Pair your caffeine with a fresh-baked pastry, settle in at a bakery or *caffè*, and take in the scene on the North End's main drag. Top choices: ❻ᴬ **Mike's Pastry,** 300 Hanover St. (℃ 617/742-3050); ❻ᴮ **Caffè Vittoria,** 296 Hanover St. (℃ 617/227-7606); and ❻ᶜ **Caffè dello Sport,** 308 Hanover St. (℃ 617/523-5063). See p. 107.

❼ **The Waterfront**

Now downtown Boston's small size pays off: In almost any direction, the gorgeous harbor is a short stroll from the North End. As the day winds down, you can take a **sightseeing cruise** ★★ (p. 176) from Long Wharf or Rowes Wharf or just a **ferry** ride from Long Wharf to Charlestown and back. If cruises aren't for you or are out of season, explore the **New England Aquarium** ★ (p. 147) or the **Children's Museum** ★★ (p. 172). If those don't appeal to you, head for the nearby Seaport District (also known as the South Boston Waterfront) and visit the **Institute of Contemporary Art** (p. 143). It's a 20- to 30-minute walk or 10-minute cab ride.

Or—it's not the Waterfront, but bear with me—abandon the sightseeing after the Paul Revere House and go **shopping** in the Back Bay, starting with a stroll along Newbury Street (see chapter 9).

Finally, head back to the hotel to wash off the grime of the day, then pick something fun from the "Suggested Evening Itineraries" box on p. 65.

3 The Best of Boston in 2 Days

Now that you have a feel for the city, it's time to explore beyond downtown and investigate subjects other than history. The Back Bay, Beacon Hill, and other attractions contrast invitingly with the colonial extravaganza of the Freedom Trail. This itinerary may require some flexibility, because you probably won't have much control over when your Duck Tour starts. Aim for tickets on a tour that starts in the afternoon, when the scene on the river is liveliest, with rowers chugging around and sailboats skimming past. If your tour falls in the morning, the rest of this itinerary easily adjusts to accommodate it. **Start:** *Museum of Fine Arts (Green Line E to Museum or Orange Line to Ruggles).*

The Best of Boston in 1, 2 & 3 Days

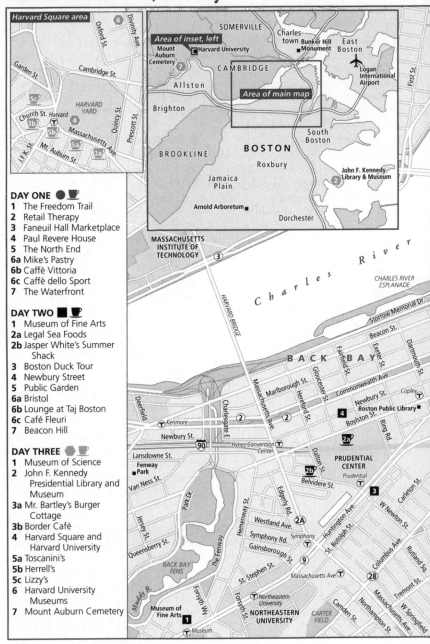

DAY ONE ● ☕🍴
1 The Freedom Trail
2 Retail Therapy
3 Faneuil Hall Marketplace
4 Paul Revere House
5 The North End
6a Mike's Pastry
6b Caffè Vittoria
6c Caffè dello Sport
7 The Waterfront

DAY TWO ■ ☕🍴
1 Museum of Fine Arts
2a Legal Sea Foods
2b Jasper White's Summer Shack
3 Boston Duck Tour
4 Newbury Street
5 Public Garden
6a Bristol
6b Lounge at Taj Boston
6c Café Fleuri
7 Beacon Hill

DAY THREE ● ☕🍴
1 Museum of Science
2 John F. Kennedy Presidential Library and Museum
3a Mr. Bartley's Burger Cottage
3b Border Café
4 Harvard Square and Harvard University
5a Toscanini's
5b Herrell's
5c Lizzy's
6 Harvard University Museums
7 Mount Auburn Cemetery

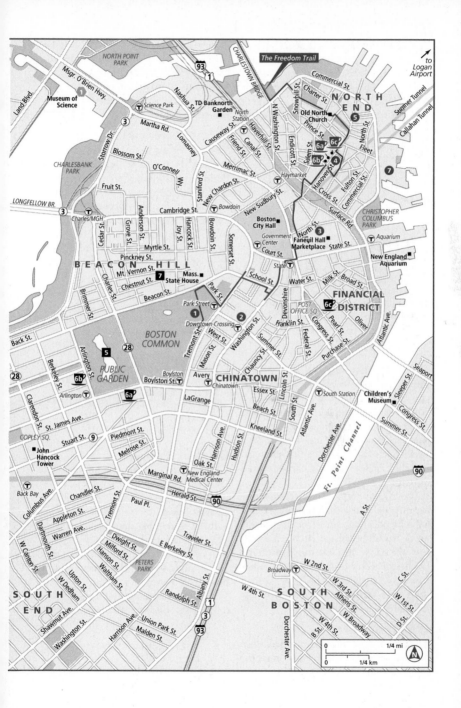

❶ Museum of Fine Arts ✦✦✦

Be at the museum when the doors open at 10am. The MFA can easily—and most enjoyably—take up a full day, but it doesn't have to. Check out the website to get some sense of what you want to see. If you prefer not to explore on your own, take the first guided tour of the day, which begins at 10:30am. The museum has a cafeteria, cafe, and restaurant, but I'd suggest saving your appetite for the next stop. See p. 145.

---

2 SHOPS AT PRUDENTIAL CENTER
One of my favorite branches of **Legal Sea Foods** ✦✦✦ (p. 106) is here, on the main level off Boylston Street. If you prefer something lighter, the **food court** is nearby. Or walk 5 minutes to the Back Bay branch of **Jasper White's Summer Shack** ✦✦. See p. 135.

---

❸ Boston Duck Tour ✦✦✦

This is the most entertaining motorized way to see the city. On a reconditioned World War II amphibious landing vehicle, you see the top attractions, pick up some historical background, and head for the water. Then, thrillingly, the Duck plunges into the Charles River and cruises around the basin. See p. 174.

Duck Tours don't operate from December through March (unless they're needed for a Patriots Super Bowl victory parade, which has happened a *lot* lately). An excellent alternative is a **Boston Symphony Orchestra** ✦✦✦ or **Boston Pops** ✦✦✦ concert at Symphony Hall (p. 224), a short walk from either the MFA or the Prudential Center (the Pru).

❹ Newbury Street

The commercial heart of the Back Bay, Newbury Street offers the best shopping in New England (see chapter 9). Familiar chains and one-of-a-kind boutiques and galleries make it a can't-miss destination for serious consumerism or just window-shopping. It's also architecturally fascinating (see "Walking Tour 1," in chapter 8).

❺ Public Garden ✦✦✦

Newbury Street begins across Arlington Street from the most beautiful park in Boston. The Public Garden (p. 163) is lovely year-round—a visit will brighten up even the grayest off-season day—and the *Make Way for Ducklings* sculptures (p. 17) are always delightful. In warm weather, leave time for a **Swan Boat** (p. 163) ride.

---

6 AFTERNOON TEA
All that walking makes a perfect excuse for a hearty meal of pastries, finger sandwiches, and, of course, tea. My favorite afternoon tea is at the **6A Bristol,** off the lobby of the Four Seasons. The **6B Lounge at the Taj Boston** and **6C Café Fleuri** in the Langham Hotel Boston also put on a good show. See "Boston Tea Party, Part 2" on p. 125.

---

❼ Beacon Hill ✦✦✦

The most picturesque neighborhood in town is a festival of red brick, cobblestones, and gorgeous architectural details. **Charles Street,** the main thoroughfare, is a lively shopping destination with a refreshing lack of chain stores. Wander on your own (see p. 169 for pointers) or seek out a guide—on summer weekdays, a **Boston By Foot** tour starts at 5:30pm.

"Suggested Evening Itineraries" (p. 65) can help you plan the rest of your day.

⟨Tips Suggested Evening Itineraries

If you're traveling as a family, you may be checking the TV listings for your evening itineraries. If not—or if you had the foresight to book a sitter— here are some suggestions. See chapter 6 for restaurant reviews and chapter 10 for nightlife listings.

- Dinner in the North End, and coffee and dessert at a *caffè*. Afterward, a show at the Comedy Connection at Faneuil Hall or the Improv Asylum, and a drink at the Cheers bar in Quincy Market.
- Dinner at Legal Sea Foods in the Prudential Center, followed (or preceded) by a visit to the 50th-floor Prudential Center Skywalk or a drink in the lounge at Top of the Hub, on the 52nd floor. If heights aren't your thing, lift a glass at the Oak Bar in the Fairmont Copley Plaza hotel.
- Summer only: Assemble a picnic and head to the Hatch Shell for music or a movie, or to Boston Common for a play or concert.
- Winter only: A Boston Symphony Orchestra or Boston Ballet performance, then late supper at Brasserie Jo or dessert at Finale.
- Dinner at Sel de la Terre or the State Street Legal Sea Foods, then a stroll along the harbor. Hit the North End or the food court at Faneuil Hall Marketplace for dessert.
- Dinner at Brasserie Jo, then a Huntington Theatre Company performance or music at Wally's Café.
- Dinner at Jasper White's Summer Shack, a stroll on Newbury Street, and a nightcap at the Bristol in the Four Seasons Hotel.
- Shopping at the Coop or the Harvard Book Store, then dinner at Mr. Bartley's Burger Cottage. Contemplate Harvard Yard from the Widener Library steps, and finish up with ice cream at Toscanini's, Herrell's, or Lizzy's or a show at Club Passim (or both).
- Dinner at Oleana or the East Coast Grill, followed by music at Scullers Jazz Club, the Regattabar, or Ryles Jazz Club.
- Dinner at Baraka Café, ice cream at Toscanini's, and music at the Middle East or T. T. the Bear's Place.
- A movie at the Kendall Square Cinema before or after dinner at the Blue Room, then music at the Cantab Lounge.
- Dinner at Redbones or Tu y Yo Mexican Fonda, and a show at Johnny D's or the Somerville Theater.

4 The Best of Boston in 3 Days

You can easily extend the suggestions for the first 2 days to fill a third—for instance, your Museum of Fine Arts admission is good for another visit within 10 days, and you haven't actually completed the Freedom Trail—but you'll probably want to branch out. Today you head for Cambridge, Dorchester, or both. This itinerary may look a little skimpy, but it's packed with interesting destinations and activities. *Start: Museum of Science (Green Line to Science Park) or Kennedy Library (Red Line to JFK/ UMass, then free shuttle bus).*

---

❶ Museum of Science ✦✦✦

❷ John F. Kennedy Presidential Library & Museum ✦✦

Although they're very different, both of these museums are well worth a trip and a full morning. The Museum of Science (p. 146), with its wealth of hands-on exhibits, is a great destination for families; adults and older kids who have studied American history can't get enough of the Kennedy Library (p. 144). Both museums open at 9am. Both have cafeterias, but I recommend that you wait to have lunch until you reach Cambridge at midday.

> **3A⁷ EAT LIKE A COLLEGE KID**
> My favorite Harvard Square lunch destinations are casual places where the sightseer's uniform of jeans or shorts and sneakers fits right in. **3B⁷ Mr. Bartley's Burger Cottage** ✦✦, 1246 Massachusetts Ave. (☏ **617/354-6559**; p. 133), is my top choice anywhere for onion rings, not to mention great burgers. The **3C⁷ Border Café**, 32 Church St. (☏ **617/864-6100**; p. 133), serves terrific Tex-Mex specialties.

❹ Harvard Square & Harvard University

I consider these two entities one big stop because the school couldn't exist without the neighborhood, and vice versa. Allow some time to wander around and enjoy the gentrified-boho atmosphere. Take a tour, which begins at the university's Information Center, or head out on your own (see "Walking Tour 2" in chapter 8). "The Square" is also a fun **shopping** destination (see chapter 9).

> **5⁷ ICE CREAM**
> Harvard Square is home to some of the best ice cream shops in this ice-cream-obsessed part of the world. I prefer **5A⁷ Toscanini's**, 1310 Massachusetts Ave. (☏ **617/354-9350**); to **5B⁷ Herrell's**, 15 Dunster St. (☏ **617/497-2179**); or **5C⁷ Lizzy's**, 29 Church St. (☏ **617/354-2911**), but that's subject to change if I see a daily special on the board that looks appealing. Take your treat to Harvard Yard.

❻ Harvard University Museums ✦

❼ Mount Auburn Cemetery ✦

Let your interests be your guide for the rest of the afternoon. Stay on campus to visit the Harvard Museum of Natural History & Peabody Museum (p. 165), which are equally welcoming to kids and adults. At the moment, highlights of the collections of the Harvard University Art Museums (p. 167) are on display at the Sackler Museum while the other two undergo renovation. (That means a relatively short visit, but that may suit you just fine.) All of the university museums close at 5pm.

A short distance from Harvard Square, Mount Auburn Cemetery is a gorgeous, fascinating destination. See p. 166.

When you've had enough, head back to the hotel. Stay in and order room service, or close your eyes and point to one of the "Suggested Evening Itineraries" on p. 65.

5

Where to Stay

The search for a hotel turns some travelers into the human equivalent of the dog in the "Far Side" cartoon who hears only her own name ("blah blah *Ginger* blah blah"). Faced with a detailed description of a potential lodging, they see only what they care about: "upstairs from the meeting that starts at 7:45am," "awards me frequent-flyer miles," "across the street from the wedding reception."

Others shop by price alone. If that describes you, be aware that the average room rate in the Boston area in 2007 topped $200, occupancy rates are high and getting higher, and just thinking about hotel parking rates can cause a nosebleed. Nevertheless, bargains are out there, particularly at slow times.

As you go through this chapter, keep Boston's relatively small size in mind, and check a map before you rule out a location. These listings use the neighborhood descriptions in chapter 4, "Suggested Boston Itineraries." Especially downtown, the neighborhoods are so small and close together that the borders are somewhat arbitrary. The division to consider is **downtown versus the Back Bay versus Cambridge,** and not, for example, the Waterfront versus the adjacent Financial District.

With enough flexibility, you probably won't have too much difficulty finding a suitable place to stay in or near the city. Year-round, it's always a good idea to **make a reservation,** and the earlier you book, the better your chances of landing a (relative) bargain. Definitely book ahead if you plan to travel between April and November, when conventions, college graduations, and vacations increase demand. During foliage season, the busiest and priciest time of year—even more expensive than the summer—plan early or risk staying far from Boston, or staying home.

Every hotel in this area accommodates both business travelers and families. That's not to say that you'll trip over a stroller in the elevator at a Hilton or a corporate takeover in the Hampton Inn lobby—you'll find a mix of guests wherever you stay in Boston. But you may feel more comfortable at the Hilton while you're executing that takeover, and more comfortable at the Hampton Inn if the stroller goes with you everywhere.

The area's lodging options reflect Boston's random geography, with properties built from the ground up in the 21st century competing against hotels in business for a century or longer. Different establishments emphasize different features; don't assume that a certain hotel, even one that's part of your favorite chain, has every option you expect. If you must swim a mile every morning or order food at 4am or hold a meeting in a conference room with Web access, always check to see whether your hotel can accommodate you. If it can't, a comparable property almost certainly can.

Most of the major hotel chains have a presence in the Boston area. Many of the larger establishments share a certain sameness, but even that comes with a

---

Tips **Tips for Last-Minute Planners**

You waited until the last minute and you can't find a room. What to do?

- Call the Hotel Hot Line (© **800/777-6001**). A service of the Greater Boston Convention & Visitors Bureau (© **888/SEE-BOSTON** or 617/536-4100; www. bostonusa.com), it can help make reservations even during the busiest times. It's staffed weekdays until 8pm, weekends until 4pm.
- If you're driving from the west, stop at a Massachusetts Turnpike rest area in Natick, Charlton, or Lee and try the reservation service at the visitor information center.
- If you arrive at Logan Airport without a room reservation (you daredevil), ask the staff at the **Visitor Service Center** in Terminal C for help.

---

potential bonus: Hotels with a common corporate parent may offer some flexibility. For instance, if one Starwood (Sheraton, Westin, or Le Méridien) property is overbooked, management can whisk you off to an affiliate and save you the trouble of calling around.

Besides Starwood, other chains operating in and around Boston include leisure-oriented Best Western, Holiday Inn, Radisson, and Ramada; boutique-hotel pioneer Kimpton; luxury operators Fairmont, Four Seasons, InterContinental, Jurys Doyle (an Irish chain), Mandarin Oriental, Ritz-Carlton, and Sonesta; and business-traveler magnets Hilton, Hyatt, and (in all its incarnations) Marriott.

The scarcest lodging option in the immediate Boston area is the moderately priced chain motel, a category almost completely driven out by soaring real estate prices. And brands that are bargains elsewhere may be pricey here—twice what you're used to paying, if not more—especially at busy times.

Rates in this chapter are for a double room; if you're traveling alone, single rates are almost always lower. The rates given here do not include the 5.7% state hotel tax. Boston and Cambridge add a 2.75% convention center tax on top of the 4% city tax, making the total tax 12.45%. Not all suburbs impose a local tax, so some towns charge only the state tax. These listings cover Boston, Cambridge, and Brookline. If you plan to visit a suburban town and want to stay overnight, see chapter 11 for suggestions.

1 Saving on Your Hotel Room

The **rack rate** is the maximum rate that a hotel charges for a room. Hardly anybody pays it, however, except sometimes in high season. To lower the cost of your room:

- **Ask for a rate,** *then* **ask about special rates or other discounts.** You may qualify for corporate, student, military, senior/AARP, AAA, or other discounts. Nail down the standard rate before you ask for your discount.
- **Book online.** Many hotels offer Internet-only discounts or supply discounted rooms to Priceline, Hotwire, or Expedia at rates much lower than the ones you can get through the hotel or chain. Some chains guarantee that the price on their websites is the lowest available; check anyway.
- **Dial direct.** When booking a room in a chain hotel, you'll often get a better deal from the hotel's reservation desk than from the chain's main number.

- **Remember the law of supply and demand.** Business-oriented hotels are busiest during the week, so you can expect discounts over the weekend. Leisure hotels are most crowded and therefore most expensive on weekends, so discounts may be available midweek.
- **Visit in the winter.** Boston-bound bargain hunters who don't mind cold and snow (sometimes *lots* of snow) aim for January through March, when hotels offer great deals, especially on weekends. The Convention & Visitors Bureau's "Boston Overnight! Just for the Fun of It" winter-weekend program targets suburbanites, but out-of-towners benefit, too.
- **Look into group or long-stay discounts.** If you come as part of a large group, you should be able to negotiate a bargain rate. If you're planning a long stay (at least 5 days), you might qualify for a discount. As a rule, expect 1 night free after a 7-night stay.
- **Avoid excess charges and hidden costs.** When you book a room, ask whether the hotel charges for parking—almost every hotel in Boston and Cambridge does. Use your cellphone, prepaid phone cards, or pay phones instead of making expensive calls from hotel phones. If you know you'll be online a lot, seek out a hotel that includes high-speed or wireless access in the room rate (a surprising number of places do; some older properties and hotels that do a lot of expense-account business don't). And don't be tempted by the minibar: Most hotels charge through the nose for water, soda, and snacks. Finally, ask about local taxes, service charges, and energy surcharges, which can increase the cost of a room by 15% or more.
- **Book an efficiency.** A room with a kitchenette allows you to shop for groceries and prepare your own meals. This is a big money saver, especially for families on long stays.
- **Consider enrolling in hotel "frequent-stay" programs,** which court repeat customers. Frequent guests can accumulate points or credits to earn free hotel nights, airline miles, in-room amenities, merchandise, tickets to concerts and events, and discounts on sporting facilities. Programs are in force not only at many chain hotels and motels (Hilton HHonors, Marriott Rewards, Starwood Preferred Guest, to name a few), but also at individual inns and B&Bs. Many chain hotels partner with other hotel chains, car-rental firms, airlines, and credit-card companies to encourage repeat business.

For tips on surfing for hotel deals online, visit www.frommers.com.

BED & BREAKFASTS

A bed-and-breakfast can be a good alternative to a chain hotel. B&Bs are usually less expensive than hotels and often more comfortable. Most are near public transportation. Because most B&Bs are small, they fill quickly. An agency can save you a lot of calling around and can match you with a lodging that accommodates your likes and dislikes, allergies, tolerance for noise and morning chitchat, and anything else you consider important. Reserve as soon as you start planning, especially if you hope to visit during fall foliage season.

Expect to pay at least $85 a night for a double in the summer and fall, and more during special events. The room rate usually includes breakfast and parking, but be sure to ask. Many lodgings require a minimum stay of at least 2 nights, and most offer good winter specials (discounts or third-night-free deals).

⌒Tips **A Note About Smoking**

Some large hotel chains and many smaller properties ban smoking throughout their premises. Still, nonsmokers shouldn't assume that they'll get a nonsmoking room without specifically requesting one. As hotels squeeze smokers into fewer rooms, the ones they use become saturated with the smell of smoke and air freshener, even in lodgings that are otherwise antiseptic. To avoid this disagreeable situation, be sure that everyone who handles your reservation knows that you need a completely nonsmoking room—or book a room at a Marriott, Westin, or (as of Jan. 1, 2009) Sheraton property.

The following organizations can help you find your ideal B&B in Boston, Cambridge, or the greater Boston area:

- **Bed & Breakfast Agency of Boston,** 47 Commercial Wharf, Boston, MA 02110 (© **800/248-9262,** 0800/89-5128 from the U.K., or 617/720-3540; fax 617/ 523-5761; www.boston-bnbagency.com)
- **Host Homes of Boston,** P.O. Box 117, Waban Branch, Boston, MA 02468 (© **800/600-1308** outside MA or 617/244-1308; fax 617/244-5156; www.hosthomesofboston.com)
- **Bed & Breakfast Reservations North Shore/Greater Boston/Cape Cod** (© **800/832-2632** outside MA, 617/964-1606, or 978/281-9505; fax 978/281-9426; www.bbreserve.com)
- **Bed and Breakfast Associates Bay Colony,** P.O. Box 57166, Boston, MA 02457 (© **888/486-6018,** 08/234-7113 from the U.K., or 781/449-5302; fax 781/455-6745; www.bnbboston.com)

2 Best Hotel Bets

- **Best Historic Hotel: The Fairmont Copley Plaza,** 138 St. James Ave. (© **800/ 257-7544**), opened in 1912 on the original site of the Museum of Fine Arts. Designed by Henry Janeway Hardenbergh (also the architect of the Plaza in New York), it has entertained presidents and celebrities since the day its magnificent gilded lobby opened. See p. 86.
- **Best for Business Travelers:** If your corporate travel department hasn't booked you into the default chain megahotel, live a little. For about the same price, enjoy posh surroundings, personalized service, and excellent business features at the **Millennium Bostonian Hotel,** 26 North St., at Faneuil Hall Marketplace (© **866/866-8086**), or the independent **Colonnade Hotel,** 120 Huntington Ave. (© **800/962-3030**). See p. 75 and p. 85.
- **Best for a Romantic Getaway:** The intimate atmosphere and elegant furnishings make a suite at the **Eliot Hotel,** 370 Commonwealth Ave. (© **800/44-ELIOT**), a great spot for a rendezvous. If you and your beloved need some time apart, close the French doors—you can be in separate rooms yet maintain eye contact. See p. 86.
- **Best for Families:** The **Doubletree Guest Suites,** 400 Soldiers Field Rd. (© **800/222-TREE**), offers two rooms for the price of one, with two TVs and a refrigerator, and a nice pool. The location, straddling Boston and Cambridge, is

especially good if you're driving from the west—you leave the turnpike before downtown traffic shatters the peace in the back of the minivan. See p. 92.

- **Best for Travelers with Disabilities:** The **Royal Sonesta Hotel,** 5 Cambridge Pkwy., Cambridge (© **800/SONESTA**), trains its staff in disability awareness and offers 18 rooms (some of which adjoin standard units) equipped for the hearing, ambulatory, and vision impaired. A wheelchair ramp for use in conference rooms is available. See p. 96. The Westin chain (© **800/WESTIN-1**) is particularly attentive to the needs of travelers with mobility issues; check out the **Westin Copley Place Boston,** 10 Huntington Ave., and the **Westin Boston Waterfront,** 425 Summer St. See p. 89 and p. 80.

- **Best Lobby for Pretending That You're Rich:** The **Boston Harbor Hotel,** Rowes Wharf (© **800/752-7077**), overlooks the harbor on one side and displays a museum-quality collection of paintings, drawings, prints, and nautical charts in its grand public spaces. See p. 71.

- **Best for Eco-Sensitive Travelers:** Listing hotels that aren't going "green" might be quicker. Every large hotel chain is boosting its environmental awareness, with **Hyatt** and **Kimpton** on the cutting edge. Boston's **Lenox Hotel,** 61 Exeter St. (© **800/225-7676;** see p. 86); **Seaport Hotel,** 1 Seaport Lane (© **877/ SEAPORT**); and **Colonnade Hotel,** 120 Huntington Ave. (© **800/962-3030**); are especially sensitive but by no means the only earth-friendly properties in town.

- **Best Pool:** The **Sheraton Boston Hotel,** 39 Dalton St. (© **800/325-3535**), has a great indoor-outdoor pool with a retractable dome. Across the river, the **Royal Sonesta Hotel,** 5 Cambridge Pkwy., Cambridge (© **800/SONESTA**), has a similarly enjoyable arrangement. See p. 89 and p. 96.

- **Best Views:** Several hotels offer impressive views of their immediate surroundings, but for a picture-postcard panorama of Boston and Cambridge, head to the upper floors of the **Westin Copley Place Boston** (© **800/WESTIN-1**). See p. 89.

3 Downtown

For the purposes of this chapter, "downtown" means most of the **Freedom Trail** and the neighborhoods defined in chapter 4 as the **Waterfront, Faneuil Hall Marketplace,** the **Financial District,** and **Downtown Crossing.** The few accommodations in the moderate price category are mostly bed-and-breakfasts; for information about B&Bs, consult the agencies listed on p. 69.

THE WATERFRONT & FANEUIL HALL MARKETPLACE

At all hotels in these neighborhoods, **ask for a room on a high floor**—the Big Dig is more or less complete, but construction continues throughout this area.

VERY EXPENSIVE

Boston Harbor Hotel ✰✰✰   The Boston Harbor Hotel is one of my favorites for its luxurious accommodations, top-notch service, abundant amenities, and great location. The landmark arch at the center of the 16-story brick complex connects the busy marina off the lobby to the Rose Kennedy Greenway and the Financial District. The clientele runs to demanding—and satisfied—business and leisure travelers who enjoy sensational views of the harbor or of the skyline and Greenway from the plush guest rooms, which start on the eighth floor. After a $12-million refurbishment completed in 2007, they have residential-style mahogany furnishings, work desks, muted

Where to Stay in Boston

Anthony's Town House **5**
Best Western Boston / The Inn at Longwood Medical **6**
Boston Harbor Hotel **50**
Boston Marriott Copley Place **22**
Boston Marriott Long Wharf **46**
Boston Park Plaza Hotel & Towers **31**
Brookline Courtyard by Marriott **2**
Bulfinch Hotel **38**
Chandler Inn Hotel **28**
Charlesmark Hotel **15**
Colonnade Hotel Boston **21**
Comfort Inn & Suites Boston / Airport **59**
Copley Square Hotel **18**
Courtyard by Marriott Boston Copley Square **17**
Doubletree Guest Suites **1**
Doubletree Hotel Boston Downtown **29**
Eliot Hotel **9**
Embassy Suites Hotel Boston at Logan Airport **57**
The Fairmont Copley Plaza Hotel **19**
Fifteen Beacon **42**
Four Seasons Hotel **32**
Hampton Inn Boston Logan Airport **58**
Harborside Inn **47**
Hilton Boston Back Bay **11**

Hilton Boston Financial District **49**
Hilton Boston Logan Airport **55**
Holiday Inn Boston at Beacon Hill **37**
Holiday Inn Boston Brookline **4**
Hostelling International–Boston **10**
Hostelling International– Boston at Fenway **7**
Hotel Commonwealth **8**
Hotel 140 **25**
Hyatt Harborside **56**
Hyatt Regency Boston Financial District **35**
InterContinental Boston **51**
The John Hancock Hotel **24**
Jurys Boston Hotel **26**
The Langham, Boston **48**
The Lenox Hotel **16**
The Liberty Hotel **36**
Longwood Inn **3**
Mandarin Oriental, Boston **13**
Marriott Residence Inn Boston Harbor **40**
The MidTown Hotel **20**
Millennium Bostonian Hotel **45**
Newbury Guest House **14**
Nine Zero **43**
Omni Parker House **44**
Onyx Hotel **39**
Radisson Hotel Boston **30**

Regent Boston **41**
Renaissance Boston Waterfront Hotel **54**
The Ritz-Carlton, Boston Common **34**
Seaport Hotel **52**
Sheraton Boston Hotel **12**
Taj Boston **33**
The Westin Boston Waterfront **53**
The Westin Copley Place Boston **23**
YWCA Boston, Berkeley Residence **27**

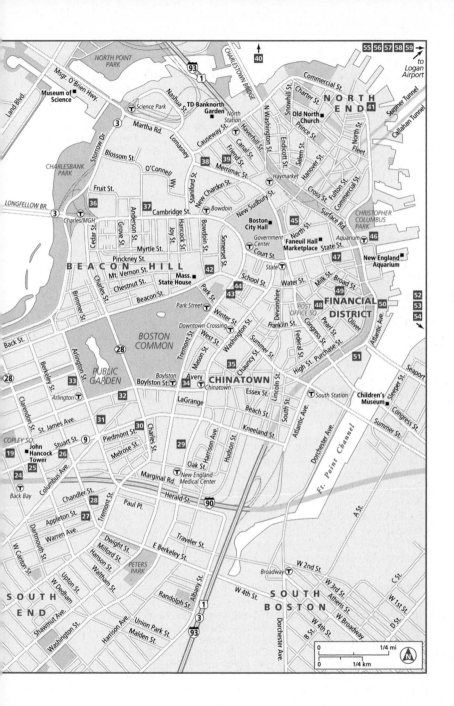

jewel-toned walls and fabrics, pillow-top mattresses, marble bathrooms, and abundant business features. Rooms with city views are less expensive, and the most desirable units (suites with private terraces) enjoy dazzling water vistas.

Rowes Wharf (entrance on Atlantic Ave.), Boston, MA 02110. ℂ **800/752-7077** or 617/439-7000. Fax 617/330-9450. www.bhh.com. 230 units. $295–$795 double; from $680 suite. Extra person $50. Children under 18 stay free in parent's room. Packages available. AE, DC, DISC, MC, V. Valet parking $37 weekdays, $26 weekends; self-parking $33 weekdays, $22 weekends. T: Red Line to South Station or Blue Line to Aquarium. Pets accepted. **Amenities:** Excellent restaurant (eclectic, w/15,000-bottle wine cellar); cafe; bar (p. 238); 60-ft. indoor lap pool; well-appointed health club and spa; concierge; courtesy car; state-of-the-art business center w/professional staff; 24-hr. room service; in-room massage; babysitting; laundry service; same-day dry cleaning; rooms for those w/limited mobility. *In room:* A/C, TV w/pay movies, high-speed Internet access ($10/day), minibar, hair dryer, iron, umbrella, robes.

Boston Marriott Long Wharf ⊛

The landmark Marriott occupies an unbeatable location a stone's throw from the New England Aquarium. It attracts business travelers with its proximity to the Financial District and families with its pool and easy access to downtown and waterfront attractions. The hotel's terraced brick exterior encloses a seven-story atrium that gives the public spaces an airy feel. Rooms, which were renovated in 2008, are large and decorated in upscale-chain-hotel style. They have cherry furnishings, either one king-size or two double beds (with pillow-top mattresses and down comforters), and a table and chairs in front of the window. Without any neighbors in the way, the building gets more natural light than any other downtown hotel. Rooms close to the water afford good views of the wharves and the waterfront; units closer to Atlantic Avenue overlook the Rose Kennedy Greenway.

296 State St. (at Atlantic Ave.), Boston, MA 02109. ℂ **800/228-9290** or 617/227-0800. Fax 617/227-2867. www.marriottlongwharf.com. 400 units. Apr–Nov $249–$629 double; Dec–Mar $159–$369 double; $450–$800 suite year-round. Weekend and family packages available. AE, DC, DISC, MC, V. Parking $34. T: Blue Line to Aquarium. **Amenities:** Restaurant (seafood); cafe and lounge; bar and grill; indoor pool; exercise room; Jacuzzi; game room; concierge; tour desk; 24-hr. business center; room service until 2am; laundry service; same-day dry cleaning; executive-level rooms; rooms for those w/limited mobility. *In room:* A/C, TV, high-speed Internet access ($10/day), fridge, coffeemaker, hair dryer, iron, safe.

InterContinental Boston ⊛

InterContinental broke into the Boston market in 2006, with the luxury brand's first New England hotel. The 22-story glass-sheathed building (the hotel occupies the bottom 12 floors) faces the Rose Kennedy Greenway, not far from the Financial District and convention center. It's about half a block from Boston Harbor, and guest rooms on the east (back) side have lovely water views. All are decorated in polished contemporary style, with plush earth-tone fabrics and dramatic artwork. Rooms are large enough to hold a comfy chaise and oversize work desk, and bathrooms are huge, with separate tubs and showers. The spa, health club, and varied dining options (not to mention the condos that share the building) amplify the residential feel. With over-the-top amenities and helpful service, the InterContinental brand consistently earns repeat business from its predominantly corporate clientele. At these prices, I'd expect nothing less.

510 Atlantic Ave., Boston, MA 02210. ℂ **800/424-6835** or 617/747-1000. Fax 617/747-5120. www.intercontinental boston.com. 424 units. $350–$600 double; $800–$6,000 suite. Children under 18 stay free in parent's room. Extra person $35. Weekend and other packages available. AE, DC, DISC, MC, V. Valet parking $39. T: Red Line to South Station. Pets under 25 lb. accepted; $100/stay. **Amenities:** Restaurant (24-hr. Provençal brasserie); 2 bars (sushi/tequila, rum/champagne); indoor pool; 24-hr. health club; spa; concierge; business center; 24-hr. room service; babysitting; laundry service; same-day dry cleaning; club-level rooms; rooms for those w/limited mobility. *In room:* A/C, TV w/pay movies, wireless Internet access ($15/day), minibar, hair dryer, iron, safe, robes.

Millennium Bostonian Hotel ★★   Three brick 19th-century buildings make up this relatively small hotel, which offers excellent service and features that make it competitive with larger rivals. It's popular with business travelers who want a break from the convention grind and with vacationers who appreciate the boutique atmosphere and access to the adjacent spa. A $25-million renovation that reconfigured the public areas should be complete by the time you visit. The redecorated guest rooms, all cool neutrals and clean lines, have Frette linens and down comforters on the pillow-top beds, and separate tubs and showers in the new bathrooms. Rooms vary in size; in half of them, French doors open onto small private balconies. My favorites overlook Faneuil Hall Marketplace, which is lively but not noisy, thanks to good soundproofing.

At Faneuil Hall Marketplace, 26 North St., Boston, MA 02109. © **866/866-8086** or 617/523-3600. Fax 617/523-2454. www.millenniumhotels.com. 201 units. $189–$449 double; $229–$489 superior double; $350–$1200 suite. Extra person $20. Children under 18 stay free in parent's room. Weekend, spa, family, and other packages available. AE, DC, DISC, MC, V. Valet parking $40. T: Green or Blue Line to Government Center, or Green or Orange Line to Haymarket. **Amenities:** Restaurant; lounge; small fitness room; access to nearby health club ($10); in-room exercise equipment delivery on request; concierge; tour desk; car-rental desk; business center; salon; 24-hr. room service; massage; babysitting; laundry service; same-day dry cleaning; executive-level rooms; rooms for those w/limited mobility. *In room:* A/C, TV w/pay movies, high-speed Internet access ($10/day), minibar, hair dryer, iron, safe, umbrella, robes.

MODERATE

Harborside Inn ★★ (*Value*   The Harborside Inn offers an unbeatable combination of location and value. The renovated 1858 warehouse is across the street from Faneuil Hall Marketplace, on the edge of the Financial District and less than 2 blocks from the harbor. The nicely appointed guest rooms, which have queen-size beds and hardwood floors, underwent renovations in 2007. Rooms surround a sky-lit atrium; units on the top floors of the eight-story building have lower ceilings but better views. Rooms that face out are more expensive but can be noisier; I have a letter here from a reader who could hear garbage trucks. You can't reserve an interior room, with windows that open only to the atrium, but you can request one at check-in if you're a light sleeper.

185 State St. (between Atlantic Ave. and the Custom House Tower), Boston, MA 02109. © **888/723-7565** or 617/723-7500. Fax 617/670-6015. www.harborsideinnboston.com. 54 units. $109–$299 double. Extra person $15. Packages and long-term rates available. Rates may be higher during special events. AE, DC, DISC, MC, V. Off-site parking $26; reservation required. T: Blue Line to Aquarium, or Blue or Orange Line to State. **Amenities:** Lounge; access to nearby health club ($15); concierge; room service until 10pm; laundry service; dry cleaning; rooms for those w/limited mobility. *In room:* A/C, TV, wireless Internet access, hair dryer, iron.

FINANCIAL DISTRICT & DOWNTOWN CROSSING

Besides being great for business travelers, the hotels in this area are closer than their Waterfront competitors to the major shopping areas and the start of the Freedom Trail. All offer excellent weekend packages, especially in the winter.

VERY EXPENSIVE

Hilton Boston Financial District ★   Contemporary yet conservative, this meticulously designed hotel delivers 21st-century technology in an Art Deco package. Like other downtown lodgings, it draws business travelers during the week and leisure travelers on weekends. The 14-story building is near Faneuil Hall Marketplace and the waterfront, but not all that close (by bratty Bostonian standards) to the T. The spacious guest rooms have 9½-foot ceilings and cordless two-line phones. The best units, on the upper floors, afford great views of the harbor and downtown. Soundproofing throughout makes the whole building—even the halls—exceptionally quiet. A rehab of a 1928 building, the Hilton opened in 1999 as the Wyndham Boston and was reflagged in 2006. The closest competitor, literally and figuratively, is the Langham, which is less convenient to public transit but has a swimming pool.

89 Broad St., Boston, MA 02110. ✆ **800/HILTONS** or 617/556-0006. Fax 617/556-0053. www.bostonfinancial. hilton.com. 362 units. $159–$499 double weekdays; $149–$399 double weekends; $234–$574 suite weekdays; $224–$474 suite weekends. Rates include continental breakfast. Children under 17 stay free in parent's room. Weekend, holiday, and family packages available. AE, DC, DISC, MC, V. Valet parking $38. T: Blue or Orange Line to State, or Red Line to South Station. **Amenities:** Restaurant (California/Italian); bar; 24-hr. exercise room; concierge; 24-hr. business center; 24-hr. room service; laundry service; same-day dry cleaning; rooms for those w/limited mobility. *In room:* A/C, TV w/pay movies, wireless Internet access ($11/day), minibar, coffeemaker, hair dryer, iron, umbrella, robes.

Hyatt Regency Boston Financial District 🖈🖈 *Value* This centrally located 22-story hotel is a busy convention and business destination during the week, and on weekends its excellent packages make it a magnet for sightseers and families. The eco-friendly Hyatt chain has spent millions upgrading the property since acquiring it in 2003, and it shows in everything from the pillow-top mattresses to the top-notch service. The building's plain exterior conceals elegant European-style appointments from the second-floor lobby on up. Guest rooms surround four atriums, creating the effect of several small hotels in one. Soft earth tones predominate, with lots of cushy upholstery and luxe linens on the king-size or (in about one-quarter of the units) two double beds. Rooms are spacious enough to hold sitting areas, desks, and settees. Ask for a unit on a high floor—adjacent Washington Street is likely to be awash in construction during your visit.

1 Ave. de Lafayette (off Washington St.), Boston, MA 02111. ✆ **800/233-1234** or 617/912-1234. Fax 617/451-0054. www.hyattregencyboston.com. 500 units. $189–$469 double; $350–$1,500 suite. Extra person $25. Children under 18 stay free in parent's room. Weekend, family, and other packages available. AE, DC, DISC, MC, V. Valet parking $41; self-parking $30. T: Red or Orange Line to Downtown Crossing, or Green Line to Park St. or Boylston. **Amenities:** Restaurant (American/Continental); bar; 52-ft. indoor pool; newly renovated health club; steam room; sauna; concierge; business center; 24-hr. room service; massage; babysitting; laundry service; same-day dry cleaning; executive-level rooms; rooms for those w/limited mobility. *In room:* A/C, TV w/pay movies, wireless Internet access ($10/day), minibar, coffeemaker, hair dryer, iron, robes.

The Langham, Boston 🖈 In the center of the Financial District, the Langham is one of the best business hotels in the city. Leisure travelers who take advantage of weekend discounts will find themselves practically on top of the waterfront and downtown attractions, and perhaps a 10-minute walk from public transit—a bit of a hike, to spoiled Bostonians. Elegantly decorated and large enough to hold a generous work area, the luxurious, regularly refurbished guest rooms have 153 configurations, including loft suites with two bathrooms. The most desirable rooms in the nine-story building overlook the lovely park in Post Office Square. The city views are engaging, but they pale in comparison to the vistas from the best units at the Langham's main competitors, the Boston Harbor Hotel and the InterContinental Boston.

250 Franklin St. (at Post Office Sq.), Boston, MA 02110. ✆ **800/791-7781** or 617/451-1900. Fax 617/423-2844. http://boston.langhamhotels.com. 325 units. $185–$495 double; $545–$2,950 suite. Extra person $30. Weekend, family, and other packages available. AE, DC, DISC, MC, V. Valet parking $39 Sun–Thurs, $25 Fri–Sat. T: Blue or Orange Line to State, or Red Line to Downtown Crossing or South Station. Pets accepted; $50 fee. **Amenities:** Restaurant (Mediterranean); cafe w/Sun jazz brunch and Sat "Chocolate Bar Buffet" (Sept–June); bar w/live piano most nights; 40-ft. indoor pool; well-equipped health club; Jacuzzi; sauna; concierge; business center; 24-hr. room service; in-room massage; laundry service; same-day dry cleaning; rooms for those w/limited mobility. *In room:* A/C, TV w/pay movies, high-speed Internet access ($10/day), minibar, coffeemaker, hair dryer, iron, safe, umbrella, robes.

Nine Zero ★★   This is anything but a traditional Boston hotel. Sleek and sophisti-cated, it feels almost like a transplant from New York or L.A.—and that's a good thing. The contemporary atmosphere distinguishes Nine Zero from its competitors, but the service is in the old-school customer-is-always-right mold. The decent-size guest rooms and oversize bathrooms contain opulent features, including luxurious linens and toiletries, down comforters, cordless two-line phones, and extensive business amenities. The 19-story hotel opened in 2002 and joined the eco-conscious luxury Kimpton chain in 2006. This neighborhood is convenient for both business and leisure travelers: It's within easy walking distance of downtown, a longer stroll from the Back Bay, and 2 blocks from the subway. Though technically in a different neigh-borhood, nearby Fifteen Beacon is Nine Zero's closest competitor; the service at both is attentive and personal, but prices here are generally a bit lower.

90 Tremont St. (near Bromfield St.), Boston, MA 02108. ✆ 866/906-9090, 800/KIMPTON, or 617/772-5800. Fax 617/772-5810. www.ninezero.com. 190 units. $289–$599 double; $500–$5,000 suite. Packages available. AE, DC, DISC, MC, V. Valet parking $38. T: Red or Green Line to Park St. Pets accepted. **Amenities:** Restaurant (steakhouse); bar; exercise room; access to nearby health club; concierge; business center; 24-hr. room service; in-room massage; babysitting; laundry service; same-day dry cleaning; rooms for those w/limited mobility. *In room:* A/C, TV w/pay movies, high-speed and wireless Internet access, minibar, coffeemaker, hair dryer, iron, safe.

EXPENSIVE

Omni Parker House ★★   The Parker House has operated continuously longer than any other hotel in America (since 1855!), but it's hardly stuck in the 19th cen-tury. Ongoing interior and exterior renovations are sprucing up the property, which was already in excellent shape; request a room removed from the work area. Most of the 50-plus configurations aren't huge, but all guest rooms are thoughtfully laid out and nicely appointed, with cherry furnishings and colorful carpeting. The hotel is popular with business travelers, who can book a unit with an expanded work area, and sightseers, who can economize by taking advantage of a weekend deal, especially in the winter, or by booking an "economy single." The closest competition is the Nine Zero, a block away, but that's an entirely different space-age animal—the Parker House is modern yet a little old-fashioned, and proud of it.

60 School St., Boston, MA 02108. ✆ 800/THE-OMNI or 617/227-8600. Fax 617/742-5729. www.omniparkerhouse.com. 551 units, some with shower only. $159–$189 economy room; $189–$289 double; $249–$399 suite. Children under 18 stay free in parent's room. Weekend packages and AARP discount available. AE, DC, DISC, MC, V. Valet park-ing $38. T: Green or Blue Line to Government Center, or Red or Green Line to Park St. Pets accepted; deposit required. **Amenities:** 2 restaurants (New England); bar; exercise room; concierge; airport shuttle; business center; 24-hr. room service; laundry service; same-day dry cleaning; executive-level rooms; rooms for those w/limited mobility. *In room:* A/C, TV w/pay movies and Nintendo, high-speed Internet access ($10/day), coffeemaker, hair dryer, iron, robes, safe.

Fun Fact **Food for Thought**

Yes, this is the Parker House of Parker House roll fame. The rolls were invented (if food is "invented") here, as was Boston cream pie.

That's not the hotel's only claim to fame. Malcolm X and Ho Chi Minh both worked here, and the room that's now Parker's Bar played host to a well-known group: Henry Wadsworth Longfellow, Oliver Wendell Holmes, Ralph Waldo Emerson, Nathaniel Hawthorne, and sometimes Charles Dickens, who made up a literary salon called the Saturday Club.

---

4 Beacon Hill/North Station/North End

Less expensive lodgings in this neighborhood are mostly B&Bs. Save time by checking with the agencies listed on p. 69.

VERY EXPENSIVE

The boutique hotel at **Battery Wharf,** off Commercial Street at Battery Street, was in search of a new operator at press time. Visit **www.batterywharf.com** for information about the property, part of a luxe-plus condo-hotel-retail development projected to open in late 2008. The only hotel in the North End, it has 150 units, abundant water views, lavish facilities (including an 18,000-sq.-ft. spa), a three-star Michelin chef in the kitchen, and prices to match.

Fifteen Beacon ✿✿ Nonstop pampering, high-tech appointments, and outrageously luxurious rooms make this *the* name to drop with the expense-be-hanged set. The meticulously maintained 10-story boutique hotel has attracted demanding travelers, especially businesspeople, since it opened in 2000. Management bends over backward to keep the loyal clientele returning, with lavish perks like business cards listing the personal phone and fax numbers guests have during their stay. The guest rooms, individually decorated in an austere but plush style that's more SoHo than Beacon Hill, contain queen-size canopy beds with Frette linens, surround-sound stereo systems, gas fireplaces, and 4-inch TVs in the bathroom. "Studio" units have a sitting area. The pricey steakhouse in the lobby is one of the best places in the city to see (or be) movers and shakers, especially at breakfast.

15 Beacon St., Boston, MA 02108. ✆ **877/XV-BEACON** or 617/670-1500. Fax 617/670-2525. www.xvbeacon.com. 60 units, some with shower only. From $395 double; from $1,200 suite. Valet parking $38. T: Red or Green Line to Park St., or Green or Blue Line to Government Center. Pets under 20 lb. accepted; refundable deposit required. **Amenities:** Restaurant (steakhouse); bar; fitness room; access to nearby health club ($15); concierge; courtesy car; 24-hr. room service; in-room massage; babysitting; laundry service; same-day dry cleaning; rooms for those w/limited mobility. *In room:* A/C, TV w/pay movies, fax/copier/printer, high-speed Internet access, minibar, hair dryer, iron, safe, umbrella, robes.

The Liberty Hotel ✿✿ A $120-million reclamation of the 1851 Charles Street Jail, the Liberty Hotel opened in 2007. A newly constructed 16-story tower complements the granite main building and holds most of the luxurious guest rooms, which boast top-of-the-line furnishings, next-gen tech, and huge bathrooms with separate tubs and showers. Catwalks encircle the 90-foot-high atrium in the original building, which holds the light-flooded public areas (with bars on the windows) and 18 guest rooms that—despite not having been "guest" accommodations before—are in high demand. Throughout, the decor combines peaceful neutrals in the rooms with colorful colonial-inspired patterns in the public areas. Striking views of the river, Beacon Hill, and (from higher floors) the Back Bay make rooms that face the Charles most desirable; elsewhere, the T station or a hospital may take center stage. My favorite units are corner rooms with a river view from the bathtub.

215 Charles St., Boston, MA 02114. ✆ **617/224-4000.** Fax 617/399-4259. www.libertyhotel.com. 298 units. $295–$550 double; $600–$1,000 suite. Children under 18 stay free in parent's room. Weekend and other packages available. AE, DC, DISC, MC, V. Valet or self-parking $40. T: Red Line to Charles/MGH. Small pets accepted. **Amenities:** 2 restaurants; bar (w/a few cell doors); 24-hr. fitness center; concierge; 24-hr. business center; 24-hr. room service; laundry service; same-day dry cleaning; rooms for those w/limited mobility. *In room:* A/C, TV w/pay movies, wireless Internet access, minibar, hair dryer, safe, robes.

EXPENSIVE

Onyx Hotel ⟨✦⟩   This plush boutique hotel opened in 2004 on a side street near North Station and TD Banknorth Garden, within easy walking distance of downtown, Beacon Hill, and the commuter rail to the North Shore. The 10-story hotel is contemporary in style, decorated in soothing jewel tones with sleek lines and high ceilings that make the decent-size rooms feel even bigger. Each unit in the hotel, an eco-friendly Kimpton property, holds a large work desk and has a well-appointed bathroom. The best accommodations are the top-floor suites, but any room with a floor-to-ceiling window feels like a mini-palace. This neighborhood is in transition, but it's improving quickly.

155 Portland St., Boston, MA 02114. ⟨⟨ 866/660-6699, 800/KIMPTON, or 617/557-9955. Fax 617/557-0005. www. onyxhotel.com. 112 units. $209–$349 double. Extra person $25. Rates include evening cocktail reception. Children under 18 stay free in parent's room. Weekend, family, and other packages, AARP and AAA discounts available. AE, DC, DISC, MC, V. Valet parking $38. T: Green or Orange Line to North Station. Pets accepted. **Amenities:** Lounge; exercise room; access to nearby health club; 24-hr. room service; massage; same-day dry cleaning; rooms for those w/limited mobility. *In room:* A/C, TV w/pay movies, high-speed and wireless Internet access, minibar, coffeemaker, hair dryer, iron, safe, umbrella, robes.

MODERATE

Bulfinch Hotel ⟨✦⟩   One block from North Station, the Bulfinch is as appealing for its design as for its convenient location and relatively reasonable rates. Every room in the 1904 building is different, with architectural details that enhance the "budget boutique" feel. Rooms are on the small side, but custom furnishings create the illusion of more space. Plush fabrics in cool neutrals and earth tones (including suede headboards), flatscreen TVs, and marble bathrooms set off the contemporary, uncluttered design. The nine-story hotel, which opened in 2004, offers business features such as work desks and cordless phones. The best units are junior suites—oversize doubles— known as "nose rooms" because they're in the pointed end of the triangular building; each has windows on three sides of the king-size bed.

107 Merrimac St., Boston, MA 02114. ⟨⟨ 617/624-0202. Fax 617/624-0211. www.bulfinchhotel.com. 80 units, most with shower only. $169–$399 double; $199–$489 junior suite. Children under 18 stay free in parent's room. Packages, AAA, AARP, and military discounts available. AE, DC, DISC, MC, V. Parking $25 in nearby garage. T: Green or Orange Line to North Station. Pets accepted; $50 fee. **Amenities:** Restaurant and lounge (tapas); exercise room; concierge; room service; same-day dry cleaning; rooms for those w/limited mobility. *In room:* A/C, TV, high-speed Internet access, coffeemaker, hair dryer, iron.

Holiday Inn Boston at Beacon Hill ⟨✦⟩   At the base of Beacon Hill, this 15-story hotel attracts both businesspeople and travelers with business at adjacent Massachusetts General Hospital; the staff is especially sensitive to the needs of patients and relatives. The location is convenient to downtown, within walking distance of the Back Bay, and not far from East Cambridge. The good-size guest rooms have contemporary furnishings and plenty of business amenities; all were refurbished in 2007. Each unit has a picture-window view of the city, the State House, or the parking structure—ask for a room on a high floor, facing Blossom Street if possible. The building is part of a small retail complex with a Whole Foods supermarket, a drugstore, and a handful of shops.

5 Blossom St., Boston, MA 02114. ⟨⟨ 800/HOLIDAY or 617/742-7630. Fax 617/742-4192. www.hisboston.com. 303 units, some with shower only. $160–$290 double; from $390 suite. Extra person $20. Rollaway $20. Children under 18 stay free in parent's room. Weekend and corporate packages and 10% AARP discount available. AE, DC, DISC, MC, V. Valet or self-parking $36. T: Red Line to Charles/MGH. **Amenities:** Restaurant (American); lounge; outdoor heated pool; small exercise room; access to nearby health club ($10); concierge; tour desk; car-rental desk; room service until 10pm; coin-op laundry; laundry service; executive-level rooms; rooms for those w/limited mobility. *In room:* A/C, TV w/pay movies, wireless Internet access, coffeemaker, hair dryer, iron.

5 Charlestown

EXPENSIVE

Marriott Residence Inn Boston Harbor ★★ *Value*   Combining the familiar sub-urban brand and a prime urban location, the Residence Inn opened in 2003. Its easy access to water transportation (water taxis serve the hotel dock) makes it competitive with more expensive downtown properties. Adjacent to the Charlestown Navy Yard, the hotel consists of studio and one- and two-bedroom suites with full kitchens; many have harbor views. Even the smallest units, studio suites, are generous in size. Most rooms in the eight-story building afford impressive views of the harbor or the Charles River and the Zakim Bridge. Patrons tend to be business travelers on weeknights (many on extended stays) and families on weekends, especially in the summer. Prices listed here are for 1 to 4 nights; longer stays mean ever-greater discounts.

Tudor Wharf, 34–44 Charles River Ave., Charlestown, MA 02129. © **866/296-2297**, 800/331-3131 (Marriott), or 617/242-9000. Fax 617/242-5554. www.marriott.com/bostw. 168 units. $199–$399 double May–Nov; $129–$229 double Dec–Apr. Rates include full breakfast. Children stay free in parent's room. Weekend, family, and other pack-ages from $129/night. AAA, government, and long-term discounts available. AE, DC, DISC, MC, V. Valet parking $29. T: Green or Orange Line to North Station, then shuttle-bus ride or 10-min. walk; Blue Line to Aquarium and ferry from Long Wharf to Navy Yard, then 5-min. walk; or Orange Line to Community College, then 10-min. walk. Pets accepted; $150 fee. **Amenities:** Cafe (New England) w/seasonal outdoor seating; indoor lap pool; exercise room; access to nearby YMCA ($8); Jacuzzi; shuttle to North Station; business center; room service until 9:30pm; coin-op laundry; laundry service; dry cleaning; rooms for those w/limited mobility. *In room:* A/C, TV w/pay movies, high-speed and wireless Internet access, kitchen, fridge, coffeemaker, hair dryer, iron.

6 South Boston Waterfront (Seaport District)

The Boston Convention and Exhibition Center, Seaport World Trade Center, Insti-tute of Contemporary Art, and Waterfront Silver Line bus (which connects South Sta-tion to the airport) are just a few of the factors helping push this neighborhood from up-and-coming to genuinely desirable. It's not quite there, though—there's no shop-ping or entertainment to speak of, and dining options are multiplying but still far from numerous. Access to the airport is excellent, but downtown is some distance away by bus and subway or on foot (Faneuil Hall Marketplace, for instance, is at least a 15-min. walk). If you're in town for a convention, thank your corporate travel agent; if you're sightseeing, budget time for public transit, money for cabs, or both.

VERY EXPENSIVE

The Westin Boston Waterfront ★★   The only hotel attached to the Boston Con-vention and Exhibition Center, the Westin opened in 2006. The state-of-the-art prop-erty offers the chain's abundant amenities, including Heavenly Beds, in its signature contemporary style. The good-size rooms have plenty of space for oversize work desks, and huge windows show off the city skyline, the water, or nearby office buildings and construction. Northeast-facing units on higher floors of the 16-story building enjoy panoramas of the action on the harbor, which—the hotel's name notwithstanding—is 2 blocks away. Bathrooms are plush, with the nicest mirrors (huge and backlit) I've ever seen in a hotel. Access to the convention center is through a weather-protected sky-bridge off the enormous lobby, which holds a bar that hops after work on weeknights.

425 Summer St., Boston, MA 02210. © **800/WESTIN-1** or 617/532-4600. Fax 617/532-4630. www.westin.com. 793 units. $259–$599 double; $359–$1,000 suite. Children under 18 stay free in parent's room. Weekend and family pack-ages available. AE, DC, DISC, MC, V. Valet parking $36; self-parking $27. T: Red Line to South Station, then Waterfront Silver Line to World Trade Center. Pets accepted. **Amenities:** 4 restaurants (contemporary American and 3 others that

were under construction at press time); lounge; coffee shop; indoor pool; state-of-the-art health club; concierge; business center; 24-hr. room service; laundry service; dry cleaning; rooms for those w/limited mobility. *In room:* A/C, TV w/pay movies, high-speed and wireless Internet access ($10/day), minibar, coffeemaker, hair dryer, iron, safe, robes.

EXPENSIVE

Renaissance Boston Waterfront Hotel ✹   In the rapidly evolving Seaport District, the Renaissance stands out: It's a hotbed of bleeding-edge tech. Lightning-fast DS-3 Internet access (the equivalent of 28 T1 lines) makes each guest room a media hub, with the capability to run everything through the 37-inch HD TV. As you'd expect within walking distance of both the convention center and the World Trade Center, the style is familiar business contemporary, all sleek silhouettes and vibrant colors, with comfy, well-appointed beds. Weeknight guests tend to be in town on business; on weekends, expect more leisure travelers and correspondingly lower prices—which seems only fair, given the distance from most attractions and dining. The glass-clad 21-story building opened in 2008, and higher you go, the better the views of the harbor, a block away, and the downtown skyline.

606 Congress St., Boston, MA 02210. (℃ **800/HOTELS-1** or 617/338-4111. Fax 617/338-4138. www.renaissance boston.com. 471 units. $169–$459 double; from $459 suite. Children under 19 stay free in parent's room. Weekend, family and other packages available. AE, DC, DISC, MC, V. Valet parking $39. T: Red Line to South Station, then Waterfront Silver Line to World Trade Center or 20-min. walk. Or water taxi to World Trade Center. Pets under 50 lb. accepted. **Amenities:** Restaurant (modern American); lounge; coffee bar; indoor pool; health club; spa; concierge; 24-hr. business center; room service until 10pm; massage; babysitting; laundry service; dry cleaning; rooms for those w/limited mobility. *In room:* A/C, TV w/pay movies, high-speed and wireless Internet access($10/night), coffeemaker, hair dryer, iron, safe, robes.

Seaport Hotel ✹✹ *(Kids)*   The independent Seaport Hotel was a pioneer on the South Boston waterfront and remains a sophisticated, eco-conscious presence in the emerging, construction-intensive neighborhood. The hotel, which opened in 1998 and was renovated in 2006, was designed and built (by Fidelity Investments) with every feature pampered, techno-savvy business travelers might dream of. The well-appointed, decent-size rooms have thoughtful features such as pillow-top mattresses, Logan Airport flight information on the TV, and fog-free bathroom mirrors. The views (of the city or harbor) from higher floors of the 18-story building are breathtaking. Across the street from and affiliated with the World Trade Center, the hotel books up unpredictably depending on the schedule there and at the nearby convention center. The kid-conscious staff, pool, weekend packages, and proximity to the Children's Museum make this a good choice for families, too.

1 Seaport Lane, Boston, MA 02210. (℃ **877/SEAPORT** or 617/385-4000. Fax 617/385-5090. www.seaportboston. com. 426 units. $189–$399 double; $450–$1,700 suite. Service charge $3 per room per night. Children under 17 stay free in parent's room. Weekend and family packages available. AE, DC, DISC, MC, V. Valet parking $39; self-parking $29. T: Red Line to South Station, then Waterfront Silver Line to World Trade Center or 20-min. walk. Or water taxi to World Trade Center. Pets under 50 lb. accepted. **Amenities:** Well-regarded restaurant (contemporary American); cafe; lounge; 50-ft. indoor pool; well-equipped health club; spa; bike rental; concierge; car-rental desk; shuttle to South Station, North Station, and State Street; 24-hr. business center w/professional staff (7am–8pm); 24-hr. room service; massage; laundry service; same-day dry cleaning; rooms for those w/limited mobility. *In room:* A/C, TV w/pay movies, high-speed and wireless Internet access, minibar, coffeemaker, hair dryer, iron, safe, robes.

7 Chinatown/Theater District

VERY EXPENSIVE

The Ritz-Carlton, Boston Common ✹   This plush, ultramodern hotel is a magnet for visiting celebrities—the state-of-the-art Sports Club/LA is a powerful draw—but

you don't have to be a movie star for the staff to treat you like one. The luxurious hotel opened in 2001 and underwent $11 million in renovations in 2007. The good-size guest rooms and huge suites feel more residential than commercial, with indulgent amenities such as luxury linens and feather duvets. Bathrooms are large, with a separate tub and shower. Rooms occupy the top four floors of the 12-story building; public spaces are at street level. You'll pay more for a room with a view of the Common. This neighborhood is convenient but not as attractive as the Back Bay, home of the Ritz's chief rival, the Four Seasons.

10 Avery St. (between Tremont and Washington sts.), Boston, MA 02111. ℭ **800/241-3333** or 617/574-7100. Fax 617/574-7200. www.ritzcarlton.com. 193 units. From $395 double; from $495 Club Level or suite. Weekend, family, and other packages available. AE, DC, DISC, MC, V. Valet parking $37. T: Green Line to Boylston. Pets accepted. **Amenities:** Restaurant (contemporary American); bar; lounge; access ($20/day) to adjoining Sports Club/LA (100,000-sq.-ft. facility w/lap pool, complete spa services, salon, regulation basketball court, 10,000-sq.-ft. weight room, steam rooms, saunas, 5 exercise studios, and 4 squash courts); concierge; courtesy car; airport shuttle; business center; 24-hr. room service; in-room massage; babysitting; laundry service; same-day dry cleaning; club-level rooms; rooms for those w/limited mobility. *In room:* A/C, TV w/pay movies, high-speed and wireless Internet access ($10/day), minibar, hair dryer, iron, safe.

EXPENSIVE

Radisson Hotel Boston ✸   Popular with business travelers, tour groups, and vacationers, this is an attractive hotel in a less-than-attractive neighborhood. The Theater District is convenient to both the Back Bay and downtown, and this would be a prime property anywhere. The Radisson's guest rooms are among the largest in the city, and each has a private balcony with great views from the higher floors. Rooms hold a king or two queen Sleep Number beds and enough space for a sitting area. The best units are the executive-level rooms on the higher floors of the 24-story building. On the premises are the **Stuart Street Playhouse** (ℭ **617/426-4499;** www.stuartstreet playhouse.com), a small theater that stages one-person and cabaret shows, and a seasonal **golf school** and practice facility (ℭ **617/457-2699;** www.healthybodies.org/ golf_school.html).

200 Stuart St. (at Charles St. S.), Boston, MA 02116. ℭ **800/333-3333** or 617/482-1800. Fax 617/451-2750. www. radisson.com/bostonma. 356 units, some with shower only. $159–$359 double. Extra person $20. Cot $20. Cribs free. Children under 18 stay free in parent's room. Weekend, theater, and other packages available. AE, DC, DISC, MC, V. Valet parking $30; self-parking $28. T: Green Line to Boylston or Orange Line to New England Medical Center. **Amenities:** 2 restaurants (cafe, Mediterranean bistro); indoor pool; exercise room; concierge; business center; room service until 11pm; in-room massage; babysitting; laundry service; same-day dry cleaning; executive-level rooms; rooms for those w/limited mobility. *In room:* A/C, TV w/pay movies, high-speed Internet access, coffeemaker, hair dryer, iron.

MODERATE

Doubletree Hotel Boston Downtown ✸ (Value   The Doubletree is conveniently located in Chinatown, within easy walking distance of both downtown and the Back Bay, and a better deal than most competitors in either of those neighborhoods. The six-story building is a former high school with high ceilings and compact, well-designed rooms. Ask for one of the units facing away from busy Washington Street; these have views of a cityscape rather than Tufts Medical Center, across the street. Nice details include Asian touches in the contemporary decor and features such as a fish tank in the lobby, installed in accordance with the principles of feng shui. Don't confuse this hotel with its all-suite corporate sibling near Cambridge (p. 92). This Doubletree adjoins the Wang YMCA of Chinatown, and room rates include access to its extensive facilities.

821 Washington St., Boston, MA 02111. © **800/222-TREE** or 617/956-7900. Fax 617/956-7901. http://doubletree. hilton.com. 267 units, some with shower only. $129–$299 double; $189–$359 suite. Extra person $10. Children under 17 stay free in parent's room. Weekend and other packages, AAA, AARP, and military discounts available. AE, DC, DISC, MC, V. Valet parking $36. T: Orange Line to New England Medical Center. **Amenities:** Restaurant and lounge (American/Asian); cafe; access to adjoining YMCA w/Olympic-size pool; concierge; business center; room service until 11:30pm; same-day dry cleaning; executive-level rooms; rooms for those w/limited mobility. *In room:* A/C, TV w/pay movies, wireless Internet access ($10/day), minibar, coffeemaker, hair dryer, iron, safe.

8 The South End

Berkeley Street runs from the Back Bay across the Mass. Pike to the most convenient corner of the sprawling South End, where you'll find these two lodgings.

MODERATE

Chandler Inn Hotel ★ *Value*   The comfortable Chandler Inn is a bargain for its location, just 2 blocks from the Back Bay. Long a popular choice with budget travelers, it underwent renovations in 2007 and 2008 that transformed the top three floors of the eight-story building. Deluxe guest rooms on these boutique floors are decorated in cool neutrals with splashes of orange; they have plasma TVs and marble bathrooms. The rest of the hotel was spruced up at the same time; guest rooms and bathrooms are small, without enough room to squeeze in a cot, but they have individual climate control and tasteful contemporary-style furniture. The staff is welcoming and helpful. This gay-friendly hotel books up early for events such as the Marathon and Boston Pride March and for foliage season.

26 Chandler St. (at Berkeley St.), Boston, MA 02116. © **800/842-3450** or 617/482-3450. Fax 617/542-3428. www. chandlerinn.com. 56 units. $109–$225 double; $179–$279 deluxe double. Children under 12 stay free in parent's room. AE, DC, DISC, MC, V. Parking $18 at nearby garage. T: Orange Line to Back Bay. Pets under 25 lb. accepted; $50 fee. **Amenities:** Lounge (Fritz; see p. 240); access to nearby health club ($10). *In room:* A/C, TV, wireless Internet access, hair dryer.

INEXPENSIVE

YWCA Boston, Berkeley Residence   This pleasant, convenient hotel and residence has a dining room, patio garden, piano, and library. Formerly for women only, it now accommodates men on one floor of the seven-story building. The dorm-style guest rooms are basic, containing little more than beds, but they're well maintained and comfortable—not plush, but not cells, either. The well-kept public areas include a 24-hour TV lounge. That description might not seem to justify the prices, but check around a little before you turn up your nose, especially if you plan to spend most of your time out and about.

40 Berkeley St., Boston, MA 02116. © **617/375-2524.** Fax 617/375-2525. www.ywcaboston.org/berkeley. 200 units, none with bathroom. $60 single; $90 double; $105 triple. Rates include full breakfast. Long-term rates available (5-week minimum). No children accepted. MC, V. No parking available. T: Orange Line to Back Bay or Green Line to Arlington. **Amenities:** Cafeteria; computer kiosk w/Internet access ($1/10 min.); coin-op laundry; rooms for those w/limited mobility. *In room:* Wireless Internet access. No phone.

9 The Back Bay

BOSTON COMMON/PUBLIC GARDEN

VERY EXPENSIVE

Four Seasons Hotel ★★★   Many luxury hotels offer exquisite service, a beautiful location, elegant guest rooms and public areas, a terrific health club, and wonderful restaurants. No other hotel in Boston—indeed, in New England—combines every element as seamlessly as the Four Seasons. If I were traveling with someone else's credit cards, I'd head straight here. Overlooking the Public Garden, the 16-story brick-and-glass building (the hotel occupies eight floors) incorporates the traditional and the contemporary. The spacious accommodations feel more like stylish apartments than hotel rooms, with lots of plush fabrics, elaborate moldings, and marble bathrooms. The best units overlook the Public Garden; city views from the back of the hotel aren't as desirable but can be engaging, especially from the higher floors. The staff is famously accommodating to businesspeople, families, and celebrities. Larger accommodations range from executive suites with parlor areas to luxurious deluxe suites with sweeping views.

200 Boylston St., Boston, MA 02116. ℰ 800/819-5053 or 617/338-4400. Fax 617/423-0154. www.fourseasons. com/boston. 273 units. $475–$600 double; from $750 1-bedroom suite; from $1,225 2-bedroom suite. Weekend and family packages available. AE, DC, DISC, MC, V. Valet parking $41. T: Green Line to Arlington. Pets under 15 lb. accepted. **Amenities:** Restaurant (Aujourd'hui, p. 125); bar (The Bristol, p. 238); 44-ft. pool and Jacuzzi overlooking the Public Garden; newly renovated health club and spa; concierge; tour desk; limo to downtown; business center; 24-hr. room service; in-room massage; babysitting; laundry service; same-day dry cleaning; rooms for those w/limited mobility. *In room:* A/C, TV w/pay movies, high-speed Internet access ($10/day), minibar, hair dryer, iron, safe, robes.

Taj Boston ⟨⟩   Better known as "the old Ritz-Carlton," Taj Boston is quickly making a name for itself. The legendary hotel overlooking the Public Garden became part of the India-based luxury chain in 2007. Completely restored for its 75th anniversary in 2002, the lovely property is undergoing regular upgrades and updates. The elegantly appointed guest rooms have dark-wood furnishings, feather duvets, crystal chandeliers, three phones (one in the marble bathroom), and windows that open. You'll pay more for a room with a view. The best units are the suites, which have wood-burning fireplaces. One of the most traditional lodgings in town, The Taj is competitive with other top-tier hotels—especially the archrival Four Seasons, 2 blocks away—on cachet alone, but state-of-the-art fitness facilities help the InterContinental and (eventually) the Mandarin Oriental mount a serious challenge.

15 Arlington St., Boston, MA 02116. ℰ 877/482-5267 or 617/536-5700. Fax 617/536-1335. www.tajhotels.com. 273 units. From $325 double; from $425 Club Level or suite. Children under 13 stay free in parent's room. Extra person $20. Weekend, family, and other packages available. AE, DC, DISC, MC, V. Valet parking $42. T: Green Line to Arlington. Pets accepted. **Amenities:** Restaurant; bar; lounge; exercise room; concierge; courtesy car; airport shuttle; business center; 24-hr. room service; in-room massage; babysitting; laundry service; same-day dry cleaning; club-level rooms; rooms for those w/limited mobility. *In room:* A/C, TV w/pay movies, high-speed Internet access ($11/day), minibar, hair dryer, iron, safe.

EXPENSIVE
Boston Park Plaza Hotel & Towers ⟨⟩   A Boston mainstay—it was built as the

Statler Hilton in 1927—the Park Plaza does a hopping convention and function business. It's the antithesis of generic, with an old-fashioned atmosphere and a cavernous, ornate lobby, yet it offers modern comforts in the guest rooms, where the design is more contemporary than in the elaborate public spaces. The latest round of renovations, upgrading the technology as well as the appointments in the guest rooms, was completed in 2005. The least expensive units here are small; if you're not a crash-and-dash traveler, the extra space might be worth the extra money. Don't expect personalized service in a hotel this large and busy. The lobby of the 15-story building is a little commercial hub, with a travel agency, pharmacy, currency exchange, and Amtrak and airline ticket offices.

64 Arlington St., Boston, MA 02116. ℰ 800/225-2008 or 617/426-2000. Fax 617/423-1708. www.bostonparkplaza. com. 941 units, some with shower only. $175–$399 double; $375–$2,000 suite. Extra person $25. Children under 18

> (*Tips* **Planning Pointer**
>
> If your trip involves a cultural event—for example, a big museum show—look into a hotel package that includes tickets. Usually offered on weekends, these deals always save time and can save money.

---

stay free in parent's room. Senior discount, weekend, and family packages available. AE, DC, DISC, MC, V. Valet parking $38. T: Green Line to Arlington. **Amenities:** 3 restaurants; nightclub; exercise room; concierge; business center; salon; 24-hr. room service; rooms for those w/limited mobility. *In room:* A/C, TV w/pay movies, high-speed Internet access ($10/day), coffeemaker, hair dryer, iron.

COPLEY SQUARE/HYNES CONVENTION CENTER
VERY EXPENSIVE

The Hong Kong–based Mandarin Oriental chain's first New England property was under construction on Boylston Street at Fairfield Street as this guide went to press. The 148-unit **Mandarin Oriental, Boston** (© 866/526-6567 or 617/531-0888; www.mandarinoriental.com/boston) is slated to open in the fall of 2008. The property is part of a 14-story hotel-condo development connected directly to the Prudential Center. It has a 16,000-square-foot spa, two restaurants (including the relocated L'Espalier), a lounge, and the ultraluxurious brand's over-the-top appointments and service.

Estimated to reopen late 2008, the **Copley Square Hotel,** 47 Huntington Ave., Boston, MA 02116 (© 800/225-7062 or 617/536-9000; www.copleysquarehotel. com), isn't just under renovation—it's closed, with walls in much of the seven-story building stripped to the studs. Opened in 1891, the 143-unit hotel is leaping straight from elaborate Edwardian decor to $14 million worth of streamlined style executed in tasteful neutrals. After the overhaul, guest rooms—some of which are quite snug—will have pillow-top beds and the latest tech accouterments; expect prices to match.

Colonnade Hotel Boston ★★ *Kids*   Adjacent to Copley Place and the Prudential Center, the independently owned Colonnade is a luxurious spot of European-style calm in the Back Bay's retail frenzy. The attentive, gracious staff caters to an international clientele of businesspeople, sightseers, shoppers, and families. An $18-million renovation completed in 2008 made the 11-story concrete-and-glass hotel even more desirable—the large guest rooms, decorated in muted earth tones, have pillow-top beds, marble-clad bathrooms, and sleek residential-style furnishings (a round table with two chairs on casters replaces the desk). Light floods through floor-to-ceiling windows, which open on the bustling Prudential Center or the South End's urban patchwork. The seasonal "rooftop resort" and swimming pool are a welcome change of pace in warm weather. Suites have dining rooms and sitting areas; my favorite is the Conductor's Suite (a nod to nearby Symphony Hall), which holds a baby grand piano.

120 Huntington Ave., Boston, MA 02116. © 800/962-3030 or 617/424-7000. Fax 617/424-1717. www.colonnade hotel.com. 285 units. $175–$459 double; $575–$1,750 suite. Children under 12 stay free in parent's room. Weekend, family, and other packages, winter and other discounts available. AE, DC, DISC, MC, V. Parking $36. T: Green Line E to Prudential. Pets accepted. **Amenities:** Restaurant (Brasserie Jo, p. 127); bar; heated outdoor rooftop pool; fitness center; concierge; 24-hr. business center; 24-hr. room service; in-room massage; babysitting; laundry service; same-day dry cleaning; rooms for those w/limited mobility. *In room:* A/C, TV/DVD w/pay movies, wireless Internet access, minibar, hair dryer, iron, safe.

Eliot Hotel 🏃🏃 This exquisite hotel combines the flavor of Yankee Boston with European-style service and abundant amenities. On tree-lined Commonwealth Avenue, the red-brick building looks more like a classy apartment building than a hotel, with a romantic atmosphere, subtle geometric and floral patterns on the rugs and upholstery, and top-notch business features. Almost every unit is a spacious suite (16 rooms are standard doubles) with antique furnishings, down comforters, and authentic botanical prints. French doors separate the living rooms and bedrooms in the suites, and all bathrooms are outfitted in Italian marble. The neo-Georgian 1925 building is near Boston University and MIT (across the river), and the location contrasts pleasantly with the bustle of Newbury Street, a block away.

370 Commonwealth Ave. (at Mass. Ave.), Boston, MA 02215. 🕐 **800/44-ELIOT** or 617/267-1607. Fax 617/536-9114. www.eliothotel.com. 95 units, 8 with shower only. $235–$395 double; $355–$545 1-bedroom suite for 2; $580–$890 2-bedroom suite. Extra person $30. Children under 18 stay free in parent's room. Packages available. AE, DC, MC, V. Valet parking $36. T: Green Line B, C, or D to Hynes Convention Center. Pets accepted. **Amenities:** Restaurant (eclectic); sashimi bar; free access to nearby health club; concierge; business center; 24-hr. room service; in-room massage; babysitting; laundry service; same-day dry cleaning; rooms for those w/limited mobility. *In room:* A/C, TV w/pay movies, wireless Internet access ($10/day), minibar, hair dryer, iron, umbrella, robes.

The Fairmont Copley Plaza 🏃🏃 The "grande dame of Boston" is a classic old-fashioned grand hotel, with opulent public spaces that recall the days when traveling was an event, not an ordeal. Built in 1912, the seven-story Renaissance-revival building faces beautiful Copley Square. The spacious, painstakingly maintained guest rooms have a residential feel, with plush draperies and upholstery and custom furnishings, including oversize desks and pillow-top mattresses. Rooms that face the square afford better views than those that overlook busy Dartmouth Street; my favorites are theme suites celebrating local treasures such as the Boston Symphony. Known for superb service, the Copley Plaza boasts countless details (inventive weekend packages, a resident black Lab guests can book for a walk or run) that have made it a favorite with generations of Bostonians and visitors.

138 St. James Ave., Boston, MA 02116. 🕐 **800/257-7544** or 617/267-5300. Fax 617/267-7668. www.fairmont.com/copleyplaza. 383 units. From $289 double; from $899 suite. Extra person $30. Weekend and other packages available. AE, DC, MC, V. Valet parking $39. T: Green Line to Copley or Orange Line to Back Bay. Pets accepted; $25/day. **Amenities:** Restaurant (steakhouse); lounge (Oak Bar, p. 238); exercise room; access to nearby health club ($15); concierge; tour desk; courtesy car; business center; 24-hr. room service; laundry service; same-day dry cleaning; concierge-level rooms; rooms for those w/limited mobility. *In room:* A/C, TV w/pay movies, high-speed Internet access ($14/day), minibar, hair dryer, iron, safe, umbrella, robes.

The Lenox Hotel 🏃🏃 The Lenox was the latest thing when it opened in 1900, and in its second century, it echoes that *fin-de-siècle* splendor everywhere, from the ornate lobby to the spacious, luxurious accommodations. The high-ceilinged guest rooms are large enough to contain sitting areas, and custom-designed wood furnishings and marble bathrooms add to the anything-but-generic vibe. My favorites are the 12 corner units with wood-burning fireplaces; rooms on the top two floors of the 11-story building enjoy excellent views. The central location makes the hotel popular with business travelers, and its relatively small size and accommodating staff make it a welcome alternative to the huge convention hotels that dominate this neighborhood. As a rule, though, those larger competitors have more extensive fitness facilities.

61 Exeter St. (at Boylston St.), Boston, MA 02116. 🕐 **800/225-7676** or 617/536-5300. Fax 617/236-0351. www.lenoxhotel.com. 212 units, some with shower only. $225–$425 double; $395–$545 junior suite; from $695 1-bedroom fireplace suite. Extra person $40. Children under 17 stay free in parent's room. Corporate, weekend, and family packages available. AE, DC, DISC, MC, V. Valet or self-parking $41. T: Green Line to Copley. **Amenities:** Well-regarded

(Kids Family-Friendly Hotels

Almost every hotel in the Boston area regularly plays host to children, and many offer special family packages. For more information, see "Family Travel," p. 47. Moderately priced chains have the most experience with youngsters, but their higher-end competitors put on a good show.

Units at the **Doubletree Guest Suites** (p. 92) are a great deal—they have two rooms in which to spread out, and they cost far less than adjoining rooms at any other hotel this nice. The in-room coffeemaker and refrigerator can help with breakfast preparation, allowing you to splurge on lunch and dinner.

In the Back Bay, the **Colonnade Hotel Boston** (p. 85) offers a family weekend package that includes parking, breakfast for two adults, up to four passes (for 2 adults and 2 children) to an attraction of your choice, and a fanny pack for younger guests that holds sunglasses, a pad and pen, a yo-yo, and a toy duck.

The **Seaport Hotel** (p. 81), near Museum Wharf, offers excellent weekend deals, splendid views of the harbor and airport, underwater music piped into the swimming pool, and even a grandparent-grandchild package.

The large rooms and proximity to downtown (15 minutes by subway) make the **Holiday Inn Boston Brookline** (p. 93) a good base for families.

In Cambridge, the **Royal Sonesta Hotel** (p. 96) is around the corner from the Museum of Science and has a large indoor/outdoor pool. It fills the vacation months with Summerfest, which includes free use of bicycles, ice cream, and boat rides along the Charles River. On off-season weekends, the Family Fun package includes four passes to the Museum of Science or the New England Aquarium.

Across the street, **Hotel Marlowe** (p. 96) boasts an excellent location, the welcoming atmosphere that family travelers have come to expect from the Kimpton chain, and special weekend packages.

The riverfront **Hyatt Regency Cambridge** (p. 97) courts families with its pool, bicycle rentals, easy access to the banks of the Charles, and discounted rates (subject to availability) on a separate room for the kids.

restaurant (contemporary American); bar; pub; small exercise room; bike rental; concierge; tour desk; car-rental desk; airport shuttle; business center; room service until 11pm; in-room massage; babysitting; laundry service; same-day dry cleaning. Rooms for those w/limited mobility and wheelchair lift to the lobby are available. *In room:* A/C, TV w/pay movies, wireless Internet access, coffeemaker, hair dryer, iron, safe, umbrella, robes.

EXPENSIVE

Hotels in this neighborhood and price category are catnip for tour groups, especially during foliage season. Consider a different location or a smaller lodging if big crowds wearing nametags bother you—but don't count on avoiding them completely.

Boston Marriott Copley Place ⟨★⟩   This 38-story tower offers something for everyone—complete business facilities, a good-size pool, and direct access to Boston's shopping wonderland. It's extremely popular with convention and meeting planners and is the hotel component of countless package deals. The contemporary-style guest rooms are large enough to hold two armchairs or an armchair and an ottoman; renovated in 2006, they have the chain's signature Revive bedding and down comforters. As at the Back Bay's other sky-high lodgings, ask for the highest possible floor and you'll enjoy excellent views. Besides booking hordes of vacationers, this Marriott and the Sheraton Boston (see below) are New England's biggest convention hotels; the Sheraton has a better pool, but both are reliable and comfortable enough that you can't go wrong by letting price and frequent-traveler points distinguish between them.

110 Huntington Ave., Boston, MA 02116. © 800/228-9290 or 617/236-5800. Fax 617/236-5885. www.copleymarriott. com. 1,147 units. $159–$329 double; $500–$1,200 suite. Children stay free in parent's room. Weekend and other packages available. AE, DC, DISC, MC, V. Valet parking $42; self-parking $32. T: Orange Line to Back Bay, Green Line to Copley, or Green Line E to Prudential. **Amenities:** Restaurant (American); heated indoor pool; well-equipped health club; Jacuzzi; sauna; game room; concierge; tour desk; car-rental desk; airport shuttle; full-service business center; 24-hr. room service; massage; laundry service; same-day dry cleaning; concierge-level rooms; rooms for those w/limited mobility. *In room:* A/C, TV w/pay movies, high-speed Internet access ($10/day), fridge, coffeemaker, hair dryer, iron, safe.

Courtyard by Marriott Boston Copley Square ✿

Opened in 2004 in a renovated 1891 apartment building on a side street off Copley Square, this 10-story limited-service hotel retains a residential atmosphere. Designed as a corporate hotel, with oversize work desks and a "library lounge" lobby that's suitable for a meeting, this place does so much leisure business that rates often rise on weekends. In the guest rooms, contemporary mahogany furnishings, subdued florals, and jewel tones create a boutique feel. I especially like the five suites; each has a sleeper sofa in the meeting-friendly living room. Without an all-day restaurant or the lavish perks of most other neighborhood hotels (including its gargantuan sister property in Copley Place), the hotel woos—and wins—repeat business with top-notch service and early-evening activities such as massages and beer tastings.

88 Exeter St., Boston, MA 02116. © 800/321-2211 or 617/437-9300. Fax 617/437-9330. www.courtyardboston. com. 81 units. $159–$399 double; from $219 suite. Children under 12 stay free in parent's room. Weekend and other packages, AAA and senior discounts available. AE, DC, DISC, MC, V. Valet parking $39. T: Green Line to Copley or Orange Line to Back Bay. **Amenities:** Restaurant (breakfast only); fitness room; access to nearby health club ($10); concierge; laundry service; dry cleaning. *In room:* A/C, TV w/pay movies, high-speed Internet access, fridge, coffeemaker, hair dryer, iron, safe.

Hilton Boston Back Bay ✿

Across the street from the Hynes Convention Center and the Prudential Center complex, the Hilton is primarily a top-notch business hotel, but vacationing families also find it convenient and comfortable. The well-maintained guest rooms were spruced up in 2007 and 2008; they're large, sound-proofed, and furnished in modern style, with oversize work desks. Units on higher floors of the 26-story tower enjoy excellent views. The weekend packages, especially in winter, can be a great deal. The atmosphere here tends to be considerably calmer than the scene at the three mega-hotels attached to the Pru and Copley Place. The closest of those, the Sheraton, is right across the street. It's three times the Hilton's size (which generally means less personalized service), has a better pool, and books more vacation and function business.

40 Dalton St., Boston, MA 02115. © 800/874-0663, 800/HILTONS, or 617/236-1100. Fax 617/867-6104. www. bostonbackbay.hilton.com. 385 units, 66 with shower only. $149–$399 double; from $450 suite. Extra person $20. Rollaway $20. Children under 18 stay free in parent's room. Packages and AAA discount available. AE, DC, DISC, MC, V. Valet parking $39; self-parking $35. T: Green Line B, C, or D to Hynes Convention Center. Pets accepted. **Amenities:** Restaurant (American/Continental); bar; indoor pool; well-equipped fitness center; concierge; courtesy car;

24-hr. business center; 24-hr. room service; laundry service; same-day dry cleaning; executive-level rooms; rooms for those w/limited mobility. *In room:* A/C, TV w/pay movies, high-speed Internet access ($10/stay), minibar, coffeemaker, hair dryer, iron.

Jurys Boston Hotel 🏨🏨 Jurys Doyle, a well-known Irish chain, isn't all that familiar in Boston, but this building is: It used to be police headquarters. These days the welcome is warmer and the business (weeknight) and leisure (weekend) clientele more satisfied than the former guests. The original 1925 limestone-and-brick building gained a wing and two floors before opening in 2004, and the public areas went from drab to dramatic. Decorated in peaceful, muted colors, the luxurious guest rooms have nice touches such as a work area with an ergonomic chair, down comforters, good-size bathrooms (not a sure thing in a renovation), and windows that open but also do a good job of muffling street noise. Still, light sleepers will want to face away from busy Berkeley Street and perhaps request a room on the second floor, where windows are smaller than elsewhere.

350 Stuart St. (at Berkeley St.), Boston, MA 02116. ✆ 866/JD-HOTELS or 617/266-7200. Fax 617/266-7203. http:// bostonhotels.jurysdoyle.com. 225 units, some with shower only. $295–$435 double; $275–$575 1-bedroom suite; from $1,150 2-bedroom suite. Children under 16 stay free in parent's room. Extra person $20. Weekend, family, and other packages available. AE, DC, DISC, MC, V. Valet parking $39. **T:** Orange Line to Back Bay, or Green Line to Arlington or Copley. **Amenities:** Restaurant (American); Irish bar; coffee and wine bar; exercise room; business center; 24-hr. room service; laundry service; same-day dry cleaning; rooms for those w/limited mobility. *In room:* A/C, TV w/pay movies, wireless Internet access, fridge, hair dryer, iron, safe, umbrella, robes.

Sheraton Boston Hotel 🏨 Its central location, range of accommodations, extensive convention and function facilities, and huge pool make this 29-story hotel one of the most popular in the city. The Sheraton attracts both business and leisure travelers with direct access to the Hynes Convention Center and the Prudential Center complex. The fairly large guest rooms, decorated in sleek contemporary style, contain the chain's signature sleigh beds with pillow-top mattresses. Units on the highest floors are club-level suites, but even standard accommodations on higher floors afford gorgeous views. Because it's so big, the Sheraton often has available rooms when smaller properties are full. If you're on a budget, shop around before you book; you may be able to find a better deal elsewhere.

39 Dalton St., Boston, MA 02199. ✆ 800/325-3535 or 617/236-2000. Fax 617/236-1702. www.sheraton.com/ boston. 1,215 units. $209–$409 double; $309–$1,800 suite. Children under 17 stay free in parent's room. Weekend packages available. 25% discount for students, faculty, and retired persons with ID, depending on availability. AE, DC, DISC, MC, V. Valet parking $39. **T:** Green Line E to Prudential, or B, C, or D to Hynes Convention Center. Dogs under 40 lb. accepted with prior approval. **Amenities:** Restaurant (New England); lounge; heated indoor/outdoor pool; well-equipped health club; Jacuzzi; sauna; concierge; airport shuttle; business center; room service until 11pm; laundry service; same-day dry cleaning; executive-level rooms; rooms for those w/limited mobility. *In room:* A/C, TV w/pay movies, high-speed Internet access ($10/day), coffeemaker, hair dryer, iron.

The Westin Copley Place Boston 🏨🏨 Towering 36 stories above Copley Square, the Westin attracts business travelers, convention-goers, sightseers, and dedicated shoppers with its great location and solicitous staff. Sky bridges link the hotel to Copley Place and the Prudential Center complex, and Copley Square is across the street from the pedestrian entrance. The spacious guest rooms—all on the eighth floor or higher—have traditional oak and mahogany furniture, Westin's beloved pillow-top mattresses, and decent-size bathrooms. Junior suites are oversized doubles with generous sitting areas, but one-bedroom suites have one of the most entertaining features around: a queen-size Murphy bed in the living room. You might not notice any of that at first—the views of downtown Boston, the airport and harbor, and the Charles River and Cambridge are spectacular.

10 Huntington Ave., Boston, MA 02116. (© **800/WESTIN-1** or 617/262-9600. Fax 617/424-7483. www.westin.com/copleyplace. 803 units. $179–$479 double; $239–$539 suite; $999–$3,300 specialty suite. Extra person $25–$50. Weekend packages available. AE, DC, DISC, MC, V. Valet parking $40. T: Green Line to Copley or Orange Line to Back Bay. Pets accepted. **Amenities:** 3 restaurants (a branch of New York's famous Palm steakhouse, Turner Fisheries, breakfast cafe); bar; indoor pool; health club and spa; children's programs; concierge; car-rental desk; airport shuttle; well-equipped business center; shopping arcade; salon; 24-hr. room service; in-room massage; laundry service; executive-level rooms. 48 rooms for those w/limited mobility adjoin standard units. *In room:* A/C, TV/VCR w/pay movies, high-speed Internet access ($16/day), minibar, coffeemaker, hair dryer, iron, safe, robes.

MODERATE

Charlesmark Hotel ★★ *Value*   In an excellent location overlooking the Boston Marathon finish line, the Charlesmark has a boutique feel and great prices. It's both luxurious and—literally, not figuratively—no frills. The sleek, contemporary design uses custom furnishings to maximize the 1892 building's compact spaces. Guest rooms are small, but they have pillow-top mattresses and enough space to hold a comfortable chair. The Charlesmark's amenities don't challenge the perks of the neighborhood's large hotels, but they're more than sufficient for most business or leisure travelers. The second-floor lobby holds a computer and printer for guests' use. Rates include breakfast, light refreshments such as bottled water and fruit, and local phone calls, all part of management's policy not to pad your bill with incidentals. The only real drawback is that the building has just one elevator—and if that's your biggest problem, you're doing pretty well.

655 Boylston St. (between Dartmouth and Exeter sts.), Boston, MA 02116. (© **617/247-1212.** Fax 617/247-1224. www.thecharlesmark.com. 33 units, most with shower only. $109–$249 double. Rates include continental breakfast. Children stay free in parent's room. AE, DC, DISC, MC, V. Self-parking $32 in nearby garage. T: Green Line to Copley. Pets accepted with prior approval. **Amenities:** Lounge; access to nearby health club ($10); laundry service; rooms for those w/limited mobility. *In room:* A/C, TV, high-speed Internet access, mini-fridge, hair dryer.

Hotel 140 *Value*   This is a textbook example of a hotel style I call "budget boutique": Rooms and bathrooms are small, amenities few, and prices reasonable. In a great location in the pricey Back Bay, Hotel 140 is a deal. The contemporary-style hotel opened in 2005 in a renovated former YWCA that dates to 1929. Rooms are on the fifth through seventh floors of the 14-story building that houses (among other things) the offices of the "Y," which owns the hotel. Each simply decorated room has a full-size or twin-size bed, without much extra space, but the hotel consistently fills with leisure and thrifty business travelers. Its main competitor is the John Hancock Hotel, a block away, which is roughly comparable but more traditional in style.

140 Clarendon St., Boston, MA 02116. (© **800/714-0140** or 617/585-5600. www.hotel140.com. 55 units (all with shower only). $119–$189 double. Rates include continental breakfast. Weekend, theater, and other packages available. AE, MC, V. Parking $20 in adjacent garage. T: Orange Line to Back Bay. **Amenities:** Exercise room; business center; rooms for those w/limited mobility. *In room:* A/C, TV, high-speed Internet access, hair dryer, iron.

The John Hancock Hotel & Conference Center *Finds*   In an unbeatable location on a dead-end street near Back Bay Station, this eight-story hotel is a hidden jewel. A limited-service lodging with an old-fashioned air and a helpful staff, it books many groups that use the abundant meeting space. The compact, comfortable guest rooms were spruced up and had their furniture replaced in 2007. Unlike the large, elaborate lobby, they're not fancy, but they're well maintained and big enough not to feel claustrophobic; bathrooms, however, are tiny. The 1925 building has been a hotel since

1986. Aramark, the national-park and sports-arena concessionaire, manages the hotel for the eponymous insurance firm, which books the whole place in the weeks before the Boston Marathon. The closest competitor, the funkier Hotel 140, sometimes beats this hotel on price.

40 Trinity Place (off Stuart St.), Boston, MA 02116. © **617/933-7700**. Fax 617/933-7709. www.jhcenter.com. 64 units. $189 double. Rates include continental breakfast. Children under 18 stay free in parent's room. Extra person $15. Off-season discounts available. AE, DC, DISC, MC, V. Parking $18 in nearby garage. Closed to the public 1st 3 weeks of Apr. T: Orange Line to Back Bay or Green Line to Copley. **Amenities:** Rooms for those w/limited mobility. *In room:* A/C, TV, wireless Internet access, hair dryer, iron.

The MidTown Hotel 🐦 (Value

This centrally located two-story hotel is popular with families, budget-conscious businesspeople, and especially tour groups. The boxy white building is on a busy street across from the Prudential Center, within walking distance of Symphony Hall and the Museum of Fine Arts. The hotel has been completely renovated since 2006 and the second floor will get its turn in 2007 and early 2008; ask for a refurbished room, and if one isn't available, be sure to request a unit away from the work area. Throughout the building, rooms are large, bright, and attractively outfitted in no-frills contemporary style, although bathrooms are on the small side. Some units have connecting doors that allow families to spread out. The best rooms are at the back of the building, away from Huntington Avenue traffic. Photocopying and fax services are available at the front desk. Although the MidTown is no longer that rarest of birds, a super-convenient hotel with free parking, the fee is the lowest around—less than one-third of the charge at some fancier lodgings.

220 Huntington Ave., Boston, MA 02445. © **800/343-1177** or 617/262-1000. Fax 617/262-8739. www.midtown hotel.com. 159 units. $119–$259 double; $139–$279 suite. Extra person $15. Children under 18 stay free in parent's room. Packages and AAA, AARP, and government discounts may be available. AE, DC, DISC, MC, V. Parking $12. T: Green Line E to Prudential or Orange Line to Mass. Ave. **Amenities:** Heated outdoor pool; access to nearby health club ($5–$10); concierge; airport shuttle; laundry service; same-day dry cleaning; rooms for those w/limited mobility. *In room:* A/C, TV w/pay movies, wireless Internet access ($10/day), coffeemaker, hair dryer, iron.

Newbury Guest House 🐦 (Value

After just a little shopping in the Back Bay, you'll appreciate what a find this cozy place is: a bargain on Newbury Street. The comfortably furnished, nicely appointed guest rooms take up three 1880s brick town houses. The largest and most expensive are the bay-window units, which overlook the lively street. Breakfast is served in the ground-level dining room, which adjoins a brick patio. The Newbury Guest House opened in 1991 and operates near capacity year-round, drawing business travelers during the week and sightseers on weekends. At these prices in this location, there's only one caveat: Reserve early.

261 Newbury St. (between Fairfield and Gloucester sts.), Boston, MA 02116. © **800/437-7668** or 617/670-6000. Fax 617/670-6100. www.newburyguesthouse.com. 32 units, some with shower only. $135–$195 double. Extra person $20. Rates include continental breakfast. Rates may be higher during special events. Minimum 2 nights on weekends. Packages available. AE, DC, DISC, MC, V. Parking $20 (reservation required). T: Green Line B, C, or D to Hynes Convention Center. **Amenities:** Access to nearby health club ($25); rooms for those w/limited mobility. *In room:* A/C, TV, wireless Internet access, hair dryer, iron.

INEXPENSIVE

Hostelling International–Boston

This eco-conscious hostel near the Berklee College of Music and Symphony Hall caters to students, youth groups, and other travelers in search of comfortable, no-frills lodging. Accommodations are dorm-style (all men, all women, or co-ed), with six beds per room. A couple of private units sleep one or two. The air-conditioned hostel has two full dine-in kitchens, 29 bathrooms (men and women have separate facilities), a large common room, and meeting and workshop space. It provides linens, or you can bring your own; sleeping bags are not permitted. The enthusiastic staff organizes free and inexpensive cultural, educational, and recreational programs on the premises and throughout the Boston area. Hostelling International also operates a summer-only hostel just outside Kenmore Square (p. 93).

12 Hemenway St., Boston, MA 02115. ✆ **888/999-4678** or 617/536-9455. Fax 617/424-6558. www.bostonhostel. org. 205 beds. Members of Hostelling International–American Youth Hostels $28–$45 per bed; nonmembers $31–$48 per bed. Members $70–$100 per private unit; nonmembers $73–$106 per private unit. Children 3–12 half-price; children under 3 free. Rates include continental breakfast. MC, V. T: Green Line B, C, or D to Hynes Convention Center. **Amenities:** Access to nearby health club ($6); shuttle; coin-op laundry; wireless Internet access. 1st-floor units and bathrooms are wheelchair accessible; wheelchair lift at building entrance. *In room:* A/C, lockers, no phone.

10 Outskirts & Brookline

What Bostonians consider "outskirts" would be centrally located in many larger cities. Brookline starts about 3 blocks beyond Boston's Kenmore Square. Staying in this area means essentially becoming a commuter to downtown Boston (unless you're in town only to visit Fenway Park or the Longwood Medical Area). It's not a great choice if your destination is Cambridge because of the unwieldy public transit connections.

VERY EXPENSIVE

Hotel Commonwealth ★★   This five-story boutique hotel in the heart of Kenmore Square boasts extensive business features as well as luxurious amenities such as Frette linens and large marble bathrooms. My favorite guest rooms are the huge Commonwealth units; each has a king bed and a heavy curtain that draws across the center of the room, separating the sleeping area and the "parlor." These rooms overlook the bustling street, outdoor restaurant seating, and the upgraded square's new bus station. You might prefer a Fenway room—they're smaller, but they face the legendary ballpark (directly across the Mass. Pike). Formerly quite scruffy, Kenmore Square has undergone a face-lift—helped immeasurably by the 2003 opening of this hotel. It draws a lot of business from nearby Boston University and from local cultural institutions.

500 Commonwealth Ave., Boston, MA 02215. ✆ **866/784-4000** or 617/933-5000. Fax 617/266-6888. www.hotel commonwealth.com. 150 units. $235–$415 standard double; $265–$485 minisuite or parlor room. Extra person $20. Children under 18 stay free in parent's room. Packages and AAA discount available. AE, DC, DISC, MC, V. Valet parking $36. T: Green Line B, C, or D to Kenmore. Pets accepted; $25 deposit. **Amenities:** 2 restaurants (seafood, bistro); lounge; exercise room; concierge; business center; room service; laundry service; same-day dry cleaning; rooms for those w/limited mobility. *In room:* A/C, TV/DVD w/pay movies, wireless Internet access, minibar, hair dryer, iron, safe, umbrella, robes.

EXPENSIVE

Doubletree Guest Suites ★★ (Kids) (Value)   This hotel is one of the best deals in town—every unit is a two-room suite with a living room, bedroom, and bathroom. Business travelers can entertain and families can spread out, making this a good choice for both. It's near Cambridge and across the street from the path that follows the Charles River, but not in an actual neighborhood. Shuttle service to local destinations makes the isolation easier to handle. The suites, which were renovated in 2007, surround a 15-story atrium. Rooms are large and attractively furnished, and most bedrooms have a king-size bed (some have two oversize twins) and a writing desk. Each living room contains a full-size sofa bed, a dining table, and a good-size refrigerator. The Hyatt Regency Cambridge, the hotel's nearest rival, is slightly more convenient than the Doubletree but generally more expensive.

400 Soldiers Field Rd., Boston, MA 02134. (C) **800/222-TREE** or 617/783-0090. Fax 617/783-0897. www.doubletree. com. 308 units. $129–$309 double. Extra person $20. Children under 18 stay free in parent's room. Packages and AARP and AAA discounts available. AE, DC, DISC, MC, V. Valet parking $27; self-parking $20. Pets accepted with prior approval. **Amenities:** Restaurant (American); lounge; excellent Scullers Jazz Club (p. 233); indoor pool; exercise room; free access to nearby health club; Jacuzzi; sauna; concierge; shuttle service to Cambridge and downtown Boston; 24-hr. business center; room service until 3am; coin-op laundry; laundry service; same-day dry cleaning; rooms for those w/limited mobility. *In room:* A/C, TV w/pay movies, wireless Internet access ($10/day), fridge, coffeemaker, hair dryer, iron.

MODERATE

The 188-room **Brookline Courtyard by Marriott,** 40 Webster St., Brookline ((C) **866/ 296-2296,** 800/321-2211, or 617/734-1393; fax 617/734-1392; www.brookline courtyard.com), is off Beacon Street in Coolidge Corner. The eight-story hotel has a breakfast cafe, an indoor pool, an exercise room, and shuttle service to the nearby Longwood Medical Area. The double rate is $159 to $399, which includes high-speed Internet access.

Best Western Boston/The Inn at Longwood Medical (ℱ)   Next to Children's Hospital in the Longwood Medical Area, this eight-story hotel is a good base for those with business at the hospitals. It's also near museums, colleges, and Fenway Park, and about 20 minutes from downtown Boston by T. The well-maintained guest rooms are quite large and furnished in colorful, contemporary style. Try to stay on the highest floor possible, not just because the views are better but because the busy intersection of Longwood and Brookline avenues is less than scenic. Suites have kitchen facilities that make them a good choice for long-term guests. The hotel adjoins the Longwood Galleria business complex, which has a food court and shops, including a drugstore.

342 Longwood Ave., Boston, MA 02115. (C) **800/GOT-BEST** or 617/731-4700, TTY 617/731-9088. Fax 617/731-4870. www.innatlongwood.com. 161 units, 18 with kitchenette. $139–$259 double; from $269 suite. Extra person $15. Children under 18 stay free in parent's room. Weekend and family packages, hospital and long-term discounts available. AE, DC, DISC, MC, V. Parking $18. T: Green Line D or E to Longwood. **Amenities:** Restaurant (international); lounge; access to nearby health club ($8); concierge; room service until 12:30am; coin-op laundry; laundry service; same-day dry cleaning; rooms for those w/limited mobility. *In room:* A/C, TV w/pay movies, high-speed and wireless Internet access, coffeemaker, hair dryer, iron.

Holiday Inn Boston Brookline (ℱ) *(Kids*   Only 15 minutes from downtown Boston on the subway, this six-story hotel is in a mostly residential area not far from the Longwood Medical Area and Boston University. Because of the location—which for many travelers is actually a plus—it charges lower prices than more centrally located hotels for comparable accommodations. Guest rooms, which were renovated in 2006, are large and well appointed, with oversize work desks. Units at the front of the building have more interesting views; they may be slightly noisier because of the busy trolley route below, but double-glazed windows keep the volume down. The bustling Coolidge Corner neighborhood is a 5-minute walk away.

1200 Beacon St., Brookline, MA 02446. (C) **800/HOLIDAY** or 617/277-1200. www.holiday-inn.com. 225 units, some with shower only. $149–$229 double; $229–$279 suite. Extra person $10. Children under 18 stay free in parent's room. AE, MC, V. Parking $15. T: Green Line C to St. Paul St. Pets accepted; $15 fee. **Amenities:** Restaurant (American); lounge; coffee shop; small indoor pool; exercise room; Jacuzzi; shuttle to hospitals; laundry service; same-day dry cleaning; club-level rooms; rooms for those w/limited mobility. *In room:* A/C, TV, high-speed and wireless Internet access, coffeemaker, hair dryer, iron.

INEXPENSIVE

A summer-only hostel occupies a former Howard Johnson hotel just outside Kenmore Square: **Hostelling International—Boston at Fenway,** 575 Commonwealth Ave.

(© **617/267-8599;** fax 617/424-6558; www.hifenway.org; T: Green Line B, C, or D to Kenmore). The 485-bed hostel offers well-equipped accommodations in a building that doubles as a Boston University dorm during the school year. Rates are $35 per bed for members of Hostelling International–American Youth Hostels, $38 for non-members. Private rooms for one to three guests cost $89 to $99.

Anthony's Town House   Many patrons at this four-story brownstone guesthouse, a family business since 1944, are Europeans accustomed to homey accommodations with shared bathrooms, and budget-minded Americans won't be disappointed. Each floor has three high-ceilinged rooms furnished in Queen Anne or Victorian style and one bathroom with an enclosed shower. Smaller rooms (one per floor) have twin beds; the large front units have bay windows. Two family units hold as many as five comfortably. Guests have the use of two refrigerators and a microwave, and the staff will supply a VCR, DVD player, hair dryer, or iron on request. The guesthouse is 1 mile from Boston's Kenmore Square, about 15 minutes from downtown by T, and 2 blocks from a busy commercial strip. There's no smoking on the premises.

1085 Beacon St., Brookline, MA 02446. © **617/566-3972**. Fax 617/232-1085. www.anthonystownhouse.com. 10 units, none with private bathroom. $78–$108 double; from $125 family room. Extra person $10. Weekly rates and winter discounts available. No credit cards. Limited free parking. T: Green Line C to Hawes St. *In room:* A/C, TV, wireless Internet access, no phone.

Longwood Inn   In a residential area 3 blocks from the Boston-Brookline border, this well-kept three-story Victorian guesthouse offers comfortable accommodations at modest rates. The interior style is homey, with accents that suit the building's architecture. Rooms were redecorated in 2007, with new furniture and crisp color schemes. Guests have use of a fully equipped kitchen, a common dining room, and a patio furnished with tables and chairs. The apartment has a private bathroom, kitchen, and balcony. Tennis courts, a running track, and a playground at the school next door are open to the public. Public transportation is nearby, and the Longwood Medical Area and busy Coolidge Corner neighborhood are within easy walking distance.

123 Longwood Ave., Brookline, MA 02446. © **617/566-8615**. Fax 617/738-1070. www.longwood-inn.com. 22 units, 19 with private bathroom, 4 with shower only. Apr–Nov $114–$134 double; Dec–Mar $79–$99 double. Extra person $5–$10. 1-bedroom apt (sleeps 4-plus) $99–$139. Weekly rates available. AE, DISC, MC, V. Free parking. T: Green Line D to Longwood or C to Coolidge Corner. **Amenities:** Coin-op laundry. *In room:* A/C, TV, wireless Internet access.

11 Cambridge

Across the Charles River from Boston, Cambridge has its own attractions and excellent hotels. Graduation season (May and early June) is especially busy, but campus events can cause high demand at unexpected times, so plan ahead.

VERY EXPENSIVE

The Charles Hotel ★★★   This nine-story brick hotel, just a block from Harvard Square, has been *the* place for business and leisure travelers to Cambridge since it opened in 1985. Much of its fame derives from its excellent restaurants, jazz bar, and day spa; the service is equally impeccable. In the guest rooms, the style is contemporary country, with custom adaptations of early American Shaker furniture. The already-posh rooms underwent a complete renovation in early 2006. Their austere design contrasts with the swanky amenities, which include down quilts and Bose Wave radios; bathrooms contain telephones and TVs (in the mirrors—cool!). And it

Where to Stay in Cambridge

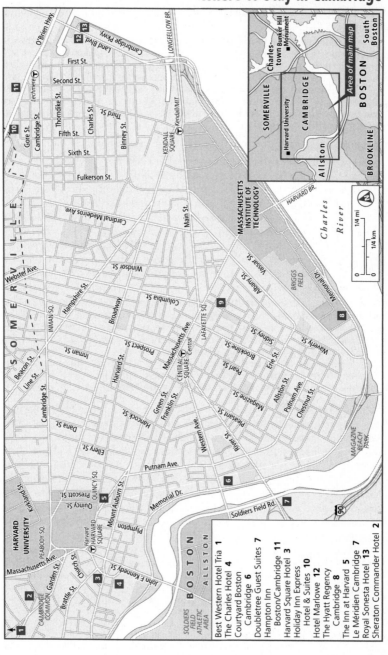

Best Western Hotel Tria **1**
The Charles Hotel **4**
Courtyard Boston
Cambridge **6**
Doubletree Guest Suites **7**
Hampton Inn
Boston/Cambridge **11**
Harvard Square Hotel **3**
Holiday Inn Express
Hotel & Suites **10**
Hotel Marlowe **12**
The Hyatt Regency
Cambridge **8**
The Inn at Harvard **5**
Le Méridien Cambridge **7**
Royal Sonesta Hotel **13**
Sheraton Commander Hotel **2**

wouldn't be Cambridge if your intellectual needs went unfulfilled—there's a library in the lobby.

1 Bennett St., Cambridge, MA 02138. © **800/882-1818** or 617/864-1200. Fax 617/864-5715. www.charleshotel. com. 293 units. $259–$599 double; $309–$4,000 suite. Extra person $20. Weekend packages available. AE, DC, MC, V. Valet or self-parking $34. T: Red Line to Harvard. Pets under 25 lb. accepted; $50 fee. **Amenities:** 2 restaurants (Rialto, one of Cambridge's best [p. 132], and Henrietta's Table, w/a lavish Sun brunch); 2 bars; Regattabar jazz club (p. 233); free access to adjacent health club w/glass-enclosed pool, Jacuzzi, and exercise room; adjacent spa and salon; concierge; car-rental desk; business center; 24-hr. room service; in-room massage; babysitting; laundry service; same-day dry cleaning; rooms for those w/limited mobility. *In room:* A/C, TV/DVD, high-speed Internet access ($11/day), minibar, hair dryer, iron, safe.

Hotel Marlowe ☆ *Kids*   Like Cambridge itself, Hotel Marlowe is fun, funky, and serious when it needs to be. The hotel opened in 2003 in a new eight-story building near the CambridgeSide Galleria mall and the Museum of Science—a great location for families—and offers abundant amenities for both business and leisure travelers. The rooms are elegantly decorated, with quirky touches like leopard-print carpeting, and large enough to hold a work desk and armchair. All have down comforters and three phones (one in the bathroom), and suites have spa tubs. Views are of the river (across the busy boulevard), a small canal, or the landscaped courtyard/driveway off the lobby. The eco-savvy hotel's closest competitor is the Royal Sonesta Hotel (see below), across the street, which has a pool and health club, better river views, and correspondingly higher prices.

25 Edwin H. Land Blvd., Cambridge, MA 02141. © **800/825-7040**, 800/KIMPTON, or 617/868-8000. Fax 617/868-8001. www.hotelmarlowe.com. 236 units, some with shower only. $199–$449 double; from $409 suite. Extra person $25. Rates include morning coffee and tea, evening wine reception, and use of bikes. Children under 18 stay free in parent's room. Weekend, family, and other packages, AARP and AAA discounts available. AE, DC, DISC, MC, V. Valet parking $28; self-parking $20. T: Green Line to Lechmere or Red Line to Kendall. Pets accepted. **Amenities:** Restaurant (American brasserie); bar; exercise room; concierge; business center; 24-hr. room service; in-room massage; laundry service; same-day dry cleaning; rooms for those w/limited mobility. *In room:* A/C, TV w/pay movies, high-speed and wireless Internet access, minibar, coffeemaker, hair dryer, iron, safe, umbrella, robes.

Royal Sonesta Hotel ☆☆ *Kids*   This luxurious hotel is close to only a few things but convenient to everything. It's popular with both business travelers and families (see "Family-Friendly Hotels," on p. 87). The CambridgeSide Galleria mall is across the street, the Museum of Science is around the corner, and Kendall Square is 10 minutes away on foot. Even in the midst of all this activity, the hotel feels serene, thanks in part to the helpful staff. Most of the good-size rooms in the 10-story building have lovely views of the river or the city (higher prices are for better views). Everything is custom-designed in modern, comfortable style and regularly refurbished. The closest competition is Hotel Marlowe (see above), across the street, which offers less extensive fitness options (there's no pool) and fewer river views.

40 Edwin H. Land Blvd., Cambridge, MA 02142. © **800/SONESTA** or 617/806-4200. Fax 617/806-4232. www.sonesta. com/boston. 400 units, some with shower only. $239–$279 standard double; $259–$299 superior double; $279–$319 deluxe double; $339–$1,000 suite. Extra person $25. Children under 18 stay free in parent's room. Weekend, family, and other packages available. AE, DC, DISC, MC, V. Valet or self-parking $27. T: Green Line to Lechmere, then a 10-min. walk. Pets accepted with prior approval. **Amenities:** Restaurant (New American/Mediterranean); cafe w/seasonal outdoor seating; heated indoor/outdoor pool w/retractable roof; well-equipped 24-hr. health club and spa; bike rental (seasonal); concierge; courtesy van; 24-hr. business center; 24-hr. room service; massage; laundry service; dry cleaning; rooms for those w/limited mobility and adjoining standard units are available; staff is trained in disability awareness. *In room:* A/C, TV w/pay movies, high-speed and wireless Internet access, minibar, coffeemaker, hair dryer, iron, safe, umbrella.

EXPENSIVE

The **Courtyard Boston Cambridge,** 777 Memorial Dr., Cambridge, MA 02139 (© **888/236-2427** or 617/492-7777; www.marriott.com), a former Radisson, opened in 2008. The 203-unit, 16-story hotel is across the street from the Charles River, meaning the views are great but public-transit access isn't. The property has a restaurant and an indoor pool; the best accommodations have private balconies. Rates for a double start at $149 and peak north of $300 in high season.

The Hyatt Regency Cambridge ✦ *(Kids*   The location of this dramatic pyramidal building is a plus and a minus. Across the street from the Charles River, the hotel is convenient to Harvard and Kendall squares and Boston University. Shuttle service and plentiful amenities help make up for the distance from the T. The spacious, well-outfitted guest rooms have pillow-top beds; most face the 16-story atrium, others overlook central Cambridge, and the best enjoy breathtaking views of Boston. A weekday business destination, the Hyatt Regency courts families (see "Family-Friendly Hotels," on p. 87) with special two-room rates, subject to availability. If you plan to rely on public transit, allow time for the bus or the hotel shuttle. If you're driving, downtown Boston is about 10 minutes away. The closest competitor is the Doubletree, which is even farther from public transit but consists of all suites.

575 Memorial Dr., Cambridge, MA 02139. © **800/233-1234** or 617/462-1234. Fax 617/491-6906. www.cambridge. hyatt.com. 469 units, some with shower only. $179–$359 double; $300–$750 suite. Extra person $25. Children under 18 stay free in parent's room. Weekend packages available. AE, DC, DISC, MC, V. Valet parking $39; self-parking $35. T: Red Line to Harvard or Kendall/MIT, then shuttle bus (no luggage permitted) or $6 cab ride. Pets under 25 lb. accepted; $50 fee. **Amenities:** Restaurant and lounge (eclectic); 75-ft. indoor lap pool; rooftop health club; Jacuzzi; sauna; bike rental; concierge; shuttle to Cambridge destinations; business center; room service until late evening; in-room massage; laundry service; same-day dry cleaning; ATM and currency exchange; rooms for those w/limited mobility. *In room:* A/C, TV w/pay movies, fax, wireless Internet access ($10/day), coffeemaker, hair dryer, iron.

The Inn at Harvard ✦✦   The red-brick Inn at Harvard looks like just another college building—it's adjacent to Harvard Yard, and its Georgian-style architecture would fit nicely on campus. Inside, however, there's no mistaking it for anything other than an elegant hotel, popular with business travelers and university visitors. Guest rooms were extensively renovated in 2006 and have pillow-top beds; each holds a work area with an Aeron chair, and a flatscreen TV. Some units have dormer windows and window seats. The four-story skylit atrium holds the "living room," a huge, well-appointed guest lounge that's suitable (in furnishings and volume level) for meeting with a visitor if you don't want to conduct business in your room.

1201 Massachusetts Ave. (at Quincy St.), Cambridge, MA 02138. © **800/458-5886** or 617/491-2222. Fax 617/520-3711. www.theinnatharvard.com. 111 units, some with shower only. $179–$419 double; $1,500 presidential suite. AAA and AARP discounts available. AE, DC, DISC, MC, V. Valet parking $45. T: Red Line to Harvard. **Amenities:** Restaurant (New England); dining privileges at the nearby Harvard Faculty Club; fitness center; room service until 10:30pm; laundry service; same-day dry cleaning; rooms for those w/limited mobility. *In room:* A/C, TV, wireless Internet access ($10/day), hair dryer, iron, umbrella, robes.

Le Méridien Cambridge ✦   The only sizable lodging close to lively Central Square, this hotel primarily attracts visitors to MIT and the tech-oriented businesses nearby. Le Méridien acquired the former Hotel@MIT in 2007 and plans to spruce it up in stages; ask for a room away from the work zone. Rooms are spacious enough to hold a small seating area, oversize desk, and decent-size bathroom. All boast the up-to-date technology you'd expect, with features such as the ability to send documents from your room to a networked laser printer. The eight-story building encloses a lovely courtyard; units facing inward are preferable to those with street views. The unusual decor—medium-tone woods, dark neutrals, and subtle patterns—includes equations printed on the quilt across the foot of the bed. That offbeat spirit extends to features such as robots in the lobby.

20 Sidney St. (at Green St., 1 block from Mass. Ave.), Cambridge, MA 02139. © 800/543-4300 or 617/577-0200. Fax 617/494-8366. www.hotelatmit.com. 210 units, 8 with shower only. $199–$419 double; $249–$519 suite. Children under 18 stay free in parent's room. Extra person $20. Weekend, family, and other packages, AAA and AARP discounts available. AE, DC, DISC, MC, V. Valet parking $28, self-parking $22. T: Red Line to Central. Pets under 50 lb. accepted. **Amenities:** Restaurant (American/Mediterranean); bar; 24-hr. fitness center; access to nearby health club; concierge; 24-hr. business center; laundry service; dry cleaning; rooms for those w/limited mobility. *In room:* A/C, TV w/pay movies, wireless Internet access, coffeemaker, hair dryer, iron, safe, robes.

Sheraton Commander Hotel ✿ This six-story hotel in the heart of Cambridge's historic district opened in 1927, and it's exactly what you'd expect of a traditional hostelry within sight of the Harvard campus. The elegant public areas and decent-size guest rooms share the colonial-style decor the regular clientele—business travelers, university guests, and visiting parents—has come to expect. Many units have canopy beds, and all have Sheraton's signature beds and plenty of accents in crimson, Harvard's school color. Ask the pleasant front-desk staff for a room facing Cambridge Common; even if you aren't on a (relatively) high floor, you'll have a pleasant view. The Sheraton Commander doesn't have the Charles Hotel's cachet and amenities, but it doesn't charge the Charles's prices, either. Plan far ahead if you're visiting during a Harvard event.

16 Garden St., Cambridge, MA 02138. © 800/325-3535 or 617/547-4800. Fax 617/234-1396. www.sheraton.com/commander. 175 units, some with shower only. $169–$375 double; $275–$1,000 suite. Extra person $20. Children under 18 stay free in parent's room. Weekend packages, AAA and AARP discounts available. AE, DC, DISC, MC, V. Valet parking $25. T: Red Line to Harvard. Dogs under 80 lb. accepted. **Amenities:** Restaurant (American); lounge; exercise room; concierge; business center; room service until 11pm; laundry service; dry cleaning; executive-level rooms; rooms for those w/limited mobility. *In room:* A/C, TV w/pay movies, high-speed Internet access ($10/day), coffeemaker, hair dryer, iron.

MODERATE

The **Hampton Inn Boston/Cambridge,** 191 Msgr. O'Brien Hwy., Cambridge (© **800/HAMPTON** or 617/494-5300; www.bostoncambridge.hamptoninn.com), is a 5-minute walk from the Green Line Lechmere stop. Rates at the 114-room hotel start at $159 for a double in high season and include parking, expanded continental breakfast, and high-speed Internet access. The Hampton Inn is a block closer to the T than the Holiday Inn Express (see listing below), but on the opposite side of a busy street from the station.

Best Western Hotel Tria ✿ This four-story establishment offers a sophisticated blend of chain-motel convenience and boutique-hotel features. Set back from the busy street in a commercial neighborhood, it offers accommodations at least one floor up from the parking lot. Guest rooms are spacious and well maintained, decorated in deep jewel tones with comfy yet sleek contemporary furnishings. Room rates include wireless Internet access and local phone calls; add the pool and continental breakfast, and the view of a traffic circle is easier to take. A 2½-mile jogging trail circles Fresh Pond, across the street, and a shopping center with a Whole Foods Market is nearby. Boston lies about a 15-minute drive or a 30-minute T ride away; Lexington and Concord are less than a half-hour away by car.

220 Alewife Brook Pkwy., Cambridge, MA 02138. ⓒ 866/333-8742 or 617/491-8000. Fax 617/491-4932. www. hoteltria.com. 69 units. Mid-Mar–Oct $149–$299 double; Nov–mid-Mar $119–$179 double. Extra person $10. Rates include continental breakfast. Rates may be higher during special events. Children under 17 stay free in parent's room. AE, DC, MC, V. Parking $12. T: Red Line to Alewife, then a 10-min. walk. Pets accepted; reservation required; $25 fee; $100 deposit. **Amenities:** Indoor pool; exercise room; Jacuzzi; tour desk; shuttle service; same-day dry cleaning. *In room:* A/C, TV, wireless Internet access, coffeemaker, hair dryer, iron, robes.

Harvard Square Hotel   The Harvard economics department could use this hotel as an illustration of the law of supply and demand: At busy times, including pretty much every night in the fall, rates seem high for such modest accommodations (supply)—but you can't beat the location (demand). Smack in the middle of "the Square," the six-story brick hotel is a favorite with visiting parents and budget-conscious business travelers. The lobby and the unpretentious guest rooms were renovated in 2006 and 2007. The rooms are relatively small but comfortable and neatly decorated in contemporary style. Each has a flatscreen TV (important when every inch counts), and some overlook Harvard Square. The front desk handles faxing and copying.

110 Mount Auburn St., Cambridge, MA 02138. ⓒ 800/458-5886 or 617/864-5200. Fax 617/492-4896. www.harvard squarehotel.com. 73 units, some with shower only. $99–$249 double. Extra person $10. Children under 17 stay free in parent's room. Corporate rates, AAA and AARP discounts available. AE, DC, DISC, MC, V. Parking $35. T: Red Line to Harvard. **Amenities:** Dining privileges at the Harvard Faculty Club; free access to nearby health club; car-rental desk; laundry service; dry cleaning; rooms for those w/limited mobility. *In room:* A/C, TV, wireless Internet access ($10/day), fridge, coffeemaker, hair dryer, iron, umbrella.

Holiday Inn Express Hotel & Suites   A limited-services lodging on a busy street, the Holiday Inn Express is comfortable and convenient—just a 5-minute walk from the Green Line—for businesspeople on a budget as well as vacationers. Each decent-size room has a fridge and microwave, making this a good choice if you plan to eat some meals in. The eight-story building sits slightly back from the street, but you'll still want to be as high up as possible to get away from traffic noise. If you're willing to do without a restaurant, business center, or exercise facility, you'll probably find that the reasonable rates, which include local phone calls and parking—a big plus in Cambridge—more than make up for the lack of extras.

250 Msgr. O'Brien Hwy., Cambridge, MA 02141. ⓒ 888/887-7690 or 617/577-7600. Fax 617/354-1313. www.hi express.com/boscambridgema. 112 units. From $140 double; from $150 suite. Rates include continental breakfast. Discounts for hospital patients and families available, subject to availability. Children stay free in parent's room. AE, DC, DISC, MC, V. Free parking. T: Green Line to Lechmere. **Amenities:** Access to nearby health club ($10); laundry service; same-day dry cleaning; rooms for those w/limited mobility. *In room:* A/C, TV w/pay movies, high-speed Internet access, fridge, microwave, coffeemaker, hair dryer, iron.

12 At & Near the Airport
VERY EXPENSIVE
Hyatt Harborside ⟨R⟩   This striking 14-story waterfront hotel on the edge of the airport offers unobstructed views of the harbor and city skyline. The good-size guest rooms afford dramatic views, especially from the higher floors. Extensively renovated in 2007, they have oversize work desks and a sophisticated no-frills style that contrasts with luxurious touches like pillow-top beds. The hotel is primarily a convention and business destination, with easy access to the airport (a 5-min. shuttle-bus ride away) and to downtown Boston—water taxis, which serve the adjacent dock, make the trip in 7 minutes. Sightseers on a tight budget for either time (on public transit) or money (for parking, cabs, or water taxis) will be better off closer to downtown. Bonus: The

building's tower is a lighthouse—the airport control tower manages the beacon so it doesn't interfere with runway lights.

101 Harborside Dr., Boston, MA 02128. © **800/233-1234** or 617/568-1234. Fax 617/567-8856. www.harborside. hyatt.com. 270 units, some with shower only. $349–$599 double high season; $199–$259 double low season; from $895 suite year-round. Children under 12 stay free in parent's room. Family packages available. AE, DC, DISC, MC, V. Valet parking $36; self-parking $32. T: Blue Line to Airport, then take shuttle bus. By car, follow signs to Logan Airport and take Harborside Dr. past car-rental area and tunnel entrance. **Amenities:** Restaurant (New England) and lounge w/seasonal outdoor seating; 40-ft. indoor pool; exercise room with harbor view; Jacuzzi; sauna; concierge; 24-hr. airport shuttle service; business center; room service until midnight; laundry service; same-day dry cleaning; executive-level rooms; rooms for those w/limited mobility. *In room:* A/C, TV w/pay movies, high-speed and wireless Internet access ($10/day), coffeemaker, hair dryer, iron.

EXPENSIVE

The **Embassy Suites Hotel Boston at Logan Airport,** 207 Porter St., Boston, MA 02128 (© **800/EMBASSY** or 617/567-5000; www.embassysuites.com), is a 273-unit hotel with an indoor pool, exercise room, and business center. Each suite in the 10-story hotel has a living room with a pullout couch. Room rates, which start at $169, include breakfast, high-speed Internet access, and shuttle service to the airport and the Airport T stop.

Hilton Boston Logan Airport ★★   Smack in the middle of the airport, the Hilton draws most of its guests from meetings, conventions, and canceled flights. It's convenient and well equipped for business travelers, and an excellent fallback for vacationers who don't mind commuting to downtown. Guest rooms are large and tastefully furnished, with business features that include two-line speakerphones and excellent soundproofing. The best units in the 10-story building (which opened in 1999 and underwent a $7 million–plus-renovation in 2007) afford sensational airport and harbor views. A shuttle bus serves all airport locations, and walkways link the building to Terminals A (nearby) and E (farther). The Hyatt Harborside (see below) is the closest competition—it's at the edge of the airport, which means less commotion outside and better water views but less convenient access to the T.

85 Terminal Rd., Logan International Airport, Boston, MA 02128. © **800/HILTONS** or 617/568-6700. Fax 617/568-6800. www.hiltonfamilyboston.com/hilton-boston-logan-airport.php. 599 units. $99–$399 double; from $500 suite. Children under 18 stay free in parent's room. Weekend and other packages available. AE, DC, DISC, MC, V. Valet parking $35; self-parking $30. T: Blue Line to Airport, then take shuttle bus. Pets accepted; deposit required. **Amenities:** Restaurant (American); Irish pub; coffee counter; indoor lap pool; health club; concierge; 24-hr. shuttle bus service to airport destinations, including car-rental offices and ferry dock, w/on-bus electronic check-in; well-equipped business center; 24-hr. room service; massage; laundry service; same-day dry cleaning; executive-level rooms. *In room:* A/C, TV w/pay movies, wireless Internet access ($10/day), minibar, coffeemaker, hair dryer, iron.

MODERATE

If you can't get a room at the Comfort Inn, consider the **Hampton Inn Boston Logan Airport,** 2300 Lee Burbank Hwy., Revere (© **800/426-7866** or 781/286-5665; www.hamptoninn.com), on a commercial-industrial strip about 3 miles north of the airport. A free shuttle bus serves the 227-room hotel, which has a pool; rates start at about $139 for a double and include continental breakfast.

Comfort Inn & Suites Boston/Airport ★ *Value*   The airport lies about 3½ miles south of the well-equipped Comfort Inn. The eight-story hotel, which opened in 2000, sits on a hill set back from the road near a busy traffic circle. It offers a good range of features for business and leisure travelers, an attentive staff, and an indoor pool. Room rates include high-speed Internet access, local phone calls, and continental breakfast. Suites are oversize rooms that contain sofa beds, and king suites have refrigerators as well. The somewhat inconvenient location translates to reasonable rates, and the North Shore is easily accessible if you plan a day trip. Revere Beach is about 2 minutes away by car.

85 American Legion Hwy. (Route 60), Revere, MA 02151. ℂ 877/485-3600 or 781/485-3600. Fax 781/485-3601. www.comfortinnboston.com. 208 units. $109–$239 double; $139–$279 suite. Rates include continental breakfast. Children under 18 stay free in parent's room. Senior and AAA discounts available. AE, DC, DISC, MC, V. Free parking. T: Blue Line to Airport; take airport shuttle bus to terminal, then hotel shuttle. Pets accepted; $20/night fee. **Amenities:** Restaurant (Mexican/American); lounge; indoor pool; exercise room; shuttle to airport; business center; room service (4–10pm); coin-op laundry; same-day dry cleaning; rooms for those w/limited mobility. *In room:* A/C, TV w/pay movies, high-speed Internet access, coffeemaker, hair dryer, iron.

6

Where to Dine

Friends tell me I'm too tough, that a so-so meal at a particular restaurant shouldn't automatically exclude it from this chapter. They want me to give their favorite neighborhood place another chance.

I think I'm not tough enough. My friends and I live here, and we can easily try that disappointing restaurant again. You're here for just a few days, and you probably don't have the time—or inclination or budget—for many second chances.

That's not to say that every restaurant in this chapter gets high marks for every aspect of every meal. If the space isn't the loveliest, the service isn't the greatest, or (rarely) the food is less impressive than some other element of the experience, I'll point that out.

The guiding thought for this chapter, without regard to price, was, "If this were your only meal in Boston, would you be delighted with it?" At all of the restaurants that follow, the answer, for one reason or another, is yes.

1 Best Restaurant Bets

- **Best Seafood: Legal Sea Foods,** 255 State St. (© 617/227-3115) and other locations, does one thing and does it exceptionally well. It's a chain for a great reason: People can't get enough of the freshest seafood around. See p. 106.
- **Best Raw Bar:** The raw bar at **Ye Olde Union Oyster House,** 41 Union St. (© 617/227-2750), is a tasty blend of new and old: The shellfish is ultrafresh, and the restaurant has been a Boston institution for the better part of 2 centuries. See p. 115.
- **Best Place for a Classic Boston Experience: Durgin-Park,** 340 Faneuil Hall Marketplace (© 617/227-2038), has packed 'em in since 1827. From tycoon to out-of-towner, everyone is happy here except the famously crotchety waitresses. It's a classic, not a relic. See p. 115.
- **Best Place for a Classic Cambridge Experience:** The **East Coast Grill & Raw Bar,** 1271 Cambridge St., Cambridge (© 617/491-6568), is a colorful blur of a place that deserves its national acclaim. When *New York Times* food critic Frank Bruni wanted "a taste of what servers go through," he spent a week on the staff here. See p. 135.
- **Best Spot for Romance:** Soaring ceilings, colorful decor, and (seasonally) a roaring fire make the atmosphere in the Monday Club Bar at **Upstairs on the Square,** 91 Winthrop St., Cambridge (© 617/864-1933), perfect for a rendezvous. See p. 130.
- **Best Spot for a Celebration:** Cool your heels at the bar at **Dalí,** 415 Washington St., Somerville (© 617/661-3254), and toast your good news with sangria while you wait for a table. The dishes on the *tapas* menu are perfect for sharing, and the atmosphere is lively and festive. See p. 134.

Tips **Time Is Money**

Lunch is an excellent, economical way to check out a fancy restaurant without breaking the bank. At restaurants that take reservations, it's always a good idea to make them, particularly for dinner. (To make reservations at any hour, visit **www.opentable.com**, which handles many local restaurants.) Boston-area restaurants are far less busy early in the week than they are Friday through Sunday. If you're flexible about when you indulge in fine cuisine and when you go for pizza and a movie, choose the low-budget option on the weekend and pamper yourself on a weeknight.

- **Best Spot for a Business Lunch:** Plenty of deals go down at private clubs and formal restaurants, but that can take hours. Leave an impression with your no-nonsense approach and a quick but delicious meal at **Così Sandwich Bar,** 53 State St. (© 617/723-4447), 14 Milk St. (© 617/426-7565), or 133 Federal St. (© 617/292-2674). See p 116.
- **Best Wine List:** Organized by characteristics (from light to rich) rather than by vintage or provenance, the excellent offerings at **The Blue Room,** 1 Kendall Sq., Cambridge (© 617/494-9034), are arranged in the most user-friendly way imaginable. See p. 134.
- **Best Value:** You'll do a double-take when the check arrives after dinner at the **Helmand,** 143 First St., Cambridge (© 617/492-4646). Yes, you're really that satisfied for that little money. See p. 136.
- **Best for Kids:** The wood-fired brick ovens of the **Bertucci's** chain are magnets for little eyes, and the pizza that comes out of them is equally enthralling. Picky parents will be happy here, too. Try the locations at Faneuil Hall Marketplace (© 617/227-7889); 43 Stanhope St., Back Bay (© 617/247-6161); 533 Commonwealth Ave., Kenmore Square (© 617/236-1030); 21 Brattle St., Harvard Square, Cambridge (© 617/864-4748); and 799 Main St., Cambridge (© 617/661-8356). See p. 124.
- **Best American Cuisine:** Maybe it's not "cuisine," but what's more American than a burger? **Mr. Bartley's Burger Cottage,** 1246 Mass. Ave., Cambridge (© 617/354-6559), is famous for its burgers, its onion rings, and a down-to-earth atmosphere that's increasingly rare in Harvard Square. See p. 133.
- **Best French Cuisine:** The bistro craze that has Boston in its grip started at **Brasserie Jo,** in the Colonnade Hotel, 120 Huntington Ave. (© 617/720-1300), and all of the copycats fall short. The long hours make it a good respite during a Back Bay shopping spree. See p. 127.
- **Best Italian Cuisine:** The best restaurant in the North End, **Mamma Maria,** 3 North Sq. (© 617/523-0077), is one of the best in town. In a lovely setting, it offers remarkable regional Italian fare in a spaghetti-and-meatballs neighborhood. See p. 107.
- **Best Brunch:** The insane displays at many top hotels are well worth the monetary and caloric compromises. If you're looking for a delicious meal that won't destroy your budget and waistline, join the throng at the **S&S Restaurant,** 1334 Cambridge St., Cambridge (© 617/354-0777). See p. 138.

2 Restaurants by Cuisine

AFGHAN

The Helmand ★★ (Cambridge, $$, p. 136)

ALGERIAN

Baraka Café ★ (Cambridge, $$, p. 136)

AMERICAN

The Bristol ★★ (Back Bay, $$$, p. 124)

Grill 23 & Bar ★ (Back Bay, $$$$, p. 123)

Hamersley's Bistro ★ (South End, $$$$, p. 121)

Jacob Wirth Company (Theater District, $$, p. 120)

Locke-Ober ★★ (Downtown Crossing, $$$$, p. 117)

Mr. Bartley's Burger Cottage ★★ (Cambridge, $, p. 133)

Troquet ★★ (Theater District, $$$$, p. 119)

Zaftigs Delicatessen (Brookline, $, p. 129)

ASIAN

Billy Tse Restaurant (North End, $$, p. 112)

BARBECUE

East Coast Grill & Raw Bar ★★ (Cambridge, $$$, p. 135)

Redbones ★ (Somerville, $$, p. 137)

CAJUN

Border Café (Cambridge, $$, p. 133)

CAMBODIAN

The Elephant Walk ★★ (Kenmore Square, $$$, p. 128)

CANTONESE

Grand Chau Chow ★ (Chinatown, $$, p. 119)

Peach Farm ★ (Chinatown, $$, p. 121)

CHINESE

Billy Tse Restaurant (North End, $$, p. 112)

Grand Chau Chow ★ (Chinatown, $$, p. 119)

Peach Farm ★ (Chinatown, $$, p. 121)

DELI

S&S Restaurant ★★ (Cambridge, $, p. 138)

Zaftigs Delicatessen (Brookline, $, p. 129)

ECLECTIC

The Blue Room ★★ (Cambridge, $$$, p. 134)

Icarus ★★ (South End, $$$$, p. 122)

Upstairs on the Square ★★ (Cambridge, $$$$, p. 130)

FRENCH

Brasserie Jo ★★ (Back Bay, $$, p. 127)

The Elephant Walk ★★ (Kenmore Square, $$$, p. 128)

Hamersley's Bistro ★ (South End, $$$$, p. 121)

La Voile ★ (Back Bay, $$$, p. 126)

L'Espalier ★★★ (Back Bay, $$$$, p. 123)

Les Zygomates ★★ (Financial District, $$$, p. 115)

Sel de la Terre ★★ (Waterfront, $$$, p. 106)

GERMAN

Jacob Wirth Company (Theater District, $$, p. 120)

INDIAN

Bombay Club (Cambridge, $$, p. 133)

ITALIAN

Artú (North End, $$, p. 111)

Così Sandwich Bar ★ (Financial District, $, p. 116)

Key to Abbreviations: $$$$ = Very Expensive $$$ = Expensive $$ = Moderate $ = Inexpensive

Daily Catch ✻ (North End, $$$,
p. 110)

Davio's Northern Italian
Steakhouse ✻✻ (Back
Bay, $$$$, p. 123)

Galleria Umberto Rosticceria (North
End, $, p. 113)

Giacomo's Ristorante ✻✻ (North
End, $$, p. 112)

Grotto ✻✻ (Beacon Hill, $$, p. 118)

La Summa ✻ (North End, $$,
p. 112)

Mamma Maria ✻✻✻ (North End,
$$$$, p. 107)

Piccola Venezia ✻ (North End, $$,
p. 113)

Rialto (Cambridge, $$$$, p. 132)

Taranta Cucina Meridionale (North
End, $$$$, p. 110)

JAPANESE

Ginza Japanese Restaurant ✻
(Chinatown, $$$, p. 119)

MEDITERRANEAN

Baraka Café ✻ (Cambridge, $$,
p. 136)

Café Jaffa (Back Bay, $, p. 128)

Casablanca ✻ (Cambridge, $$$,
p. 130)

La Voile ✻ (Back Bay, $$$, p. 126)

Oleana ✻✻ (Cambridge, $$$, p. 136)

MEXICAN

Casa Romero ✻ (Back Bay, $$$,
p. 125)

Tu y Yo Mexican Fonda (Cambridge,
$$, p. 137)

MIDDLE EASTERN

Café Jaffa (Back Bay, $, p. 128)

NEW ENGLAND

Durgin-Park ✻✻✻ (Faneuil Hall, $$,
p. 115)

Henrietta's Table ✻ (Cambridge, $$$,
p. 132)

L'Espalier ✻✻✻ (Back Bay, $$$$,
p. 123)

Ye Olde Union Oyster House ✻
(Faneuil Hall, $$$, p. 115)

PERUVIAN

Taranta Cucina Meridionale (North
End, $$$$, p. 110)

PIZZA

Picco (South End, $, p. 123)

Pizzeria Regina ✻✻ (North End, $,
p. 114)

SANDWICHES

Così Sandwich Bar ✻ (Financial
District, $, p. 116)

SEAFOOD

Barking Crab ✻ (Waterfront, $$,
p. 107)

Daily Catch ✻ (North End, $$$,
p. 110)

East Coast Grill & Raw Bar ✻✻
(Cambridge, $$$, p. 135)

Giacomo's Ristorante ✻✻ (North
End, $$, p. 112)

Jasper White's Summer Shack ✻✻
(Back Bay, Cambridge, $$$,
p. 135)

Legal Sea Foods ✻✻✻ (Waterfront,
$$$, p. 106)

Neptune Oyster ✻ (North End, $$$,
p. 110)

Peach Farm ✻ (Chinatown, $$,
p. 121)

Ye Olde Union Oyster House ✻
(Faneuil Hall, $$$, p. 115)

SPANISH

Dalí ✻✻ (Cambridge, $$$, p. 134)

STEAKS

Davio's Northern Italian
Steakhouse ✻✻ (Back
Bay, $$$$, p. 123)

Grill 23 & Bar ✻ (Back Bay, $$$$,
p. 123)

SUSHI

Billy Tse Restaurant (North End, $$,
p. 112)

Ginza Japanese Restaurant ⍟
(Chinatown, $$$, p. 119)

TEX-MEX

Border Café (Cambridge, $$, p. 133)
Fajitas & 'Ritas ⍟ (Downtown
Crossing, $, p. 117)

THAI

Bangkok City ⍟ (Back Bay, $$,
p. 127)

TUNISIAN

Baraka Café ⍟ (Cambridge, $$,
p. 136)

VEGETARIAN/VIETNAMESE

Buddha's Delight ⍟ (Chinatown, $,
p. 121)

WINE BARS

Les Zygomates ⍟⍟ (Financial
District, $$$, p. 115)
Troquet ⍟⍟ (Theater District, $$$$,
p. 119)

3 The Waterfront

EXPENSIVE

Legal Sea Foods ⍟⍟⍟ SEAFOOD   Out-of-towners sometimes react suspiciously when I recommend Legal's—they're expecting a secret insider tip, and I'm suggesting a place they've already heard of. Just remember that this family-owned business enjoys an international reputation for serving only the freshest, best-quality fish and shellfish, which it processes at its own state-of-the-art plant. The menu includes regular selections (scrod, haddock, bluefish, salmon, shrimp, calamari, and lobster, among others) plus whatever was at the market that morning, prepared in every imaginable way, and it's all splendid. The clam chowder is great, the fish chowder lighter but equally good. Entrees run the gamut from grilled fish served plain or with Cajun spices (try the arctic char) to seafood fra diavolo on fresh linguine to salmon baked in parchment with vegetables and white wine. Or go the luxurious route and order a mammoth lobster. The classic dessert is ice cream bonbons, but the Boston cream pie is so good that you might come back just for that. And the wide-ranging, reasonably priced wine list is exceptional—a friend who makes his living as a wine writer tells me it's the best restaurant-chain wine list in the country.

My favorite branch is at Long Wharf, tantalizingly close to the fish at the New England Aquarium. A close runner-up is the location in the Prudential Center, 800 Boylston St. (© **617/266-6800;** T: Green Line B, C, or D to Hynes Convention Center, or E to Prudential). Other Boston branches are at 26 Park Square, between Columbus Avenue and Stuart Street (© **617/426-4444;** T: Green Line to Arlington); at Copley Place, 2nd level (© **617/266-7775;** T: Orange Line to Back Bay or Green Line to Copley); and in the three domestic terminals at Logan Airport. In Cambridge, branches are in the courtyard of the Charles Hotel, 20 University Rd. (© **617/491-9400;** T: Red Line to Harvard); and at 5 Cambridge Center (© **617/864-3400;** T: Red Line to Kendall/MIT).

255 State St. © **617/742-5300.** www.legalseafoods.com. Reservations recommended. Main courses $11–$19 at lunch, $14–$35 at dinner; lobster market price. AE, DC, DISC, MC, V. Mon–Thurs 11am–10pm; Fri–Sun 11am–11pm. T: Blue Line to Aquarium.

Sel de la Terre ⍟⍟ FRENCH   A stone's throw from Boston Harbor, Sel de la Terre is a peaceful slice of southern France. The kitchen uses fresh local ingredients in its subtly flavorful food: scallops handled so gently that they're still sweet, skillet-roasted duck atop jewel-toned winter vegetables, luscious salmon with French lentils and caramelized cauliflower. Banquettes, earth tones, and professional service attract a go-go business-lunch crowd (dinner is calmer). The unusual pricing structure—the same amount for almost every dish—feels like a deal when you're tucking into a generous portion of braised short ribs, less of a bargain if you're eating pasta. Whatever you order, accompany it with a side of sublime *pommes frites* (french fries). The *boulangerie* (bakery) at the entrance sells out-of-this-world breads, salads, and pastries, and there's seasonal outdoor seating.

255 State St. (© 617/720-1300. www.seldelaterre.com. Reservations recommended. Lunch main courses $15, sandwiches $9, 3-course prix fixe menu $19. Dinner main courses $26; additional charge for some items. Children's menu $7–$9. AE, DISC, MC, V. Mon–Fri 11:30am–2:30pm, Sat–Sun (brunch) 11am–2:30pm; daily 5–10pm. Afternoon menu daily 2:30–5pm, late-night menu Wed–Sat 10pm–12:30am. Valet parking available at dinner. T: Blue Line to Aquarium.

MODERATE

Barking Crab *Kids* SEAFOOD   The Barking Crab is a clam shack overlooking the water. That wouldn't be a big deal on the coast of Maine or the shores of the Chesapeake Bay, but in downtown Boston, it's beyond cool. A wooden building perched above Fort Point Channel (which separates downtown from South Boston), this extremely casual restaurant has a colorful interior, a lively bar scene, and a clientele of regulars from local offices and families visiting the nearby Children's Museum. The place to be in the summer is at a picnic table on the deck, which might require a wait at busy times; in the off season, the indoor dining room, which has a cheery wood-burning stove, is a cozy oasis. The menu includes the usual clam chowder, fried-seafood plates, and lobsters, with a handful of more creative options (such as spicy fried calamari and a yummy crab-cake burger) and enough non-seafood dishes to keep vegetarians from starving. The food is fine, and overall quite good, but that's not really the point. This is a *downtown* clam shack—what a concept.

88 Sleeper St. (© 617/426-2722. www.barkingcrab.com. Reservations accepted only for parties of 6 or more. Main courses $9–$24; sandwiches $9–$14; fresh seafood market price. AE, DC, MC, V. Sun–Wed 11:30am–11pm, Thurs–Sat 11am–1am. T: Red Line to South Station and Waterfront Silver Line to Courthouse, or Blue Line to Aquarium.

4 The North End

Boston's Italian-American enclave has dozens of restaurants; many are tiny and don't serve dessert and coffee. Hit the *caffès* for an espresso or cappuccino and fresh pastry in an atmosphere where lingering is welcome. My favorite dessert destinations are **Caffè Vittoria,** 296 Hanover St. (© **617/227-7606;** www.vittoriacaffe.com), and **Caffè dello Sport,** 308 Hanover St. (© **617/523-5063**). There's also table service at **Mike's Pastry,** 300 Hanover St. (© **617/742-3050;** www.mikespastry.com), a bakery that's famous for its bustling takeout business and its cannoli. If you plan to eat in, find what you want in the cases first, then take a seat and order from the server. For gelato, head to **Gelateria,** 272 Hanover St. (© **617/720-4243;** www.depasqualeventures.com), which serves 50 flavors of the Italian version of ice cream as well as pastries, coffee, and Italian soft drinks.

VERY EXPENSIVE

Mamma Maria NORTHERN ITALIAN   Upscale restaurants have been popping up on the North End's family-style dining scene for a couple of years now, piquing my curiosity. Off I go to check out each new addition, enjoying the fashionable bars, puzzling over the wild menus, yelling in the noisy dining rooms. And every time someone with a generous budget asks for a recommendation, I land here. In a

Where to Dine in Boston

Abe & Louie's **16**
Artú (Beacon Hill) **58**
Aujourd'hui **43**
Bangkok City **7**
Barking Crab **81**
Ben & Jerry's (Newbury St.) **25**
Ben & Jerry's (Park Plaza) **40**
Bertucci's (Back Bay) **29**
Bertucci's (Faneuil Hall) **70**
Bertucci's (Kenmore Square) **5**
Boston Public Library **23**
Brasserie Jo **20**
The Bristol **38**
Buddha's Delight **49**
Café Fleuri **77**
Café Jaffa **14**
Capital Grille **8**
Casa Romero **11**
Chacarero **66**
Charlie's Sandwich Shoppe **27**
Chau Chow City **50**
China Pearl **52**
Cosí Sandwich Bar (Federal St.) **78**
Cosí Sandwich Bar (Milk St.) **67**
Cosí Sandwich Bar (State St.) **76**
Daily Catch (Harborwalk) **82**
Davio's Northern Italian
  Steakhouse **37**
Durgin-Park **72**
The Elephant Walk **4**
Emack & Bolio's (Newbury St.) **12**

Emack & Bolio's (State St.) **75**
Empire Garden Restaurant **48**
Fajitas & 'Ritas **64**
Figs **61**
Finale (Brookline) **2**
Finale (Theater District) **41**
Fleming's Prime Steakhouse &
  Wine Bar **44**
Ginza Japanese Restaurant
  (Brookline) **3**
Ginza Japanese Restaurant
  (Chinatown) **54**
Grand Chau Chow **51**
Grill 23 & Bar **34**
Grotto **63**
Hamersley's Bistro **30**
Hei La Moon **55**
Icarus **32**
Intrigue **79**
Jacob Wirth Company **47**
Jasper White's Summer Shack **10**
JP Licks **9**
La Voile **16**
Legal Sea Foods (Copley Place) **26**
Legal Sea Foods (Park Square) **39**
Legal Sea Foods (Prudential) **18**
Legal Sea Foods (Waterfront) **74**
L'Espalier **19**
Les Zygomates **56**
Locke-Ober **65**
The Lounge at Taj Boston **36**

Maggiano's Little Italy **42**
McCormick & Schmick's
  (Faneuil Hall) **71**
McCormick & Schmick's
  (Park Plaza) **38**
Miel **80**
Morton's of Chicago (Back Bay) **22**
Morton's of Chicago (Seaport) **83**
Oak Room **28**
The Palm **24**
The Paramount **60**
Parish Café and Bar **35**
Peach Farm **53**
P. F. Chang's China Bistro **45**
Picco **31**
Ruth's Chris Steak House **68**
Savenor's Market **59**
Sel de la Terre **73**
Smith & Wollensky **33**
Sorriso Trattoria **57**
Spike's Junkyard Dogs **6**
Stephanie's on Newbury **21**
Sugar Heaven **17**
Tapéo **15**
Trader Joe's **13**
Troquet **46**
The Upper Crust (Beacon Hill) **62**
Ye Olde Union Oyster House **69**
Zaftigs Delicatessen **1**

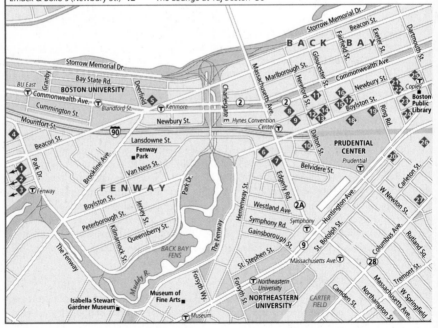

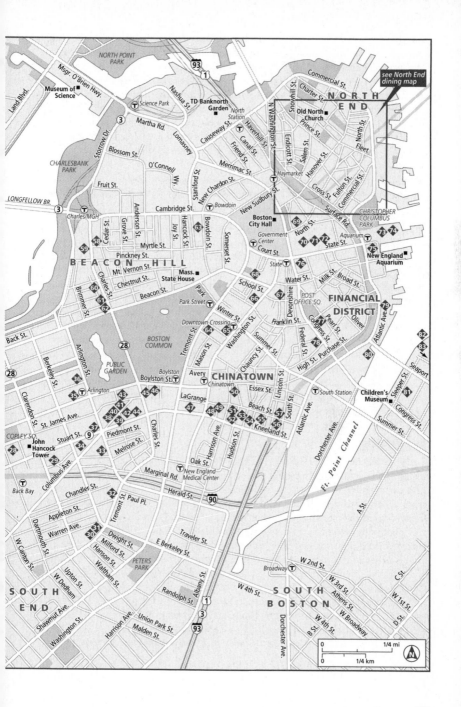

town house overlooking North Square and the Paul Revere House, the best restaurant in the North End offers innovative cuisine in a sophisticated yet comfortable setting. The menu changes seasonally. Start with excellent soup, risotto, or a pasta special. The superb entrees are unlike anything else in this neighborhood, except in size—portions are more than generous. Fork-tender *osso buco*, a limited-quantity nightly special, is almost enough for two, but you'll want it all for yourself. You can't go wrong with main-course pastas, either, and the steaks, chops, and fresh seafood specials, all with creative accompaniments (say, local cod with Maine shrimp, calamari, and risotto), are uniformly marvelous. The pasta, bread, and desserts are homemade, and the wine list is excellent.

3 North Sq. ℂ 617/523-0077. www.mammamaria.com. Reservations recommended. Main courses $26–$40. AE, DC, DISC, MC, V. Sun–Thurs 5–9:30pm; Fri–Sat 5–10:30pm. Valet parking available. T: Green or Orange Line to Haymarket.

Taranta Cucina Meridionale ⭐⭐ SOUTHERN ITALIAN/PERUVIAN   This unlikely-sounding combination is actually a kick-yourself-for-not-thinking-of-it great idea. Chef-owner Jose Duarte's creations incorporate the flavors of his native Peru, ingredients (notably peppers) you won't see on other Boston menus, and classic Italian preparations. The dining room is a typical upscale North End space, with exposed-brick walls, an open kitchen, and tables just a bit too close together. Servers are friendly and eager to explain the unusual cuisine. The risk-averse can opt for pasta with tomato sauce—a good rendition, but not the reason to come here. Pasta in garlic–white wine sauce with *aji amarillo* pepper–spiced sausage; salmon in a macadamia crust with pisco–Incan goldenberry sauce; and espresso-crusted filet mignon are the sort of dishes that make Taranta a standout. The signature dish is a Flintstone-esque pork chop with a sweet-hot glaze of sugar cane and *rocoto* pepper; it's not unusual to see everyone at a table of businessmen who appear to be retired NFL linemen ordering it. Desserts are as accomplished as the rest of the food, so try to save some room.

210 Hanover St. ℂ 617/720-0052. www.tarantarist.com. Reservations recommended. Main courses $18–$34. AE, DC, MC, V. Daily 5:30–10pm. T: Green or Orange Line to Haymarket.

EXPENSIVE

Daily Catch ⭐ SOUTHERN ITALIAN/SEAFOOD   About the size of a large kitchen (it seats just 20), this storefront restaurant packs a wallop—of garlic. A North End favorite since 1973, it offers excellent food, chummy service, and very little elbow room. The surprisingly varied menu includes an impressive variety of calamari (try it fried, in squid-ink pasta puttanesca, or stuffed with bread crumbs, parsley, and garlic) and a tempting selection of broiled, fried, and sautéed fish and shellfish. One of the pickiest eaters I know comes here from New York just for the monkfish Marsala. All food is prepared to order, and some dishes arrive at the table still in the frying pan.

This is the original Daily Catch. The **Harborwalk** branch, at the Moakley Federal Courthouse, 2 Northern Ave., on the South Boston waterfront (ℂ 617/772-4402; T: Silver Line to Courthouse), is open Monday through Thursday 11am to 10pm, Friday until 11pm, and weekends 4 to 10pm, and accepts credit cards (AE, MC, V).

323 Hanover St. ℂ 617/523-8567. www.dailycatch.com. Reservations not accepted. Main courses $17–$27. No credit cards. Sun–Thurs 11:30am–10pm; Fri–Sat 11:30am–11pm. T: Green or Orange Line to Haymarket.

Neptune Oyster ⭐ SEAFOOD   Tiny and cramped, with a red-leather banquette and a marble-topped bar down either side of a narrow room, Neptune feels like one of those off-the-radar places out-of-towners fantasize about—or it would, if it weren't so crowded. Super-fresh, inventively prepared seafood keeps this restaurant busy and

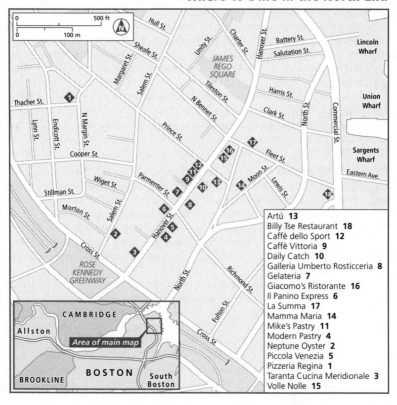

Artú **13**
Billy Tse Restaurant **18**
Caffè dello Sport **12**
Caffè Vittoria **9**
Daily Catch **10**
Galleria Umberto Rosticceria **8**
Gelateria **7**
Giacomo's Ristorante **16**
Il Panino Express **6**
La Summa **17**
Mamma Maria **14**
Mike's Pastry **11**
Modern Pastry **4**
Neptune Oyster **2**
Piccola Venezia **5**
Pizzeria Regina **1**
Taranta Cucina Meridionale **3**
Volle Nolle **15**

loud almost all the time, and not just with North Enders sick of chicken parm; even in the winter, I suggest planning for lunch or an early dinner on a weekday if you don't enjoy waiting. Check out the daily specials listed on the chalkboard and mirrors, then start with oysters, comparing specimens from both coasts (Pacific Northwest Kumamotos, which taste the way the ocean smells, are my favorite). Main courses include some menu standards, at least two of which aren't seafood, and dishes that make good use of whatever's fresh that day. You might find something unfamiliar like cod cheeks, exotic like sea urchin, or even familiar, like a lobster roll (cold with mayonnaise or hot with butter—quite the dilemma). Neptune is a few steps off the Freedom Trail and easy to find: Look for the eye-catching display of ice, lemons, and oysters in the front window and the crowd inside.

63 Salem St. ✆ **617/742-3474**. www.neptuneoyster.com. Reservations not accepted. Main courses $13–$34; lobster market price. AE, MC, V. Sun–Wed 11:30am–10pm; Thurs–Sat 11:30am–midnight. T: Green or Orange Line to Haymarket.

MODERATE

Artú ITALIAN   Plates of roasted vegetables draw your eye to the front window, and the accompanying aromas will reel in the rest of you. Don't resist—this is a neighborhood favorite for a reason, and a good stop for Freedom Trail walkers. The best appetizer is a sampler of those gorgeous veggies. Move on to superb roasted meats or bounteous home-style pasta dishes. Roast lamb, *penne alla puttanesca*, and chicken stuffed with ham and cheese are all terrific. Panini (sandwiches) are big in size and fla-vor—the prosciutto, mozzarella, and tomato is sublime, and chicken parmigiana is tender and filling. Originally a little takeout place, Artú now fills three storefronts, one of which holds a marble-topped bar. It isn't a great place for quiet conversation, espe-cially during dinner in the noisy main room, but do you really want to talk with your mouth full?

There's another Artú on **Beacon Hill** at 89 Charles St. (© **617/227-9023**). It keeps the same hours, except that it opens at noon on Sunday and 5pm on Monday.

6 Prince St. © 617/742-4336. www.artuboston.com. Reservations recommended at dinner. Main courses $8–$14 at lunch, $14–$23 at dinner; sandwiches $6–$8. AE, MC, V. Daily 11am–11pm; bar menu until 1am. T: Green or Orange Line to Haymarket.

Billy Tse Restaurant CHINESE/PAN-ASIAN/SUSHI   An Asian restaurant on the edge of the Italian North End might seem incongruous, but this casual spot fits right in. It serves excellent renditions of the usual dishes, and the kitchen also has a flair for fresh seafood. The pan-Asian selections and sushi are as enjoyable as the Chi-nese classics. Start with wonderful soup, sinfully good crab Rangoon, or fried calamari with garlic and pepper. Main dishes range from nine kinds of fried rice to scallops with garlic sauce to the signature "Ocean Three Treasures," shrimp, calamari, and scallops in a scrumptious sake sauce.

Be sure to ask about the daily specials—bitter Chinese broccoli, when it's available, is deftly prepared. Most lunch specials, served until 4pm, include vegetable fried rice or vegetable lo mein; I'm hooked on the udon noodles with shrimp in miso broth. You can eat in the comfortable main dining room or near the bar, which has French doors that open to the street. Although it's opposite a trolley stop, Billy Tse isn't especially touristy—the neighbors obviously welcome a break from pizza and pasta.

240 Commercial St. © 617/227-9990. www.billytserestaurant.com. Reservations recommended at dinner on week-ends. Main courses $8–$38 (most items less than $20); lunch specials $7–$9; sushi from $3.75. AE, DC, DISC, MC, V. Mon–Thurs 11:30am–11:30pm; Fri–Sat 11:30am–midnight; Sun 11:30am–11pm. Closed 1 week in Feb. T: Green or Orange Line to Haymarket, or Blue Line to Aquarium.

Giacomo's Ristorante ★★ ITALIAN/SEAFOOD   Fans of Giacomo's seem to have adopted the U.S. Postal Service's motto: They brave snow, sleet, rain, and gloom of night. The line forms early and grows long, especially on weekends. No reservations, cash only, a tiny dining room with an open kitchen—what's the attraction? The food is terrific, there's plenty of it, and the we're-all-in-this-together atmosphere certainly helps. My dad is a New York ethnic-dining snob, and this is his favorite Boston restaurant.

The fried calamari appetizer, served with marinara sauce, is ultralight and crisp. You can take the chef's advice or put together your own main dish from the list of ingredi-ents on a board on the wall. The best suggestion is salmon and sun-dried tomatoes in tomato cream sauce over fettuccine; any dish with shrimp is delectable, too. Non-seafood offerings such as butternut squash ravioli in mascarpone cheese sauce are equally memorable. Service is friendly but incredibly swift, and lingering is not encouraged—but unless you have a heart of stone, you won't want to take up a table when people are standing outside waiting for your seat in sweltering heat or (no kidding) an ice storm.

355 Hanover St. © 617/523-9026. Reservations not accepted. Main courses $14–$18; specials market price. No credit cards. Mon–Thurs 5–10pm; Fri–Sat 5–10:30pm; Sun 4–10pm. T: Green or Orange Line to Haymarket.

La Summa ★ SOUTHERN ITALIAN   Because La Summa isn't on the restaurant rows of Hanover and Salem streets, it maintains a cozy neighborhood atmosphere.

Finds **Go Straight to the Source**

The tiramisu at many North End restaurants comes from **Modern Pastry**, 257 Hanover St. (© 617/523-3783). The surreally good concoction ($3.50 a slice at the shop) makes an excellent picnic dessert in the summer—head 4 blocks down Richmond Street to eat in Christopher Columbus Waterfront Park, off Atlantic Avenue.

Unlike some neighborhood places, it's friendly to outsiders—you'll feel welcome even if your server doesn't greet you by name. La Summa is worth seeking out just for the wonderful homemade pasta and desserts, and the more elaborate entrees are scrumptious, too. You might start with salad, ravioli, or soup (our waitress one night didn't know exactly what was in the excellent butternut squash soup because, and I quote, "My mother made it").

Try any seafood special, *pappardelle e melanzane* (strips of eggplant tossed with ethereal fresh pasta in a light marinara sauce), shrimp in light marinara sauce over linguini, or the house special—veal, chicken, sausage, shrimp, artichokes, *pepperoncini* (pickled hot peppers), olives, and mushrooms in white-wine sauce. Desserts, especially tiramisu, are terrific.

30 Fleet St. © **617/523-9503**. Reservations recommended on weekends. Main courses $11–$24. AE, DC, DISC, MC, V. Sun–Fri 4:30–10:30pm; Sat 4:30–11pm. T: Green or Orange Line to Haymarket.

Piccola Venezia ITALIAN   The glass front wall of Piccola Venezia ("little Venice") shows off the exposed-brick dining room, decorated with photos and posters and filled with happy locals and out-of-towners. Portions are large, and the homey food tends to be heavy on red sauce. You might begin with the appetizer sampler, an artery-clogging delight featuring fried calamari, garlic bread with cheese, mozzarella sticks, and sautéed shrimp; a more traditional starter is tasty *pasta e fagioli* (bean and pasta soup). Then dig into a big plate of chicken parmigiana, eggplant rolatini, or grilled pork chops with vinegar peppers. This is a good place to try traditional Italian-American favorites such as polenta (home-style, not the yuppie croutons available at so many other places) and *baccala* (reconstituted salt cod).

263 Hanover St. © **617/523-3888**. Reservations recommended at dinner. Main courses $13–$26; lunch specialties $5–$10. AE, DISC, MC, V. Sun–Thurs 11:30am–9:30pm, Fri–Sat 11:30am–10:30pm (lunch Mon–Sat until 3pm). Validated parking available. T: Green or Orange Line to Haymarket.

INEXPENSIVE

Galleria Umberto Rosticceria *Value* ITALIAN   The long, fast-moving line snaking toward the door is your first clue that this cafeteria-style spot just off the Freedom Trail is a bargain. Then you notice that most of the customers are locals and businesspeople. The food is worth the wait. You can fill up on a couple of slices of pizza, but for the true experience, try *arancini* (a deep-fried rice ball filled with ground beef, peas, and cheese). Calzones—ham and cheese; spinach; spinach and cheese; or spinach, sausage, and cheese—and mozzarella-stuffed potato croquettes *(panzarotti)* are also tasty. Study the cases of food while you wait and be ready to order at once when you reach the head of the line. Pause for a quick lunch and get on with your sightseeing.

289 Hanover St. © **617/227-5709**. All items less than $4. No credit cards. Mon–Sat 10:45am–2:30pm. Closed July. T: Green or Orange Line to Haymarket.

Breakfast & Sunday Brunch

Several top hotels serve Sunday brunch buffets of monstrous proportions—outrageous displays that are outrageously expensive. They're worth the investment for a special occasion, but you can have a less incapacitating experience for considerably less money.

My top choice is in Cambridge: the **S&S Restaurant** (p. 138), a family-run operation that never sends anyone away hungry. In Boston, **Charlie's Sandwich Shoppe,** 429 Columbus Ave. (℗ **617/536-7669**), is a longtime South End favorite not far from the Back Bay—just the right distance to walk off some blueberry-waffle calories—that's closed Sunday and doesn't accept credit cards. The **Paramount,** 44 Charles St., Beacon Hill (℗ **617/720-1152;** www.paramountboston.com), is a classic destination for eggs and a glimpse of the real community behind the neighborhood's red-brick facade. At the **Centre Street Café,** 669 Centre St., Jamaica Plain (℗ **617/524-9217;** www.centrestcafe.com), locals tough out long weekend waits for strong coffee and delicious specials made (when possible) with local and organic ingredients.

My favorite hotel buffet brunch is the manageable spread at **Intrigue,** in the Boston Harbor Hotel, Rowes Wharf (℗ **617/856-7744**), served on weekends from 7 to 11:30am. It costs $25 for adults, $13 for children—a steal compared to the big boys. For them, make reservations (especially on holidays) but do *not* make elaborate dinner plans. **Aujourd'hui** (p. 125), in the Four Seasons Hotel, 200 Boylston St. (℗ **617/351-2037**), charges $65 for adults, $32.50 for children; at **Café Fleuri,** in the Langham Hotel Boston, 250 Franklin St. (℗ **617/956-8751**), adults pay $50, children $18.

Pizzeria Regina ★★ PIZZA   Regina's looks almost like a movie set, but look a little closer—this local legend is the place the movie sets are trying to re-create. It's been in business since 1926, and the only thing that's changed recently is the end of the cash-only policy in 2008. As it has for decades, the line stretches up the street on busy nights, but even at off hours, business is seldom slow. Locals often call for take-out; if you borrow that tactic, though, you'll miss the full experience. Busy waitresses who might call you "dear" weave through the boisterous dining room, shouting orders and questions as they deliver peerless pizza steaming hot from the brick oven. (You can also drop in for a slice, weekdays at lunch only.) Let it cool a little before you dig in. Nouveau ingredients such as sun-dried tomatoes appear on the list of toppings, but that's not authentic. House-made sausage, maybe some pepperoni, and a couple of beers—now, *that's* authentic.

11½ Thacher St. ℗ **617/227-0765.** www.pizzeriaregina.com. Reservations not accepted. Pizza $10–$17. AE, MC, V. Mon–Thurs 11am–11:30pm; Fri–Sat 11am–midnight; Sun noon–11pm. T: Green or Orange Line to Haymarket.

5 Faneuil Hall Marketplace & the Financial District

EXPENSIVE

The national chain **McCormick & Schmick's Seafood Restaurant** has a branch at Faneuil Hall Marketplace in the North Market Building (℗ **617/720-5522**).

Tips   **It's Nothing Personal**

State law requires the scary disclaimer that appears on menus to alert you to the potential danger of eating raw or undercooked meat (such as rare burgers), seafood (such as raw oysters), poultry, or eggs.

Les Zygomates ★★ FRENCH BISTRO/WINE BAR   Tucked away near South Station, this delightful place is worth seeking out; Bostonians have found their way here since 1994. The bar in the high-ceilinged, brick-walled space serves a great selection of wine, available by the bottle, the glass, and the 2-ounce "taste." The efficient staff will guide you to a good accompaniment for the delicious food. Salads are excellent, lightly dressed and garden fresh, and main courses are hearty and filling but not heavy. Seared duck breast with pomegranate *jus* and wild-rice pilaf was a satisfying combination of textures and flavors, and I'd come back just for the pan-seared wild striped bass. For dessert, try not to fight over warm chocolate cake. A popular business-lunch destination, Les Zygomates has a chic, romantic atmosphere at night, when live jazz (in its own dining room) helps set the mood.

Up the street and under the same management, **Sorriso Trattoria,** 107 South St. (© **617/259-1560;** www.sorrisoboston.com), serves sophisticated country Italian cuisine, including brick-oven pizza. It's open for lunch weekdays and dinner nightly. The name is a clever tribute to the original restaurant: *Les zygomates* is French for the muscles that make you smile; *sorriso* is Italian for "smile."

129 South St. © 617/542-5108. www.winebar.com. Reservations recommended. Main courses $10–$15 at lunch, $24–$36 (most less than $29) at dinner; lunch prix fixe $17. AE, DC, DISC, MC, V. Mon–Fri 11:30am–1am (lunch until 2pm, dinner until 10:30pm); Sat 6pm–1am (dinner until 11:30pm). Valet parking available at dinner. T: Red Line to South Station.

Ye Olde Union Oyster House ★ NEW ENGLAND/SEAFOOD   America's oldest restaurant in continuous service, the Union Oyster House opened in 1826. The food is tasty, traditional New England fare, popular with visitors walking on the adjacent Freedom Trail and savvy locals. They're not looking for anything fancy, and you shouldn't, either—simple, classic preparations account for the restaurant's staying power. At the crescent-shaped oyster bar on the lower level of the cramped, low-ceilinged building (a National Historic Landmark "where Daniel Webster drank many a toddy in his day"), try oyster stew or the cold seafood sampler of oysters, clams, and shrimp to start. Follow with a broiled or grilled dish such as scrod or salmon, or perhaps fried seafood or grilled pork loin. A "shore dinner" of chowder, steamers or mussels, lobster, corn, potatoes, and dessert is an excellent introduction to local favorites. For dessert, try gingerbread with whipped cream. *Tip:* A plaque marks John F. Kennedy's favorite booth (no. 18), where he often sat to read the Sunday papers.

41 Union St. (between North and Hanover sts.). © 617/227-2750. www.unionoysterhouse.com. Reservations recommended. Main courses $8–$22 at lunch, $17–$29 at dinner; lobster market price. Children's menu $5–$12. AE, DC, DISC, MC, V. Sun–Thurs 11am–9:30pm (lunch menu until 5pm); Fri–Sat 11am–10pm (lunch until 6pm). Union Bar daily 11am–midnight (lunch until 3pm, late supper until 11pm). Validated and valet parking available. T: Green or Orange Line to Haymarket.

MODERATE

Durgin-Park ★★★ *Kids* NEW ENGLAND   For huge portions of delicious food, a rowdy atmosphere where CEOs share tables with students, and run-ins with the

---

Tips **Boston Restaurant Weeks**

During Boston Restaurant Week, dozens of terrific spots serve a three-course *prix-fixe* lunch for the decimal equivalent of the year—in 2009, $20.09—and many offer dinner for just $10 more. The third week of August was the original Restaurant Week; it's now 2 weeks, as is the March incarnation. I find the latter less enjoyable because late winter's seasonal ingredients are, to put it nicely, dull, but the price is right. Popular places book up quickly, so plan accordingly. The Convention & Visitors Bureau (© **888/SEE-BOSTON;** www.bostonusa.com) lists names of participating restaurants and individual numbers to call for reservations. Ask whether the menu is set yet, and seek out restaurants that really get into the spirit by offering more than just a couple of choices for each course. If you don't, you're going to experience more chicken, salmon, and begrudging service than anyone deserves.

---

famously cranky waitresses, people have poured into Durgin-Park since 1827. A tourist magnet that attracts many locals, it's everything it's cracked up to be. Approximately 2,000 people a day join the line that stretches down a flight of stairs to the first floor of Faneuil Hall Marketplace's North Market building. The queue moves quickly, and you'll probably wind up seated at a long table with other people (smaller tables are available).

The food is wonderful, and there's plenty of it—prime rib the size of a hubcap, lamb chops, fried seafood, huge salads, and juicy roast turkey are sure bets. The cooks broil steaks and chops on an open fire over wood charcoal. Fresh seafood arrives twice daily, and fish dinners are broiled to order. Every meal starts with a square of dense, rich cornbread. Boston baked beans are a signature dish, and this is the best place to try them. For dessert, strawberry shortcake is justly celebrated, and Indian pudding (molasses and cornmeal baked for hours and served with ice cream) is a New England classic. So is backtalk from the waitresses, but don't be disappointed if your server doesn't deliver—everyone has an off day sometimes.

340 Faneuil Hall Marketplace. © **617/227-2038.** www.durgin-park.com. Reservations accepted only for parties of 15 or more. Main courses $7–$11 at lunch, $10–$25 at dinner; specials $19–$40. Children's menu $8–$9. AE, DC, DISC, MC, V. Mon–Sat 11:30am–10pm, Sun 11:30am–11pm; lunch menu daily until 2:30pm. Validated parking available. T: Green or Blue Line to Government Center, Green or Orange Line to Haymarket, or Blue Line to Aquarium.

INEXPENSIVE

Così Sandwich Bar ⊕ SANDWICHES/ITALIAN   Flavorful fillings on delectable bread make Così (inexplicably pronounced "cozy") a downtown lunch hot spot. This location, right on the Freedom Trail, makes a delicious refueling stop. Italian flatbread baked fresh all day—so tasty that it's even good plain—gets split open and filled with your choice of meat, fish, vegetables, cheese, and spreads. Soups and salads are good, too, and pizzas with flatbread as the crust are tasty, but for me, this place is all about the sandwiches. The more fillings you choose, the more you pay; the total can really climb, so don't go wild if you're on a budget. Tandoori chicken is sensational, as is roast beef with wasabi mayonnaise. For dessert, order s'mores, and a staffer will bring you a contraption that holds an actual fire.

Other branches are at 14 Milk St. (© **617/426-7565**), near Downtown Crossing, and 133 Federal St. (© **617/292-2674**), which has patio seating in warm weather.

53 State St. (at Congress St.). ℂ **617/723-4447.** www.getcosi.com. Sandwiches $6–$10; soups and salads $5–$8. AE, DC, MC, V. Mon–Thurs 7am–6pm; Fri 7am–5pm. T: Orange or Blue Line to State.

6 Downtown Crossing

VERY EXPENSIVE

Locke-Ober ★★ NEW AMERICAN   "Locke's" is *the* traditional Boston restaurant, a power-broker favorite since 1875. Famed Boston restaurateur Lydia Shire bought it in 2001, but if the ghosts who surely hang around here mind having a woman in charge, you'd never know it. In an alley off the Winter Street pedestrian mall, the wood-paneled restaurant entertainingly evokes a Waspy men's club. The long, mirrored downstairs bar dates from 1880, and the service is 19th-century-style courtly.

The food deftly combines old-fashioned and contemporary. Traditional fish cakes sit alongside new-fangled jasmine rice, red-pepper aioli comes with Maine crab cakes, and delectable scalloped potatoes accompany the signature roast beef hash. Other traditions, including excellent steaks and chops, Wiener schnitzel a la Holstein, lobster Savannah, and broiled scrod with brown bread, endure. So does Locke-Ober, an "only in Boston" experience if ever there was one.

3 Winter Place. ℂ **617/542-1340.** www.lockeober.com. Reservations recommended. No denim, shorts, or sneakers. Main courses $11–$32 at lunch; $28–$62 at dinner. AE, DISC, MC, V. Mon–Fri 11:30am–2:30pm; Mon–Thurs 5:30–10pm, Fri–Sat 5:30–11pm. Valet parking available at dinner. T: Red or Orange Line to Downtown Crossing, or Green Line to Park St.

INEXPENSIVE

There's a **Così Sandwich Bar** (see above) at 14 Milk St. (ℂ **617/426-7565**).

Fajitas & 'Ritas ★ TEX-MEX   This colorful, entertaining restaurant is one of the most fun places around. It serves nachos, quesadillas, burritos, and, of course, fajitas, exactly the way you want them. You mark your food and drink selections on a checklist, and a member of the busy staff quickly returns with big portions of tasty food. You can also try barbecue items, such as smoked brisket or pulled pork, or tequila-marinated chicken wings. There's nothing particularly exotic—beef, chicken, shrimp, beans, and so

---

⌐*Tips* The Lunch Line

Try to be near Downtown Crossing at lunchtime at least once during your visit and seek out at **Chacarero,** 26 Province St., between School and Bromfield streets (ℂ **617/367-1167;** www.chacarero.com). It serves other things, but the line is so long because of the scrumptious Chilean sandwiches, served on house-made bread. Order chicken, beef, or vegetarian, ask for it "with everything"—tomatoes, cheese, avocado, hot sauce, and (unexpected but delicious) green beans—and dig in. I've never detected much difference in flavor between "original" and "b-b-que," but many fans swear by the latter, and I've never seen anyone other than a starving teenager finish a large—even a small is a lot of food. And for less than $8, you feel like a savvy Bostonian. Chacarero started as a counter in the exterior wall of a department store, and the line was long. Now it's indoors, in a bright, colorful storefront, and the line is long. Another location, at 101 Arch St., off Summer Street, is in the works at press time, and there'll probably be a line there, too.

forth——but it's all super-fresh, because this place is too busy to let anything sit around for very long. As the name indicates, 'ritas (margaritas) are a house specialty. Primarily a casual business destination at lunch, it's livelier at dinner (probably thanks to the margaritas) and a perfect stop before or after a movie at the nearby AMC Loews Boston Common theater.

25 West St. (between Washington and Tremont sts.). ℂ 617/426-1222. www.fajitasandritas.com. Reservations accepted only for parties of 8 or more. Main dishes $5–$9 at lunch, $6–$13 at dinner. AE, DC, DISC, MC, V. Mon–Tues 11:30am–9pm; Wed–Thurs 11:30am–10pm; Fri–Sat 11:30am–11pm; Sun noon–8pm. T: Red or Green Line to Park St., or Red or Orange Line to Downtown Crossing.

7 Beacon Hill

MODERATE

Artú (p. 111) has a branch at 89 Charles St. (ℂ **617/227-9023**). It's open Sunday and Monday from 4 to 11pm, Tuesday through Saturday from 11am to 11pm.

Grotto ★★ (Value) ITALIAN   When I feel like cheating on the North End, I leave my Italian-American neighborhood and head for Beacon Hill. Grotto's shadowy subterranean dining room is a cozy retreat, with contemporary art on the exposed-brick walls and overtaxed servers bustling around the small, crowded space. Chef-owner Scott Herritt has fun with seasonal local ingredients, beginning his regularly changing menu with imaginative soups and ending with fruit desserts, and his three-course set-price dinner is one of the best deals around. You might see seared diver scallops with morel mushrooms, baby leeks, and corn in the spring; apple-stuffed duck breast in the winter; or spaghetti and meatballs "with Grotto's insanely fabulous tomato sauce" anytime. The first dish that got my attention here was hearty gnocchi with braised short ribs, Gorgonzola, and mushrooms; it was a summer night, and I cleaned my plate. Desserts are indulgent but not overwhelming—a friend who's usually indifferent to sweets (where do I find these people?) devoured banana bread pudding with caramel ice cream. Good—more chocolate cake for me.

37 Bowdoin St. ℂ 617/227-3434. www.grottorestaurant.com. Reservations recommended at dinner. Main courses $8–$13 at lunch, $20–$27 at dinner; 3-course fixed-price dinner $35. AE, MC, V. Mon–Fri 11:30am–3pm; daily 5–10pm. T: Green or Red Line to Park St., or Blue Line to Bowdoin (weekdays only).

8 Chinatown/Theater District

The most entertaining and delicious introduction to Chinatown's cuisine is **dim sum** (see "Yum, Yum, Dim Sum," below). If you're eating dinner, you should know that many restaurants have a second menu for Chinese patrons (often written in Chinese). You can ask for it or tell your waiter that you want your meal Chinese-style.

If you're serious about sweets, consider ending—or even beginning—your meal at **Finale** (p. 229), 1 Columbus Ave. (ℂ **617/423-3184**; www.finaledesserts.com).

The area around Park Square (Columbus Ave. and South Charles St., between the Theater District and the Public Garden) is a hotbed of upscale national chain restaurants. None of these places offers a unique or even unusual experience, but they're all reliable destinations if you're feeling unadventurous. They include **Fleming's Prime Steakhouse & Wine Bar,** 217 Stuart St. (ℂ **617/292-0808**); **Maggiano's Little Italy,** 4 Columbus Ave. (ℂ **617/542-3456**); **McCormick & Schmick's Seafood Restaurant,** 34 Columbus Ave., in the Boston Park Plaza Hotel (ℂ **617/482-3999**); and **P. F. Chang's China Bistro,** 8 Park Plaza (ℂ **617/573-0821**).

VERY EXPENSIVE

Troquet ✿✿ NEW AMERICAN/WINE BAR   Troquet is French slang for "small wine cafe," and it's a good name for this sophisticated two-level restaurant. The second-floor dining room overlooks Boston Common, and the ground floor is a lounge that serves "creative cocktails" and small plates to a chic after-work and pre- and post-theater crowd. Troquet offers 40-plus wines by the 2- or 4-ounce glass and hundreds more by the bottle. Because the markup is lower than usual, sampling several selections is surprisingly affordable. The menu recommends pairings, and you'll want just the right thing to complement the exceptional cuisine, which emphasizes seasonal ingredients and never overwhelms the wine. The word that keeps coming back to me is *subtle*—a salad of marinated beets over baby greens was flavorful but not overpowering; pan-roasted rib steak with root vegetables and potato purée was rich and earthy; panko-crusted cod seemed perfumed rather than punched up with red curry and kaffir lime. Best of all, whether you're a novice or a pro, the staff offers as much wine advice as you need. I'll offer some dessert advice: sticky toffee pudding.

140 Boylston St. ✆ 617/695-9463. www.troquetboston.com. Reservations recommended. Main courses $26–$38; lounge menu $9–$22. AE, DC, DISC, MC, V. Dining room Tues–Sat 5–10:30pm; lounge daily 5pm–1am (food served until midnight). T: Green Line to Boylston.

EXPENSIVE

There's a branch of **Legal Sea Foods** (p. 106) at 26 Park Sq., between Columbus Avenue and Stuart Street (✆ **617/426-4444;** www.legalseafoods.com).

Ginza Japanese Restaurant ✿ JAPANESE/SUSHI   On a side street in Chinatown, you'll find one of the city's best Japanese restaurants. Track down the nondescript entrance up the street from the Chinatown arch, settle into one of the two rooms (in a booth, if you're lucky), and watch as kimono-clad waitresses glide past, bearing sushi boats the size of small children. Ginza is a magnet for Japanese expatriates, sushi-lovers, and, in the wee hours, club-hoppers. It's not the only place in town where expert chefs work wonders with ocean-fresh ingredients, but it serves some of the most creative creations (including "spider maki," a soft-shelled crab fried and tucked into a seaweed wrapper with avocado, cucumber, and flying-fish roe). An excellent starter is edamame—addictive boiled and salted soybeans served in the pod (you pull the beans out with your teeth). Then let your imagination run wild, or trust the chefs to assemble something dazzling. Green-tea ice cream makes an unusually satisfying dessert, but nobody will blame you for finishing with another round of California maki.

Ginza has a branch just over the **Brookline** border at 1002 Beacon St. (✆ **617/566-9688**) that's open until 1:30am on Friday and Saturday nights, 10pm the rest of the week.

14 Hudson St. ✆ 617/338-2261. www.ginzaboston.com. Reservations accepted only for parties of 6 or more. Sushi from $3.50; lunch specials $10–$17; main courses $14–$23. AE, DC, MC, V. Mon–Fri 11:30am–2:30pm; Mon–Thurs 5–11pm; Fri 5pm–3:30am; Sat 11:30am–3:30am; Sun 11:30am–11pm. T: Orange Line to New England Medical Center.

MODERATE

Grand Chau Chow ✿ CANTONESE/CHINESE   This is one of the best and busiest restaurants in Chinatown. It offers niceties that the smaller restaurants don't, such as tablecloths and tuxedoed waiters, as well as a nearly encyclopedic menu. Clams with black-bean sauce is a signature dish, as is gray sole with fried fins and bones. If you have the heart, you can watch your dinner swimming around in the large fish

Yum, Yum, Dim Sum

Many Chinatown restaurants offer **dim sum,** the traditional midday meal featuring appetizer-style dishes. You'll see steamed buns *(bao)* filled with pork or bean paste; meat, shrimp, and vegetable dumplings; sticky rice dotted with sausage and vegetables; shrimp-stuffed eggplant; spring rolls; sweets such as sesame balls and coconut gelatin; and more. Waitresses wheel carts laden with tempting dishes to your table, and you order by pointing (unless you know Chinese). The waitress then stamps your check with the symbol of the dish, adding about $1 to $3 to your tab for each selection. Unless you order a la carte items from the regular menu or the steam table off to the side in most dining rooms, the total usually won't be more than about $10 to $12 per person.

Dim sum varies from restaurant to restaurant, chef to chef, and even day to day; if something looks familiar, don't be surprised if it's different from what you're accustomed to and equally good. This is a great group activity, especially on weekends. The selection is wider than on weekdays, the turnover is faster (which means fresher food), and you'll often see three generations of families sharing large tables. Even picky children can usually find something they enjoy. If you don't eat pork and shrimp, be aware that many, but not all, dishes include one or the other; calorie counters should know that many dishes (again, not all) are fried.

Asked to name a favorite destination, I tend to favor the last place I went, which at the moment is **China Pearl** ✸✸, 9 Tyler St., 2nd floor (✆ **617/426-4338**). Other good destinations are **Chau Chow City** ✸✸, 83 Essex St. (✆ **617/338-8158**), **Empire Garden Restaurant** ✸, also known as Emperor's Garden, 690–698 Washington St., 2nd floor (✆ **617/482-8898**), and **Hei La Moon,** 88 Beach St. (✆ **617/338-8813**).

tanks, both salt- and freshwater. Stick to seafood and you can't go wrong. Lunch specials are a great deal, but skip the *chow fun,* which quickly turns gelatinous. If you're in town during Chinese New Year celebrations, phone ahead and request a multi-course banquet for your group (about $25 a person).

45 Beach St. ✆ **617/292-5166**. Reservations accepted only for parties of 10 or more. Main courses $6–$24; lobster and some fish dishes market price. AE, DC, DISC, MC, V. Sun–Thurs 10am–2:30am; Fri–Sat 10am–3:30am. T: Orange Line to Chinatown.

Jacob Wirth Company GERMAN/AMERICAN   In the heart of the Theater District, "Jake's" has been serving Bostonians since 1868—even before there were theaters here. The wood floor and brass accents give the spacious room the feeling of a saloon, and the menu incorporates traditional pub grub and more contemporary fare. The hearty German specialties include Wiener schnitzel, mixed grills, bratwurst, knock-wurst, and potato pancakes. Daily specials, comfort-food favorites like chicken pot pie, and a large variety of sandwiches and salads round out the menu. Service at lunchtime is snappy, but if you want to be on time for the theater, be ready to remind your server. On Friday after 8pm, a live pianist leads sing-along night, which has something of a chicken-and-egg connection to the huge selection of beers on tap.

31–37 Stuart St. ℂ 617/338-8586. www.jacobwirth.com. Reservations recommended at dinner. Main courses $8– $28 (most items less than $20). AE, DC, DISC, MC, V. Tues–Thurs 11:30am–11pm; Fri–Sat 11:30am–midnight; Sun 11:30am–8pm. Validated parking available. T: Green Line to Boylston or Orange Line to New England Medical Center.

Peach Farm ✿ SEAFOOD/CANTONESE/SZECHUAN   Chinatown's go-to place for fresh seafood is a subterranean hideaway with no decor to speak of. You won't be looking around much anyway—the service is so fast that just saying "calamari" seems to make spicy dry-fried salted squid appear on your table. Gobble it up while it's hot, then turn to the delicious dishes that follow in lightning-quick order: messy clams with black-bean sauce, braised chicken hot pot, an emerald-green pile of stir-fried pea-pod stems. Spicy salt shrimp—you can eat them whole, shells, heads, and all—is only the most recent commendable dish I've tried here; my favorite is that same spicy salt preparation applied to meltingly tender scallops. Fair warning to the soft-hearted: Order the Cantonese classic fresh fish steamed with ginger and scallions, and the waiter brings the poor creature to your table thrashing in a plastic bucket; it reappears moments later, perfectly cooked. Peach Farm is virtually indistinguishable from the rest of the little restaurants that dot Chinatown's narrow side streets, except that it's so crowded—savvy locals and celebratory groups fill both compact dining rooms every night.

4 Tyler St. ℂ 617/482-3332. Reservations recommended for large groups at dinner. Main courses $5–$34 (most items less than $15); fresh seafood market price. MC, V. Daily 11am–3am. T: Orange Line to Chinatown.

INEXPENSIVE

Buddha's Delight ✿ ⓥalue VEGETARIAN/VIETNAMESE   Fresh and healthy intersect with cheap and filling at this busy restaurant. Brave the run-down stairwell, ask for a table near the window, and be ready to experiment. The menu lists "chicken," "shrimp," "pork," and even "lobster"—in quotes because the kitchen doesn't use meat, poultry, fish, or dairy (some beverages have condensed milk). The chefs fry and barbecue tofu and gluten into more-than-reasonable facsimiles using techniques owner Cuong Van Tran learned from Buddhist monks in a temple outside Los Angeles. Between trying to figure out how they do it and savoring Vietnamese cuisine's strong, clear flavors, you might not miss your usual protein. To start, try fried "pork" dumplings or a delectable salad. Move on to "shrimp" with rice noodles, any of the house specialties, or excellent *chow fun*.

3 Beach St., 2nd floor. ℂ 617/451-2395. Main courses $6–$13; lunch specials $6.50. MC, V. Sun–Thurs 11am– 9:30pm, Fri–Sat 11am–10:30pm. T: Orange Line to Chinatown.

9 The South End

VERY EXPENSIVE

Hamersley's Bistro ✿ FRENCH/AMERICAN   This is the place that put the South End on Boston's culinary map, a pioneering restaurant (it opened in 1987) that's both classic and contemporary. It's one of the most beloved special-occasion restaurants in the Boston area yet somehow manages to feel like a neighborhood hangout, mostly thanks to the huge volume of repeat business. The husband-and-wife team of Gordon and Fiona Hamersley presides over a long dining room with lots of soft surfaces that absorb sound, so you can see but not quite hear what's going on at the tables around you. That means you'll have to quiz one of the courteous servers about the dish that just passed by—perhaps a starter of rabbit pâté or smoked-trout salad with beets.

Tips **Where's the Beef?**

Say "Boston," think "seafood," right? Apparently not. Branches of most of the national steakhouse chains dot the city, and they're all at the top of their game—a rising tide lifts all boats, as the seafood folks say.

The local favorites are **Grill 23 & Bar** (p. 123); the **Oak Room,** in the Fairmont Copley Plaza Hotel, 138 St. James Ave. (✆ **617/267-5300; www.theoakroom. com**); and **Abe & Louie's,** 793 Boylston St. (✆ **617/536-6300; www.abeand louies.com**). Devotees of the national chains can choose from the **Palm,** in the Westin Copley Place Boston, 200 Dartmouth St. (✆ **617/867-9292; www.the palm.com**); the **Capital Grille,** 359 Newbury St. (✆ **617/262-8900; www.the capitalgrille.com**); **Fleming's Prime Steakhouse & Wine Bar,** 217 Stuart St. (✆ **617/ 292-0808; www.flemingssteakhouse.com**); **Morton's of Chicago** (**www.mortons. com**), 1 Exeter Plaza, Boylston Street at Exeter Street (✆ **617/266-5858**), and World Trade Center East, 2 Seaport Lane (✆ **617/526-0410**); **Ruth's Chris Steak House** (✆ **800/544-0808; www.ruthschris.com**), in Old City Hall, 45 School St.; and **Smith & Wollensky,** 101 Arlington St. (✆ **617/432-1112; www.smithand wollensky.com**).

The menu changes seasonally and offers about a dozen carefully considered entrees noted for their emphasis on local ingredients and classic preparations. I find the famed roast chicken with garlic, lemon, and parsley a bit tame, but the inventive seafood dishes have no such problem; a memorable dish of peppered tuna with spicy cauliflower and fennel warmed a recent chilly night. For meat-eaters, cassoulet with pork, duck confit, and garlic sausage is a gorgeously executed combination of flavors and textures. The wine list is excellent, and there's seasonal outdoor seating.

553 Tremont St. ✆ 617/423-2700. www.hamersleysbistro.com. Reservations recommended. Main courses $26– $42; tasting menu varies. AE, DISC, MC, V. Mon–Fri 6–10pm; Sat 5:30–10:30pm; Sun 11am–2pm (brunch) and 5:30– 9:30pm. Closed Jan 1–12. Valet parking available. T: Orange Line to Back Bay.

Icarus ⭐⭐ ECLECTIC   This shamelessly romantic subterranean restaurant is perfect for everything from helping a friend heal a broken heart to celebrating a milestone anniversary. Marble accents and dark-wood trim lend an elegant air to the two-level dining room, and the service is efficient but not formal. Chef and co-owner Chris Douglass uses choice local seafood, poultry, meats, and produce to create his imaginative dishes. The menu changes regularly. You might start with braised exotic mushrooms atop polenta, succulent avocado soup, or the daily "pasta whim" (but make sure the server quotes the price, which can be extravagant). Move on to seared duck breast and roasted duck leg served with wild-rice pancakes, or a scrumptious seafood special like sautéed black cod with local clams, white beans, and morels. Finally, save room for dessert: The trio of seasonal fruit sorbets is one of the best non-chocolate desserts I've ever tasted. And on Friday from 7 to 11pm, the bar schedules live jazz.

3 Appleton St. ✆ 617/426-1790. www.icarusrestaurant.com. Reservations recommended. Main courses $28–$41. AE, DC, DISC, MC, V. Mon–Thurs 6–9:30pm; Fri 6–10pm; Sat 5:30–10pm; Sun 5:30–9pm. Valet parking available. T: Green Line to Arlington or Orange Line to Back Bay.

INEXPENSIVE

Picco PIZZA   The cutesy name—short for "Pizza and Ice Cream Company"—may seem like a red flag. Ignore it. Picco serves traditional and yuppified pizza and phenomenal ice cream in an airy space up the street from the Boston Center for the Arts. The pizza menu ranges from traditional Margherita (tomato, basil, and cheese) to the "Alsatian variation," topped with a lip-smacking combo of caramelized onions, bacon, sour cream, roasted garlic, and Gruyère. The crust—a little smoky from the wood-fired oven, blistered in spots, thin but not crackery—is as good as the toppings. If you're not in a pizza mood, the menu includes a selection of calzones, soups, salads, and sandwiches. Somewhat unexpectedly, Picco also has a fantastic wine list. And what about the "IC" part of the name? The ice cream sandwich didn't do it for me because the cookies weren't nearly as good as the filling, but all of the other sweets—including a huge brownie sundae, ice cream sodas, and even a dish of plain old vanilla—were scrumptious.

513 Tremont St. (℃ **617/927-0066**. www.piccorestaurant.com. Reservations accepted only for parties of 8 or more. Pizza $9.50 and up; main courses $9–$13. MC, V. Daily 11am–11pm. T: Orange Line to Back Bay.

10 The Back Bay

VERY EXPENSIVE

In 2008, **L'Espalier** (℃ **617/262-3023;** www.lespalier.com) moved from a town house off Newbury Street to Boylston Street's new Mandarin Oriental, Boston (p. 85). One of Boston's favorite special-occasion restaurants, it combines French technique and ingredients from all over—notably small New England purveyors—to create prix fixe menus of three or more courses that make dinner more event than meal. You'll pay at least $75 a head, and you won't mind a bit.

Davio's Northern Italian Steakhouse 𝒢𝒢 STEAKS/CREATIVE NORTHERN ITALIAN   A cavernous space with a surprisingly comfortable vibe, Davio's offers robust cuisine that contrasts delightfully with the business-chic setting. It's stylish but not trendy: Owner-chef Steve DiFillippo built the restaurant's excellent reputation on its top-notch kitchen and dedicated staff. Straight-up Northern Italian cuisine shares the menu with steakhouse offerings such as picture-perfect steaks, chops, and seafood, as well as inventive-comfort-food sides. The traditional dishes—homemade sausage, savory soups, out-of-this-world risotto (I'd walk a mile for the lobster version), and pasta—are equally superb, making Davio's a great compromise for hard-core carnivores dining with Italophiles. The exceptional wine list includes some rare and expensive Italian vintages, and the excellent breads and desserts are made in-house. Despite the open kitchen, the bar in the middle of the room, and the lively lounge area, the noise level allows for conversation, even at busy times. Bonus, if you're into that sort of thing: When the Yankees are in town to play the Red Sox, you can often see at least a few of them here.

75 Arlington St. (℃ **617/357-4810**. www.davios.com. Reservations recommended. Main courses $9–$43 at lunch (most less than $25), $21–$52 at dinner; 5-course tasting menu $95. AE, DC, DISC, MC, V. Mon–Fri 11:30am–3pm; Sun–Tues 5–10pm (lounge menu until 11pm), Wed–Sat 5–11pm (lounge menu until midnight). Validated and valet parking available. T: Green Line to Arlington.

Grill 23 & Bar 𝒢 STEAKS/AMERICAN   The best steakhouse in town, Grill 23 is a wood-paneled, glass-walled place with a businesslike air. A briefcase-toting crowd fills its two levels and chows down on traditional slabs of beef and chops, traditional steakhouse side dishes, and sophisticated yet traditional desserts. The meat is of the

Kids Family-Friendly Restaurants

Like chocolate and champagne, well-behaved children are welcome almost everywhere. Most Boston-area restaurants can accommodate families, and many youngsters can be stunned into tranquility if a place is fancy enough. If your kids can't or won't sign a good-conduct pledge, here are some suggestions.

The nonstop activity and smart-mouthed service at **Durgin-Park** (p. 115) will entrance any child, and parents of picky eaters appreciate the straightforward New England fare. Other good non-chain choices are **Redbones** (p. 137), the **Barking Crab** (p. 107), and **Jasper White's Summer Shack** (p. 135)—especially the Cambridge location.

The **Bertucci's** chain of pizzerias (www.bertuccis.com) appeals to children and adults equally, with wood-fired brick ovens that are visible from many tables, great rolls made from pizza dough, and pizzas and pastas that range from basic to sophisticated. There are convenient branches at Faneuil Hall Marketplace (© 617/227-7889), on Merchants Row off State Street; in the Back Bay at 43 Stanhope St. (© 617/247-6161); at 533 Commonwealth Avenue, Kenmore Square (© 617/236-1030); and in Cambridge at 21 Brattle St., Harvard Square (© 617/864-4748), and 799 Main St. (© 617/661-8356), a short walk from Central Square

---

highest quality, expertly prepared. Steak au poivre and lamb chops are perfectly grilled, crusty, juicy, and tender. Fish dishes aren't quite as memorable as the meat offerings, but hey, it's a steakhouse. The bountiful a la carte sides include out-of-this-world garlic mashed potatoes, ginger beets, and "tater tots" drizzled with truffle oil. Desserts are toothsome but (this is *not* your father's steakhouse) don't always include cheesecake. The service is exactly right for the setting, helpful but not familiar.

Caveats: The excellent wine list is pricey, and the noise level rises as the evening progresses. Still, you probably won't realize that you're shouting until you're outside yelling about what a good meal you had.

161 Berkeley St. © 617/542-2255. www.grill23.com. Reservations recommended. Main courses $25–$49 (most more than $33); Kobe beef $59. AE, DC, DISC, MC, V. Mon–Thurs 5:30–10:30pm; Fri–Sat 5:30–11pm; Sun 5:30–10pm. Valet parking available. T: Green Line to Arlington.

EXPENSIVE

Tapéo, 266 Newbury St. (© 617/267-4799), has the same owners and menu as **Dalí** (p. 134). **Jasper White's Summer Shack** (p. 135) has a branch at 50 Dalton St. (© 617/867-9955), across the street from the Sheraton Boston Hotel and the Hynes Convention Center.

The Bristol AMERICAN   The Bristol is to a regular restaurant as the Four Seasons is to a regular hotel: It looks about the same, but everything is just *better.* Columns and cushy banquettes break up a large space with floor-to-ceiling windows, red-leather accents, and plenty of wood paneling; there's seating in the lively bar and the stylish dining area. The all-day menu extends from pricey breakfast items to tasty bar bites to sophisticated versions of classic dishes. The juicy burgers are famous, the soups and salads depend on what's fresh and seasonal, and the main courses are top-of-the-line comfort food (seared cod, roasted chicken, creamy lobster risotto). Desserts are inventive versions of apple pie, fudge cake, cheesecake, and other traditional favorites. In keeping with the quality of every other element of the experience, the service is fantastic.

The hotel's fine-dining restaurant, **Aujourd'hui** (© **617/351-2037**), is one of Boston's top special-occasion and expense-account destinations. In a gorgeous second-floor space overlooking the Public Garden, it serves modern French cuisine (main courses $26–$42) Tuesday through Saturday from 5:30 to 10:30pm and Sunday 6 to 10pm, and a bountiful New England Sunday brunch buffet ($65 adults, $32.50 children) from 11am to 3pm. Reservations are strongly recommended.

In the Four Seasons Hotel, 200 Boylston St. © 617/351-2037. www.fourseasons.com/boston. Reservations recommended. Main courses $14–$28 at lunch, $16–$33 at dinner; bar menu $8–$27. AE, DC, DISC, MC, V. Mon–Thurs 6:30am–11:30pm; Fri–Sat 6:30am–12:30am; Sun 10am–12:30am. Valet parking available. T: Green Line to Arlington.

Casa Romero *Finds* MEXICAN   Restaurants in alleys have that certain something. They feel like secret clubs, and finding one can make a hungry diner feel like a daring explorer. Casa Romero is just such a place. The tiled floor, rustic wood furnishings, dim lighting, and clay pots lend an authentic feel—you're definitely not at the

---

Finds Boston Tea Party, Part 2

In Boston, the only city that has a tea party named after it, the tradition of afternoon tea at a posh hotel is alive and well. At all of them, reservations are strongly recommended; at the Bristol and Taj Boston, they're pretty much mandatory.

The best afternoon tea in town is at the **Bristol** in the Four Seasons Hotel, 200 Boylston St. (© **617/351-2037**). The gorgeous room, lovely view, and courtly ritual elevate scones, pastries, tea sandwiches, and nut bread from delicious to unforgettable. The Bristol serves tea ($28) every day from 3 to 4:30pm. My second choice is a bit of a sleeper: **Intrigue,** in the Boston Harbor Hotel, Rowes Wharf (© **617/856-7744**), serves tea daily from 2:30 to 4pm in an elegant space that faces the harbor. It's just $18.50 per person, $26 if you add a glass of Champagne.

The **Langham, Boston,** 250 Franklin St. (© **617/956-8751**), serves afternoon tea daily from 3 to 4:30pm. The chain's flagship is in London, and as you'd expect, this is a proper British experience. The price is $18, $24, or $36 per person, plus $2 to $5 for premium teas. Taj Boston, 15 Arlington St. (© **617/598-5255**), serves tea in the celebrated **Lounge** at 2 and 4pm; it's available Wednesday through Sunday in the winter, Friday through Sunday the rest of the year. The price is $22 for tea and pastries, $30 to add sandwiches.

It's neither a hotel nor in Boston, but beloved Cambridge restaurant **Upstairs on the Square** (p. 130) makes a wonderful destination. Zebra Tea ($25) is a three-tiered wonder that lets the inventive kitchen cut loose on a small scale. Food and drinks are also available a la carte, and the Grand Peppermint Tea ($18) combines minty sweets and a pot of the headliner. Tea is served Friday and Saturday (Thurs–Sun in Dec) from 3 to 5pm.

Quick Bites & Picnic Provisions

Takeout food particularly appeals to two kinds of out-of-towners: eat-and-run sightseers and picnickers looking to take advantage of the acres of waterfront property in Boston and Cambridge. Here are some suggestions.

If you're walking the Freedom Trail, pick up food at **Faneuil Hall Market-place** and stake out a bench. Or buy a tasty sandwich in the North End at **Volle Nolle**, 351 Hanover St. (© 617/523-0003), or **Il Panino Express**, 266 Hanover St. (© 617/720-5720), and stroll down Fleet or Richmond streets toward the harbor. Eat at the park on Sargent's Wharf, behind 2 Atlantic Ave., or in Christopher Columbus Waterfront Park, overlooking the marina (which is also an option if you stocked up at Faneuil Hall Marketplace).

Two neighborhoods abut the Charles River Esplanade, a great destination for a picnic, concert, or movie. In the **Back Bay,** stop at **Trader Joe's,** 899 Boylston St. (© 617/262-6505), for prepared food, or **Spike's Junkyard Dogs,** 1076 Boylston St. (© 617/266-0909), for some of the tastiest hot dogs, chicken sandwiches, and "poodle" (curly) fries around. At the foot of **Beacon Hill,** pick up all you need for a do-it-yourself feast at **Savenor's Market,** 160 Charles St. (© 617/723-6328). Or call ahead for pizza from the original location of the **Upper Crust** chain, 20 Charles St. (© 617/723-9600), or **Figs,** 42 Charles St. (© 617/742-3447), a minuscule pizzeria that's an offshoot of the celebrated Olives. The upscale fare at these places isn't cheap, but avoiding the lines is worth the price—as is the delectable pizza.

On the Cambridge side of the river, **Harvard Square** is close enough to the water to allow a riverside repast. About 5 minutes from the heart of the Square and well worth the walk, **Darwin's Ltd.,** 148 Mount Auburn St. (© 617/354-5233; www.darwinsltd.com), serves excellent gourmet sandwiches and salads. Take yours to John F. Kennedy Park, on Memorial Drive and Kennedy Street, or right to the riverbank, a block away. Nowhere near the Charles, there's a branch at 1629 Cambridge St. (© 617/491-2999), in Inman Square.

local Tex-Mex counter. The food is excellent, with generous portions of spicy-hot and milder dishes; the friendly staff will help you navigate the menu. To start, count yourself lucky if the soup of the day is garlic, or try a refreshing cactus-and-tomato salad. Main-dish specialties include several kinds of enchiladas, traditional preparations of fresh fish and shellfish, at least two vegetarian options, and the restaurant's signature dish, succulent pork tenderloin marinated with oranges and chipotle peppers. The walled garden is the "find" here; on a summer evening, it's a peaceful retreat.

30 Gloucester St., side entrance. © 617/536-4341. www.casaromero.com. Reservations recommended. Main courses $15–$28. DISC, MC, V. Mon–Thurs 5–10pm; Fri–Sat 5–11pm; Sun noon–10pm (brunch until 2:30pm). Validated parking available. T: Green Line B, C, or D to Hynes Convention Center.

La Voile ✿ FRENCH/MEDITERRANEAN   Talk about authentically French: The owners created La Voile by shutting down La Voile au Vent in Cannes and shipping it to Boston, complete with chef and decor. Red velvet banquettes soften the tile-floored space, which is littered with model sailboats (the name means "the sail"), but don't mind the goofy theme: La Voile is a revelation. Start with a house-made terrine, or surrender to the Gallic vibe and order bone marrow to smear on bread and dot with sea salt. Now that you're in the mood, try *blanquette de veau* (veal in cream sauce, which doesn't even begin to do it justice), *choucroute Alsacienne* (the bistro standby of sausages over sauerkraut), or roasted chicken, which gets a goose-fat bath before going in the oven. It's not perfect: One night as I deconstructed a lamb shank with just the edge of my fork, I realized my companion was only picking at the bouillabaisse—it comes in a gravy-like sauce, so watch out if you're expecting broth. The biggest drawback here is the somewhat scatterbrained service, but to be fair, I did my research within a few months of La Voile's opening in late 2007. By the time you visit, the kinks should be worked out, a new pastry chef (imported, of course) should be in the kitchen, and lunch should be available.

261 Newbury St. ℂ **617/587-4200**. www.lavoileboston.net. Reservations recommended. Main courses $15–$43 (most less than $26). AE, MC, V. Tues–Sun 5:30–10:30pm. Valet parking available. T: Green Line to Copley.

MODERATE

Bangkok City ⚝ THAI In a neighborhood loaded with Thai restaurants, this is my top choice. In the large dining room, the cordial staff and tempting aromas greet you as you check out the exotic decor and lengthy menu. Appetizers are the usual dumplings and satays, plus unique items like "Boston triangles" (tasty fried pork-and-shrimp patties). Entrees range from mild pad Thai to blow-your-hair-back curries, with many vegetarian options. The mix-and-match selection of proteins and sauces is larger than at many other Thai restaurants, so you can let your palate's imagination run wild. (Oh, great—now I want some tamarind duck.) Hot tip: The friend who steered me to this place comes here just for the zesty salt-and-pepper squid.

167 Massachusetts Ave. ℂ **617/266-8884**. www.bkkcityboston.com. Reservations recommended before Symphony and Pops performances. Main courses $7–$10 at lunch; $8–$17 at dinner. AE, DC, DISC, MC, V. Mon–Sat 11:30am–3pm; Mon–Thurs 5–10pm; Fri 5–10:30pm; Sat 3–10:30pm; Sun 5–10pm. T: Green Line B, C, or D to Hynes Convention Center.

Brasserie Jo ⚝⚝ REGIONAL FRENCH One of the most discriminating diners I know lit up like a marquee upon hearing that Boston has a branch of this Chicago favorite. The food is classic—house-made pâtés, fresh baguettes, superb shellfish, salade Niçoise, Alsatian onion tart, *choucroute*, coq au vin—but never boring. The house beer, an Alsace-style draft, is a good accompaniment. The casual, all-day French brasserie and bar fits well in this neighborhood, where shoppers can always use a break but might not want a full meal. It's also a good bet before or after a Symphony or Pops performance, and it's popular for business lunches. The noise level can be high when the spacious room is full—have your tête-à-tête at a table near the bar.

⸨Tips⸩ Beat the Rush

If you plan to dine in a neighborhood that's near a performing arts or sports venue, try to arrive after the performance or game begins so you don't get caught in the frenzy. This is especially true in the Symphony Hall area and the Theater District, as well as Harvard Square, the North End (when there's an event at the Garden), and Kenmore Square (during baseball season).

Finds How Sweet It Is

What a world! The low-carb craze just won't go away, but a place with the delightfully unsubtle name **Sugar Heaven** is thriving. The self-serve calorie castle at 218 Newbury St. (© **617/266-6969;** www.sugarheaven.us) carries hundreds of confections, makes its own cotton candy, and stays open till midnight daily. That sound you hear is your dentist whimpering.

In the Colonnade Hotel, 120 Huntington Ave. © 617/425-3240. www.brasseriejoboston.com. Reservations recommended at dinner. Main courses $6–$15 at lunch, $15–$27 at dinner; *plats du jour* $18–$32. AE, DC, DISC, MC, V. Mon–Fri 6:30am–11pm; Sat 7am–11pm; Sun 7am–10pm; late-night menu daily until 1am. Valet and garage parking available. T: Green Line E to Prudential.

INEXPENSIVE

The Boston Public Library, 700 Boylston St. (© **617/536-5400;** www.bpl.org), is home to a restaurant, **Novel,** that serves lunch and afternoon tea on weekdays only, and the self-service **Sebastian's Map Room Café,** which serves meals and snacks Monday through Saturday from 9am to 5pm.

Café Jaffa MIDDLE EASTERN/MEDITERRANEAN A long, narrow brick room with a glass front, Café Jaffa looks more like a snazzy pizza place than the excellent Middle Eastern restaurant it is. The reasonable prices, high quality, and large portions draw hordes of students and other thrifty diners for traditional Middle Eastern offerings such as falafel, baba ghanouj, and hummus, as well as burgers and steak tips. Lamb, beef, and chicken kabobs come with Greek salad, rice pilaf, and pita bread. For dessert, try the baklava if it's fresh (give it a pass if not).

48 Gloucester St. © 617/536-0230. Main courses $5–$18. AE, DC, DISC, MC, V. Mon–Thurs 11am–10:30pm; Fri–Sat 11am–11pm; Sun 1–10pm. T: Green Line B, C, or D to Hynes Convention Center.

11 Kenmore Square to Brookline

EXPENSIVE

Ginza Japanese Restaurant (p. 119) has a branch at 1002 Beacon St., Brookline (© **617/566-9688**). Unlike the Boston location, the Brookline restaurant doesn't cater to a wee-hours crowd; its late nights are Friday and Saturday, when closing time is 1:30am (which is very late for Brookline).

The Elephant Walk ★★ FRENCH/CAMBODIAN France meets Cambodia on the menu at this madly popular spot, 4 blocks from Kenmore Square and decorated with lots of pachyderms. The menu is French on one side and Cambodian on the other, but the boundary is quite porous. Many Cambodian dishes have part-French names, such as *poulet à la citronelle* (chicken sautéed with lemongrass) and *mee siem,* a tangle of rice noodles, sliced omelet, tofu, chicken, and picture-perfect vegetables. My mouth is still burning from *loc lac,* fork-tender beef cubes in addictively spicy sauce. On the French side, you'll find *poulet rôti* (roasted chicken) and top-notch steak frites. Many dishes are available with tofu substituted for animal protein, and this is one of the best destinations in the Boston area if you can't have gluten. The pleasant staff members will help if you need guidance. Ask to be seated in the plant-filled front room, which is less noisy than the main dining room and has a view of the street. *Tip:* Sunday brunch, which includes the prettiest omelets I've ever seen, is worth checking out.

The **Cambridge** location of the Elephant Walk is just outside Porter Square, at 2067 Massachusetts Ave. (© **617/492-6900**). It serves dinner only in a high-ceilinged room decorated with fewer, bigger elephants than the Boston restaurant and offers free parking.

900 Beacon St., Boston. © 617/247-1500. www.elephantwalk.com. Reservations recommended at dinner Sun–Thurs, not accepted Fri–Sat. Main courses $7–$26 at lunch (most items less than $11); $14–$28 at dinner; tasting menus $30 and $40. AE, DC, DISC, MC, V. Mon–Fri 11:30am–2:30pm; Sun–Thurs 5–10pm; Fri–Sat 5–11pm; Sun brunch 11am–3pm. Valet parking available at dinner. T: Green Line C to St. Mary's St.

MODERATE

There's a branch of **Finale** (p. 229) at 1306 Beacon St., just outside Coolidge Corner, Brookline (© **617/232-3233;** www.finaledesserts.com).

INEXPENSIVE

Zaftigs Delicatessen DELI/AMERICAN   The magical phrase "breakfast served all day" might be enough to lure you to this bustling restaurant, but even breakfast haters will be happy at Zaftigs. The name, Yiddish for "pleasingly plump," is no joke—portions are more than generous. Try fluffy pancakes, challah French toast, or a terrific omelet. They share the menu with wonderful overstuffed deli sandwiches as well as entrees that seem basic but demonstrate a certain flair. Roasted chicken is juicy and flavorful, meatloaf and gravy equally enjoyable. The knock on Boston-area deli food is that (well, duh) it's not New York, but the hard-core deli items here are more

---

The Great Outdoors: Alfresco Dining

Cambridge is a better destination for outdoor dining than Boston, where an alarming number of tables sit unpleasantly close to busy traffic, but both cities offer agreeable spots to lounge under the sun or stars.

Across the street from the Charles River near Kendall Square, the **Sail Loft**, 1 Memorial Dr. (© 617/225-2222), opens onto a leafy plaza that usually picks up a breeze from the water. Both restaurant patios at the **Royal Sonesta Hotel**, 5 Cambridge Pkwy. (© 617/491-3600), have great views. The hotel's **Gallery Café** is casual; **Marco's** is fancier. On one of Harvard Square's main drags, **Shay's Pub & Wine Bar**, 58 John F. Kennedy St. (© 617/864-9161), has a small, lively seating area. More peaceful are the patios at **Henrietta's Table** (p. 132) and **Oleana** (p. 136).

On the other side of the river, try the airy terrace at **Miel** (© 617/217-5151), in the InterContinental Boston hotel, which overlooks Fort Point Channel. Most bars and restaurants in **Faneuil Hall Marketplace** offer outdoor seating and great people-watching. In the Back Bay, Newbury Street is similarly diverting; a good vantage point is **Stephanie's on Newbury**, 190 Newbury St. (© 617/236-0990). A popular shopping stop and after-work hangout is the **Parish Café and Bar**, 361 Boylston St. (© 617/247-4777), where the sandwich menu is a "greatest hits" roster of top local chefs' creations. A laid-back alternative in this area is the hideaway garden at **Casa Romero** (p. 125).

than acceptable. The gefilte fish is light, citrus twinkles in the blintz filling, and—the true test—the chicken soup is excellent. Weekend lunch here is comically crowded; be early or late, or expect to wait a while.

335 Harvard St., Brookline. © 617/975-0075. www.zaftigs.com. Reservations recommended at dinner; limited number accepted. Main courses $8–$17; sandwiches $7–$15; breakfast items $3.50–$11. AE, DISC, MC, V. Daily 8am–10pm. T: Green Line C to Coolidge Corner.

12 Cambridge

The dining scene in Cambridge, as in Boston, offers something for everyone, from penny-pinching students to the tycoons that many of them aspire to become. The Red Line runs from Boston to Harvard Square, and many of the restaurants listed here are within walking distance of the square; others (including a couple of real finds over the Somerville border) are under the heading "Outside Harvard Square."

To locate the restaurants reviewed in this section, see the "Where to Dine in Cambridge" map on p. 131.

HARVARD SQUARE & VICINITY

A brilliant idea cooked up by a pair of Harvard Business School students, **Finale** (p. 229), 30 Dunster St. (© **617/441-9797**), specializes in dessert.

VERY EXPENSIVE

Upstairs on the Square ★★ ECLECTIC   Overlooking a little park just off Harvard Square, Upstairs on the Square is the perfect combination of comfort food and fine dining. It consists of two lovely spaces; I prefer the more casual one to its fancier counterpart. The second-floor Monday Club Bar dining room is a relaxed yet romantic space where firelight flickers on jewel-toned walls. The food—unusual salads and sandwiches, satisfying soups, a daily pizza option (at lunch), fried chicken, inventive pastas, steak with ever-changing versions of potatoey goodness—is homey and satisfying, and the bar is a tweedy Cambridge scene. The top-floor Soirée Room, a jewel box of pinks and golds under a low, mirrored ceiling, is the place for that big anniversary dinner. The menu is enjoyably old-fashioned, with straightforward main courses (a slab of halibut, juicy grilled lamb loin) that contrast with bolder starters—delectable Jerusalem artichoke or watercress soup, simple but superb salads and shellfish. Tasting menus, for vegetarians and carnivores, let the kitchen show off. In both rooms, you'll find outstanding wine selections and desserts.

91 Winthrop St. © 617/864-1933. www.upstairsonthesquare.com. Reservations recommended. Main courses $10–$28 downstairs, $25–$42 upstairs; prix fixe lunch (downstairs only) $20; tasting menus (upstairs only) $50–$86. AE, DC, DISC, MC, V. Downstairs Mon–Fri 11:30am–2:30pm; Sat–Sun brunch 10am–3pm; afternoon tea Fri–Sat 3–5pm; daily 5pm–2am (dinner until 11pm). Upstairs Mon–Thurs 5:30–10pm; Fri–Sat 5:30–11pm. Validated and valet parking available. T: Red Line to Harvard.

EXPENSIVE

There's a **Legal Sea Foods** (p. 106) in the Charles Hotel courtyard, 20 University Rd. (© **617/491-9400**).

Casablanca ★ MEDITERRANEAN   This old-time Harvard Square favorite (the restaurant dates to 1977, the bar all the way to 1955) is a landmark for a reason, and it's not just the hopping bar scene. The walls of the long, sky-lit dining room and crowded, noisy bar sport murals of scenes from the movie *Casablanca*. Humphrey Bogart looks as though he might lean down to ask for a taste of your crispy eggplant

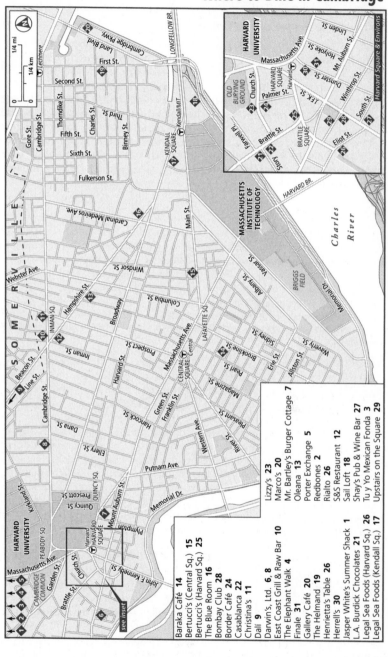

Baraka Café **14**
Bertucci's (Central Sq.) **15**
Bertucci's (Harvard Sq.) **25**
The Blue Room **16**
Bombay Club **28**
Border Café **24**
Casablanca **22**
Christina's **11**
Dalí **9**
Darwin's, Ltd. **6, 8**
East Coast Grill & Raw Bar **10**
The Elephant Walk **4**
Finale **31**
Gallery Café **20**
The Helmand **19**
Henrietta's Table **26**
Herrell's **30**
Jasper White's Summer Shack **1**
L.A. Burdick Chocolates **21**
Legal Sea Foods (Harvard Sq.) **26**
Legal Sea Foods (Kendall Sq.) **17**

Lizzy's **23**
Marco's **20**
Mr. Bartley's Burger Cottage **7**
Oleana **13**
Porter Exchange **5**
Redbones **2**
Rialto **26**
S&S Restaurant **12**
Sail Loft **18**
Shay's Pub & Wine Bar **27**
Tu Yo Mexican Fonda **3**
Upstairs on the Square **29**

Kids The Scoop on Ice Cream

No less an expert than Ben Cohen of Ben & Jerry's has described Boston as "a great place for ice cream." That goes for Cambridge, too—residents of both cities famously defy even the most frigid weather to get their fix. I like Cambridge better: Try **Christina's,** 1255 Cambridge St., Inman Square (© **617/492-7021); Herrell's,** 15 Dunster St., Harvard Square (© **617/497-2179);** or **Lizzy's,** 29 Church St. (© **617/354-2911).** Favorite Boston destinations include **Emack & Bolio's,** 290 Newbury St. (© **617/536-7127)** and 255 State St., across from the New England Aquarium (© **617/367-0220); Ben & Jerry's,** 174 Newbury St. (© **617/536-5456)** and 20 Park Plaza (© **617/426-0890);** and **JP Licks,** 352 Newbury St. (© **617/236-1666)** and 659 Centre St., Jamaica Plain (© **617/524-6740).**

---

with herbed ricotta or roasted leg of lamb with charred tomatoes. The appetizers and tapas are so good that you might want to assemble them into a meal—start with the Turkish meze plate or fried calamari. Just be sure to leave room for dessert; I don't usually have much use for fruit when there's chocolate around, but the spice cake here made me reconsider. I also usually go nuts when service is this erratic (it's better at lunch than at dinner), but somehow that's not the impression that sticks.

40 Brattle St. © 617/876-0999. www.casablanca-restaurant.com. Reservations recommended at dinner. Main courses $10–$14 at lunch, $24–$29 at dinner; *tapas* and small plates $5–$14. AE, DC, MC, V. Mon–Sat 11:30am–2:30pm; Sun brunch 11am–2:30pm; Sun–Thurs 5:30–10pm; Fri–Sat 5:30–11pm. Validated parking available. T: Red Line to Harvard.

Henrietta's Table ⧊⧊★ NEW ENGLAND   It figures that the Charles Hotel, which looks utilitarian at first and turns out to be luxurious, has a similarly deceptive restaurant. Decorated in upscale farmhouse style, Henrietta's Table serves (and prices) "supper" side dishes a la carte—I didn't see the appeal. Baked scrod, roasted chicken, pot roast? Show me an American city that *doesn't* have a "sophisticated comfort food" restaurant. But I'm sold on the concept, hooked by the fresh, usually local, often organic provisions chef Peter Davis uses to create his . . . oh, fine: sophisticated comfort food. Complementing the top-of-the line meats, fish, and poultry are terrific breads and an impressive variety of gorgeous produce, prepared to let the quality of the ingredients take center stage. I especially like the bounteous salads and tasty desserts, but try any dish with ingredients you like: mysterious additions aren't a problem here. Given a choice, go for lunch over dinner, when service can be scattered and running up an unexpectedly large bill is unexpectedly easy. There's seasonal outdoor seating in the pleasant courtyard.

The hotel's fine-dining restaurant, **Rialto** (© **617/661-5050;** www.rialto-restaurant. com), serves dinner daily. Rialto made its reputation as a special-occasion favorite in the days when it served a Mediterranean menu, and the handful of hold-overs from the old days are the only surefire options today. The cuisine otherwise is exclusively Italian, presented in a style that seems designed to appeal to other chefs, culinary purists, and diners with small appetites and big wallets.

In the Charles Hotel, 1 Bennett St. © 617/661-5005. www.henriettastable.com. Reservations recommended. Main courses $11–$19 at lunch, $14–$19 at dinner. AE, DC, MC, V. Mon–Fri 6:30–11am, Sat 7–11am, Sun 7–10:30am; daily noon–3pm (Sat a la carte brunch; Sun buffet brunch); daily 5:30–10pm. Valet and validated parking available. T: Red Line to Harvard.

MODERATE

Bombay Club *Value* INDIAN   This second-floor spot overlooking Harvard Square gained fame through its lunch buffet, a generous assortment of some of the best items on the menu. The buffet's reasonable price and the lively scene make midday the best time to dine here. At all times, the food is flavorful and fresh, with yogurt and cheese made in-house daily. The family-run restaurant, in business since 1991, serves a broad selection of typical dishes from across the subcontinent—Bombay fish curry, a lamb specialty from Delhi, Kerala-style grilled shrimp, numerous vegetarian selections. The breads, baked to perfection in a traditional charcoal-fired clay oven, and the lamb offerings are especially tasty. The "chef's recommendations," platters of assorted meat or vegetarian dishes, make good samplers if you're new to the cuisine or can't make up your mind. If grazing isn't your thing, *rogan josh* (lamb in garlicky tomato sauce) and fiery chicken, lamb, or shrimp vindaloo all merit full portions.

57 John F. Kennedy St. © 617/661-8100. www.bombayclub.com. Lunch buffet $9 Mon–Fri, $12 Sat–Sun; main courses $5–$9 at lunch, $9–$18 at dinner. AE, DC, MC, V. Daily 11:30am–11pm (lunch until 3pm). Discounted parking available. T: Red Line to Harvard.

Border Café TEX-MEX/CAJUN   When you first see the Border Café, your thoughts might turn to, of all people, baseball Hall of Famer Yogi Berra. He supposedly said, "Nobody goes there anymore; it's too crowded." Yogi was talking about a New York nightclub, but people have been saying the same thing about this Harvard Square hangout since 1987. Patrons loiter at the bar for hours, enhancing the festival atmosphere. Many are waiting to be seated for generous portions of tasty (if not completely authentic) food. The menu features Tex-Mex, Cajun, and Caribbean specialties, with plenty of vegetarian options, and the beleaguered staff keeps the chips—fried after you order them—and fresh house-made salsa coming. When you shout your order over the roar of the crowd, try an excellent chorizo appetizer, enchiladas (Gulf coast seafood is particularly delectable), any kind of tacos, or popcorn shrimp. Fajitas for one or two, sizzling noisily, are also a popular choice. Set aside a couple of hours, get into a party mood, and ask to be seated downstairs if you want to be able to hear your companions. **Tip for parents:** Although there's no children's menu, this place is great for kids—even the risk-averse will devour chips—but only if you eat early (you do that anyway, right?).

32 Church St. © 617/864-6100. www.bordercafe.com. Reservations not accepted. Main courses $7–$18. AE, MC, V. Daily 11am–11pm. T: Red Line to Harvard.

INEXPENSIVE

Mr. Bartley's Burger Cottage ✿✿ AMERICAN   Great burgers and the best onion rings in the world make Bartley's a perennial favorite with a cross-section of Cambridge. In increasingly generic Harvard Square, it's a beacon of originality.

Tips Sweet-Tooth Alert

As a rule, nonfranchise businesses that carve out a niche in Harvard Square do one thing and do it extremely well. Case in point: **L.A. Burdick Chocolates,** 52D Brattle St., Cambridge (© **617/491-4340**; www.burdickchocolate.com; T: Red Line to Harvard). The amazing confections include sublime hot chocolate to stay or go.

Founded in 1960, the family business isn't a cottage, but a crowded, high-ceilinged room (there's also a small outdoor seating area) plastered with signs, posters, and memorabilia. Burgers bear the names of local and national celebrities, notably political figures; the names change almost as quickly as a cable-news crawl, but the ingredients stay the same.

Anything you can think of to put on your personal 7 ounces of house-ground beef is available, from American cheese to guacamole to grilled pineapple. Good dishes that don't involve meat include veggie burgers, huge salads, and creamy, garlicky hummus. Bartley's also serves sandwiches and comfort-food dinners, and it's one of the only places in the area that still serves a real raspberry lime rickey (raspberry syrup, lime juice, lime wedges, and club soda). It's a taste of summer even in the dead of winter.

1246 Massachusetts Ave. ℂ 617/354-6559. www.bartleysburgers.com. Burgers $9–$13; main courses, salads, and sandwiches $5–$9. Children's menu $4–$5. No credit cards. Mon–Sat 11am–9pm. Closed Memorial Day, July 4, Labor Day, Dec 25–Jan 1. T: Red Line to Harvard.

OUTSIDE HARVARD SQUARE
EXPENSIVE

There's a **Legal Sea Foods** (p. 106) at 5 Cambridge Center, Kendall Square (ℂ **617/ 864-3400**). The **Elephant Walk** (p. 128) has a branch outside Porter Square, at 2067 Massachusetts Ave. (ℂ **617/492-6900**).

The Blue Room 𝕽𝕽 ECLECTIC   The Blue Room sits below plaza level in an office-retail complex, a slice of foodie paradise in high-tech heaven. Its out-of-the-way location means that it doesn't get as much publicity as it deserves, but it's well worth a trip to East Cambridge, perhaps combined with a movie at the Kendall Square Cinema. The regularly changing menu combines top-notch ingredients and layers of aggressive flavors, and the crowded dining room isn't as noisy as you might fear when you first spy the open kitchen through the glass front wall. (Upholstery and carpeting help soften the din.)

Appetizers range from imaginative salads to steamed mussels with chorizo and saffron aïoli to delectable pizza. Most entrees are grilled over a wood fire, roasted, or braised, with at least one well-conceived vegetarian choice. Roast chicken with Moroccan spices, served with garlic mashed potatoes, is fantastic. Seafood is always a wise choice (grilled branzino—yum!), and pork chops are juicy and succulent. In warm weather, there's seating on the brick patio.

1 Kendall Sq. ℂ 617/494-9034. www.theblueroom.net. Reservations recommended. Main courses $21–$26. AE, DC, DISC, MC, V. Sun–Thurs 5:30–10pm; Fri–Sat 5:30–11pm; Sun brunch 11am–2:30pm. Closed 1st week of July. Validated parking available. T: Red Line to Kendall/MIT, then a 10-min. walk.

Dalí 𝕽𝕽 SPANISH   This festive restaurant casts an irresistible spell—it's noisy and inconvenient, accepts only limited reservations, and still fills with people cheerfully waiting an hour or more for a table. The bar offers plenty to look at while you wait, including gorgeous tiles, carved wood, and eclectic artwork. The payoff is authentic Spanish food, notably *tapas*—little plates of hot or cold creations that burst with flavor.

Entrees include excellent paella, but most people come with friends and explore the three dozen or more *tapas* offerings, all perfect for sharing. They include *patatas ali-oli* (garlic potatoes), *albóndigas de salmón* (salmon balls with not-too-salty caper sauce), *setas al ajillo* (sautéed mushrooms), and *lomito al cabrales* (pork tenderloin with blue goat cheese and mushrooms), plus monthly specials such as beef and sweet potato pie. The helpful staff sometimes seems rushed but never fails to supply bread for sopping up juices and sangria for washing it all down. Finish with "ubiquitous flan" or luscious *tarta de chocolates.*

The owners of Dalí also run **Tapéo** at 266 Newbury St. (© **617/267-4799**), between Fairfield and Dartmouth streets in Boston's **Back Bay.** It offers the same menu and similarly wacky decor in a more sedate two-level setting.

415 Washington St., Somerville. © **617/661-3254.** www.dalirestaurant.com. Reservations recommended; accepted Sun–Thurs until 6:30pm, Fri until 6pm, Sat for parties of 6 or more until 6pm. *Tapas* $4.50–$16 (most less than $10); main courses $20–$25; late-night menu $4.50–$9. AE, DC, MC, V. Daily 5:30–11pm; bar serves food until 12:30am. T: Red Line to Harvard, then follow Kirkland St. to intersection of Washington and Beacon sts. (20-min. walk or $6 cab ride).

East Coast Grill & Raw Bar ★★ SEAFOOD/BARBECUE   Huge portions, a dizzy-ing menu, and funky decor have made the East Coast Grill madly popular since 1985. Just walking into the colorful, noisy restaurant is exciting, but the legions of repeat customers know that the real excitement is on the menu. The kitchen handles fresh seafood (an encyclopedic variety), barbecue, and grilled fish and meats with equal authority and imagination. The influence of founder Chris Schlesinger, a national expert on grilling and spicy food, is apparent in the exuberant menu descriptions ("super-fresh catch o' the moment," "wings of mass destruction"). To start, consider the raw-bar offerings, or try the sublime fried oysters. The seafood entrees are excep-tional—always check the specials board, because you may luck into something memo-rable, like 13-spice grilled monkfish. Barbecue comes on abundant platters in three styles: Texas beef, Memphis spareribs, and North Carolina pork. Vegetarians can opt for the "all-vegetable experience of the day." Desserts are tasty, but if you've played your cards right, you won't have room. *A note to parents:* Because there's no children's menu, I don't feel comfortable adding a "Kids" icon, but the menu includes plenty of options for less adventuresome palates, and when I dined here (anonymously, as always) with two well-behaved but active little boys, the staff couldn't have been nicer.

1271 Cambridge St., Inman Sq. © **617/491-6568.** www.eastcoastgrill.net. Reservations accepted only for parties of 5 or more, Sun–Thurs. Main courses $15–$30; fresh seafood market price. AE, MC, V. Sun–Thurs 5:30–10pm; Fri–Sat 5:30–10:30pm; Sun brunch 11am–2:30pm. Validated parking available. T: Red Line to Harvard, then no. 69 (Harvard-Lechmere) bus to Inman Sq.; or Red Line to Central, then a 10-min. walk on Prospect St.

Jasper White's Summer Shack ★★ *Kids* SEAFOOD   An enormous space with a lobster tank in the middle of the floor, the Summer Shack feels like an overgrown sea-side clam shack—but one that's been to cooking school. All the basics are here: raw bar, excellent french fries, out-of-this-world tuna burger, lobster roll, and even a clam-bake (a lobster, clams, mussels, potatoes, sausage, and corn on the cob). But check the name again—Jasper White is nationally renowned for seafood, and his pan-roasted lobster, on the aptly named "big bucks lobster" section of the menu, has been a local foodie favorite for nearly 3 decades (since his days at the fine-dining restaurant Jasper's). Yes, the contrast is incongruous, but it works. You might find yourself sitting between a kid chowing down on a corn dog and a suburban couple savoring wok-seared lobster with ginger and scallions or steamed mussels in wine-and-herb broth—and they'll all be equally happy. You'll be able to hear them exclaiming, too: When it's full, this is one of the loudest restaurants in the Boston area. Arrive early, ask to sit on the second level (just a few steps up, but much quieter), and you might be able to have a conversation.

The Summer Shack in Boston's **Back Bay,** at 50 Dalton St. (© **617/867-9955**), is especially popular before and after Red Sox games and Symphony performances. It also accepts reservations for parties of any size. From April through October, it's open

11:30am to 10pm Sunday through Wednesday, until 11pm Thursday through Saturday. In the winter, the weekday opening time is 5pm. Year-round, the bar serves food until 12:30am. Other branches are at **Logan Airport,** in Terminal A (© **617/569-9695**), and at the Mohegan Sun casino in Connecticut.

149 Alewife Brook Pkwy. © 617/520-9500. www.summershackrestaurant.com. Reservations accepted only for parties of 8 or more. Main courses $8–$36 (most $25 or less); sandwiches $5–$15; lobster and specials market price. AE, DISC, MC, V. Mon–Thurs 11:30am–9:30pm (lunch menu until 5pm); Fri 11:30am–10:30pm (lunch menu until 5pm); Sat noon–10:30pm; Sun noon–9pm. Free parking. T: Red Line to Alewife.

Oleana ⭐⭐ MEDITERRANEAN   Both casual neighborhood place and culinary travelogue, Oleana occupies a cozy space outside Inman Square and another one close to my heart. The wonderful food and welcoming atmosphere make it one of the best restaurants in the Boston area. The seasonal menu, which features cuisine typical of and inspired by the Mediterranean—not just the usual suspects, either; Turkey and Armenia figure prominently—relies on fresh ingredients and chef and co-owner Ana (short for Oleana) Sortun's signature unusual flavors. Tempting aromas signal the arrival of Moroccan-spiced grouper, which might land next to a plate of succulent lemon chicken; poultry is often the dull option on even the most adventuresome menu, but here it's a match for the most exotic dishes. Even better is spicy tuna, in a peppery sauce that trades intense heat for intense flavor, a perfect match for the meaty fish. Portions are generous, vegetarians are happy, and the dessert menu is heavy on house-made ice cream. My only caveat is that at busy times, the servers tend to fall behind. In warm weather, there's seating on the peaceful patio—and it can't be reserved, so try to eat early.

134 Hampshire St., Inman Sq. © 617/661-0505. www.oleanarestaurant.com. Reservations recommended; not accepted for patio. Main courses $22–$30; vegetarian tasting menu $42. AE, MC, V. Sun–Thurs 5:30–10pm; Fri–Sat 5:30–11pm. Free parking. T: Red Line to Central, then a 10-min. walk.

MODERATE

Baraka Café ⭐ ALGERIAN/TUNISIAN/MEDITERRANEAN   On a run-down side street off Central Square, Baraka Café is a tiny, aromatic destination for adventurous diners. Flavorful, highly spiced (though not necessarily hot) food served in an elaborately decorated dining room makes it a favorite with local foodies. They talk about it as though it's a secret, but one look at the line that forms on weekend evenings will tell you it's not. The drawbacks—no alcohol, cash only, tiny dining room, deliberate service—are insignificant when the food is this good. Start with house-made breads and appetizers such as spicy merguez sausage and *bedenjal mechoui* (Algerian baba ghanouj, more or less). Main courses include fantastic couscous, fork-tender lamb chops, and eggplant stuffed with a tasty concoction of olives, spinach, scallions, and two cheeses. Be sure to ask about daily specials, which show off the kitchen's considerable abilities better than the limited regular menu. The signature beverage is lemonade with rose petals—it tastes like soap to me, but its legions of fans strenuously disagree.

80½ Pearl St., Central Sq. © 617/868-3951. www.barakacafe.com. Reservations not accepted. Main courses $5–$9 at lunch, $9–$16 at dinner. No credit cards. Tues–Sat 11:30am–3pm; Tues–Sun 5:30–10pm. T: Red Line to Central.

The Helmand ⭐⭐ AFGHAN   Newshounds will recognize Helmand as a region and river in Afghanistan; Boston-area foodies know it as a restaurant that's both low-profile and always crowded. Definitely make a reservation. The elegant setting belies the reasonable prices at this spacious spot near the CambridgeSide Galleria mall. The delectable flavors and textures evoke Middle Eastern, Indian, and Pakistani cuisine. Many dishes are vegetarian, and meat is often one element of a dish rather than the centerpiece. Every meal comes with delectable bread made fresh in a wood-fired brick oven near the entrance. Service could be more attentive, but with food this good, that's a minor quibble.

To start, you might try slightly sweet baked pumpkin topped with spicy ground meat sauce—a great contrast of flavors and textures—or *aushak*, "Afghan ravioli" filled with leeks or potatoes and buried under a sauce of either meat or split peas and carrots. Main courses include grilled meats, poultry, and fish, plus several versions of what Americans would call stew. *Kourma challow,* an excellent mélange of lamb, potatoes, onion, tomatoes, and green beans, comes with flavorful, cumin-scented rice. For dessert, don't miss the Afghan version of baklava.

143 First St. ✆ **617/492-4646**. www.helmandrestaurantcambridge.com. Reservations recommended. Main courses $12–$20. AE, MC, V. Sun–Thurs 5–10pm; Fri–Sat 5–11pm. T: Green Line to Lechmere.

Redbones ✪ *Kids* BARBECUE Geographically, this raucous restaurant is in Somerville, but in spirit it's on a Southern back road where the sun is hot, the beer is cold, and a slab of meat is done to a turn. Barbecued ribs (Memphis-, Texas-, and Arkansas-style), smoked beef brisket, fried Louisiana catfish, and grilled chicken come with appropriate side dishes such as coleslaw and beans. The chummy staff can help you choose sweet, hot, mild, or vinegar sauce. The best non-barbecue dish is a starter or dinner of succulent buffalo shrimp, swimming in hot sauce. Portions are large, so pace yourself. You'll want to try the appetizers and sides—catfish "catfingers," succotash, corn pudding, and collard greens, just to name a few; if you're with enough other people, the appetizer samplers are a good deal. The only less-than-tasty dish I've had here was watery broccoli. The beer selection is huge, and there's valet parking for your bike. Given a choice, sit upstairs—Underbones, downstairs, is a noisy bar.

55 Chester St. (off Elm St.), Somerville. ✆ **617/628-2200**. www.redbones.com. Reservations accepted only for parties of 10 or more, Sun–Thurs before 7pm. Main courses $8–$19; sandwiches $6–$8; children's menu $5. AE, MC, V. Mon–Thurs 11:30am–10:30pm; Fri–Sat 11:30am–11pm; Sun 11am–10:30pm (brunch until 3pm); lunch Mon–Sat until 4pm, Sun noon–4pm; late-night menu daily until 12:30am. T: Red Line to Davis.

Tu y Yo Mexican Fonda REGIONAL MEXICAN A large, colorful storefront near the Tufts University campus, Tu y Yo specializes in authentic Mexican food in a style that dates to the 16th century. Settlers lived and ate at *fondas,* or boarding houses, that served home-style cooking. They ate well, too—I've never had a disappointing meal here. The menu looks short, but many dishes are available with a choice of beef, chicken, pork, sausage, shrimp, or fish, and in vegetarian versions. Weekly specials expand your options further. To start, try *sopes* (fried disks of *masa,* or corn flour) topped with beans, cheese, and onions, or cheese-filled plantain empanadas. Many main-course descriptions include the dish's date and place of origin—owner Epi Guzman's family figures prominently—but even the options that have no pedigree are delicious. I especially like spinach a la Carlos (with potatoes in garlic sauce) and *chile relleno en nogada* (poblano with a flavorful ground-beef stuffing and creamy pomegranate sauce). For the full experience, try one of the three versions of sangria and finish with cinnamon-infused coffee and unbelievable flan.

858 Broadway, Powderhouse Sq., Somerville. ✆ **617/623-5411**. www.tuyyomexicanfonda.com. Reservations recommended; accepted Sun–Thurs. Main courses $13–$19; brunch items $4–$11. MC, V. Mon–Thurs 5–10pm; Fri 4–11pm; Sat 10am–11pm (brunch until 2pm); Sun 10am–9pm (brunch until 2pm). T: Red Line to Davis, then a 10-min. walk (follow College Ave. to the traffic circle and take sharp left).

INEXPENSIVE

The food court on the lower level of the **Porter Exchange** mall, 1815 Massachusetts Ave., Porter Square, is home to half a dozen or so Japanese businesses that attract expats from all over the Boston area. The super-authentic dining options are mostly fast-food counters with small seating areas in front; wander around until you see a dish that strikes your fancy. All open in the late morning and close by 9pm. Start at **Cafe Mami** (© 617/547-9130), but also check out **Tampopo** (© 617/868-5457), **Sapporo Ramen** (© 617/876-4805), and **Ittyo** (© 617/354-5944). **Kotobukiya** is both a sushi bar (© 617/492-4655) and Japanese grocery (© 617/354-6914; www. kotobukiyamarket.com). Afterward, hit **Japonaise Bakery** (© 617/547-5531) for French- and Japanese-style pastries, notably the items that incorporate adzuki cream.

S&S Restaurant ✸✸ DELI   *Es* is Yiddish for "eat," and this Cambridge classic is as straightforward as its name ("eat and eat"). Founded in 1919 by the great-grandmother of the current owners, the wildly popular brunch spot draws what seems to be half of Cambridge at busy times on weekends. It's northeast of Harvard Square, west of MIT, and worth a visit during the week, too. Light-flooded, with lots of light wood and plants, it looks contemporary, but the brunch offerings are huge portions of traditional dishes such as pancakes, waffles, and omelets. The bagels and cinnamon rolls are among the best in the area; you'll also find traditional deli items (corned beef, pastrami, tongue, potato pancakes, and blintzes), yummy house-made corned beef hash, and breakfast anytime. Be early for brunch, or plan to spend a good chunk of your Saturday or Sunday standing around people-watching and getting hungry—I'll be right there with you. Or dine on a weekday and soak up the neighborhood atmosphere.

1334 Cambridge St., Inman Sq. © 617/354-0777. www.sandsrestaurant.com. Main courses $4–$18. AE, MC, V. Mon–Wed 7am–10pm; Thurs–Fri 7am–11pm; Sat 8am–11pm; Sun 8am–10pm; brunch Sat–Sun until 4pm. Free parking; ask cashier for token on weekends. T: Red Line to Harvard, then no. 69 (Harvard-Lechmere) bus to Inman Sq.; or Red Line to Central, then a 10-min. walk on Prospect St.

7

What to See & Do in Boston

Whether you want to immerse yourself in the colonial era or just cruise around the harbor, you can do it—and plenty more—in Boston. Throw out your preconceptions of the city as an open-air history museum (although that's certainly one of the guises it can assume), and allow your interests to dictate where you go.

It's possible but not advisable to take in most of the major attractions in 2 or 3 days if you don't linger anywhere too long. For a more enjoyable, less rushed visit, plan fewer activities and spend more time on them. For descriptions of suggested itineraries, see p. 55.

Mergers and budget cuts have slashed corporate and government contributions to many cultural organizations. Admissions fees and hours in this chapter are current at press time, but establishments that rely heavily on outside aid may cost a bit more or be keeping shorter hours by the time you visit. And prices for attractions that use fuel—such as tours and cruises—are subject to changes or surcharges depending on the fluctuating energy market. If you're on a tight schedule or budget, check ahead.

For security reasons, some attractions require adult patrons to show ID before entering. Double-check that you have your license or passport before you leave the hotel.

In 2009, observations of the **bicentennial of Abraham Lincoln's birth** will take place all over the United States; the holiday is in February, and events will stretch throughout the year. Another 1809 baby, **Park Street Church** (p. 151), is planning its own birthday celebration; check ahead for information about special events. Also wearing a pointy hat and blowing out candles: the **New England Aquarium** (p. 147), which turns 40 in 2009. The National Park Service opened a new **Charlestown Navy Yard Visitor Center** in 2008; visit Building 5, between the entrance and the warship "Old Ironsides," to check out the new facility and enjoy the air-conditioning.

In 2008, two of the three **Harvard Art Museums** (p. 167) closed for renovations. Check ahead for details about the greatest-hits displays in the one that remains open, the Arthur M. Sackler Museum. At press time, the **Boston Tea Party Ship & Museum** (© 617/269-7150; www.boston teapartyship.com), which closed after a fire in 2001, was scheduled to reopen in mid-2009. Chronically delayed plans in place since shortly after a devastating fire in 2001 called for the construction of two more ships, doubling the size of the museum, and addition of a tearoom. Check at your hotel or call ahead before setting out.

1 The Top Attractions

The attractions in this section are easily accessible by **public transportation;** given the difficulty and expense of parking, it's preferable to take the T everywhere. Even the Kennedy Library, which has a large free parking lot, operates a free shuttle bus that

Boston Attractions

Abiel Smith School **12**
African Meeting House **12**
BosTix **8, 18**
Boston Athenaeum **14**
Boston Children's Museum **23**
Boston Public Library **7**
Boston Tea Party Ship & Museum **22**
Faneuil Hall Marketplace **18**
Fenway Park **1**
Foster's Rotunda **20**
Gibson House Museum **9**
Independence Wharf
   (470 Atlantic Ave.) **21**
Institute of Contemporary Art **25**
Isabella Stewart Gardner Museum **2**
John Adams Courthouse **15**

Moakley Federal Courthouse **24**
Mary Baker Eddy Library /
   Mapparium **5**
Museum of African American
   History **12**
Museum of Fine Arts **3**
Museum of Science **10**
New England Aquarium **19**
Nichols House Museum **13**
Otis House Museum **11**
Paul Revere House **17**
Prudential Center Skywalk
   Observatory **6**
Sports Museum of New England
   (TD Banknorth Garden) **16**
Symphony Hall **4**

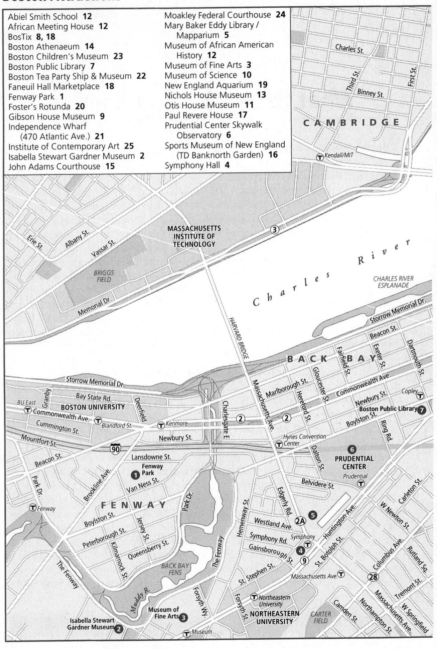

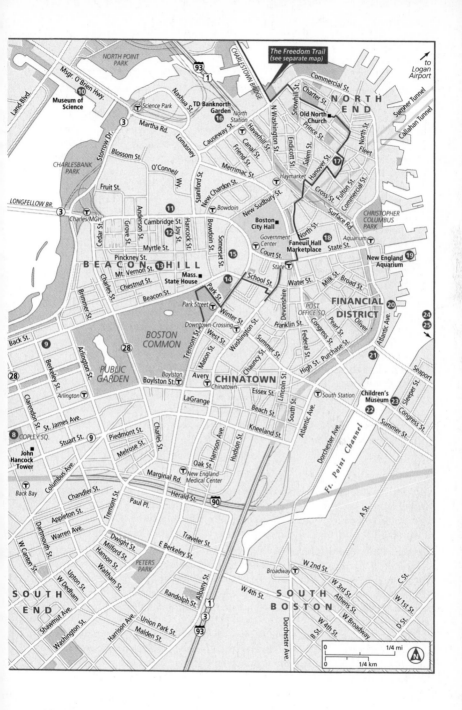

Value **Let's Make a Deal**

As you plan your sightseeing, consider these money-saving options. Check their respective websites for info about buying each pass.

If you concentrate on the included attractions, a **CityPass** (© 888/330-5008; www.citypass.com) offers great savings. It's a booklet of tickets (so you can go straight to the entrance) to the Harvard Museum of Natural History, the Kennedy Library, the New England Aquarium, the Museum of Fine Arts, the Museum of Science, and the Prudential Center Skywalk Observatory. If you visit all six, the price gives adults a nearly 50% savings—which feels like an even better deal on a steamy day when the line at the aquarium is long. At press time, the cost was $44 for adults, $24 for youths 3 to 11, subject to change as admission prices rise. The passes, good for 9 days from first use (except in the winter, when they're good for up to 3½ months), also include discounts good at other local businesses.

The main competition for CityPass is the **Go Boston Card** (© 800/887-9103; www.gobostoncard.com). The original Go Boston card includes admission to more than 60 Boston-area and New England attractions, plus dining and shopping discounts, a guidebook, and a 2-day trolley pass. If you strategize wisely, this card can be a great value. It costs $55 for 1 day, $85 for 2 days, $115 for 3 days, $155 for 5 days, and $195 for 7 days, with discounts for children and winter travelers (some of the included businesses close in the winter). A spin-off, the Explorer Pass, lets you select three of the nine included attractions and is good for 30 days. It costs $59 for adults and $39 for children—a potentially good deal, but do a little math before committing.

The MBTA's 7-day **LinkPass** (© 877/927-7277 or 617/222-4545; www.mbta.com) can be a good deal—but only if you plan to use public transit often enough. See p. 37.

---

connects it to the Red Line. To maximize your enjoyment, try to visit these attractions during relatively slow times. If possible, especially in the summer, sightsee on weekdays; if you're traveling without children, aim for times when school is in session. And if you're in town on a July or August weekend, resign yourself to lines and crowds.

Faneuil Hall Marketplace *(★★ (Kids)* Since Boston's most popular attraction opened in 1976, cities all over the country have imitated the "festival market" concept. Each complex of shops, food counters, restaurants, bars, and public spaces reflects its city, and Faneuil Hall Marketplace is no exception. Its popularity with visitors and suburbanites is so great that you might understandably think the only Bostonians in the crowd are employees.

The marketplace includes five buildings—the central three-building complex is on the National Register of Historic Places—set on brick and stone plazas that teem with crowds shopping, eating, performing, watching performers, and just people-watching. In warm weather, it's busy from just after dawn until well past dark. **Quincy Market** (you'll also hear the whole complex called by that name) is the central three-level Greek revival–style building. It reopened after extensive renovations on August 26,

1976, 150 years after Mayor Josiah Quincy opened the original market. The **South Market building** reopened on August 26, 1977, the **North Market building** on August 26, 1978.

The central corridor of Quincy Market is the food court, where you can find anything from a cream puff to a full Greek dinner, a slice of pizza to a fresh-shucked oyster. On either side, under glass canopies, are full-service restaurants as well as pushcarts that sell everything from crafts created by New England artisans to hokey souvenirs. Here you'll find a bar that exactly replicates the set of the TV show *Cheers.* In the plaza between the **South Canopy** and the South Market building is an **information kiosk,** and throughout the complex you'll find a mix of predictable chain stores and unique shops (see chapter 9). On warm evenings, the tables that spill outdoors from the restaurants and bars fill with people. One constant since the year after the market—the *original* market—opened is **Durgin-Park** ✹✹✹ (p. 115), a traditional New England restaurant with traditionally crabby waitresses.

The original **Faneuil Hall** ✹ sometimes gets overlooked, but it's well worth a visit. See p. 154 for a full description.

Between North, Congress, and State sts. and Atlantic Ave. ⓒ 617/523-1300. www.faneuilhallmarketplace.com. Marketplace Mon–Sat 10am–9pm, Sun noon–6pm. Food court opens earlier; some restaurants close later. T: Green Line to Government Center, Orange Line to Haymarket or State, or Blue Line to Aquarium or State.

Institute of Contemporary Art ✹✹   Even if you think contemporary art isn't for you, the ICA is a blast. The city's first new art museum in nearly a century is a work of art in its own right. The cantilevered building—designed by the New York firm Diller Scofidio + Renfro, whose work on this landmark project helped boost its growing reputation—juts out above the harbor, affording dizzying views of the water, the waterfront, and the airport. Besides being an irresistible draw, the architecture reflects the institution's curatorial philosophy that art is inseparable from everyday life, rather than a singular experience reserved for special occasions and field trips. The ICA showcases 20th- and 21st-century art in every imaginable medium, including film and video, music, literature, and dance. Opened in 2006, the 65,000-square-foot museum gives the institution the space it needs to create a permanent collection for the first time since its founding (under a different name) in 1936. Visitors have already enjoyed works by Louise Bourgeois and Anish Kapoor that wouldn't have fit in (literally or figuratively) elsewhere in Boston, and the schedule of events, concerts, films, and other activities seemingly can't expand quickly enough. Special exhibitions during

Tips **Let's All Go for a Harborwalk**

The concept is irresistible: The **Harborwalk** is a pathway that traces 47 miles of Boston's shoreline, allowing public access to multimillion-dollar views of the water. In theory, the Harborwalk extends from East Boston to Dorchester; in practice, the pathway isn't continuous. Distinctive royal blue signs with a white logo and text point the way along the Harborwalk, which is an ideal route to take from downtown to the Institute of Contemporary Art, on the South Boston waterfront. The ambitious project has been in the works since 1984 and is more than three-quarters complete. Learn more by visiting the website, **www.boston harborwalk.com,** which features a map and a downloadable audio tour.

the lifespan of this book include **Tara Donovan** (Oct 10, 2008–Jan 4, 2009) and **Damián Ortega** (May 22–Sept 7, 2009). The cafe overlooks the water and offers outdoor seating in fine weather, and the gift shop is spectacular.

100 Northern Ave. Ⓒ 617/478-3100. www.icaboston.org. Admission adults $12, seniors and students $10, free for children under 18 and those visiting only the cafe. Free to all Thurs after 5pm and to families (up to 2 adults with children under 13) last Sat of each month. Sat–Sun, Tues–Wed, and some Mon holidays 10am–5pm; Thurs–Fri 10am–9pm. T: Red Line to South Station, then Waterfront Silver Line bus to World Trade Center.

Isabella Stewart Gardner Museum ★★

Isabella Stewart Gardner (1840–1924) was an incorrigible individualist long before strong-willed behavior was acceptable for women in polite Boston society, and her legacy is a treasure for art lovers. "Mrs. Jack" designed her exquisite home in the style of a 15th-century Venetian palace and filled it with European, American, and Asian paintings and sculptures, much of it chosen with the help of her friend and protégé Bernard Berenson. You'll see works by Titian, Botticelli, Raphael, Rembrandt, Matisse, and Mrs. Gardner's friends James McNeill Whistler and John Singer Sargent. Titian's magnificent *Europa,* which many scholars consider his finest work, is one of the most important Renaissance paintings in the United States. I took a casual poll of local travel experts while writing the 2005 edition of this book, and the Gardner was the most popular museum.

The building, which opened to the public after Mrs. Gardner's death, holds a glorious hodgepodge of furniture and architectural details imported from European churches and palaces. The *pièce de résistance* is the magnificent skylit courtyard, filled year-round with fresh flowers from the museum greenhouse. Although the terms of Mrs. Gardner's will forbid changing the arrangement of the museum's content, there has been some evolution: A special exhibition gallery features two or three changing shows a year, often by contemporary artists in residence.

See p. 226 for a description of the **concert series** ★ (Ⓒ **617/278-5102** [info line] or 617/278-5156 [box office]). The cafe serves lunch and desserts, and there's an excellent gift shop.

280 The Fenway. Ⓒ **617/566-1401.** www.gardnermuseum.org. Admission adults $12, $10 seniors, $5 college students with ID, free for children under 18 and adults named Isabella with ID. Tues–Sun (and some Mon holidays) 11am–5pm. Closed Thanksgiving, Dec 25, and Dec 31. T: Green Line E to Museum.

John F. Kennedy Presidential Library and Museum ★★ *Kids*

The Kennedy era springs to life at this dramatic library, museum, and educational research complex overlooking Dorchester Bay. It captures the 35th president's accomplishments and legacy in video and sound recordings and fascinating displays of memorabilia and photos. Far from being a static experience, it changes regularly, with temporary shows and reinterpreted displays that highlight and complement the permanent installations.

> **More JFK**
>
> For details about visiting President Kennedy's birthplace in suburban Brookline, see p. 161.

Your visit begins with a 17-minute film narrated by John F. Kennedy—a detail that seems eerie for a moment, then perfectly natural. Through skillfully edited audio clips, he discusses his childhood, education, war experience, and early political career. Then you enter the museum to spend as much time as you like on each exhibit. Starting with the 1960 presidential campaign, the displays immerse you in the era. The galleries hold campaign souvenirs, film of Kennedy debating Richard Nixon and delivering his inaugural address, a replica of the Oval Office, gifts from foreign dignitaries, letters, documents, and keepsakes. There's a film about the Cuban Missile Crisis and displays on Attorney General Robert F. Kennedy, First Lady Jacqueline Bouvier Kennedy, the civil rights movement, the Peace Corps, the space program, and the Kennedy family. As the tour winds down, you pass through a darkened chamber where news reports of John Kennedy's assassination and funeral play. The final room, the soaring glass-enclosed pavilion that is the heart of the I. M. Pei design, affords a glorious view of the water and the Boston skyline.

Columbia Point. Ⓒ **866/JFK-1960** or 617/514-1600. www.jfklibrary.org. Admission $12 adults; $10 seniors and students with ID; $9 youths 13–17; free for children under 13. Surcharges may apply for special exhibitions. Daily 9am–5pm (last film begins at 3:55pm). Closed Jan 1, Thanksgiving, and Dec 25. T: Red Line to JFK/UMass, then take free shuttle bus, which runs every 20 min. By car, take Southeast Expressway (I-93/Rte. 3) south to Exit 15 (Morrissey Blvd./JFK Library), turn left onto Columbia Rd., and follow signs to free parking lot.

Museum of Fine Arts ✦✦✦ *Kids*   One of the world's great art museums, the MFA works nonstop to become even more accessible and interesting. Every installation reflects a curatorial attitude that makes even those who go in with a feeling of obligation leave with a sense of discovery and wonder. That includes children, who can launch a scavenger hunt, admire the mummies, or participate in family-friendly programs scheduled year-round (and extra offerings during school vacations).

Among the numerous highlights of the magnificent collections are the **Impressionist** ✦✦✦ paintings (including one of the largest collections of Monets outside of Paris), Asian and Old Kingdom Egyptian collections, classical art, Buddhist temple, and medieval sculpture and tapestries.

The works that you might find most familiar are paintings and sculpture by Americans and Europeans. Some favorites: Renoir's *Dance at Bougival,* Childe Hassam's *Boston Common at Twilight,* Gilbert Stuart's 1796 portrait of George Washington, John Singleton Copley's 1768 portrait of Paul Revere (which looks suspiciously like the Samuel Adams beer logo), a bronze casting of Edgar Degas's sculpture *Little Dancer,* John Singer Sargent's *The Daughters of Edward Darley Boit,* Gauguin's *Where Do We Come From? What Are We? Where Are We Going?,* and several Luminist masterpieces by Fitz Henry Lane (formerly known as Fitz Hugh Lane). There are also outstanding holdings of prints, photographs, furnishings, and decorative arts, including the finest collection of Paul Revere silver in the world.

None of this comes cheap: The MFA's adult admission fee (which covers two visits within 10 days) is among the highest in the country. A Boston CityPass or Go Boston card (see the "Let's Make a Deal" box on p. 142) is a bargain if you plan to visit enough of the other included attractions.

(Tips   MFA FYI

The Museum of Fine Arts entrance through the West Wing is usually much busier than Huntington Avenue entrance and the Fenway entrance, which reopened in 2008 as part of the ongoing expansion project. To soak up the drama of the older entrances, check the website to see which one is in use, and walk back along Huntington Avenue or the Fenway after you leave the T. Inside, in the Upper Rotunda between the two original entrances, are the museum's famed John Singer Sargent murals.

Kids **On Top of the World**

The **Prudential Center Skywalk Observatory** ★★, 800 Boylston St. (© **617/ 859-0648**; www.topofthehub.net), offers a 360-degree view of Boston and far beyond. From the enclosed observation deck on the 50th floor of the Prudential Tower, you can see for miles, even (when it's clear) as far as the mountains of southern New Hampshire to the north and the beaches of Cape Cod to the south. Away from the windows, interactive audiovisual exhibits chronicle the city's history. The admission price includes a narrated audio tour, available in versions targeted to adults and children. *Wings Over Boston*, a dramatic aerial video tour of the city, screens in the on-site theater. Also here are fascinating exhibits, including video presentations about refugees, on the history of immigration to Boston. Call before visiting, because the space sometimes closes for private events. Hours are 10am to 10pm daily. Admission is $11 for adults, $9 for seniors and college students with ID, and $7.50 for children under 12; adults must show a photo ID to enter the building.

To begin, pick up a floor plan at the information desk or take a free guided tour (weekdays except Mon holidays 10:30am–3pm, Wed at 6:15pm, and Sat–Sun 11am–3pm). The I. M. Pei–designed West Wing (1981) contains the main entrance, an auditorium, and an atrium with a tree-lined "sidewalk" cafe. There are also a restaurant and a cafeteria. The excellent Museum Shop carries abundant souvenirs and a huge book selection.

An ambitious expansion project began in 2005. While construction proceeds, the museum is rearranging some collections and closing some exhibition spaces. Check ahead before visiting if you have your heart set on seeing a particular piece of art.

Three special exhibitions scheduled to coincide with the lifespan of this book highlight the MFA's particular strengths: current events viewed through the prism of antiquity in *Art & Empire: Treasures from Assyria in the British Museum* (Sept 22, 2007–Jan 13, 2008); iconic photography in *Karsh 100: A Biography in Images* (Sept 23, 2008–Jan 18, 2009); and a fresh perspective on beloved artists in *Titian, Tintoretto, Veronese: Rivals in Renaissance Venice* (Mar 15–July 19, 2009).

465 Huntington Ave. © 617/267-9300. www.mfa.org. Admission $17 adults, $15 students and seniors when entire museum is open; or $15 and $13, respectively, when only West Wing is open. Children 7–17 $6.50 on school days 10am–3pm, otherwise free. Free for children under 7. Admission good for 2 visits within 10 days. Contribution welcome ($17 suggested) Wed 4–9:45pm. Surcharges may apply for special exhibitions. No admission fee for Museum Shop, library, restaurants, or auditoriums. Entire museum Sat–Tues 10am–4:45pm, Wed 10am–9:45pm, Thurs–Fri 10am–5pm; West Wing only, Thurs–Fri 5–9:45pm. Closed Jan 1, Patriots Day, July 4, Thanksgiving, and Dec 25. T: Green Line E to Museum or Orange Line to Ruggles.

Museum of Science ★★★ *Kids*　For the ultimate pain-free educational experience, head to the Museum of Science. The demonstrations, experiments, and interactive displays introduce facts and concepts so effortlessly that everyone winds up learning something. Take a couple of hours or a whole day to explore the permanent and temporary exhibits, most of them hands-on and all of them great fun.

Among the 500-plus exhibits, you might meet a dinosaur or a live butterfly, find out how much you'd weigh on the moon, battle urban traffic (in a computer model), or climb into a space module. Activity centers and exhibits focus on fields of interest—natural history (with live animals), computers, the human body—while others take an interdisciplinary approach. **Investigate!** teaches visitors to think like scientists, formulating questions, finding evidence, and drawing conclusions through activities such as strapping on a skin sensor to measure reactions to stimuli or sifting through an archaeological site. **Beyond the X-Ray** explores medical-imaging techniques and allows would-be diagnosticians to try to figure out what's ailing their "patients." The **Science in the Park** exhibit introduces the concepts of Newtonian physics through familiar objects such as playground equipment and skateboards. Temporary exhibits change regularly, and just about any **major touring show** (national or international) that focuses on a scientific topic stops here. The separate-admission **theaters** are worth planning for. Even if you're skipping the exhibits, try to see a show. If you're making a day of it, buy all your tickets at once—shows sometimes sell out. The **Mugar Omni Theater** ★★★, which shows IMAX movies, is an intense experience, bombarding you with images on a five-story domed screen and digital sound. The engulfing sensations and steep pitch of the seating area will have you hanging on for dear life, whether the film is about Bengal tigers; the Nile; or volcanoes, earthquakes, and tornados. Features change every 4 to 6 months. The **Charles Hayden Planetarium** ★★ takes visitors into space with daily star shows and shows on special topics that change several times a year. On weekends, rock-music laser shows take over. At the entrance is a hands-on astronomy exhibit called **Welcome to the Universe.**

The museum has a terrific gift shop, with toys and games that promote learning without lecturing. The ground-floor Galaxy Cafés have spectacular views of the sky-line and river. There's a parking garage on the premises, but it's on a busy street, and entering and exiting can be harrowing; take the T.

Science Park, off O'Brien Hwy. on bridge between Boston and Cambridge. (℃) 617/723-2500. www.mos.org. Admission to exhibit halls $17 adults, $15 seniors, $14 children 3–11, free for children under 3; to Butterfly Garden or 3-D Digital Cinema (available only with exhibit hall admission) $4 adults, $3.50 seniors, $3 children 3–11. Admission to Mugar Omni Theater, Hayden Planetarium, or laser shows $9 adults, $8 seniors, $7 children 3–11, free for children under 3. Discounted combination tickets available. July 5–Labor Day Sat–Thurs 9am–7pm, Fri 9am–9pm; day after Labor Day–July 4 Sat–Thurs 9am–5pm, Fri 9am–9pm. Check ahead for extended hours during school vacations. Closed Thanksgiving and Dec 25. T: Green Line to Science Park.

New England Aquarium ★ (Kids)   This complex is home to more than 15,000 fish and aquatic mammals, and at busy times, it seems to contain at least that many people—in July and August, try to make this your first stop of the morning, especially on weekends. Pause as you enter to visit with the **harbor seals,** who frolic in a free outdoor enclosure just past the ticket booth. Inside, **penguins** from three continents greet

---

(Finds Gone Fishing

The Museum of Science's **Virtual FishTank** ★★★ uses 3-D computer graphics and character-animation software that allows visitors to design their own virtual fish. You can even "build" fish on your home computer (visit www.virtualfishtank.com) and launch them at the museum.

visitors as they enter. The focal point of the aquarium is the four-story, 200,000-gallon **Giant Ocean Tank.** A four-story spiral ramp encircles the tank, which contains a replica of a Caribbean coral reef and an assortment of sea creatures that seem to coexist amazingly well. Part of the reason for the peace might be that scuba divers feed the sharks twice a day. The two-floor **Amazing Jellies** exhibit is home to hundreds of eye-catching jellyfish. At the **Edge of the Sea** exhibit, visitors can touch the sea stars, sea urchins, and horseshoe crabs in the tide pool. The **Medical Center** is especially involving: It's a working veterinary hospital. Other exhibits show off tropical sea creatures (including clownfish—you know, Nemo), freshwater specimens, denizens of the Amazon, marine life in the Gulf of Maine, and the ecology of Boston Harbor.

The **Simons IMAX Theatre** ✸✸✸, which has its own building, hours, and admission fees, is worth planning for, too. Its 85-foot-by-65-foot screen shows 3-D films with digital sound that concentrate on the natural world. It's an impressive experience.

The **aquarium turns 40** in 2009; the big day is June 29, but check ahead all year for special exhibits, events, and activities.

I suggest starting your day here because you'll want to spend at least half a day, and huge afternoon crowds can make getting around painfully slow. Discounts are available when you combine a visit to the aquarium with an IMAX film or a **whale watch** (p. 178). Also consider investing in a Boston CityPass or Go Boston card (see the "Let's Make a Deal" box on p. 142); either one allows you to skip the ticket line, which can be uncomfortably long, and may represent a savings on the steep admission charge.

Central Wharf (off State St. and Atlantic Ave.). © **617/973-5200.** www.newenglandaquarium.org. Admission $19 adults, $11 children 3–11. Free for children under 3 and for those visiting only the outdoor exhibits, cafe, and gift shop. July–Labor Day Mon–Thurs 9am–6pm, Fri–Sun and holidays 9am–7pm; day after Labor Day–June Mon–Fri 9am–5pm, Sat–Sun and holidays 9am–6pm. Simons IMAX Theatre: © **866/815-4629** or 617/973-5206. Tickets $10 adults, $8 children 3–11. Thurs–Sat 10am–8pm; Sun–Mon 10am–6pm. Closed Dec 25 and until noon Jan 1. T: Blue Line to Aquarium.

2 The Freedom Trail

A line of red paint or red brick on the sidewalk, the 2½-mile **Freedom Trail** ✸✸✸ links 16 historic sites, many of them associated with the Revolution and the early days of the United States. The route cuts across downtown, passing through the busy shopping area around Downtown Crossing, the Financial District, and the North End, on the way to Charlestown. Markers identify the stops, and plaques point the way from one to the next.

This section lists the stops on the trail in the customary order, from Boston Common to the Bunker Hill Monument. It's important to remember that this is the *suggested* route, and nobody's checking up on you. You don't have to visit every stop or even go in order—you can skip around, start in Charlestown and work backward, visit different sights on different days, or even (horrors!) omit some sights. Here's a suggestion: If you find yourself sighing and saying "should" a lot, take a break.

A hard-core history fiend who peers at every artifact and reads every plaque can easily spend 4 hours along the trail. A family with restless children will probably appreciate the enforced efficiency of a free 90-minute ranger-led tour.

The excursions, from the **Boston National Historical Park Visitor Center,** 15 State St. (© **617/242-5642;** www.nps.gov/bost), cover the "heart" of the trail, from the Old South Meeting House to the Old North Church. From April through mid-June, they begin weekends at 10 and 11am and 2pm, weekdays at 2pm only. From mid-June through September, starting times are daily at 10 and 11am and 2pm. The

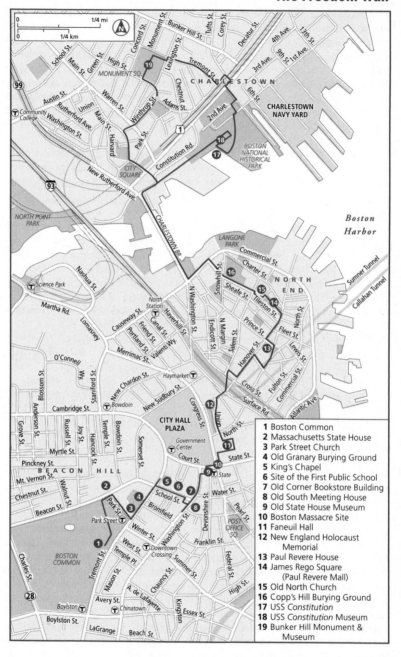

1 Boston Common
2 Massachusetts State House
3 Park Street Church
4 Old Granary Burying Ground
5 King's Chapel
6 Site of the First Public School
7 Old Corner Bookstore Building
8 Old South Meeting House
9 Old State House Museum
10 Boston Massacre Site
11 Faneuil Hall
12 New England Holocaust
   Memorial
13 Paul Revere House
14 James Rego Square
   (Paul Revere Mall)
15 Old North Church
16 Copp's Hill Burying Ground
17 USS *Constitution*
18 USS *Constitution* Museum
19 Bunker Hill Monument &
   Museum

first-come-first-served tours are limited to 30 people (rangers distribute stickers starting 30 min. before tour time) and not available in bad weather. No tours October through March.

The nonprofit **Freedom Trail Foundation** (© 617/357-8300; www.thefreedom trail.org) is an excellent resource as you plan your visit. The foundation's costumed **Freedom Trail Players** lead 90-minute tours ($12 adults, $10 seniors and students, $6 children under 13) on two different, overlapping routes around downtown and the North End. Make reservations online, allowing time to explore the interactive website. It lists a plethora of other activities, including a pub crawl (participants must be 21 years old) and holiday stroll.

The best time to start on the trail is in the morning. During the summer and fall, aim for a weekday if possible. Try not to set out later than midafternoon, because attractions will be closing and you'll run into the evening rush hour.

Boston Common   In 1634, when their settlement was just 4 years old, the town fathers paid the Rev. William Blackstone £30 for this property. In 1640 it was set aside as common land. The 45 or so acres of the country's oldest public park have served as a cow pasture, a military camp, and the site of hangings, protest marches, and visits by dignitaries. Today the Common is a bit run-down, especially compared with the adjacent Public Garden, but an overhaul began in 2007. Even with large parcels of land roped off for renovation, the Common buzzes with activity all day. You might see a demonstration, a musical performance, a picnic lunch, or a game of tag—almost anything but a cow. Cows have been banned since 1830, which seems to be one of the few events related to the Common that isn't commemorated with a plaque.

One of the loveliest markers is on this route; head up the hill inside the fence, walking parallel to Park Street. At Beacon Street is a **memorial** ★★★ designed by Augustus Saint-Gaudens to celebrate the deeds (indeed, the very existence) of Col. Robert Gould Shaw and the Union Army's **54th Massachusetts Colored Regiment,** who fought in the Civil War. You might remember the story of the first American army unit made up of free black soldiers from the movie *Glory.*

To continue on the Freedom Trail: Cross Beacon Street.

Between Beacon, Park, Tremont, Boylston, and Charles sts. Visitor information center: 146 Tremont St. © 888/SEE-BOSTON or 617/536-4100. www.bostonusa.com. Mon–Sat 8:30am–5pm; Sun 9am–5pm. T: Green or Red Line to Park St.

Massachusetts State House   Boston is one of the only American cities where a building whose cornerstone was laid in 1795 (by Gov. Samuel Adams) would be called the "new" anything. Nevertheless, this is the new State House, as opposed to the Old State House (see below). The great Federal-era architect Charles Bulfinch designed the central building of the state capitol, and in 1802 copper sheathing manufactured by Paul Revere replaced the shingles on the landmark dome. Gold leaf now covers the dome; during World War II blackouts, it was painted black. The state legislature, or Massachusetts General Court, meets here. The House of Representatives congregates under a wooden fish, the **Sacred Cod,** as a reminder of the importance of fishing to the local economy. Take a self-guided tour or call ahead to schedule a conducted tour.

Whether or not you go inside, be sure to study some of the many statues outside. Subjects range from **Mary Dyer,** a Quaker hanged on the Common in 1660 for refusing to abandon her religious beliefs, to Pres. **John F. Kennedy.** The 60-foot monument at the rear (off Bowdoin St.) illustrates Beacon Hill's original height, before the top was shorn off to use in 19th-century landfill projects.

(Finds) **Listen Up: The Audio Freedom Trail**

A 2-hour tour narrative commissioned by the **Freedom Trail Foundation** (℃ **617/357-8300;** www.thefreedomtrail.org) includes interviews, sound effects, and music that help bring the sites to life. It costs $15 (credit cards only); buy it as an mp3 download, or rent a handheld digital audio player, for use with or without headphones, that can be picked up at the Boston Common Visitor Center, 146 Tremont St. (and dropped off there or at several other locations).

To continue on the Freedom Trail: Walk down Park Street (which Bulfinch laid out in 1804) to Tremont Street.

Beacon St. at Park St. ℃ 617/727-3676. www.mass.gov/statehouse. Mon–Fri 9am–5pm. Free tours Mon–Fri 10am–3:30pm. T: Green or Red Line to Park St., or Blue Line to Bowdoin (weekdays only).

Park Street Church   Henry James described this 1809 structure with a 217-foot steeple as "the most interesting mass of bricks and mortar in America." The church has accumulated an impressive number of firsts: The first Protestant missionaries to Hawaii left from here in 1819; the prominent abolitionist William Lloyd Garrison gave his first antislavery speech here on July 4, 1829; and "America" ("My Country 'Tis of Thee") was first sung here on July 4, 1831. You're standing on **"Brimstone Corner,"** named either for the passion of the Congregational ministers who declaimed from the pulpit or for the fact that gunpowder (made from brimstone) was stored in the basement during the War of 1812. This was part of the site of a huge granary that became a public building after the Revolutionary War. In the 1790s, the sails for USS *Constitution* ("Old Ironsides") were manufactured in that building.

In 2009, Park Street Church will celebrate its bicentennial. Visit **www.parkstreet 200.org** for information about concerts, lectures, exhibits, children's activities, and more, starting February 27 and continuing all year.

To continue on the Freedom Trail: Walk away from the Common on Tremont Street.

1 Park St. ℃ 617/523-3383. www.parkstreet.org. Tours mid-June to Aug Tues–Sat 9am–3pm. Sun services year-round 8:30 and 11am, 4 and 6pm. T: Green or Red Line to Park St.

Old Granary Burying Ground ⚜   This cemetery, established in 1660, was once part of Boston Common. You'll see the graves of patriots **Samuel Adams, Paul Revere, John Hancock,** and **James Otis;** merchant **Peter Faneuil** (spelled "Funal"); and Benjamin Franklin's parents. Also buried here are the victims of the **Boston Massacre** (see below) and the wife of Isaac Vergoose, who is believed to be **"Mother Goose"** of nursery rhyme fame. Note that gravestone rubbing, however tempting, is illegal in Boston's historic cemeteries.

To continue on the Freedom Trail: Turn left as you leave the cemetery and continue 1½ blocks on Tremont Street. En route to King's Chapel, you'll pass a 21st-century phenomenon: **Studio 73,** in the lobby of 73 Tremont St. and visible from the sidewalk. Suffolk University broadcast journalism and communications students staff the high-def TV studio.

Tremont St. at Bromfield St. Daily 9am–5pm (until 3pm in winter). T: Green or Red Line to Park St.

King's Chapel and Burying Ground   Architect Peter Harrison sent the plans for this Georgian-style building from Newport, Rhode Island, in 1749. Rather than replacing the existing wooden chapel, the granite edifice was constructed around it. Completed in 1754, it was the first Anglican church in Boston. George III sent gifts, as did Queen Anne and William and Mary, who presented the communion table and chancel tablets (still in use today) before the church was even built. The Puritan colonists had little use for the royal religion; after the Revolution, this became the first Unitarian church in the new nation. Today, the church conducts Unitarian Universalist services using the Anglican Book of Common Prayer and schedules public concerts (p. 227) every Tuesday at 12:15pm and some Sundays at 5pm.

The **burying ground** ★★, on Tremont Street, is the oldest in the city; it dates to 1630. Among the scary colonial headstones (winged skulls are a popular decoration) are the graves of **John Winthrop,** the first governor of the Massachusetts Bay Colony; **William Dawes,** who rode with Paul Revere; **Elizabeth Pain,** the model for Hester Prynne in Nathaniel Hawthorne's novel *The Scarlet Letter;* and **Mary Chilton,** the first female colonist to step ashore on Plymouth Rock.

To continue on the Freedom Trail: Follow the trail back along Tremont Street and turn left onto School Street.

58 Tremont St. ⓒ 617/227-2155. www.kings-chapel.org. Chapel: Year-round Sat 10am–4pm. Summer Sun 1:30–4pm; Mon and Thurs–Sat 10am–4pm; Tues–Wed 10–11:15am and 1:30–4pm. Check website for up-to-date spring and fall hours. Closed to visitors during religious services. $2 donation suggested. Services Wed 12:15pm, Sun 11am. Burying ground: Daily 8am–5:30pm (until 3pm in winter). T: Green or Blue Line to Government Center.

First Public School/Benjamin Franklin Statue   A colorful folk-art mosaic in the sidewalk marks the site of the first public school in the country. It was founded in 1634, 2 years before Harvard College. Samuel Adams, Benjamin Franklin, John Hancock, and Cotton Mather studied there. The original building (1645) was demolished to make way for the expansion of King's Chapel, and the school moved across the street. Other alumni include Charles Bulfinch, Ralph Waldo Emerson, George Santayana, Arthur Fiedler, and Leonard Bernstein. Now called Boston Latin School, the prestigious institution later moved to the Fenway neighborhood and started admitting girls.

Behind the fence in the courtyard to your left is the **Benjamin Franklin statue,** the first portrait statue erected in Boston (1856). Franklin was born in Boston in 1706 and was apprenticed to his half-brother James, a printer, but they got along so poorly that in 1723 Benjamin ran away to Philadelphia. Plaques on the base of the statue describe Franklin's numerous accomplishments. The lovely granite building behind the statue is **Old City Hall** (1865), designed in Second Empire style by Arthur Gilman (who laid out the Back Bay) and Gridley J. F. Bryant. The administration moved to Government Center in 1969, and the building now houses commercial tenants.

To continue on the Freedom Trail: Follow School Street to Washington Street.

School St. at City Hall Ave. (between Tremont and Washington sts.). T: Blue or Orange Line to State.

Old Corner Bookstore Building   Built in 1718, this building stands on a plot of land that was once home to the religious reformer Anne Hutchinson, who was excommunicated and expelled from Boston in 1638 for heresy. In the middle of the 19th century, the little brick building held the publishing house of Ticknor & Fields, which effectively made this the literary center of America. Publisher James Fields, known as "Jamie," counted among his friends Henry Wadsworth Longfellow, James Russell Lowell, Henry David Thoreau, Ralph Waldo Emerson, Nathaniel Hawthorne, and

Harriet Beecher Stowe. For many years this was the Globe Corner Bookstore, which is now in Harvard Square (p. 206).

To continue on the Freedom Trail: Turn right and walk 1 block.

3 School St. T: Blue or Orange Line to State.

Old South Meeting House ☆   Look for the clock tower that tops this religious and political gathering place, best known as the site of an important event leading to the Revolution. On December 16, 1773, a restive crowd of several thousand, too big to fit into Faneuil Hall, gathered here. They were waiting for word from the governor about whether three ships full of tea—priced to undercut the cost of smuggled tea and force the colonists to trade with merchants approved by the Crown—would be sent back to England from Boston. The ships were not, and revolutionaries haphazardly disguised as Mohawks cast the tea into the harbor. The meeting house commemorates that uprising, the **Boston Tea Party.** You can even see a vial of the tea.

Originally built in 1670 and replaced by the current structure in 1729, the building underwent extensive renovations in the 1990s. In 1872, a devastating fire that destroyed most of downtown stopped at Old South, a phenomenon considered evidence of the building's power. An interactive multimedia exhibit, ***Voices of Protest,*** tells the story of the events that took place here.

The meeting house frequently schedules speeches, readings, panel discussions, and children's activities, often with a colonial theme. Each December, it stages a reenactment of the debate that led to the tea party—it's especially fun for kids, who can participate in the heated debate. Check ahead for schedules.

To continue on the Freedom Trail: Exit through the gift shop and look across Milk Street to see **Benjamin Franklin's birthplace.** In a little house at 17 Milk St., Franklin was born in 1706, the 15th child of Josiah Franklin. The house is long gone, but look across at the second floor of what's now 1 Milk St. When the building went up after the fire of 1872, the architect guaranteed that the Founding Father wouldn't be forgotten: A bust and the words BIRTHPLACE OF FRANKLIN adorn the facade.

Now backtrack on Washington Street (passing Spring Lane, one of the first streets in Boston and originally the site of a real spring) and follow it to State Street.

310 Washington St. ℂ **617/482-6439.** www.oldsouthmeetinghouse.org. Admission $5 adults, $4 seniors and students with ID, $1 children 6–18, free for children under 6. Freedom Trail ticket (with Old State House and Paul Revere House) $11 adults, $3 children. Daily Apr–Oct 9:30am–5pm; Nov–Mar 10am–4pm. Closed Jan 1, Thanksgiving, Dec 24–25. T: Blue or Orange Line to State St.

Old State House Museum   Built in 1713, this brick structure served as the seat of colonial government before the Revolution and as the state capitol until 1798. From its balcony, the Declaration of Independence was first read to Bostonians on July 18, 1776. In 1789, Pres. George Washington reviewed a parade from here. The exterior decorations are particularly interesting—the clock was installed in place of a sundial, and the gilded lion and unicorn are reproductions of the original symbols of British rule that were ripped from the facade and burned the day the Declaration of Independence was read.

Inside is the **Bostonian Society's museum** ☆ of the city's history. The society was founded in 1881 to save this building, which was badly deteriorated and, incredibly, was about to be sold and shipped to Chicago. Two floors of exhibits focus on the role of the city and the building in the Revolution and the events that led to it—a Paul Revere print depicting the Boston Massacre and tea from the Boston Tea Party are on

Moments   Trail Mix

Faneuil Hall Marketplace is a great spot for a break. Time your walk right, and it can be the starting point of a picnic lunch. Visit the **Quincy Market** food court for takeout, then head across Atlantic Avenue toward the water. **Christopher Columbus Waterfront Park,** on the left-hand side of the Marriott Long Wharf hotel, is a popular place to picnic, watch the action at the marina, and play in the playground.

As you walk from Faneuil Hall to the Paul Revere House, you'll find yourself in the midst of **Haymarket.** On Friday and Saturday, the bustling open-air market on Hanover and Blackstone streets consists of stalls piled high with produce, seafood, and flowers. Shoppers aren't allowed to touch anything they haven't bought, a rule you might learn from a hollering vendor or a cutthroat customer. It's a great scene and a favorite with photographers.

---

view—but this experience is anything but a static history lesson. A multimedia presentation helps visitors learn about the Boston Massacre, an interactive display helps recount the story of the building, and changing exhibits focus on other topics, such as the Great Fire of 1872, using vintage photographs and artifacts from the society's collections.

To continue on the Freedom Trail: Leave the building, turn left, and walk half a block.

206 Washington St. ℂ 617/720-1713, ext. 21. www.bostonhistory.org. Admission $5 adults, $4 seniors and students, $1 children 6–18, free for children under 6. Freedom Trail ticket (with Old South Meeting House and Paul Revere House) $11 adults, $3 children. July–Aug daily 9am–6pm, Feb–June and Sept–Dec daily 9am–5pm, Jan daily 9am–4pm. T: Blue or Orange Line to State.

Boston Massacre Site   A ring of cobblestones on a traffic island marks the location of the skirmish that helped consolidate the spirit of rebellion in the colonies. On March 5, 1770, angered at the presence of royal troops in Boston, colonists threw snowballs, garbage, rocks, and other debris at a group of redcoats. The soldiers panicked and fired into the crowd, killing five men. Their graves, including that of Crispus Attucks, the first black man to die in the Revolution, are in the Old Granary Burying Ground.

To continue on the Freedom Trail: Turn left onto Congress Street and walk down the hill, covering 1 long block. Faneuil Hall will be on your right.

State St. at Devonshire St. T: Blue or Orange Line to State.

Faneuil Hall 🐦   Built in 1742 (and enlarged using a Charles Bulfinch design in 1805), this building was a gift to Boston, which was then just a town, from prosperous merchant Peter Faneuil. This "Cradle of Liberty" rang with speeches by orators such as Samuel Adams—whose statue stands outside the Congress Street entrance—in the years leading to the Revolution. Abolitionists, temperance advocates, and suffragists also used the hall as a pulpit. The upstairs is still a public meeting and concert hall, and downstairs holds retail space, all according to Faneuil's will. The grasshopper **weather vane,** the sole remaining detail from the original building, is modeled after the weather vane on London's Royal Exchange.

National Park Service rangers give **free historical talks** every half-hour from 9am to 5pm in the second-floor auditorium. On the top floor is a small museum that houses the weapons collection and historical exhibits of the **Ancient and Honorable Artillery Company of Massachusetts.**

To continue on the Freedom Trail: Leave Faneuil Hall, cross North Street, and follow the trail through the "Blackstone Block." These buildings, among the oldest in the city, give a sense of the scale of 18th- and 19th-century Boston. In the park at the corner of North and Union streets are two sculptures of legendary Boston mayor (and Congressman, and federal prisoner) **James Michael Curley,** the inspiration for the protagonist of Edwin O'Connor's *The Last Hurrah.* Pause on Union Street.

Dock Sq. (Congress St. and North St.). (*C*) **617/242-5675.** Free admission. Daily 9am–5pm; no public access during special events. T: Green or Blue Line to Government Center, or Orange Line to Haymarket.

The New England Holocaust Memorial ⟨★★⟩
Erected in 1995, these six glass towers spring up in the midst of attractions that celebrate freedom, reminding visitors of the consequences of a world without it. The pattern on the glass, which at first appears merely decorative, is actually 6 million random numbers, one for each Jew who died during the Holocaust. As you pass through, pause to read the inscriptions.

To continue on the Freedom Trail: You now pass through an area that encapsulates the benefits and drawbacks of the Big Dig. The Rose Kennedy Greenway—the strip of parkland that runs perpendicular to this section of the Freedom Trail—is part garden, part road, part construction site. Follow Hanover Street across the Greenway to reach the North End, which begins at Cross Street. Take Hanover Street 1 block to Richmond Street, passing the post office on your right. Turn right, go 1 block, and turn left.

Union St. between North and Hanover sts. (*C*) **617/457-8755.** www.nehm.org. T: Orange or Green Line to Haymarket.

Paul Revere House ⟨★★★⟩
One of the most pleasant stops on the Freedom Trail, this 2½-story wood structure presents history on a human scale. Revere was living here when he set out for Lexington on April 18, 1775, a feat immortalized in Henry Wadsworth Longfellow's poem "Paul Revere's Ride" ("Listen, my children, and you shall hear / of the midnight ride of Paul Revere"). It holds neatly arranged and identified 17th- and 18th-century furnishings and artifacts, including the famous Revere silver, considered some of the finest anywhere. The oldest house in downtown Boston, it was built around 1680, bought by Revere in 1770, and put to a number of uses before being turned into a museum in 1908.

The thought-provoking tour is self-guided, with staff members around in case you have questions. The format allows you to linger on the artifacts that hold your interest. Revere had 16 children (he called them "my lambs")—eight with each of his two wives—and supported the family with a thriving silversmith's trade. At his home, you'll get a good sense of the risks he took in the events that led to the Revolutionary War. If you're visiting in 2008, check ahead for info about special events celebrating the building's 100th anniversary as a museum.

Across the courtyard is the home of Revere's Hichborn cousins, the **Pierce/Hichborn House** ⟨★⟩. The 1711 Georgian-style home is a rare example of 18th-century middle-class architecture. It's suitably furnished and shown only by guided tour (usually twice a day at busy times). Call the Paul Revere House for schedules and reservations.

Before you leave North Square, look across the cobblestone plaza at **Sacred Heart Church.** It was established in 1833 as the Seamen's Bethel, a church devoted to the needs of the mariners who frequented the area. Wharves ran up almost this far in colonial days; in the 19th century, this was a notorious red-light district.

⟮Moments   Church Chat

One surefire way to announce yourself as an out-of-towner is to pause on Hanover Street between Prince and Fleet streets and proclaim that you see the Old North Church. The first house of worship you see is **St. Stephen's,** the only Charles Bulfinch–designed church still standing in Boston. It was Unitarian when it was dedicated in 1804. The next year, the congregation bought a bell (still in use) from Paul Revere's foundry for $800. The design is a paragon of Federal-style symmetry. St. Stephen's became Roman Catholic in 1862. During refurbishment in 1964 and 1965, it regained its original appearance, with clear glass windows, white walls, and gilded organ pipes. It's one of the plainest Catholic churches you'll ever see.

To continue on the Freedom Trail: The trail leaves the square on Prince Street and runs along Hanover Street past Clark Street. Before turning onto Prince Street, take a few steps down Garden Court Street and look for no. 4, on the right. The private residence was the birthplace of Rose Fitzgerald (later Kennedy).

19 North Sq. ✆ 617/523-2338. www.paulreverehouse.org. Admission $3 adults, $2.50 seniors and students, $1 children 5–17, free for children under 5. Freedom Trail ticket (with Old South Meeting House and Old State House) $11 adults, $3 children. Daily Apr 15–Oct 9:30am–5:15pm; daily Apr 1–14 and Nov–Dec 9:30am–4:15pm; Jan–Mar Tues–Sun 9:30am–4:15pm. Closed Jan 1, Thanksgiving, and Dec 25. T: Green or Orange Line to Haymarket, Blue Line to Aquarium, or Green or Blue Line to Government Center.

James Rego Square (Paul Revere Mall)   A pleasant little brick-paved park also known as "the Prado," the mall holds a famous equestrian statue of Paul Revere—a great photo op. Take time to read some of the **tablets** ✿ on the left-hand wall that describe famous people and places in the history of the North End.

To continue on the Freedom Trail: Walk around the fountain and continue to Salem Street, heading toward the steeple of the Old North Church.

Hanover St. at Clark St. T: Green or Orange Line to Haymarket.

Old North Church ✿   Look up! In this building's original steeple, sexton Robert Newman hung two lanterns on the night of April 18, 1775, to signal Paul Revere that British troops were setting out for Lexington and Concord in boats across the Charles River, not on foot. We know that part of the story in Longfellow's words: "One if by land, and two if by sea."

Officially named Christ Church, this is the oldest church building in Boston (1723). The design is in the style of Sir Christopher Wren. The steeple fell in hurricanes in 1804 and 1954; the current version is an exact copy of the original. The 190-foot spire, long a reference point for sailors, appears on navigational charts to this day. And how's this for a coincidence: Newman was a great-grandson of George Burroughs, one of the victims of the Salem witch trials of 1692.

Members of the Revere family attended this church (their plaque is on pew 54); famous visitors have included Presidents James Monroe, Theodore Roosevelt, Calvin Coolidge, Franklin D. Roosevelt, and Gerald R. Ford, and Queen Elizabeth II. There are markers and plaques throughout; note the bust of George Washington, reputedly the first memorial to the first president. The **gardens** ✿ on the north side of the church (dotted with more plaques) are open to the public. On the south side of the church, volunteers maintain an 18th-century garden.

Free tours of the church begin every 15 minutes, year-round. The 50-minute **behind-the-scenes tour** ($8 adults, $5 children under 17), which includes visits to the steeple and the crypt, is available on weekdays and on weekend afternoons from June to October, and the rest of the year by appointment. Tickets are available for advance purchase online.

To continue on the Freedom Trail: Cross Salem Street onto Hull Street and walk uphill toward Copp's Hill Burying Ground. On the left you'll pass 44 Hull St., a private residence that's the narrowest (10 ft. wide) house in Boston.

193 Salem St. ⓒ 617/523-6676. www.oldnorth.com. $3 donation requested. June–Oct daily 9am–5pm; March–May and Nov daily 9am–5pm; Dec daily 10am–5pm; Jan–Feb Tues–Sun 10am–4pm. Sun services (Episcopal) 9 and 11am. T: Orange or Green Line to Haymarket.

Copp's Hill Burying Ground ⚐   The second-oldest cemetery (1659) in the city is the burial place of Cotton Mather and his family, Robert Newman, and Prince Hall. Hall, a prominent member of the free black community that occupied the north slope of the hill in colonial times, fought at Bunker Hill and established the first black Masonic lodge. The highest point in the North End, Copp's Hill was the site of a windmill and of the British batteries that destroyed the village of Charlestown during the Battle of Bunker Hill on June 17, 1775. Charlestown is clearly visible (look for the masts of the USS *Constitution*) across the Inner Harbor. No gravestone rubbing is allowed.

To continue on the Freedom Trail: Follow Hull Street down the hill to Commercial Street (be careful crossing Commercial at the dangerous intersection with Hull) and follow the trail to North Washington Street and across the bridge. Follow signs and the trail to the Charlestown Navy Yard.

Off Hull St. near Snowhill St. Daily 9am–5pm (until 3pm in winter). T: Green or Orange Line to North Station.

USS *Constitution* ⚐⚐ *Kids*   **"Old Ironsides,"** one of the U.S. Navy's six original frigates, never lost a battle. A tour, led by an active-duty sailor in an 1812 dress uniform, is an excellent introduction to an era when the future of the new nation was anything but certain. The ship was constructed in the North End from 1794 to 1797 at a cost of $302,718, using bolts, spikes, and other fittings from Paul Revere's foundry. As the United States built its naval and military reputation, the *Constitution* played a key role, battling French privateers and Barbary pirates, repelling the British fleet during the War of 1812, participating in 40 engagements, and capturing 20 vessels. The frigate earned its nickname during a battle on August 19, 1812, when shots from HMS *Guerriere* bounced off its thick oak hull as if it were iron.

(*Tips*   **Security on "Old Ironsides"**

The Charlestown Navy Yard, home to USS *Constitution* and the Constitution Museum, is a heavily guarded area. At press time, a visitor center that incorporates a screening facility is in the works and scheduled to open in the summer of 2008. Regardless of the security arrangements during your visit, expect a search of your bags and a trip through a metal detector. And call ahead if the national terror alert is high; the navy yard closes to civilians at the first sign of a serious threat.

Retired from combat in 1815, the *Constitution* was rescued from destruction when Oliver Wendell Holmes's poem "Old Ironsides" launched a preservation movement in 1830. The frigate was completely overhauled for its bicentennial in 1997, when it sailed under its own power for the first time since 1881, drawing international attention. Tugs tow the *Constitution* into the harbor every **Fourth of July** for its celebratory "turnaround cruise," and for occasional events around the harbor. If you see TV helicopters circling over the water, wander down and take a look.

Adjacent to the ship, National Park Service rangers staff the **Charlestown Navy Yard Visitor Center** (© 617/242-5601), which opened in 2008, and give free 1-hour guided tours of the base.

To continue on the Freedom Trail: Walk straight ahead to the museum entrance.

Charlestown Navy Yard. © 617/242-7511. www.oldironsides.com. Free tours. Apr–Oct Tues–Sun 10am–6pm; tours every 30 min. 10am–3:30pm. Nov–Mar Thurs–Sun 10am–4pm; tours every 30 min. 10am–3:30pm. Closed Jan 1, Presidents Day, Thanksgiving, and Dec 25. T: Ferry from Long Wharf; or Green or Orange Line to North Station, then a 10-min. walk.

USS *Constitution* **Museum** ★ *Kids* *Value*   Just across from the vessel, the museum features engaging participatory exhibits that allow visitors to hoist a sail, fire a cannon, swing in a hammock, and learn about life onboard the ship during the War of 1812. The interactive computer displays—including a Barbary War exhibit that asks you to decide whether to risk a ship in the Mediterranean—and naval artifacts appeal to visitors of all ages. The museum's collections include more than 3,000 items, arranged and interpreted to put them in context, and staff members and volunteers conduct interesting talks (I've seen one every time I've been in the galleries) that expand on the exhibits. In February and March, special displays and activities focus on ship models.

To continue on the Freedom Trail: Follow the trail up Constitution Road, crossing Chelsea Street, and continue to the Bunker Hill Monument. A more interesting, slightly longer route runs from Chelsea Street and Rutherford Avenue (back at the bridge) across City Square Park.

Off First Ave., Charlestown Navy Yard. © 617/426-1812. www.ussconstitutionmuseum.org. Free admission; donations encouraged. Daily May–Oct 15 9am–6pm; Oct 16–Apr 10am–5pm. Closed Jan 1, Thanksgiving, and Dec 25. T: Ferry from Long Wharf (Blue Line Aquarium stop), or Green or Orange Line to North Station, then a 10-min. walk.

Bunker Hill Monument   The 221-foot granite obelisk, a landmark that's visible from miles away, honors the memory of the colonists who died in the Battle of Bunker Hill on June 17, 1775. The rebels lost the battle, but nearly half the British troops were killed or wounded, a loss that contributed to the redcoats' decision to abandon Boston 9 months later. The Marquis de Lafayette, the celebrated hero of the American and French revolutions, helped lay the monument's cornerstone in 1825. He is buried in Paris under soil taken from the hill. A punishing flight of 294 steps—imagine your worst StairMaster experience, then imagine not being able to stop in the middle—leads to the top of the monument. It's not a can't-miss experience unless you're traveling with children you'd like to tire out. There's no elevator, and although the views of the harbor and the Zakim–Bunker Hill Bridge are good, the windows are quite small.

Across the street is the **Bunker Hill Museum,** which opened in 2007 after extensive renovations to the monument and grounds. The ranger-staffed museum, at the corner where Monument Avenue enters Monument Square, holds dioramas, a cyclorama mural, and other exhibits about the battle and the community.

Monument Sq., Charlestown. © 617/242-5641. www.nps.gov/bost. Free admission. Exhibits daily 9am–5pm; monument daily 9am–4:30pm (until 5:30pm July–Aug). T: Orange Line to Community College.

Tips **Trailing Off**

If you don't feel like retracing your steps at the end of the Freedom Trail, you have two public transit options. Return to the Charlestown Navy Yard for the **ferry** to Long Wharf, which leaves every half-hour from 6:45am to 8:15pm on weekdays (every 15 min. 6:45–9:15am and 3:45–6:45pm), and every half-hour on the quarter-hour from 10:15am to 6:15pm on weekends. The 10-minute trip costs $1.70 (or show your 7-day LinkPass), and the dock is an easy walk from Old Ironsides. Alternatively, walk to the foot of the hill; on Main Street, take **bus no. 92 or 93** to Haymarket (Green or Orange Line).

3 More Museums & Attractions

Boston Athenæum 🏛 Both a private library and an art gallery, the Athenæum gives outsiders an insider's perspective on Boston Brahmin society. The city's leading families founded the members-only library in 1807 to make "the great works of learning and science in all languages" available to members. The arts component was added in 1827, and the building is now filled with artwork. Only the first floor is open to the public, but that's plenty—you'll get a sense of the spirit of self-improvement that inspired the members. Docent-led tours (offered twice weekly, by reservation only; ℂ **617/227-0270,** ext. 279) show off the Palladian-inspired sandstone building, replete with soaring galleries and hideaway nooks, that backs up to the Old Granary Burying Ground. Completed in 1849 and expanded in 1913–15, it was extensively renovated around the turn of the 21st century. Offerings within usually include exhibits in the compact art gallery; sometimes there are also readings, concerts, and, on rare occasions, public viewings of the library's most famous holding: an 1847 volume bound in the author's skin.

10½ Beacon St. ℂ **617/227-0270.** www.bostonathenaeum.org. Free admission. Year-round Mon 9am–8pm, Tues–Fri 9am–5:30pm; Sept–May Sat 9am–4pm. Free tours (reservations required) Tues and Thurs 3pm. Closed Sat June–Aug, Sun and major holidays year-round. T: Red or Green Line to Park St.

Boston Public Library The central branch of the city's library system is an architectural and intellectual monument. The original 1895 building, a National Historic Landmark designed by Charles F. McKim, is an Italian Renaissance–style masterpiece that fairly drips with art. The **lobby doors** are the work of Daniel Chester French (who also designed the Abraham Lincoln statue in the memorial in Washington, the *Minute Man* statue in Concord, and the John Harvard statue in Cambridge). The **murals** are by John Singer Sargent and Pierre Puvis de Chavannes, among others. Visit the lovely **courtyard** 🏛 or peek at it from a window on the stairs. The adjoining addition, of the same height and material (pink granite), was designed by Philip Johnson and opened in 1972. The lobby holds changing exhibits. The restaurant, **Novel,** serves lunch and afternoon tea Monday through Friday, and **Sebastian's Map Room Café** is open 9am to 5pm Monday through Saturday.

Free **Art & Architecture Tours** (www.bpl.org/guides/tours.htm) begin Monday at 2:30pm, Tuesday and Thursday at 6pm, Friday and Saturday at 11am, with an additional tour October through May on Sunday at 2pm. Visit the website and click "Guides to the Library" to find information about the McKim building. Call ℂ **617/536-5400,** ext. 2216, to arrange group tours.

Moments Eyes in the Skies

For a smashing view of the airport, the harbor, and the South Boston water-front, stroll along the harbor or Atlantic Avenue to Northern Avenue. On either side of this intersection are buildings with free observation areas. Be ready to show an ID to gain entrance. The first, on the 14th floor of Independence Wharf, 470 Atlantic Ave., is open daily from 11am to 5pm. The other, Foster's Rotunda, is on the ninth floor of 30 Rowes Wharf, in the Boston Harbor Hotel complex. It's open Monday to Friday from 11am to 4pm.

700 Boylston St., Copley Sq. (C) 617/536-5400. www.bpl.org. Free admission. Year-round Mon–Thurs 9am–9pm, Fri–Sat 9am–5pm; Oct–May Sun 1–5pm. Closed Sun June–Sept and legal holidays. T: Green Line to Copley.

Mary Baker Eddy Library/Mapparium *Kids*   The Mary Baker Eddy Library, a research center with two floors of interactive exhibits, aims to explore ideas such as liberty and spirituality through history, with a central role for Mary Baker Eddy, the founder of Christian Science. The most intriguing artifact is the **Mapparium** ✦, a unique hollow globe 30 feet across. A work of both art and history, it consists of a bronze framework that connects 608 stained-glass panels. Because sound bounces off the nonporous surfaces, the acoustics are as unusual as the aesthetics. As you cross the glass bridge just south of the equator, you'll see the political divisions of the world from 1932 to 1935, when the three-story globe was constructed.

World Headquarters of the First Church of Christ, Scientist, 200 Massachusetts Ave. (C) **888/222-3711** or 617/450-7000. www.mbelibrary.org. Admission $6 adults; $4 seniors, students, and children 6–17. Tues–Sun 10am–4pm. Closed Jan 1, Thanksgiving, and Dec 25. MBTA: Green Line E to Symphony; Green Line B, C, or D to Hynes Convention Center; or Orange Line to Mass. Ave. Parking $5.

Museum of African American History ✦✦   In Revolutionary War–obsessed New England, the history of the black community that thrived in Boston from early colonial times gets short shrift, with some notable exceptions. The final stop on the **Black Heritage Trail** (p. 162), this museum is one of those exceptions, presenting a comprehensive look at the history and contributions of blacks in Boston and Massachusetts. It occupies the **Abiel Smith School** (1834), the first American public grammar school for African-American children, and the **African Meeting House,** 8 Smith Court. Changing and permanent exhibits use art, artifacts, documents, historic photographs, and other objects—including many family heirlooms—to explore an important era in the country's history. The oldest standing black church in the United States, the meeting house opened in 1806. William Lloyd Garrison founded the New England Anti-Slavery Society in this building, where Frederick Douglass made some of his great abolitionist speeches. Once known as the "Black Faneuil Hall," it also schedules lectures, concerts, and church meetings. The museum (formerly the Museum of Afro-American History) will mount the temporary exhibit *Black Entrepreneurs of the 18th and 19th Centuries* beginning in the fall of 2008.

46 Joy St. (C) 617/725-0022. www.afroammuseum.org. Free admission; suggested donation $5. Mon–Sat 10am–4pm. Closed Jan 1, Thanksgiving, and Dec 25. MBTA: Red or Green Line to Park Street, or Red Line to Charles/MGH.

4 Historic Houses

The home in Boston imbued with the most history is the **Paul Revere House** (p. 155). A visit brings the legendary revolutionary to life. For information on the **Longfellow National Historic Site,** see p. 164.

On **Beacon Hill,** you'll find houses that are as interesting for their architecture as for their occupants. The south slope, facing Boston Common, has been a fashionable address since the 1620s; excellent tours of two houses (one on the north slope) focus on the late 18th and early 19th centuries. The architect of the homes was Charles Bulfinch; he also designed the State House, which sits at the hill's summit.

Historic New England (formerly the Society for the Preservation of New England Antiquities) owns and operates the Otis House Museum (see below) and dozens of other historic properties throughout New England. Contact the organization (© 617/227-3956; www.historicnewengland.org) for information on its properties, visiting hours, and admission fees.

Gibson House Museum   The Gibson House is an 1859 brownstone that embodies the word "Victorian." Forget you've ever heard the phrase "less is more"—the ornate furnishings and abundant accessories permit a compelling look at the domestic life of a socially prominent family in the then-new Back Bay neighborhood. You'll see decorations of all kinds, including family photos and portraits, petrified-wood hat racks, a sequined red-velvet pagoda for the cat, a Victrola, and an original icebox. Check ahead for the schedule of lectures and other special events.

137 Beacon St. © 617/267-6338. www.thegibsonhouse.org. Admission $7. Tours on the hour Wed–Sun 1–3pm. Closed Jan 1, July 4, Thanksgiving, and Dec 25. T: Green Line to Arlington.

John F. Kennedy National Historic Site   The 35th president's birthplace is a modest 1909 house in a quiet residential neighborhood. The president's mother, Rose Fitzgerald Kennedy, collected many of the items on display and helped with the restoration; the current configuration is her recollection of the house's appearance around 1917, when "Jack," her second child, was born. The tour, led by a National Park Service ranger, discusses domestic life of the period and the roots of the Kennedy family. If you miss the last guided tour, ask about the self-guided option, which is available in English, French, German, Japanese, and Spanish. One-hour walking tours of the neighborhood take place several times each weekend.

83 Beals St., Brookline. © 617/566-7937. www.nps.gov/jofi. Tours $3 adults, free for children under 18. May–early Oct Wed–Sun 10am–4:30pm. Tours every 30 min. 10am–3:30pm. Call ahead to double-check hours and tour schedules, especially early and late in the season. Closed mid-Oct to Apr. T: Green Line C to Coolidge Corner, then walk 4 blocks north on Harvard St. and turn right.

Nichols House Museum ⊛   A stroll around Beacon Hill leaves many visitors pining to know what the stately homes look like inside. This is one of the only places to satisfy that curiosity. The 1804 home holds beautiful antique furnishings, art, carpets, and tapestries collected by several generations of the Nichols family. Its most prominent occupant, Rose Standish Nichols, was a suffragist and a pioneering landscape designer. Her legacy includes not just family heirlooms but objects she brought back from her many travels to the thoroughfare Henry James (who lived at no. 131) reputedly called "the only respectable street in America."

55 Mount Vernon St. © 617/227-6993. www.nicholshousemuseum.org. Admission $7. Apr–Oct Tues–Sat noon–4pm; Nov–Mar Thurs–Sat noon–4pm; tours every 30 min. T: Red or Green Line to Park St.

Otis House Museum ✯✯   Legendary architect Charles Bulfinch designed this gorgeous 1796 mansion for his friends Harrison Gray Otis, an up-and-coming young lawyer who later became mayor of Boston, and his wife, Sally. The restoration was one of the first in the country to use computer analysis of paint, and the result was revolutionary: It revealed that the walls were drab because the paint had faded, not because the colors started out dingy. Furnished in the style to which a wealthy family in the young United States would have been accustomed, the Federal-style building is a colorful, elegant treasure. Guided tours (the only way to see the property) discuss the architecture of the house and post-Revolutionary social, business, and family life, and touch on the history of the neighborhood.

141 Cambridge St. ⟲ **617/227-3956.** www.historicnewengland.org. Guided tour $8. Tours every 30 min. Wed–Sun 11am–4:30pm. T: Blue Line to Bowdoin (weekdays only), Green or Blue Line to Government Center, or Red Line to Charles/MGH.

5 African-American History

The 1.6-mile **Black Heritage Trail** ✯✯ covers sites on Beacon Hill that preserve the history of 19th-century Boston. The neighborhood was the center of the free black community, and the trail links stations of the Underground Railroad, homes of famous citizens, and the first integrated public school in the city. You can take a free 2-hour guided tour with a ranger from the National Park Service's **Boston African American National Historic Site** (⟲ **617/742-5415;** www.nps.gov/boaf). Tours start at the **Robert Gould Shaw Memorial,** on Beacon Street across from the State House. They're available Monday through Saturday from Memorial Day to Labor Day, and by request at other times; call ahead for a reservation. Or go on your own, using a brochure (available at the Museum of African American History and the Boston Common and State Street visitor centers) that includes a map and descriptions of the buildings. The only buildings on the trail that are open to the public are the **African Meeting House** and the **Abiel Smith School,** which make up the **Museum of African American History** (p. 160). Check ahead for special programs in February.

Across the river, the **Cambridge African American Heritage Trail** focuses on significant sites in the history of the city's large black community. To buy the guide, visit the office on the second floor of 831 Massachusetts Ave., download an order form from the website, or send a check for $3.50 (includes shipping), payable to the

Focus on Women's History

The **Boston Women's Heritage Trail** (⟲ **617/522-2872;** www.bwht.org) creates walking tours with stops at homes, churches, and social and political institutions associated with women who made great contributions to society. Subjects include Julia Ward Howe, social reformer Dorothea Dix, colonial religious leader Anne Hutchinson, and less famous Bostonians such as Phillis Wheatley, a slave who became the first African-American published poet, and abolitionist and feminist Lucy Stone. You can buy a guidebook at the National Park Service Visitor Center at 15 State St., at some local historic sites and bookstores, or online.

Cambridge Historical Society, to the **Cambridge Historical Commission,** 831 Massachusetts Ave., Cambridge, MA 02139 (© **617/349-4683;** www.ci.cambridge.ma. us/~historic).

6 Parks & Gardens

Green space is an important part of Boston's appeal, and the public parks are hard to miss. The world-famous **Emerald Necklace,** Frederick Law Olmsted's vision for a loop of green spaces, runs through the city. See p. 174 for information on seeing part or all of the Emerald Necklace with a Boston park ranger.

The best-known park, for good reason, is the spectacular **Public Garden** ★★★, bordered by Arlington, Boylston, Charles, and Beacon streets. Something lovely is in bloom at the country's first botanical garden at least half the year. The spring flowers are particularly impressive, especially if your visit happens to coincide with the first really warm days of the year. It's hard not to enjoy yourself when everyone around you seems ecstatic just to be seeing the sun.

For many Bostonians, the official beginning of spring coincides with the return of the **Swan Boats** ★★ (© **617/522-1966;** www.swanboats.com). The pedal-powered vessels—the attendants pedal, not the passengers—plunge into the lagoon on the Saturday before Patriots Day, the third Monday of April. The surrounding greenery and placid water help lend a 19th-century aura to the attraction, which the Paget family has operated since 1877. Although the Swan Boats don't move fast, they'll transport you. They operate daily from 10am to 5pm in the summer, daily from 10am to 4pm in the spring, and weekdays noon to 4pm and weekends 10am to 4pm from Labor Day to mid-September. The cost for the 15-minute ride is $2.75 for adults, $2 for seniors, and $1.25 for children 2 to 15.

Across Charles Street is **Boston Common,** the country's first public park and the first site on the **Freedom Trail** (p. 148). The property was purchased in 1634 and officially set aside as public land in 1640, so if it seems a bit run-down (especially compared to the Public Garden), it's no wonder. A rehab project that began in 2007 may be bearing fruit—or closing off whole sections of the park, or both—by the time you visit. The Frog Pond, where there really were frogs at one time, makes a pleasant spot to splash around in the summer and skate in the winter. At the Boylston Street side of the Common is the **Central Burying Ground,** where you can see the grave of famed portraitist Gilbert Stuart. There's also a bandstand where you might take in a free concert or play, and many beautiful shade trees.

The most spectacular garden in town is the **Arnold Arboretum** ★★, 125 Arborway, Jamaica Plain (© **617/524-1718;** www.arboretum.harvard.edu), which Frederick Law Olmsted designed as the final link in the Emerald Necklace. One of the oldest parks in the United States, founded in 1872, it is open daily from sunrise to sunset. Its 265 acres contain more than 15,000 ornamental trees, shrubs, and vines from all over the world. In the spring, the grounds are ablaze with blossoming dogwood, azaleas, and rhododendrons, and the air fills with the dizzying scent of hundreds of varieties of lilacs, for which the arboretum is especially famous. This is definitely a place to take a camera—but not food. Lilac Sunday, in May, is the only time the arboretum allows picnicking.

There is no admission fee for this National Historic Landmark, which Harvard University administers in cooperation with the Boston Department of Parks and Recreation. To get there, take the MBTA Orange Line to the Forest Hills stop and follow signs to the entrance. The visitor center is open weekdays from 9am to 4pm,

Saturday 10am to 4pm, and Sunday noon to 4pm (closed major holidays). Call or visit the website for information about educational programs and driving directions.

7 Cambridge

Boston and Cambridge are so closely associated that many people believe they're the same place—a notion that both cities' residents and politicians are happy to dispel. Cantabrigians are often considered more liberal and better educated than Bostonians, which is another idea that's sure to get you involved in a lively discussion. Take the Red Line across the river and see for yourself.

For a good overview, begin at the main Harvard T entrance. Follow our Harvard Square walking tour (p. 193), or set out on your own. At the **information booth** (© **617/497-1630**) in the middle of Harvard Square at the intersection of Mass. Ave., John F. Kennedy Street, and Brattle Street, trained volunteers dispense maps and brochures and answer questions Monday through Saturday from 9am to 5pm and Sunday from 1 to 5pm. From mid-June to Labor Day, **guided tours** explore the entire old Cambridge area. Check at the booth for rates, meeting places, and times, or call ahead. If you prefer to sightsee on your own, you can buy the Cambridge Historical Commission's *Revolutionary Cambridge* walking guide ($2).

Whatever you do, spend some time in **Harvard Square.** It's a hodgepodge of college and high school students, professors and instructors, commuters, street performers, and sightseers. Stores and restaurants line all three streets that spread out from the center of the square and the streets that intersect them. If you follow **Brattle Street** to the residential area just outside the square, you'll arrive at a part of town known as **"Tory Row"** because the residents were loyal to King George during the Revolution.

The yellow mansion at 105 Brattle St. is the **Longfellow National Historic Site** ✦ (© **617/876-4491;** www.nps.gov/long), the longtime home of Henry Wadsworth Longfellow (1807–82). The poet first lived here as a boarder in 1837. When he and Fanny Appleton married in 1843, her father made the house a wedding present. The furnishings and books in the stately home are original to Longfellow, who lived here until his death, and his descendants. During the siege of Boston in 1775–76, the house served as the headquarters of Gen. George Washington, with whom Longfellow was fascinated. On a tour—the only way to see the house—you'll learn about the history of the building and its famous occupants.

The house is usually open June through October Wednesday through Sunday from 10am to 4:30pm, but always check ahead. Tours begin at 10:30 and 11:30am, and 1, 2, 3, and 4pm. Admission is $3 for adults, free for children under 16.

Farther west, near where Brattle Street and Mount Auburn Street intersect, is **Mount Auburn Cemetery** (see the box titled "Celebrity Cemetery"). It's a pleasant but long walk; you might prefer to drive or take a bus from Harvard station.

HARVARD UNIVERSITY

Our Harvard Square walking tour (p. 193) describes many of the buildings you'll see on the Harvard campus. Free student-led tours leave from the **Information Center** in Holyoke Center, 1350 Massachusetts Ave. (© **617/495-1573**). They operate during the school year twice a day on weekdays and once on Saturday, except during vacations, and during the summer four times a day Monday through Saturday. Call or surf ahead for exact times; reservations aren't necessary. The Information Center has maps, illustrated booklets, and self-guided walking-tour directions, as well as a bulletin board

Harvard Square Attractions

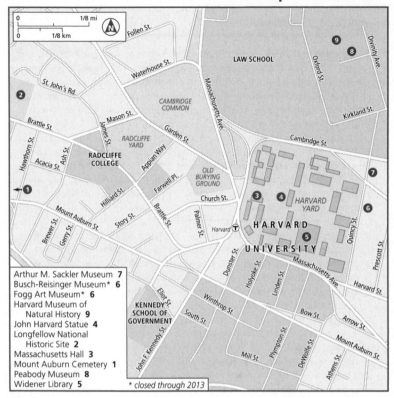

Arthur M. Sackler Museum **7**
Busch-Reisinger Museum* **6**
Fogg Art Museum* **6**
Harvard Museum of
    Natural History **9**
John Harvard Statue **4**
Longfellow National
    Historic Site **2**
Massachusetts Hall **3**
Mount Auburn Cemetery **1**
Peabody Museum **8**
Widener Library **5**

closed through 2013

where flyers publicize campus activities. You might want to check out the university website (www.harvard.edu) before you visit.

The best-known part of the university is **Harvard Yard,** which consists of two large quadrangles. Daniel Chester French's **John Harvard statue,** a rendering of one of the school's original benefactors, is in the Old Yard, which dates to the college's founding in 1636. Most first-year students live in the dormitories here—even in the school's oldest building, **Massachusetts Hall** (1720). "Mass. Hall" also holds the university president's office, which gained a female occupant for the first time in 2007. The other side of the Yard (sometimes called Tercentenary Theater because the college's 300th-anniversary celebration was held there) is home to the imposing **Widener Library,** named after a Harvard graduate who perished when the *Titanic* sank.

Also on campus are two engaging museum complexes:

Harvard Museum of Natural History and Peabody Museum of Archaeology & Ethnology ★ *Kids*   These fascinating museums house the university's collections of items and artifacts related to the natural world. Just about everyone finds something interesting here, be it a 42-foot-long dinosaur skeleton, the largest turtle shell in the world, an exploration of climate science, a Native American artifact, or the **Museum of Natural History**'s world-famous Glass Flowers.

Celebrity Cemetery

Three important colonial burying grounds—Old Granary, King's Chapel, and Copp's Hill—are in Boston on the Freedom Trail (see "The Freedom Trail," earlier in this chapter), but the most famous cemetery in the area is in Cambridge.

Mount Auburn Cemetery ★, 580 Mount Auburn St. (© **617/547-7105;** www.mountauburn.org), the final resting place of many well-known people, is also famous simply for existing. Dedicated in 1831, it was the first of America's rural, or garden, cemeteries. The establishment of burying places removed from city centers reflected practical and philosophical concerns: Development was encroaching on urban graveyards, and the ideas associated with Transcendentalism and the Greek revival dictated that communing with nature take precedence over organized religion. Since the day it opened, Mount Auburn has been a popular place to retreat and reflect.

Visitors to this National Historic Landmark find history and horticulture coexisting with celebrity. The graves of Henry Wadsworth Longfellow, Oliver Wendell Holmes, Julia Ward Howe, and Mary Baker Eddy are here, as are those of Charles Bulfinch, James Russell Lowell, Winslow Homer, Transcendentalist leader Margaret Fuller, and abolitionist Charles Sumner. In season you'll see gorgeous flowering trees and shrubs (the Massachusetts Horticultural Society had a hand in the design).

Stop at the **visitor center** in Story Chapel (daily 9am–4pm Apr–Oct except during burials; closed Sun Nov–Mar) for an overview and a look at the changing exhibits, or ask at the office or front gate for brochures and a map. You can rent an audiotape tour ($7; a $15 deposit is required) and listen in your car or on a portable tape player; there's a 60-minute driving tour and two 75-minute walking tours. The **Friends of Mount Auburn Cemetery** conduct workshops and lectures and coordinate walking tours; call the main number for topics, schedules, and fees.

The cemetery is open daily from 8am to 5pm October through April, 8am to 7pm May through September; admission is free. Animals and recreational activities such as jogging, biking, and picnicking are not allowed. MBTA bus nos. 71 and 73 start at Harvard station and stop near the cemetery gates; they run frequently on weekdays and less often on weekends. By car (5 min.) or on foot (30 min.), take Mount Auburn Street or Brattle Street west from Harvard Square; just after the streets intersect, the gate is on the left.

The **Glass Flowers** ★★★ are 3,000 models of more than 840 plant species devised between 1887 and 1936 by the German father-and-son team of Leopold and Rudolph Blaschka. You may be skeptical, but it's true: They look real. Children love the **zoological collections** ★★, where dinosaurs share space with preserved and stuffed insects and animals that range in size from butterflies to giraffes. Arthropods—insects, centipedes, spiders, and other creepy-crawlies—have their own multimedia installation. The **mineralogical collections** are the most specialized but can be just as interesting as the rest, especially if gemstones hold your interest.

Language of Color, an exhibit opening Sept. 28, 2008, looks at the world through the prism of animals—not just what they look like but what they perceive.

The **Peabody Museum of Archaeology & Ethnology** ⊕ boasts the **Hall of the North American Indian,** where 500 artifacts representing 10 cultures are on display. Photographs, textiles, pottery, and art and crafts of all ages and descriptions fill the galleries, spanning six continents and countless years.

One of the university's most popular attractions, this complex is also a world-famous academic resource; interdisciplinary programs and exhibitions tie in elements of all the associated fields. Check ahead for special events, including family programs and lectures by celebrated scientists, during your visit.

Harvard Museum of Natural History: 26 Oxford St. © 617/495-3045. www.hmnh.harvard.edu. Peabody Museum: 11 Divinity Ave. © 617/496-1027. www.peabody.harvard.edu. Admission to both $9 adults, $7 seniors and students, $6 children 3–18, free for children under 3. Free to Mass. residents Sun until noon and Wed 3–5pm. Daily 9am–5pm. Closed Jan 1, Thanksgiving, Dec 24–25. T: Red Line to Harvard. Cross Harvard Yard, keeping John Harvard statue on right. Before reaching Science Center entrance, turn right and quickly turn left (onto Oxford St.). Check website for parking info.

Harvard Art Museums

In June 2008, Harvard's Fogg and Busch-Reisinger museums closed for renovations scheduled to last 5 years. The Sackler Museum will stay open and show highlights from all three institutions' collections. Before you add this stop to your itinerary, check the website for specifics of what's on exhibit—I for one can't wait to see what kind of lemonade the inventive curators will make from this lemon-scented situation, but you may feel differently.

The collections of the Fogg, Busch-Reisinger, and the Sackler museums encompass a quarter-million works, from ancient sculptures to contemporary photos. The **Arthur M. Sackler Museum** houses Harvard's world-famous collections of Asian, ancient, Islamic, and Later Indian art. Here you'll find internationally renowned Chinese jades, superb Roman sculpture, Greek vases, Korean ceramics, Japanese woodblock prints, and Persian miniature paintings and calligraphy. The **Fogg Museum's** holdings include everything from 17th-century Dutch and Flemish landscapes to Impressionist masterpieces to contemporary sculpture. The **Busch-Reisinger Museum's** specialty is the art of northern and central Europe, specifically Germany; the early-20th-century holdings are particularly notable. Exhibit spaces also serve as teaching and research facilities; keep an ear out for instructors leading classes.

485 Broadway. © 617/495-9400. www.artmuseums.harvard.edu. Admission fees not set at press time; check ahead. Mon–Sat 10am–5pm; Sun 1–5pm. Closed major holidays. T: Red Line to Harvard, cross Harvard Yard diagonally from the T station and exit onto Quincy St., turn left, and walk to the next corner. Or turn your back on the Coop and follow Mass. Ave. to Quincy St., then turn left and walk 1 long block.

MASSACHUSETTS INSTITUTE OF TECHNOLOGY (MIT)

The public is welcome at the Massachusetts Institute of Technology campus, a mile or so from Harvard Square, across the Charles River from Beacon Hill and the Back Bay. Visit the **Information Office,** 77 Mass. Ave. (© 617/253-4795), to take a free guided tour (weekdays at 10am and 2pm) or to pick up a copy of the *Walk Around MIT* map and brochure. At the same address, the **Hart Nautical Galleries** (open daily 9am–8pm) contain ship and engine models that illustrate the development of marine engineering.

MIT's campus is known for its art and architecture. The excellent **outdoor sculpture** collection includes works by Picasso and Alexander Calder, and notable modern buildings include designs by Frank Gehry, Eero Saarinen, and I. M. Pei. Gehry designed the **Stata Center** (http://web.mit.edu/evolving/buildings/stata), a curvilinear landmark that

---

Moments **Hey There, You with the Stars in Your Eyes**

Two local colleges have on-campus observatories that allow the public a look at the skies above Boston—through a telescope. This is a good activity for high school students as well as adults. The Judson B. Coit Observatory at **Boston University,** 725 Commonwealth Ave. (© **617/353-2630;** www.bu.edu/astronomy/opennight.html), throws open its doors on most Wednesdays, year-round. The **Harvard College Observatory,** 60 Garden St. (© **617/495-9059;** http://cfa-www.harvard.edu/events) schedules a lecture and quality time with a telescope on the third Thursday of each month.

---

opened on Vassar Street off Main Street in 2004. Visit the information desk on the ground floor to pick up a pamphlet describing a self-guided tour.

Engaging holography displays and robots are the hallmarks of the **MIT Museum,** 265 Massachusetts Ave. (© **617/253-4444;** http://web.mit.edu/museum), where you'll also find works in more conventional media, such as kinetic sculpture. This is a good place to participate in activities and programs that explore the role of science and technology in society. The museum and its entertaining gift shop are open Tuesday through Friday (plus Mon July–Aug) from 10am to 5pm, weekends from noon to 5pm (closed on major holidays). Admission is $5 for adults, $2 for seniors, and $1 for students and children 5 to 17. The school's contemporary art repository, the **List Visual Arts Center,** in the atrium of the Wiesner Building, 20 Ames St. (© **617/253-4680;** http://web.mit.edu/lvac), is open Tuesday through Sunday from noon to 6pm, until 8pm on Friday. Admission and gallery tours are free.

To get to MIT, take the MBTA Red Line to Kendall/MIT. The scenic walk from the Back Bay takes you along Mass. Ave. over the river straight to the campus. By car from Boston, cross the river at the Museum of Science, Cambridge Street, or Mass. Ave. and follow signs to Memorial Drive, where you can usually find parking during the day.

8 Boston Neighborhoods to Explore

Boston is a city of neighborhoods, some of which I've described in talking about the Freedom Trail (see "The Freedom Trail," earlier in this chapter) and in the walking tours in chapter 8. Here are several other areas that are fun to explore. Bear in mind that many of the buildings you will see are private homes, not tourist attractions. See chapter 6 for dining suggestions and chapter 9 for shopping tips.

BEACON HILL ✦✦✦

The original Boston settlers, clustered around what are now the Old State House and the North End, considered Beacon Hill far distant. Today the distance is a matter of atmosphere; climbing "the Hill" is like traveling back in time. Lace up your walking shoes (the brick sidewalks gnaw at anything fancier, and driving is next to impossible), wander the narrow streets, and admire the brick and brownstone architecture.

At Beacon and Park streets is a figurative high point (literally, it's *the* high point): Charles Bulfinch's magnificent **State House.** The 60-foot **monument** at the rear illustrates the hill's original height, before the top was shorn off to use in 19th-century landfill projects. **Beacon and Mount Vernon streets** run downhill to commercially dense **Charles Street,** but if ever there was an area where there's no need to head in a straight line, it's this one. Your travels might take you past the former homes of Louisa May Alcott (10 Louisburg Sq.), Henry Kissinger (1 Chestnut St.), Julia Ward Howe (13 Chestnut St.), Edwin Booth (29A Chestnut St.), and Robert Frost (88 Mount Vernon St.). One of the oldest black churches in the country, the **African Meeting House** (p. 160), is at 8 Smith Court.

These days, Alcott probably wouldn't be able to afford even the rent for a home on **Louisburg Square** (say "Lewis-burg"), better known today as the home of John and Teresa Heinz Kerry. Twenty-two homes where a struggling writer would more likely be an employee than a resident surround the lovely park. The iron-railed square is open only to residents with keys.

Your wandering will probably lead you down to Charles Street. After you've had your fill of the shops and restaurants there, you might want to investigate the architecture of the **"flats,"** between Charles Street and the Charles River. Built on landfill,

Welcome to the North End

The Paul Revere House and the Old North Church are the best-known buildings in the **North End** ★★★, Boston's "Little Italy" (although it's *never* called that). Home to natives of Italy and their assimilated children, numerous Italian restaurants and private social clubs, and many historic sites, this is one of the oldest neighborhoods in the city. It was home in the 17th century to the **Mather family** of Puritan ministers, who certainly would be shocked to see the merry goings-on at the festivals and street fairs that take over different areas of the North End on weekends in July and August.

The Italians (and their yuppie neighbors who have made inroads since the 1980s) are only the latest immigrant group to dominate the North End. In the 19th century, this was an Eastern European Jewish enclave and later an Irish stronghold. In 1890, President Kennedy's mother, Rose Fitzgerald, was born on Garden Court Street and baptized at St. Stephen's Church.

Modern visitors might be more interested in a Hanover Street *caffè*, the perfect place to have coffee or a soft drink and feast on sweets. **Mike's Pastry** ★★★, 300 Hanover St. (② **617/742-3050**; www.mikespastry.com), is a bakery that does a frantic takeout business and has tables where you can sit down and order one of the confections on display in the cases. The signature item is cannoli (tubes of crisp-fried pastry filled with sweetened ricotta cheese); the cookies, cakes, and other pastries are excellent, too. You can also sit and relax at **Caffè dello Sport** or **Caffè Vittoria,** on either side of Mike's.

Before you leave the North End, stroll down toward the water and see whether there's a **bocce** game going on at the courts on Commercial Street near Hull Street. The European pastime is both a game of skill and an excuse to hang around and shoot the breeze—in Italian and English—with the locals (mostly men of a certain age). It's so popular that the neighborhood has courts both outdoors, in the Langone Playground at Puopolo Park, and indoors, at the back of the Steriti Rink, 561 Commercial St.

Tips   A Different Voice

Mytown multicultural youth walking tours (📞 **617/536-8696,** ext. 11; www. mytowninc.org) offers tours led by a local high school student. The Youth Guide program trains participants in historical research and encourages them to put a personal spin on their narration. The result is a uniquely fascinating take on the city. Tours ($15) operate from late April to October; check ahead for tour details, meeting times, and reservations.

---

the buildings here are younger than those higher up, but many are just as eye-catching. MTV fans might recognize the converted firehouse at Mount Vernon and River streets as a former *Real World* location (it's also a one-time *Spenser: For Hire* set).

T: Red Line to Charles/MGH, Green Line to Park Street, or Blue Line to Bowdoin (weekdays only).

THE SOUTH END 🏵🏵

One of Boston's most diverse neighborhoods is also one of its largest, but fans of Victorian architecture won't mind the sore feet they'll have after trekking around the South End.

The neighborhood was laid out in the mid–19th century, before the Back Bay. While the newer area's grid echoes the boulevards of Paris, the South End tips its hat to London. The main streets are broad, and pocket parks dot the side streets. Late-20th-century gentrification saw many South End brownstones reclaimed from squalor and converted into luxury condominiums, driving out many longtime residents and making construction materials as widespread as falling leaves. Even on the few remaining run-down buildings, you'll see wonderful details.

With Back Bay Station to your left, walk down **Dartmouth Street,** crossing Columbus Avenue. Proceed on Dartmouth and explore some of the streets that extend to the left, including **Chandler, Lawrence, and Appleton streets.** This area is known as **Clarendon Park.** Turn left on any of these streets and walk to **Clarendon Street.** Its intersection with Tremont Street is the part of the South End you're most likely to see if you're not out exploring. This is the area where businesses and restaurants surround the **Boston Center for the Arts** (p. 221). The BCA's **Cyclorama** building (the interior is dome-shaped), at 539 Tremont St., is listed on the National Register of Historic Places. Here you can see a show, have a meal, or continue your expedition, perhaps to do a little shopping on Tremont Street, Shawmut Avenue, or Washington Street. You can wander and explore all the way to Mass. Ave. From there, take the no. 1 bus to the Back Bay or into Cambridge, or the Orange Line downtown.

T: Orange Line to Back Bay or Green Line to Copley.

JAMAICA PLAIN 🏵

You can combine a visit to the Arnold Arboretum (p. 163) with a stroll around Jamaica Pond or along Centre Street. Culturally diverse Jamaica Plain abounds with interesting architecture and open space. The pond is especially pleasant in good weather, when people walk, run, skate, fish, picnic, and sunbathe. Many of the 19th-century mansions overlooking the pond date to the days when families fled the oppressive heat downtown and moved to the "country" for the summer.

After you've had your fill of nature (or before you set out), Centre Street makes a good destination for wandering and snacking. The AIDS Action Committee's excellent resale shop, **Boomerangs,** 716 Centre St. (© **617/524-5120**), is worth a look for upscale merchandise and reasonable prices. A favorite among the neighborhood's countless dining destinations is **JP Licks Homemade Ice Cream,** 674 Centre St. (© **617/524-6740**). Across the street from the T stop is the **Dogwood Café,** 3712 Washington St. (© **617/522-7997**), a family-friendly bar and restaurant with plenty of beers on tap and tasty pizza.

T: Orange Line to Forest Hills.

9 Especially for Kids

What can the children do in Boston? A better question might be "What *can't* the children do in Boston?" Just about every major attraction in the city either is specifically designed to appeal to youngsters or can easily be adapted to do so.

The following attractions are covered extensively elsewhere in this chapter; here's the boiled-down version for busy parents.

Destinations with something for every member of the family include **Faneuil Hall Marketplace** (© **617/338-2323;** p. 142) and the **Museum of Fine Arts** (© **617/ 267-9300;** p. 145), which offers special weekend and after-school programs.

Hands-on exhibits and large-format films are the headliners at the **New England Aquarium** (© **617/973-5200;** p. 147), where you'll find the Simons IMAX Theatre, and at the **Museum of Science** (© **617/723-2500;** p. 146), home to the Mugar Omni Theater as well as the Hayden Planetarium.

You might get your hands on a baseball at a **Red Sox game** (p. 185) or the **Sports Museum of New England** (© **617/624-1234;** p. 185).

The allure of seeing people the size of ants draws young visitors to the **Prudential Center Skywalk Observatory** (© **617/859-0648;** p. 146). And they can see actual ants—although they might prefer the dinosaurs—at the **Harvard Museum of Natural History** (© **617/495-3045;** p. 165).

Older children who have studied modern American history will enjoy a visit to the **John F. Kennedy Presidential Library and Museum** (© **617/929-4523;** p. 144). Middle-schoolers who enjoyed Esther Forbes's *Johnny Tremain* will probably get a kick

---

Tips More Kid Stuff

For more suggestions, check (or let the kids check) elsewhere in this book. Chapter 10 lists nightlife destinations for all ages. Before night falls (and sometimes afterward), the whole family can have a great time at the **Hard Rock Cafe** (food and music), **Club Passim** (folk music; no alcohol), *Shear Madness* (audience-participation theater), **Blue Man Group** (performance art), and the **Puppet Showplace Theater.**

Turn to chapter 9 for shopping recommendations—**Beadworks,** the **CambridgeSide Galleria** mall, **Curious George Books & Toys, Pearl Art & Craft Supplies,** and the various **college bookstores** can be almost as fun as all-toy stores.

Finally, check chapter 11 for information about day trips. Fun destinations include **Salem, Plymouth,** and (for *Little Women* fans) **Concord.**

out of the **Paul Revere House** (*©* **617/523-2338;** p. 155). Young visitors who have read Robert McCloskey's classic *Make Way for Ducklings* will relish a visit to the **Public Garden** (p. 163), and fans of E. B. White's *The Trumpet of the Swan* certainly will want to ride on the **Swan Boats** (*©* **617/522-1966;** p. 163). Considerably less tame (and much longer) are **whale watches** (p. 178).

   Boston Harbor Cruises, 1 Long Wharf (*©* **877/SEE-WHALE** or 617/227-4321; www.bostonharborcruises.com), offers a cruise called **Codzilla,** which it bills as a "high-speed thrill boat ride." It leaves Long Wharf on the hour from 10am to 4pm daily in the summer; from the shore, you may be able to hear delighted screaming. Tickets cost $19 for adults, $17 for seniors, and $15 for children 4 to 12; reservations are recommended.

   Note: At press time, the **Boston Tea Party Ship & Museum** (*©* **617/269-7150;** www.bostonteapartyship.com) was under renovation and scheduled to reopen in the summer of 2009. The expanded museum complements full-size replicas of the three merchant ships that were raided during the colonial uprising in December 1773. I've written this paragraph at least once a year since a devastating fire shuttered the attraction in 2001, so definitely check ahead before heading out.

WALKING TOURS

Boston By Foot 🔍🔍 (*©* **617/367-2345,** or 617/367-3766 for recorded information; www.bostonbyfoot.com) has a special walk, **"Boston By Little Feet,"** that's geared to children 6 to 12 years old. The 60-minute walk gives a child's-eye view of the architecture along the Freedom Trail and of Boston's role in the American Revolution. Children must be accompanied by an adult, and a map is provided. Tours run from May through October and begin at the statue of Samuel Adams on the Congress Street side of Faneuil Hall, Friday and Saturday at 10am, Sunday at 2pm, rain or shine. The cost is $8 per person.

Blue Hills Trailside Museum *Kids*   At the foot of Great Blue Hill, a 20-minute drive south of Boston, this museum is fun for all ages and especially popular with the under-10 set. Here you'll see replicas of the natural habitats found in the area, displays about Native Americans, and live animal exhibits. Resident animals include owls, honeybees, otters, foxes, snakes, opossum, and turtles. Children can feed the ducks and turkeys. Other activities include climbing the lookout tower and hiking around the 7,500-acre Blue Hills Reservation recreation area. On weekends, there's story time at 11am and natural-history programs at 12:30 and 2pm. Special events and family programs change with the seasons; call ahead to register.

1904 Canton Ave., Milton. *©* 617/333-0690. www.massaudubon.org. Admission $3 adults, $2 seniors, $1.50 children 3–12, free for children under 3 and Massachusetts Audubon Society members. Wed–Sun and Mon holidays 10am–5pm. By car, take I-93 south to Exit 2B (Rte. 138 north).

Boston Children's Museum 🔍🔍 *Kids*   As you approach the Children's Museum, look for the 40-foot-high red-and-white milk bottle out front—and for children and their chronological-adult companions racing each other to the entrance. The under-11 set is the target audience for this delightful museum, but it appeals to the little kid in everyone.

   The museum reopened in April 2007 after an ambitious expansion project added 23,000 square feet of space and overhauled the 75,000-square-foot interior of the converted wool warehouse. As they explore, beginning in the glass-enclosed lobby, young visitors can stick with their adults or wander on their own, learning, doing, and role-playing. A three-story-high climbing structure, the **New Balance Climb,** incorporates motor skills and problem-solving. Other favorite hands-on exhibits include physical experiments (such as creating giant soap bubbles) in **Science Playground; Johnny's Workbench,** a souped-up version of puttering in the garage; and **Boats Afloat,** which has a replica of the bridge of a working boat and an 800-gallon play tank modeled after the Fort Point Channel, in front of the museum. You can explore **Boston Black,** which celebrates Boston's black history and culture; the **Japanese House,** a 2-story replica of a residence in Kyoto (Boston's sister city); or, from May 2008 through January 4, 2009, an exhibit that introduces the children of Boston to the **Children of Hangzhou, China.** Children under 4 and their caregivers have a special room, **Playspace,** that's packed with toys and activities.

Check ahead for information about traveling exhibitions and special programs. And be sure to check out the excellent gift shop (as if you have a choice).

300 Congress St. (Museum Wharf). © 617/426-8855. www.bostonchildrensmuseum.org. Admission $10 adults, $8 children 2–15 and seniors, $2 children age 1, free for children under 1; Fri 5–9pm $1 for all. Sat–Thurs 10am–5pm; Fri 10am–9pm. Closed Thanksgiving, Dec 25, and until noon Jan 1. T: Red Line to South Station, from South Station walk north on Atlantic Ave. 1 block (past Federal Reserve Bank), turn right onto Congress St., then walk 2 blocks (across bridge). Or Silver Line to Courthouse; walk toward downtown and turn left at the Fort Point Channel. Call for information about discounted parking.

Franklin Park Zoo *(Kids)*   This enjoyable, engaging attraction lies some distance from downtown Boston; animal-mad families won't mind the cab ride or trek on public transit. The centerpiece is the **Tropical Forest** exhibit, a sprawling complex that houses more than 50 species of animals. Here you might have a close encounter with a Western lowland gorilla (Little Joe, who made international headlines by literally going over the wall in 2003, is secure in a redesigned enclosure) or see a pygmy hippo. Kids find the hands-on **Franklin Farm** both entertaining and educational. **Tigers, lions,** and **giraffes** (with their zebra friends) have their own turf, and the **Serengeti Crossing** and **Outback Trail** exhibits assemble species from their respective continents—African zebras, ibex, and ostriches, and Australian kangaroos, emus, and cockatoos. From June to September, you can visit the popular, colorful **Butterfly Landing** enclosure.

Allow at least half a day for a visit, and try to budget for a cab ride in at least one direction. Franklin Park is 40 minutes from downtown by subway and bus, and the walk from the main gate and parking area to the entrance is fairly long.

1 Franklin Park Rd. © 617/541-LION. www.franklinparkzoo.org. Admission $11 adults, $9.50 seniors, $6 children 2–12, free for children under 2; first Sat of the month half-price for all. Apr–Sept Mon–Fri 10am–5pm, Sat–Sun and holidays 10am–6pm; Oct–Mar daily 10am–4pm. T: Orange Line to Forest Hills or Red Line to Andrew, then bus no. 16 to the main entrance, or a $15 cab ride from central Boston. Check website for driving directions and information about winter discounts.

10 Organized Tours

ORIENTATION TOURS

GUIDED WALKING TOURS   Even if you usually prefer to explore on your own, I heartily recommend a walking tour with **Boston By Foot** *(star star)*, 77 N. Washington St. (© 617/367-2345, or 617/367-3766 for recorded information; www.bostonby foot.com). From May to October, the nonprofit educational corporation conducts historical and architectural tours that focus on particular neighborhoods or themes. The rigorously trained guides are volunteers who encourage questions. Buy tickets

($12 adults, $8 children 6–12) from the guide; reservations are not required. The 90-minute tours take place rain or shine.

Note: All excursions from Faneuil Hall start at the statue of Samuel Adams on Congress Street.

The **Heart of the Freedom Trail** tour starts at Faneuil Hall daily at 10am and on Saturday at 2pm. Tours of **Beacon Hill** begin at the foot of the State House steps on Beacon Street weekdays at 5:30pm, Saturday at 10am, and Sunday at 2pm. Other tours and meeting places are **Victorian Back Bay,** on the front steps of Trinity Church, 5:30pm Monday and 10am Friday and Sunday; the **North End,** at Faneuil Hall, 2pm Friday and Saturday, 1pm Sunday; and **Literary Landmarks,** in front of Borders, 10–24 School St., 10am Saturday.

Boston Underfoot looks at subterranean technology, including the subway and the depression of the Central Artery. It starts at Faneuil Hall Sunday at 2pm and costs $14 (including subway fare). On the last Sunday of each month, a special tour ($15) covers a particular subject or area such as Art Deco design or Harvard Square. In addition, the company offers themed holiday strolls and off-season group tours.

For information about other guided walking tours of the **Freedom Trail** (with a costumed Freedom Trail Player, or free with a National Park Service ranger) see the section "The Freedom Trail," on p. 148.

The **Boston Park Rangers** (© 617/635-7383; www.cityofboston.gov/parks) offer free guided walking tours. The best-known focus is the **Emerald Necklace,** a loop of green spaces designed by pioneering American landscape architect Frederick Law Olmsted, including Boston Common, the Public Garden, the Commonwealth Avenue Mall, the Muddy River in the Fenway, Olmsted Park, Jamaica Pond, the Arnold Arboretum, and Franklin Park. The full walk takes 6 hours; a typical offering is a tour of one of the sites. Call or surf ahead for schedules.

"DUCK" TOURS   The most unusual and enjoyable way to see Boston is with **Boston Duck Tours** ✸✸✸ (© 800/226-7442 or 617/267-DUCK; www.bostonduck tours.com). The tours, offered late March through November only, are pricey but great fun. Sightseers board a "duck," a reconditioned World War II amphibious landing craft, behind the Prudential Center on Huntington Avenue or at the Museum of Science. The 80-minute narrated tour begins with a quick but comprehensive jaunt around the city. Then the duck lumbers down a ramp, splashes into the Charles River, and goes for a spin around the basin.

Tickets, available at the Prudential Center, the Museum of Science, and Faneuil Hall, are $29 for adults, $25 for seniors and students, $19 for children 3 to 11, and

---

Finds **Behind the Scenes at the BSO**

From October through early May, free volunteer-led tours of **Symphony Hall,** 301 Massachusetts Ave. (© **617/266-1492;** www.bso.org), take visitors all around the landmark building and relate the Boston Symphony Orchestra's fascinating history. The 1-hour tours start on Wednesday at 4:30pm, except during the last 3 weeks of December, and on the first Saturday of each month at 1:30pm. Reservations aren't necessary; meet in the lobby at the Mass. Ave. entrance. For information about performances, see p. 224.

(*Moments* Moon River, Moon Harbor

Fire up the camera as you approach the water. Every **bridge** that crosses the river between Boston and Cambridge affords an excellent perspective. If your travels take you to the area around the Esplanade or Kendall Square (T: Red Line to Charles/MGH or Kendall/MIT), wander out onto the **Longfellow Bridge,** especially at twilight—the views of the river are splendid, and if you hit it just right, the moon appears to shine out of the Hancock Tower.

In warm weather, check the papers for the time of moonrise and stroll down to the plaza at the end of **Long Wharf** (T: Blue Line to Aquarium). The full moon appears to rise out of the Boston Harbor Islands, and because it's so close to the horizon, it looks huge. For astronomical reasons, this only works in the summer, but boy, is it cool.

$5 for children under 3. Tours run every 30 or 60 minutes from 9am to 30 minutes before sunset, and they usually sell out. You can buy tickets online or in person. Try to buy same-day tickets early in the day, or ask about the limited number of tickets available starting 30 days in advance. Reservations are accepted only for groups of 20 or more. No tours December through mid-March.

TROLLEY TOURS   The ticket vendors who clamor for your business wherever tourists gather will claim that no visit is complete without a day on a trolley. Sometimes that's true: if you're unable to walk long distances, are short on time, or are traveling with children. A narrated tour on a trolley (actually a bus chassis with a trolley body) can give you an overview of the city before you focus on specific attractions, or you can use the all-day pass to hit as many places as possible in 8 hours or so. In some neighborhoods, notably the North End, the trolleys stop some distance from the attractions—don't believe a ticket seller who tells you otherwise. Because Boston is so pedestrian-friendly, a trolley tour isn't the best choice for the able-bodied and unencumbered making a long visit, but it can save time and effort. For those who are physically able, I can't say this enough: *Climb down and look around.*

The business is extremely competitive, with various firms offering different stops in an effort to distinguish themselves from the rest. All cover the major attractions and offer informative narratives and anecdotes in their 90- to 120-minute tours; most offer free reboarding if you want to visit the attractions. Each tour is only as good as its guide, and quality varies widely—every few years a TV station or newspaper runs an "exposé" of the wacky information a tour guide is passing off as fact. Have a grain of salt ready. If you have time, you might even chat up guides in the waiting area and choose the one you like best.

Trolley tickets cost $29 to $40 for adults, $16 or less for children. Most companies offer online discounts and reservations, and you may find discount coupons at visitor information centers and hotel-lobby brochure racks. Boarding spots are at hotels, historic sites, and tourist information centers. Busy waiting areas are near the New England Aquarium, the Park Street T stop, and the corner of Boylston Street and Charles Street South, across from Boston Common. Each company paints its cars a different color. They include orange-and-green **Old Town Trolley Tours** (© **617/269-7150;** www.trolleytours.com); **Beantown Trolleys** (© **800/343-1328** or 781/986-6100; www.grayline.com), which say "Gray Line" but are red; and silver **CityView Trolleys**

(© 617/363-7899; www.cityviewtrolleys.com). The **Super Trolley Tours** (© 617/742-1440; www.bostonsupertrolleytours.com) vehicle is white; its narration is available translated into Japanese, Spanish, French, German, and Italian.

SIGHTSEEING CRUISES

Take to the water for a taste of Boston's rich maritime history or a daylong break from walking and driving. You can cruise around the harbor or go all the way to Provincetown. The **sightseeing cruise** ★★ season runs from **April through November,** with spring and fall offerings often restricted to weekends. Check websites for discount coupons before you leave home. If you're traveling in a large group, call ahead for information about reservations and discounted tickets. If you're prone to seasickness, check the size of the vessel for your tour before buying tickets; larger boats provide more cushioning and comfort than smaller ones.

Tip: Before taking a cruise just for the sake of taking a cruise, weigh the investment of time and money against your group's interests. Especially if kids are along, you might be better off with an excursion that targets a destination—the Charlestown Navy Yard (see the box titled "On the Cheap"), the Boston Harbor Islands (see the box titled "A Vacation in the Islands" on p. 183), or Boston Light (see the box titled "Trip the Light Fantastic" on p. 177)—than with a pricey narrated cruise.

The largest company is **Boston Harbor Cruises,** 1 Long Wharf (© 877/SEE-WHALE or 617/227-4321; www.bostonharborcruises.com). Ninety-minute **historic sightseeing cruises,** which tour the Inner and Outer harbors, depart from Long Wharf daily May through September at 11am, 1pm, and 3pm, with extra excursions at busy times. Tickets are $19 for adults, $17 for seniors, and $15 for children 4 to 12; tickets for the sunset cruise (6 or 7pm) are $1 more. The 45-minute **USS *Constitution* cruise** takes you around the Inner Harbor and docks at the Charlestown Navy Yard so that you can go ashore and visit "Old Ironsides." Tours leave Long Wharf daily May through November hourly from 10:30am to 4:30pm, and on the hour from the Navy Yard from 11am to 5pm. The cruise is $14 for adults, $12 for seniors, and $10 for children.

Massachusetts Bay Lines (© 617/542-8000; www.massbaylines.com) offers 55-minute **harbor tours** from Memorial Day to Columbus Day. Cruises leave Rowes Wharf on the hour from 11am to 6pm (there's no 6pm cruise after Labor Day); the price is $16 for adults, $12 for children and seniors. The 90-minute sunset cruise leaves nightly at 7pm from Memorial Day to September 1, and at 6pm through mid-October. The 90-minute moonlight cruise leaves at 8:45pm on Friday and Saturday from mid-June to early September; call for times in early summer and fall. Sunset and moonlight cruises costs $19 for adults, $16 for seniors and children.

The **Charles Riverboat Company** (© 617/621-3001; www.charlesriverboat.com) offers 60-minute narrated cruises from the CambridgeSide Galleria mall daily May through October. Tours of the **lower Charles River basin** start at 11:30am and 12:45,

---

Value **On the Cheap**

You don't have to take a tour to take a cruise. The MBTA runs a **ferry** that connects Long Wharf and the Charlestown Navy Yard. It costs $1.70, is included in the MBTA's 7-day LinkPass, and makes a good final leg of the Freedom Trail.

Finds Trip the Light Fantastic

North America's oldest lighthouse, **Boston Light** ✸✸, is the only lighthouse in the country that's still staffed (by the Coast Guard). Built on **Little Brewster Island** in 1716, it fell to the British in 1776 and was rebuilt in 1783. Excursions to the 102-foot lighthouse include a narrated cruise, 90 minutes to explore the island, and a chance to climb the spiral stairs to the top (you must be 50-in. tall). The 3½-hour tours leave from the Moakley Courthouse at Fan Pier, 2 Northern Ave., from late June to early October on Thursday at 10am and Friday through Sunday at 10am and 1:30pm. Tickets cost $28 for adults, $25 for seniors and students, $17 for children 3 to 11, free for children under 3. Only 48 people may take each tour; reservations (✆ **617/223-8666;** www.bostonislands.com) are strongly recommended.

2, 3:15, and 4:30pm. A tour of the **Charles River lock system and Boston Harbor** begins at 10am. The **sunset cruise** runs daily from June through August; call to confirm times. Tickets cost $13 for adults, $10 for seniors, and $6 for children 2 to 12.

DAY TRIPS   Two companies serve **Provincetown** ✸✸✸, at the tip of Cape Cod. On a day trip, you'll have time for world-class people-watching, strolling around the novelty shops and art galleries, lunching on seafood, and—if you're quick—a trip to the famous beaches. However, you'll have to forgo the hopping gay nightlife scene unless you've planned a longer excursion. (For in-depth coverage of Provincetown and other Cape Cod locales, consult *Frommer's Cape Cod, Nantucket & Martha's Vineyard* or *Frommer's New England*.)

Bay State Cruise Company (✆ **866/90-FERRY** or 617/748-1428; www.baystate cruises.com) operates high-speed and conventional service to Provincetown. High-speed service takes half as long and costs twice as much as the conventional excursion, which is a time-honored New England tradition that's especially popular with families. Trips leave from the Seaport World Trade Center Marine Terminal, 200 Seaport Blvd. To get to the pier, take the Silver Line bus from South Station to the World Trade Center stop, the $10 water taxi (✆ **617/422-0392;** www.citywatertaxi.com) from locations around the harbor, or a regular taxi (when you reserve your cruise, ask the clerk for the best way to reach the pier from your hotel).

Fast ferry service on the *Provincetown III* takes 90 minutes and operates 3 times a day from mid-May to mid-October. The round-trip fare is $71 for adults, $65 for seniors, and $50 for children 3 to 12, plus $5 each way for your bike. Reservations are recommended. **M/V *Provincetown II*** sails weekends only from late June through early September. It leaves at 9:30am for the 3-hour trip to Provincetown, at the tip of Cape Cod. The return trip leaves at 3:30pm, giving you 3 hours for shopping and sightseeing in P-town. The same-day round-trip fare is $33 for adults, free for children. Bringing a bike costs $5 extra each way.

Boston Harbor Cruises, 1 Long Wharf (✆ **877/SEE-WHALE** or 617/227-4321; www.bostonharborcruises.com), operates catamarans that make the trip in just 90 minutes. They operate daily Memorial Day through Columbus Day, twice a day Monday through Wednesday and three times daily Thursday to Sunday, with extra runs on summer weekends. The round-trip fare is $71 for adults, $65 for seniors, and $60 for children 4 to 12.

WHALE WATCHING

For whale-watching trips from Cape Ann, see the box titled "A Whale of an Adventure" on p. 265.

The **New England Aquarium** (© 617/973-5200 for information, 617/973-5206 for tickets; www.newenglandaquarium.org; p. 147) runs **whale watches** 🦑🦑 daily from May through mid-October and on weekends in April and late October. You'll travel several miles out to sea to Stellwagen Bank, the feeding ground for the whales as they migrate from Newfoundland to Provincetown. Allow 3½ to 5 hours. Tickets are $36 for adults, $33 for seniors and college students, $30 for children 3 to 11. Children must be 3 years old and at least 30 inches tall. Reservations are strongly recommended; you can also buy tickets online, subject to a service charge.

With its onboard exhibits and vast experience, the aquarium offers the best whale watches in Boston. If they're booked, other companies offer whale watches: **Boston Harbor Cruises** (© 877/SEE-WHALE or 617/227-4321; www.bostonharbor cruises.com), which operates up to five trips a day on its two high-speed catamarans, trimming the excursion time to 3 hours total; and **Massachusetts Bay Lines** (© 617/542-8000; www.massbaylines.com).

SPECIALTY TOURS

Two excellent resources to investigate before you leave home are the **Boston Center for Adult Education** (© 617/267-4430; www.bcae.org) and the **Cambridge Center for Adult Education** (© 617/547-6789; www.ccae.org). Multiple-week courses are the norm, but both schools also schedule single-day classes that last 2 hours or longer. The expert-led offerings include walking tours (often with a focus on local architecture), cooking classes and wine tastings, and workshops about everything from poetry to gardening. Prices start at $23, and preregistration is required.

The **French Library Alliance Française** (© 617/912-0400; www.frenchlib.org) is a cultural center that offers cooking classes as well as intensive language instruction.

FOR HISTORY BUFFS   Historic New England 🌟 (© 617/227-3956; www. historicnewengland.org) offers a fascinating tour that describes and illustrates life in the mansions and garrets of Beacon Hill in 1810. The 2-hour program, "Magnificent and Modest," costs $12 and starts at the Otis House Museum, 141 Cambridge St., at 11am on Saturdays from May to October. The price includes a tour of the museum, and reservations are recommended.

A map of the self-guided tour created by the **Boston Irish Tourism Association** (© 617/696-9880; www.irishheritagetrail.com) is available at the Boston Common and Prudential Center visitor centers. Check the website for an interactive map with pop-ups describing the sites and information about guided tours, which were in the planning stages at press time.

FOR ARCHITECTURE BUFFS   **Check ahead for walking tours and classes with the **Boston Center for Adult Education or **Cambridge Center for Adult Education** (see above).

FOR CRIMINAL-JUSTICE MAJORS   **Free guided tours of the **John Joseph Moakley Federal Courthouse, 1 Courthouse Way, show off the waterfront building's dramatic architecture and introduce visitors to the workings of the justice system. You may even see part of a trial. Docents from **Discovering Justice** (© 617/748-4185; www.discoveringjustice.org) lead the tours (45 min.), which are available to

---

Tips **Missing This Would Be a Crime**

A bailiff at the adjacent Suffolk County Courthouse tipped me off to the wonders of the **John Adams Courthouse,** one of the most beautiful buildings in Boston. Constructed between 1886 and 1894 and expanded in 1910, the courthouse recalls an era when public buildings were more like cathedrals. It is the suitably impressive home of the Supreme Judicial Court, or SJC, the highest court in the Massachusetts system and the oldest (1692) appellate court in the Western Hemisphere. The French Second Empire facade of the courthouse conceals an almost unbelievably elaborate interior dripping with frescoes, moldings, paintings, and sculptures, all surrounding the soaring central space, the Great Hall, which sits beneath a richly decorated vaulted ceiling. The galleries on either side of the lowest level hold exhibits relating to history and the courts; *The Case of Sacco and Vanzetti: Justice on Trial* will be on display during your visit.

Early in the 21st century, the courthouse underwent a complete restoration that transformed it into one of the city's most interesting destinations. The public is welcome to look around or to attend a court session if one is going on. The building is open Monday through Friday from 9am to 5pm, and you and your bags must be inspected before entering. The entrance is at 1 Pemberton Square, hidden in plain sight behind the curving Center Plaza complex on Cambridge Street, across from City Hall Plaza and the Government Center T stop. Head to the second floor and ask for a brochure from the helpful staff of the Public Information Office (© 617/557-1114; www.mass.gov/courts/jaceducation), or arrange in advance to take a tour with **Discovering Justice** (© 617/557-1031; jonhadams@discoveringjustice.org).

---

individuals and groups by appointment only Tuesday through Thursday from 9am to 4pm throughout the year (reserve 2 weeks in advance).

The courthouse is on Fan Pier, off Old Northern Avenue across the Fort Point Channel from the Coast Guard building at 408 Atlantic Ave. You can walk from downtown or take the Silver Line bus from South Station. To enter the heavily guarded courthouse, adults must show two forms of ID (one of which must have a photo), and everyone must temporarily surrender his or her cellphone. You don't have to take a tour to enter—local office workers often visit the second-floor cafeteria, which has decent food and a breathtaking view.

FOR PEDAL PUSHERS   A group bicycle tour with **Urban AdvenTours** (© 800/979-3370 [tickets] or 617/233-7595 [info]; www.urbanadventours.com) covers more in 2½ to 3 hours than you could ever see on foot. The diverse offerings include an "insider's" overview as well as tours that focus on a particular neighborhood, art and architecture, and photography. You can also request a customized special-interest excursion. Prices begin at $50 per person and include bicycle and helmet rental. You get a break on the price if you supply your own bike or if you opt for the self-guided option, but I can't recommend that for out-of-towners—the supervision of a guide who's experienced in Boston's terrifying traffic is well worth the money.

FOR SHUTTERBUGS   The unusual offerings of **PhotoWalks** (© 617/851-2273; www.photowalks.com) combine narrated walking tours with photography tips. On a 2-hour stroll around Beacon Hill, the Public Garden, or the Freedom Trail, visitors learn to look at Boston from (literally) a different angle—that of a creative photographer. Adults pay $30, students with ID $20, and youths 12 to 17 $15. Tours run several times a week from April through October, and by appointment during the winter. Call or surf ahead for reservations.

FOR MOVIE FANS   Boston Movie Tours (© 866/MOVIE-45; www.boston movietours.net) boast that they offer "behind-the-scenes trivia and insider gossip" about the city's incarnations on the silver and small screens—a busy undertaking now that there's film production going on all over the state. Guides offer regularly updated info about the local color in *The Departed, Good Will Hunting, Mystic River, Legally Blonde,* and, of course, *Cheers,* among other projects. The 90-minute walking tours ($20 adults, $17 seniors and students, $10 children 6–12) and 2½-hour mini-coach or "Theater-on-Wheels" tours ($35 adults, $32 seniors and students, $25 children) operate Wednesday through Monday from April through October. Check start times and locations when you make reservations, which are strongly recommended.

FOR HORROR-MOVIE FANS   Ghosts & Gravestones (© 617/269-3626; www. ghostsandgravestones.com) covers burial grounds and other shiver-inducing areas in a trolley and on foot, with a guide dressed as a gravedigger. The 2-hour tour starts at dusk on weekends in April and May, nightly from Memorial Day weekend through October. It costs $34 for adults, $21 for children 3 to 12. Reservations are required.

FOR FOODIES   A cooking or wine-tasting class makes an excellent, if pricey, break from shopping and sightseeing. Resources to check out before you leave home include: **Boston University's** Seminars in the Arts and Culinary Arts (© 617/353-9852; www.bu.edu/foodandwine); the **Cambridge School of Culinary Arts** (© 617/354-2020; www.cambridgeculinary.com); the **Boston Vegetarian Society** (© 617/424-8846; www.bostonveg.org); the **Elephant Walk** restaurant (see p. 128; © 617/285-0410 or 617/285-1056; www.elephantwalk.com/Classes); and **Stir,** which is run by Barbara Lynch of No. 9 Park fame (© 617/423-STIR; www.stirboston.com). Winter visitors can check ahead for classes during the **Boston Wine Festival** (see p. 26; © 888/660-WINE; bostonwinefestival.net).

A neighborhood resident offers **North End Market Tours** (© 617/523-6032; www.northendmarkettours.com), 3½-hour excursions that stop at many of the shops in the legendary Italian-American stronghold. Tours include product tastings, shopping and cooking tips, and plenty of local lore. They cost $50 (including tax) per person. The same company offers a 3½-hour **Chinatown Market Tour;** the $60 fee includes a dim sum lunch. Visit the website to register and pay in advance.

Old Town Trolley (© 617/269-7010; www.historictours.com) offers the 3-hour **Boston Chocolate Tour** on weekends from January through mid-April. The $75 tour includes three restaurants noted for their chocolate desserts; reservations are required.

11 Outdoor Pursuits

The **Department of Conservation & Recreation,** or DCR (© 617/626-1250; www. state.ma.us/dcr), oversees outdoor activities on public lands across the state through its divisions of Urban Parks & Recreation and State Parks & Recreation. (The Division of Urban Parks & Recreation replaced the Metropolitan District Commission, a name that still appears on many signs.) The incredibly helpful website includes descriptions of properties and activities, and has a planning area to help you make the most of your time.

BEACHES

The beaches in Boston proper are not worth the trouble. Besides being bone-chilling, Boston Harbor water is subject to being declared unsafe for swimming. If you want to swim, book a hotel with a pool. If you want the sand-between-your-toes experience, visit the North Shore or Walden Pond in Concord. See chapter 11 or consult the DCR (see the introduction to this section) for information on suburban beaches.

BIKING

Even the few expert cyclists who feel comfortable with Boston's layout will be better off in Cambridge, which has many bike lanes (Boston's first are in the planning stage), or on the area's many bike paths. State law requires that children under 12 wear helmets. Bicycles are forbidden on buses and the Green Line at all times and during rush hours on the other lines of the subway system.

On summer Sundays from 11am to 7pm, a flat 1½-mile stretch of **Memorial Drive** ⊛ in Cambridge, from Western Avenue to the Eliot Bridge (Central Sq. to west Cambridge), closes to cars. It's also popular with pedestrians and in-line skaters, and it can get quite crowded. The **Dr. Paul Dudley White Charles River Bike Path** ⊛⊛ is an 18-mile circuit that begins at Science Park (near the Museum of Science) and runs along both sides of the river as far as Watertown. You can enter and exit at many points along the way. Bikers share the path with joggers and in-line skaters, especially in Boston near the Esplanade and in Cambridge near Harvard Square. The DCR (see the introduction to this section) maintains this path and the 5-mile **Pierre Lallement Bike Path,** in Southwest Corridor Park, which starts behind Copley Place and runs through the South End and Roxbury along the route of the MBTA Orange Line to Franklin Park. The 11-mile **Minuteman Bikeway** ⊛⊛ (www.minutemanbikeway. org) starts at Alewife station at the end of the Red Line in Cambridge. It runs through Arlington and Lexington to Bedford along an old railroad bed and is a wonderful way to reach the historic sites in Lexington.

Rental shops require you to show a driver's license or passport and leave a deposit using a major credit card. Back Bay Bicycles offers hourly rentals for around $10 an hour, with a minimum of 2 hours. Daily flat rates start at $25. Check out **Back Bay Bicycles,** 366 Commonwealth Ave., near Mass. Ave. (© **617/247-2336;** www.back baybicycles.com); **Boston Bicycle,** 842 Beacon St., about 3 blocks from Kenmore Square (© **617/236-0752;** www.cambridgebicycle.com); and **Cambridge Bicycle,** 259 Massachusetts Ave. (© **617/876-6555;** www.cambridgebicycle.com), near MIT. For additional information, contact **MassBike** (© **617/542-BIKE;** www.massbike.org).

GOLF

You won't get far in the suburbs without seeing a golf course, and given the sport's popularity, you won't be the only one looking. If possible, opt for the lower prices and smaller crowds that you'll find on weekdays. The **Massachusetts Golf Association** (© **800/356-2201** or 774/430-9100; www.mgalinks.org) represents more than 400 golf courses around the state. It has a searchable online database and will send you a list of courses on request.

One of the best public courses in the area, **Newton Commonwealth Golf Course,** 212 Kenrick St., Newton (© **617/630-1971;** www.sterlinggolf.com), is a challenging

18-hole Donald Ross design. It's 5,305 yards from the blue tees, par is 70, and greens fees are $30 on weekdays, $37 on weekends.

Within the city limits is the legendary 6,009-yard **William J. Devine Golf Course,** in Franklin Park, Dorchester (© **617/265-4084**). As a Harvard student, Bobby Jones sharpened his game on the 18-hole, par-70 course, which is managed by the city parks department. Greens fees are $39 on weekdays, $48 on weekends.

Less challenging but with more of a neighborhood feel is the 9-hole, par-35 **Fresh Pond Golf Course,** 691 Huron Ave., Cambridge (© **617/349-6282**; www.fresh pondgolf.com). The 3,161-yard layout adjoins the Fresh Pond Reservoir, and there's water on four holes. It charges $22, or $32 to go around twice, on weekdays; $26 and $38, respectively, on weekends.

GYMS

If your hotel doesn't have a health club, your best bet is to ask the concierge or front desk staff to recommend one nearby; you may receive a pass good for free or discounted admission. Guests at the **Ritz-Carlton, Boston Common,** have the use of the over-the-top facilities at the 100,000-square-foot Sports Club/LA, which is otherwise closed to nonmembers. Other hotels with good health clubs (see chapter 5) include the **Boston Harbor Hotel,** the **Charles Hotel,** the **Four Seasons Hotel,** the **Hilton Boston Logan Airport,** the **InterContinental Boston,** and the **Royal Sonesta Hotel.**

The "Y" (www.ymcaboston.org) offers the best combination of facilities and value. The **Wang YMCA of Chinatown,** 8 Oak St. W., off Washington St. (© **617/426-2237**), is convenient to downtown; the **Central Branch YMCA,** 316 Huntington Ave. (© **617/536-7800**), is near Symphony Hall. A 1-day pass costs $10 ($5 if you belong to the Y at home) and includes the use of the pool, gym, weight room, and fitness center. **Fitcorp** (© **617/375-5600;** www.fitcorp.com) charges $20 for a guest pass and offers well-equipped facilities but no pool. It has a dozen area branches, including 1 Beacon St., near Government Center (© **617/248-9797**); 125 Summer St., in the Financial District (© **617/261-4855**); and 197 Clarendon St. (© **617/933-5090**) and 800 Boylston St., in the Prudential Center (© **617/262-2050**), both in the Back Bay. A day pass costs $20 at women-only, no-pool **Healthworks** (www.healthworksfitness.com), which has well-equipped facilities in the Back Bay at 441 Stuart St. (© **617/859-7700**) and in Cambridge at the Porter Square Shopping Center, 35 White St. (© **617/497-4454**).

HIKING

For information about hiking in state parks and forests, visit **www.massparks.org**. The **Boston Harbor Islands** offer great hiking; circling the largest island, Peddocks, takes half a day. See the box, "A Vacation in the Islands," p. 183.

ICE SKATING & IN-LINE SKATING

The outdoor ice-skating season runs from mid-November to mid-March, weather permitting. Check ahead for open hours and closures for private events.

The rink at the Boston Common **Frog Pond** ⟨⟨ (© **617/635-2120;** www.cityof boston.gov/parks) is an extremely popular cold-weather destination. It's an open surface with an ice-making system and a clubhouse. Admission is $4 for adults and free for children under 14; skate rental costs $8 for adults, $5 for kids. The rink gets unbelievably crowded on weekend afternoons, so try to go in the morning or on a weekday.

Finds **A Vacation in the Islands**

Majestic ocean views, hiking trails, historic sites, rocky beaches, nature walks, campsites, and picnic areas abound in New England. To find them all together, head east (yes, east) of Boston to the **Boston Harbor Islands** (© 617/223-8666; www.bostonislands.com). The national park area's unspoiled beauty is a welcome break from the urban landscape, and the islands are not well known, even to many longtime Bostonians. Thirty-four islands dot the Outer Harbor, and at least a half dozen are open for exploring, camping, swimming, and more. Bring a sweater or jacket. Plan a day trip or even an overnight trip, but note that only Georges Island has fresh water, and management strongly suggests bringing your own.

Ferries run to **Georges Island,** home of Fort Warren (1833), which held Confederate prisoners during the Civil War. You can investigate on your own or take a ranger-led tour. The island has a visitor center, refreshment area, fishing pier, picnic area, and wonderful view of Boston's skyline. Allow at least half a day, longer if you plan to take the free water taxi to **Lovell, Peddocks, Bumpkin,** or **Grape Island,** all of which have picnic areas and campsites. Lovell Island also has the remains of a fort (Fort Standish). **Spectacle Island,** which opened to the public in 2006, holds more than 3 million cubic yards of material dug up during the Big Dig—then sealed, covered with topsoil, and landscaped to allow recreational use.

Harbor Express (© 617/222-6999; www.harborexpress.com) serves Georges Island (30 min. or less) and Spectacle Island (15 min.) from Long Wharf. Round-trip tickets cost $14 for adults, $10 for seniors, $8 for children 3 to 11; the island-to-island fare is $5. Cruises depart daily on the hour from 9am to 5pm in the summer, more often on weekends, less frequently in the spring and fall. In the off season, check ahead for winter wildlife excursions (scheduled occasionally). Water taxis and admission to the islands are free.

A public-private National Park Partnership administers the Boston Harbor Islands National Recreation Area (www.nps.gov/boha). For more information, visit the website, consult the staff at the **kiosk on Long Wharf,** or contact the **Friends of the Boston Harbor Islands** (© 617/740-4290; www.fbhi. org). The Friends coordinate a variety of cruises on and around the harbor throughout the summer and fall; check ahead for details.

Kendall Square Community Skating, 300 Athenaeum St., East Cambridge (© 617/492-0941; www.paddleboston.com), is an open rink in a courtyard not far from MIT. It charges $3 for adults, $2 for seniors and students, $1 for children under 11; skate rentals are $5. Validated discounted parking is available.

A favorite spot for in-line skaters is the **Esplanade,** between the Back Bay and the Charles River. It continues onto the bike path that runs to Watertown and back (p. 181), but after you leave the Esplanade, the pavement isn't totally smooth, which can lead to mishaps. Your best bet is to wait for a Sunday in the summer, when **Memorial Drive** near Harvard Square in Cambridge closes to traffic from 11am to

7pm. It's a perfect surface. Unless you're confident of your ability and your knowledge of Boston traffic, stay off the streets.

To rent skates or blades, visit the **Beacon Hill Skate Shop,** 135 Charles St. S. (*©* **617/482-7400**). It's not on Beacon Hill but near the Theater District, not too far from the Esplanade, and has a knowledgeable staff. Expect to pay about $15 a day. The **InLine Club of Boston's** website (www.sk8net.com) offers up-to-date event and safety information.

JOGGING

The **Dr. Paul Dudley White Charles River Bike Path** *©©* is also a jogging route. The 18-mile loop along the water is extremely popular because it's car-free (except at intersections), scenic, and generally safe. The bridges that connect Boston and Cambridge allow for circuits of various lengths. Be careful around abutments, where you can't see far ahead. Don't jog at night, and try not to go alone. Visit the DCR website (see the introduction to this section) to view a map that gives distances. If the river's not convenient, the concierge or desk staff at your hotel probably can provide a map with suggested jogging routes. As in any other city, stay out of park areas at night.

SAILING

Sailboats fill the Charles River basin all summer and skim across the Inner Harbor in all but the coldest weather. Your options during a short stay aren't especially cost-effective, but they are fun.

The best deal is with **Community Boating,** 21 David Mugar Way, on the Esplanade (*©* **617/523-1038;** www.community-boating.org). Visitors pay $100 for 2 days of unlimited use in the Charles River Basin, a gorgeous but congested patch of water between the Back Bay and Cambridge's Kendall Square. The oldest public sailing facility in the country offers lessons and boating programs for children and adults from April through November. The fleet includes 13- to 23-foot sailboats as well as Windsurfers and kayaks. The **Boston Sailing Center,** Lewis Wharf, off Atlantic Avenue (*©* **617/227-4198;** www.bostonsailingcenter.com), offers lessons for sailors of all ability levels. The center is open year-round (even for "frostbite" racing in the winter). The least expensive 30-day mini-membership costs $350.

TENNIS

Public courts are available throughout the city at no charge. Well-maintained courts that seldom get busy until after work are at several spots on the Southwest Corridor Park in the **South End** (there's a nice one near **West Newton St.**). The courts on **Boston Common** and in **Charlesbank Park,** overlooking the river next to the bridge to the Museum of Science, are more crowded during the day. To find the court nearest you, ask the concierge or desk staff at your hotel or visit the DCR website (www. state.ma.us/dcr).

12 Spectator Sports

Boston has long enjoyed a well-deserved reputation as a great sports town. The Red Sox, Celtics, and New England Patriots have been more successful and popular than the Bruins recently, but local fans are nothing if not loyal—just ask all those Celtics fans who waited 22 years between NBA championships. Fans are also passionate about college sports, particularly hockey, in which the Division I schools are fierce rivals.

The **TD Banknorth Garden,** 100 Legends Way (Causeway St.; © **617/624-1000** for events line or 617/931-2000 for Ticketmaster; www.tdbanknorthgarden.com), is open for tours on the hour from 11am to 3pm daily, depending on the arena schedule. Tours concentrate on the displays in the fifth- and sixth-floor concourses, where the **Sports Museum of New England** (© **617/624-1235;** www.sportsmuseum.org) celebrates local teams and athletes of all ages—especially the Celtics and Bruins, who play in the building. Tickets cost $6 for adults, $4 for seniors and children 6 to 17, free for children under 6. Always call ahead; there's no access during events. *Note:* Visitors may not bring any bags, including backpacks and briefcases, into the arena.

Beyond the "big four" professional sports and dozens of college options, several lower-profile pro franchises call the Boston area home. The New England Revolution (© **877/438-7387;** www.revolutionsoccer.net) of **Major League Soccer** plays at Gillette Stadium on Route 1 in Foxboro from April through October. Tickets cost $19 to $37 and are available through Ticketmaster (© **617/931-2000;** www.ticketmaster.com). The Boston Cannons of **Major League Lacrosse** (© **888/847-9700** or 617/746-9933; www.bostoncannons.com) play at Harvard Stadium from mid-May through mid-August; tickets cost $10 to $20. The **Boston Breakers** of Women's Professional Soccer (WPS; © **877/439-2732** or 781/251-2100; www.womensprosoccer.com/boston) plan to resume play in April 2009. The team, a WUSA franchise before that league went under, will play at Harvard Stadium beginning in April 2009; check the website for updates.

BASEBALL

Ho-hum, another World Series championship—that's something you'll *never* hear from a true **Boston Red Sox** fan. The baseball world was still pinching itself over the team's 2004 title, which ended an 86-year dry spell, when the Sox brought home the 2007 crown. "Home" is legendary **Fenway Park** ✪✪✪, and no other experience in all of sports matches watching a game there. Fenway was already selling out well before the 2004 Series, and tickets remain a precious commodity, sky-high prices notwithstanding.

The season runs from early April to early October, later if the team makes the playoffs. The quirkiness of the oldest park in the major leagues (1912), rich with history and atmosphere, only adds to the mystique. A hand-operated scoreboard fronts the 37-foot left-field wall, or "Green Monster." Watch carefully during a pitching change—the left fielder from either team might suddenly disappear into a door in the wall to get out of the sun. Most seats are narrow and uncomfortable, but also gratifyingly close to the field.

One of the most imaginative management teams in baseball strives to make visiting Fenway worth the big bucks. Yawkey Way turns into a sort of carnival midway for ticketholders before games, with concession stands, live music, and other diversions. New sections of seats keep cropping up in previously unused areas of the ballpark, notably including the section *above* the Green Monster.

Practical concerns: Compared with its modern brethren, Fenway is tiny. Tickets are the most expensive in the majors—a few upper bleacher seats go for $12, but most are in the $25-to-$90 range, with the best dugout boxes topping $300, and that's *if* you pay face value. They go on sale in December; order early. Forced to choose between seats in a low-numbered grandstand section—say, 10 or below—and in the bleachers, go for the bleachers. They can get rowdy during night games, but the view is better from there than from deep in right field. "Monster" seats top out at $120 and go on sale by lottery in batches throughout the season; check the website. A limited

Moments Play Ball!

Fenway Park tours (© 617/226-6666) take visitors around the legendary ball-park. This is an excellent alternative if your budget or schedule doesn't allow for attending a game. Depending on what's going on at the park, a tour may include a walk on the warning track, a stop in the press box, and a visit to the Red Sox Hall of Fame. Tours start on the hour Monday through Saturday from 9am to 4pm, Sunday from noon to 3pm (or 3 hr. before game time, whichever is earlier), in the summer; winter hours end 1 hour earlier, with no tours on Sunday. There are no tours on holidays or before day games. Admission is $12 for adults, $11 for seniors, and $10 for children under 15, and advance individual sales aren't available.

number of same-day standing-room tickets ($20–$30) are available before each game, and fans sometimes return presold tickets, especially if a rainout causes rescheduling. It can't hurt to check, particularly if the team isn't playing well; visit the website and navigate to "Red Sox Replay," or check at the ticket office.

The **Fenway Park ticket office** (© 877/REDSOX-9; www.redsox.com; T: Green Line B, C, or D to Kenmore, or D to Fenway) is at 4 Yawkey Way, near the corner of Brookline Avenue. Tickets for people with disabilities and in no-alcohol sections are available. Smoking is not allowed in the park.

BASKETBALL

The **Boston Celtics** raised their 17th National Basketball Association championship banner to the rafters of the TD Banknorth Garden in 2008. The team's unlikely run to the title captivated even the most jaded fans. The Celtics play from early October to April or May; when a top contender is visiting, getting tickets may be tough. Prices are as low as $10 for some games and top out at $275 ($750 for floor seats). For information, call the Garden (© 617/624-1000; www.nba.com/celtics); for tickets, contact Ticketmaster (© 617/931-2000; www.ticketmaster.com). To reach the Garden, take the MBTA Green or Orange Line or commuter rail to North Station. *Note:* Spectators may not bring any bags, including backpacks and briefcases, into the arena.

FOOTBALL

The **New England Patriots** (© 800/543-1776; www.patriots.com) were playing to standing-room-only crowds even before they won three Super Bowls in 4 years (2002, 2004, and 2005) and famously fizzled out in 2008. The Pats play from August through December or January at Gillette Stadium on Route 1 in Foxboro, about a 45-minute drive south of Boston. Tickets ($49–$169) sell out well in advance, often as part of season-ticket packages. Call or check the website for information on individual ticket sales and resales and public-transit options.

Boston College, another tough ticket, is the state's only Division I-A team. The Eagles play at Alumni Stadium in Chestnut Hill (© 617/552-GOBC; www.bceagles.collegesports.com). The area's Division I-AA teams are **Harvard University,** Harvard Stadium, North Harvard Street, Allston (© 877/GO-HARVARD or 617/495-2211; www.gocrimson.com), and **Northeastern University,** Parsons Field, Kent Street, Brookline (© 617/373-4700; www.gonu.com).

GOLF TOURNAMENTS

At least two of the major tours get within an hour of downtown Boston. Over Labor Day weekend, the **PGA Tour** (www.pgatour.com) visits the Tournament Players Club of Boston, which is actually in suburban Norton (*C* **508/285-3200;** www.thetpcof boston.com). The senior golfers on the **Champions Tour** (www.pgatour.com/s) swing by in late June or July, landing at Nashawtuc Country Club in Concord (*C* **978/610-2700;** www.nashawtuc.com). The senior women on the **Legends Tour** (www.the legendstour.com) stop at suburban Quincy's Granite Links Golf Club (*C* **617/689-1900;** www.granitelinksgolfclub.com) in August. Check ahead for exact dates and other information on golf events, and to see whether the **LPGA** (www.lpga.com) tournament circuit will return to eastern Massachusetts. The *Globe* and *Herald* regularly list numerous amateur events for fun and charity.

HOCKEY

Tickets to see the **Boston Bruins,** one of the NHL's original six teams, are expensive but worth it for hard-core fans. For information, call the TD Banknorth Garden (*C* **617/624-1000;** www.bostonbruins.com); for tickets, contact Ticketmaster (*C* **617/931-2000;** www.ticketmaster.com). To reach the Garden, take the MBTA Green or Orange Line or commuter rail to North Station. *Note:* Spectators may not bring any bags, including backpacks and briefcases, into the arena.

Budget-minded fans who don't have their hearts set on seeing a pro game will be pleasantly surprised by the quality of local **college hockey** *R*. Even for sold-out games, standing-room tickets are usually available the night of the game. The local teams regularly hit the national rankings; they include **Boston College,** Conte Forum, Chestnut Hill (*C* **617/552-GOBC;** www.bceagles.collegesports.com); **Boston University,** Agganis Arena, 928 Commonwealth Ave. (*C* **617/353-3838;** www.bu.edu/ athletics); **Harvard University,** Bright Hockey Center, North Harvard Street, Allston (*C* **877/GO-HARVARD** or 617/495-2211; www.gocrimson.com); and **Northeastern University,** Matthews Arena, St. Botolph Street (*C* **617/373-4700;** www.gonu. com). These four are the Beanpot schools, whose men's teams play a tradition-steeped tournament on the first two Mondays of February at the TD Banknorth Garden. Women's games don't normally sell out; the exception will be the **2009 NCAA Women's Frozen Four** (national semifinals and finals), at Agganis arena on March 20 and 22.

HORSE RACING

Suffolk Downs *R*, 111 Waldemar Ave., East Boston (*C* **617/567-3900;** www. suffolkdowns.com), is one of the best-run smaller tracks in the country. The legendary Seabiscuit raced here; a marker commemorates his storied career. In addition to extensive simulcasting options day and night year-round, the live racing season runs from May to November. The Massachusetts Handicap, or **MassCap,** is an important Breeders' Cup prep race run in late September. General admission and weekend preferred parking for live racing cost $2 each. General parking is free all week.

The day's entries appear in the *Globe* and *Herald.* The track is off Route 1A, about 2 miles north of Logan Airport. The MBTA Blue Line has a Suffolk Downs station; wait for the shuttle bus or walk about 10 minutes to the track entrance.

THE MARATHON

Every year on Patriots Day—the third Monday in April—the **Boston Marathon** *RRR* rules the roads from suburban Hopkinton to Copley Square in Boston. Cheering fans line the entire route. An especially nice place to watch is tree-shaded Commonwealth Avenue between Kenmore Square and Mass. Ave., but you'll be in a crowd wherever you stand, particularly near the finish line in front of the Boston Public Library. For information about watching, ask the staff at your hotel or check the daily papers. For information about qualifying, contact the **Boston Athletic Association** (© 617/236-1652; www.bostonmarathon.org).

ROWING

In late October, the **Head of the Charles Regatta** (© 617/868-6200; www.hocr.org) attracts more rowers than any other crew event in the country. Some 4,000 oarsmen and -women race against the clock for 4 miles from the Charles River basin to the Eliot Bridge in west Cambridge. Hundreds of thousands of spectators socialize and occasionally watch the action, which runs nonstop on Saturday afternoon and all day Sunday.

Spring crew racing is more exciting than the "head" format; the course is 2,000m (1¼ miles), and races last just 5 to 7 minutes. Men's and women's collegiate events take place on Saturday mornings in April and early May in the Charles River basin. You'll have a perfect view of the finish line from Memorial Drive between the MIT boathouse and the Hyatt Regency Cambridge hotel. To find out who's racing, check the Friday *Globe* sports section.

8

Boston Strolls

Walking is the best way to see Boston. The narrow, twisting streets that make driving such a headache are a treat for pedestrians, who are never far from something worth seeing. The central city is compact—walking quickly from one end to the other takes about an hour—and abounds with historically and architecturally interesting buildings and neighborhoods.

In this chapter you'll find a tour of Boston's **Back Bay** and one of **Harvard Square** in Cambridge. For information on Boston's most famous walking tour, the 2½-mile **Freedom Trail** ⟨⟨⟨, see chapter 7.

Be sure to wear comfortable shoes, and if you're not inclined to pay designer prices for designer water, bring your own bottle and fill it at your hotel.

WALKING TOUR 1   THE BACK BAY

Start:	The Public Garden (T: Green Line to Arlington).
Finish:	Copley Square.
Time:	2 hours if you make good time, 3 if you detour to the Esplanade, and longer if you do a lot of shopping.
Best Time:	Any time before late afternoon.
Worst Time:	Late afternoon, when people and cars pack the streets. And don't attempt the detour on July 4th, when concertgoers jam the neighborhood. This walk is mostly outdoors, so if the weather is bad, you may find yourself in lots of shops. You decide whether that makes an overcast day a "best" or "worst" time.

The Back Bay is the youngest neighborhood in central Boston, the product of a massive landfill project that transformed the city from 1835 to 1882. It's flat, symmetrical, logically designed—the names of the cross streets go in alphabetical order—and altogether anomalous in Boston's crazy-quilt geography.

Begin your walk in the:

❶ Public Garden

Before the Back Bay was filled in, the Charles River flowed right up to Charles Street, which separates Boston Common from the Public Garden. On the night of April 18, 1775, British troops bound for Lexington and Concord boarded boats to Cambridge ("two if by sea") at the foot of the Common and set off across what's now the Public Garden.

Explore the lagoon, the trees and other flora, and the statuary. Take a ride on the **Swan Boats** (mid-Apr to mid-Sept), and then make your way toward the corner of Charles and Beacon streets, inside the Public Garden (follow the sound of delighted children).

Here you'll see a 35-foot strip of cobblestones topped with the bronze figures that immortalize Robert McCloskey's book:

❷ Make Way for Ducklings

Installed in 1987 and wildly popular since the moment they were unveiled, Nancy Schön's renderings of Mrs. Mallard and her eight babies are irresistible. Mrs. Mallard is 38 inches tall, making her back a bit higher than a tricycle seat, but that doesn't keep people of all ages from climbing on. If you don't know the story of the family's perilous trip to meet Mr. Mallard at the lagoon, ask one of the parents or children you'll find here.

The city bought the site of the Public Garden from private interests in 1824. Planting began in 1837, but it wasn't until the late 1850s that Arlington Street was built and the land permanently set aside. George F. Meacham executed the design.

Cross the lagoon using the little suspension bridge and look for the statue of:

❸ George Washington

Unveiled in 1875, this was Boston's first equestrian statue. It stands 38 feet tall and is considered an excellent likeness of the first president of the United States, an outstanding horseman. The artist, Thomas Ball, was a Charlestown native who worked in Italy. Among his students was noted sculptor Daniel Chester French. Pass through the gate onto Arlington Street. Before you begin exploring in earnest, this is a good place to detour.

TAKE A BREAK
Turn right and walk up Arlington Street to Beacon Street. On your right, across the busy intersection, is **Cheers**, 84 Beacon St. (© **617/227-9605**; www.cheersboston.com), originally the Bull & Finch Pub. The food is tasty enough, but remember: The bar looks nothing like its TV offspring (you'll find a replica of the set at Faneuil Hall Marketplace), and the clientele generally consists of people from everywhere else in the universe except Boston.

Alternatively, turn right on Beacon Street and walk 1 long block to Charles Street. You can pick up food to go at **Panificio**, 144 Charles St. (© **617/227-4340**), or indulge in a delicious French-style pastry at **Cafe Vanille**, 70 Charles St. (© **617/523-9200**). This street is also a promising place for a **shopping** break (see chapter 9).

Once you've picked up something to eat, backtrack along Beacon Street past Arlington Street to Embankment Road and turn right. Take the Arthur Fiedler Footbridge across Storrow Drive to the Esplanade, and unpack your food near the giant head of:

❹ Arthur Fiedler

Installed in 1985, this sculpture by Ralph Helmick consists of sheets of aluminum that eerily capture the countenance of the legendary conductor of the Boston Pops, who died in 1979. The amphitheater to the right is the **Hatch Shell,** where the Pops perform free during the week leading up to and including July 4th.

When you're ready, retrace your steps to the corner of Arlington Street and Commonwealth Avenue. This is the:

❺ Boston Center for Adult Education

Constructed in 1904 as a private home, this building at 5 Commonwealth Ave., known as the Gamble Mansion, gained a huge ballroom in 1912. The building went up for sale in 2007, shortly before the bottom started falling out of the real estate market, so you may have to admire it from outside. If you can gain entry and the ornate ballroom is not in use for a class or a function (it's popular for weddings), you're welcome to have a look. The BCAE (© **617/267-4430;** www.bcae.org), established in 1933, is the oldest continuing-education institution in New England.

You're now on the 8-block **Commonwealth Avenue Mall.** This graceful promenade is the centerpiece of architect Arthur Gilman's design of the Back Bay.

Walking Tour 1: The Back Bay

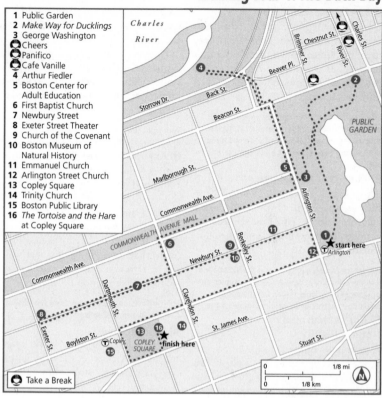

1 Public Garden
2 *Make Way for Ducklings*
3 George Washington
Cheers
Panifico
Cafe Vanille
4 Arthur Fiedler
5 Boston Center for Adult Education
6 First Baptist Church
7 Newbury Street
8 Exeter Street Theater
9 Church of the Covenant
10 Boston Museum of Natural History
11 Emmanuel Church
12 Arlington Street Church
13 Copley Square
14 Trinity Church
15 Boston Public Library
16 *The Tortoise and the Hare* at Copley Square

Charles River

PUBLIC GARDEN

Chestnut St.
Charles St.
Brimmer St.
River St.
Beaver Pl.
Back St.
Storrow Dr.
Beacon St.
Marlborough St.
Commonwealth Ave.
COMMONWEALTH AVENUE MALL
Arlington St.
★ start here
Arlington
Newbury St.
Berkeley St.
Commonwealth Ave.
Dartmouth St.
Clarendon St.
St. James Ave.
Stuart St.
Exeter St.
Boylston St.
Copley
COPLEY SQUARE ★ finish here

0   1/8 mi
0   1/8 km

Take a Break

The mall is 100-feet wide (the entire street is 240 ft.) and stretches to Kenmore Square. The elegant Victorian mansions on either side—almost all divided into apartments or in commercial or educational use—are recognized as a great asset, but the apparently random collection of sculptures along the mall is less acclaimed. Judge for yourself as you inspect the art, starting with **Alexander Hamilton,** across Arlington Street from **George Washington.** The most moving sculpture is at Dartmouth Street: The **Vendome Memorial** honors the memory of the nine firefighters who lost their lives in a blaze at the Hotel Vendome in 1972.

Two blocks from the Public Garden, at 110 Commonwealth Ave., at the corner of Clarendon Street, is the:

⑥ First Baptist Church

Built from 1870 to 1872 of Roxbury puddingstone, it originally housed the congregation of the Brattle Street Church (Unitarian), which had been downtown, near Faneuil Hall.

At Clarendon Street or Dartmouth Street, turn left and walk 1 block to:

⑦ Newbury Street

Commonwealth Avenue is the architectural heart of the Back Bay, and Newbury Street is the commercial center. Take some time to roam around here (see chapter 9 for pointers), browsing in the galleries, window-shopping at the boutiques, and watching the chic shoppers.

Walk down Newbury Street to Exeter Street. At 26 Exeter St. is the building that was once the:

❽ Exeter Street Theater

Designed in 1884 as the First Spiritualist Temple, it was a movie house from 1914 to 1984. Once known for the crowds flocking to *The Rocky Horror Picture Show*, it now houses offices and a TGI Friday's restaurant.

When you're ready to continue your stroll (or when your credit cards cry for mercy), turn back toward the Public Garden and seek out three of Newbury Street's oldest buildings, starting with the:

❾ Church of the Covenant

This Gothic revival edifice at 67 Newbury St. was designed by Richard Upjohn and completed in 1867. The stained-glass windows are the work of Louis Comfort Tiffany.

Across the street, set back from the sidewalk at 234 Berkeley St., an opulent store occupies an opulent setting. Now the clothing emporium Louis Boston, this is the original home of the:

❿ Boston Museum of Natural History

A forerunner of the Museum of Science, it was built according to William Preston's French Academic design. The 1864 structure, originally two stories high, still has its original roof, preserved when the building gained a third floor.

Cross Newbury Street again and continue walking toward the Public Garden. On your left, at 15 Newbury St., is:

⓫ Emmanuel Church

The first building completed on Newbury Street, in 1862, this Episcopal church ministers through the arts, so there might be a concert (classical to jazz, solo to orchestral) going on during your visit. Check ahead (© 617/536-3355; www.emmanuel-boston.org) for schedules.

Now you're almost back at the Public Garden. On your left is the swanky Taj Boston hotel, which until 2007 was known as the original **Ritz-Carlton** (1927).

Turn right onto Arlington Street and walk 1 block. On your right, at 351 Boylston St., is the:

⓬ Arlington Street Church

This is the oldest church in the Back Bay, completed in 1861. An interesting blend of Georgian and Italianate details, it's the work of architect Arthur Gilman, who laid out this whole neighborhood. Here you'll find more Tiffany stained glass. Step inside to see the pulpit that was in use in 1788 when the congregation worshipped downtown on Federal Street.

Follow Boylston Street away from the Public Garden. Two blocks up is:

⓭ Copley Square

Enjoy the fountain and visit the farmers' market, which operates Tuesday and Friday afternoons from July through November.

Overlooking the square is one of the most famous church buildings in the United States. This is:

⓮ Trinity Church

H. H. Richardson's Romanesque masterpiece, completed in 1877, is to your left. The church, 206 Clarendon St. (© 617/536-0944; www.trinitychurchboston.org), was built on 4,502 pilings driven into the mud that was once the Back Bay.

⌒Fun Fact The Shape of Things to Come

The **First Baptist Church** is a fine building, but the design is notable mainly because its creators went on to much more famous projects. The architect, **H. H. Richardson,** is best known for nearby **Trinity Church.** The artist who created the frieze, which represents the sacraments, was **Frédéric Auguste Bartholdi,** who designed the **Statue of Liberty.**

> **Fun Fact It's All French to Me**
>
> As you explore the Boston area, you'll keep hearing the name of sculptor **Daniel Chester French**. French (1850–1931) was responsible for the gorgeous doors on the Dartmouth Street side of the **Boston Public Library,** the statue of **John Harvard** in Harvard Yard, and the *Minute Man* statue near the North Bridge in Concord. If you're not a parochial Bostonian, you probably know him best as the sculptor of the seated Abraham Lincoln in the presidential memorial in Washington.

Brochures and guides are available to help you find your way around a building considered one of the finest examples of church architecture in the country. Tours cost $5. It's open daily from 8am to 6pm. Friday organ recitals begin at 12:15pm.

Across Dartmouth Street is the:

⓯ Boston Public Library

The work of architect Charles Follen McKim and many others, the Renaissance revival building was completed in 1895 after 10 years of construction. Its design reflects the significant influence of the Bibliothèque Nationale in Paris. Wander up the steps to check out the building's impressive interior (p. 159). **Daniel Chester French** designed the doors.

Head across the street to Copley Square. In a sense, you've come full circle; as at the Public Garden, you'll see another playful and compelling sculpture by Nancy Schön:

⓰ *The Tortoise & Hare* at Copley Square

Designed to signify the end of the **Boston Marathon** (the finish line is on Boylston St. between Exeter and Dartmouth sts.), this work was unveiled for the 100th anniversary of the event in 1996.

From here you're in a good position to set out for any other part of town or walk a little way in any direction and continue exploring. Copley Place and the Shops at Prudential Center are nearby, Newbury Street is 1 block over, and there's a Green Line T station at Boylston and Dartmouth streets.

WALKING TOUR 2 ⬛ HARVARD SQUARE

Start:	Harvard Square (T: Red Line to Harvard).
Finish:	John F. Kennedy Park.
Time:	2–4 hours, depending on how much time you spend in shops and museums.
Best Time:	Almost any time during the day. The Harvard University Art Museums are free on Saturday morning.
Worst Time:	The first full week of June. You might have trouble gaining admission to Harvard Yard during commencement festivities. The ceremony is Thursday morning; without a ticket, you won't be allowed in.

Popular impressions to the contrary, Cambridge is not exclusively Harvard. In fact, even Harvard Square isn't exclusively Harvard. During a walk around the area, you'll see historic buildings and sights, interesting museums, and notable architecture on and off the university's main campus.

Impressions

One emerged, as one still does, from the subway exit in the Square and faced an old red-brick wall behind which stretched, to my fond eye, what remains still the most beautiful campus in America, the Harvard Yard. If there is any one place in all America that mirrors better all American history, I do not know of it.

—Theodore H. White, *In Search of History* (1978)

Leave the T station by the main entrance (use the ramp to the turnstiles, then take the escalator) and emerge in the heart of:

❶ Harvard Square

Town and gown meet at this lively intersection, where you'll get a taste of the improbable mix of people drawn to the crossroads of Cambridge. To your right is the landmark **Out of Town News** kiosk (© **800/862-5678**). It stocks newspapers and magazines from all over the world and tons of souvenirs (beefed up when the rise of the Internet cut into the demand for non-virtual journalism). At the colorful kiosk in front of you, you can request information about the area. Step close to it so that you're out of the flow of pedestrian traffic and look around.

The store across Mass. Ave. is the **Harvard Coop.** It rhymes with *hoop*—say "co-op" and risk being taken for a Yalie. On the far side of the intersection, at the corner of John F. Kennedy and Brattle streets, is a sign reading DEWEY CHEETHAM & HOWE (say it out loud) on the third floor of the brick building. National Public Radio's "Car Talk" originates here.

Turn around so that the Coop is at your back and walk half a block, crossing Dunster Street. Across the way, at 1341 Massachusetts Ave., you'll see:

❷ Wadsworth House

Most of the people waiting for the bus in front of this yellow wood building probably don't know that it was built in 1726 as a residence for Harvard's fourth president—but then, neither do most Harvard students. Its biggest claim to fame is a classic: George Washington slept here.

Cross the street, pass through the gate, and continue until you're at the edge of a sweeping lawn crisscrossed with walking paths. This is:

❸ Harvard Yard/Johnston Gate

You're standing in the oldest part of "the Yard." It was a patch of grass with animals grazing on it when Harvard College was established in 1636 to train young men for the ministry, and it wasn't much more when the Continental Army spent the winter of 1775–76 here. Harvard is the oldest college in the country, with the most competitive admissions process, and if you suggest aloud that it's not the best, you might encounter the attitude that inspired the saying "You can always tell a Harvard man, but you can't tell him much."

Harvard, a private institution since 1865, includes the college and 10 graduate and professional schools. It owns more than 400 buildings in Boston and Cambridge; some of the most interesting surround this quad.

Walk forward until you see majestic Johnston Gate on your left and take in the classroom and administration buildings and dormitories that make up the:

❹ Old Yard

Just inside the gate stands **Massachusetts Hall.** Built in 1720, this National Historic Landmark is the university's oldest surviving building. First-year students share "Mass. Hall" with the first-floor office of the university president (or perhaps it's the other way around), whom they traditionally invite upstairs for tea once a year. Across the way is **Harvard Hall,** a classroom building constructed in

Walking Tour 2: Harvard Square

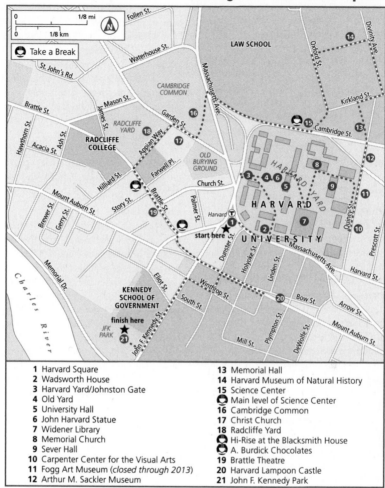

1 Harvard Square
2 Wadsworth House
3 Harvard Yard/Johnston Gate
4 Old Yard
5 University Hall
6 John Harvard Statue
7 Widener Library
8 Memorial Church
9 Sever Hall
10 Carpenter Center for the Visual Arts
11 Fogg Art Museum (*closed through 2013*)
12 Arthur M. Sackler Museum
13 Memorial Hall
14 Harvard Museum of Natural History
15 Science Center
🅒 Main level of Science Center
16 Cambridge Common
17 Christ Church
18 Radcliffe Yard
🅒 Hi-Rise at the Blacksmith House
🅒 A. Burdick Chocolates
19 Brattle Theatre
20 Harvard Lampoon Castle
21 John F. Kennedy Park

1765. Walk along the Yard side of Harvard Hall until you reach matching side-by-side buildings, **Hollis** and **Stoughton halls.** Hollis dates to 1763 (Stoughton "only" to 1805) and has been home to many students who went on to great fame, among them Ralph Waldo Emerson, Henry David Thoreau, and Charles Bulfinch. Almost hidden across the tiny lawn between these two buildings is **Holden Chapel,** a Georgian-style gem completed in 1744. It has been an anatomy lab, a classroom building, and, of course, a chapel, and it is now home to the Harvard Glee Club.

Cross the Yard to the building opposite Johnston Gate. This is:

❺ University Hall

Designed by Charles Bulfinch and constructed of granite quarried in suburban Chelmsford, the 1813 structure is the college's main administration building. In 1969, students protesting the Vietnam War occupied it.

University Hall is best known as the backdrop of the:

⑥ John Harvard Statue

This is one of the most photographed objects in the Boston area. Daniel Chester French designed it in 1884.

Walk around University Hall into the adjoining quad. This is still the Yard, but it's the **"New Yard,"** sometimes called **Tercentenary Theater** because the college's 300th-anniversary celebration was held here in 1936. Commencement and other university-wide ceremonies take place here.

On your right is:

⑦ Widener Library

The centerpiece of the world's largest university library system was built in 1913 as a memorial to Harry Elkins Widener, Harvard class of 1907. Legend has it that he died when the *Titanic* sank in 1912 because he was unable to swim 50 yards to a lifeboat, and his mother donated $2 million for the library on the condition that every undergraduate prove his ability to swim 50 yards. Today the library holds more than 3 million volumes, including 3,500 rare volumes collected by Harry Elkins Widener, on 50 miles of shelves. Don't even think about swiping Harry's Gutenberg Bible. The last person to try, in 1969, gained access from above but couldn't climb out. With the 70-pound Bible in his knapsack, he fell six stories to the courtyard below.

Horace Trumbauer of Philadelphia designed the library. His primary design assistant was Julian Francis Abele, a student of architecture at the University of Pennsylvania and the first black graduate of L'Ecole des Beaux Arts in Paris. The lobby—which sits within view of the locked memorial room that holds Widener's collection—is not open to the public, but you may be able to talk your way in if you're affiliated (student or staff) with another university; visit the office to the left of the main entrance. If you're not allowed to take a peek, pause at the top of the outside staircase and enjoy the view.

Facing the library is:

⑧ Memorial Church

Built in 1931, the church is topped with a tower and weather vane 197-feet tall. You're welcome to look around this Georgian revival–style edifice unless services are going on, or to attend them if they are. Morning prayers run daily from 8:45 to 9am, and the Sunday service is at 11am. Weddings and funerals also take place here. The entrance is on the left. Inside, on the south wall (toward the Yard), panels bear the names of Harvard alumni who died in the world wars, Korea, and Vietnam. One is Joseph P. Kennedy, Jr., the president's brother, class of 1938.

Facing Widener Library with Memorial Church behind you, turn left toward:

⑨ Sever Hall

H. H. Richardson, architect of Boston's Trinity Church, designed this classroom

---

⟨Fun Fact⟩ Nothing But the Truth

The likeness of **John Harvard** outside University Hall is known as the "Statue of Three Lies" because the inscription reads "John Harvard/Founder/1638." In fact, the college was founded in 1636; Harvard (one of many benefactors) didn't establish it, but donated money and his library; and this isn't John Harvard anyway. No portraits of him survive, so the model for this benevolent-looking bronze gentleman was, according to various accounts, either his nephew or a student.

Moments Pssst . . . Check This Out

Climb the front steps of **Sever Hall** and scoot to the side, out of the way of passing students. The doorway is set in a "whispering gallery." Stand on one side of the arch, station a friend or willing passerby on the opposite side, and speak softly into the facade. Someone standing next to you can't hear you, but the person at the other side of the arch can.

---

building (1880). Surveys of architects and designers consistently name the deceptively simple structure one of the professionals' favorite buildings in the Boston area. Notice the gorgeous brickwork that includes rolled moldings around the doors, the fluted brick chimneys, and the arrangement of the windows.

Facing Sever Hall, turn right and go around to the back. The building on your right is Emerson Hall, which appeared in the movie *Love Story* as Barrett Hall, named after the family of Ryan O'Neal's character. Cross this quad and exit through the gate onto Quincy Street.

On your right on the other side of the street, about 100 yards up, at 24 Quincy St., is the:

⑩ Carpenter Center for the Visual Arts

Art exhibitions occupy the lobby, the Harvard Film Archive shows movies in the basement (pick up a schedule on the main floor), and the concrete-and-glass building is itself a work of art. Opened in 1963, it was designed by the Swiss-French architect Le Corbusier and the team of Sert, Jackson, and Gourley. It's the only Le Corbusier design in North America.

Just up Quincy Street, opposite the gate you used to leave the Yard, is the:

⑪ Fogg Art Museum

Founded in 1895, the museum has been at 32 Quincy St. since the building was completed in 1927. Visitors after June 2008 will find this building and the adjacent Busch-Reisinger Museum closed for extensive renovations, and highlights of

the excellent collections on display at our next stop. See chapter 7 for details.

Continue on Quincy Street and cross Broadway to reach the:

⑫ Arthur M. Sackler Museum

The British architect James Stirling (who described this part of the campus as an "architectural zoo") designed the Sackler, at 485 Broadway. It normally houses the university's spectacular collection of Asian art; during your visit, look for a "greatest hits" selection of work from Harvard's three art museums.

Continue on Quincy Street. As you cross Cambridge Street, watch out for confused drivers emerging from the underpass to your left. Filling the block between Cambridge and Kirkland streets is:

⑬ Memorial Hall

This imposing Victorian structure, known to students as "Mem Hall," was completed in 1874. Enter from Cambridge Street and investigate the hall of memorials, a transept where you can read the names of the Harvard men who died fighting for the Union during the Civil War—but not of their Confederate counterparts. (The name of Col. Robert Gould Shaw, Matthew Broderick's character in the movie *Glory*, is halfway down on the right.) To the right is **Sanders Theatre**, prized as a performance space and lecture hall for its excellent acoustics and clear views. To the left is **Annenberg Hall.** It's a dining hall that's closed to visitors, but you may be able to sneak a look at the gorgeous stained-glass windows. Harvard graduates William Ware and

Henry Van Brunt won a design competition for Memorial Hall, which was constructed for a total cost of $390,000 (most of it donated by alumni). The colorful tower is a replica of the original, which was destroyed by fire in 1956 and rebuilt in 1999.

Facing in the same direction you were when you entered, walk through the transept and exit onto Kirkland Street. Turn left and quickly right, onto Oxford Street. One block up on the right, at 26 Oxford St., you'll see an entrance to the:

⑭ Harvard Museum of Natural History

Adjoining the **Peabody Museum of Archaeology & Ethnology** at 11 Divinity Ave., the Museum of Natural History entertainingly presents the university's collections and research relating to the natural world. See p. 165 for a full description.

Leave through the back door of 11 Divinity Ave. and look around. Across the street at 6 Divinity Ave. is the **Semitic Museum** (✆ **617/495-4631**), where the second- and third-floor galleries hold displays of archaeological artifacts and photographs from the Near and Middle East. Horace Trumbauer, the architect of Widener Library, designed the building next door, 2 Divinity Ave. It's home to the **Harvard-Yenching Institute,** which promotes East Asian studies and facilitates scholar-exchange programs. For every person who can tell you that, there are several thousand who know this building for the pair of **Chinese stone lions** flanking the front door.

Turn right and return to Kirkland Street, then go right. You'll pass Memorial Hall as you proceed to the intersection of Kirkland and Oxford streets. At Zero Oxford St. is the university's:

⑮ Science Center

The 10-story monolith is said to resemble a Polaroid camera (Edwin H. Land, founder of the Polaroid Corporation, was one of its main benefactors). The Spanish architect Josep Lluís Sert designed the

Science Center, which opened in 1972. Sert, the dean of the university's Graduate School of Design from 1953 to 1969, was a disciple of Le Corbusier (who designed the Carpenter Center for the Visual Arts). On the plaza between the Science Center and the Yard is the **Tanner Rock Fountain,** a group of 159 New England boulders arranged around a small fountain. Since 1985 this has been a favorite spot for students to relax and watch unsuspecting passersby get wet: The fountain sprays a fine mist, which begins slowly and gradually intensifies.

TAKE A BREAK
The **main level of the Science Center** is open to the public and has several options if you want a soft drink, gourmet coffee, or sandwich. Go easy on the sweets, though, in anticipation of the next break.

Leave the Science Center near the fountain and turn right. Keeping the underpass on your left, follow the walkway for the equivalent of 1½ blocks as it curves around to the right. The Harvard Law School campus is on your right. You're back at Mass. Ave. Cross carefully to:

⑯ Cambridge Common

Memorials and plaques dot this well-used plot of greenery and bare earth. Follow the sidewalk along Mass. Ave. to the left, and after a block or so you'll walk near or over horseshoes embedded in the concrete. This is the path William Dawes, Paul Revere's fellow alarm-sounder, took from Boston to Lexington on April 18, 1775. Turn right onto Garden Street and continue following the Common for 1 block. On your right you'll see a monument marking the place where General George Washington took control of the Continental Army on July 3, 1775. The elm under which he reputedly assumed command is no longer standing.

Fun Fact Play It, Sam

The **Brattle Theatre,** one of the oldest independent movie houses in the country, started the *Casablanca* revival craze, which explains the name of the restaurant in the basement.

Cross Garden Street and backtrack to Zero Garden St. This is:

🄱 Christ Church

Peter Harrison of Newport, Rhode Island (also the architect of King's Chapel in Boston), designed the oldest church in Cambridge, which opened in 1760. Note the square wooden tower. Inside the vestibule you can still see bullet holes made by British muskets. At one time the church was used as the barracks for troops from Connecticut, who melted down the organ pipes to make ammunition. The graveyard on the Mass. Ave. side of the building, the **Old Burying Ground,** is the oldest in Cambridge, dating to 1635. It's the final resting place of nine Harvard presidents as well as many early settlers and at least two black Revolutionary War soldiers.

Facing Christ Church, turn right and follow Garden Street to the next intersection. This is Appian Way. Turn left and take the first right into:

🄱 Radcliffe Yard

Radcliffe College was founded in 1879 as the "Harvard Annex" and named for Ann Radcliffe, Lady Mowlson, Harvard's first female benefactor. Undergraduate classes merged with Harvard's in 1943, Radcliffe graduates first received Harvard degrees in 1963, and Harvard officially assumed responsibility for educating undergraduate women in 1977. Radcliffe was an independent corporation until 1999; it's now the university's Radcliffe Institute for Advanced Study. The institute's first dean, Drew Gilpin Faust, became the university's first woman president in 2007. After you've strolled around, return to Appian Way and turn right. You'll emerge on Brattle Street.

A visit to the **Longfellow National Historic Site,** 105 Brattle St. (© 617/876-4491; www.nps.gov/long; p. 164), makes an interesting detour and adds about an hour to your walk. If you don't detour, turn left and continue walking along Brattle Street. Excellent shops are on both sides of the street.

TAKE A BREAK
Hi-Rise at the Blacksmith House, 56 Brattle St. (© 617/492-3003), a branch of a well-known local artisan bread company, handles the baking for this legendary house, made famous by a Longfellow poem. "Under the spreading chestnut tree," stuff yourself with delectable pastry. Or sate your sweet tooth with something from the celebrated New Hampshire–based confectioner **L. A. Burdick Chocolates,** 52 Brattle St. (© 617/491-4340; www.burdick chocolate.com).

Down the street, at 40 Brattle St., is the:

🄱 Brattle Theatre

Opened in 1890 as Brattle Hall, the theater (© 617/876-6837; www.brattle film.org) was founded by the Cambridge Social Union and used as a cultural and entertainment venue. It became a movie hall in 1953 and gained a reputation as Cambridge's center for art films.

You're now in the **Brattle Square** part of Harvard Square. You might see street performers, a protest, a speech, or more shopping opportunities. Facing Dickson Brothers Hardware, cross Brattle Street, bear right, and follow the curve of the building all the way around the corner so that you're on Mount Auburn Street. Stay on the left-hand side of the street as you cross John F. Kennedy, Dunster, Holyoke, and Linden streets. On your left between Dunster and Holyoke streets is **Holyoke Center,** an administration building designed by Josep Luis Sert that has commercial space on the ground floor.

The corner of Mount Auburn and Linden streets offers a good view of the:

⑳ Harvard Lampoon Castle

Constructed in 1909, designed by Wheelwright & Haven (architects of Boston's Horticultural Hall), and listed on the National Register of Historic Places, this is the home of Harvard's undergraduate humor magazine, the *Lampoon.* The main tower resembles a face, with windows as the eyes, nose, and mouth, topped by what looks like a miner's hat. All five of the building's addresses have been mentioned on "The Simpsons," which draws many of its writers from the staff. The *Lampoon* and the daily student newspaper, the *Crimson,* share a long history of reciprocal pranks and vandalism. Elaborate security measures notwithstanding, *Crimson* editors occasionally make off with the bird that you might see atop the castle (it looks like a crane but is actually an ibis), and *Lampoon* staffers have absconded with the huge wooden president's chair from the *Crimson.*

You'll pass the *Crimson* on your right if you detour to the **Harvard Book Store** (turn left onto Plympton St. and follow it to the corner of Mass. Ave.). Otherwise, cross Mount Auburn Street and walk away from Holyoke Center on Holyoke Street or Dunster Street to get a sense of some of the rest of the campus. The tower directly in front of you sits atop Lowell House, one of a dozen residences for upperclassmen (first-year students live in and around Harvard Yard).

Turn right on Winthrop Street or South Street, and proceed to Kennedy Street. Turn left and follow Kennedy Street toward the Charles River. On your right at Memorial Drive is:

㉑ John F. Kennedy Park

In the 1970s, when the search was on for a site for the Kennedy Library, this lovely parcel of land was an empty plot near the MBTA train yard (the Red Line then ended at Harvard). Traffic concerns led to the library's being built in Dorchester, but the **Graduate School of Government** and this adjacent park bear the president's name. Walk away from the street to enjoy the fountain, which is engraved with excerpts from JFK's speeches. This is a great place to take a break and plan the rest of your day.

9

Shopping

If you turned straight to this chapter, you're in good company: Surveys of visitors to Boston consistently show that shopping is their most popular activity, beating museum-going by a comfortable margin.

Boston-area shopping represents a tempting blend of classic and contemporary. Boston and Cambridge teem with tiny boutiques and sprawling malls, esoteric bookshops and national chain stores, exclusive galleries and snazzy secondhand-clothing outlets.

One of the most popular shopping destinations in New England will most likely be closed during your visit: **Filene's**

Basement temporarily shuttered its flagship store in 2007 to make way for extensive renovations and construction in the building upstairs, which will last until 2009. Ask at your hotel to see whether the retail landmark has reopened, or check out the Back Bay branch (p. 208), which doesn't offer the original's automatic-markdown policy.

This chapter concentrates on only-in-Boston businesses, and it also includes many national (and international) names that are worth a visit. I'll point you to areas that are great for shop-hopping and toward specific destinations that are great for particular items.

1 The Shopping Scene

One of the best things about shopping in Massachusetts is that there's **no sales tax** on clothing priced below $175 or on food items. All other items are taxed at 5% (as are restaurant meals and takeout food). Just about every store will ship your purchases home for a fee, but if the store is part of a chain that operates in your home state, you'll probably have to pay that sales tax. Be sure to ask.

In the major shopping areas, stores usually open at 10am and close at 6 or 7pm Monday through Saturday. On Sunday, most open at 11am or noon and close at 5 or 6pm, but some don't open at all. Closing time may be later 1 night a week, usually Wednesday or Thursday. Malls keep their own hours (noted below), and some smaller shops open later. Days and hours can vary in winter. Year-round, many art galleries close on Monday. In short, if a store sounds too good to pass up, call to make sure it's open before you head out.

GREAT SHOPPING AREAS

The area's premier shopping district is Boston's **Back Bay**, where dozens of upmarket galleries, shops, and boutiques make **Newbury Street** a world-famous destination. Parallel to Newbury is retail-rich **Boylston Street.**

Stretching from Boylston Street past Huntington Avenue, the **Shops at Prudential Center** and **Copley Place** (linked by an enclosed walkway across Huntington) bookend a giant retail complex that includes the posh department stores **Neiman Marcus,**

Lord & Taylor, and **Saks Fifth Avenue.** A branch of **Barneys New York,** the luxe fashion wonderland, is in Copley Place. The adjacent **South End,** though less commercially dense, boasts a number of art galleries and quirky shops; it's a great destination for strolling, shopping, and snacking.

Another popular destination is chain-heavy **Faneuil Hall Marketplace.** The shops, boutiques, and pushcarts at Boston's busiest attraction sell everything from candles to costume jewelry, sweaters to souvenirs. Nearby, the **North End** has augmented its dozens of Italian restaurants a limited but fun retail scene.

Beacon Hill is a classic shopping destination. Picturesque **Charles Street,** at the foot of the hill, is a short but retail-heavy street noted for its excellent gift shops and antiques dealers.

One of Boston's oldest shopping areas is **Downtown Crossing,** a traffic-free pedestrian mall along Washington, Winter, and Summer streets near Boston Common. With construction raging at the site of the old Filene's building (temporarily driving out the century-old Filene's Basement flagship), the center of this area can be something of a mess. But you'll still find **Macy's,** Swedish fashion phenomenon **H&M,** tons of smaller clothing and shoe stores, food and merchandise pushcarts, and a **Borders** bookstore.

Harvard Square in Cambridge, with its bookstores, boutiques, and T-shirt shops, is about 15 minutes from downtown Boston by subway. Despite the neighborhood association's efforts, chain stores have swept over "the Square." You'll find a mix of national and regional outlets, and more than a few persistent independent retailers.

For a less generic experience, stroll from Harvard Square along shop-lined **Mass. Ave.** toward **Porter Square** to the north or **Central Square** to the southeast. About 10 minutes up Prospect Street from Central Square is **Inman Square,** home to a number of vibrant independent retailers. Another neighborhood with a well-deserved reputation for shopping variety is Brookline's **Coolidge Corner,** which is worth a trip (on the Green Line C train).

2 Shopping A to Z

Here I've singled out establishments that I especially like and neighborhoods that suit shoppers interested in particular types of merchandise. Addresses are in Boston unless otherwise indicated.

ANTIQUES & COLLECTIBLES

No antiques hound worthy of the name will leave Boston without an expedition along both sides of **Charles Street** ★★, with a detour to **River Street** (parallel to Charles, 1 block closer to the river).

Bromfield Pen Shop ★   This shop's selection of antique pens will thrill any collector. It also sells new pens—including Mont Blanc, Pelikan, Waterman, and Omas—gifts, and the full Filofax line. Closed Sunday. 5 Bromfield St. ✆ 617/482-9053. www. bromfieldpenshop.com. T: Red or Orange Line to Downtown Crossing.

Cambridge Antique Market ★★ (Finds   As you navigate the enormous variety of merchandise spread over five floors (don't forget to check out the basement), you may feel as though you're on a treasure hunt—and really, aren't you? Weekends, especially Saturday, are when most of the 100-plus dealers are likeliest to be open. Prices are better than in Boston, but the selection is more catch-as-catch-can. Closed Monday. 201 Msgr. O'Brien Hwy., Cambridge. ✆ 617/868-9655. www.marketantique.com. T: Green Line to Lechmere.

Back Bay Shopping

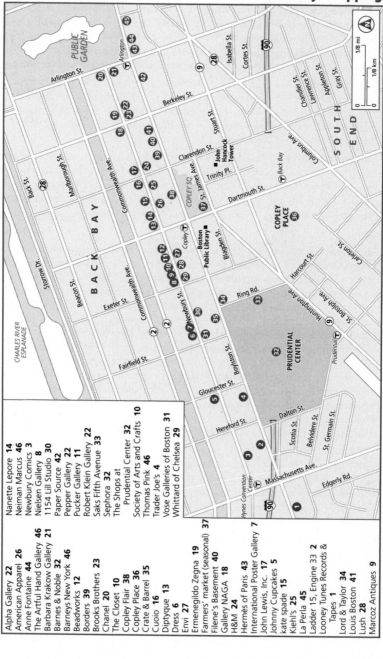

PUBLIC GARDEN

CHARLES RIVER ESPLANADE

BACK BAY

COPLEY SQ

SOUTH END

COPLEY PLACE

PRUDENTIAL CENTER

John Hancock Tower

Boston Public Library

Hynes Convention Center

1/8 mi
1/8 km

Alpha Gallery **22**
American Apparel **26**
Anne Fontaine **44**
The Artful Hand Gallery **46**
Barbara Krakow Gallery **21**
Barnes & Noble **32**
Barneys New York **46**
Beadworks **12**
Borders **39**
Brooks Brothers **23**
Chanel **20**
The Closet **10**
Copley Flair **38**
Copley Place **36**
Crate & Barrel **35**
Cuoio **16**
Diptyque **13**
Dress **6**
Envi **27**
Ermenegildo Zegna **19**
Farmers' market (seasonal) **37**
Filene's Basement **40**
Gallery NAGA **18**
H&M **24**
Hermès of Paris **43**
International Poster Gallery **7**
John Lewis, Inc. **17**
Johnny Cupcakes **5**
kate spade **15**
Kiehl's **25**
La Perla **45**
Ladder 15, Engine 33 **2**
Looney Tunes Records & Tapes **1**
Lord & Taylor **34**
Louis Boston **41**
Lush **28**
Marcoz Antiques **9**

Nanette Lepore **14**
Neiman Marcus **46**
Newbury Comics **3**
Nielsen Gallery **8**
1154 Lill Studio **30**
Paper Source **42**
Pepper Gallery **22**
Pucker Gallery **11**
Robert Klein Gallery **22**
Saks Fifth Avenue **33**
Sephora **32**
The Shops at Prudential Center **32**
Society of Arts and Crafts **10**
Thomas Pink **46**
Trader Joe's **4**
Vose Galleries of Boston **31**
Whittard of Chelsea **29**

203

Danish Country Antique Furniture ⍟   Owner James Kilroy specializes in Scandinavian antiques dating from the 1700s onward. In this mahogany-intensive neighborhood, the light woods are a visual treat. You'll also see folk art, lovely Mora clocks, Royal Copenhagen porcelain, and antique Chinese furniture and home accessories. 138 Charles St. © 617/227-1804. www.europeanstyleantiques.com. T: Red Line to Charles/MGH.

Marcoz Antiques ⍟   The specialty here is 18th- through 20th-century European pieces, mainly in room arrangements that make you suspect you've wandered into an Edith Wharton novel. Lovely home accessories and textiles complement stately furnishings, and the gorgeous jewelry is worth a visit on its own. 177 Newbury St. © 617/262-0780. T: Green Line to Copley.

Upstairs Downstairs Antiques ⍟⍟⍟ *Finds*   It's a cliché to say that antiques remind you of your grandmother's furniture. Here that's less trite because the merchandise displays are room arrangements that change with the seasons. From huge sideboards to delicate side tables to books and doilies, it's more evocative than a madeleine. 93 Charles St. © 617/367-1950. T: Red Line to Charles/MGH.

ART

The greatest concentration of galleries lines **Newbury Street,** at street level and above; budget some time for exploring. Browsers and questions are welcome. Most galleries are open Tuesday through Saturday or Sunday from 10 or 11am to 5:30 or 6pm. Exhibitions typically change once a month, and the public is welcome at most opening receptions. They generally begin after business hours on the first Friday or Saturday of the month. For specifics, visit individual websites or pick up a copy of the free monthly *Gallery Guide,* available at many businesses along Newbury Street.

The **SoWa district**—short for "south of Washington Street"—centers on Bernard Toale Gallery (see below). The Back Bay and South End don't have a monopoly, either; real estate prices being what they are, artists tend to crop up in even the unlikeliest-looking areas.

An excellent way to see artists at work is to visit during neighborhood **open studio** days. Artists' communities throughout the Boston area stage the weekend events once or twice a year. You might be asked for a contribution to a charity in exchange for a map of the studios. Check listings in the *Globe* and *Herald* or visit www.cityofboston.gov/arts for information.

Alpha Gallery ⍟   The Alpha Gallery specializes in contemporary American paintings, sculpture, and works on paper, as well as modern master paintings and prints. Established in 1967, this is a family operation: Director Joanna E. Fink is founder Alan Fink's daughter. Closed Sunday and Monday. 38 Newbury St., 7th floor. © 617/536-4465. www.alphagallery.com. T: Green Line to Arlington.

Barbara Krakow Gallery ⍟   This prestigious gallery, founded in 1964, is as cutting-edge as they come. It specializes in paintings, sculptures, drawings, and prints created after 1945. Closed Sunday and Monday. 10 Newbury St., 5th floor. © 617/262-4490. www.barbarakrakowgallery.com. T: Green Line to Arlington.

Bernard Toale Gallery ⍟   One of the Boston area's most celebrated galleries was a pioneer in the "SoWa" (south of Washington St.) section of the South End in the late '90s. It shows exclusively contemporary art, in every medium and by artists at all stages of their careers. Closed Sunday and Monday; closed August except by appointment. 450 Harrison Ave. (between Randolph and Thayer sts.). © 617/482-2477. www.bernardtoalegallery.com. T: Orange Line to New England Medical Center or Back Bay, then 15-min. walk; or Washington St. Silver Line bus from Temple Pl. (Downtown Crossing) to E. Berkeley St., then 5-min. walk.

Gallery NAGA ★★   In the neo-Gothic Church of the Covenant, Gallery NAGA exhibits contemporary paintings, photography, and studio furniture, often by New England artists. A stop here is a must if you want to see holography (trust me, you do). Closed Sunday and Monday. 67 Newbury St. © 617/267-9060. www.gallerynaga.com. T: Green Line to Arlington.

International Poster Gallery ★★★ *Finds*   Yes, posters are art—as you'll see before you even cross the threshold of this extraordinary gallery. It features extensive collections of French, Swiss, Soviet, and Italian vintage posters, and thousands of other posters, including originals from around the world. The accommodating staff will comb its databases (cyber and cerebral) to help you find the exact image you want, and the website is a great resource. The theme of the works on display changes three or four times a year. Prices start at $50, with most between $500 and $2,000. 205 Newbury St. © 617/375-0076. www.internationalposter.com. T: Green Line to Copley.

Nielsen Gallery ★   Owner Nina Nielsen personally selects the contemporary artists who exhibit in her gallery (which opened in 1963), and she has great taste. You might see the work of a young, newly discovered talent or that of a more established artist. Closed Sunday and Monday. 179 Newbury St. © 617/266-4835. www.nielsengallery.com. T: Green Line to Copley.

Pepper Gallery ★★   I wandered in here after visiting the Robert Klein Gallery (see below) and found myself captivated by the top-notch work of living contemporary artists, especially representational painters. You may see prints, photographs, and abstract work as well. Closed Sunday and Monday. 38 Newbury St., 4th floor. © 617/236-4497. www.peppergalleryboston.com. T: Green Line to Arlington.

Pucker Gallery ★★   The eclectic offerings here include African, Asian, Inuit, and Israeli art; contemporary paintings, prints, drawings, sculpture, and ceramics by regional and international artists; and excellent photographs. The staff is eager to discuss the art, which spreads over five floors. 171 Newbury St. © 617/267-9473. www.puckergallery.com. T: Green Line to Copley.

Robert Klein Gallery ★   For 19th- to 21st-century photography, head here. Among the dozens of artists represented are Diane Arbus, Robert Mapplethorpe, Man Ray, and Ansel Adams. Closed Sunday and Monday. 38 Newbury St., 4th floor. © 617/267-7997. www.robertkleingallery.com. T: Green Line to Arlington.

Vose Galleries of Boston ★   One of Vose's specialties is Hudson River School paintings—fitting, because the business and the mid-19th-century movement are about the same age. The Vose family (now in its sixth generation) runs the oldest continuously operating gallery in the United States, which opened in 1841. You'll see works of the Boston School and American Impressionists among the 18th-, 19th-, and early-20th-century American paintings, as well as contemporary pieces by American realists. Closed Sunday. 238 Newbury St. © 617/536-6176. www.vosegalleries.com. T: Green Line to Copley, or Green Line B, C, or D to Hynes Convention Center.

BOOKS

The Boston area is a book-lover's paradise. It's an important stop on most author tours; check the local papers or stop by any store that sells new books for details on **readings and book-signings.**

Barnes & Noble   The well-stocked Prudential Center branch of the national chain offers both a cafe and plenty of kids' events. Barnes & Noble runs most of the college

bookstore operations around town (see "College Merchandise," below). Shops at Pruden-
tial Center, 800 Boylston St. ℂ 617/247-6959. www.barnesandnoble.com. T: Green Line E to Prudential,
Green Line to Copley, or Green Line B, C, or D to Hynes Convention Center. 325 Harvard St., Brookline.
ℂ 617/232-0594. T: Green Line C to Coolidge Corner.

Borders   All three local branches make good places to retreat when you've had
enough of the abundant shopping around them. The sprawling Downtown Crossing
store contains two levels of books and one of music, the Back Bay location has an
entrance off Newbury Street, and the Cambridge Borders is one of the only quiet
places in the mall. 10–24 School St. ℂ 617/557-7188. www.bordersstores.com. T: Orange or Blue
Line to State. 511 Boylston St. ℂ 617/236-1444. T: Green Line to Copley. CambridgeSide Galleria mall,
Cambridge. ℂ 617/679-0887. T: Green Line to Lechmere.

Brattle Book Shop 𝕏𝕏   Bibliophiles who start here might not get any other shopping done. This marvelous store near Macy's buys and sells used, rare, and out-of-print
titles, and second-generation owner Kenneth Gloss does free appraisals. Be sure to
check the outdoor carts and shelves for good deals on books of all ages. Closed Sunday. 9 West St. ℂ 800/447-9595 or 617/542-0210. www.brattlebookshop.com. T: Red or Orange Line
to Downtown Crossing, or Green Line to Park St.

Brookline Booksmith 𝕏𝕏𝕏   The huge, varied selection makes this store a poly-
math's dream. The employees have excellent taste—look for their recommendations.
A great gift-and-card section, a small but choice used-book selection in the basement,
and tons of events are among the offerings. 279 Harvard St., Brookline. ℂ 617/566-6660.
www.brooklinebooksmith.com. T: Green Line C to Coolidge Corner.

Curious George Books & Toys   No, it's not just Curious George books and merchandise. Here you'll find a superlative selection of children's books and gifts, including stuffed animals and games. Check downstairs for items that suit older kids, with
an emphasis on old and new classics. 1 John F. Kennedy St. ℂ 617/498-0062.
www.curiousg.com. T: Red Line to Harvard.

Globe Corner Bookstore 𝕏   The offspring of the dear departed original on the
Freedom Trail, the Globe Corner carries huge selections of travel guides and essays,
maps, atlases, and globes. Check ahead for special events, such as the annual adven-
ture-travel lecture series. 90 Mount Auburn St., Cambridge. ℂ 800/358-6013617/497-6277.
www.globecorner.com. T: Red Line to Harvard.

Grolier Poetry Book Shop   Shelves packed with poetry line this tiny space from
floor to high, high ceiling. Grolier carries just what the name says: only poetry, and
lots of it. 6 Plympton St., Cambridge. ℂ 617/547-4648. T: Red Line to Harvard.

Harvard Book Store 𝕏𝕏   On the main level of this shop, readers peruse an excellent scholarly selection and discounted bestsellers. The basement is the draw for those
in the know: Prices on remainders are good, and used paperbacks (many bought for
classes and hardly opened) are 50% off their original prices. Check ahead for information on readings and other special events. 1256 Massachusetts Ave., Cambridge. ℂ 800/542-
READ or 617/661-1515. www.harvard.com. T: Red Line to Harvard.

Porter Square Books   A well-stocked independent bookstore with everything
from the latest best-sellers to esoteric academic tomes to a great children's department—it's a dying breed. If they were all run as well as this one, with staffs this helpful and selections this brain-tickling, the species would be anything but endangered.

In the Porter Square Shopping Center, 25 White St., Cambridge. ✆ 617/491-2220. www.portersquare books.com. T: Red Line to Porter.

Schoenhof's Foreign Books ✪   The oldest foreign-language bookseller in the country stocks volumes for adults and children in more than 50 languages. It also carries dictionaries and language-learning materials for 700-plus languages and dialects, plus quirky gift items (haven't you always wanted a Hannah Arendt T-shirt?) and translations of children's classics. Closed Sunday. 76A Mt. Auburn St., Cambridge. ✆ 617/547-8855. www.schoenhofs.com. T: Red Line to Harvard.

COLLEGE MERCHANDISE

The big names are BU and Harvard (you'll see Boston College merchandise downtown, too), but there are so many more insignia to explore. Look like an insider with a T-shirt from the **Emerson College Bookstore,** 114 Boylston St. (✆ **617/824-8696;** T: Green Line to Boylston); the **MIT Coop,** 3 Cambridge Center (✆ **617/499-3200;** T: Red Line to Kendall/MIT); the **Northeastern University Bookstore,** 360 Huntington Ave. (✆ **617/373-2286;** T: Green Line E to Northeastern); or the **Suffolk University Bookstore,** 148 Cambridge St., Beacon Hill (✆ **617/227-4085;** T: Blue Line to Bowdoin or Green Line to Government Center).

Barnes & Noble at Boston University   The BU crest, terrier mascot, or name appears on at least a floor's worth of clothing and just about any other item with room for a logo. The book selection is huge, and the author series brings writers to campus year-round. 660 Beacon St. ✆ 617/267-8484. www.bu.bkstore.com. T: Green Line B, C, or D to Kenmore.

The Harvard Coop ✪   The Coop (rhymes with *hoop*), or Harvard Cooperative Society, is student-oriented but not a run-of-the-mill college bookstore. You'll find Harvard insignia merchandise, stationery, prints, and posters. As at BU, Barnes & Noble runs the book operation. 1400 Massachusetts Ave., Cambridge. ✆ 617/499-2000. www.thecoop.com. T: Red Line to Harvard.

CRAFT GALLERIES

The Artful Hand Gallery ✪   The Artful Hand specializes, as you might guess, in handcrafted items. It sells wonderful work by an excellent roster of artists: jewelry, ceramics, blown glass, wood pieces (including boxes), and sculpture, plus furniture, folk art, and books. Copley Place. ✆ 617/262-9601. T: Orange Line to Back Bay or Green Line to Copley.

Society of Arts and Crafts ✪✪   Contemporary American work is the focus at the oldest nonprofit craft organization in the country. The exquisite jewelry, furniture, home accessories, glass, ceramics, and fiber art range from practical to purely decorative; the second floor holds a gallery that mounts four shows a year. 175 Newbury St. ✆ 617/266-1810. www.societyofcrafts.org. T: Green Line to Copley.

CRAFT SUPPLIES

See "Jewelry," later in this chapter, for information about **Beadworks.**

Blick Art Materials   The extensive selection of art supplies and equipment, plus teachers' materials and unusual gift items, almost make up for the somewhat inconvenient location. Prices are higher than at Pearl, the other big national name in this market, but not bad. In the Landmark Center, 401 Park Dr. ✆ 617/247-3322. www.dickblick.com. T: Green Line D to Fenway.

Paper Source ✪✪   Gorgeous paper (writing and wrapping), cards, pens, ink, stamps, books, stickers, unusual gifts, and custom invitations make these well-organized stores

---

Tips Present at the Creation: Craft Shows

New England is a hotbed of fine crafts, and the Boston area affords many opportunities to explore the latest trends in every imaginable medium and style. Prominent artisans often have exclusive relationships with galleries; an excellent way to get an overview is to attend a show and sale. The best-known exhibitions are prestigious weekend events that benefit nonprofit organizations. **Crafts at the Castle** (✆ **617/523-6400**, ext. 5987; www.fsgb.org/catc.htm) takes place in late November or early December at the Hynes Convention Center. **CraftBoston** (✆ **617/266-1810**; www.craftboston.org) is in April or May at the Seaport World Trade Center.

---

magnets for anyone with a thing for stationery. Be sure to check out the handmade paper from around the world. A crafty friend swears by the Boston location, but all three are delightful. 338 Boylston St. ✆ 617/536-3444. www.paper-source.com. T: Green Line to Arlington. 1810 Massachusetts Ave., Cambridge. ✆ 617/497-1077. T: Red Line to Porter. 1361 Beacon St., Brookline. ✆ 617/264-2800. T: Green Line C to Coolidge Corner.

Pearl Art & Craft Supplies ⟨⁂⟩   The Central Square branch of the national discount chain stocks everything you need to do it yourself, from pens and pencils to stamps and stencils to cards and canvas. 579 Massachusetts Ave., Cambridge. ✆ 617/547-6600. www.pearlpaint.com. T: Red Line to Central.

Windsor Button   The name doesn't come close to telling the whole story of this 70-plus-year-old business. It's known for its impressive range of yarn and knitting and crochet patterns and accessories; the helpful staff is a great resource for everyone from beginners to experts. Also in stock are thousands of buttons, from utilitarian to ultra-fancy, as well as ribbon, trim, notions, and needlework kits. Closed Sunday. 35 Temple Place. ✆ 617/482-4969. www.windsorbutton.com. T: Red or Green Line to Park St., or Orange Line to Downtown Crossing.

DISCOUNT SHOPPING

City Sports   The regional athletic-apparel retailer City Sports carries clothing, footwear, and some sports equipment. The crowded lower level of this store—also a regular retail location—stocks a constantly changing selection of out-of-season merchandise at excellent prices. 11 Bromfield St. ✆ 617/423-2015. www.citysports.com. T: Red or Orange Line to Downtown Crossing.

DSW Shoe Warehouse   Here you'll find two large floors of discounted women's and men's shoes, boots, sandals, and sneakers. Check the clearance racks for the real deals. 385 Washington St. ✆ 617/556-0052. www.dswshoe.com. T: Red or Orange Line to Downtown Crossing.

Eddie Bauer Outlet   Not what you might expect from an outlet—the prices aren't breathtaking (they're lowest during January and August end-of-season sales), but the quality and selection are good. 500 Washington St. ✆ 617/423-4722. www.eddiebaueroutlet.com. T: Red or Orange Line to Downtown Crossing.

Filene's Basement ⟨⁂⟩   New England's most famous discount retailer opened at Downtown Crossing in 1908 (it's now a subsidiary of a Midwestern chain). At press time, that location, the only one where the celebrated automatic-markdown pricing policy applies, was closed for construction and not expected to reopen until 2009. The

Back Bay store is many things the original isn't (well lit and scrubbed clean, just to name two), but I find the merchandise roughly equivalent to the stock at other branches. Still, in this neighborhood, any store that acknowledges the concept of discounts is definitely worth a look. 497 Boylston St. ℂ **800/843-8474** or 617/424-5520. www. filenesbasement.com. T: Green Line to Copley.

FASHION

In addition, see "Shoes & Boots" and "Vintage & Secondhand Clothing" later in this chapter.

ADULTS

The **Back Bay** is New England's top destination for swanky boutiques and if-you-have-to-ask-you-can't-afford-it designer shops. Definitely check out the second level of **Copley Place,** but don't go anywhere until you've explored the retail fantasyland that is **Newbury Street.** Bring your platinum card to (take a deep breath) **Chanel,** 15 Arlington St., in the Taj Boston (ℂ 617/859-0055); **Ermenegildo Zegna,** 39 Newbury St. (ℂ 617/424-6657); **Hermès of Paris,** 22 Arlington St. (ℂ 617/482-8707); **kate spade,** 117 Newbury St. (ℂ 617/262-2632); **La Perla,** 250 Boylston St. (ℂ 617/423-5709); and **Nanette Lepore,** 119 Newbury St. (ℂ 617/421-9200).

American Apparel ⭐⭐ A leading light of the anti-sweatshop movement, American Apparel is so sincere that you might expect the clothes to be the fabric equivalent of Brussels sprouts. But the women's and men's T-shirts, underwear, and other fashionable knits—all manufactured in downtown L.A.—are fun, gorgeous, or both. www.americanapparel.net. 138 Newbury St. ℂ **617/536-4768.** T: Green Line to Arlington. 47 Brattle St. ℂ **617/661-2770.** T: Red Line to Harvard.

Anne Fontaine ⭐ This was the first U.S. outlet for the designer's "perfect white blouse collection from Paris." I wanted to laugh, but then I saw for myself—almost every item *is* a perfect (for one reason or another) white blouse. Prices start at $80. Closed Sunday. Heritage on the Garden, 318 Boylston St. (at Arlington St.) ℂ **617/423-0366.** www.annefontaine.com. T: Green Line to Arlington.

Brooks Brothers Would-be "proper Bostonians" head here for blue blazers, gray flannels, seersucker suits, and less conservative business and casual wear for men and women. Brooks is the only place for exactly the right preppy shade of pink button-down oxford shirts—something I've never seen at the outlet stores. 46 Newbury St. ℂ **617/267-2600.** www.brooksbrothers.com. T: Green Line to Arlington. 75 State St. ℂ **617/261-9990.** T: Orange or Blue Line to State.

Dress Think of the verb, not the noun. This airy boutique stocks women's fashion (including dresses), jeans, shoes, and jewelry. Many pieces are the work of designers whose creations aren't available elsewhere in Boston—always the goal on Newbury Street. 221 Newbury St. ℂ **617/424-7125.** www.dressboston.com. T: Green Line to Copley.

Envi "Eco-conscious" doesn't have to mean "lumpy sweatshirt and shapeless jeans," and the stylish merchandise here proves it. Envi carries sweatshop-free, sustainably manufactured women's clothing that's more comfortable than corporate—but never dowdy. 164 Newbury St. ℂ **617/267-3684.** www.shopenvi.com. T: Green Line to Copley.

H&M ⭐ The Swedish discount-fashion juggernaut is a terrific place to look for cheap, stylish clothing and accessories. The Downtown Crossing store outfits women, men, and kids; the Cambridge branch concentrates on fashions for women (including underwear) and teens of both sexes. 350 Washington St. ℂ **617/482-7001.** www.hm.com. T: Red or Orange Line to Downtown Crossing. 100 Newbury St. (tel) **617/859-3192**). T: Green Line to Copley. CambridgeSide Galleria, 100 CambridgeSide Place, Cambridge. ℂ **617/225-0895**. T: Green Line to Lechmere, or Red Line to Kendall/MIT and free shuttle bus (every 10–20 min.).

Injeanius   The North End doesn't have a bookstore, but it does have a designer-jean boutique—and it's a good one. Owner Alison Barnard and her staff will find just the right fit for you in their well-edited selection of pricey denim; the tops, shoes, and bags represent an impressive variety of hard-to-find-in-Boston brands. The nearby sister shop, **Twilight,** 12 Fleet St. (ℂ **617523-8008**), carries a gorgeous, ever-changing selection of party dresses and suitable accessories. 441 Hanover St. ℂ **617/523-5326**. www.injeanius.com. T: Green or Orange Line to Haymarket.

Jean Therapy ⨁   Designer dungarees are the raison d'être of this spendy boutique in a fancy hotel. Jean Therapy prides itself on its discriminating selection and on customer service so good that it eases the stress of checking out your own butt in public. Nearby sibling **Therapy,** 152 Brookline Ave. (ℂ **617/266-6501**), stocks well-edited selections of fashionable business clothes and chic home accessories. In the Hotel Commonwealth, 524 Commonwealth Ave. ℂ **617/266-6555**. www.jean-therapy.com. T: Green Line B, C, or D to Kenmore.

Johnny Cupcakes   There's no food in the bakery cases at this adorable shop—just limited-edition, custom-designed T-shirts made in the USA. They're pricey but adorable, with clever designs that often play off the cupcake theme. And yes, there really is a Johnny (his last name is really Earle). 279 Newbury St. ℂ **617/375-0100**. www.johnnycupcakes.com. T: Green Line B, C, or D to Hynes Convention Center.

1154 Lill Studio ⨁⨁ (Finds)   Shoppers at this adorable design-your-own-handbag shop have a lot of decisions to make, starting with a big one: instant or delayed gratification? Bags of all sizes are on display; you can walk out with one or, if you don't see *exactly* what you want, customize your own using an impressive variety of materials, from fabric to straps to lining. It arrives at your home a month or so later, built from scratch just as you imagined it. This is the third branch in a mini-chain with locations in Chicago and Kansas City. Prices run $25 to $150. 220 Newbury St. ℂ **617/247-1154**. www.1154lillstudio.com. T: Green Line B, C, or D to Hynes Convention Center.

Louis Boston   Louis (pronounced "Louie's") enjoys a well-deserved reputation for offering cutting-edge New York style in a traditional Boston setting. The ultra-prestigious store sells men's designer suits, handmade shirts, silk ties, and Italian shoes; the women's fashions are equally elegant. The merchandise represents a mix of big names, emerging stars, and the celebrated house label. Also on the premises are an "apothecary" department, a full-service salon, and a restaurant that serves lunch and dinner. 234 Berkeley St. ℂ **800/225-5135** or 617/262-6100. www.louisboston.com. T: Green Line to Arlington.

Thomas Pink   The London-based haberdasher carries top-quality men's (mostly) and women's dress shirts, both off the rack and made to order. The merchandise is just as lovely and the prices less tic-inducing during periodic sales. And you get to say "haberdasher." The Downtown Crossing location closes Sunday. Copley Place. ℂ **617/267-0447**. www.thomaspink.com. T: Orange Line to Back Bay. 280 Washington St. ℂ **617/426-7859**. T: Blue or Orange Line to State.

Turtle   The eclectic selection of clothing, jewelry, and accessories by up-and-coming designers and artists (they're coming out of their shells—get it?) makes this a good destination for fashion plates who want to be absolutely sure no one else will be

---

Tips **An Outlet Excursion**

If you can't get through a vacation without some outlet shopping, the fact that you left the car at home doesn't have to stop you. **Brush Hill Tours** (② 800/ 343-1328 or 781/986-6100; www.brushhilltours.com) operates daily service to **Wrentham Village Premium Outlets** (② 508/384-0600; www.premium outlets.com), a huge complex about 45 minutes south of Boston. Its dozens of outlet stores include—and this is merely scratching the surface—Anne Klein, Banana Republic, Barneys New York, Juicy Couture, Kenneth Cole, Nike, Polo Ralph Lauren, Reebok, Timberland, Tommy Hilfiger, and Versace. Shoppers leave Boston around 10am; the return trip departs at 5pm. The round-trip fare is $36 for adults, $20 for children 5 to 11; reservations are required.

---

wearing the same outfit (or gorgeous shoes, or unusual necklace, or . . .). 619 Tremont St. ② 617/266-2610. www.turtleboston.com. T: Orange Line to Back Bay.

Wish   The interior is stark, the service chilly, the prices high—and the designer fashions unbeatable. Wish is a default destination for an incredible number of stylish Bostonians and suburbanites, not because the labels are unusual but because the selection is so painstaking. The January and July sales are worth waiting for. 49 Charles St. ② 617/227-4441. www.wishboston.com. T: Orange Line to Back Bay.

CHILDREN

Bird by Bird ⊕   This "urban boutique," the brainchild of two local moms, stocks everything you need to turn your youngster into a teeny-tiny fashionista and offers classes (such as yoga and massage) for kids as well as adults. Closed Monday. 1361 Cambridge St., Inman Sq., Cambridge. ② 617/497-1361. www.mybirdbybird.com. T: Red Line to Central; 10-min. walk.

Calliope ⊕⊕ *Finds*   The must-see window displays at this Harvard Square shop use stuffed animals, clothes, and toys to illustrate sayings and proverbs, often twisted into hilarious puns. The merchandise inside, for children up to age 6, is equally delightful. You'll find clothing and accessories, European shoes, and unusual gifts, including a huge selection of plush animals. 33 Brattle St., Cambridge. ② 617/876-4149. T: Red Line to Harvard.

The Red Wagon ⊕   Just about everything in this boutique is as cute as a kitten, from the baby duds to the big trike, which is irresistible to older kids. Busy parents cherish this Beacon Hill mainstay for its wide selection of American and European clothing and shoes (through size 8) and the fact that it's also a well-stocked toy shop— two errands in one stop. 69 Charles St. ② 617/523-9402. www.theredwagon.com. T: Red Line to Charles/MGH.

FOOD & CANDY

Beacon Hill Chocolates   Off Charles Street, this little shop turning out artisan creations has been a hot topic on the chocoholic grapevine since it opened in 2006. The special-occasion selections in handmade boxes are as beautiful as they are delicious. 92B Pinckney St. ② 617/725-1900. www.beaconhillchocolates.com. T: Red Line to Charles/MGH.

Cardullo's Gourmet Shoppe   A veritable United Nations of fancy food, this Harvard Square landmark carries specialties (including beer, wine, and a huge variety of

---

Finds Fired Up

A good souvenir is something you'd never find anywhere else, and a **Boston Fire Department T-shirt** is a great one. They cost about $15 at most neighborhood firehouses. The handiest for out-of-towners are Engine 8, Ladder 1, on Hanover Street at Charter Street in the North End (off the Freedom Trail), and Engine 33, Ladder 15, on Boylston Street at Hereford Street in the Back Bay (near the Hynes Convention Center).

---

candy) from just about everywhere. If you can't afford the big-ticket items, order a tasty sandwich to go. 6 Brattle St., Cambridge. ✆ 617/491-8888. T: Red Line to Harvard.

Penzeys 🌟🌟   The Wisconsin-based purveyor of spices, herbs, flavorings, and spice rubs attracts delighted cooks and foodies from miles around (the closest branch is in Connecticut) with its huge, reasonably priced selection. Getting here is a pain, but it's absolutely worth the trip. 1293 Massachusetts Ave., Arlington. ✆ 800/741-7787 or 781/646-7707. www.penzeys.com. T: Red Line to Harvard or Porter, then no. 77 bus.

Salumeria Italiana 🌟   The city's premier Italian grocer caters to picky North Enders and foodies from all over the Boston area. Owner Gaetano Martignetti, the son of the founder, prides himself on his selection of meats, cheeses, olives, olive oils, vinegars, pastas, and more. The store is small, the variety huge. 151 Richmond St. ✆ 617/523-8743. www.salumeriaitaliana.com. T: Green or Orange Line to Haymarket.

Savenor's Market   Both gourmet shop and posh meat market, Savenor's is the perfect place to provision yourself before a concert or movie on the nearby Esplanade (or a really pricey cookout; Kobe beef, anyone?). And it's *the* local purveyor of exotic meats—if you crave buffalo or rattlesnake, this is the place. The original location, in Cambridge, was a favorite of Julia Child's. 160 Charles St. ✆ 617/723-6328. www.savenorsmarket.com. T: Red Line to Charles/MGH. 92 Kirkland St., Cambridge. ✆ 617/576-6328. T: Red Line to Harvard, then a 10-min. walk.

Trader Joe's 🌟   The celebrated California-based retailer stocks a large selection of prepared foods, cheese, nuts, baked goods, natural and organic products, and other edibles, all at excellent prices. Get a preview on the website or just ask devotees—they can't shut up about it. The Cambridge location (which sells alcohol, as does the Brookline store) is a good place to stop for picnic provisions if you're driving, but it's not convenient to public transit. 899 Boylston St. ✆ 617/262-6505. www.traderjoes.com. T: Green Line B, C, or D to Hynes Convention Center. 1317 Beacon St., Brookline. ✆ 617/278-9997. T: Green Line C to Coolidge Corner. 748 Memorial Dr., Cambridge. ✆ 617/491-8582.

Whittard of Chelsea   The venerable British tea and coffee—and hot chocolate!—merchant used Boston as an entry point for the American market. Whittard (accent on the second syllable) dates to 1886 and prides itself, rightly, on personalized service. A Faneuil Hall Marketplace branch is in the works. 170 Newbury St. ✆ 617/536-5200. www.whittard.co.uk. T: Green Line to Copley.

GIFTS & SOUVENIRS

Boston has dozens of shops and pushcarts that sell T-shirts, hats, and other souvenirs. At the stores listed here, you'll find gifts that say Boston without actually *saying* "Boston" all over them. Remember to check out museum shops for unique items, including crafts and games. Particularly good outlets include those at the **Museum of Fine Arts,** the **Museum of Science,** the **Isabella Stewart Gardner Museum,** the **Institute of Contemporary Art,** the **Concord Museum,** and the **Peabody Essex Museum** in Salem. The online-only merchandise of the **Boston Public Library** (www.bpl.org) incorporates images from the library's vast holdings, including historic maps, photos, and even sports memorabilia—and you don't have to take up space in your carry-on to get your souvenirs home.

Aunt Sadie's   Brimming with perhaps the most miscellaneous merchandise in the South End (which is saying something), Aunt Sadie's started out as a candle shop and now carries inventive gifts and accessories for home, bath, kitchen, adults, children, pets, and maybe even your own Aunt Sadie. 18 Union Park St. (off Tremont St.). ℂ 617/357-7117. www.auntsadiesinc.com. T: Orange Line to Back Bay.

Black Ink ⭐⭐   The wacky wares here defy categorization, but they all fit comfortably under the umbrella of "oh, cool." Rubber stamps, stuffed animals, and doll figurines from Japan caught my eye recently; greeting cards, desktop accessories, and retro toys are equally appealing. Under the same management, the **Museum of Useful Things,** 49 Brattle St. (ℂ 617/576-3322; www.themut.com), up the street from the Harvard Square location, is a festival of industrial design for home and office. 101 Charles St. ℂ 617/723-3883. www.blackinkboston.com. T: Red Line to Charles/MGH. 5 Brattle St., Cambridge. ℂ 866/497-1221 or 617/497-1221. T: Red Line to Harvard.

Buckaroo's Mercantile ⭐   Proclaiming your business a "pop culture superstore" might sound like overreaching, but this place delivers. The wild selection of vintage and retro-style contemporary gifts, home accessories, clothing, and gadgets—there's a nun candle in my living room, and I have my eye on a mirror with mermaid drawings arranged around it—changes regularly. 5 Brookline St., Cambridge. ℂ 617/492-4792. www.buckmerc.com. T: Red Line to Central.

Copley Flair   Late for a party, unwilling to give the birthday girl an unwrapped book or resort to the drugstore card aisle *again,* I realized for the umpteenth time how great these little shops are. Both are crammed with high-quality greeting cards, wrapping paper, ribbons and bows, stationery, and unusual gifts and novelty items. 11 School St. ℂ 617/367-7170. www.copleyflair.com. T: Orange or Blue Line to State. 583 Boylston St. ℂ 617/247-1648. T: Green Line to Copley.

Cross ⭐   The Rhode Island–based pen company's first retail outlet proves that good things come in small packages. The tiny store carries a surprisingly large selection of beautiful stationery and cards, gift items such as journals and picture frames, and office accessories. Oh, right—pens, too. Zero Brattle St., Cambridge. ℂ 617/868-7020. www.cross.com. T: Red Line to Harvard.

Joie de Vivre ⭐⭐⭐ *Finds*   When I'm stumped for a present for a person who has everything, I head to this delightful little shop, which has been here since 1984. Joie de Vivre's constantly changing selection of gifts and toys for adults and sophisticated children is beyond compare. The kaleidoscope collection alone is worth the trip; you'll also find jewelry, note cards, puzzles, music boxes, clocks, stuffed animals, and even salt and pepper shakers. 1792 Massachusetts Ave., Cambridge. ℂ 617/864-8188. www.joiede vivre.net. T: Red Line to Porter.

Museum of Fine Arts Gift Shop ⭐   For those without the time or inclination to visit the museum, the satellite shop carries posters, prints, cards and stationery, books, educational toys, scarves, mugs, T-shirts, and reproductions of jewelry in the museum's collections. You might even be inspired to pay a call on the real thing. 3 South Market Building, Faneuil Hall Marketplace. ℂ 617/720-1266. www.mfashop.org. T: Green or Blue Line to Government Center.

Shake the Tree   Tucked in among the North End's innumerable restaurants is this appealing boutique. It's artsier than a lot of gift shops, with an ever-changing stock of handmade jewelry, clothing, handbags, baby presents, home accessories, candles, and soaps. Closed Sunday in winter. 67 Salem St. ℂ 617/742-0484. www.shakethetreeboston.com. T: Green or Orange Line to Haymarket.

WardMaps.com   A "ward map" shows municipal divisions, usually on a grid and often bound into an atlas. WardMaps.com is an entrancing little place just outside Harvard Square. It carries maps and prints in various sizes and conditions, plus an excellent selection of gift items—coasters, puzzles, mugs, notebooks, and more—printed with (can you guess?) maps. 12 Bow St., Cambridge. ℂ 617/497-0737. www.wardmaps.com. T: Red Line to Harvard.

HOME & GARDEN

Boutique Fabulous ⟨⋆   The name, a classic case of truth in advertising, only partly conveys the fun of exploring this jam-packed emporium of home accessories, antiques, cosmetics, tableware, memorabilia, greeting cards, vintage fashion, and (in case this isn't implied) offbeat gifts. A visit to Boutique Fabulous is the perfect after-dinner treat on a visit to Inman Square—it's open until 10pm Sunday through Friday, 11pm on Sat. 1309 Cambridge St., Cambridge. ℂ 617/864-0656. www.boutiquefabulous.com. T: Red Line to Central, 10-min. walk on Prospect St.

Crate & Barrel ⟨⋆⋆   This is wedding-present heaven, packed with contemporary and classic housewares. The merchandise, from juice glasses and linen napkins to top-of-the-line knives and roasting pans, includes items to suit any budget. The Boylston Street location (which also stocks the full line of housewares) and the Mass. Ave. store carry furniture and home accessories. South Market Building, Faneuil Hall Marketplace. ℂ 617/742-6025. www.crateandbarrel.com. T: Green or Blue Line to Government Center. 777 Boylston St. ℂ 617/262-8700. T: Green Line to Copley. 48 Brattle St., Cambridge. ℂ 617/876-6300. T: Red Line to Harvard. 1045 Massachusetts Ave., Cambridge. ℂ 617/547-3994. T: Red Line to Harvard.

Diptyque   I'm not a candle person, but even I admire the subtly fragrant offerings at this Parisian outpost. The shop carries other scented products, such as soaps and room sprays, and other brands, but if you're looking for a hostess gift with off-the-charts snob appeal, you can't go wrong with a Diptyque candle. 123 Newbury St. ℂ 617/351-2430. www.diptyqueparis.com. T: Green Line to Copley.

Greenward   A quick glance reveals what appears to be an upscale boutique that may be taking the description "colorful" a bit too literally, but that's part of what makes Greenward so ingenious. The merchandise—home goods, fashion accessories (including jewelry), products for cleaning your home and yourself, kids' clothing and toys, and more—are both desirable and eco-conscious (organic, handmade, recycled, recyclable, generally virtuous). 1776 Massachusetts Ave., Cambridge. ℂ 617/395-1338. www.greenwardshop.com. T: Red Line to Porter.

Koo De Kir ⟨⋆⋆   In the heart of 19th-century Beacon Hill, Koo De Kir is a splash of modern style. Creative director Kristine Irving has a great eye, and her selection of contemporary home accessories, furniture, lighting, sculpture, and gifts at every price point—from impulse to investment—ranges from classics-to-be to downright whimsical. 65 Chestnut St. (at Charles St.). ℂ 617/723-8111. www.koodekir.com. T: Red Line to Charles/MGH.

Lekker *Lekker* is Dutch for "tempting," which this striking store certainly is. A perfect fit for the modish South End, it features contemporary home accessories and furniture as well as a delightful selection of gifts for adults and children. Closed Monday. 1317 Washington St. ✆ **877/7-LEKKER** or 617/542-6464. www.lekkerhome.com. T: Orange Line to Back Bay and 10-min. walk, or Washington St. Silver Line to Union Park St.

West Elm The minimalist purveyor of furniture, home accessories, linens, and textiles (also known as Williams Sonoma's answer to Crate & Barrel) operates its first Boston branch in a somewhat inconvenient location near Fenway Park. If this is your style—for decorating or daydreaming—it's worth the time. 160 Brookline Ave. ✆ **888/ 922-4119** or 617/450-9500. www.westelm.com. T: Green Line D to Fenway.

JEWELRY

Beadworks The jewelry at these shops will suit you exactly—you make it yourself. Prices for the dazzling variety of raw materials start at 5¢ a bead, findings (hardware) are available, and you can assemble your finery at the in-store worktable. Beadworks also carries ready-made pieces and schedules jewelry-making workshops; check ahead for details. 167 Newbury St. ✆ **617/247-7227**. www.beadworksboston.com. T: Green Line to Copley. 23 Church St., Cambridge. ✆ **617/868-9777**. T: Red Line to Harvard.

High Gear Jewelry 🐸🐸 The biggest jewelry snob I know makes up excuses to visit the North End just so she can stop in here. This eye-catching shop right on the Freedom Trail carries an impressive selection of reasonably priced costume jewelry, watches, and hair accessories. If you don't see what you want, ask the friendly staff for help—the owner recently turned a pair of pierced earrings into clip-ons for my sister in a matter of seconds, for no extra charge. 204 Hanover St. ✆ **617/523-5804**. T: Green or Orange Line to Haymarket.

John Lewis, Inc. 🐸🐸 *Finds* John Lewis's imaginative women's and men's jewelry— crafted on the premises—suits both traditional and avant-garde tastes. The wide selection of silver, gold, and platinum items and unusual colored stones add to the museum-like shop's appeal. The pieces that mark you as a savvy Bostonian are earrings, necklaces, and bracelets made of hammered metal circles. Closed Sunday and Monday. 97 Newbury St. ✆ **617/266-6665**. www.johnlewisinc.com. T: Green Line to Arlington.

MALLS & SHOPPING CENTERS

CambridgeSide Galleria This three-level mall houses two large department stores— **Macy's** (✆ **617/621-3800**) and **Sears** (✆ **617/252-3500**)—and more than 100 specialty stores. Pleasant but quite generic, it might be the bargaining chip you need to lure your teenager to the nearby Museum of Science.

There's trendy sportswear at **Abercrombie & Fitch** (✆ 617/494-1338) and **H&M** (p. 209), electronics at **Cambridge SoundWorks** (✆ 617/225-3900) and the **Apple Store** (✆ 617/225-0442), casual clothing at **J. Crew** (✆ 617/225-2739), and music and appliances at **Best Buy** (✆ 617/225-2004). The mall also has a branch of **Borders** (p. 206), three restaurants, a food court, and seating along a pleasant canal.

Strollers and wheelchairs are available. Open Monday through Saturday from 10am to 9:30pm, Sunday from 11am to 7pm. 100 CambridgeSide Place, Cambridge. ✆ **617/ 621-8666**. www.shopcambridgeside.com. T: Green Line to Lechmere, or Red Line to Kendall/MIT and free shuttle bus (every 10–20 min.). Garage parking from $1/hr.

Copley Place Copley Place has set the standard for upscale shopping in Boston since 1985. Connected to the Westin and Marriott hotels and the Prudential Center, it's a crossroads for office workers, out-of-towners, and enthusiastic consumers. You can while away a couple of hours or a whole day shopping and dining here and at the adjacent Shops at the Prudential Center (see below) without ever going outdoors.

Some of Copley Place's 100-plus shops will be familiar from the mall at home, but this is emphatically not a suburban shopping complex that happens to be in the city. You'll see high-end stores that don't have another branch in Boston, including **Christian Dior** (© 617/927-7577), **Gucci** (© 617/247-3000), **Jimmy Choo** (© 617/927-9570), **Louis Vuitton** (© 617/437-6519), and **Tiffany & Co.** (© 617/353-0222). The anchor department stores here are **Barneys New York** and **Neiman Marcus.** Also here are the **Artful Hand Gallery** (p. 207) and a branch of **Legal Sea Foods** (p. 106).

Open Monday through Saturday from 10am to 9pm, Sunday from 11am to 7pm. Some stores have longer or shorter hours, and most restaurants are open through late evening. 100 Huntington Ave. © **617/369-5000.** www.simon.com. T: Orange Line to Back Bay or Green Line to Copley. Discounted validated parking with purchase.

Faneuil Hall Marketplace 🏵🏵   The original festival market hall is both wildly popular and widely imitated, and Faneuil Hall Marketplace changes constantly to appeal to visitors as well as locals wary of its touristy reputation. The original part of **Faneuil Hall** itself dates to 1742, and the lower floors preserve the building's retail roots. The **Quincy Market Colonnade,** in the central building, houses a gargantuan selection of food and confections. The bars and restaurants always seem to be crowded, and the shopping is terrific, if generic.

In and around the five buildings, the shops combine "only in Boston" with "only at every mall in the country." **Marketplace Center** and the ground floors of the **North Market** and **South Market buildings** have lots of chain outlets. Most of the unique offerings are under the Quincy Market canopies, where crafts and gifts spill off dozens of **pushcarts,** and upstairs and downstairs in the market buildings.

Shop hours are Monday through Saturday from 10am to 9pm and Sunday from noon to 6pm. The Colonnade opens earlier, and most bars and restaurants close later. If you must drive, many businesses offer a discount at the 75 State St. Garage; there's also parking in the Government Center garage off Congress Street and the marketplace's crowded garage off Atlantic Avenue. Between North, Congress, and State sts. and Atlantic Ave. © **617/338-2323.** www.faneuilhallmarketplace.com. T: Green or Blue Line to Government Center or Orange Line to Haymarket.

The Shops at Prudential Center   The main level of the city's second-tallest tower holds this sprawling complex. In addition to **Saks Fifth Avenue** (© **617/262-8500**), there are dozens of shops and boutiques, a large **Barnes & Noble** (p. 205), a food court, a post office, and five restaurants, including **Legal Sea Foods** (p. 106) and the Cheesecake Factory. Also here are Boston's branches of **Club Monaco** (© **617/ 262-2658**) and **Sephora** (p. 218), and one of a handful of retail outlets for the upscale office and home accessories that **Levenger** (© **800/667-8934** or 617/536-3434;

Tips **Flying Lobsters**

Why go to the trouble of sending a postcard? Send a lobster instead. **James Hook & Co.,** 15 Northern Ave. at Atlantic Avenue (© **617/423-5500;** T: Red Line to South Station), and **Legal Sea Foods Fresh by Mail,** Logan Airport Terminal B and C (© **800/343-5804,** 617/568-2811, or 617/568-2800; www.sendlegal.com; T: Blue Line to Airport), do overnight shipping.

www.levenger.com) calls "tools for serious readers." Vendors sell gifts, souvenirs, and novelty items off carts and kiosks in the arcades, the Greater Boston Convention & Visitors Bureau operates an **information booth,** and there's outdoor space if you need some fresh air.

Hours are Monday through Saturday from 10am to 9pm, Sunday from 11am to 6pm. Restaurant hours vary. 800 Boylston St. ✆ **800/SHOP-PRU.** www.prudentialcenter.com. T: Green Line E to Prudential, Green Line to Copley, Orange Line to Back Bay, or Green Line B, C, or D to Hynes Convention Center. Discounted validated parking with purchase.

MARKETS

Massachusetts farmers and growers under the auspices of the state **Department of Food and Agriculture** (✆ **617/227-3018;** www.mass.gov/agr) dispatch trucks filled with whatever's in season to the heart of the city from July through November. Depending on the time of year, you'll have your pick of berries, herbs, tomatoes, squash, pumpkins, apples, corn, and more, all fresh and reasonably priced. Visit the website for a complete list of state-sponsored markets. In Boston, you can stop by City Hall Plaza on Monday or Wednesday (T: Green or Blue Line to Government Center) or Copley Square on Tuesday or Friday (T: Green Line to Copley or Orange Line to Back Bay). In Cambridge, head to Parking Lot 5, a block from Mass. Ave., in Central Square on Monday (T: Red Line to Central).

The **Boston Public Market** (✆ **617/263-3355;** www.bostonpublicmarket.org) is the first major step in a drive for a permanent public market à la Philadelphia's or Seattle's. Open from mid-June through early November, it offers a tasty mix of farm products and specialty foods at Dewey Square, an open area on the sidewalk on Atlantic Avenue across the street from South Station (Mon, Wed–Thurs 11:30am–6:30pm; T: Red Line to South Station).

The funky, fashionable **SoWa Open Market** (✆ **617/481-2257;** www.southendopen market.com) operates Sunday 10am to 5pm from late May through October in the parking lot at 540 Harrison Ave. in the South End (T: Orange Line to Back Bay, then a 10-min. walk). Originally the South End Open Market, it features numerous craftspeople as well as food merchants in a neighborhood you may not have a chance to explore otherwise.

MUSIC

Looney Tunes Records & Tapes   Where there are college students, there are pizza places, copy shops, and used-CD (and record) stores. Looney Tunes, adjacent to the Berklee College of Music, specializes in classical, jazz, and rock, and sells tons of other tunes at excellent prices. 1106 Boylston St. ✆ **617/247-2238.** www.vinylhigh.com. T: Green Line B, C, or D to Hynes Convention Center.

Newbury Comics   A quickly adapting survivor of the downloading revolution, Newbury Comics is a funky local chain of what were originally record stores; it now stocks a wide selection of posters, gifts, novelty items, T-shirts—and, of course, comics. You'll also still find CDs (and tapes!) of particularly cutting-edge music, with lots of independent labels and imports. 332 Newbury St. ✆ **617/236-4930.** www.newbury.com. T: Green Line B, C, or D to Hynes Convention Center. 1 Washington Mall, off State St. at Washington St. ✆ **617/248-9992.** T: Orange or Blue Line to State. 36 John F. Kennedy St., Cambridge ✆ **617/491-0337.** T: Red Line to Harvard.

Stereo Jack's   I love music; I'm not obsessed, but I can recognize people who are, and the staff here qualifies. If you just can't get enough jazz, blues, and R&B (new and used), you'll feel right at home. 1686 Massachusetts Ave. ✆ **617/497-9447.** www.stereojacks.com. T: Red Line to Porter.

PERFUME & COSMETICS

Colonial Drug ⊛⊛ (Finds) The perfume counter at this family business puts the "special" in "specialize." You can choose from more than 1,000 fragrances—plus cosmetics, soap, and countless other body-care products—with the help of the gracious staff members. They remain unflappable even during Harvard Square's equivalent of rush hour, Saturday afternoon. No credit cards; closed Sunday. 49 Brattle St., Cambridge. ℂ 617/864-2222. T: Red Line to Harvard.

Kiehl's ⊛ Lots of trends originate in New York, but few of them develop this kind of cult following. Customers wax evangelical over the skin, hair, and body products from Kiehl's ("since 1851"), which straddle the line between cosmetics and pharmaceuticals. 112 Newbury St. ℂ 617/247-1777. www.kiehls.com. T: Green Line to Copley.

Lush ⊛⊛⊛ Of all the lotions-and-potions purveyors in the Boston area, this is my favorite. It smells great, and the enthusiastic staff is entirely attitude-free. U.K.-based Lush specializes in fresh, organic, natural products, notably "bath bombs" (solid bubble bath) and solid shampoo priced by the pound. 166 Newbury St. ℂ 617/375-5874. www.lush.com. T: Green Line to Copley. 30 John F. Kennedy St. ℂ 617/497-5874. T: Red Line to Harvard.

Sephora ⊛ This European phenomenon is a fashionista magnet. You'll find an encyclopedic, international selection of manufacturers and products in a well-lit, well-organized space overflowing with testers. Everything is self-service, and the staff provides as much help as you want. Shops at Prudential Center, 800 Boylston St. ℂ 617/262-4200. www.sephora.com. T: Green Line E to Prudential, Green Line to Copley, or Green Line or B, C, or D to Hynes Convention Center.

SHOES & BOOTS

Also see the listing for **DSW Shoe Warehouse** under "Discount Shopping," earlier in this chapter.

Berk's Shoes "Trendy" doesn't adequately describe the wares at this Harvard Square institution. College students and people who want to look like them come here to stock up on whatever's fashionable right this red-hot minute. 50 John F. Kennedy St. ℂ 888/GO-BERKS or 617/492-9511. www.berkshoes.com. T: Red Line to Harvard.

Cuoio The enormous selections of designer footwear at these compact boutiques are dream fuel for the truly fetishistic (you know who you are). Be sure to check out the dramatically discounted clearance merchandise. 115 Newbury St. ℂ 617/859-0636. T: Green Line to Arlington. 170 Faneuil Hall Marketplace. ℂ 617/742-4486. T: Blue Line to Aquarium or Green Line to Government Center.

Helen's Leather Shop ⊛ Homesick Texans visit Helen's just to gaze upon the boots. Many are handmade from exotic leathers, including ostrich, buffalo, and snakeskin. The shop carries brands such as Lucchese and Tony Lama, along with a large selection of other leather goods, Western shirts, belts and buckles, and Stetson hats. Closed Tuesday. 110 Charles St. ℂ 617/742-2077. www.helensleather.com. T: Red Line to Charles/MGH.

Moxie ⊛ A chic little shop with an unbelievable selection of designer shoes, Moxie may look like an intimidating boutique, but it so isn't. The welcoming, helpful staff will help you put together an ensemble of accessories (shoes, handbag, jewelry) that makes you feel like a princess—while making you feel like a princess. 51 Charles St. ℂ 617/557-9991. www.moxieboston.com. T: Red Line to Charles/MGH.

TOYS & GAMES

A number of businesses listed earlier in this chapter are good places to look for toys. They include most of the shops under "Gifts & Souvenirs," **Curious George Books & Toys** (see "Books"), and **Calliope** (see "Fashion"). Also be sure to check out the gift shops at the **Children's Museum, Museum of Science,** and **New England Aquarium.**

The Games People Play ⭐ Just outside Harvard Square, this 30-plus-year-old business carries enough board games (foreign as well as domestic) to outfit every country, summer, and beach house in New England. Also check out the puzzles, playing cards, role-playing games, Steiff toys, and chess and backgammon sets. 1100 Massachusetts Ave., Cambridge. ℂ 800/696-0711 or 617/492-0711. T: Red Line to Harvard.

Stellabella Toys ⭐⭐ Both retro (lots of wooden toys) and modern (no guns), Stellabella is a welcoming destination for parents and kids alike. It carries everything from baby strollers to craft supplies and costumes for big kids, and the friendly staff can lend a hand if you need help maintaining your status as the cool aunt or uncle. 1360 Cambridge St., Inman Sq., Cambridge. ℂ 617/491-6290. www.stellabellatoys.com. T: Red Line to Central, then 10-min. walk on Prospect St. 1967 Massachusetts Ave., Cambridge. ℂ 617/864-6290. T: Red Line to Porter.

VINTAGE & SECONDHAND CLOTHING

Bobby From Boston ⭐ Boston's vintage clothing scene tends to be light on men's options (but not on whining about it). The perfect antidote is this off-the-beaten-track shop run by a veteran dealer who specializes in supplying wardrobe for period films. The focus is the 1940s through '70s. Open by appointment only. 19 Thayer St. ℂ 617/423-9299. T: Silver Line bus from Temple Pl., Downtown Crossing, to E. Berkeley St. Or Orange Line to New England Medical Center and 10-min. walk.

The Closet This is the not-very-secret weapon of many a chic shopper. One of Boston's best consignment shops, it offers "gently worn" (not vintage) high-end designer clothing and accessories (be sure to check out the shoes and bags) for women and men at drastically reduced prices. 175 Newbury St. ℂ 617/536-1919. T: Green Line to Copley.

The Garment District ⭐ You're hitting the clubs and you want to look cool, but money is tight. You'll be right at home among the shoppers here, paying great prices for a huge selection of contemporary and vintage clothing, costumes, and accessories. "Dollar a pound" merchandise on the first floor actually costs $1.50 a pound. And Boston Costume, which is on the premises, is *the* go-to place for rental, retail, and vintage costumes, which are available year-round. 200 Broadway, Cambridge. ℂ 617/876-5230. www.garmentdistrict.com. T: Red Line to Kendall/MIT.

Oona's ⭐⭐ From funky accessories and costume jewelry to vintage dresses nice enough to get married in, Oona's carries an extensive selection of "experienced clothing" at good prices. The Harvard Square stalwart, which opened in 1973, is especially busy at Halloween but great fun anytime. 1210 Massachusetts Ave., Cambridge. ℂ 617/491-2654. T: Red Line to Harvard.

Velvet Fly The merchandise here isn't exclusively vintage, but even the newest pieces share that sensibility—you definitely won't see your outfit on anyone else. Unusual accessories complement the flirty fashions. The Velvet Fly is one of the little boutiques that's helping the North End develop its own quirky fashion sense; it's on the main drag past where the restaurants peter out. 424 Hanover St. ℂ 617/557-4359. www.thevelvetfly.com. T: Green or Orange Line to Haymarket.

10

Boston After Dark

Countless musicians, actors, and comedians went to college or got their start in the Boston area, and it's a great place to check out rising stars and promising unknowns. You might get an early look at the next Branford Marsalis, Matt Damon, Bonnie Raitt, or Yo-Yo Ma. And you'll certainly be able to enjoy the work of many established artists.

The nightlife scene is, to put it mildly, lame. You can be home from a night on the town when your friends in New York are still drying their hair. (In fact, flying to New York after work and taking the first shuttle back the next morning isn't unheard of.) Clubs close at 2am, which means packing a lot into 4 hours or less.

For up-to-date entertainment listings, consult the "Sidekick" section in the daily *Boston Globe,* the "Edge" section of Friday's *Boston Herald,* and the Sunday arts sections of both papers. Four free publications, available at newspaper boxes around town, publish good nightlife listings: the weekly *Boston Phoenix* and *Weekly Dig,* and the biweekly *Stuff@ Night* (a *Phoenix* offshoot) and *Improper Bostonian.* The *Phoenix* website (www. bostonphoenix.com) archives the paper's season-preview issues; especially before a summer or fall visit, it's a valuable planning tool.

1 Getting Tickets

Some companies and venues sell tickets over the phone or the Internet; many will refer you to a ticket agency. Two major agencies serve Boston: **Ticketmaster** (© 617/ 931-2000; www.ticketmaster.com) and **Telecharge** (© 800/447-7400 or TTY 888/ 889-8587; www.telecharge.com). Many smaller venues use independent companies that don't charge as much. To avoid fees—and possible losses if your plans change and you can't get your money back—visit the box office in person. *Tip:* If you wait until the day before or day of a performance, you'll sometimes have access to tickets that were held back for some reason and have just gone on sale.

2 The Performing Arts

PERFORMANCE VENUES

The **Hatch Shell** on the Esplanade (© 617/727-5215; www.mass.gov/dcr/hatch_ events.htm; T: Red Line to Charles/MGH or Green Line to Arlington) is an amphitheater best known for the Boston Pops' Fourth of July concerts. On many summer nights, free music and dance performances and films take over the stage, to the delight of crowds on the lawn.

Agganis Arena at Boston University BU's hockey arena is also a popular midsize concert venue. The facility, which opened in 2005, seats 6,300 to 7,200. It books rock and pop concerts and ice shows, such as Santana and *Sesame Street Live* (not at the same

(*Value* **Let's Make a Deal**

Yankee thrift gains artistic expression at the **BosTix** booths at Faneuil Hall Marketplace, on the south side of Faneuil Hall (T: Green or Blue Line to Government Center, or Orange Line to Haymarket), and in Copley Square at the corner of Boylston and Dartmouth streets (T: Green Line to Copley or Orange Line to Back Bay). Same-day tickets to musical and theatrical performances are half price, subject to availability. You must pay cash in person, and there are no refunds or exchanges. Check the board or the website for the day's offerings. The booths are also Ticketmaster outlets. Both are open Tuesday through Saturday from 10am to 6pm (half-price tickets go on sale at 11am), and Sunday from 11am to 4pm. The Copley Square location is also open Monday from 10am to 6pm.

   BosTix (© **617/262-8632;** www.artsboston.org) also offers full-price advance tickets; discounts on more than 100 theater, music, and dance events; and tickets for trolley tours. *Tip:* Sign up for email updates (you can always unsubscribe after you return home).

time), as well as sporting events. 925 Commonwealth Ave. © **617/353-4628** (ticket office) or 617/931-2000 (Ticketmaster). www.agganisarena.com. T: Green Line B to St. Paul St. or Pleasant St.

Bank of America Pavilion   One of the most pleasant venues in the area, this giant white tent encloses a 5,000-seat waterfront pavilion. It schedules pop, rock, country, rap, folk, and jazz on evenings from May through September. Check ahead for information about water transportation. 290 Northern Ave., South Boston. © **617/728-1600** or 617/931-2000 (Ticketmaster). www.bankofamericapavilion.com. T: Waterfront Silver Line bus to Silver Line Way.

Berklee Performance Center   The Berklee College of Music's theater features professional artists (many of them former Berklee students, both alumni and dropouts), instructors, and students. Offerings are heavy on jazz and folk, with plenty of other options. 136 Massachusetts Ave. © **617/747-8890** or 617/747-2261 (box office). www.berkleebpc.com. T: Green Line B, C, or D to Hynes Convention Center.

Boston Center for the Arts   Multiple performance spaces and an anything-goes booking policy make the BCA a leading venue for contemporary theater, music and dance performances, and visual arts exhibitions. The BCA and the Huntington Theatre Company (see "Theater," below) are partners in the Theatre Pavilion, which incorporates 350- and 200-seat theaters. 539 Tremont St. © **617/426-5000.** www.bcaonline.org. T: Orange Line to Back Bay.

Cambridge Multicultural Arts Center   Concerts, plays, art and photography exhibits, dance performances, and films jam the schedule at this renovated courthouse not far from the CambridgeSide Galleria mall. CMAC is also home to the **Real Deal Jazz Club & Cafe** (© **617/876-7777;** www.concertix.com), a 200-seat cabaret that books local, national, and international performers. 41 Second St., Cambridge © **617/577-1400.** www.cmacusa.org. T: Green Line Lechmere.

Citi Wang Theatre   This Art Deco palace books numerous and varied national companies. Through the end of the 2008–09 season, it's home to **Boston Ballet** (except for *The Nutcracker*). Part of Citi Performing Arts Center, it's sometimes still called the Wang Center, its pre-Citicorp name. 270 Tremont St. © **800/447-7400** (Telecharge) or 617/482-9393. www.citicenter.org. T: Green Line to Boylston or Orange Line to New England Medical Center.

Boston After Dark

Agganis Arena **2**
AMC Loews Boston Common **61**
Bank of America Pavilion **87**
The Bar at Taj Boston **27**
The Beehive **38**
Berklee Performance Center **19**
Bill's Bar **9**
The Black Rose **83**
Blackman Theater
　(Northeastern U.) **13**
Bob's Southern Bistro **14**
BosTix (Copley Sq.) **32**
BosTix (Faneuil Hall) **81**
Boston Beanstock Coffee Co.
　(North End) **77**
Boston Beanstock Coffee Co.
　(High St.) **65**
Boston Beer Works
　(Brookline Ave.) **3**
Boston Beer Works (Canal St.) **73**
Boston Billiard Club **4**
Boston Center for the Arts **38**
Boston Harbor Hotel **86**
Brasserie Jo **23**
The Bristol **43**
C. Walsh Theatre (Suffolk U.) **70**
Caffè Pompei **76**
Cask 'n Flagon **6**
Charles Playhouse **51**
Cheers (Beacon Hill) **26**
Cheers (Faneuil Hall) **82**
Citi Wang Theatre **54**
Club Café **35**
Colonial Theatre **46**

The Comedy Connection
　at Faneuil Hall **82**
Commonwealth Shakespeare
　Company **44**
Copley Theatre **29**
Cutler Majestic Theatre **48**
Davio's Northern Italian
　Steakhouse **40**
DeLux Cafe **36**
Emmanuel Music **28**
The Estate **47**
Felt **63**
Finale **42**
The Fours **72**
Fritz **39**
Game On! Sports Cafe **5**
Ginza Japanese Restaurant **57**
The Grand Canal **74**
Hard Rock Cafe **80**
Hatch Shell **25**
House of Blues (*opening 2009*) **8**
Huntington Theatre Company **17**
Icarus **40**
Improv Asylum **78**
Isabella Stewart Gardner
　Museum **11**
Jacob Wirth **56**
Jacques **49**
Jillian's Boston **10**
Kings **21**
King's Chapel **68**
Les Zygomates **60**
Lucky Strike Lanes **9**
Lyric Stage **34**

Mr. Dooley's Boston Tavern **85**
Museum of Fine Arts **12**
New England Conservatory **16**
News Restaurant & Lounge **58**
Oak Bar **33**
Old South Church **24**
Opera House **62**
Orpheum Theater **66**
Paradise Rock Club **1**
Pho Republique **37**
Pizzeria Regina **75**
The Place **84**
The Purple Shamrock **79**
Radius **84**
Rowes Wharf Bar **86**
The Roxy **53**
Shubert Theatre **52**
Silvertone Bar & Grill **67**
South Street Diner **59**
Stuart Street Playhouse **50**
Symphony Hall **18**
TD Banknorth Garden **71**
Tealuxe **30**
Top of the Hub **22**
Trident Booksellers & Café **20**
Trinity Church **31**
Troquet **45**
21st Amendment **69**
Via Matta **41**
Wally's Café **15**
Wilbur Theater **55**

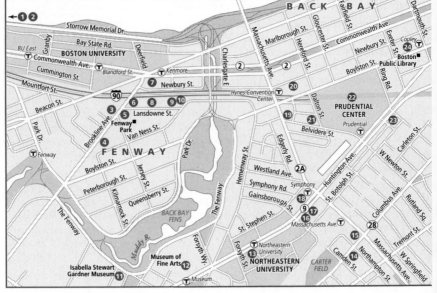

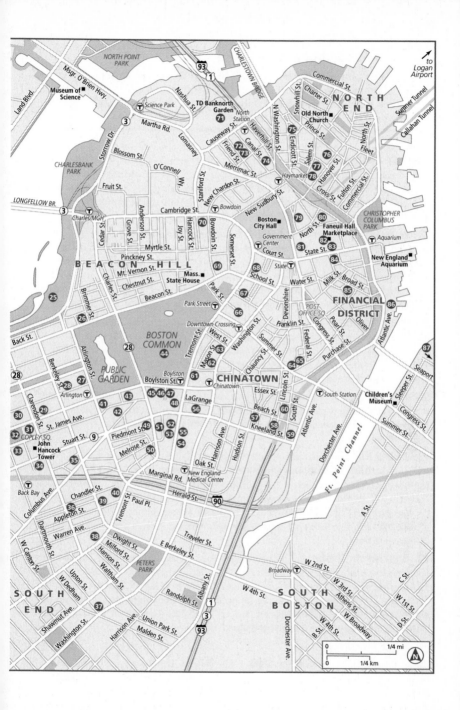

Tips **Music Under the Sky & Stars**

The **Boston Landmarks Orchestra** (📞 **617/520-2200**; www.landmarksorchestra. org) performs free in parks around town, including the Hatch Shell, on evenings from July through September. A concert is a great excuse to visit a pretty park and hear some excellent music.

Comcast Center   When a mainstream act's summer schedule says "Boston," that often means this bucolic setting about an hour south of town. A sheltered (it has a roof but no sides) auditorium surrounded by a lawn, the Comcast Center features rock, pop, folk, country, and light classical artists. Shows go on rain or shine. 885 S. Main St. (Rte. 140), Mansfield. 📞 **508/339-2331** or 617/931-2000 (Ticketmaster). www.livenation.com.

Cutler Majestic Theatre   A popular dance, music, and opera performance space, the Cutler Majestic is the home stage of several small arts companies. The gorgeous theater also books a diverse slate of touring shows, groups, and companies as well as Emerson College student productions. Check the website for the schedule of tours ($5) of the building, a 1903 Beaux Arts landmark. 219 Tremont St. 📞 **800/233-3123** (Telecharge) or 617/824-8000 (information). www.maj.org. T: Green Line to Boylston or Orange Line to Chinatown.

Orpheum Theater   Although it's old (1852) and cramped, the Orpheum offers an intimate setting for big-name performers. It books top local acts, popular up-and-coming artists, and international icons, recently including Ray Davies, James Blunt, and KT Tunstall. 1 Hamilton Place (off Tremont St., across from Park St. Church). 📞 **617/679-0810** or 617/931-2000 (Ticketmaster). www.livenation.com. T: Red or Green Line to Park St.

Sanders Theatre   A landmark space in Harvard's Memorial Hall, Sanders Theatre schedules big names in classical, folk, and world music, as well as student performances. 45 Quincy St. (at Cambridge St.), Cambridge. 📞 **617/496-4595**. www.fas.harvard.edu/~memhall. T: Red Line to Harvard.

Symphony Hall   Acoustically perfect Symphony Hall, which opened in 1900, is the home of the **Boston Symphony Orchestra** and the **Boston Pops.** When they're away, top-notch classical, chamber, world, and popular music artists from elsewhere take over. For information on free tours of Symphony Hall, see p. 174. 301 Massachusetts Ave. (at Huntington Ave.). 📞 **617-266-1492** or 617/266-2378 (concert information). SymphonyCharge 📞 **888/266-1200** or 617/266-1200. www.bostonsymphonyhall.org. T: Green Line E to Symphony or Orange Line to Mass. Ave.

TD Banknorth Garden   This state-of-the-art facility is home to the Bruins (hockey), the Celtics (basketball), the circus (in Oct), ice shows (at least twice a year), and touring rock and pop artists of all stripes. Concerts in the 19,600-seat Garden— "Gah-den," in Bostonian—are in the round or in the arena stage format. 100 Legends Way (Causeway St.) 📞 **617/624-1000** (events line) or 617/931-2000 (Ticketmaster). www.tdbanknorth garden.com. T: Orange or Green Line to North Station.

CLASSICAL MUSIC

Boston Symphony Orchestra ★★★   The Boston Symphony, one of the world's greatest, was founded in 1881. The repertoire includes contemporary music, but classical is the BSO's calling card—you might want to schedule your trip to coincide with a particular performance or with a visit by a celebrated guest artist. Illustrious conductor

James Levine is the music director (he holds the same title with New York City's Metropolitan Opera).

The season runs from October to April, with performances most Tuesday, Thursday, and Saturday evenings; Friday afternoons; and some Friday evenings. Thirty-minute explanatory talks (included in the ticket price) begin 1 hour and 15 minutes before the curtain rises. If you aren't able to get tickets in advance, check at the box office for returns from subscribers 2 hours before show time. A limited number of same-day **rush tickets** (one per person) are available for Tuesday and Thursday evening and Friday afternoon, and some Wednesday evening and Thursday morning rehearsals are open to the public. Symphony Hall, 301 Massachusetts Ave. (at Huntington Ave.). ℂ 617/266-1492 or 617/CONCERT (program information). SymphonyCharge ℂ 888/266-1200 or 617/266-1200. www.bso.org. Tickets $29–$114. Rush tickets $9 (on sale Fri 10am; Tues, Thurs 5pm). Rehearsal tickets $19. T: Green Line E to Symphony or Orange Line to Mass. Ave.

Boston Pops ⭐⭐ "It's nice to eat a good hunk of beef," longtime Boston Pops conductor Arthur Fiedler once said, "but you want a light dessert, too." The Pops are the dessert to the BSO's beef. From early May to early July, tables and chairs replace the floor seats at Symphony Hall, and drinks and light refreshments are served. Under the direction of conductor Keith Lockhart, the Pops play a range of music from light classical to show tunes to popular (hence the name), often with celebrity guest stars of both the Broadway and Top 40 variety. Performances are Tuesday through Sunday evenings. Special holiday performances in December ($32–$118) usually sell out well in advance, but it can't hurt to check; tickets go on sale in late October.

The regular season ends with two **free outdoor concerts at the Hatch Shell** on the Esplanade along the Charles River. The traditional **Fourth of July** concert is a mob scene; the rehearsal the night before is merely very crowded. Both are great fun. Performing at Symphony Hall, 301 Mass. Ave. (at Huntington Ave.). ℂ 617/266-1492 or 617/CONCERT (program information). SymphonyCharge ℂ 888/266-1200 or 617/266-1200. www.bso.org. Tickets $40–$87 for tables, $19–$52 for balcony seats. T: Green Line E to Symphony or Orange Line to Mass. Ave.

Handel & Haydn Society ⭐⭐ The Handel & Haydn Society uses period instruments and techniques in its orchestral, choral, and opera performances, yet it's as cutting-edge as any other ensemble in town. Established in 1815, it's the oldest continuously performing arts organization in the country. The company prides itself on its creative programming of "historically informed" concerts, which it stages from September through mid-May, with most performances at Symphony Hall and New England Conservatory's Jordan Hall. Works by Handel and Haydn predominate but don't take up the entire schedule.

⟮Tips⟯ A Major Music Festival in the Bucolic Berkshires

When the Boston Symphony Orchestra goes away for the summer, it goes to **Tanglewood** (ℂ 413/637-5165 or 617/266-1492 out of season; www.tanglewood.org), in Lenox, Massachusetts, a 2½-hour drive from Boston. Weekend concerts sell out in advance, but tickets to weeknight performances and Saturday morning rehearsals are usually available at the box office. If you can't get a seat inside, bring a blanket and picnic on the lawn. (Consult *Frommer's New England* for in-depth coverage of western Massachusetts.)

H&H was the first American group to perform Handel's *Messiah,* in 1818, and has made it an annual holiday tradition since 1854. If you'll be in town in December, check for ticket availability as soon as you start planning your trip. 300 Massachusetts Ave. ℭ 617/266-3605. www.handelandhaydn.org. Tickets $15–$83. T: Green Line E to Symphony or Orange Line to Mass. Ave.

ADDITIONAL OFFERINGS

The **Boston Lyric Opera** (ℭ **800/447-7400** Telecharge or 617/542-6772; box office, 270 Tremont St.; www.blo.org) nurtures and showcases emerging talent in its classical and contemporary productions. The season runs from November to May at Citi Performing Arts Center's Shubert Theatre, 265 Tremont St. Tickets cost $34 to $126.

Less familiar works make up the repertoire of **Opera Boston** (ℭ **800/432-7250** Telecharge or 617/451-3388; www.operaboston.org), which performs at the Cutler Majestic Theatre, 219 Tremont St. Tickets go for $29 to $114.

Boston Baroque (ℭ **617/484-9200;** www.bostonbaroque.org), a Grammy-nominated period orchestra with a chamber chorus, performs at New England Conservatory's Jordan Hall and Harvard's Sanders Theatre. Tickets cost $25 to $72.

CONCERT & PERFORMANCE SERIES

The starriest names in classical music, dance, theater, jazz, opera, and world music play Boston as part of the **Celebrity Series** (ℭ **617/482-2595** or 617/482-6661 for Celebrity Charge; www.celebrityseries.org). It's a subscription series that also offers tickets to individual events, which go on sale in September. Performances take place at Symphony Hall, New England Conservatory's Jordan Hall, the Wang and Shubert theaters, and other venues.

World Music (ℭ **617/876-4275;** www.worldmusic.org) showcases top-flight musicians, dance troupes, and other performers from around the globe. Shows (70 a year) are at the Somerville Theater, the Berklee Performance Center, Sanders Theatre, the Cutler Majestic Theatre, and other venues.

The **Isabella Stewart Gardner Museum,** 280 The Fenway (ℭ **617/278-5102** [info line] or 278-5156 [box office]; www.gardnermuseum.org; T: Green Line E to Museum), features music in the Tapestry Room most Sundays at 1:30pm and some Thursdays at 7pm from September through May. Sunday performances are chamber music by the museum orchestra, professionals, and students; on Thursdays, jazz and new music take over. Tickets (including museum admission) are $23 adults, $18 seniors, $10 students with ID, $5 children 5 to 17 (children under 5 not admitted). Free podcasts are available through the website. See p. 144 for a full museum listing.

FREE (& ALMOST FREE) CONCERTS

Radio stations sponsor free outdoor music all summer. Specifics change frequently, but you can count on hearing oldies, pop, jazz, alternative, rock, and classical music at various convenient venues, including City Hall Plaza, Copley Square, and the Hatch Shell, at lunch, after work, and in the evening. Check the papers when you arrive, listen to a station that sounds good to you, or just follow the crowds.

Students and faculty members at two prestigious musical institutions perform frequently during the academic year; admission is usually free. For information, contact the **New England Conservatory of Music,** 290 Huntington Ave. (ℭ **617/585-1260;** http://concerts.newenglandconservatory.edu), or the **Longy School of Music,** 1 Follen St., Cambridge (ℭ **617/876-0956,** ext. 500; www.longy.edu). Also check listings for free or cheap student performances at other area colleges.

Emmanuel Music ⟨★★⟩   The gorgeous building fills with equally exquisite music every Sunday from mid-September through mid-May. Emmanuel Music's orchestra and chorus perform Bach cantatas during the 10am service. 15 Newbury St. ⟨ℂ⟩ 617/ 536-3356. www.emmanuelmusic.org. Free-will offering. T: Green Line to Arlington.

Fridays at Trinity   This landmark church features 30-minute organ recitals by local and visiting artists on Fridays at 12:15pm. Trinity Church, 206 Clarendon St., Copley Sq. ⟨ℂ⟩ 617/536-0944. www.trinitychurchboston.org. $5 donation suggested. T: Green Line to Copley or Orange Line to Back Bay.

King's Chapel Noon Hour Recitals   Organ, instrumental, and vocal classical, jazz, and folk music fills this historic building with music and makes for a pleasant break along the Freedom Trail. Concerts begin at 12:15pm on Tuesday and last 30 to 40 minutes. 58 Tremont St. ⟨ℂ⟩ 617/227-2155. www.kings-chapel.org. $3 donation requested. T: Red or Green Line to Park St.

Old South Church   The church choir sings at the 11am Sunday service, accompanied by a Skinner organ, and a 1-hour jazz service begins every Thursday at 6pm. The congregation dates to 1669, the elaborate Northern Italian Gothic building to 1875, and the 7,625-pipe organ to 1921. 645 Boylston St. ⟨ℂ⟩ 617/536-1970. www.oldsouth.org. Voluntary offering. T: Green Line to Copley.

DANCE

The **Celebrity Series** and **World Music** (see Concert & Performance Series, above) schedule numerous touring dance troupes; check ahead when you're planning your trip.

Boston Ballet ⟨★★⟩   Boston Ballet's reputation seems to jump a notch every time someone says, "So it's not just *The Nutcracker.*" One of the top dance companies in the country, Boston Ballet performs an eclectic mix of classic story ballets and contemporary works during the rest of the season (Oct–May). The holiday classic runs from Thanksgiving to New Year's at the **Opera House,** 539 Washington St. Beginning in the fall of 2009, the Opera House will be the company's full-time home, which is great news for dance aficionados. The current venue, the **Citi Wang Theatre,** was originally a movie theater, and the pitch of the seats makes the top two balconies less than ideal for watching ballet. Paying more for a better seat is a good investment. *Nutcracker* tickets go on sale in early July; for the rest of the season, in September. Performing at the Citi Wang Theatre, 270 Tremont St., and the Opera House, 539 Washington St. ⟨ℂ⟩ 800/447-7400 (Telecharge) or 617/695-6955. www.bostonballet.org. Tickets $45–$110. Senior, student, and child rush tickets (2 hr. before curtain) $20, except for *Nutcracker.* T: Green Line to Boylston.

THEATER

Local and national companies, professional and amateur actors, and classic and experimental drama combine to make the local theater scene a lively one. Call or surf ahead, or check the papers or BosTix (see "Let's Make a Deal," on p. 142) after you arrive.

Boston is one of the last cities for pre-Broadway tryouts, allowing an early look at a classic (or a catastrophe) in the making. It's also a popular destination for touring companies of established hits. The promoter is often **Broadway Across America** (⟨ℂ⟩ 866/523-7469; www.broadwayacrossamerica.com). You'll find most of the shows headed to or coming from Broadway in the Theater District, at the **Colonial Theatre,** 106 Boylston St. (⟨ℂ⟩ 617/426-9366); the **Opera House,** 539 Washington St. (⟨ℂ⟩ 617/880-2400); the **Shubert Theatre,** 265 Tremont St. (⟨ℂ⟩ 617/482-9393); the **Citi Wang Theatre,** 270 Tremont St. (⟨ℂ⟩ 617/482-9393); and the **Wilbur Theater,**

246 Tremont St. (© **617/423-4008**). The Citi Performing Arts Center operates the Wang and the Shubert.

The excellent local theater scene boasts two nationally acclaimed repertory companies that stage classic and contemporary productions. The **Huntington Theatre Company** performs at the Boston University Theatre, 264 Huntington Ave. (© **617/ 266-0800;** www.huntingtontheatre.org). The **American Repertory Theatre,** or ART (pronounced A-R-T), which makes its home at Harvard University's **Loeb Drama Center,** 64 Brattle St., Cambridge (© **617/547-8300;** www.amrep.org), also books the **Zero Arrow Theatre,** 0 Arrow Street at Mass. Ave.

The **Lyric Stage,** 140 Clarendon St. (© **617/585-5678;** www.lyricstage.com), mounts contemporary and modern works in an intimate second-floor setting. The **Stuart Street Playhouse,** 200 Stuart St., in the Radisson Hotel Boston (© **617/426-4499;** www.stuartstreetplayhouse.com), books one-person shows and revues.

The innumerable college options include Suffolk University's **C. Walsh Theatre,** 55 Temple St., Beacon Hill (© **617/573-8680**); various performance spaces at **Boston University** (© **617/266-0800**), **Harvard** (© **617/495-8676;** www.fas.harvard.edu/~ofa), and **MIT** (© **617/253-4003;** web.mit.edu/arts); and Northeastern's **Blackman Theater,** 360 Huntington Ave. (© **617/373-2247**).

FAMILY THEATER/AUDIENCE PARTICIPATION

Charles Playhouse *(Kids)*   The off-Broadway sensation **Blue Man Group** *★★* began selling out the Charles Playhouse's Stage I as soon as it arrived in 1995. The trio of cobalt-colored entertainers backed by a rock band uses music, percussion, food, and audience members in its performance. It's not recommended for children under 8, but older kids will love it. Shows are usually at 7:30pm Wednesday and Thursday; 7 and 10pm Friday; 4, 7, and 10pm Saturday; and 1 and 4pm Sunday (with extra performances during the holidays and school vacations). Tickets are available at the box office and through Ticketmaster.

Shear Madness *★*, on Stage II (downstairs), is the longest-running nonmusical play in theater history. Since January 1980, the zany "comic murder mystery" has turned the stage into a unisex hairdressing salon—and crime scene. The show's never the same twice; one of the original audience-participation productions, the play changes as spectator-investigators question suspects, reconstruct events, and then name the murderer. Performances are Tuesday through Friday at 8pm, Saturday at 6 and 9pm, and Sunday at 3 and 7pm. 74 Warrenton St. © 617/426-6912 (Blue Man Group) and 617/426-5225 *(Shear Madness).* www.blueman.com and www.shearmadness.com. Blue Man Group $58

Finds **A Summer Theater Treat**

The **Commonwealth Shakespeare Company** *★★★* (© **617/482-9393;** www.free shakespeare.org) usually performs free on Boston Common Tuesday through Sunday nights in late July and early August. Bring a picnic and blanket, rent a chair ($5 or so) if you don't want to sit on the ground, and enjoy the sunset and a high-quality performance. The company, which is affiliated with the Citi Performing Arts Center, is about half Equity actors, and the sets are spectacular. Maintenance work on the Common may affect the schedule during your visit; check ahead.

Finds Dessert Alert

Finale is one of the best debuts Boston's Theater District has seen in many years. It's a "desserterie" that serves a mouth-watering variety of glorious desserts in elegant, romantic surroundings with lots of velvet and soft lighting. Yes, it's a tad expensive. No, this is not a balanced meal. But the sweet tooths (sweet teeth?) who flock here don't care. The original is at 1 Columbus Ave., in the pointy end of the Park Plaza Building (*©* **617/423-3184;** www.finaledesserts.com), with branches at 30 Dunster St., Harvard Square (*©* **617/441-9797**), and 1306 Beacon St., Coolidge Corner, Brookline (*©* **617/232-3233**). Finale also serves real food, such as salads and pizzas, but the desserts are the real draw.

---

and $48; student rush $25 when available. *Shear Madness* $40; student rush $20 when available. T: Green Line to Boylston.

Le Grand David and His Own Spectacular Magic Company *☆* *Kids* Three generations of magicians make up this company, a nationally acclaimed troupe of illusionists that has delighted families since 1977. The ever-changing 2-hour shows, directed by master magician Marco the Magi, take place on Sunday afternoon and Thursday evening at two historic theaters in Beverly, about 40 minutes from Boston by car. It makes a perfect stop after a sightseeing excursion to the North Shore (see chapter 11). Cabot Street Cinema Theater, 286 Cabot St., Beverly; and Larcom Theatre, 13 Wallis St., Beverly. *©* **978/927-3677.** www.legranddavid.com. Tickets $20 adults, $12 children under 12.

Puppet Showplace Theatre *Kids* The Puppet Showplace presents favorite fables, ethnic legends, and folktales and fairy tales from around the world. Professional puppeteers put on creative, engaging shows year-round in a lovely 100-seat theater. The theater displays historic puppets and puppet posters, offers puppet-making workshops, and sells toy puppets. Family performances take place on weekends, with shows for toddlers on weekdays. Adult-oriented "Puppets at Night" shows play this theater and at other local venues. Call for schedules and reservations. 32 Station St., Brookline. *©* **617/731-6400.** www.puppetshowplace.org. Tickets $10 for children's shows, $13–$20 for adult shows. T: Green Line D to Brookline Village.

3 The Club & Music Scene

The Boston-area club scene is multifaceted and constantly changing. As a rule, live music is more compelling than the dance-club scene by several orders of magnitude, but somewhere out there is a good time for anyone, regardless of age, musical taste, or budget. Check the "Sidekick" section of the daily *Globe*, the "Edge" section of Friday's *Herald*, the *Phoenix*, *Stuff@Night*, or the *Improper Bostonian* for ideas.

Clubs cluster on **Lansdowne Street**, near Boston's Kenmore Square, and on **Boylston Place**, off Boylston Street near Boston Common. The center of the local live-music universe is **Central Square** in Cambridge. Rowdy college bars and clubs abound near the intersection of Harvard and Brighton avenues in **Allston** (T: Green Line B to Harvard Ave.). That makes club-hopping easy, but it also means dealing with swarms of teenagers, students, and recent college grads. To steer clear, stick to slightly more upscale and less centrally located nightspots. If you do like teenagers

---

Tips Got a Light? Not So Fast!

Massachusetts state law forbids smoking in all workplaces, including bars, nightclubs, and restaurants.

(or you are one), seek out a place where admission is 18- or 19-plus. Policies change regularly, sometimes from night to night, so check ahead.

A night on the town in Boston and Cambridge is brief: Most bars close by 1am, clubs close at 2am, and the T shuts down between 12:30 and 1am. The drinking age is 21; a valid driver's license or passport is required as proof of age, and the law is strictly enforced, especially near college campuses.

COMEDY CLUBS

The annual **Boston International Comedy & Movie Festival** (© 617/782-8100; www.bostoncomedyfestival.com) attracts big-name national performers, local up-and-comers, and films. The increasingly popular weeklong event takes place all over town in early to mid-September; check ahead for schedules and venues.

The Comedy Connection at Faneuil Hall ★★ A large room with a clear view from every seat, the oldest original comedy club in town (established in 1978) draws top-notch talent from near and far. Opening acts are usually local and hilarious; national headliners you'll recognize from late-night TV break loose from the censors and draw enthusiastic crowds. There's one show a night Sunday through Thursday, two shows Friday and Saturday (times vary, so call ahead for specifics). The cover charge seldom tops $20 during the week but jumps for big names appearing on weekends. *This just in:* Check ahead—by the time you read this, the Comedy Connection may be at the historic Wilbur Theatre, 246 Tremont St., in the Theater District. 245 Quincy Market Place (2nd floor, off the rotunda). © 617/248-9700. www.comedyconnectionboston.com. Cover $15–$45, 2-item minimum. T: Green or Blue Line to Government Center, or Orange Line to Haymarket. Validated parking available.

The Comedy Studio ★★ *Finds* Nobody here is a sitcom star—yet. With a stellar reputation for searching out undiscovered talent, the no-frills Comedy Studio draws a savvy crowd of comedy connoisseurs, college students, and network scouts. It's not just setup–punch line–laugh, either; sketches and improv spice up the standup. Shows are Tuesday (magicians—really) through Sunday at 8pm. At the Hong Kong restaurant, 1238 Massachusetts Ave., Cambridge. © 617/661-6507. www.thecomedystudio.com. Cover $8–$10. T: Red Line to Harvard.

Improv Asylum The posters that catch your eye on the Freedom Trail might draw you back to the North End later for raucous improv and sketch comedy in a subterranean setting. Performances are Wednesday through Saturday evenings, and buying tickets in advance is recommended. 216 Hanover St. © 617/263-6887. www.improvasylum.com. Tickets $15–$20. T: Green or Orange Line to Haymarket. Validated parking available.

DANCE CLUBS

Most clubs enforce a **dress code** that forbids athletic wear (including game jerseys), sneakers, jeans, Timberland boots, and ball caps—or some combination thereof—on everyone, as well as tank tops on men. Some places require that men wear a shirt with a collar, and a few require a jacket. Check ahead. The local club scene is in transition at press time, with a chunk of Lansdowne Street under construction and the city cracking down on venues in the Theater District after a scary spate of closing-time violence. The *Improper Bostonian* and the *Phoenix* club listings are good resources, but a savvy concierge is even better. *Tip:* While you're visiting websites, note that some clubs will let you put your name on the VIP list online. Can't hurt, might help.

The Estate   The Estate opened in 2007 and quickly established itself as a can't-miss destination for visiting "celebrities," such as Paris Hilton. A cavernous space with a balcony overlooking the large dance floor, it attracts a lively 20-something crowd with well-known local DJs and an excellent sound system. The lower level is the **Suite**—all house music, all the time. In both clubs, the dress code is "casual chic and fashionable," which appears to mean shirts with collars on men and something tight and black on women. The key to jumping the inevitable line is to reserve a table and look sharp. Open Thursday through Sunday (both are gay nights); check ahead for specifics. 1 Boylston Place. ℂ 617/351-7000. www.theestateboston.com. Cover $10–25. T: Green Line to Boylston.

The Roxy ⭑⭑   This former hotel ballroom boasts excellent DJs and all sorts of live music, a huge dance floor, a stage, and a balcony that's perfect for checking out the action below. Concerts (recently, Elliott Yamin and Spoon) and occasional boxing cards take good advantage of the sight lines. Offerings change regularly, so call or surf for the latest schedule. Open at 10pm Friday and Saturday, and other days depending on bookings. In the Courtyard Boston Tremont hotel, 279 Tremont St. ℂ 617/338-7699. www.roxy plex.com. Cover $10–$20. T: Green Line to Boylston or Orange Line to New England Medical Center.

ECLECTIC

Johnny D's Uptown Restaurant & Music Club ⭑⭑⭑ *Finds*   This family-owned and -operated establishment is one of the best places in the area for live music. You'll kick yourself if you don't at least check the lineup while you're in town. Johnny D's draws a congenial, low-key crowd for acts on international tours as well as artists who haven't been out of eastern Massachusetts. The music ranges from zydeco to rock, rockabilly to jazz, blues to ska. The veggie-friendly food's good, too; try the weekend brunch. The club, which opened in 1969, is worth a long trip, but it's only two stops past Harvard on the Red Line (about a 15-min. ride at night). Most shows are 21-plus; some are all ages. Open daily from 12:30pm to 1am. Brunch starts at 9am on weekends; dinner runs from 4:30 to 9:30pm Tuesday through Saturday, with lighter fare until 11pm. *Tip:* Make a dinner reservation, and you're guaranteed a seat for the show. 17 Holland St., Davis Sq., Somerville. ℂ 617/776-2004 or 617/776-9667 (concert line). www.johnnyds.com. Cover $3–$20, usually $8–$12. T: Red Line to Davis.

Lizard Lounge ⭑⭑   In the basement of the Cambridge Common restaurant, this way-cool, cozy-but-not-cramped room features well-known local rock and folk musicians (and the occasional classical interloper) who play right out on the floor. The Lizard Lounge draws a postcollegiate-and-up crowd (Harvard Law School is next door). Shows are daily at 8 and 9:30pm. Sunday is poetry jam night; Monday is open-mic night. 1667 Massachusetts Ave., Cambridge. ℂ 617/547-0759. www.lizardloungeclub.com. Cover for late show $5–$12. T: Red Line to Harvard.

T.T. the Bear's Place ⭑   A mainstay of the Central Square live-music scene since it opened in 1985, "T.T.'s" has an uncanny knack for booking hot new talent. A friendly, no-frills spot, it generally attracts a young, savvy crowd, but 30-somethings will feel comfortable, too. Bookings—three or four per night—range from cutting-edge alternative and roots music to up-and-coming indie-rock acts. New bands predominate early in the week, with more established artists on weekends. Open until 1am Sunday to Wednesday, 2am Thursday through Saturday. 10 Brookline St., Cambridge. ℭ **617/492-0082** or 617/492-BEAR (concert line). www.ttthebears.com. Cover $3–$17. T: Red Line to Central.

The Western Front ⟨✯⟩   A 30-ish friend swears by this legendary reggae club for one reason: "You're never the oldest one there." Open since 1968, it's a casual, friendly spot on a nondescript street south of Central Square. Integrated crowds flock here for world-beat music, blues, jazz, hip-hop, salsa, and especially reggae. Open Thursday through Saturday from 8pm to 2am; live entertainment usually begins at 9pm. 343 Western Ave., Cambridge. ℭ **617/492-7772.** www.thewesternfrontclub.com. Cover $5–$10. T: Red Line to Central.

FOLK

Boston is one of the only cities where folk musicians consistently sell out large venues that usually book rock and pop performers. If an artist you want to see is touring, check ahead for Boston-area dates. The annual **Boston Folk Festival** (ℭ **617/ 287-6911;** www.bostonfolkfestival.org) is a 2-day event in mid-September on the UMass-Boston campus in Dorchester.

The music listings in the "Sidekick" section of Thursday's *Globe* include information about **coffeehouses,** the area's main outlets for folk. Probably the best known of these, the 4-decade-old **Nameless Coffeehouse** (ℭ **617/864-1630;** www.nameless coffeehouse.org), puts on one show a month in the First Parish Church, 3 Church St., Harvard Square, Cambridge. The streets around **Harvard Square** are another promising venue—Tracy Chapman is just one famous graduate of the scene.

Also see the **Lizard Lounge** (p. 231).

Club Passim ⟨✯✯✯⟩   Passim has launched more careers than the mass production of acoustic guitars—Joan Baez, Shawn Colvin, and Tom Rush started out here, and this is where you'll find Arlo Guthrie and Ellis Paul when they're in town. In a basement on a Harvard Square side street, the legendary coffeehouse (which doesn't serve alcohol) enjoys an international reputation built on 4 decades of nurturing new talent and showcasing established musicians. Patrons who have been regulars since day one mix with college students. There's live music nightly, and coffee and vegetarian food until 10:30pm. Tuesday is open-mic night. Open Sunday through Thursday from 11am to 11pm, Friday and Saturday from 11am to midnight. Most shows start at 8pm; on two-show nights, starting times are 7 and 10pm. 47 Palmer St., Cambridge. ℭ **617/ 492-7679.** www.passimcenter.org. Cover $5–$27; most shows $15 or less. T: Red Line to Harvard.

JAZZ & BLUES

JazzWeek (www.jazzboston.org) is a 10-day event in late April and early May at multiple venues. Surf around the JazzBoston website for an introduction to the local scene. The **Beantown Jazz Festival** (ℭ **617/267-2244;** www.beantownjazzfestival.com), in late September, draws tens of thousands of aficionados to Columbus Avenue in the South End for a full afternoon of free music. Check the website for details.

Restaurants that offer jazz along with excellent food include **Icarus** (p. 122; Fri only) and **Les Zygomates** (p. 115). The theater at the Cambridge Multicultural Arts Center (p. 221) becomes the **Real Deal Jazz Club & Cafe** at least a couple of times a month, year-round.

Kids Theme a Little Theme

The **Hard Rock Cafe**, 24 Clinton St. (© **617/424-ROCK;** www.hardrock.com), is a fun link in the fun chain—just ask the other tourists all around you. The memorabilia that covers the walls celebrates rock musicians, and the kid-friendly menu features salads, burgers, sandwiches, and barbecue. The Hard Rock moved from the Back Bay to this cavernous space across the street from Faneuil Hall Marketplace in 2007.

On summer Thursdays at 6pm, the **Boston Harbor Hotel** (© **617/491-2100;** www.bhh.com) sponsors free performances on the "Blues Barge," behind the hotel.

Cantab Lounge ⊛ Follow your ears to this friendly neighborhood bar, which attracts a lively three-generation crowd. When the door swings open at night, deafening music—usually blues, rock, or folk—spills out. Downstairs is the Cantab Underground, which schedules bluegrass on Tuesday, poetry on Wednesday, and improv on Thursday. 738 Massachusetts Ave., Cambridge. © 617/354-2685. www.cantab-lounge.com. Cover $3–$10. T: Red Line to Central.

Regattabar ⊛⊛ The Regattabar's selection of local and international jazz artists is often considered the best in the area, but be sure you check the lineup at Scullers Jazz Club (see below) before you make up your mind. Irma Thomas, Madeleine Peyroux, and McCoy Tyner have appeared recently. The large third-floor room holds about 200. Buy tickets in advance or try your luck at the door an hour before show time. Open Tuesday through Saturday and some Sundays, with one or two performances per night, but frequently closed for private events. In the Charles Hotel, 1 Bennett St., Cambridge. © 617/661-5000 or 617/395-7757 for tickets. www.regattabarjazz.com. Tickets $12–$35. T: Red Line to Harvard.

Ryles Jazz Club ⊛ This popular spot, which doubles as a barbecue joint, books a wide variety of excellent blues, jazz, R&B, world beat, and Latin in two rooms. Sunday jazz brunch runs from 10am to 3pm. Open Tuesday through Sunday at 5pm; shows start at 9pm. 212 Hampshire St., Inman Sq., Cambridge. © 617/876-9330. www.ryles.com. Cover for music $8–$20 (usually $12 or less). T: Red Line to Central, then a 10-min. walk.

Scullers Jazz Club ⊛⊛⊛ Overlooking the Charles River, Scullers is a lovely, comfortable room with a top-notch sound system. The club celebrates its 20th anniversary in 2009; check ahead for celebratory events. It books acclaimed singers and instrumentalists—recent notables include Tower of Power, Abbey Lincoln, Herb Alpert, and Bobby Caldwell. Patrons tend to be more hard-core than the crowds at the Regattabar (above), but it depends on who's performing. There are usually two shows a night Tuesday through Saturday; the box office is open Monday through Saturday from 11am to 6pm. Ask about dinner packages ($47–$75 per person), which include preferred seating and a three-course meal, and overnight packages (from $99). In the Doubletree Guest Suites hotel, 400 Soldiers Field Rd. © 617/562-4111. www.scullersjazz.com. Tickets $15–$50. Validated parking available.

Wally's Cafe ⊛⊛ This Boston institution, near a busy corner in the South End, opened in 1947. Its New Orleans–style all-about-the-music atmosphere draws a notably diverse crowd—black, white, straight, gay, affluent, indigent. Live jazz, by local ensembles, students and instructors from the Berklee College of Music, and the occasional local or international star, starts every night at 9pm. Monday is blues night. Open daily until 2am. *Tip:* I can't promise anything, but big-name performers in town to play bigger venues have been known to turn up at Wally's afterward. 427 Massachusetts Ave. ℭ **617/424-1408.** www.wallyscafe.com. No cover; 1-drink minimum. T: Orange Line to Mass. Ave.

ROCK

Bill's Bar   Long known as the only real hangout on Lansdowne Street, Bill's has a friendly atmosphere and a great beer menu. It books lots of live performers, including local favorites like the Dropkick Murphys, and reggae on Sunday. Open nightly from 9pm to 2am. 5½ Lansdowne St. ℭ **617/421-9678.** www.billsbar.com. Cover $5–$15, usually $10 or less. T: Green Line B, C, or D to Kenmore.

The Middle East 🎯🎯🎯   The best rock club in the area and one of the best in New England, the Middle East books an impressive variety of progressive and alternative artists in two rooms (upstairs and downstairs) every night. Showcasing top local talent as well as bands with local roots and international reputations, it's a popular hangout that gets crowded, hot, and *loud.* The Middle East is the heart of a complex that incorporates the **Corner,** a former bakery that features acoustic artists most of the time and belly dancers on Sunday and Wednesday, and **ZuZu,** a Middle Eastern restaurant that has its own music schedule and gallery space with rotating art exhibits. Most shows are 18-plus (ZuZu is 21-plus); the age of the crowd varies with the performer. 472–480 Massachusetts Ave., Central Sq., Cambridge. ℭ **617/864-EAST** or 617/931-2000 (Ticketmaster). www.mideastclub.com. Cover $7–$15 (ZuZu cover $3 Fri–Sat only). T: Red Line to Central.

Paradise Rock Club 🎯   Hard by the Boston University campus, the medium-size Paradise draws enthusiastic, student-intensive crowds for top local rock and alternative performers. You might see national names who want a relatively small venue and others who aren't ready to headline a big show on their own (lately, Fountains of Wayne, the Donnas, and the Lemonheads). Most shows are 18-plus. 967–969 Commonwealth Ave. ℭ **617/562-8800** or 617/423-NEXT for tickets. www.thedise.com. T: Green Line B to Pleasant St.

Toad 🎯🎯 *(Value)*   Essentially a bar with a stage, this narrow, high-ceilinged space draws a savvy three-generation clientele attracted by local big-name performers—rock, rockabilly, and sometimes blues—and the lack of a cover charge. Toad enjoys good acoustics but not much elbow room—a plus when restless performers wander into the crowd. 1912 Massachusetts Ave., Cambridge. ℭ **617/497-4950** (info line). www.toadcambridge.com. T: Red Line to Porter.

Tips Rock of Ages

Bring your driver's license or passport when you go club-hopping, no matter how old you think you look—you must be 21 to drink alcohol, and the law is strictly enforced. Most bouncers won't risk a fine or license suspension, especially at 18-plus shows.

---

4 The Bar Scene

Bostonians had some quibbles with the TV show *Cheers,* but no one complained that the concept of a neighborhood bar where everybody knows your name was implausible. This tends to be a fairly insular scene—as a stranger, don't assume that you'll get a warm welcome. This is one area where you can and probably should judge a book by its cover: If you peek in and see people who look like you and your friends, give it a whirl.

BARS & LOUNGES

The Beehive A funky two-level space beneath the Boston Center for the Arts (p. 221), this restaurant and lounge was all the buzz in summer 2007 and has since settled down a bit. The Beehive schedules live music, usually jazz, every night. Early in the week, the crowd tends toward laid-back and local; weekends are more of a see-and-be-seen scene for suburbanites. 541 Tremont St. ✆ **617/423-0069.** www.beehiveboston.com. T: Orange Line to Back Bay.

Casablanca ✪✪ Students and professors jam this legendary Harvard Square watering hole, especially on weekends. You'll find excellent food (p. 130), an excellent jukebox, and excellent eavesdropping. 40 Brattle St., Cambridge. ✆ **617/876-0999.** T: Red Line to Harvard.

Cask 'n Flagon ✪ A long fly ball away from Fenway Park, "the Cask," which opened in 1969, is one of the best-known sports bars in this sports-mad city. It's much bigger than it looks from Brookline Avenue, but lines on game days are still comically long. The crowds watching major events on numerous TVs in the memorabilia-drenched bar are large and enthusiastic year-round. 62 Brookline Ave. ✆ **617/536-4840.** www.casknflagon.com. T: Green Line B, C, or D to Kenmore.

Cheers (Beacon Hill) If you're out to impersonate a native, try not to be shocked when you enter "the *Cheers* bar" and the inside looks nothing like the bar on the TV show. (A spin-off in Faneuil Hall Marketplace fills that niche—see the listing below.) Formerly the Bull & Finch Pub, this really is a neighborhood bar, but it's far better known for attracting legions of out-of-towners, who find good pub grub and plenty of souvenirs. There's food from 11am until late evening and a kids' menu ($4–$5). 84 Beacon St. ✆ **617/227-9605.** www.cheersboston.com. T: Green Line to Arlington.

Cheers (Faneuil Hall Marketplace) Blatantly but good-naturedly courting fans of the sitcom, this bar's interior is an exact replica of the *Cheers* TV set. It serves pub fare starting at 11am and schedules live entertainment on weekend nights. Memorabilia on display includes Sam Malone's Red Sox jacket. Bring a camera. Quincy Market Building, South Canopy, Faneuil Hall Marketplace. ✆ **617/227-0150.** www.cheersboston.com. T: Green or Blue Line to Government Center, or Orange Line to Haymarket.

DeLux Cafe ✪✪ One of the coolest places in the increasingly yuppified South End, the DeLux is the epitome of a classy dive. The funky decor, selection of microbrews, and veggie-friendly ethnic menu attract a cross-section of the neighborhood. Part of the appeal is the decor, a scrapbook of 20th-century pop culture (posters, photos, postcards, and such)—check out the Elvis shrine. 100 Chandler St. ✆ **617/338-5258.** T: Orange Line to Back Bay.

The Fours ✪ One of Boston's best and best-known sports bars—*Sports Illustrated* says it's the best in the *country*—the Fours is about one football field away from the

Garden. Festooned with sports memorabilia and TVs, it's a madhouse before Celtics and Bruins games—and a promising place to pick up an extra ticket. 166 Canal St. ℂ 617/720-4455. www.thefours.com. T: Green or Orange Line to North Station.

Game On! Sports Cafe   Yes, it's actually *in* Fenway Park, and no, you can't just sneak into the stands. The overgrown sports bar and restaurant boasts the latest techno toys, including high-def TVs and a booming sound system, on two deafeningly loud levels of a onetime bowling alley. On game days, the line stretches out the door. 82 Lansdowne St. ℂ 617/351-7001. www.gameonboston.com. T: Green Line D to Fenway, or B, C, or D to Kenmore.

Grafton Street   Deftly accommodating party-hearty students and demanding Cantabrigians, this Harvard Square veteran is a classy watering hole with a superb beer selection. It's also a busy restaurant, but I prefer a snack or sandwich at the bar to a meal in the dining room. Open daily until 2am. 1230 Massachusetts Ave., Cambridge. ℂ 617/497-0400. www.graftonstreetcambridge.com. T: Red Line to Harvard.

Grendel's Den 𝕗   A vestige of pre-franchise Harvard Square, this cozy subterranean space is *the* place to celebrate turning 21. Recent grads and grad students dominate, but Grendel's has been so popular for so long that it also gets its share of Gen Y's parents. The food is tasty, with loads of vegetarian dishes, and the fireplace enhances the comfy atmosphere. 89 Winthrop St., Cambridge. ℂ 617/491-1160. www.grendelsden.com. T: Red Line to Harvard.

The Hong Kong   This fun hangout is a retro Chinese restaurant on the first floor, a bar on the second floor, and a small dance club (starting at 11pm nightly) on the third floor. It's also the home of the scorpion bowl, a rum-based concoction that has contributed to the destruction of countless Ivy League brain cells. Nevertheless, you might see Harvard football players here. Never mind how I know. 1236 Massachusetts Ave., Cambridge. ℂ 617/864-5311. www.hongkongharvard.com. T: Red Line to Harvard.

Pho Republique   The chic factor soars as the numbers on Washington Street get higher. The lounge is the place to be at this trendy Vietnamese restaurant, which serves creative cocktails and pan-Asian nibbles to a stylish after-work crowd. 1415 Washington St. ℂ 617/262-0005. www.phorepublique.net. T: Silver Line bus to Union Park St.

The Place 𝕗   Is it a Financial District hangout? A sports bar on (pardon the expression) steroids, with flatscreen TVs all over? An after-work destination for bankers and lawyers and the men and women who love them? Yes, yes, and yes. 2 Broad St. ℂ 617/523-2081. www.theplaceboston.com. Cover $5 Thurs–Sat after 9pm. T: Orange or Blue Line to State. Validated parking available.

The Purple Shamrock   Across the street from Faneuil Hall Marketplace, the Purple Shamrock packs in wall-to-wall tourists of all ages. This is a rowdy, fun place that schedules DJs and cover bands. 1 Union St. ℂ 617/227-2060. www.irishconnection.com. Cover $5–$10 Thurs–Sat. T: Green or Blue Line to Government Center, or Orange Line to Haymarket.

Radius   The high-tech bar at this hot, *haute* restaurant offers almost everything the dining room does—the chic crowd, the noise, the perfect martinis—without the sky-high food bill. The bar snacks are pricey but worth every penny. 8 High St. ℂ 617/426-1234. www.radiusrestaurant.com. T: Red Line to South Station.

Silvertone Bar & Grill 𝕗   One of the few real hangouts in the Downtown Crossing area, this tiny, subterranean bar attracts an incredibly loud after-work crowd. The dining room is noted for reasonably priced comfort food (try the sublime macaroni

---

---

and cheese). Closed Sunday. 69 Bromfield St. © **617/338-7887.** www.silvertonedowntown.com. T: Red or Green Line to Park Street.

Top of the Hub ★★★ Boasting a panoramic view of greater Boston, Top of the Hub is 52 stories above the city; the view is especially beautiful at sunset. It's an elegant destination and a favorite with couples out on a big date or celebrating a special occasion. Take a turn around the dance floor or just enjoy the live jazz and the late-night menu, which features superb desserts. Dress is casual but neat (no jeans). Open until 1am Sunday through Wednesday, 2am Thursday through Saturday. You must have a photo ID to enter the building. Prudential Center, 800 Boylston St. © **617/536-1775.** www.selectrestaurants.com. T: Green Line E to Prudential. Validated parking available.

21st Amendment A Beacon Hill standby, this tavern looks like a regular old neighborhood bar and restaurant—unless the Legislature is in session. Then it turns into an annex of the State House, just across the street, and the entertainment value of the conversation jumps dramatically. (In case you were absent that day, the 21st Amendment repealed Prohibition.) 150 Bowdoin St. © **617/227-7100.** www.21stboston.com. T: Red Line to Park Street.

Via Matta This chic Italian restaurant's equally stylish bar and divine wine list make this a perfect place to recharge after an afternoon of hard work or hard shopping—Newbury Street is 3 blocks away. 79 Park Plaza (Arlington St. and Columbus Ave.). © **617/422-0008.** www.viamattarestaurant.com. T: Green Line to Arlington.

BREWPUBS

Boston Beer Works Across the street from Fenway Park, this cavernous space is frantic before and after Red Sox games. Don't plan to be able to hear anything your friends are saying. It has a full food menu and 14 brews on tap, including excellent bitters and ales. The sweet-potato fries make a terrific snack. The **North Station** branch, near the TD Banknorth Garden, is smaller but equally loud and has a couple of pool tables. Open daily from 11:30am to 1am. 61 Brookline Ave. © **617/536-BEER.** www.beerworks.net. T: Green Line B, C, or D to Kenmore. 110 Canal St. © **617/896-BEER.** T: Green or Orange Line to North Station.

John Harvard's Brew House ★★ This subterranean Harvard Square hangout, the flagship of the regional chain, pumps out terrific English-style brews in a clublike setting and prides itself on its food. The brewed-on-the-premises beer selection changes regularly. Order a sampler if you can't decide, and while you wait, try to find the sports figures in the stained-glass windows. Open Monday through Thursday from 11:30am to 12:30am, Friday and Saturday until 2am, Sunday until midnight, with food service until 11:30pm. 33 Dunster St., Cambridge. ⓒ 617/868-3585. www.johnharvards. com. T: Red Line to Harvard.

HOTEL BARS & LOUNGES

Many popular nightspots are associated with hotels and restaurants (see chapters 5 and 6); as a rule, these are the only watering holes in town where you don't have to shout to be heard. The following are particularly agreeable, albeit expensive, places to while away an hour or three.

The Bar at Taj Boston 𝆏 The Bar at the Ritz, this lovely space's predecessor, established it as *the* place to go for a classic martini. The cushy seating, crackling fire, impeccable service, and view of the Public Garden have made it a favorite with generations of Bostonians. In the Taj Boston hotel, 15 Arlington St. ⓒ 617/536-5700. T: Green Line to Arlington.

Boston Harbor Hotel 𝆏 You have two appealing options on the ground floor. **Intrigue** looks like a comfortable living room, serves food all day, and boasts a harbor view, and the businesslike **Rowes Wharf Bar** makes a serious martini. Rowes Wharf (entrance on Atlantic Ave.). ⓒ 617/439-7000. T: Red Line to South Station.

The Bristol 𝆏𝆏𝆏 This is a perfect choice after the theater, after work, or after anything else. An elegant room with soft lounge chairs, a fireplace, and fresh flowers, it features a fabulous Viennese Dessert Buffet on Friday and Saturday from 9pm to midnight. There's live jazz every evening. Food is available until 11:30pm (12:30am Fri–Sat). In the Four Seasons Hotel, 200 Boylston St. ⓒ 617/351-2037. T: Green Line to Arlington.

Eastern Standard A cavernous brasserie with a mile-long marble bar, Eastern Standard is an all-things-to-all-people destination. It serves three meals daily, offers outdoor seating, and has a hopping bar scene every night during the week and almost all day on weekends. The specialty cocktails are numerous and diverse, and the bartenders know their way around the wine list. On Red Sox game nights, be ready to stand. In the Hotel Commonwealth, 528 Commonwealth Ave. ⓒ 617/532-9100. www.easternstandard boston.com. T: Green Line B, C, or D to Kenmore.

Oak Bar 𝆏𝆏 This paneled, high-ceilinged room feels like an old-fashioned men's club—but one that welcomes women. The lighting is muted, the leather seating soft and welcoming, and the raw bar picture-perfect. There's live entertainment on weekends. Proper dress (no shorts or sneakers) is required. Open Sunday through Thursday until midnight, Friday and Saturday until 1am. In the Fairmont Copley Plaza Hotel, 138 St. James Ave. ⓒ 617/267-5300. www.theoakroom.com. T: Green Line to Copley or Orange Line to Back Bay.

Finds Make Some Noise in a Museum

Two proper museums become spirited nightlife destinations at least once a month. These events cater to 20- and 30-somethings with live music, cocktails, food, and mingling; a visit is an equally good couple or group activity. On the first Friday of each month—and every Friday in the summer—the **Museum of Fine Arts,** 465 Huntington Ave. (ⓒ 617/267-9300; www.mfa.org), schedules "mfafirstfridays" from 5:30 to 9:30pm. General admission to the museum ($15 after 5pm) includes admission to the evening event. The **Isabella Stewart Gardner Museum's** "Gardner After Hours" series, from 5 to 9pm on the third Thursday of each month, includes self-guided tours and gallery talks. Admission is $12.

IRISH BARS

The Black Rose   Purists might sneer at the Black Rose's touristy location, but performers don't. Sing along with the authentic entertainment at this jam-packed pub and restaurant at the edge of Faneuil Hall Marketplace. You might even be able to make out the tune on a fiddle over the din. 160 State St. ℭ 617/742-2286. www.irishconnection. com. Cover $3–$5. T: Orange or Blue Line to State.

The Burren ℳ   The expatriate Irish community has found the Burren an antidote to homesickness since 1996, and you will, too. There's traditional music in the front room, acoustic rock in the large back room, and good food. 247 Elm St., Somerville. ℭ 617/776-6896. www.burren.com. Cover (back room only) $5–$10. T: Red Line to Davis.

The Grand Canal   No, it's not Italian (the namesake waterway connects Dublin to the Shannon River). This atmospheric pub and restaurant boasts an excellent beer selection, good food, a 12-foot TV screen, and Irish or rock cover bands or DJs Thursday through Saturday nights. French windows that open to the street make it a popular after-work spot in good weather. 57 Canal St. ℭ 617/523-1112. www.thegrandcanalboston.com. Cover $5 for music. T: Green or Orange Line to Haymarket or North Station.

Mr. Dooley's Boston Tavern ℳℳ   Sometimes an expertly poured Guinness is all you need. If one of the nicest bartenders in the city pours it, and you enjoy it in an authentically decorated room, so much the better. This Financial District spot offers a wide selection of imported beers on tap, live Irish music, and a menu of pub favorites at lunch and dinner. 77 Broad St. ℭ 617/338-5656. www.somerspubs.com. Cover (Fri–Sat only) $3–$5. T: Orange Line to State or Blue Line to Aquarium.

The Plough & Stars ℳ   Although it's tiny, the Plough is a huge presence on the local pub scene. A neighborhood hangout during the day, it's a hipster magnet at night. Live music is a regular feature and a big draw; Saturday is bluegrass night. 912 Massachusetts Ave., Cambridge. ℭ 617/576-0032. www.ploughandstars.com. Cover $6 or less. T: Red Line to Central or Harvard.

GAY & LESBIAN BARS & CLUBS

In addition to the clubs listed here, some mainstream venues schedule a weekly gay night. The particulars are current at press time, but always check ahead. Avalon Sunday, the city's biggest gay night, moved to the **Estate** (p. 231) after its namesake closed. The Estate also plays host to **Glamlife** (www.chrisharrispresents.com) on Thursday; **Epic Saturday** is at the Roxy (p. 231). **Tribe** (www.tribenightclub.com) is a Thursday dance party for women that moves around; at press time it's at Felt, 533 Washington St. (ℭ 617/350-5555; www.feltboston.com).

On the first Friday of each month, the Boston chapter of **Guerrilla Queer Bar** (www.bostonguerrilla.com) stages a flash mob–style takeover of a straight bar just for the night. Visit the website to sign up for a notification email.

For up-to-date listings, check *Bay Windows,* the *Improper Bostonian,* and the *Phoenix.* Worthwhile websites include www.edgeboston.com and http://boston.lesbian nightlife.com.

Club Café ℳℳ   This fun South End spot draws a chic crowd of men and women for conversation (the noise level is reasonable), dining, live music in the front room, and video entertainment in the back room. Thursday is the busiest night. Open daily until 2am; the restaurant, 209 Boston, serves Sunday brunch, dinner nightly, and a light bar menu daily starting at noon. 209 Columbus Ave. ℭ 617/536-0966. www.clubcafe.com. T: Green Line to Arlington or Orange Line to Back Bay.

Fritz   This popular South End hangout is a neighborhood favorite that serves brunch on weekends. The friendly crowd bonds over sports on the plasma satellite TVs. In the Chandler Inn Hotel, 26 Chandler St. ℂ 617/482-4428. T: Orange Line to Back Bay.

Jacques ⟨★   The only drag venue in town, Jacques draws a friendly crowd of gay and straight patrons who mix with the "girls" and sometimes engage in a shocking activity—that's right, disco dancing. The eclectic entertainment includes live music (on weekends), performance artists, and, of course, drag shows. Open daily from noon to midnight; no credit cards. 79 Broadway, Bay Village. ℂ 617/426-8902. www.jacquescabaret.com. Cover $6–$10. T: Green Line to Arlington.

Paradise   Not to be confused with the Boston rock club (well, you can, but it won't be quite the same experience), the Paradise attracts an all-ages male crowd. There's a stripper every evening. Thursday is college night. Open Sunday through Wednesday until 1am, Thursday through Saturday until 2am. 180 Massachusetts Ave., Cambridge. ℂ 617/868-3000. www.paradisecambridge.com. T: Red Line to Central, then a 10-min. walk.

5 More Entertainment Options

COFFEEHOUSES & TEA SALONS

As in most other American cities, you won't get far without seeing a Starbucks. I'll submit to the passive-aggressive counter routine if it ends in a frozen drink, but for coffee, tea, and hanging out, there are plenty of less generic options. Many are in the North End (see chapter 6); other favorites are listed here. At all of them, hours are long and loitering is encouraged—these are good places to bring your journal.

Algiers Café & Restaurant ⟨★   Middle Eastern food and music, plain and flavored coffees, and the legendary atmosphere make this a classic Harvard Square hangout. Your "quick" snack or drink (try the mint coffee) might turn into a longer stay as the sociologist in you studies the would-be intellectuals. This is a good spot to eavesdrop while you sample terrific soups, sandwiches, homemade sausages, falafel, and hummus. 40 Brattle St., Cambridge. ℂ 617/492-1557. T: Red Line to Harvard.

BeanTowne Coffee House   A splash of the bohemian in a buttoned-up office-retail complex, this is a good stop before or after a film at the Kendall Square Cinema. Order from the extensive beverage menu or the tempting selection of soups, salads, and sandwiches. There's only one problem with this little place—it's too popular. If a table empties, move in fast. 1 Kendall Sq., Cambridge. ℂ 617/621-7900. www.beantownecambridge.com. T: Red Line to Kendall.

Boston Beanstock Coffee Co. ⟨★   Most of the other coffee places in the North End are right out of a Scorsese movie. This is a yuppier caffeine-delivery system, with free wireless Internet and a menu of delectable baked goods and hearty sandwiches. It seems a bit incongruous at first, but it's always crowded. The **Financial District** location, 10 High St., off Summer Street (ℂ **617/695-9700**), closes on weekends. 97 Salem St. ℂ 617/723-0040. www.bostonbeanstock.com. T: Green or Orange Line to Haymarket.

Tealuxe   Tealuxe pulls in connoisseurs with its selection of 100-plus teas, dispensed by unfortunately named "tea-tenders." The Harvard Square location is the original in the chain, which thrives on a combination of hard-to-find selections and comfortable atmosphere. www.tealuxe.com. 108 Newbury St. ℂ 617/927-0400. T: Green Line to Arlington. Zero Brattle St., Cambridge. ℂ 617/441-0077. T: Red Line to Harvard.

1369 Coffee House ⚔ A long, narrow room with a colorful clientele, the 1369 offers excellent baked goods, a dazzling selection of premium teas and coffees, and great people-watching. There's also a light lunch menu and a pleasant outdoor seating area. The equally enjoyable original location is at 1369 Cambridge St., Inman Square (*(C)* **617/576-1369**). 757 Massachusetts Ave., Central Sq., Cambridge. *(C)* **617/576-4600**. www. 1369coffeehouse.com. T: Red Line to Central.

Trident Booksellers & Café ⚔⚔ This Back Bay institution is more than just a cafe. The veggie-friendly menu (including breakfast served all day) complements the free Wi-Fi access, thoughtful book selection, and casual, New Age-y atmosphere. Open 9am to midnight daily. 338 Newbury St. *(C)* **617/267-8688**. www.tridentbookscafe.com. T: Green Line B, C, or D to Hynes Convention Center.

POOL & BOWLING

These establishments aren't the divey hangouts you remember from your misspent youth; they're upscale destinations with prices to match. For pool, expect to pay at least $12 an hour on weekend evenings, with weekday and daytime discounts. Bowlers can count on parting with at least $6 per person per game.

Boston Billiard Club A large, clubby space decorated with brass sconces and a mahogany bar, this club has 55 tables, tasty bar food, and full liquor service. If you don't want to wait for a table, ask about reserving a private room (from $30/hr.). Like other establishments in this neighborhood, it's a madhouse on Red Sox game days and nights. Open daily from noon to 2am. 126 Brookline Ave. *(C)* **617/536-POOL**. www.boston billiardclub.com. T: Green Line B, C, or D to Kenmore, or D to Fenway.

Flat Top Johnny's ⚔⚔ I blink like a geisha every time I walk in here—I can't believe such a cool, funky spot is this close to MIT. A spacious, loud room with a bar and 12 red-topped pool tables, Flat Top Johnny's has a casual neighborhood feel despite being in a rather sterile office-retail complex. Open weekdays noon to 1am, weekends 3pm to 1am. 1 Kendall Sq., Cambridge. *(C)* **617/494-9565**. www.flattopjohnnys.com. T: Red Line to Kendall/MIT.

Jillian's Boston *(Kids* The 70,000-square-foot Jillian's complex, which anchors the Lansdowne Street strip, offers billiards on 52 tables, an upscale bowling alley (part of the Lucky Strike Lanes chain), a spring break–themed dance club (Tequila Rain), tons of plasma TVs, five full bars, and two restaurants. If you can't scare up some fun here, check your pulse. Open Monday through Saturday from 11am to 2am, Sunday from noon to 2am. Children under 18 accompanied by an adult are admitted before 8pm Sunday through Thursday; on Friday and Saturday, Jillian's is 21-plus after 8pm. 145 Ipswich St. *(C)* **617/437-0300**. www.jilliansboston.com or www.luckystrikeboston.com. Valet parking available Wed–Sun after 6pm, except during Red Sox games. T: Green Line B, C, or D to Kenmore.

Kings ⚔ In a former movie theater across from the Hynes Convention Center, Kings is a popular date destination that attracts the occasional pro athlete or celebrity. It has 20 bowling lanes (4 of them private) and an eight-table billiards room. It's open Monday 5pm to 2am, Tuesday through Sunday 11:30am to 2am; after 6pm, patrons must be at least 21. 50 Dalton St. *(C)* **617/266-BOWL**. www.backbaykings.com. T: Green Line B, C, or D to Hynes Convention Center.

FILMS

Free Friday Flicks at the Hatch Shell ⚔⚔⚔ (*(C)* **617/787-7200**) are family films shown on a large screen in the amphitheater on the Esplanade. On the lawn in front of the Hatch Shell, hundreds of people picnic until the sky grows dark and the credits roll. In the last few years, the films have tended toward recent releases (no big thrill for anyone with a Netflix subscription), but the movie is only part of the experience. *Tip:* Bring sweaters in case the breeze off the river grows chilly.

Revival houses—they feature lectures and live performances in addition to foreign and classic films—include the **Brattle Theatre,** 40 Brattle St., Cambridge (© 617/876-6837; www.brattlefilm.org; T: Red Line to Harvard), and the **Coolidge Corner Movie Theater,** 290 Harvard St., Brookline (© 617/734-2500; www.coolidge.org; T: Green Line C to Coolidge Corner). The Coolidge also schedules midnight shows. Classic and foreign films are the tip of the iceberg at the quirky **Harvard Film Archive,** 24 Quincy St., Cambridge (© 617/495-4700; http://hcl.harvard.edu/hfa; T: Red Line to Harvard), which also shows student films.

For first-run independent and foreign films, head to the **Kendall Square Cinema,** 1 Kendall Sq., Cambridge (© 617/499-1996; www.landmarktheatres.com; T: Red Line to Kendall/MIT). The best movie theater in the immediate Boston area, it offers discounted parking in the adjoining garage. Second-run current releases at discount prices are the usual fare at the **Somerville Theater,** 55 Davis Sq. (© 617/625-5700; www.somervilletheatreonline.com; T: Red Line to Davis), which schedules occasional concerts, too. A great place to see mainstream releases is the 19-screen **AMC Loews Boston Common,** 175 Tremont St. (© 617/423-5801; www.amctheatres.com; T: Green Line to Boylston), which has stadium seating and digital sound.

LECTURES & READINGS

The Thursday *Globe* "Sidekick" section is the best place to check for listings of lectures, readings, and talks on a wide variety of subjects, often at local colleges and libraries. Many are free or charge a small fee. Most of the bookstores listed in chapter 9 sponsor author readings; check their websites or in-store displays, or surf ahead.

6 Late-Night Bites

To be frank, Boston's late-night scene needs to climb a couple of notches to reach pathetic, and Cambridge's wee-hour diversions are even skimpier. The only plus is that just about every cab driver out cruising knows how to reach the places that are still open. In the late evening, especially on weekends, you have it a bit easier: Hit a restaurant (see chapter 6) that keeps long hours. They include **Brasserie Jo, Davio's, Jacob Wirth, Jasper White's Summer Shack, Pizzeria Regina,** and the lounge at **Troquet.**

A number of **Chinatown** restaurants (see chapter 6) don't close until 3 or 4am. Asking for "cold tea" might—*might*—get you a teapot full of beer. The hottest scene is at **Ginza Japanese Restaurant,** 14 Hudson St. (© 617/338-2261). In the North End, **Caffe Pompei,** 280 Hanover St. (© 617/523-9438), draws club-hoppers and neighborhood shift workers until 3:30am. Or make like a college student and road-trip to the **International House of Pancakes** at 1850 Soldiers Field Rd. in Brighton (© 617/787-0533). It's open 24 hours daily.

Two other late-night destinations are on the edge of Chinatown, not far from South Station. The **South Street Diner,** 178 Kneeland St. (© 617/350-0028; www.south streetdiner.com), is a '50s-style joint with a wine and beer license and a jukebox; it's open 24 hours and is a popular morning-after destination. The upscale **News Restaurant & Lounge,** 150 Kneeland St. (© 617/426-6397; www.newsboston.com), is open until 4am on weeknights, 5am on weekends.

11

Side Trips from Boston

In addition to being, in Oliver Wendell Holmes's words, "the hub of the solar system," Boston is the hub of a network of delightful excursions. The destinations in this chapter—**Lexington** and **Concord,** the **North Shore** and **Cape Ann,** and **Plymouth**—make fascinating, manageable day trips and offer enough diversions to fill several days.

Like Boston, the suburbs are home to many attractions that rely heavily on aid from outside sources. Admission fees in this chapter are current at press time, but the double whammy of funding cuts and energy prices may have nudged admission fees higher by the time you visit. If you're on a tight budget, call ahead.

1 Lexington & Concord

The shooting stage of the Revolutionary War began here, and parts of the towns still look much as they did in April 1775, when the fight for independence began. Start your visit in **Lexington,** where colonists and British troops first clashed. Spend some time at **Minute Man National Historical Park,** on the border with **Concord,** investigating the battle that raged there. Decide for yourself where the "shot heard round the world" rang out—bearing in mind that **Ralph Waldo Emerson,** who wrote those words, lived in Concord. Emerson's house and **Louisa May Alcott's** nearby family home are just two of the fascinating destinations in this area.

Some attractions close from late fall to March, April, or mid-April (opening after **Patriots Day,** the third Monday in April). Information about both towns is available from the **Greater Merrimack Valley Convention & Visitors Bureau,** 9 Central St., Suite 201, Lowell, MA 01852 (© **800/443-3332** or 978/459-6150; www.merrimackvalley.org).

LEXINGTON ✪
6 miles NW of Cambridge, 9 miles NW of Boston

A country village turned prosperous suburb, Lexington takes great pride in its history. It's a pleasant town with some engaging destinations, but it lacks the atmosphere and abundant attractions of nearby Concord. Making sure to leave time for a tour of the Buckman Tavern, you can schedule as little as a couple of hours to explore downtown Lexington, possibly en route to Concord; a visit can also fill a half or full day. The town contains part of **Minute Man National Historical Park** (see "Exploring the Area" in the "Concord" section, below), which is definitely worth a visit.

British troops marched from Boston to Lexington late on April 18, 1775 (no need to memorize the date; you'll hear it everywhere). Tipped off, patriots Paul Revere and William Dawes rode ahead to sound the warning. Members of the local militia, known as "Minutemen" for their ability to assemble quickly, were waiting at the **Buckman Tavern.** John Hancock and Samuel Adams, leaders of the revolutionary movement,

Tips　Poetry in Motion

Before you visit Lexington and Concord, you might want to read **"Paul Revere's Ride,"** Henry Wadsworth Longfellow's classic but historically questionable poem that dramatically chronicles the events of April 18 and 19, 1775.

were sleeping (or trying to) at the nearby **Hancock-Clarke House.** The warning came around midnight, followed about 5 hours later by some 700 British troops, en route to Concord, where they planned to destroy the rebels' military supplies. Ordered to disperse, the colonists—fewer than 100, and some accounts say 77—stood their ground. Nobody knows who started the shooting, but when it was over, eight militia members lay dead, including a drummer boy, and 10 were wounded.

ESSENTIALS

GETTING THERE　From downtown Boston, take Storrow Drive or Memorial Drive to Route 2. Take Route 2 from Cambridge through Belmont, exit at Route 4/225, and follow signs to the center of Lexington. Or take Route 128 (I-95) to Exit 31A and follow the signs. Massachusetts Avenue—the same "Mass. Ave." you saw in Boston and Cambridge—runs through Lexington. There's metered parking on the street and in several municipal lots, and free parking at the National Heritage Museum and the National Historical Park.

The **MBTA** (© **617/222-3200;** www.mbta.com) runs bus route nos. 62 (Bedford) and 76 (Hanscom) to Lexington from Alewife station, the last stop on the Red Line. The one-way fare is $1.25 with a CharlieCard or $1.50 with a CharlieTicket, and the trip takes about 25 minutes. Buses leave every hour during the day and every half-hour during rush periods, Monday through Saturday, with no service on Sunday. They pass the Munroe Tavern and the National Heritage Museum, if you prefer not to walk from the center of town. There's no public transit between Lexington and Concord, but the seasonal Liberty Ride tour connects the towns.

VISITOR INFORMATION　The **Chamber of Commerce Visitor Center,** 1875 Massachusetts Ave., Lexington, MA 02420 (© **781/862-1450;** www.lexingtonchamber. org), distributes sketch maps and information. It's open daily from 9am to 5pm (10am–4pm Dec–Mar).

EXPLORING THE TOWN

Minute Man National Historical Park is in Lexington, Concord, and Lincoln. At the Lexington end of the park is the **Minute Man Visitor Center** ⊛, off Route 2A, about ½ mile west of I-95 Exit 30B (© **781/674-1920;** www.nps.gov/mima). This area of the park includes the first 4 miles of the Battle Road, the route the defeated British troops took as they left Concord. The rangers recommend that you begin your visit here by watching "The Road to Revolution," a fascinating multimedia program that explains Paul Revere's ride and the events of April 19, 1775. (Winter visitors can start in Concord.) Also here are informational displays and a 40-foot mural illustrating the battle. On summer weekends, rangers lead tours of the park; call ahead for times. The **Battle Road Trail,** a 5½-mile interpretive path, carries pedestrian, wheelchair, and bicycle traffic. Panels and granite markers along the trail display information about the military, social, and natural history of the area. In season (Oct–Apr), this center is open daily from 9am to 5pm, but schedules vary. Call ahead (use the phone number for the North

Lexington

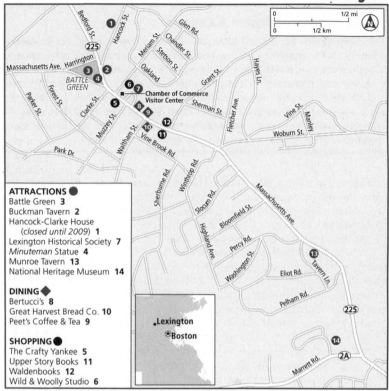

ATTRACTIONS ●
Battle Green **3**
Buckman Tavern **2**
Hancock-Clarke House
  (*closed until 2009*) **1**
Lexington Historical Society **7**
Minuteman Statue **4**
Munroe Tavern **13**
National Heritage Museum **14**

DINING ◆
Bertucci's **8**
Great Harvest Bread Co. **10**
Peet's Coffee & Tea **9**

SHOPPING ●
The Crafty Yankee **5**
Upper Story Books **11**
Waldenbooks **12**
Wild & Woolly Studio **6**

Bridge Visitor Center, ☏ 978/369-6993, if there's no answer here) for open days and hours. For more information, see "Concord," below.

Start your visit to downtown Lexington at the **visitor center,** on the town common, better known as the Battle Green. It's open daily from 9am to 5pm (10am–4pm Dec–Mar). A **diorama** and accompanying narrative illustrate the Battle of Lexington. The *Minuteman* **statue** on the Green is of Capt. John Parker, who commanded the militia. When the British confronted his troops, Parker called: "Stand your ground. Don't fire unless fired upon, but if they mean to have a war, let it begin here!" Allow about 30 minutes to look around the visitor center and the Green.

Lexington Historical Society ✸✸ *(Kids)*   The historical society's signature properties were among the country's first **historic houses** when restoration of the three buildings began around the turn of the 20th century. A guided tour (30–45 min.) is the only way to see the houses.

Across from the Battle Green is the **Buckman Tavern** ✸✸, 1 Bedford St., built around 1710. If time is short and you have to pick just one house to visit, make it this one. The interior of the tavern has been restored to approximate its appearance on the day of the battle. The colonists gathered here to await word of British troop movements, and they brought their wounded here after the conflict. The tour of the tavern, by guides in period dress, is educational and entertaining.

Tips **Touring Lexington & Concord**

The **Liberty Ride** (© **781/862-0500**, ext. 702; www.libertyride.us) is a 90-minute trolley tour, narrated by a costumed guide, that connects the attractions in both towns. It operates from 10:30am to 4:30pm Saturday and Sunday of Patriots Day weekend and daily from Memorial Day weekend through late October; check ahead for schedules and to confirm that it's running. The fare (good for a full day) is $20 for adults, $10 for children 5 to 17, free for children under 5. There's free parking at the National Heritage Museum and the national park, and your ticket entitles you to discounts at local attractions.

Within easy walking distance, the **Hancock-Clarke House,** 36 Hancock St., is where Samuel Adams and John Hancock were staying when Paul Revere arrived. They fled to nearby Woburn. The 1698 house with a 1738 addition contains some original furnishings as well as artifacts of the Battle of Lexington. *Note:* This house will close for restoration in 2008, reopening for the 2009 season.

The British took over the **Munroe Tavern** ⚐, 1332 Massachusetts Ave. (about 1 mile from the Green), to use as their headquarters and, after the battle, as their field hospital. In this building (1690), you'll learn more about the royal troops and see furniture carefully preserved by the Munroe family, including the table and chair President George Washington used when he dined here in 1789. The historically accurate gardens in the rear (free admission) are beautifully planted and maintained.

The historical society makes its headquarters downtown in the 1846 Lexington Depot, where changing exhibits on local history are open to the public.

Depot Square (off Mass. Ave. near the Battle Green). © **781/862-1703** or 781/862-5598 for information about group tours, offered by appointment only. www.lexingtonhistory.org. **Buckman Tavern:** Daily Apr–Oct. 10am–4pm. Tours every 30 min. Closed Nov–Mar. **Hancock-Clarke House:** Sat–Sun Apr to mid-June, daily mid-June to Oct. 11am–2pm. Tours every 30 min. Closed Nov–Mar. **Munroe Tavern:** Sat–Sun Apr to mid-June, daily mid-June to Oct. 11am–3pm. Tours every 30 min. Closed Nov–Mar. Admission $6 adults for 1 house, $8 for 2, $10 for all 3; $4 children 6–16 for 1 house, $5 for 2, $7 for all 3.

National Heritage Museum ⚐⚐ *Kids*   The fascinating exhibits at this unusual museum explore American history and culture. Its focus on everyday life makes an entertaining complement to the colonial-history focus of the rest of the town. The installations in the six exhibition spaces change regularly. You can start with another dose of the Revolution, the permanent exhibit **Sowing the Seeds of Liberty,** which tells the story of that tumultuous period through the lives of Lexington residents. Other topics of exhibits have ranged from Paul Revere to 19th-century inventions to early photos of Elvis, Dylan, and the Beatles. The museum schedules lectures, concerts, and family programs, and the cafe in the atrium serves lunch Tuesday through Saturday. The Scottish Rite of Freemasonry sponsors the museum.

33 Marrett Rd. (Route 2A), at Mass. Ave. © **781/861-6559**. www.nationalheritagemuseum.org. Free admission. Mon–Sat 10am–5pm, Sun noon–5pm. Closed Jan 1, Thanksgiving, and Dec 24–25. From downtown Lexington, follow Mass. Ave. east to intersection with Route 2A; enter from Route 2A.

SHOPPING

A stroll along **Mass. Ave.** near the center of town won't disappoint. Check out **Walden-books,** 1713 Massachusetts Ave. (© **781/862-7870**); **Upper Story Books,** 1730 Massachusetts Ave. (© **781/862-0999**); and the **Crafty Yankee,** 1838 Massachusetts

Concord

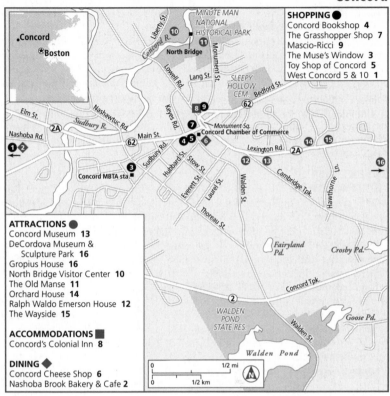

SHOPPING ●
Concord Bookshop **4**
The Grasshopper Shop **7**
Mascio-Ricci **9**
The Muse's Window **3**
Toy Shop of Concord **5**
West Concord 5 & 10 **1**

ATTRACTIONS ●
Concord Museum **13**
DeCordova Museum &
Sculpture Park **16**
Gropius House **16**
North Bridge Visitor Center **10**
The Old Manse **11**
Orchard House **14**
Ralph Waldo Emerson House **12**
The Wayside **15**

ACCOMMODATIONS ■
Concord's Colonial Inn **8**

DINING ◆
Concord Cheese Shop **6**
Nashoba Brook Bakery & Cafe **2**

Ave. (© **781/861-1219**). One of the best-known yarn shops in eastern Massachusetts
is **Wild & Woolly Studio,** 7A Meriam St., off Mass. Ave. (© **781/861-7717**).

WHERE TO DINE

If you're not continuing to Concord, which has more interesting dining options, Lexington offers some pleasant choices. The fresh soups and sandwiches at the cafe at the
National Heritage Museum (see above) are popular for lunch; it's open Tuesday
through Saturday from 11:30am to 2:30pm. **Peet's Coffee & Tea,** 1749 Massachusetts Ave. (© **781/357-2090**), is a good place for a pick-me-up. **Bertucci's,** 1777
Massachusetts Ave. (© **781/860-9000**), is a branch of the family-friendly pizzeria
chain. For a muffin or scone and a hot drink, seek out Lexington's branch of **Great
Harvest Bread Co.,** 1736 Massachusetts Ave. (© **781/861-9990**).

CONCORD ✩✩✩

18 miles NW of Boston, 15 miles NW of Cambridge, 6 miles W of Lexington

Concord (say "conquered") revels in its legacy as a center of groundbreaking thought
and its role in the country's political and intellectual history. The first official battle of
the Revolutionary War took place in 1775 at the North Bridge (now part of Minute
Man National Historical Park); less than a century later, Concord was an important literary and intellectual center. A visit can easily fill a day; if your interests are specialized

or time is short, a half-day excursion is reasonable. For an excellent overview of town history, start at the **Concord Museum.**

After just a little time in this lovely town, you might find yourself adopting the local attitude toward two famous residents: **Ralph Waldo Emerson,** who comes across as a respected uncle figure, and **Henry David Thoreau,** everyone's favorite eccentric cousin. The contemplative writers wandered the countryside and did much of their work in Concord, forming the nucleus of a group of important writers who called the town home. By the mid–19th century, Concord was the center of the Transcendentalist movement. Sightseers can tour the former **homes of Emerson, Thoreau, Nathaniel Hawthorne,** and **Louisa May Alcott,** and visit their graves at **Sleepy Hollow Cemetery.**

ESSENTIALS

GETTING THERE   From Lexington, take Route 2A west from Mass. Ave. (Route 4/225) at the National Heritage Museum; follow the BATTLE ROAD signs. From Boston and Cambridge, take Route 2 into Lincoln and stay in the right lane. Where the main road makes a sharp left, go straight onto Cambridge Turnpike. Signs that point to HISTORIC CONCORD lead downtown. To go straight to Walden Pond, use the left lane, take the main road (Route 2/2A) another mile or so, and turn left onto Route 126. There's parking throughout town and at the attractions.

The **commuter rail** (© **617/222-3200;** www.mbta.com) takes about 45 minutes from North Station in Boston, with a stop at Porter Square in Cambridge. The round-trip fare is $13. The station is about three-quarters of a mile over flat terrain from the town center. There is no bus service from Boston to Concord, and no public transportation between Lexington and Concord. The **Liberty Ride** tour (see p. 246) operates in the summer and fall.

VISITOR INFORMATION   The **Chamber of Commerce,** 15 Walden St., Suite 7, Concord, MA 01742 (© **978/369-3120;** www.concordchamberofcommerce.org), maintains a visitor center at 58 Main St., next to Middlesex Savings Bank, 1 block south of Monument Square. It's open daily 10am to 4pm from April through October; public restrooms in the same building are open year-round. Ninety-minute guided walking tours ($18 adults, $12 seniors and students 13–18, $10 children 6–12, free for children under 6) are available Friday through Monday from mid-March through October. Tours start at the visitor center. Group tours are available by appointment. The chamber office is open year-round Monday through Friday; hours vary, so call ahead.

The town website, **www.concordma.gov,** has an area with visitor information.

EXPLORING THE AREA

Minute Man National Historical Park ★★ (Kids)   This 970-acre park preserves the scene of the first Revolutionary War battle at Concord on (all together now) April 19, 1775. After the skirmish at Lexington, the British continued to Concord in search of stockpiled arms (which militia members had already moved). Warned of the advance, the colonists prepared to confront the troops. The Minutemen crossed the North Bridge, evading the regular standing guard, and waited on a hilltop for reinforcements. The British searched nearby homes and burned any guns they found. The colonials saw the smoke and, mistakenly thinking that the troops were torching the town, attacked the soldiers at the bridge. The gunfire that ensued is remembered as "the shot heard round the world," the opening salvo of the Revolution.

The park is open daily, year-round. A visit can take as little as half an hour for a jaunt to the North Bridge (a reproduction) or as long as half a day or more, if you stop at both visitor centers and perhaps participate in a ranger-led program. The rangers suggest beginning your visit at the Minute Man Visitor Center (see "Lexington," above), which is closed in the winter. Alternatively, start at the **North Bridge Visitor Center** ✪, 174 Liberty St., off Monument Street (✆ **978/369-6993;** www.nps.gov/mima), which overlooks the Concord River and the bridge. A diorama and video program illustrate the battle, and exhibits include uniforms, weapons, and tools of colonial and British soldiers. Park rangers are on duty if you have questions. Outside, picnicking is allowed, and the scenery is lovely, especially in the fall. The center is open daily from 9am to 5pm (11am–3pm in winter) and is closed January 1 and December 25.

To go straight to the bridge, follow Monument Street out of Concord Center until you see the parking lot on the right. Park and walk a short distance to the bridge, stopping along the unpaved path to read the narratives and hear the audio presentations. On one side of the bridge is a plaque commemorating the British soldiers who died in the Revolutionary War; on the other is Daniel Chester French's famed *Minute Man* statue, a photograph of which is in the color insert at the beginning of this guidebook.

Walden Pond State Reservation ✪✪   The conservation movement started here, in a small wooden structure where a misunderstood social activist moved to "live deliberately." A pile of stones marks the site of the cabin where Henry David Thoreau lived from 1845 to 1847. Today the picturesque park is an extremely popular destination for walking (a path circles the pond), swimming, and fishing. Although crowded, it's well preserved and insulated from development, making it less difficult than you might expect to imagine Thoreau's experience. Call for the schedule of ranger-led interpretive programs. No dogs or bikes are allowed. In good weather, the parking lot fills early every day—call before setting out, because the rangers turn away visitors once the park reaches capacity (1,000).

Visitors Center: 915 Walden St. (Rte. 126). ✆ **978/369-3254.** www.mass.gov/dcr/parks/walden. Free admission. Parking $5 (cash only). Daily 8am–sunset. From downtown Concord, take Walden St. (Rte. 126) south, cross Rte. 2, and follow signs to the parking lot.

Museums & Literary Sites

Concord Museum ✪✪ *Kids*   Just when you're (understandably) suspecting that everything interesting in this area started on April 18, 1775, and ended the next day, this superb museum sets you straight. It's a great place to start your visit to the town.

The **History Galleries** ✪✪ explore the question "Why Concord?" Artifacts, murals, films, maps, documents, and other exhibits illustrate the town's changing roles. It has been a Native American settlement, Revolutionary War battleground, 19th-century intellectual center, and focal point of the 20th-century historic preservation movement.

Items on display include silver from colonial churches, a fascinating collection of embroidery samplers, 19th-century clocks (Concord was a center of clock making), and rooms furnished with period furniture and textiles. Explanatory text places the objects in context. One of the **lanterns** immortalized by Longfellow in "Paul Revere's Ride" ("one if by land, two if by sea") is on display. You'll also see the contents of **Ralph Waldo Emerson's study,** arranged the way it was at his death in 1882, and a large collection of **Henry David Thoreau's belongings.**

Pick up a **family activity pack** ✦ as you enter; kids can use the games and reproduction artifacts (including a quill pen and powder horn) to get a hands-on feel for life in the past. The museum also mounts changing exhibits in the New Wing, offers special events such as story hour and "tea and tour" (call for reservations), and has an outstanding gift shop.

Cambridge Turnpike at Lexington Rd. ☎ **978/369-9609** (recorded info) or 978/369-9763. www.concordmuseum. org. Admission $10 adults, $8 seniors and students, $5 6–18, free for children under 6. June–Aug daily 9am–5pm; Apr–May and Sept–Dec Mon–Sat 9am–5pm, Sun noon–5pm; Jan–Mar Mon–Sat 11am–4pm, Sun 1–4pm. Closed Easter, Thanksgiving, and Dec 25. Parking allowed on road. Follow Lexington Rd. out of Concord Center and bear right at museum onto Cambridge Tpk.; entrance is on left.

The Old Manse ✦   The engaging history of this home touches on the military and the literary, but it's mostly the story of a family. The Rev. William Emerson built the Old Manse in 1770 and watched the Battle of Concord from the yard. He died during the Revolutionary War, and for almost 170 years the house was home to his widow, her second husband (Rev. Ripley), their descendants, and two famous friends. Nathaniel Hawthorne and his bride, Sophia Peabody, moved in after their marriage in 1842 and stayed for 3 years. As a wedding present, Henry David Thoreau sowed a vegetable garden; today, a re-creation of that garden is part of a self-guided tour of the grounds. William Emerson's grandson Ralph Waldo Emerson wrote the essay "Nature" here, in the same study where Hawthorne later toiled. On the guided tour (the only way to visit the house), you'll see mementos and memorabilia of the Emerson and Ripley families and of the Hawthornes, who scratched notes on two windows with Sophia's diamond ring.

269 Monument St. (at North Bridge). ☎ **978/369-3909.** www.oldmanse.org. Guided tour $8 adults, $7 seniors and students, $5 children 6–12, $25 families. Patriots Day weekend to Columbus Day Mon–Sat 10am–5pm, Sun and holidays noon–5pm (last tour at 4:30pm). Closed mid-Oct to mid-Apr. From Concord Center, follow Monument St. to North Bridge parking lot (on right); Old Manse is on left.

Orchard House ✦✦✦ *Kids*   *Little Women* (1868), Louisa May Alcott's best known and most popular work, was written and set at Orchard House. Seeing the Alcotts' home brings the author and her family to life for legions of female visitors and their pleasantly surprised male companions. Fans won't want to miss the excellent tour (the only way to explore the house), copiously illustrated with heirlooms. Serious buffs can check ahead for information on the extensive schedule of special events and seasonal and holiday programs, some of which require reservations.

Louisa's father, Amos Bronson Alcott, was a writer, educator, and philosopher, and the leader of the Transcendentalist movement. He created Orchard House by joining and restoring two homes on 12 acres of land that he bought in 1857. Bronson and his wife, the social activist Abigail May Alcott, and their family lived here from 1858 to 1877, socializing in the same circles as Emerson, Thoreau, and Hawthorne.

Their daughters inspired the characters in *Little Women.* Anna ("Meg"), the eldest, was an amateur actress, and May ("Amy") was a talented artist. "Jo" was Louisa's alter ego, and Elizabeth ("Beth"), a gifted musician, died before the family moved to this house, which has been open to the public since 1911.

399 Lexington Rd. ℂ 978/369-4118. www.louisamayalcott.org. Guided tours $9 adults, $7 seniors and students, $5 children 6–17, $25 families. Apr–Oct Mon–Sat 10am–4:30pm, Sun 1–4:30pm; Nov–Mar Mon–Fri 11am–3pm, Sat 10am–4:30pm, Sun 1–4:30pm. Closed Jan 1–15, Easter, Thanksgiving, and Dec 25. Follow Lexington Rd. out of Concord Center and bear left at Concord Museum; house is on the left. Overflow parking lot is across the street.

Ralph Waldo Emerson House   This house offers an instructive look at the days when a philosopher could attain the status we now associate with rock stars. Emerson, also an essayist and poet, lived here from 1835 until his death, in 1882. He moved in after marrying his second wife, Lydia Jackson, whom he called Lydian; she called him Mr. Emerson, as the staff still does. The tour (the only way to enter the house) gives an affectionate look at Emerson's personal side and at the fashionably ornate interior decoration of the time. You'll see original furnishings and some of Emerson's personal effects. The contents of his study from the time of his death are in the Concord Museum (p. 249).

28 Cambridge Tpk. ℂ 978/369-2236. www.rwe.org/emersonhouse. Guided tours $7 adults, $5 seniors and students, free for children under 7. Call to arrange group tours (10 people or more). Patriots Day weekend–late Oct Thurs–Sat 10am–4:30pm, Sun 1–4:30pm. Closed late Oct to mid-Apr. Follow Cambridge Tpk. out of Concord Center; just before Concord Museum, house is on right.

Sleepy Hollow Cemetery ⓚ   Follow the signs for AUTHOR'S RIDGE and climb the hill to the graves of some of the town's literary lights, including the Alcotts, Emerson, Hawthorne, and Thoreau. Emerson's bears no religious symbols; the marker is an uncarved quartz boulder. Thoreau is buried nearby; at his funeral, in 1862, his old friend Emerson concluded his eulogy with these words: " . . . wherever there is knowledge, wherever there is virtue, wherever there is beauty, he will find a home."

Entrance on Rte. 62 W. ℂ 978/318-3233. www.concordma.gov. Daily 7am–dusk, weather permitting. No buses allowed.

The Wayside ⓚ   The Wayside was Nathaniel Hawthorne's home from 1852 until his death in 1864. The Alcotts also lived here (the girls called it "the yellow house"), as did Harriett Lothrop, who wrote the *Five Little Peppers* books under the pen name Margaret Sidney and owned most of the current furnishings. The Wayside is part of Minute Man National Historical Park, and the fascinating 45-minute ranger tour (the only way to see the house) illuminates the occupants' lives and the house's crazy-quilt architecture. The exhibit in the barn (free admission) consists of audio presentations and figures of Hawthorne, Louisa May and Bronson Alcott, and Sidney. Call ahead to double-check hours, which are subject to change.

455 Lexington Rd. ℂ 978/318-7863. www.nps.gov/mima. Guided tours $5 adults, free for children under 17. May–Oct; open days and hours vary. Closed Nov–Apr. Follow Lexington Rd. out of Concord Center past Concord Museum and Orchard House. Park across the street.

NEARBY SIGHTS

DeCordova Museum and Sculpture Park ✰✰　Indoors and out, this dramatic museum shows the work of American contemporary and modern artists, with an emphasis on living New England residents. The imaginative curatorial staff builds exhibits around themes as well as the work of individual artists—shows during the lifespan of this book will focus on (among other things) contemporary American drawings, recent work by New England artist Laylah Ali, and prints by Vermont artists. The main building, on a leafy hilltop, overlooks the outdoor public sculpture park. The museum also has a sculpture terrace that displays the work of one sculptor per year. The prestigious **DeCordova Annual Exhibition** (May–Aug) is a group show of recent work in various media by a select group of New England artists.

Allow at least half a day, perhaps including lunch. Picnicking is allowed in the sculpture park; bring food or buy it at the cafe (open Tues noon–3pm, Wed–Sun 11am–4pm). Free guided tours of the main galleries start at 1pm Thursday and 2pm Sunday, year-round; sculpture-park tours run May through October on weekends at 1pm. Be sure to check out the excellent gift shop.

51 Sandy Pond Rd., Lincoln. ℂ 781/259-8355. www.decordova.org. Admission $9 adults; $6 seniors, students, and children 6–12. Admission to sculpture park free when museum is closed. Museum: Tues–Sun and some Mon holidays 10am–5pm. Closed Jan 1, July 4, Thanksgiving, and Dec 25. Sculpture park: Daily daylight hours. From Rte. 2 E., take Rte. 126 south to Baker Bridge Rd. (1st left after Walden Pond). When it ends, go right onto Sandy Pond Rd.; museum is on the left. From I-95, take Exit 28B, follow Trapelo Rd. 2½ miles to Sandy Pond Rd., then follow signs.

Gropius House ✰　Architect Walter Gropius (1883–1969), founder of the Bauhaus school of design, built this hilltop home for his family in 1938 after accepting a job at the Harvard Graduate School of Design. He used traditional materials such as clapboard, brick, and fieldstone, with components then seldom seen in domestic architecture, including glass blocks and chrome (on the banisters). Marcel Breuer designed many of the furnishings, which were made for the family at the Bauhaus. Decorated as it was in the last decade of Gropius's life, the house affords a revealing look at his life, career, and philosophy. Call for information on workshops and special tours; evening tours (reservation required) take place throughout the year.

68 Baker Bridge Rd., Lincoln. ℂ 781/259-8098. www.historicnewengland.org. Guided tours $10 adults, $9 seniors, $5 students with ID and children. Tours on the hour June–Oct 15 Wed–Sun 11am–4pm; Oct 16–May Sat–Sun 11am–4pm. From Rte. 2 E., take Rte. 126 south to Baker Bridge Rd. (1st left after Walden Pond); house is on the right. From I-95, take Exit 28B, follow Trapelo Rd. to Sandy Pond Rd., go left onto Baker Bridge Rd.; house is on the left.

SHOPPING

Downtown Concord, off **Monument Square,** is a terrific shopping destination. Here you'll find the **Toy Shop of Concord,** 4 Walden St. (ℂ **978/369-2553**); the **Grasshopper Shop,** 36 Main St. (ℂ **978/369-8295**), which carries women's clothing and accessories; jewelry at **Mascio-Ricci,** at Concord's Colonial Inn, 48 Monument Sq. (ℂ **978/371-1191**); and the **Concord Bookshop,** 65 Main St. (ℂ **978/369-2405**). At the Concord Depot, the **Muse's Window,** 84 Thoreau St. (ℂ **978/287-5500**), is an excellent fine-crafts gallery. The compact shopping district in **West Concord,** along Route 62, boasts the old-fashioned **West Concord 5 & 10,** 106 Commonwealth Ave. (ℂ **978/369-9011**), which carries everything from light bulbs to lace.

WHERE TO STAY & DINE

Consider taking a **picnic** to the North Bridge, Walden Pond, or another spot that catches your eye. Stock up at **Nashoba Brook Bakery** (see below) or downtown at the **Cheese Shop,** 25–31 Walden St. (ℂ **978/369-5778**).

Concord's Colonial Inn ⍟   The main building of the Colonial Inn has overlooked Monument Square since 1716. Like many historic inns, it's not luxurious, but it is comfortable, centrally located, and possibly haunted. Additions since it became a hotel in 1889 have made the inn large enough to offer modern conveniences (including wireless Internet access) and small enough to feel friendly. The 15 original guest rooms—one of which (no. 24) supposedly is home to a ghost—are in great demand. Reserve early if you want to stay in the main inn, which is decorated (surprise, surprise) in colonial style. Rooms in the 1970 Prescott House have country-style decor, as do the one-, two-, and three-bedroom suites (available for long-term stays) in four freestanding buildings. The amenities, variety of rooms, and accommodating staff make the inn popular with business travelers as well as vacationers, especially during foliage season.

The two lounges serve light meals; ask for an outdoor table, and you'll have a front-row seat for the action on Monument Square. The restaurant serves salads, sandwiches, and pasta at lunch and traditional American fare at dinner. Afternoon tea ($25) is served Friday through Sunday; reservations (℃ **978/369-2373**) are required.

48 Monument Sq., Concord, MA 01742. ℃ **800/370-9200** or 978/369-9200. Fax 978/371-1533. www.concords colonialinn.com. 56 units, some with shower only. Apr–early Sept $179–$229 main inn, $149–$199 Prescott House; mid-Sept to Oct $199–$249 main inn, $169–$219 Prescott House; Nov–Mar from $159 main inn, from $129 Prescott House. Long-term rates from $50/day. AE, DC, DISC, MC, V. **Amenities:** Restaurant (American); 2 lounges; bar w/live jazz and blues on weekends; access to nearby health club ($10); concierge; tour desk; business center; same-day dry cleaning; executive-level rooms, rooms for those w/limited mobility. *In room:* A/C, TV/DVD, wireless Internet access, coffeemaker, hair dryer, iron.

Nashoba Brook Bakery & Café ⍟⍟ AMERICAN   True story: A friend living in Australia recently returned home for a visit craving two things: a nap and a visit here. The enticing variety of fresh artisan breads, scrumptious baked goods and pastries, and made-from-scratch soups, salads, and sandwiches makes the airy cafe a popular destination throughout the day. It offers a good break from the sightseeing circuit. The industrial-looking building off West Concord's main street backs up to little Nashoba Brook, which is visible through the glass back wall. Order and pick up at the counter, and then grab a seat along the window or near the children's play area. You can also order takeout—this is great picnic food—or a loaf of crusty bread. On weekend mornings, the cafe serves scrumptious homemade Belgian waffles.

152 Commonwealth Ave., West Concord. ℃ **978/318-1999.** www.slowrise.com. Sandwiches $7; other menu items $2–$8. MC, V. Mon–Fri 7am–5:30pm, Sat 7am–5pm, Sun 8am–5pm. From Concord Center, follow Main St. (Rte. 62) west, across Rte. 2; bear right at traffic light in front of train station and go 3 blocks. To reach overflow parking, turn right onto Commonwealth Ave. and take first right into lot on Winthrop St.; walk across bridge over brook.

2 The North Shore & Cape Ann

The areas north of Boston abound with historic sights and gorgeous ocean vistas. Cape Ann is a rocky peninsula so enchantingly beautiful that when you hear the slogan "Massachusetts's *Other* Cape," you might forget what the first one was. Cape Ann and Cape Cod do share some attributes—scenery, shopping, seafood, and traffic. Its proximity to Boston and manageable scale make Cape Ann a wonderful day trip as well as a good choice for a longer stay.

If possible, explore the North Shore by car. Public transportation in this area is good, but it doesn't go everywhere, and in some towns the train station is some distance from the attractions. For the full day-trip experience, try to visit on a spring,

> **Tips You Do the Math**
>
> The **MBTA** (℃ 800/392-6100 or 617/222-3200; www.mbta.com) serves most of the destinations in this chapter, but public transit isn't necessarily cheaper than renting a car for a day. For example, suppose you're visiting Gloucester with three other adults, each paying a total of $15 to ride the commuter rail. Even allowing for gas prices, a good deal on a rental car will be cheaper than $60 in train fares. What's more, having a car allows you to make your own schedule instead of being tethered to the train's timetable—and you don't have to leave from North Station. Just make sure that the car-rental company accepts returns at the time you anticipate returning to Boston, so that you don't get stuck with the car and pricey overnight parking.

summer, or fall weekday; traffic is brutal on warm weekends. Many areas are practically ghost towns from November through March, but all of the destinations in this chapter have enough of a year-round community to make an off-season excursion worthwhile.

The **North of Boston Convention & Visitors Bureau,** 17 Peabody Sq., Peabody, MA 01960 (℃ **800/742-5306** or 978/977-7760; www.northofboston.org), publishes a map and a visitor guide that covers 34 municipalities, including Salem, Marblehead, and all of Cape Ann. It also coordinates **Escapes North** (www.escapesnorth.com), a clearinghouse for arts- and culture-oriented travel throughout the area. The **Cape Ann Chamber of Commerce** information center (see "Gloucester," later in this chapter) is another good resource.

MARBLEHEAD 🐦🐦🐦
15 miles NE of Boston

Like an attractive person with a great personality, Marblehead has it all. Scenery, history, architecture, and shopping combine to make this one of the area's most popular day trips for both locals and visitors. It's even polite—many speed-limit signs say PLEASE. Allow at least a full morning, but be flexible, because you might want to hang around.

One of the most picturesque neighborhoods in New England is **Old Town** 🐦🐦🐦, where narrow, twisting streets lead down to the magnificent harbor that helps make this the self-proclaimed "Yachting Capital of America." As you stroll the downtown historic district, you'll see plaques on the houses bearing the date of construction, as well as the names of the builder and original occupant—a history lesson without studying. Many of the houses have stood since before the Revolutionary War, when Marblehead was a center of merchant shipping. Two historic homes are open to the public (see "Exploring the Town," below).

ESSENTIALS
GETTING THERE By car, take Route 1A north through Revere and Lynn; bear right at the signs for Nahant and Swampscott. Follow Lynn Shore Drive through Swampscott to Route 129, which runs into town. Or take I-93 or Route 1 to Route 128, then follow Route 114 through Salem into Marblehead. Parking is tough, especially in Old Town—grab the first spot you see.

Marblehead

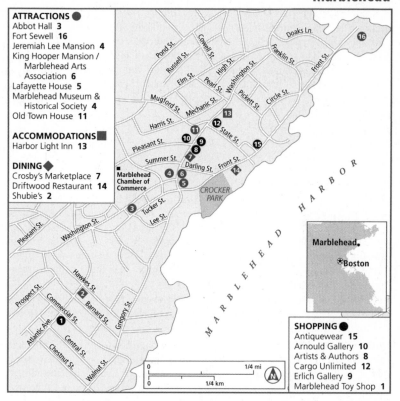

ATTRACTIONS ●
Abbot Hall **3**
Fort Sewell **16**
Jeremiah Lee Mansion **4**
King Hooper Mansion /
   Marblehead Arts
   Association **6**
Lafayette House **5**
Marblehead Museum &
   Historical Society **4**
Old Town House **11**

ACCOMMODATIONS ■
Harbor Light Inn **13**

DINING ◆
Crosby's Marketplace **7**
Driftwood Restaurant **14**
Shubie's **2**

SHOPPING ●
Antiquewear **15**
Arnould Gallery **10**
Artists & Authors **8**
Cargo Unlimited **12**
Erlich Gallery **9**
Marblehead Toy Shop **1**

MBTA (*☎* **617/222-3200;** www.mbta.com) bus no. 441/442 runs from Haymarket (Orange or Green line) to downtown Marblehead. During rush periods on weekdays, the no. 448/449 connects Marblehead to Downtown Crossing. The trip takes about an hour, and the one-way fare is $2.80 with a CharlieCard, $3.50 with a CharlieTicket.

VISITOR INFORMATION   The **Marblehead Chamber of Commerce,** 62 Pleasant St., Marblehead, MA 01945 (*☎* **781/631-2868;** www.visitmarblehead.com), is open weekdays from 9am to 5pm. The **information booth** (*☎* **781/639-8469**), on Pleasant Street near Spring Street, is open mid-May through October, Monday to Friday noon to 5pm, Saturday and Sunday 10am to 6pm. The chamber publishes a visitor guide and map that includes a calendar of events; before you visit, download a description of a walking tour.

SPECIAL EVENTS   Sailing regattas take place in the outer harbor all summer. The biggie, the **National Offshore One Design (NOOD) Regatta,** also known as Race Week, falls in mid- to late July and attracts enthusiasts from all over the country. The **Christmas Walk,** on the first weekend in December, incorporates music, arts and crafts, shopping, and Santa Claus, who arrives by lobster boat.

EXPLORING THE TOWN

Marblehead is a wonderful place for aimless wandering; to add some structure, consult the walking tour described on the chamber of commerce's website. Whatever else you do, be sure to spend some time in **Crocker Park** 🌟🌟, on the harbor off Front Street. Especially in the warmer months, when boats jam the water nearly as far as the eye can see, the view is breathtaking. The park has benches and a swing, and it's a great place for a picnic. The view from **Fort Sewall,** at the other end of Front Street, is equally mesmerizing.

Just inland, the **Lafayette House** is at the corner of Hooper and Union streets. A corner of the private home was chopped off to make room for the passage of the Marquis de Lafayette's carriage when he visited the town in 1824. In Market Square on Washington Street, near the corner of State Street, is the **Old Town House,** in use for meetings and gatherings since 1727.

Abbot Hall   A 5-minute stop here (look for the clock tower) is just the ticket if you want to be able to say you did some sightseeing. The town offices and historical commission share Abbot Hall with Archibald M. Willard's famous painting *The Spirit of '76* 🌟, on display in the Selectmen's Meeting Room. The thrill of recognizing the ubiquitous drummer, drummer boy, and fife player is the main reason to stop here. Cases in the halls contain objects and artifacts from the collections of the Marblehead Historical Society and other organizations.

Washington Sq. ⓒ 781/631-0528. www.marblehead.org. Free admission. Year-round Mon–Tues and Thurs 8am–5pm, Wed 7:30am–7:30pm, Fri 8am–1pm; May–Oct Fri 1–5pm, Sat 9am–6pm, Sun 11am–6pm. From the historic district, follow Washington St. up the hill.

Jeremiah Lee Mansion 🌟🌟   Built in 1768 for one of the wealthiest merchants in the colonies, the Lee Mansion is internationally recognized as an extraordinary example of pre-Revolutionary Georgian architecture. The attraction for aficionados is the excitement of seeing original hand-painted wallpaper in an 18th-century home, but the friendly, knowledgeable guides make visitors of all interest levels feel welcome, fielding questions about the history of the home and the town. Rococo woodcarving and other details complement historically accurate room arrangements, and ongoing restoration and interpretation by the Marblehead Museum & Historical Society place the 18th- and 19th-century furnishings and artifacts in context. The peaceful gardens are open to the public.

Across the street is a visitor center (free admission) that houses two galleries. One displays paintings by the noted early-20th-century folk artist J. O. J. Frost, a Marblehead native; the other mounts changing exhibits, which will include a display of wooden decoys in late 2008. Call ahead for the schedule of **summer walking tours** of Marblehead.

(Fun Fact **Architectural Details**

On the hill between the Jeremiah Lee Mansion and Abbot Hall, notice the private homes at 185, 181, and 175 Washington St. Like the Lee mansion—and hundreds of other residences in the tiny downtown area—these are good original examples of the architecture of the colonial period.

> ## Finds For the Birds
>
> Marblehead Neck, an upscale neighborhood across the causeway from Dev-
> ereux Beach, is home to a **Massachusetts Audubon Society bird sanctuary**
> (© **800/AUDUBON** or 781/259-9500; www.massaudubon.org). Turn east on
> Ocean Avenue south of downtown and follow it less than a mile until you see
> a small sign to the left at Risley Avenue. Park in the small lot and follow the
> path into the sanctuary, where you can see the varied species of birds that use
> the Atlantic flyway, especially in spring and fall. Admission is free. To return to
> Marblehead proper, continue on Ocean Avenue, which becomes Harbor
> Avenue and forms a loop. En route, at the end of "the Neck," you can park
> near the decommissioned lighthouse and take in a breathtaking view.

161 Washington St. © **781/631-1768**. www.marbleheadmuseum.org. Guided tours $5 adults, $4.50 seniors and students. June–Oct Tues–Sat 10am–4pm. Closed Nov–May. Visitor center: 170 Washington St. Free admission. June–Oct Tues–Sat 10am–4pm; Nov–May Tues–Fri 10am–4pm. From Abbot Hall, follow Washington St. down the hill; mansion is on left.

King Hooper Mansion/Marblehead Arts Association & Gallery   Shipping
tycoon Robert Hooper got his nickname because he treated his sailors so well, but it's
easy to think he was called "King" because he lived like royalty—his house has both a
wine cellar and a ballroom. Around the corner from the home of Jeremiah Lee (whose
sister-in-law was the second of Hooper's four wives), the 1728 mansion gained a Georgian addition sometime after 1745. The **Marblehead Arts Association** bought the
building in 1938 and now stages monthly exhibits (with a public reception on the first
Sunday of every month from 2–4pm), schedules special events, and sells members'
work in the gift shop. The mansion has a lovely garden; enter through the gate at the
right of the house.

8 Hooper St. © **781/631-2608**. www.marbleheadarts.org. Free admission. May–Oct Tues–Sat 11am–5pm, Sun noon–5pm; Nov–Apr Tues–Sat noon–4pm, Sun 1–5pm. Where Washington St. curves at the foot of hill near Lee man-sion, look for the colorful sign.

SHOPPING
Marblehead is a legendary (or notorious, if you're on a budget) shopping destination.
Shops, boutiques, and galleries abound in **Old Town** and on **Atlantic Avenue** and the
east end of **Pleasant Street.** The most unusual shop in town is **Antiquewear,** 82 Front
St. (© **781/639-0070;** www.antiquewear.com), near the town pier, which sells 19th-
century buttons ingeniously fashioned into women's and men's jewelry of all descriptions. Other good stops include **Arnould Gallery & Framery,** 111 Washington St.
(© **781/631-6366**); **Artists & Authors,** 108 Washington St. (© **781/639-0400;**
www.artists-authors.com), which carries rare books and fine art; **Cargo Unlimited,**
118 Washington St. (© **781/631-1112;** www.cargounlimited.com), for home furnishings and accessories; **Erlich Gallery,** 96 Washington St. (© **781/631-1202;** www.
erlichgallery.com); and the beloved **Marblehead Toy Shop,** 44–48 Atlantic Ave.
(© **781/631-9900**).

WHERE TO STAY
This is B&B heaven. Space considerations preclude listing the numerous small inns and
bed-and-breakfasts, but the accommodations listings of the **Marblehead Chamber of**

Commerce, 62 Pleasant St., Marblehead, MA 01945 (© **781/631-2868;** www.visit marblehead.com), include many of them. Check the website, call or write for a visitor guide, or consult one of the B&B agencies listed on p. 70.

Harbor Light Inn 🐦🐦   A stone's throw from the Old Town House, two Federal-era mansions make up this gracious inn, which is much bigger and more luxurious than its austere facade suggests. From the wood floors to the 1729 beams (in a third-floor room) to the swimming pool, it's both historic and relaxing. Rooms are comfortably furnished in period style, with some lovely antiques; most have canopy or four-poster beds. Eleven hold working fireplaces, and five have double Jacuzzis. VCRs and free video rentals are available. The best rooms, on the top floor at the back of the building, away from the street, have gorgeous harbor views. The undeniably romantic inn, a popular honeymoon and weekend-getaway destination, shifts gears seamlessly to attract weekday business travelers with its wireless Internet access and meeting space.

58 Washington St., Marblehead, MA 01945. © **781/631-2186.** Fax 781/631-2216. www.harborlightinn.com. 21 units, 7 with shower only. $145–$335 double; $195–$375 suite. Rates include breakfast buffet, afternoon refreshments, and use of bikes. Corporate rate available midweek. 2-night minimum stay weekends, 3-night minimum holiday and high-season weekends. AE, MC, V. Free parking. **Amenities:** Bar; heated outdoor pool; access to nearby health club ($5); Jacuzzi; concierge; airport shuttle; in-room massage. *In room:* A/C, TV/VCR, wireless Internet access, hair dryer, iron, robes.

WHERE TO DINE

Marblehead has a number of serviceable dining options, plus a ton of bars that serve decent food. You're probably better off heading to Salem if you want a sit-down meal, but I prefer sitting down outdoors—for a picnic. You can stock up at a number of places in Old Town. **Crosby's Marketplace,** 118 Washington St. (© **781/631-1741**), is a full-service market with a large prepared-food section. **Shubie's,** 32 Atlantic Ave. (© **781/631-0149**), carries a good selection of specialty foods. Another excellent option is to hit the road early and have breakfast near the harbor.

Driftwood Restaurant 🐦 DINER/SEAFOOD   At the foot of State Street, next to Clark Landing (the town pier), is an honest-to-goodness local hangout that serves excellent food. Join the crowd at a table or the counter for a mug of strong coffee and generous portions of breakfast (served all day) or lunch. Try pancakes or hash, chowder or a seafood roll—a hot dog bun filled with, say, fried clams or lobster salad. The house specialty, served on weekends and holidays, is fried dough, which is sort of a solid doughnut, as crispy as a good New Orleans beignet. At busy times, you may have to wait outside for a while.

63 Front St. © **781/631-1145.** Main courses $3–$12; breakfast items less than $7. No credit cards. Daily 5:30am–2pm.

SALEM 🐦🐦
17 miles NE of Boston, 4 miles NW of Marblehead

Settled in 1626, 4 years before Boston, Salem later enjoyed international renown as a center of merchant shipping, but today it's famous around the world because of a 7-month episode in 1692. The witchcraft trial hysteria led to 20 deaths, 3-plus centuries of notoriety, countless lessons on the evils of prejudice, and innumerable bad puns ("Stop by for a spell" is a favorite slogan).

Unable to live down the association, and never forgetting the victims, Salem embraces its reputation. The high school sports teams are the Witches, and the *Salem Evening News* logo is a silhouette of a sorceress. The city abounds with witch-associated

Salem

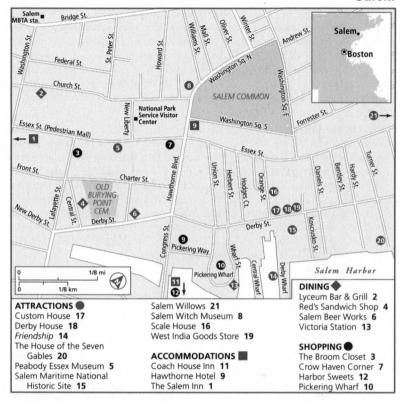

ATTRACTIONS ●
Custom House **17**
Derby House **18**
Friendship **14**
The House of the Seven
    Gables **20**
Peabody Essex Museum **5**
Salem Maritime National
    Historic Site **15**

Salem Willows **21**
Salem Witch Museum **8**
Scale House **16**
West India Goods Store **19**

ACCOMMODATIONS ■
Coach House Inn **11**
Hawthorne Hotel **9**
The Salem Inn **1**

DINING ◆
Lyceum Bar & Grill **2**
Red's Sandwich Shop **4**
Salem Beer Works **6**
Victoria Station **13**

SHOPPING ●
The Broom Closet **3**
Crow Haven Corner **7**
Harbor Sweets **12**
Pickering Wharf **10**

attractions, plus nearly as many reminders of Salem's seagoing legacy. Most are historically accurate, but you'll also see a fair number of goofy souvenirs and opportunistic tourist traps. An excellent antidote to the latter is the **Peabody Essex Museum.** Salem is a family-friendly destination that's worth at least a half-day visit (perhaps after a stop in Marblehead) and can easily fill a day.

ESSENTIALS

GETTING THERE   By car from Marblehead, follow Route 114 west. From Boston, take Route 1A north to Salem, being careful in Lynn, where the road turns left and immediately right. You can also take I-93 or Route 1 to Route 128 and then Route 114 into downtown Salem. There's metered street parking and a reasonably priced municipal garage across the street from the National Park Service Regional Visitor Center.

From Boston, the **MBTA** (© **617/222-3200;** www.mbta.com) operates commuter trains from North Station and bus no. 450 from Haymarket (Orange or Green line). The train is more comfortable than the bus but runs less frequently. It takes 30 to 35 minutes; the round-trip fare is $11. The station is about 5 blocks from the downtown area. The one-way fare for the 35- to 55-minute bus trip is $2.80 with a CharlieCard, $3.50 with a CharlieTicket.

The **Salem Ferry** (© 978/741-0220; www.salemferry.com) operates daily from Memorial Day weekend through October. The 50-minute catamaran trip connects Central Wharf, next to Boston's New England Aquarium (T: Blue Line to Aquarium) to the Blaney Street Wharf, off Derby Street, a 15-minute walk or quick hop on the Salem Trolley (see below) from downtown Salem. The peak adult fare (before 4pm from late June–early September) is $13 one-way, $23 round-trip, with discounts for seniors, children, families, and evening passengers. The one-way off-season fare is $10 for all.

VISITOR INFORMATION   A good place to start your visit is the **National Park Service Regional Visitor Center,** 2 New Liberty St. (© 978/740-1650; www.nps. gov/sama), open daily from 9am to 5pm. Exhibits highlight early settlement, maritime history, and the leather and textiles industries. The center also distributes brochures and pamphlets, including one that describes a **walking tour** of the historic district, and has an auditorium where a free film on Essex County provides an overview.

The city's Office of Tourism, **Destination Salem** (© 877/SALEM-MA or 978/744-3663; www.salem.org), produces and distributes a free visitor guide that includes an excellent map. The **Salem Chamber of Commerce,** 265 Essex St., Salem, MA 01970 (© 978/744-0004; www.salem-chamber.org), maintains a large rack of brochures and pamphlets, and the staff is up on the latest events. It's open weekdays from 9am to 5pm.

The municipal website (www.salem.com) and an excellent community website (www.salemweb.com) offer information for out-of-towners.

GETTING AROUND   In the congested downtown area, **walking** is the way to go, but you might not want to hoof it to all the sights, especially if it's hot. At the Essex Street side of the visitor center, you can board the **Salem Trolley** ⟨★ (© 978/744-5469; www.salemtrolley.com) for a 1-hour narrated tour, and reboard as often as you like at any of the 12 stops. It's a good deal if you're spending the day and don't want to keep moving the car or carrying leg-weary children. The trolley operates from 10am to 5pm (last tour at 4pm) daily April through October; check ahead for hours in November. Tickets ($12 adults, $10 seniors, $5 children 6–14) are good all day; they're available onboard, from the Trolley Depot shop, 191 Essex St. at Central Street, on the pedestrian mall, and at the Park Service visitor center. A sister company, Salem Historical Tours (same phone; www.salemhistoricaltours.com), offers a number of excursions, the best known of which is the **Haunted Footsteps Ghost Tour.** A 90-minute exploration of the spooky and paranormal, the tour runs nightly from April through October and costs $14 for adults, $10 for seniors and students, $8 for children 6 to 14.

SPECIAL EVENTS   The city's month-long Halloween celebration, **Haunted Happenings** ★★ (www.hauntedhappenings.org), includes parades, parties, tours, and a ceremony on the big day. In August, the 2-day **Salem Maritime Festival** fills the area around the Salem Maritime National Historic Site (see listing below) with live music, food, and demonstrations of nautical crafts. The festival kicks off **Heritage Days,** a weeklong event when the city celebrates its multicultural history with musical and theatrical performances, a parade, and fireworks. Contact Destination Salem (see "Visitor Information," above) or Escapes North (www.escapesnorth.com) for details.

EXPLORING THE TOWN
The historic district extends well inland from the waterfront. Many 18th-century houses, some with original furnishings, still stand. Ship captains lived near the water

at the east end of downtown, in relatively small houses crowded close together. The captains' employers, the shipping company owners, built their homes away from the water (and the accompanying aromas). Many of them lived on **Chestnut Street** ★★, now a National Historic Landmark. Residents along the grand thoroughfare must, by legal agreement, adhere to colonial style in their decorating and furnishings. Ask at the visitor center for the pamphlet that describes a walking tour of the historic district.

By car or trolley, the **Salem Willows** (© 978/745-0251; www.salemwillows.com) amusements are 5 minutes away; many signs point the way. The strip of rides and snack bars has a honky-tonk air, and the waterfront park is a good place to bring a picnic and wander along the shore. There's no admission fee; meter parking is available. To enjoy the great view without the arcades and rides, have lunch one peninsula over at **Winter Island Park.**

The House of the Seven Gables ★ *Kids* Nathaniel Hawthorne's cousin lived here, and stories and legends of the house and its inhabitants inspired the author's 1851 book. If you haven't read the eerie novel, don't let that keep you away—begin your visit with the audiovisual program, which tells the story. The house, built by Capt. John Turner in 1668, contains six rooms of period furniture, including pieces referred to in the book, and a secret staircase. Tours include a visit to Hawthorne's birthplace (built before 1750 and moved to the grounds) and describe what life was like for the house's 18th-century inhabitants. The costumed guides are well versed in the history of the buildings and artifacts, and eager to answer questions. The site, a National Historic Landmark District overlooking Salem Harbor, also holds period gardens, the **Retire Beckett House** (1655), the **Hooper-Hathaway House** (1682), and a **counting house** (1830) where children find hands-on activities related to Salem's maritime legacy.

115 Derby St. © 978/744-0991. www.7gables.org. Guided tour of house and grounds $12 adults, $11 seniors and AAA members, $7.25 children 5–12, free for children under 5. Surcharges may apply for special exhibitions. July–Oct daily 10am–7pm (until 11pm Oct weekends); Nov–June daily 10am–5pm. Closed 1st 2 weeks of Jan, Thanksgiving, and Dec 25. From downtown, follow Derby St. east 3 blocks past Derby Wharf.

Peabody Essex Museum ★★ *Kids* Now in its third century, the Peabody Essex Museum has transformed itself into a national presence. All by itself, this captivating museum is reason enough to visit Salem.

Impressive collections of art from New England and around the world are the Peabody Essex's calling card, but they're just part of the story. The museum owns two dozen houses, including a well-preserved 18th-century Qing dynasty house, **Yin Yu Tang** ★, that was shipped here from China and reassembled. The only example of Chinese domestic architecture outside that country, the house captures 2 centuries of rural life. It's part of a huge wing designed by Moshe Safdie that opened in 2003.

The 1.4 million other items in the museum's permanent collections blend contemporary acquisitions with "the natural and artificial curiosities" that Salem's sea captains and merchants brought back from around the world to the Peabody Museum (1799) and local and domestic objects collected by the Essex Institute (1821), the county historical society. The displays help visitors understand the significance of each object, and interpretive materials (including interactive and hands-on activities) let children get involved. You might see objects related to the history of the port of Salem (including gorgeous furniture) or to the whaling trade (such as amazing scrimshaw). Other noteworthy collections include American, African, Indian, Asian, and East Asian art and objects; photography; and the practical arts and crafts of East Asian, Pacific

Island, and Native American peoples. Portraits of area residents include Charles Osgood's omnipresent rendering of Nathaniel Hawthorne.

Special exhibitions during the period covered by this book include **Stage Idols: Japanese Kabuki Theater** (through Jan 25, 2009) and **To the Ends of the Earth: Painting the Polar Landscape** (Nov 8, 2008–Mar 1, 2009).

To explore the museum, take a guided or self-guided gallery tour. The cafe keeps the same hours as the museum, and the restaurant serves lunch Wednesday through Sunday and afternoon tea on weekends.

East India Sq. © 866/745-1876 or 978/745-9500. www.pem.org. Admission $15 adults, $13 seniors, $11 students, free for children under 17. Yin Yu Tang admission $4 with museum admission. Surcharges may apply for special exhibitions. Daily 10am–5pm. Take Hawthorne Blvd. to Essex St., following signs for visitor center. Enter on Essex St. or New Liberty St.

Salem Maritime National Historic Site ⟨𝓡⟩ *(Kids)*   An entertaining introduction to Salem's seagoing history, this complex includes an exciting attraction: a real live ship. The **Friendship** ⟨𝓡𝓡⟩ is a full-size replica of a 1797 East Indiaman merchant vessel, a three-masted 171-footer that disappeared during the War of 1812. The tall ship is a faithful replica with some concessions to the modern era, such as diesel engines. The **guided ranger tour** includes a tour of the ship.

With the decline of merchant shipping in the early 19th century, Salem's wharves fell into disrepair. In 1938, the National Park Service took over a small piece of the waterfront, **Derby Wharf.** It's now a finger of parkland extending into the harbor, part of the 9 acres that make up the historic site. On adjacent **Central Wharf** is a warehouse, built around 1800, that houses the orientation center. Tours, which vary seasonally, explore Salem's maritime history. Yours might include the **Derby House** (1762), a wedding gift to shipping magnate Elias Hasket Derby from his father, and the **Custom House** (1819). Legend—myth, really—has it that Nathaniel Hawthorne was working here when he found an embroidered scarlet "A." If you prefer to explore on your own, you can see a free film and wander around **Derby Wharf,** the **West India Goods Store,** the **Bonded Warehouse,** the **Scale House,** and Central Wharf. Check ahead for lectures and other special events that focus on topics related to Salem's seagoing legacy.

193 Derby St. © **978/740-1660.** www.nps.gov/sama. Free admission. Guided tours $5 adults, $3 seniors and children 6–16. Daily 9am–5pm. Closed Jan 1, Thanksgiving, and Dec 25. Take Derby St. east; just past Pickering Wharf, Derby Wharf is on the right.

Salem Witch Museum ⟨𝓡𝓡⟩ *(Kids)*   This is one of the most memorable attractions in eastern Massachusetts—it's both interesting and scary. The main draw of the museum (a former church) is a three-dimensional audiovisual presentation with life-size figures. The show takes place in a huge room lined with displays that are lighted in sequence. The 30-minute narration tells the tale of the witchcraft trials and the accompanying hysteria. The well-researched presentation recounts the story accurately, if somewhat

---

(Fun Fact **A Face in the Crowd**

On the traffic island across from the entrance to the **Salem Witch Museum** is a statue that's easily mistaken for a witch. It's really **Roger Conant,** who founded Salem in 1626.

Finds Confection Connection

Shops throughout New England sell the chocolate confections of **Harbor Sweets** ★★, Palmer Cove, 85 Leavitt St., off Lafayette Street (✆ **978/745-7648**; www.harborsweets.com). The retail store overlooks the floor of the factory. The deliriously good sweets are expensive, but candy bars and small assortments are available. Closed Sunday.

---

overdramatically. One of the victims was crushed to death by rocks piled on a board on his chest—smaller kids might need a reminder that he's not real. The narration is available translated into French, German, Italian, Japanese, and Spanish. There's also a small exhibit that traces the history of witches, witchcraft, and witch hunts.

19½ Washington Sq., on Rte. 1A. ✆ **978/744-1692**. www.salemwitchmuseum.com. Admission $8 adults, $7 seniors, $5.50 children 6–14. Daily July–Aug 10am–7pm; Sept–June 10am–5pm; check ahead for extended Oct hours. Closed Jan 1, Thanksgiving, and Dec 25. Follow Hawthorne Blvd. to the northwest corner of Salem Common.

SHOPPING

Pickering Wharf (✆ **978/740-6990**; www.pickeringwharf.com), at the corner of Derby and Congress streets, is a waterfront complex of shops, boutiques, restaurants, and condos. It's popular for strolling, snacking, and shopping, and the central location makes it a local landmark.

Several shops specialize in witchcraft accessories. Bear in mind that Salem is home to many practicing witches who take their beliefs very seriously. The **Broom Closet,** 3 Central St. (✆ **978/741-3669**; www.broomclose.com), and **Crow Haven Corner,** 125 Essex St. (✆ **978/745-8763**; www.crowhavencorner.net), stock everything from crystals to clothing.

WHERE TO STAY

The busiest and most expensive time of year is Halloween week, followed closely by the rest of October; it's not unusual for the whole city to be sold out months in advance.

Coach House Inn   Built in 1879 for a ship's captain, this welcoming inn is in a historic district 2 blocks from the harbor and 9 blocks from downtown. The three-story mansion, set back from the street behind a well-kept lawn, is elegantly furnished in just-frilly-enough style. All of the good-size rooms have high ceilings, period antiques, four-poster beds, and Oriental rugs, and most have (nonworking) fireplaces. Breakfast arrives at your door in a basket—a nice perk if dining-room chitchat isn't your thing. The Coach House Inn is 20 minutes on foot or 5 minutes by car from the center of town, and just up the street from Salem State College.

284 Lafayette St. (Rtes. 1A and 114), Salem, MA 01970. ✆ **800/688-8689** or 978/744-4092. Fax 978/745-8031. www.coachhousesalem.com. 11 units, 9 with bathroom, 2 with shower only. $105–$185 double; $165–$240 2-room suite. Rates include continental breakfast. Minimum 2- or 3-night stay weekends and holidays. AE, DISC, MC, V. Free parking. *In room:* A/C, TV, fridge, coffeemaker.

Hawthorne Hotel ★ *(Kids)*   This historic hotel, built in 1925, is both convenient and comfortable. It books business travelers as well as vacationers, and it's popular for functions. The six-story building is centrally located and well maintained, with an ornate lobby that evokes the building's Roaring Twenties origins. The well-kept guest rooms vary in size from snug to spacious. All are attractively furnished with reproduction Federal-style pieces, but bathrooms can be small. The best units, on the Salem Common (north) side of the building, have better views than rooms that overlook the street. Whatever direction you face, ask to be as high up as possible, because the neighborhood is busy. If you're traveling with children, ask about "Family Fun" packages, which include discounted tickets to area museums.

18 Washington Sq. W. (at Salem Common), Salem, MA 01970. © 800/729-7829 or 978/744-4080. Fax 978/745-9842. www.hawthornehotel.com. 89 units, 30 with shower only. $107–$209 double; $209–$315 suite. Extra person $12. Children under 16 stay free in parent's room. 2-night minimum stay May–Oct weekends. Off-season discounts, senior discount, and weekend and other packages available. AE, DC, DISC, MC, V. Limited self-parking. Pets accepted; $100 deposit and $10/day fee. **Amenities:** Restaurant (American); tavern; exercise room; access to nearby heath club w/pool; concierge; airport shuttle; business center; room service until 11pm; laundry service; same-day dry cleaning; rooms for those w/limited mobility. *In room:* A/C, TV, wireless Internet access, hair dryer, iron, umbrella.

Salem Inn 𝄂𝄂 The Salem Inn occupies the comfortable niche between too-big hotel and too-small B&B. Its clientele includes honeymooners as well as sightseers and families, and the variety of rooms means that the innkeepers can make a good match of guest and accommodations. The inn consists of three properties. The 1834 West House and the 1854 Curwen House, former homes of ship captains, are listed on the National Register of Historic Places. The best units are the honeymoon and family suites (which have kitchenettes) in the 1874 Peabody House. Guest rooms are large and tastefully decorated; some have fireplaces, canopy beds, and whirlpool baths. The peaceful rose garden at the rear of the main building is open to all guests.

7 Summer St. (Rte. 114), Salem, MA 01970. © 800/446-2995 or 978/741-0680. Fax 978/744-8924. www.salem innma.com. 40 units, some with shower only. Nov–Sept $119–$179 double; $169–$229 suite; Oct $180–$225 double, $225–$295 suite. Rates include continental breakfast. Extra person $15–$25. Minimum stay 2–3 nights during special events and holidays. Winter and family packages available. AE, DC, DISC, MC, V. Free parking. Pets accepted by prior arrangement; $15/night Nov–Sept, $25/night Oct. *In room:* A/C, TV, wireless Internet access, coffeemaker, hair dryer, iron.

WHERE TO DINE

Pickering Wharf has a food court as well as a restaurant, **Victoria Station** (© 978/744-7644; www.victoriastationinc.com), where the deck has a great view of the marina and the menu emphasizes seafood and traditional American dishes. **Red's Sandwich Shop,** 15 Central St. (© 978/745-3527; www.redssandwichshop.com), is a local favorite that serves diner-style breakfast and lunch daily. The restaurant and cafe at the **Peabody Essex Museum** (p. 261) serve lunch.

Lyceum Bar & Grill 𝄂𝄂 CONTEMPORARY AMERICAN The elegance of the Lyceum's high-ceilinged front rooms and glass-walled back rooms matches the sky-high quality of the food, which attracts local businesspeople as well as out-of-towners. Grilling is the signature cooking technique, but the kitchen is adept with the full range of preparations and delectable (local, when possible) ingredients. Bounteous chicken salad with unusual slaw or the inventive risotto of the day makes a substantial but not incapacitating lunch in the middle of sightseeing; "penne from heaven," goofy name

---

Fun Fact Party Line

Alexander Graham Bell made the first telephone call from the building that now holds the Lyceum Bar & Grill.

(Kids) A Whale of an Adventure

The depletion of New England's fishing grounds has led to the rise of another important seagoing industry, **whale watching** ★★. The waters off the coast of Massachusetts are prime territory, and Gloucester is a center of whale-watching cruises. Stellwagen Bank, which runs from Gloucester to Provincetown about 27 miles east of Boston, is a rich feeding ground for the magnificent mammals. Species spotted in the area are mainly humpback, finback, and minke whales, who dine on sand eels and other fish that gather along the ridge. The whales often perform for their audience by jumping out of the water, and dolphins occasionally join the show. Naturalists onboard narrate the trip for the companies listed here, pointing out the whales and describing birds and fish that cross your path.

Whale watching is not particularly time- or cost-effective, especially if restless children are along, but it's so popular for a reason: The payoff is, literally and figuratively, huge. This is an "only in New England" experience that kids (and adults) will remember for a long time.

The season runs from April or May through October. Bundle up, even in the middle of summer—it's much cooler at sea than on land. Wear a hat and rubber-soled shoes, and take sunglasses, sunscreen, a hat, and a camera. If you're prone to motion sickness, take precautions, because you'll be at sea for 3½ to 5 hours. If you plan to take Dramamine, take it before you depart.

This is an extremely competitive business—they'd deny it, but the companies are virtually indistinguishable. Most guarantee sightings, offer a morning and an afternoon cruise as well as deep-sea fishing excursions and charters, honor other firms' coupons, and offer AAA and AARP discounts. Check ahead for sailing times, prices (at least $40 for adults, slightly less for seniors and children), and reservations, which are strongly recommended. If you're on a budget, ask whether the company imposes a fuel surcharge, and double-check the cut-off ages for kids and seniors.

In downtown Gloucester, **Cape Ann Whale Watch** (© **800/877-5110** or 978/283-5110; www.caww.com) is the best-known operation. Also downtown are **Capt. Bill & Sons Whale Watch** (© **800/33-WHALE** or 978/283-6995; www.captbillandsons.com) and **Seven Seas Whale Watch** (© **888/283-1776** or 978/283-1776; www.7seas-whalewatch.com). At the Cape Ann Marina, off Route 133, is **Yankee Whale Watch** (© **800/WHALING** or 978/283-0313; www.yankeefleet.com).

aside, is terrific. Sunday brunch here is an unexpected treat, with superb egg dishes and a good range of entrees for the breakfast averse. At dinner, flavorful meat and fish dishes, such as roasted duck breast with port-wine sauce and grilled peaches or oven-roasted cod over white-bean succotash, are equally delicious. Try to save room for a traditional yet sophisticated dessert—the brownie sundae is out of this world.

43 Church St. (at Washington St.). © **978/745-7665**. www.lyceumsalem.com. Reservations recommended. Main courses $8–$14 at lunch, $17–$29 at dinner. AE, DISC, MC, V. Mon–Fri 11:30am–3pm; Sun brunch 11am–3pm; daily 5:30–10pm. Validated parking available.

Salem Beer Works PUB GRUB   Beer is the headliner at this popular downtown restaurant (a sibling of Boston Beer Works, p. 237), but the food is also worth mentioning. Piled-high burgers, salads, sandwiches, and buckets of fried delicacies such as onion rings, jalapeño poppers, and pickles (yes, fried pickles) complement the house-made brews.

278 Derby St. © 978/745-BEER. www.beerworks.net. Main courses $6–$17. AE, DISC, MC, V. Sun–Thurs 11:30am–midnight; Fri–Sat 11:30am–1am.

A DETOUR TO ESSEX

If you approach or leave Cape Ann on Route 128, head west on Route 133 to **Essex.** It's a beautiful little town known for Essex clams, salt marshes, a long tradition of ship-building, an incredible number of antiques shops, and one celebrated restaurant.

Legend has it that **Woodman's of Essex** 🏵🏵🏵, 121 Main St. (© **800/649-1773** or 978/768-6057; www.woodmans.com), was the birthplace of the fried clam in 1916. Today, the thriving family-owned eatery is a great spot to join legions of locals and visitors from around the world for lobster "in the rough," chowder, steamers, corn on the cob, onion rings, and (you guessed it) superb fried clams. In warm weather, people from all over the world flock here, especially on the way back from the beach. In the winter, the crowd is mostly locals desperate for a taste of summer (pass me a moist towelette, please). The line is long, but it moves quickly and offers a good view of the regimented commotion in the food-prep area. Eat inside, upstairs on the deck, or out back at a picnic table. You'll want to be well fed before you set off to explore the numerous antiques shops along Main Street. Long a cash-only business, Woodman's now accepts credit cards (AE, MC, V). Open daily in the summer from 11am to 10pm; winter, Sunday to Thursday from 11am to 8pm, Friday and Saturday 11am to 9pm.

As with most cult-favorite foods, the fashion is to be contrarian and say that Woodman's is too crowded and too many people know about it. I disagree, but if you're interested in comparison shopping—in the interest of science, of course—two other excellent destinations are **J. T. Farnham's,** 88 Eastern Ave., Essex (© **978768-6643**), about a mile east of Woodman's; and the **Clam Box,** 246 High St. (© **978/356-9707;** www.ipswichma.com/clambox), a little over 7 miles northwest of Woodman's.

GLOUCESTER 🏵🏵

33 miles NE of Boston, 16 miles NE of Salem

The ocean has been Gloucester's lifeblood since long before the first European settlement in 1623. The French explorer Samuel de Champlain called the harbor "Le Beauport" when he came across it in 1606, some 600 years after the Vikings. The harbor's configuration and proximity to good fishing gave it the reputation it enjoys to this day. If you read or saw *The Perfect Storm,* you'll have a sense of what to expect here.

Gloucester (which rhymes with "roster") is a working city, not a cutesy tourist town. It's home to one of the last commercial fishing fleets in New England, an internationally celebrated artists' colony, a large Portuguese-American community, and just enough historic attractions. Allow at least half a day, perhaps combined with a visit to the tourist magnet of Rockport; a full day would be better, especially if you plan a cruise or whale watch.

Gloucester

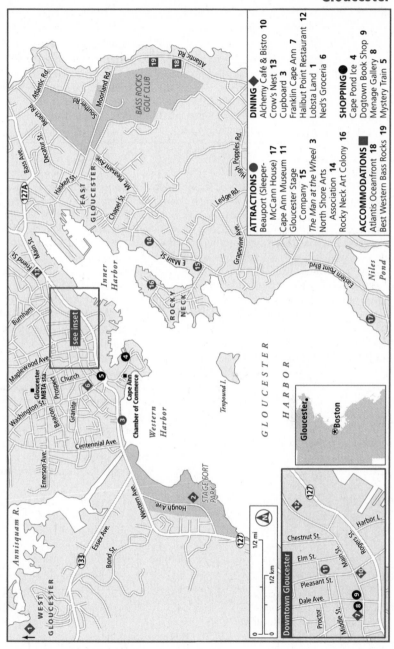

ATTRACTIONS ●
Beauport (Sleeper-
  McCann House) **17**
Cape Ann Museum **11**
Gloucester Stage
  Company **15**
The Man at the Wheel **3**
North Shore Arts
  Association **14**
Rocky Neck Art Colony **16**

ACCOMMODATIONS ■
Atlantis Oceanfront **18**
Best Western Bass Rocks **19**

DINING ◆
Alchemy Café & Bistro **10**
Crow's Nest **13**
Cupboard **3**
Franklin Cape Ann **7**
Halibut Point Restaurant **12**
Lobsta Land **1**
Ned's Groceria **6**

SHOPPING ●
Cape Pond Ice **4**
Dogtown Book Shop **9**
Menage Gallery **8**
Mystery Train **5**

Moments Down by the Sea

On Stacy Boulevard west of downtown Gloucester is a reminder of the sea's danger. Leonard Craske's bronze statue of the **Gloucester Fisherman,** known as "The Man at the Wheel," bears the inscription "They That Go Down to the Sea in Ships 1623–1923" (the phrase is from the 107th Psalm). Several hundred yards west is a memorial to the women and children who waited at home. As you take in the glorious view, consider this: More than 10,000 fishermen lost their lives during the city's first 300 years.

ESSENTIALS

GETTING THERE   From Salem, follow Route 1A across the bridge to Beverly, pick up Route 127, and take it through Manchester (near, not on, the water) to Gloucester. From Boston, the quickest path is I-93 or Route 1 to Route 128, which runs directly to Gloucester. Route 128 is mostly inland; to take in more scenery, leave Route 128 at Manchester and continue to Gloucester on Route 127. There's street parking (metered and not), and a free lot on the causeway to Rocky Neck.

The **commuter rail** (© 617/222-3200; www.mbta.com) runs from Boston's North Station. The trip takes about an hour; the round-trip fare is $15. The station is across town from downtown, so allow time for getting to the waterfront area. The **Cape Ann Transportation Authority,** or CATA (© 978/283-7916; www.canntran. com), runs buses from town to town on Cape Ann and operates special routes during the summer.

VISITOR INFORMATION   The **Gloucester Tourism Office,** City Hall, 9 Dale Ave., Gloucester, MA 01930 (© 800/649-6839 or 978/281-8865; www.gloucester ma.com), operates the excellent Visitors Welcoming Center at Stage Fort Park, off Route 127 at Route 133. It's open during the summer daily from 9am to 5pm; closed in winter. The **Cape Ann Chamber of Commerce,** 33 Commercial St., Gloucester, MA 01930 (© 800/321-0133 or 978/283-1601; www.capeannvacations.com), is open year-round (summer weekdays 8am–6pm, Sat 10am–6pm, Sun 10am–4pm; winter weekdays 8am–5pm) and has a helpful staff. It also operates a seasonal information booth on Rogers Street at Harbor Loop. Call or write for the chamber's four-color map and brochure.

SPECIAL EVENTS   Gloucester holds festivals and street fairs on weekends throughout the summer. Check in advance to find out what's up when you'll be in town. The best-known event is **St. Peter's Fiesta,** a colorful 4-day celebration at the end of June. The Italian-American fishing colony's festival has more in common with a carnival midway than a religious observation, but it's great fun. There are parades, games, music, food, sporting events, and, on Sunday, the blessing of the fleet. The **Schooner Festival,** a floating party with plenty of land-based revelry, takes place over Labor Day weekend; the 2009 event is the 25th annual.

EXPLORING THE TOWN

Business isn't nearly what it once was, but fishing is still Gloucester's leading industry (as your nose will tell you). Tourism is a very close second, and the city is an exceptionally welcoming destination—residents seem genuinely happy to see out-of-towners and to offer directions and insider info. The **"Gloucester Maritime Trail"** brochure, available at visitor centers, describes four excellent self-guided tours.

Stage Fort Park, off Route 127 at Route 133, offers a superb view of the harbor and has a busy snack bar (summer only). It's a good spot for picnicking, swimming, or playing on the cannons in the Revolutionary War fort.

To reach **East Gloucester,** follow signs as you leave downtown or go directly from Route 128, Exit 9. On East Main Street, you'll see signs for the world-famous **Rocky Neck Art Colony** ★★, the oldest continuously operating art colony in the country. Park in the lot on the tiny causeway and head west along Rocky Neck Avenue, which abounds with studios, galleries, restaurants, and people. The draw is the presence of working artists, not just shops that happen to sell art. Most galleries are open daily in the summer 10am to 10pm.

The prestigious **North Shore Arts Association,** Pirate's Lane, 197R E. Main St. (© 978/283-1857; www.northshoreartsassoc.org), was founded in 1922 to showcase local artists' work. The exhibits are worth a visit before or after your excursion across the causeway. The building is open late May through Columbus Day, Monday through Saturday from 10am to 5pm, Sunday noon to 5pm. Admission is free.

Also in East Gloucester, the **Gloucester Stage Company** ★, 267 E. Main St. (© 978/281-4099; www.gloucesterstage.com), is one of the best repertory troupes in New England. It schedules six plays a season (late May–early Sept); tickets cost $35.

NARRATED CRUISES   For information on whale watches, see the box "A Whale of an Adventure" (p. 265).

The schooner *Thomas E. Lannon* ★ (© 978/281-6634; www.schooner.org) is a gorgeous reproduction of a Gloucester fishing vessel. The 65-foot tall ship sails from Seven Seas Wharf downtown; 2-hour excursions ($38 for adults, $33 for seniors, $25 for children under 17) leave about four times daily from mid-June to mid-September, less often on weekends from mid-May to mid-June and mid-September to mid-October. Reservations are recommended. The company also offers music and dining cruises, including sunset lobster bakes.

The two-masted schooner *Adventure* ★ (© 978/281-8079; www.schooner-adventure.org), a 122-foot fishing vessel built in Essex in 1926, was completing an extensive restoration project at press time and is expected to be sailing again in 2009.

⌒Moments *The Perfect Storm*

Long after the release of the blockbuster movie, Sebastian Junger's best-selling book *The Perfect Storm* remains a popular reason to visit Gloucester. The thrilling but tragic true account of the "no-name" hurricane of 1991 centers on the ocean and a neighborhood tavern. The **Crow's Nest,** 334 Main St. (© 978/ 281-2965), a bit east of downtown, is a no-frills place with a horseshoe-shaped bar and a crowd of regulars who seem amused that their hangout is a tourist attraction. The Crow's Nest plays a major role in Junger's story, but its ceilings weren't high enough for it to be a movie set, so the film crew built an exact replica nearby. If you admired the movie's wardrobe design, check out the shirts and caps at **Cape Pond Ice,** 104 Commercial St., near the Chamber of Commerce (© 978/283-0174; www.capepondice.com).

The "living museum," a National Historic Landmark, is open to the public and on view at Rowe's Wharf downtown; check ahead for details and schedules of dockside programs, open days and hours, and prices.

Beauport (Sleeper-McCann House) ⚜⚜   The rough-and-tumble fishing port of Gloucester has another face: exclusive summer community. Aficionados of house tours will want to build their schedules around a visit to this magnificent property on the stylish Back Shore, the product of a uniquely creative mind. Pioneering interior designer and antiquarian Henry Davis Sleeper created Beauport, transforming it into a repository for his vast collection of American and European decorative arts and antiques. From 1907 to 1934, he built and expanded the house, which has more than 40 rooms, and decorated many of the chambers to illustrate literary and historical themes. The entertaining tour concentrates more on the gorgeous house and rooms in general than on the countless objects on display, which remain virtually as Sleeper left them. You'll see architectural details rescued from other buildings, magnificent arrangements of colored glassware, secret staircases, the "Red Indian Room" (with a majestic view of the harbor), the "Master Mariner's Room" (overflowing with nautical items), and even the kitchen and servants' quarters. Beauport, a National Historic Landmark, also schedules events such as afternoon tea, wine tastings, and specialty tours throughout the season.

75 Eastern Point Blvd. ⓒ 978/283-0800. www.historicnewengland.org. Guided tour $10 adults, $9 seniors, $5 students and children 6–12. Tours on the hour June to mid-Oct Tues–Sat 10am–4pm. Closed mid-Oct to May and Sun–Mon year-round. Take E. Main St. to Eastern Point Blvd. (a private road), continue ½ mile to house, park on left.

Cape Ann Historical Museum ⚜   This meticulously curated museum makes an excellent introduction to Cape Ann's history and artists. It devotes an entire gallery to the extraordinary work of **Fitz Henry Lane** ⚜⚜⚜ (formerly known as Fitz Hugh Lane), the Luminist painter whose light-flooded canvases show off the best of his native Gloucester. The nation's largest collection of his paintings and drawings is here. Other galleries feature works on paper by 20th-century artists such as Maurice Prendergast and Milton Avery, work by other contemporary artists, and granite-quarrying tools and equipment. There's also an outdoor sculpture court. On display in the maritime and fisheries galleries are entire vessels (including one about the size of a station wagon that crossed the Atlantic), exhibits on the fishing industry, ship models, and historic photographs and models of the Gloucester waterfront. The **Capt. Elias Davis House** (1804), decorated and furnished in Federal style with furniture, silver, and porcelains, is part of the museum.

27 Pleasant St. ⓒ 978/283-0455. www.capeannmuseum.org. Admission $8 adults, $6 seniors and students, free for children under 12. Mar–Jan Tues–Sat 10am–5pm, Sun 1–4pm. Closed Feb. Follow Main St. west through downtown and turn right onto Pleasant St.; museum is 1 block up on right. Metered parking on street or in lot across street.

SHOPPING

Rocky Neck (see "Exploring the Town," above) offers great browsing. Downtown, **Main Street** between Pleasant and Washington streets is a good destination. Agreeable stops include **Mystery Train,** 21 Main St. (ⓒ 978/281-8911; www.mysterytrain records.com), which carries a huge variety of used music and films; the **Ménage Gallery,** 134 Main St. (ⓒ 877/283-6030 or 978/283-6030; www.menagegallery. com), which shows varied works by artists and artisans, including gorgeous furniture; and the **Dogtown Book Shop,** 132 Main St. (ⓒ 978/281-5599; www.dogtown books.com), noted for its used and antiquarian selection.

WHERE TO STAY

Gloucester abounds with B&Bs; for guidance, check with the Cape Ann Chamber of Commerce (© 978/283-1601) or consult one of the agencies listed on p. 70.

Atlantis Oceanfront Motor Inn   This motor inn with an outdoor pool and helpful staff sits across the street from the water, affording stunning views from every window. The good-size guest rooms are decorated in comfortable, contemporary style; about half were renovated before the 2008 season, and the rest will follow before the 2009 season. Each room has a terrace or balcony and a small table and chairs. Second-floor accommodations are slightly preferable because the view is a little better. The Atlantis doesn't have the resort feel of its more expensive neighbor, the Bass Rocks Ocean Inn, but the views are the same. Beach parking discount vouchers are available to guests.

125 Atlantic Rd., Gloucester, MA 01930. © **800/732-6313** or 978/283-0014. Fax 978/281-8994. www.atlantis motorinn.com. 40 units, 7 with shower only. Late June–Labor Day $165–$195 double; spring and fall $140–$170 double. Extra person $10. Rollaway or crib $15. Children under 13 stay free in parent's room. Minimum stay may be required. Off-season midweek discounts available. AE, MC, V. Closed Nov–late Apr. Take Rt. 128 to the end (Exit 9, East Gloucester), turn left onto Bass Ave. (Rte. 127A), and follow it ½ mile. Turn right and follow Atlantic Rd. **Amenities:** Coffee shop (breakfast only); heated outdoor pool. *In room:* A/C, TV, wireless Internet access, fridge, coffeemaker, hair dryer, iron.

Best Western Bass Rocks Ocean Inn   The Bass Rocks Ocean Inn offers gorgeous ocean views, spacious guest rooms, a heated pool, and modern accommodations. Across the road from the rocky shore, the sprawling, comfortable two-story motel has been a family operation since 1946. A Colonial Revival mansion built in 1899 and known as the "wedding-cake house" holds a handful of one-bedroom suites and the public areas, including a billiard room and a library. The 1960s-era guest rooms are up-to-date, but overall the property feels like an old-fashioned resort, which distinguishes it from the neighboring Atlantis. Each motel room has sliding glass doors that open onto a balcony or patio, and a king bed or two double beds. Second-floor rooms have slightly better views. In the afternoon, the staff serves coffee, tea, lemonade, and chocolate-chip cookies.

107 Atlantic Rd., Gloucester, MA 01930. © **800/WESTERN** or 978/283-7600. Fax 978/281-6489. www.bassrocks oceaninn.com. 48 units. Summer $239–$350 double; $450 suite. Spring and fall $159–$229 double, $300–$350 suite. Extra person $10. Children under 13 stay free in parent's room. Rollaway or crib $12. Rates include continental breakfast, afternoon refreshments, and use of bikes. Minimum 3-night stay summer weekends, some spring and fall weekends. AAA and AARP discounts available. AE, DC, DISC, MC, V. Closed Nov–late Apr. Follow Rte. 128 to the end (Exit 9, East Gloucester), turn left onto Bass Ave. (Rte. 127A), and follow it ½ mile. Turn right and follow Atlantic Rd. **Amenities:** Heated outdoor pool; game room. *In room:* A/C, TV/VCR, wireless Internet access, fridge, coffeemaker, hair dryer, iron.

WHERE TO DINE

See "A Detour to Essex," on p. 266, for information about the celebrated **Woodman's of Essex,** which is about 20 minutes from downtown Gloucester. The Stage Fort Park snack bar, the **Cupboard,** 41 Hough Ave. (© **978/281-1908**), serves excellent fried seafood and blue-plate specials in the summer. **Lobsta Land,** 10 Causeway St., near Exit 12 off Route 128 (© **978/281-0415**), is a summer-only destination for familiar and unusual seafood dishes and amazing french fries. If you're in town just for a day, consider sticking around for dinner at the **Franklin Cape Ann,** 118 Main St. (© **978/283-7888;** www.franklincafe.com). It serves excellent bistro cuisine daily from 5pm to midnight (but unfortunately not at lunch). **Ned's Groceria,** 24 Washington St.

North Shore Beaches

North of Boston, sandy beaches complement the predominantly rocky coastline. Things to know: The water is *cold* (optimistic locals say "refreshing"). Parking can be scarce, especially on weekends, and pricey—the $25-per-car barrier fell in 2007. If you can't set out early, wait until midafternoon and hope that the people who arrived in the morning have had their fill. During the summer, lifeguards are on duty from 9am to 5pm at larger public beaches. Surfing is generally permitted outside of those hours. The beaches listed here all have bathhouses and snack bars. Swimming or not, watch out for greenhead flies in July and August. They don't sting—they take little bites of flesh. Bring or buy insect repellent.

The best-known North Shore beach is **Singing Beach** 🏖🏖, off Masconomo Street in Manchester-by-the-Sea. Because it's accessible by public transportation, it attracts the most diverse crowd—carless singles, local families, and other beach bunnies of all ages. They walk ½ mile on Beach Street from the train station to find sparkling sand and lively surf. Take the commuter rail (© **617/222-3200;** www.mbta.com) from Boston's North Station.

Nearly as famous and popular is **Crane Beach** 🏖, off Argilla Road in Ipswich, part of a 1,400-acre barrier beach reservation. Fragile dunes and a white sand beach lead down to Ipswich Bay. The surf is calmer than that at less sheltered Singing Beach, but it's still quite chilly. Pick up Argilla Road south of Ipswich Center near the intersection of Routes 1A and 133 or take the Cape Ann Transportation Authority's summer-only, weekend-only Ipswich Essex Explorer bus service (www.ipswich-essexexplorer.com) from the Ipswich train station. Also on Ipswich Bay is Gloucester's **Wingaersheek Beach** 🏖, on Atlantic Street off Route 133. It has its own exit (no. 13) off Route 128, about 15 minutes away on winding roads with low speed limits. When you finally arrive, you'll find beautiful white sand, a glorious view, and more dunes. Because these beaches are harder to get to, they attract more locals—but also lots of day-tripping families. At the east end of Route 133, the beaches and snack bar in Gloucester's easily accessible **Stage Fort Park** are popular local hangouts.

(© **978/290-9800;** www.nedsgroceria.com), is a gourmet grocery that makes a great pre-picnic stop.

Alchemy Café and Bistro 🏖 CREATIVE AMERICAN   An unusually varied menu is usually a red flag, but not here. Friends who live in Gloucester tipped me off to this funky-yet-elegant place on a little side street downtown. They rave about inventive cocktails, creative flavors, and a vegetarian-friendly menu that offers something for everyone (up went the red flag). Could the French onion soup really be as good as the pizza? Could a kitchen that produces mouthwatering meatloaf also crank out perfect seared tuna? Do nachos even belong in the same restaurant as triple vanilla crème brûlée? In a word, yes. Alchemy is a good destination for lunch (try a fish taco or pulled-pork sandwich), cocktails and appetizers, or a special dinner. The service could be a bit more polished, but it's hard to quibble when even the pickiest eater in your party can find just the right dish.

3 Duncan St., off Main St. ✆ **978/281-3997**. www.alchemybistro.com. Reservations recommended at dinner. Main courses $7–$16 at lunch, $12–$26 at dinner; pizza $10 and up. Children's menu $6. AE, MC, V. Sun–Thurs 11:30am–9:30pm, Fri–Sat 11:30am–10pm (lunch served until 4pm). From intersection of Rogers and Main sts. (just north of downtown), follow Main St. south ½ mile; Duncan St. is on left.

Halibut Point Restaurant ✿ SEAFOOD/AMERICAN   A local legend for its chowders and burgers, Halibut Point is a friendly tavern that serves generous portions of good food. The "Halibut Point Special"—a cup of chowder, a burger, and a beer—hits the high points. The clam chowder is terrific, and the spicy Italian fish chowder is so good that some people come to Gloucester just for a bowlful of that. There's also a raw bar. Main courses are simple (mostly sandwiches) at lunch and more elaborate at dinner. Be sure to check the specials board—you didn't come all this way to a fishing port not to have fresh fish, did you?

289 Main St. ✆ **978/281-1900**. www.halibutpoint.com. Main courses $5–$13 at lunch, $9–$18 at dinner. AE, DISC, MC, V. Daily 11:30am–11pm.

ROCKPORT
40 miles NE of Boston, 7 miles N of Gloucester

This lovely little town at the tip of Cape Ann was settled in 1690. Over the years it has been an active fishing port, a center of granite excavation and cutting, and a thriving summer community whose specialty appears to be selling fudge and refrigerator magnets to out-of-towners. Rockport is an entertaining half-day trip, perhaps combined with a visit to Gloucester.

There's more to Rockport than just gift shops. It's home to a lovely state park, and it's popular with photographers, painters, jewelry designers, and sculptors. Winslow Homer, Fitz Henry Lane, and Childe Hassam are among the famous artists who have captured the local color. At times, however, especially on summer weekends, you'll be hard pressed to find much local color in this tourist-weary destination. But for every year-round resident who seems genuinely startled when legions of people with cameras around their necks descend on Rockport each June, there are dozens who are proud to show off their town.

Out of season, especially January through mid-April, Rockport is pretty but somewhat desolate, though some businesses stay open and keep reduced hours.

ESSENTIALS
GETTING THERE   Rockport is north of Gloucester along Route 127 or 127A. At the end of Route 128, turn left at the signs for Rockport to take Route 127, which is shorter but more commercial. To take Route 127A, which runs near the east coast of Cape Ann, continue on Route 128 until you see the sign for East Gloucester and turn left. Parking is tough, especially on summer Saturday afternoons, but metered spots are available throughout downtown. Make one loop around downtown and then head to the free parking lot on Upper Main Street (Rte. 127). The shuttle bus to downtown costs $1.

The **commuter rail** (✆ **617/222-3200;** www.mbta.com) runs from Boston's North Station. The trip takes 60 to 70 minutes, and the round-trip fare is $16. The station is about 6 blocks from the downtown waterfront. The **Cape Ann Transportation Authority,** or CATA (✆ **978/283-7916;** www.canntran.com), runs buses from town to town on Cape Ann.

VISITOR INFORMATION   The **Rockport Chamber of Commerce,** 3 Whistlestop Mall (*©* **888/726-3922** or 978/546-6575; www.rockportusa.com), is open weekdays from 9am to 5pm. The chamber operates an information booth on Upper Main Street (Rte. 127) daily from July 1 through Labor Day and on weekends from mid-May to June and early September through mid-October. It's about a mile from the town line and a mile from downtown—look for the WELCOME TO ROCKPORT sign on the right as you head north. At either location, ask for the pamphlet *Rockport: A Walking Guide,* which contains a good map and descriptions of three short walking tours. The Rockport Chamber is a division of the Cape Ann Chamber of Commerce (see "Gloucester," earlier in this chapter), which is also a good source of information.

SPECIAL EVENTS   The **Rockport Chamber Music Festival** (*©* **978/546-7391;** www.rcmf.org) takes place in June at the Rockport Art Association, 12 Main St. It's a good excuse to see the lovely town before the tourist season gets wild. In addition to performances by promising young musicians and family-oriented concerts (tickets $20–$35), events include free lectures and discussions.

The annual **Christmas pageant,** on Main Street in December, is a crowded, kid-friendly event with carol singing and live animals.

EXPLORING THE TOWN

The most famous sight in Rockport has something of an "Emperor's New Clothes" aura—it's a wooden fish warehouse on the town wharf, or T-Wharf, in the harbor. The barn-red shack known as **Motif No. 1** is the most frequently painted and photographed object in a town filled with lovely buildings and surrounded by breathtaking rocky coastline. The color certainly catches the eye against the neutrals of the seascape, but you might find yourself wondering what the big deal is. Originally constructed in 1884 and destroyed during the blizzard of 1978, Motif No. 1 was rebuilt using donations from residents and tourists. It stands on the same pier as the original, duplicated in every detail and reinforced to withstand storms.

Nearby is a phenomenon whose popularity is easier to explain. **Bearskin Neck,** named after an unfortunate ursine visitor who drowned and washed ashore in 1800, has perhaps the highest concentration of gift shops anywhere. It's a narrow peninsula with one main street (South Rd.) and several alleys crammed with galleries, snack bars, antiques shops, and ancient houses. The peninsula ends in a plaza with a magnificent water view.

Throughout the town, more than two dozen **art galleries** *♠* display the works of local and nationally known artists. The **Rockport Art Association,** 12 Main St. (*©* **978/546-6604;** www.rockportartassn.org), sponsors major exhibitions and special shows. It's open daily mid-morning to late afternoon in the summer (except on Sun, when it opens at noon); in the winter, it's open mid-morning to late afternoon Tuesday through Saturday and noon to late afternoon Sunday.

To get a sense of the power of the sea, take Route 127 north of town to the tip of Cape Ann. Turn right on Gott Avenue to reach **Halibut Point State Park** *♠♠* (*©* **978/546-2997;** www.mass.gov/dcr). The park is a great place to wander around and admire the gorgeous scenery. On a clear day, you can see Maine. It has a staffed visitor center, walking trails, and tidal pools. Swimming in the water-filled quarries is absolutely forbidden. You can climb around on giant boulders on the rocky beach or climb to the top of the World War II observation tower. To take a self-guided tour, pick up a brochure at the visitor center or the Chamber of Commerce. Guided quarry

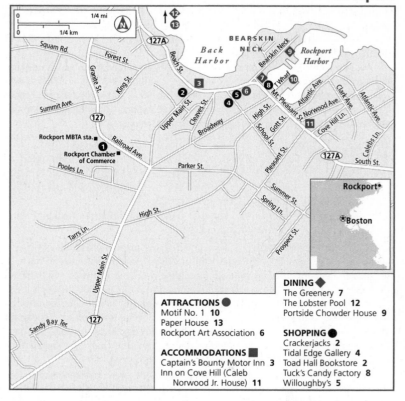

DINING ◆
The Greenery **7**
The Lobster Pool **12**
Portside Chowder House **9**

ATTRACTIONS ●
Motif No. 1 **10**
Paper House **13**
Rockport Art Association **6**

SHOPPING ●
Crackerjacks **2**
Tidal Edge Gallery **4**
Toad Hall Bookstore **2**
Tuck's Candy Factory **8**
Willoughby's **5**

ACCOMMODATIONS ■
Captain's Bounty Motor Inn **3**
Inn on Cove Hill (Caleb
Norwood Jr. House) **11**

tours and stone-splitting demonstrations take place on summer Saturdays at 10am. Check ahead for information about other special programs, scheduled from May through September. The park is open daily from Memorial Day to Labor Day 8am to 8pm, otherwise daily dawn to dusk; parking costs $2 from Memorial Day to Columbus Day.

If the mansions of Gloucester were too plush for you, or if you want some recycling tips, visit the **Paper House,** 52 Pigeon Hill St., Pigeon Cove (© **978/546-2629;** www.paperhouserockport.com). A genuinely wacky attraction, it was built beginning in 1922 entirely out of 100,000 newspapers—walls, furniture, even a newspaper-covered piano. Creator Elis Stenman made every item from papers of a different period. The house is open daily April through October from 10am to 5pm (closed Nov–Mar). Admission is $1.50 for adults, $1 for children 6 to 14. Follow Route 127 north out of downtown about 1½ miles until you see signs at Curtis Street pointing to the left, then go left on Pigeon Hill Street.

SHOPPING

Bearskin Neck is the obvious place to start. Dozens of little shops stock clothes, gifts, toys, jewelry, souvenirs, inexpensive novelties, and expensive handmade crafts and paintings. Another enjoyable stroll is along **Main** and **Mount Pleasant streets.** Good stops include the nonprofit **Toad Hall Bookstore,** 47 Main St. (℃ **978/546-7323;** www.toadhallbooks.org); **Tidal Edge Gallery,** 3 School St., off Main St. (℃ **978/ 546-3196;** www.tidaledgegallery.com); and **Willoughby's,** 20 Main St. (℃ **978/546-9820**), a women's clothing and accessories shop.

Two of my favorite stops are retro delights. Downtown, you can watch taffy being made at **Tuck's Candy Factory,** 7 Dock Sq. (℃ **800/569-2767** or 978/546-6352; www.tuckscandy.com), a local landmark that turns 80 in 2009. Near the train station, **Crackerjacks,** 27 Whistlestop Mall, off Railroad Avenue (℃ **978/546-1616**), is an old-fashioned variety store with a great crafts department.

WHERE TO STAY

When Rockport is busy, it's very busy—and when it's not, it's practically empty. The town's dozens of B&Bs fill in good weather and empty or even close in the winter. Make summer reservations well in advance or cross your fingers and call the Chamber of Commerce (p. 274) to ask about availability.

If you're traveling by train, call ahead to request pick-up at the Rockport station, which most lodgings in town offer at no charge.

Captain's Bounty Motor Inn   This modern, well-maintained motor inn is on the water. In fact, it's almost *in* the water, and nearly as close to the center of town as to the harbor. Each room in the three-story building overlooks the water and has its own balcony and sliding glass door; all were renovated in 2006 and 2007. Rooms are spacious and soundproofed, with good cross-ventilation but no air-conditioning. Each has a microwave and fridge in case you want to eat some meals in; kitchenette units are available. The best rooms are on the adults-only top floor. Although it's hardly plush and the pricing structure is a bit peculiar (note the charge for children), you can't beat the location. All rooms and decks are no-smoking.

1 Beach St., Rockport, MA 01966. ℃ 978/546-9557. Fax 978/546-9993. www.captainsbountymotorinn.com. 24 units. Late May–late Sept $160 double, $170 efficiency, $200 efficiency suite; spring and fall $115–$135 double, $125–$140 efficiency, $145–$155 efficiency suite. Extra adult $10; $5 for each child. Minimum 2-night stay weekends, 3-night stay holiday weekends. MC, V. Closed Nov–Mar. Pets accepted; $10/night. First-floor units are wheelchair accessible. *In room:* TV/DVD, wireless Internet access, fridge.

Inn on Cove Hill (Caleb Norwood, Jr., House) 🖈   This attractive Federal-style inn was built in 1771 using the proceeds of pirates' gold found nearby. Although it's just 2 blocks from the town wharf, the inn is set back from the road and has a delightful hideaway feel. Innkeeper Betsy Eck overhauls one guest room each winter, decorating them in exquisite period style; most have colonial furnishings and handmade quilts, and some have canopy beds. Water views from the windows and good-size decks at the back of the house are worth the climb to the third floor. The generous breakfast is served in the dining room or, in good weather, in the pleasant garden. Guests have the use of a phone in the living room. A harbor-view apartment across the street is available for long-term (1 week or more) stays.

37 Mount Pleasant St., Rockport, MA 01966. ℃ 888/546-2701 or 978/546-2701. Fax 978/546-1095. www.innon covehill.com. 7 units, some with shower only. $120–$175 double. Extra person $25. Rates include continental breakfast. 2-night minimum mid-May to mid-Oct and most weekends. MC, V. *In room:* A/C, TV, no phone.

WHERE TO DINE

Because Rockport was "dry" until 2005, the dining scene isn't as sophisticated as Gloucester's; if you're not ravenous, head there or to **Woodman's of Essex** (p. 266).

Follow Route 127 north along the peninsula past Halibut Point State Park and you'll soon see the **Lobster Pool,** 329 Granite St. (© **978/546-7808;** www.lobster poolrestaurant.com). The family-run self-service restaurant is a classic clam shack, with picnic tables, spectacular water views, and huge weekend crowds. It serves seafood "in the rough" as well as soup, salads, sandwiches, and homemade desserts. It's open only from Memorial Day weekend through Labor Day weekend, daily from 11:30am to 8:30pm, and extremely crowded on weekends. No credit cards. Off Bearskin Neck, the **Portside Chowder House,** 7 Tuna Wharf (© **978/546-7045**), serves a variety of chowders, fresh seafood, salads, and sandwiches in its harbor-view dining room.

The Greenery SEAFOOD/AMERICAN   In a great location at the head of Bearskin Neck, the Greenery is a tad pricey, but you're paying for the great view. The cafe at the front serves light fare to stay or to go; the dining rooms, at the back, over-look the harbor. The food ranges from tasty quiche at lunch to lobster at dinner to steamers and fresh-caught fish anytime. As in any town with a fishing fleet, check out the daily specials. All baking is done in-house, which explains the lines at the front counter for muffins and pastries. When the restaurant is busy, the usually cheerful service tends to drag. This is a good place to launch a picnic lunch on the beach, and an equally good spot for lingering over coffee and dessert and watching the action around the harbor.

15 Dock Sq. © **978/546-9593**. www.greenery-restaurant.com. Reservations recommended at dinner. Main courses $6–$23 at lunch, $10–$25 at dinner; breakfast items $2–$14. Fresh seafood market price. AE, DC, DISC, MC, V. Spring–fall daily 8am–9:30pm; call for winter hours.

3 Plymouth ★★

40 miles SE of Boston

Everyone educated in the United States knows at least a little about Plymouth—about how the Pilgrims, fleeing religious persecution, left Europe on the *Mayflower* and landed at Plymouth Rock in December 1620. Many also know that the Pilgrims endured disease and privation, and that just 51 people from the original group of 102 celebrated the first Thanksgiving in 1621 with Squanto, a Pawtuxet Indian associated with the Wampanoags, and his cohorts.

What you won't know until you visit is how small everything was. The *Mayflower* (a replica) seems perilously tiny, and when you contemplate how dangerous life was at the time, it's hard not to marvel at the settlers' accomplishments. One of their descen-dants' accomplishments is this: Plymouth is in many ways a model destination, where the 17th century coexists with the 21st, and most historic attractions are both educa-tional and fun. Tourists jam the downtown area in the summer, but the year-round population is so large that Plymouth feels more like the working community it is than like a warm-weather day-trip destination. It's a manageable 1-day excursion from Boston, particularly enjoyable if you're traveling with children. It also makes a good stop between Boston and Cape Cod.

ESSENTIALS

GETTING THERE   By car, follow the Southeast Expressway (I-93) south from Boston to Route 3. Take Exit 6A and then Route 44 east and follow signs to the his-toric attractions. The trip from Boston takes 45 to 60 minutes if it's not rush hour.

Take Exit 5 to the **Regional Information Complex** for maps, brochures, and information. To go directly to **Plimoth Plantation,** take Exit 4. There's metered parking throughout town.

The **commuter rail** (© 617/222-3200; www.mbta.com) serves Cordage Park, on Route 3A north of downtown, from Boston's South Station four times a day on weekdays and three times a day on weekends (at other times, service is to nearby Kingston). The round-trip fare is $16. Plymouth and Brockton **buses** (© 508/746-4795 or 508/746-0378; www.p-b.com) take about an hour from South Station. They run more often than the train, but they cost more ($13 one-way, $23 round-trip) and drop off and pick up passengers at the park-and-ride lot at Route 3 Exit 5. The **Plymouth Area Link** bus (© 508/746-0378; www.gatra.org/pal.html) connects the train station and bus stop with downtown. The fare is $1, free for children under 7.

VISITOR INFORMATION If you haven't visited the Regional Information Complex (see above), pick up a map at the **visitor center** (© 508/747-7525), open seasonally at 130 Water St., across from the town pier. To plan ahead, contact **Destination Plymouth** (Plymouth Visitor Information), 170 Water St., Suite 10C, Plymouth, MA 02360 (© 800/USA-1620 or 508/747-7533; www.visit-plymouth.com), and request information. The **Plymouth County Convention & Visitors Bureau,** 170 Water St., Suite 24, Plymouth, MA 02360 (© 800/231-1620 or 508/747-0100; www.see plymouth.com), publishes a vacation guide and several other brochures.

GETTING AROUND The downtown attractions are easily accessible on foot. A shallow hill slopes from the center of town to the waterfront.

Plymouth Rock Trolley (© 800/698-5636 or 508/747-4161; www.plymouth rocktrolley.com) offers a 40-minute narrated tour with unlimited reboarding, daily from Memorial Day to October and weekends through Thanksgiving. It serves marked stops downtown every 20 minutes and stops at Plimoth Plantation once an hour in the summer. Tickets are $15 for adults, $12 for children 3 to 12.

SEEING THE SIGHTS

The logical place to begin (good luck talking children out of it) is where the Pilgrims first set foot—at **Plymouth Rock** 🌟🌟. The rock, accepted as the landing place of the

---

Tips **A Presidential History Twofer**

A worthwhile detour en route to Plymouth is the **Adams National Historical Park** in Quincy, about 10 miles south of Boston. The park preserves the birthplaces of Presidents John Adams and John Quincy Adams, the house where four generations of the family lived, and eight other buildings associated with the political dynasty. A trolley connects the buildings, which are open for guided tours daily from 9am to 5pm in season (mid-Apr to mid-Nov). Admission is $5 for adults, free for children under 16. The grounds and the visitor center, 1250 Hancock St. (© 617/770-1175; www.nps.gov/adam), are open in the winter Tuesday through Friday 10am to 4pm. The center is across the street from the Quincy Center stop on the Red Line; call or surf ahead for driving directions.

Plymouth

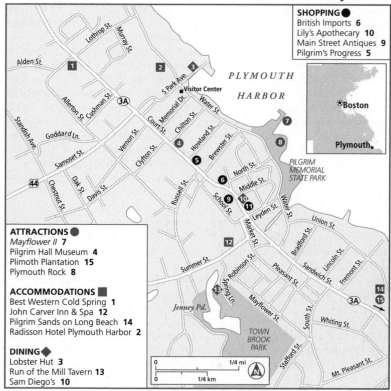

SHOPPING ●
British Imports **6**
Lily's Apothecary **10**
Main Street Antiques **9**
Pilgrim's Progress **5**

PLYMOUTH

HARBOR

☀Boston

Plymouth.

PILGRIM
MEMORIAL
STATE PARK

ATTRACTIONS ●
Mayflower II **7**
Pilgrim Hall Museum **4**
Plimoth Plantation **15**
Plymouth Rock **8**

ACCOMMODATIONS ■
Best Western Cold Spring **1**
John Carver Inn & Spa **12**
Pilgrim Sands on Long Beach **14**
Radisson Hotel Plymouth Harbor **2**

DINING ◆
Lobster Hut **3**
Run of the Mill Tavern **13**
Sam Diego's **10**

TOWN
BROOK
PARK

0   1/4 mi
0   1/4 km

Mayflower passengers, was originally 15 feet long and 3 feet wide. It was moved on the eve of the Revolution and several times thereafter. In 1867, it assumed its present permanent position at tide level. The rock itself isn't much to look at, but the accompanying descriptions are interesting, and the atmosphere is curiously inspiring.

The Colonial Dames of America commissioned the portico around the rock, designed by McKim, Mead & White and erected in 1920. The remnants of a renovation project slated to begin and end in early 2008 may still be evident during your visit.

The park just south of the Rock (which is technically in its own little state park) is **Brewster Gardens,** a lovely green space that traces Town Brook. This is a good shortcut to **Jenney Pond,** in Town Brook Park, across Summer Street from the John Carver Inn. A short distance from the bustle of the waterfront, the park has plenty of room to run around as well as a pond with ducks and geese.

GUIDED TOURS   To walk in the Pilgrims' footsteps, take a **Colonial Lantern Tour** ⭐ (© **508/747-4161** or 774/454-8126 for reservations; www.lanterntours. com). Participants carry pierced-tin lanterns on a 90-minute walking tour of the original settlement, conducted by a knowledgeable guide. It might seem a bit hokey at first, but it's fascinating. Tours run nightly from April to Thanksgiving. The standard history tour begins at 7:30pm; the "Ghostly Haunts & Legends" tour starts at 9pm.

Tickets are $15 for adults, $12 for seniors and children 6 to 16, and free for children under 6; check the meeting place when you call for reservations. The company also offers special tours for Halloween and Thanksgiving.

Narrated cruises run from April through November from State Pier and Town Wharf; check the departure point when you make reservations, which are always recommended. **Capt. John Boats** (© **800/242-2469** or 508/746-2643; www.captjohn. com) offers several entertaining options, including 75-minute narrated **harbor tours** on the *Pilgrim Belle* paddle wheeler ($14 adults, $12 seniors, $10 children 2–12) and **whale watches** ($37 adults, $31 seniors, $25 children 4–12). Dining, entertainment, and sunset cruises and seasonal service to Provincetown are also available. Tours with **Lobster Tales** (© **508/746-5342;** www.lobstertalesinc.com) include **lobster excursions** ($15 adults, $13 seniors, $11 children under 12), which give passengers the chance to haul up traps and handle the feisty crustaceans, and kid-friendly **pirate cruises** ($18 per person), with music, singing, and dancing by the crew and hats for the young buccaneers.

Mayflower II ℛ *(Kids)*   Berthed a few steps from Plymouth Rock, the *Mayflower II* is a full-scale reproduction of the type of ship that brought the Pilgrims from England to America in 1620. Even though it's full-scale, the 106½-foot vessel, constructed in England from 1955 to 1957, is remarkably small. Although little technical information about the original *Mayflower* survives, William A. Baker, designer of the *Mayflower II,* incorporated the few references in Governor Bradford's account of the voyage with other research to re-create it as authentically as possible.

Costumed guides provide interesting first-person narratives about the vessel and voyage, and other interpreters provide a contemporary perspective. Displays describe and illustrate the journey and the Pilgrims' experience, and include exhibits about 17th-century navigation techniques, stocking the ship with food and other provisions, and the history of the *Mayflower II.* Plimoth Plantation (below) owns and maintains the vessel and offers combined admission discounts. Alongside the ship are museum shops that replicate early Pilgrim dwellings.

State Pier. © 508/746-1622. www.plimoth.org. Admission $10 adults, $9 seniors, $7 children 6–12. Plimoth Plantation (good for 2 consecutive days) and *Mayflower II* admission $28 adults, $25 seniors and students, $18 children 6–12, $110 families (2 adults and up to 4 children 6–17; not available online). Free for children under 6. Apr–Nov daily 9am–5pm. Closed Dec–Mar.

Pilgrim Hall Museum ℛ *(Kids)*   This is a great place to get a sense of the day-to-day lives of Plymouth's first European residents. Many original possessions of the early Pilgrims and their descendants are on display, including one of Myles Standish's swords, Governor Bradford's Bible, and an uncomfortable chair (you can sit in a replica) that belonged to William Brewster. Regularly changing exhibits explore aspects of the settlers' lives, such as home construction or maritime history, and hands-on activities such as treasure hunts get kids interested. Built in 1824, the Pilgrim Hall Museum is the oldest public museum in the United States. Check ahead for information about exhibits that make use of the new wing completed in 2008.

75 Court St. © 508/746-1620. www.pilgrimhall.org. Admission $7 adults, $6 seniors and AAA members, $4 children 5–17, $20 families. Feb–Dec daily 9:30am–4:30pm. Closed Jan, Dec 25. From Plymouth Rock, walk north on Water St. and up the hill on Chilton St.

Plimoth Plantation ℛℛ *(Kids)*   Allow at least half a day to explore this re-creation of the 1627 English village, which children and adults find equally interesting. Enter by the hilltop fort that protected the village and walk down the hill to the farm area, visiting homes and gardens constructed with careful attention to historic detail. Although the experience is a bit disorienting at first, talking to the "Pilgrims" is great fun. They're actors who, in speech, dress, and manner, assume the personalities of members of the original community. You can watch them framing a house, splitting wood, shearing sheep, preserving foodstuffs, or cooking a pot of fish stew over an open hearth, all as it was done in the 1600s and using only the tools and cookware available then. Sometimes you can join the activities—perhaps planting, harvesting, witnessing a trial, or visiting a wedding party. Wear comfortable shoes, because you'll be walking a lot.

The plantation is as accurate as research can make it. The planners combined accounts of the original colony with archaeological research, old records, and the history written by the Pilgrims' leader, William Bradford (who often used the spelling "Plimoth"). There are daily militia drills with matchlock muskets that are fired to demonstrate the community's defense system. In fact, little defense was needed, because the Native Americans were friendly. Local tribes included the Wampanoags, who are represented near the village at a replica of a homesite (included in plantation admission), where staff members show off native foodstuffs, agricultural practices, and crafts.

At the main entrance are two modern buildings that house exhibits, a gift shop, a bookstore, a cafeteria, and an auditorium where visitors can view a film produced by the History Channel. There's also a picnic area. Call or surf ahead for information about the numerous special events, lectures, tours, workshops, theme dinners, and children's and family programs offered throughout the season.

137 Warren Ave. (Rte. 3). (℃ **508/746-1622.** www.plimoth.org. Admission (good for 2 consecutive days) $24 adults, $22 seniors, $14 children 6–12. Plimoth Plantation and *Mayflower II* admission $28 adults, $25 seniors and students, $18 children 6–12, $110 families (2 adults and up to 4 children 6–17; not available online). Free for children under 6. Apr–Nov daily 9am–5pm. Closed Dec–Mar. From Rte. 3, take Exit 4, Plimoth Plantation Hwy.

SHOPPING

Water Street, along the harbor, boasts an inexhaustible supply of souvenir shops. A less kitschy destination, just up the hill, is Route 3A, known as Court, Main, and Warren Street as it runs through town. **Lily's Apothecary,** 6 Main St. extension, in the old post office (℃ **508/747-7546;** www.lilysapothecary.com), stocks a big-city-style selection of skin- and hair-care products for women and men. Closed Wednesday and Sunday. **Main Street Antiques,** 46 Main St. (℃ **508/747-8887**), is home to dozens of dealers, and **Pilgrim's Progress,** 13 Court St. (℃ **508/746-6033;** www.pilgrims progressclothing.com), carries stylish women's and men's clothing and accessories. After a stop in **British Imports,** 1 Court St. (℃ **508/747-2972;** www.britishsupplies. com), which attracts homesick Marmite fans from miles around, you'll be able to write your own English food joke.

WHERE TO STAY

On busy summer weekends, it's not unusual for every room in town to sell out. Make reservations well in advance. Whenever you travel, don't book a room without checking for special packages and offers. Just about every establishment in town participates in a **Destination Plymouth** (℃ **800/USA-1620;** www.visit-plymouth.com) program that piles on deals and discounts in an effort to turn day-trippers into overnight guests.

The **Radisson Hotel Plymouth Harbor,** 180 Water St. (℃ **800/333-3333** or 508/747-4900; www.radisson.com), is the only chain hotel downtown. The 175-unit hotel, on a hill across the street from the waterfront, offers all the usual chain amenities, including a swimming pool in the atrium lobby. Doubles in high season start at $139. The **Hilton Garden Inn,** 4 Home Depot Dr. (℃ **877/782-9444** or 508/830-0200; www.hiltongardeninn.com), is Route 3 Exit 5, about 10 minutes from downtown. The hotel has an exercise room, an indoor pool, and extensive business features; doubles go for $139 and up in high season.

Best Western Cold Spring ⭐   This pleasant motel and its adjacent cottages surround landscaped lawns. Rooms are attractively decorated and big enough for a family to spread out in; if the adults want some privacy, book a two-bedroom cottage. The fastidiously maintained property has a good-sized outdoor pool, and about half of the guest rooms have wired high-speed Internet access (there's wireless throughout the property). I especially like the location, in a quiet, mostly residential part of town convenient to downtown and the historic sights. The tolerable distance from the water is what makes the Cold Spring a good deal. The two-story complex is 1 long block inland, set back from the street.

188 Court St. (Rte. 3A), Plymouth, MA 02360. ℃ **800/678-8667** or 508/746-2222. Fax 508/746-2744. www.bwcold spring.com. 58 units, 10 with shower only, 2 2-bedroom cottages. Apr–Nov $99–$159 double; $139–$199 suite; $109–$159 cottage. Extra person $10. Rollaway $10. Crib $5. Children under 12 stay free in parent's room. Rates include continental breakfast. Packages and AAA and off-season discounts available. AE, DC, DISC, MC, V. Closed Dec–Mar. Pets accepted; $10 fee. **Amenities:** Outdoor pool; rooms for those w/limited mobility. *In room:* A/C, TV, wireless Internet access, coffeemaker, hair dryer, iron.

John Carver Inn & Spa *(Kids*   A three-story colonial-style building with a landmark portico, this hotel offers comfortable, modern accommodations and plenty of amenities, including a full-service spa. The indoor "theme pool," a big hit with families, has a large water slide and a Pilgrim ship model. The good-size guest rooms are regularly renovated and decorated in colonial style. The best units are the lavishly appointed two-room suites, with fireplaces, two TVs, and private Jacuzzis; I like the "four-poster" rooms, which have king beds. The inn is on the edge of the downtown business district, within walking distance of the main attractions. Business features and meeting space make this hotel the Radisson's main competition for corporate travelers. Always check ahead for packages, which can be a great deal.

25 Summer St., Plymouth, MA 02360. ℃ **800/274-1620** or 508/746-7100. Fax 508/746-8299. www.johncarverinn. com. 80 units. Early Apr to mid-June and mid-Oct to Nov $119–$219 double, $259–$299 suite; mid-June to mid-Oct $159–$249 double, $299–$329 suite; Dec–early Apr $109–$199 double, $239–$279 suite. Extra person $20. Rollaway $20. Cribs free. Children under 19 stay free in parent's room. Packages and senior and AAA discounts available. AE, DC, DISC, MC, V. **Amenities:** Restaurant (American/seafood); indoor pool; fitness center; game room; Jacuzzi; concierge; business center; room service until 10pm; laundry service; dry cleaning; rooms for those w/limited mobility. *In room:* A/C, TV w/pay movies, wireless Internet access, hair dryer, iron.

Pilgrim Sands on Long Beach ⭐⭐ *(Kids*   This attractive motel sits on its own beach 3 miles south of town, within walking distance of Plimoth Plantation. Right smack on the water, it's an excellent choice if you want to avoid the bustle of downtown. The well-maintained, regularly updated property has an indoor and an outdoor pool if you don't care for ocean swimming, wireless Internet access in one wing and the lobby, and a small business center. The helpful staff is eager to offer sightseeing and dining advice. The good-size guest rooms are tastefully furnished and well maintained; all but four are set aside for nonsmokers. Most have two double or queen beds.

If you can swing it, book a beachfront room—the view is worth the money, especially when the surf is rough.

150 Warren Ave. (Rte. 3A), Plymouth, MA 02360. (Ⓒ) 800/729-7263 or 508/747-0900. Fax 508/746-8066. www. pilgrimsands.com. 64 units. Summer $155–$195 double; spring and early fall $114–$169 double; Apr and late fall $94–$134 double; Dec–Mar $84–$99 double. $159–$309 suite year-round. Extra person $6–$8 (suite $10–$15). Up to 2 children under 7 stay free in parent's room. Rates include continental breakfast. Minimum 2-night stay holiday weekends. Rates may be higher on holiday weekends. AE, DC, DISC, MC, V. **Amenities:** Coffee shop; indoor and outdoor pools; access to nearby health club ($10); Jacuzzi; small business center; private beach; rooms for those w/limited mobility. *In room:* A/C, TV, wireless Internet access, fridge, hair dryer.

WHERE TO DINE

Plimoth Plantation (p. 280) has a cafeteria and a picnic area, and occasionally schedules theme dinners. Should you happen to reach the "seafood again?" stage (it happens), a good destination downtown is **Sam Diego's,** 15 Main St. (Ⓒ **508/747-0048;** www.samdiegos.com), a cheerful Tex-Mex restaurant and bar in a renovated firehouse. It serves tasty renditions of exactly what you'd expect and offers a kids' menu and seasonal outdoor seating. Hours are 11:30am to midnight daily.

Lobster Hut ⭐ SEAFOOD   A busy self-service restaurant with a great view, the Lobster Hut is popular with both sightseers and, despite its touristy location, hungry locals. Order and pick up at the counter, then head to an indoor table or out onto the large deck that overlooks the action on the bay. This isn't an elegant place, but the food is ultra-fresh and expertly prepared. To start, try clam chowder or lobster bisque. The seafood rolls (hot dog buns with your choice of filling) are excellent. The many fried seafood options include clams, scallops, shrimp, and haddock. You can also opt for broiled fish and shellfish, burgers, chicken tenders—or lobster, of course. Beer and wine are served, but only with meals.

25 Town Wharf. (Ⓒ) 508/746-2270. Reservations not accepted. Lunch specials (available Mon–Fri until 4pm) $8–$11; main courses $6–$19; sandwiches $3–$11 (most under $8); clams and lobster priced daily. MC, V. Summer daily 11am–9pm; winter daily 11am–7pm. Closed Jan.

Run of the Mill Tavern ⭐ AMERICAN   This friendly restaurant sits 3 blocks inland, across from Town Brook Park. You won't mind not having a water view—the food is tasty and reasonably priced, and the comfortable post-and-beam tavern is a popular hangout. The unconventional clam chowder, made with red potatoes, is fantastic. Other appetizers include nachos, potato skins, buffalo wings, and mushrooms. Entrees are well-executed versions of familiar meat, chicken, and fish dishes, plus burgers, fresh seafood (fried, broiled, or baked), and sandwiches (at lunch). On some Saturday nights, there's live Irish music.

6 Spring Lane, off Summer St. (Ⓒ) 508/830-1262. Reservations accepted only for parties of 6 or more. Main courses $8–$19; children's menu $4–$6. AE, DC, DISC, MC, V. Sun–Thurs 11:30am–9:30pm, Fri–Sat 11:30am–10pm (lunch menu until 4pm). Bar closes at 1am.

Appendix:
Fast Facts, Toll-Free
Numbers & Websites

1 Fast Facts: Boston

American Express Offices are at 1 State St., opposite the Old State House (© **617/723-8400**); 170 Federal St., Financial District (© **617/439-4400**); 432 Stuart St., Back Bay (© **617/236-1331**); and 39 John F. Kennedy St., Harvard Square, Cambridge (© **617/868-2600**).

Area Codes Boston proper, **617** and **857**; immediate suburbs, **781** and **339**; northern and western suburbs, **978** and **351**; southern suburbs, **508** and **774**. *Note:* To make a local call, you must dial the 3-digit area code and the 7-digit number.

ATM Networks/Cashpoints See "Money & Costs," p. 43.

Automobile Organizations Motor clubs will supply maps, suggested routes, guidebooks, accident and bail-bond insurance, and emergency road service. The **American Automobile Association (AAA)** is the major auto club in the United States. If you belong to a motor club in your home country, inquire about AAA reciprocity before you leave. You may be able to join AAA even if you're not a member of a reciprocal club; to inquire, call AAA (© **800/222-4357**; www.aaa. com). AAA is actually an organization of regional motor clubs, so look under "AAA Automobile Club" in the White Pages of the telephone directory. AAA has a nationwide emergency road service telephone number (© 800/AAA-HELP).

Babysitters Many hotels maintain lists of babysitters; check at the front desk or with the concierge. Local agencies aren't a cost-effective option; most charge a steep annual fee on top of the daily referral charge and the sitter's hourly wage and expenses. If you're in town on business, ask whether the company you're visiting has a corporate membership in an agency.

Business Hours Offices are usually open weekdays from 9am to 5 or 6pm. Banks are open weekdays from 9am to 4pm or later and sometimes on Saturday morning; most offer 24-hour access to automated teller machines (ATMs). Stores typically open between 9 and 10am and close at between 6pm (neighborhood shops) and 9pm (mall and shopping center locations) from Monday through Saturday. Sunday hours for shops that have them are usually noon to 5 or 6pm.

Car Rentals See "Toll-Free Numbers & Websites," p. 292.

Drinking Laws The legal age for purchase and consumption of alcoholic beverages is 21. Proof of age is required and often requested at bars, nightclubs, and restaurants, particularly near college campuses (in the Boston area, that's everywhere), so it's always a good idea to bring ID when you go out. At sporting events, everyone buying alcohol must show ID. Liquor stores and a few supermarkets and convenience stores sell alcohol. Liquor stores and the liquor sections of other stores are open Monday though Saturday; in communities where it's legal, open at noon on Sunday. Serving alcohol before noon on Sunday is technically illegal, which you may find out if you try to order a drink at a morning brunch. Most restaurants have full liquor licenses; some serve only beer, wine, and cordials. Last call typically is 30 minutes before closing time (1am in bars, 2am in clubs).

Do not carry open containers of alcohol in your car or any public area that isn't zoned for alcohol consumption. The police can fine you on the spot. And nothing will ruin your trip faster than getting a citation for DUI ("driving under the influence"), so don't even think about driving while intoxicated.

Driving Rules   See "Getting There and Getting Around," p. 32.

Drugstores   Downtown Boston has no 24-hour pharmacy. The **CVS** at 587 Boylston St., off Copley Square in the Back Bay (© 617/437-8414), is open 24 hours, 7 days a week, as is its pharmacy. The same goes for two CVS locations in Cambridge: 1426 Massachusetts Ave., Harvard Square (© 617/354-4420), and 36 White St., off Mass. Ave. in the Porter Square Shopping Center (© 617/876-5519). The Back Bay **Walgreens,** 841 Boylston St. (© 617/236-1692), is open 24 hours, and its pharmacy is open until 10pm on weeknights, 7pm on weekends.

Electricity   Like Canada, the United States uses 110–120 volts AC (60 cycles), compared to 220–240 volts AC (50 cycles) in most of Europe, Australia, and New Zealand. Downward converters that change 220–240 volts to 110–120 volts are difficult to find in the United States, so bring one with you.

Pack a **connection kit** of the right power and phone adapters, a spare phone cord, and a spare Ethernet network cable—or find out whether your hotel supplies them to guests.

Embassies & Consulates   All **embassies** are in the nation's capital, Washington, D.C. Most nations have a mission to the United Nations in New York City. The countries listed below have **consulates** in major American cities; check embassy websites for details. If your country isn't listed below, call directory information in Washington, D.C. (© 202/555-1212) or check **www.embassy.org/embassies**.

The embassy of **Australia** is at 1601 Massachusetts Ave. NW, Washington, DC 20036 (© 202/797-3000; www.austemb.org). The office of the local part-time **honorary consul** is at 55 Thomson Pl., Boston, MA 02210 (© 617/261-5555).

The embassy of **Canada** is at 501 Pennsylvania Ave. NW, Washington, DC 20001 (© 202/682-1740; www.canadianembassy.org). The local **Canadian consulate** is at 3 Copley Place, Suite 400, Boston, MA 02116 (© 617/262-3760).

The embassy of **Ireland** is at 2234 Massachusetts Ave. NW, Washington, DC 20008 (© 202/462-3939; www.irelandemb.org). The local **Irish consulate** is at 535 Boylston St., Boston, MA 02116 (© 617/267-9330).

The embassy of **New Zealand** is at 37 Observatory Circle NW, Washington, DC 20008 (© 202/328-4800; www.nzembassy.com). Contact the **honorary consul** to the Boston area at P.O. Box 1318, 57 N. Main St., Concord, NH 03302 (© 603/225-8228).

The embassy of the **United Kingdom** is at 3100 Massachusetts Ave. NW, Washington, DC 20008 (© 202/588-7800; www.britainusa.com). The Boston-area **British consulate** is at 1 Memorial Dr., 15th floor, Cambridge, MA 02142 (© 617/245-4500).

Emergencies Call © **911** for fire, ambulance, or the police. This is a free call from pay phones. For the state police, call © **617/523-1212.** Dialing 911 on a cellphone connects you to the state police; the Boston police direct emergency number is © 617/343-4911.

Gasoline (Petrol) At press time, in the U.S., the cost of gasoline (also known as gas, but never petrol), is abnormally high. You'll pay at least $4, and possibly much more, per gallon. The posted price includes taxes. One U.S. gallon equals 3.8 liters or .85 imperial gallons. Fill-up locations are known as gas or service stations.

Holidays Banks, government offices, post offices, and many stores, restaurants, and museums are closed on the following legal national holidays: January 1 (New Year's Day), the third Monday in January (Martin Luther King, Jr., Day), the third Monday in February (Presidents' Day), the last Monday in May (Memorial Day), July 4 (Independence Day), the first Monday in September (Labor Day), the second Monday in October (Columbus Day), November 11 (Veterans' Day/ Armistice Day), the fourth Thursday in November (Thanksgiving Day), and December 25 (Christmas). The Tuesday after the first Monday in November is Election Day, a federal government holiday in presidential-election years (held every 4 years, and next in 2008). In Massachusetts, state offices close for **Patriots Day** on the third Monday in April, and Suffolk County offices (including Boston City Hall and the public libraries) close on March 17 for **Evacuation Day.**

For more information on holidays, see "Calendar of Events," in Chapter 3 (p. 26).

Hospitals Massachusetts General Hospital, 55 Fruit St. (© **617/726-2000;** www.massgeneral.org), and **Tufts Medical Center,** 800 Washington St. (© **617/636-5000;** www.tufts-nemc. org), are closest to downtown.

At the Harvard Medical Area on the Boston-Brookline border are **Beth Israel Deaconess Medical Center,** 330 Brookline Ave. (© **617/667-7000;** www. bidmc.harvard.edu); **Brigham and Women's Hospital,** 75 Francis St. (© **617/732-5500;** www.brighamand womens.org); and **Children's Hospital Boston,** 300 Longwood Ave. (© **617/ 355-6000;** www.childrenshospital.org).

In Cambridge are **Mount Auburn Hospital,** 330 Mount Auburn St. (© **617/ 492-3500;** www.mountauburn.caregroup. org), and **Cambridge Hospital,** 1493 Cambridge St. (© **617/655-1000;** www. challiance.org/cambridge/index.shtml).

For more information, see "Health," p. 44.

Hotlines AIDS Hotline (© 800/235-2331), **Poison Control Center** (© 800/ 682-9211), **Rape Crisis** (© 877/627-7700 or 617/492-7273), **Samaritans Suicide Prevention** (© 617/247-0220), **Samariteens** (© 800/252-8336 or 617/ 247-8050).

Insurance Medical Insurance Although it's not required of travelers, health insurance is highly recommended. Most health insurance policies cover you if you get sick away from home—but check your coverage before you leave.

International visitors to the U.S. should note that unlike many European countries, the United States does not usually offer free or low-cost medical care to its citizens or visitors. Doctors and hospitals are expensive, and most require advance payment or proof of coverage before they render their services. Good policies will cover the costs of an accident, repatriation, or death. Packages such as **Europ Assistance's "Worldwide Healthcare Plan"** are sold by European automobile clubs and travel agencies at attractive rates. **Worldwide Assistance Services, Inc.** (© **800/777-8710;** www. worldwideassistance.com) is the agent for Europ Assistance in the United States.

Though lack of health insurance may prevent you from being admitted to a hospital in nonemergencies, don't worry about being left on a street corner to die: The American way is to fix you now and bill the daylights out of you later.

If you're ever hospitalized more than 150 miles from home, **MedjetAssist** (© **800/ 527-7478;** www.medjetassistance.com) will pick you up and fly you to the hospital of your choice in a medically equipped and staffed aircraft 24 hours day, 7 days a week. Annual memberships are $225 individual, $350 family; you can also purchase short-term memberships.

Canadians should check with their provincial health plan offices or call **Health Canada** (© **866/225-0709;** www.hc-sc.gc.ca) to find out the extent of their coverage and what documentation and receipts they must take home in case they are treated in the United States.

Travelers from the U.K. should carry their European Health Insurance Card (EHIC), which replaced the E111 form as proof of entitlement to free/reduced cost medical treatment abroad (© **0845/ 606-2030;** www.ehic.org.uk). Note, however, that the EHIC only covers "necessary medical treatment." For repatriation costs, lost money, baggage, or cancellation, seek travel insurance from a reputable company (www.travel insuranceweb.com).

As a safety net, you may want to buy travel medical insurance, particularly if you're traveling to a remote or high-risk area where emergency evacuation might be necessary. If you require additional medical insurance, try **MEDEX Assistance** (© **410/453-6300;** www.medex assist.com) or **Travel Assistance International** (© **800/821-2828;** www.travel assistance.com; for general information on services, call the company's **Worldwide Assistance Services, Inc.,** © **800/ 777-8710**).

Travel Insurance The cost of travel insurance varies widely, depending on the destination, the cost and length of your trip, your age and health, and the type of trip you're taking, but expect to pay between 5% and 8% of the vacation itself. You can get estimates from various providers through **InsureMyTrip.com**. Enter your trip cost and dates, your age, and other information, for prices from more than a dozen companies.

U.K. citizens and their families who make more than one trip abroad per year may save money by buying an annual travel insurance policy. Check **www. moneysupermarket.com**, which compares prices across a wide range of providers for single- and multi-trip policies.

Most big travel agents offer their own insurance and will probably try to sell you their package when you book a holiday. Think before you sign. **Britain's Consumers' Association** recommends that you insist on seeing the policy and reading the fine print before buying travel insurance. **The Association of British Insurers** (© **020/7600-3333;** www.abi. org.uk) gives advice by phone and publishes *Holiday Insurance,* a free guide to policy provisions and prices. You might also shop around for better deals: Try **Columbus Direct** (© **0870/033-9988;** www.columbusdirect.net).

Trip Cancellation Insurance Trip-cancellation insurance will help retrieve your money if you have to back out of a trip or depart early, or if your travel supplier goes bankrupt. Trip cancellation traditionally covers such events as sickness, natural disasters, and State Department advisories. The latest news in trip-cancellation insurance is the availability of **expanded hurricane coverage** and **"any-reason"** cancellation coverage—which costs more but covers cancellations made for any reason. You'll get back a substantial portion, though not 100%, of your pre-paid trip cost. **TravelSafe** (© **888/885-7233;** www.travelsafe.com) offers both types of coverage. Expedia also offers any-reason cancellation coverage for its air-hotel packages. For details, contact one of the following recommended insurers: **Access America** (© 866/807-3982; www.accessamerica.com); **Travel Guard International** (© 800/826-4919; www.travelguard.com); **Travel Insured International** (© 800/243-3174; www.travel insured.com); and **Travelex Insurance Services** (© 888/457-4602; www.travelex-insurance.com).

Internet Access   Tech-happy Boston has relatively few dedicated cybercafes but makes up for the lack with tons of Wi-Fi (some free, some not). Many hotels have a wired terminal for guests' use, and most offer on-premises wireless. To find public Wi-Fi hotspots, go to **www.jiwire.com**; its Hotspot Finder holds the world's largest directory of public wireless hotspots. Other resources are the **Boston Wireless Advocacy Group's** directory (www.bostonwag.org/projects/hotspots.php) and **Hotspotr** (http://hotspotr.com/wifi), a Google Maps mash-up that indexes user-generated listings. **Tech Superpowers,** 252 Newbury St., 3rd floor (© **617/267-9716;** www.newbury open.net), offers access by the hour ($5/hr.; $3/15 min. minimum) with or without a computer, and provides the free wireless you'll find in most businesses on the upper end of Newbury Street. The city of Boston coordinates free Wi-Fi at a number of locations around town, including Faneuil Hall Marketplace (the rotunda of Quincy Market) and Christopher Columbus Waterfront Park; visit **www.cityofboston.gov/wireless** for more information. For wired access, the ubiquitous **FedEx Kinko's** (www.fedex kinkos.com) charges 10¢ to 20¢ a minute. Locations include 2 Center Plaza, Government Center (© **617/973-9000**); 10 Post Office Sq., Financial District (© **617/482-4400**); 187 Dartmouth St., Back Bay (© **617/262-6188**); and 1 Mifflin Place, off Mount Auburn Street near Eliot Street, Harvard Square (© **617/497-0125**).

For more information, see "Staying Connected," p. 52.

Legal Aid   If you are "pulled over" for a minor infraction (such as speeding), never attempt to pay the fine directly to a police officer; this could be construed as attempted bribery, a much more serious crime. Pay fines by mail, or directly into the hands of the clerk of the court. If accused of a more serious offense, say and do nothing before consulting a lawyer. Here the burden is on the state to prove a person's guilt beyond a reasonable doubt, and everyone has the right to remain silent, whether he or she is suspected of a crime or actually arrested. Once arrested, a person can make one telephone call to a party of his or her choice. International visitors should call your embassy or consulate.

Lost & Found   Be sure to tell all of your credit card companies the minute you discover your wallet has been lost or stolen, and file a report at the nearest police precinct. Your credit-card com-pany or insurer may require a police report number or record of the loss. Most card issuers have an emergency toll-free number to call if your card is lost or stolen; they may be able to wire you a cash advance immediately or deliver an emergency credit card in a day or two. Visa's U.S. emergency number is © **800/847-2911** or 410/581-9994. American Express cardholders and traveler's check holders should call © **800/221-7282.** MasterCard holders should call © **800/307-7309** or 636/722-7111. For other credit cards, call the toll-free number directory at © **800/555-1212.**

If you need emergency cash on a weekend or holiday when banks and American Express offices are closed, you can have money wired to you through **Western Union** (© **800/325-6000;** www.western union.com).

If you lose something in a cab, contact the Boston Police Department's **Hackney Unit** (© **617/343-4475;** www.cityof boston.gov/police).

Mail At press time, domestic postage rates were 27¢ for a postcard and 42¢ for a letter. For international mail, a first-class letter of up to 1 ounce costs 94¢ (72¢ to Canada and Mexico); a first-class postcard costs the same as a letter. For more information, go to **www.usps.com** and click on "Calculate Postage."

If you aren't sure what your address will be in the United States, mail can be sent to you, in your name, c/o General Delivery at the main post office of the city or region where you expect to be. (Call © **800/275-8777** for information on the nearest post office.) The addressee must pick up mail in person and must produce proof of identity (driver's license, passport, etc.). Most post offices will hold your mail for up to 1 month, and are open Monday to Friday from 8am to 6pm, and Saturday from 9am to 3pm.

Always include zip codes when mailing items in the U.S. If you don't know your zip code, visit www.usps.com/zip4.

Maps To supplement the maps provided with this guide, pick up free maps of downtown Boston and the subway lines at visitor information centers around the city, from hotel concierge desks and pamphlet racks, and from most trolley operators (ask the ticket seller). **National Park Service** maps, available from the visitor centers at 15 State St. and the Charlestown Navy Yard, are especially useful. *Where* magazine, available free at most hotels, contains maps of central Boston and the T.

Measurements See the chart on the inside front cover of this book for details on converting metric measurements to nonmetric equivalents.

Medical Conditions If you have a medical condition that requires **syringe-administered medications,** carry a valid signed prescription from your physician; syringes in carry-on baggage will be inspected. Insulin in any form should have the proper pharmaceutical documentation. If you have a disease that requires treatment with **narcotics,** you should also carry documented proof with you—smuggling narcotics aboard a plane carries severe penalties in the U.S.

For **HIV-positive visitors,** requirements for entering the United States are somewhat vague and change frequently. For up-to-the-minute information, contact **AIDSinfo** (© **800/448-0440** or 301/ 519-6616 outside the U.S.; www.aidsinfo. nih.gov) or the **Gay Men's Health Crisis** (© **212/367-1000;** www.gmhc.org).

Newspapers & Magazines The daily *Boston Globe, Boston Herald, New York Times, USA Today,* and *Wall Street Journal* are available at convenience stores, newsstands, some supermarkets, and sidewalk newspaper boxes all over the Boston area. National newsweeklies include *Newsweek, Time,* and *U.S. News & World Report.* The free, arts-oriented *Boston Phoenix,* published on Thursday, has extensive entertainment and restaurant listings.

Where, a monthly magazine available free at most hotels, lists information about shopping, nightlife, attractions, and current shows at museums and art galleries. Newspaper boxes dispense free copies of *Stuff@Night,* a biweekly *Phoenix* offshoot with selective listings and arts coverage; the irreverent *Weekly Dig,* which covers news, entertainment, and dining; the biweekly *Improper Bostonian,* with extensive event and restaurant listings; and the weekly *Tab,* which lists neighborhood-specific event information. Available on newsstands, *Boston* magazine is a lifestyle-oriented monthly with cultural and restaurant listings.

Newsstands with good selections of international periodicals include **Out of Town News,** Zero Harvard Square, Cambridge (© 617/354-7777); **Nini's Corner,** across the street at 1394 Massachusetts Ave. (© 617/547-3558); and the newsstand on the street level of Faneuil Hall.

Passports The websites listed provide downloadable passport applications as well as the current fees for processing applications. For an up-to-date, country-by-country listing of passport requirements around the world, go to the "International Travel" tab of the U.S. State Department site at **http://travel. state.gov**. International visitors to the U.S. can obtain a visa application at the same website. *Note:* Children are required to present a passport when entering the United States at airports. If you're traveling with your child but not your spouse, it's a good idea to carry a notarized letter from the spouse granting permission to travel and a copy of his or her passport (to allay suspicions of custody interference).

For Residents of Australia You can pick up an application from your local post office or any branch of Passports Australia, but you must schedule an interview at the passport office to present your application materials. Within Australia, contact the **Australian Passport Information Service** (© 131-232; www. passports.gov.au). If you're already abroad, contact an Australian diplomatic or consular mission.

For Residents of Canada Passport applications are available at travel agencies throughout Canada or from the central **Passport Office,** Department of Foreign Affairs and International Trade, Ottawa, ON K1A 0G3 (© 800/567-6868; www.ppt.gc.ca). *Note:* Canadian

children who travel must have their own passport. However, if you hold a valid Canadian passport issued before December 11, 2001, that bears the name of your child, the passport remains valid for you and your child until it expires.

For Residents of Ireland You can apply for a 10-year passport at the **Passport Office,** Setanta Centre, Molesworth Street, Dublin 2 (© **01/671-1633;** www. irlgov.ie/iveagh). Those under age 18 and over 65 must apply for a 3-year passport. You can also apply at 1A South Mall, Cork (© **21/494-4700**), or at most main post offices.

For Residents of New Zealand You can pick up a passport application at any New Zealand Passports Office or download it from their website. Contact the **Passports Office** (© **0800/225-050** in New Zealand or 04/474-8100; www. passports.govt.nz).

For Residents of the United Kingdom To pick up an application for a standard 10-year passport (5-yr. passport for children under 16), visit your nearest passport office, major post office, or travel agency or contact the **United Kingdom Passport Service** (© **0870/521-0410;** www.ukpa.gov.uk).

Police Call © **911** for emergencies. The Boston police emergency line to call from a cellphone is © **617/343-4911.**

Smoking In a word, no. State law bans smoking in all workplaces, including restaurants, bars, and clubs, and the MBTA forbids smoking in subway stations. A growing number of hotel chains ban smoking in all guest rooms.

Taxes The United States has no value-added tax (VAT) or other indirect tax at the national level. Every state, county, and city may levy its own local tax on all purchases, including hotel and restaurant checks and airline tickets. These taxes will not appear on price tags. The 5% state sales tax in Massachusetts does not apply to groceries, prescription drugs, newspapers, or clothing that costs less than $175. The tax on meals and takeout food is 5%. The lodging tax is 12.45% in Boston and Cambridge.

Telephones   For information about making local, long-distance, and international calls, please turn to "Staying Connected," p. 52.

Telegraph, Telex & Fax   The primary provider of **telegraph and telex services** is **Western Union** (© 800/325-6000; www.westernunion.com). You can telegraph (wire) money, or have it telegraphed to you, very quickly over the Western Union system, but this service can cost as much as 20 percent of the amount sent.

Most hotels have **fax machines** available for guest use (be sure to ask about the charge to use it). Many hotel rooms are wired for guests' fax machines. A less expensive way to send and receive faxes may be at stores such as **The UPS Store.**

Time   Boston is in the Eastern time zone. The continental United States is divided into **four time zones:** Eastern Time (ET), Central Time (CT), Mountain Time (MT), and Pacific Time (PT). Alaska and Hawaii have their own zones. For example, when it's 9am in Los Angeles (PT), it's 7am in Honolulu (HT), 10am in Denver (MT), 11am in Chicago (CT), noon in Boston and New York (ET), 5pm in London (GMT), and 2am the next day in Sydney.

Daylight saving time is in effect from 1am on the second Sunday in March to 1am on the first Sunday in November, except in Arizona, Hawaii, the U.S. Virgin Islands, and Puerto Rico. Daylight saving time moves the clock 1 hour ahead of standard time.

Tipping   Tips are a very important part of certain workers' income, and gratuities are the standard way of showing appreciation for services provided. (Tipping is certainly not compulsory if the service is poor!) In hotels, tip **bellhops** at least $1 per bag ($2–$3 if you have a lot of luggage) and tip the **chamber staff** $1 to $2 per day (more if you've left behind a big mess). Tip the **doorman** or **concierge** only if he or she has provided a specific service (for example, calling a cab for you or obtaining difficult-to-get theater tickets). Tip the **valet-parking attendant** $1 every time you get your car.

In restaurants, bars, and nightclubs, tip **service staff** 15% to 20% of the check, tip **bartenders** 10% to 15%, tip **checkroom attendants** $1 per garment, and tip **valet-parking attendants** $1 per vehicle.

As for other service personnel, tip **cab drivers** 15% of the fare; tip **skycaps** at airports at least $1 per bag ($2–$3 if you have a lot of luggage); and tip **hairdressers** and **barbers** 15% to 20%.

Toilets   You won't find public toilets or "restrooms" on the streets in most U.S. cities, but they can be found in hotel lobbies, bars, restaurants, museums, department stores, railway and bus stations, and service stations. The visitor center at 15 State St. has a public restroom, as do the CambridgeSide Galleria, Copley Place, Prudential Center, and Quincy Market shopping areas. The central branch of the Boston Public Library, in Copley Square, has toilets in the basement. Large hotels, coffee bars, and fast-food restaurants are often the best bet for clean facilities. Businesses in popular tourist areas such as downtown Boston may reserve their restrooms for patrons.

You'll find freestanding, self-cleaning **pay toilets** (25¢) at locations around downtown. These include City Hall Plaza, Congress Street behind City Hall, the plaza in front of the New England Aquarium, and Commercial Street at Snowhill Street, just off the Freedom Trail. Check these facilities carefully before using them or sending a child in alone; despite regular patrols, IV-drug users have been known to take advantage of the generous time limits.

Useful Phone Numbers   MBTA (subways, local buses, commuter rail) ℭ 800/392-6100 or 617/222-3200.

Massachusetts Port Authority (airport) ℭ 800/23-LOGAN.

Greater Boston Convention & Visitors Bureau (visitor info) 888/SEE-BOSTON or 617/536-4100.

U.S. Dept. of State Travel Advisory ℭ 202/647-5225 (staffed 24 hrs.).

U.S. Passport Agency ℭ 202/647-0518.

U.S. Centers for Disease Control International Traveler's Hotline: ℭ 404/332-4559.

Visas   For information about U.S. Visas go to **http://travel.state.gov** and click on "Visas." Or go to one of the following websites:

Australian citizens can obtain up-to-date visa information from the **U.S. Embassy Canberra,** Moonah Place, Yarralumla, ACT 2600 (ℭ **02/6214-5600**) or by checking the U.S. Diplomatic Mission's website at **http://us embassy-australia.state.gov/consular**.

British subjects can obtain up-to-date visa information by calling the **U.S. Embassy Visa Information Line** (ℭ **0891/200-290**) or by visiting the "Visas to the U.S." section of the American Embassy London's website at **www.usembassy.org.uk**.

Irish citizens can obtain up-to-date visa information through the **Embassy of the USA Dublin,** 42 Elgin Rd., Dublin 4, Ireland (ℭ **353/1-668-8777**), or by checking the "Consular Services" section of the website at **http://dublin.usembassy.gov**.

Citizens of **New Zealand** can obtain up-to-date visa information by contacting the **U.S. Embassy New Zealand,** 29 Fitzherbert Terrace, Thorndon, Wellington (ℭ **644/472-2068;** http://wellington.usembassy.gov).

2 Toll-Free Numbers & Websites

MAJOR U.S. AIRLINES
(*flies internationally as well)

AirTran
ℭ 800/247-8726
www.airtranairways.com

Alaska Airlines/Horizon Air*
ℭ 800/252-7522
www.alaskaair.com

American Airlines*
ℭ 800/433-7300 (in U.S. and Canada)
ℭ 020/7365-0777 (in U.K.)
www.aa.com

Cape Air
ℭ 800/352-0714
www.flycapeair.com

Continental Airlines*
ℭ 800/523-3273 (in U.S. and Canada)
ℭ 084/5607-6760 (in U.K.)
www.continental.com

Delta Air Lines*
ℭ 800/221-1212 (in U.S. and Canada)
ℭ 084/5600-0950 (in U.K.)
www.delta.com

JetBlue Airways
ℭ 800/538-2583 (in U.S.)
ℭ 080/1365-2525 (in U.K. and Canada)
www.jetblue.com

Midwest Airlines
ℭ 800/452-2022
www.midwestairlines.com

Northwest/KLM*
ℭ 800/225-2525 (in U.S.)
ℭ 870/0507-4074 (in U.K.)
www.nwa.com

Spirit Airlines
ℭ 800/772-7117
www.spiritair.com

United Airlines*
© 800/864-8331 (in U.S. and Canada)
© 084/5844-4777 in U.K.
www.united.com

US Airways*
© 800/428-4322 (in U.S. and Canada)
© 084/5600-3300 (in U.K.)
www.usairways.com

Virgin America*
© 877/359-8474
www.virginamerica.com

MAJOR INTERNATIONAL AIRLINES

Aer Lingus
© 800/2474-7424 (in U.S.)
© 0818/365-000 (in Ireland)
www.aerlingus.com

Air Canada
© 888/247-2262 (U.S. and Canada)
© 0871/220-1111 (in U.K.)
www.aircanada.com

Air France
© 800/237-2747 (in U.S.)
© 800/375-8723 (U.S. and Canada)
© 087/0142-4343 (in U.K.)
www.airfrance.com

Alitalia
© 800/223-5730 (in U.S.)
© 800/361-8336 (in Canada)
© 087/0608-6003 (in U.K.)
www.alitalia.com

American Airlines
© 800/433-7300 (in U.S. and Canada)
© 020/7365-0777 (in U.K.)
www.aa.com

British Airways
© 800/247-9297 (in U.S. and Canada)
© 087/0850-9850 (in U.K.)
www.british-airways.com

Continental Airlines
© 800/523-3273 (in U.S. and Canada)
© 084/5607-6760 (in U.K.)
www.continental.com

Delta Air Lines
© 800/221-1212 (in U.S. and Canada)
© 084/5600-0950 (in U.K.)
www.delta.com

Finnair
© 800/950-5000 (in U.S. and Canada)
© 087/0241-4411 (in U.K.)
www.finnair.com

Iberia Airlines
© 800/722-4642 (in U.S. and Canada)
© 087/0609-0500 (in U.K.)
www.iberia.com

Icelandair
© 800/223-5500 ext. 2 prompt 1
    (in U.S. and Canada)
© 084/5758-1111 (in U.K.)
www.icelandair.com
www.icelandair.co.uk (in U.K.)

Lufthansa
© 800/399-5838 (in U.S.)
© 800/563-5954 (in Canada)
© 087/0837-7747 (in U.K.)
www.lufthansa.com

SATA
© 800/762-9995
© 707/22-7282 (in Portugal)
www.sata.pt

Swiss Air
© 877/359-7947 (in U.S. and Canada)
© 084/5601-0956 (in U.K.)
www.swiss.com

United Airlines*
© 800/864-8331 (in U.S. and Canada)
© 084/5844-4777 (in U.K.)
www.united.com

US Airways*
© 800/428-4322 (in U.S. and Canada)
© 084/5600-3300 (in U.K.)
www.usairways.com

Virgin Atlantic Airways
© 800/821-5438 (in U.S. and Canada)
© 08705/747-747 (in U.K.)
www.virgin-atlantic.com

BUDGET AIRLINES

Aer Lingus*
© 800/474-7424 (in U.S. and Canada)
© 087/0876-5000 (in U.K.)
www.aerlingus.com

AirTran Airways
© 800/247-8726
www.airtran.com

JetBlue Airways
© 800/538-2583 (in U.S.)
© 801/365-2525 (in U.K. and Canada)
www.jetblue.com

Southwest Airlines
© 800/435-9792 (in U.S., U.K., and Canada)
www.southwest.com

Spirit Airlines
© 800/772-7117
www.spiritair.com

CAR-RENTAL AGENCIES

Alamo
© 800/GO-ALAMO (800/462-5266)
www.alamo.com

Avis
© 800/331-1212 (in U.S. and Canada)
© 084/4581-8181 (in U.K.)
www.avis.com

Budget
© 800/527-0700 (in U.S.)
© 087/0156-5656 (in U.K.)

© 800/268-8900 (in Canada)
www.budget.com

Dollar
© 800/800-4000 (in U.S.)
© 800/848-8268 (in Canada)
© 080/8234-7524 (in U.K.)
www.dollar.com

Enterprise
© 800/261-7331 (in U.S.)
© 514/355-4028 (in Canada)
© 012/9360-9090 (in U.K.)
www.enterprise.com

Hertz
© 800/645-3131
© 800/654-3001 (for international reservations)
www.hertz.com

National
© 800/CAR-RENT (800/227-7368)
www.nationalcar.com

Rent-A-Wreck
© 800/944-7501
www.rentawreck.com

Thrifty
© 800/367-2277
© 918/669-2168 (international)
www.thrifty.com

Index

See also Accommodations and Restaurant indexes, below.

GENERAL INDEX

A
AA (American Automobile Association), 284
Abbot Hall (Marblehead), 256
Abiel Smith School, 160
Academic trips, 51–52
Access America, 288
Accommodations, 67–101. *See also* Accommodations Index
  The Back Bay, 83–92
  bars and lounges at, 238
  Beacon Hill/North Station/North End, 78–80
  best, 5, 70–71
  Cambridge, 94–99
  Charlestown, 80
  Chinatown/Theater District, 81–83
  Copley Square and Hynes Convention Center, 85–92
  downtown, 71–77
  family-friendly, 87
  Financial District & Downtown Crossing, 75–77
  Gloucester, 271
  with gyms, 182
  for last-minute planners, 68
  Marblehead, 257–258
  at and near the airport, 99–101
  outskirts and Brookline, 92–94
  Plymouth, 281–283
  Rockport, 276
  Salem, 263–264
  saving on, 68–69
  South Boston Waterfront (Seaport District), 80–81
  The South End, 83
  The Waterfront & Faneuil Hall Marketplace, 71–75
  what's new in, 1–2
Adams, Samuel, 151
Adams National Historical Park (Quincy), 278
Adventure trips, 52

African-American History Month, 27
African-Americans, 162–163
  Abiel Smith School, 160
  African Meeting House, 160
  Black Heritage Trail, 160, 162
  Black Nativity, 31
  54th Massachusetts Colored Regiment, 150
  Martin Luther King, Jr., Birthday Celebration, 26
African Meeting House, 160, 169
Afternoon tea, 125
Agganis Arena at Boston University, 220–221
AIDS Hotline, 286
AIDSinfo, 289
Airport Accessible Van, 46
Airports, 31. *See also* Logan International Airport
Air travel, toll-free numbers and websites for airlines, 292–294
Alcott, Louisa May, 250–251
Algiers Café & Restaurant (Cambridge), 240
Ambassador Brattle (Cambridge), 38
AMC Loews Boston Common, 242
American Airlines Vacations, 50
American Apparel (Cambridge), 209
American Automobile Association (AAA), 34, 284
American Eagle, 36
American Express, 284
American Repertory Theatre (Cambridge), 228
American Revolution
  Cambridge, 164
  Freedom Trail, 148–159
America the Beautiful—National Park and Federal Recreational Lands Pass
  Access Pass, 46
  Senior Pass, 47

Amtrak, 34–35
Amtrak Vacations, 51
Ancient and Honorable Artillery Company of Massachusetts, 155
An Evening with Champions, 30
Anne Fontaine, 209
Annenberg Hall (Cambridge), 197–198
Antiques and collectibles, 202, 205
  Plymouth, 281
Antiquewear (Marblehead), 257
Appalachian Mountain Club, 52
Aquarium, New England, 147–148, 171
Architectural walking tours and classes, 178
Area codes, 284
Arlington Street Church, 192
Arnold Arboretum, 163–164
Art & Architecture Tours, 159
The Artful Hand Gallery, 207
Arthur M. Sackler Museum (Cambridge), 167, 197
Art museums
  Arthur M. Sackler Museum (Cambridge), 167, 197
  Boston Athenæum, 159
  DeCordova Museum and Sculpture Park (Lincoln), 252
  Fogg Art Museum (Cambridge), 167, 197
  Institute of Contemporary Art, 143–144
  Isabella Stewart Gardner Museum, 144, 226, 238
  Museum of Fine Arts, 145–146, 171, 238
  North Shore Arts Association (Gloucester), 269
  Peabody Essex Museum, 259, 261–262

ATMs (automated teller machines), 43–44, 284
Attucks, Crispus, 12, 154
August Moon Festival, 30
Aunt Sadie's, 213
Australia
  customs regulations, 25
  embassy and consul, 285
  passports, 290
  visas, 292
Auto insurance, 40–41

Babysitters, 284
The Back Bay, 59
  accommodations, 83–92
  restaurants, 123–128
  shopping, 209
  walking tour, 189–193
Back Bay Bicycles, 181
Back Bay Station, 34
Bank of America Pavilion, 221
The Bar at Taj Boston, 238
Barnes & Noble, 205–206
Barnes & Noble at Boston University, 207
Bars, 235–240
  brewpubs, 237–238
  hotel bars and lounges, 238
  Irish, 239
Baseball, 185
Basketball, 186
Battle Road Trail, 244–245
Bay State Cruise Company, 177
Beaches, 181
  the North Shore, 272
Beacon Hill, 58
  accommodations, 78–80
  exploring, 168–170
  historic houses, 161
  restaurants, 118
Beacon Hill Chocolates, 211
Beacon Hill Skate Shop, 184
Beacon Street, 168–169
Beadworks, 215
BeanTowne Coffee House (Cambridge), 240
Beantown Jazz Festival, 232
Beantown Trolleys, 175
Bearskin Neck (Rockport), 274
Beauport (Sleeper-McCann House; Gloucester), 270
Bed & breakfasts (B&Bs), 69
The Beehive, 235
Ben & Jerry's (Cambridge), 132
Berklee Performance Center, 221
Berk's Shoes (Cambridge), 218
Beth Israel Deaconess Medical Center (Cambridge), 286

Big Apple Circus, 27
Biking, 42, 181
  tours, 179
Bill's Bar, 234
Bird by Bird (Cambridge), 211
Bird-watching, Marblehead, 257
Bisexual Resource Center, 46
Black Heritage Trail, 160, 162
Black Ink (Cambridge), 213
Blackman Theater, 228
Black Nativity, 31
The Black Rose, 239
Blick Art Materials, 207
Blue Hills Trailside Museum, 172
Blue Man Group, 228
Boat trips and cruises
  from the airport, 33
  Boston Duck Tours, 174–175
  Boston Harbor Islands, 183
  Gloucester, 269
  Plymouth, 280
  sightseeing cruises, 176–177
  whale-watching, 178
Bobby From Boston, 219
BoltBus, 35
Bonanza, 36
Books, recommended, 17
Bookstores, 205–207
Boomerangs, 171
Borders, 206
BosTix, 221
Boston African American National Historic Site, 162
Boston Alliance of Gay and Lesbian Youth, 46
Boston Athenæum, 159
Boston Ballet, 221, 227
Boston Baroque, 226
Boston Beanstock Coffee Co., 240
Boston Beer Works, 237
Boston Bicycle, 181
Boston Billiard Club, 241
Boston Breakers, 185
Boston Bruins, 187
Boston By Foot, 172, 173–174
Boston By Little Feet, 172
Boston Cab, 38, 46
Boston Cannons, 185
Boston Celtics, 186
Boston Center for Adult Education, 178, 190
Boston Center for the Arts, 170, 221
Boston Children's Museum, 172–173
Boston Chocolate Tour, 180

Boston College
  football, 186
  hockey, 187
Boston Common, 150, 163
  accommodations, 83–85
  garage under, 42
  tennis courts, 184
Boston Common Information Center, 22
Boston Duck Tours, 174–175
Boston Film Festival, 30
Boston Fire Department T-shirt, 212
Boston Folk Festival, 232
Boston Harbor Cruises, 172, 176–178
Boston Harborfest, 29–30
Boston Harbor Hotel, nightlife, 233, 238
Boston Harbor Islands, 182, 183
Boston Harbor Water Taxi, 33, 38
Bostonian Society's museum, 153–154
Boston International Comedy & Movie Festival, 230
Boston Irish Tourism Association, 178
Boston Landmarks Orchestra, 224
Boston Light, 177
Boston Lyric Opera, 226
Boston Marathon, 28, 187–188, 193
Boston Massacre, 151
Boston Massacre Site, 154
Boston Movie Tours, 180
Boston Museum of Natural History, 192
Boston National Historical Park Visitor Center, 21, 148
Boston Park Rangers, 174
Boston Pops, 224, 225
  Concert and Fireworks Display, 29
Boston Pride March, 29
Boston Public Library, 159–160, 193
Boston Public Market, 217
Boston Red Sox, 185–186
  Opening Day, 27
Boston Sailing Center, 184
Boston Symphony Orchestra, 224–225
Boston Tea Party, 153
Boston Tea Party Reenactment, 31
Boston Underfoot, 174

Boston University, 168, 187, 228
Boston Vegetarian Society, 180
Boston Wine Festival, 26–27, 180
Boston Women's Heritage Trail, 162
Boutique Fabulous (Cambridge), 214
Brattle Book Shop, 206
Brattle Square (Cambridge), 199
Brattle Street (Cambridge), 164
Brattle Theatre (Cambridge), 199, 242
Brewpubs, 237–238
Brewster Gardens (Plymouth), 279
Bridges, 175
Brigham and Women's Hospital, 286
Brimstone Corner, 151
The Bristol, 238
British Imports (Plymouth), 281
Broadway Across America, 227
Bromfield Pen Shop, 202
Brookline accommodations, 92–94
Brookline Booksmith, 206
Brooks Brothers, 209
Broom Closet (Salem), 263
Brush Hill Tours, 36, 51, 211
Buckaroo's Mercantile (Cambridge), 213
Buckman Tavern (Lexington), 243, 245
Bulfinch, Charles, 150–152, 154, 156, 161, 162, 166, 168, 195
Bunker Hill Monument, 158
Bunker Hill Museum, 158
The Burren, 239
Busch-Reisinger Museum (Cambridge), 167
Business hours, 284
Bus travel
from the airport, 33
to Boston, 35–36
within Boston, 37–38
wheelchair-accessible, 46

C. Walsh Theatre, 228
Cabs, 38
from the airport, 33
wheelchair-accessible, 46
Calendar of events, 26–32
Calliope (Cambridge), 211

Cambridge
accommodations, 94–99
picnic provisions, 126
restaurants, 130–138
for outdoor dining, 129
sights and attractions, 164–168
Cambridge African American Heritage Trail, 162–163
Cambridge Antique Market, 202
Cambridge Bicycle, 181
Cambridge Center for Adult Education, 178
Cambridge Common, 198
Cambridge Hospital, 45, 286
Cambridge Multicultural Arts Center, 221
Cambridge Office for Tourism, 21
Cambridge River Festival, 29
Cambridge School of Culinary Arts, 180
CambridgeSide Galleria, 215
Canada
customs regulations, 25
embassy and consulate, 285
health insurance, 287
passports, 290
Canoeing, Concord, 249
Cantab Lounge, 233
Cape Ann, 253, 265, 268
Cape Ann Chamber of Commerce, 254
Cape Ann Historical Museum (Gloucester), 270
Cape Pond Ice (Gloucester), 269
Capt. Elias Davis House (Gloucester), 270
Cardullo's Gourmet Shoppe (Cambridge), 211–212
Carpenter Center for the Visual Arts (Cambridge), 197
Car rentals, 40–41
toll-free numbers and websites, 294
Car travel
to Boston, 34
within Boston, 40–42
Casablanca (Cambridge), 235
Cask 'n Flagon, 235
Celebrity Series, 226
Cellphones, 53
Central Branch YMCA, 182
Central Burying Ground, 163
Central Square World's Fair (Cambridge), 29
Central Wharf (Salem), 262

Chamber of Commerce (Concord), 248
Chamber of Commerce Visitor Center (Lexington), 244
Champions Tour, 187
Chanel, 209
Charlesbank Park, tennis courts, 184
Charles Hayden Planetarium, 147
Charles Playhouse, 228
Charles Riverboat Company cruises, 176–177
Charles River lock system and Boston Harbor, tour of, 177
Charles Street, 169
Charlestown accommodations, 80
Charlestown Navy Yard, 22
Charlestown Navy Yard Visitor Center, 158
CharlieCard, 36
CharlieTicket, 36
Cheers (Beacon Hill), 235
Cheers (Faneuil Hall Marketplace), 235
Cheese Shop (Concord), 252
Chestnut Street (Salem), 261
Children, families with
accommodations, 87
best activities for, 7–8
information and resources, 47
restaurants, 124
shopping
clothing, 211
toys and games, 219, 252, 257
Children's Hospital Boston, 286
Children's Museum, 27
Chilton, Mary, 152
Chinatown
accommodations, 81–83
restaurants, 118–121
Chinatown bus, 35
Chinatown Market Tour, 180
Chinese New Year, 27
Chinese stone lions (Cambridge), 198
Chocolate Tour, 180
Christ Church (Cambridge), 199
Christ Church (Old North Church), 156
Christina's (Cambridge), 132
Christmas pageant (Rockport), 274
Christmas Revels, 32
Christmas Walk (Marblehead), 255
Christopher Columbus Waterfront Park, 154

Church of the Covenant, 192
Citi Wang Theatre, 221, 227
City Cab, 38
CityPass, 142
City Sports, 208
CityView Trolleys, 175–176
City Water Taxi, 33, 38
Clarendon Park, 170
Classical music, 224–226
The Closet, 219
Club and music scene, 229–234
Club Café, 239
Club Passim (Cambridge), 232
Coffeehouses and tea salons, 240–241
College merchandise, 207
College Sports Extravaganza, 27
Collette Vacations, 51
Colonial Drug (Cambridge), 218
Colonial Lantern Tour (Plymouth), 279
Colonial Theatre, 227
Comcast Center, 224
Comedy clubs, 230
The Comedy Connection at Faneuil Hall, 230
The Comedy Studio (Cambridge), 230
Commonwealth Avenue Mall, 190
Commonwealth Shakespeare Company, 228
Community Boating, 184
Concord, 247–253
Concord Bookshop, 252
Concord Museum, 248–250
Concord Trailways, 36
Constitution, USS ("Old Ironsides"), 157–158
    cruises, 176
    Museum, 158
Consulates, 285
Coolidge Corner Movie Theater, 242
Copley Flair, 213
Copley Place, 209, 215–216
    garage at, 42
Copley Square, 192
    accommodations, 85–92
Copp's Hill Burying Ground, 157
Corner (Cambridge), 234
Counting house (Salem), 261
Crackerjacks (Rockport), 276
CraftBoston, 208
Craft galleries, 207
Crafts at the Castle, 208
Craft supplies, 207–208
Crane Beach (Ipswich), 272

Crate & Barrel, 214
Credit cards, 44
Crocker Park (Marblehead), 256
Crosby's Marketplace (Marblehead), 258
Cross (Cambridge), 213
Crow Haven Corner (Salem), 263
Crow's Nest (Gloucester), 269
Cuoio, 218
Curious George Books & Toys (Cambridge), 206
Curley, James Michael, 155
Currency and currency exchange, 44
Custom House (Salem), 262
Customs regulations, 25
Cutler Majestic Theatre, 224
CVS, 285
Cyclorama, 170

Dance clubs, 230–231
Dance performances, 227
Dawes, William, 152
Daylight saving time, 291
Debit cards, 44
DeCordova Museum and Sculpture Park (Lincoln), 252
DeLux Cafe, 235
Derby House (Salem), 262
Derby Wharf (Salem), 262
Destination Plymouth, 281
Destination Salem, 260
Dining, 102–138. See also Restaurant Index
    afternoon tea, 125
    alfresco, 129
    the Back Bay, 123–128
    Beacon Hill, 118
    best, 5–6, 102–103
    for breakfast and Sunday brunch, 114
    Cambridge, 130–138
    Chinatown/Theater District, 118–121
    by cuisine, 104–106
    dim sum, 120
    Downtown Crossing, 117–118
    family-friendly, 124
    Faneuil Hall Marketplace & the Financial District, 114–117
    Gloucester, 271–273
    Kenmore Square to Brookline, 128–130
    late-night, 242
    Lexington, 247
    Marblehead, 258
    the North End, 107–114

Plymouth, 283
    for, quick bites, 126
    Rockport, 276–277
    Salem, 264
    the South End, 121–123
    steakhouses, 122
    The Waterfront, 106–107
    what's new in, 2
Diptyque, 214
Disabilities, travelers with, 45–46
Discount shopping, 208–209
Discovering Justice, 178, 179
Dogtown Book Shop (Gloucester), 270
Downtown accommodations, 71–77
Downtown Crossing, 58
    accommodations, 75–77
    restaurants, 117–118
Dr. Paul Dudley White Charles River Bike Path, 181, 184
Dragon Boat Festival, 29
Dress, 209
Drinking laws, 284–285
Driving rules, 42
Drugstores, 285
DSW Shoe Warehouse, 208
Duck Tours, 64
Dyer, Mary, 150

Eastern Standard, 238
East Gloucester, 269
Eddie Bauer Outlet, 208
Eddy, Mary Baker, Library, 160
Elderhostel, 52
Electricity, 285
Elephant Walk, 180
1154 Lill Studio, 210
Eliot House (Cambridge), 30
Emack & Bolio's (Cambridge), 132
Embassies and consulates, 285
Emerald Necklace, 163, 174
Emergencies, 286
Emerson, Ralph Waldo, 248, 250
    House (Concord), 251
Emerson College Bookstore, 207
Emerson Hall (Cambridge), 197
Emmanuel Church, 192
Emmanuel Music, 227
Entry requirements, 24–25
Envi, 209
Ermenegildo Zegna, 209
Escapes North, 254
Escorted general-interest tours, 51

The Esplanade, in-line skating, 183
Essex, 266
The Estate, 231
Evacuation Day, 286
Exeter Street Theater, 192

Families with children
accommodations, 87
best activities for, 7–8
information and resources, 47
restaurants, 124
shopping
clothing, 211
toys and games, 219, 252, 257
theater, 228
Faneuil, Peter, 151
Faneuil Hall, 154–155
Faneuil Hall Marketplace, 58, 142, 154, 171, 216
accommodations, 71–75
Casa Romero, 129
information booth at, 22
Parish Café and Bar, 129
picnic provisions, 126
restaurants, 114–117
with outdoor seating, 129
Stephanie's on Newbury, 129
Fashions (clothing), 209–211
vintage and secondhand, 219
Fax machines, 291
Fenway Park, 185
ticket office, 186
tours, 186
Ferries, 38, 176
Salem, 260
Festivals and special events, 26–32
Fiedler, Arthur, 190
54th Massachusetts Colored Regiment, 150
Filene's Basement, 208–209
Film festivals, 28, 30
Films, 241–242
The Financial District, 58
accommodations, 75–77
restaurants, 114–117
First Baptist Church, 191, 192
First Night, 32
First Public School, 152
Fitcorp, 182
Flat Top Johnny's (Cambridge), 241
Fogg Art Museum (Cambridge), 167, 197
Folk music, 232

Food and cuisine, 19–20
classes and tours for foodies, 180
shopping, 211
Football, 186
Fort Sewall (Marblehead), 256
The Fours, 235–236
Fourth of July, 158
Boston Pops concert, 225
Franklin, Benjamin
birthplace, 153
Statue, 152
Franklin Park Zoo, 173
Freedom Trail, 22, 174
The Freedom Trail, 148–159
audio tour narrative, 151
Freedom Trail Foundation, 150
Freedom Trail Players, 150
Freedom Trail Week, 28
Free Friday Flicks at the Hatch Shell, 241–242
Free or almost free activities, best, 6–7
French, Daniel Chester, 193, 196
French Library Alliance Française, 178
Fresh Pond Golf Course (Cambridge), 182
Fridays at Trinity, 227
Fritz, 240
Frog Pond, 182
Frommers.com, 50
Fung Wah, 35

Gallery NAGA, 205
Game On! Sports Cafe, 236
The Garment District (Cambridge), 219
Garrison, William Lloyd, 14, 151, 160
Gasoline, 286
Gay, Lesbian, Bisexual and Transgender Helpline, 46
Gay Men's Health Crisis, 289
Gays and lesbians, 46
bars and clubs, 239–240
Boston Pride March, 29
Georges Island, 183
Ghosts & Gravestones tour, 180
Gibson House Museum, 161
Gifts and souvenirs, 212–214
Glass Flowers (Cambridge), 166
Globe Corner Bookstore (Cambridge), 206
Globus and Cosmos, 51
Gloucester, 266–273

Gloucester Stage Company, 269
Go Boston Card, 142
Golf, 181–182
tournaments, 187
Government Center, 58
Grafton Street (Cambridge), 236
The Grand Canal, 239
Grasshopper Shop (Concord), 252
Greater Boston Convention & Visitors Bureau, 21, 22, 26
Greenward, 214
Grendel's Den (Cambridge), 236
Grolier Poetry Book Shop (Cambridge), 206
Gropius House (Lincoln), 252
GSM (Global System for Mobile Communications), 53
Guerrilla Queer Bar, 239
Gyms, 182

Habitat for Humanity, 52
Halibut Point State Park (Rockport), 274–275
Hall of the North American Indian (Cambridge), 167
Hamilton, Alexander, statue of, 191
Hancock, John, 151
Hancock-Clarke House (Lexington), 244, 246
Handel & Haydn Society, 225–226
H&M, 209
Harbor Express, 183
Harborfest, 29–30
Harbor Sweets (Salem), 263
Harborwalk, 143
Hard Rock Cafe, 233
Hart Nautical Galleries (Cambridge), 167
Harvard, John, Statue of (Cambridge), 165, 196
Harvard Art Museums (Cambridge), 167
Harvard Book Store (Cambridge), 200, 206
Harvard College Observatory (Cambridge), 168
The Harvard Coop (Cambridge), 207
Harvard Film Archive (Cambridge), 242
Harvard Hall (Cambridge), 194–195

Harvard Lampoon Castle (Cambridge), 200
Harvard Museum of Natural History, 198
Harvard Museum of Natural History (Cambridge), 165–167, 171
Harvard Square (Cambridge), 164, 194
  information kiosk, 22
  restaurants, 130–134
  walking tour, 193–200
Harvard University (Cambridge), 164–167, 186, 187, 228
Harvard Yard (Cambridge), 165, 194
Harvard-Yenching Institute (Cambridge), 198
Hatch Shell, 190, 220
  Free Friday Flicks at the, 241–242
Haunted Footsteps Ghost Tour (Salem), 260
Haunted Happenings (Salem), 260
Hawthorne, Nathaniel, 262
  The House of the Seven Gables (Salem), 261
  The Wayside (Concord), 251
Haymarket, 154
Head of the Charles Regatta, 30, 188
Health concerns, 44–45
Health insurance, 286–287
Healthworks, 182
Helen's Leather Shop, 218
Heritage Days (Salem), 260
Hermès of Paris, 209
Herrell's (Cambridge), 132
High Gear Jewelry, 215
Hiking, 182
Hi-Rise at the Blacksmith House (Cambridge), 199
Historic houses, 161–162
Historic New England, 161
  tours, 178
History of Boston, 9–16
HIV-positive visitors, 289
Hockey, 187
Holden Chapel (Cambridge), 195
Holidays, 286
Hollis Hall (Cambridge), 195
Holyoke Center (Cambridge), 200
Home and garden products, 214
The Hong Kong (Cambridge), 236

Hooper-Hathaway House (Salem), 261
Horse racing, 187
Hospitals, 45, 286
Hotel Hot Line, 68
Hotels, 67–101. See also Accommodations Index
  The Back Bay, 83–92
  bars and lounges at, 238
  Beacon Hill/North Station/North End, 78–80
  best, 5, 70–71
  Cambridge, 94–99
  Charlestown, 80
  Chinatown/Theater District, 81–83
  Copley Square and Hynes Convention Center, 85–92
  downtown, 71–77
  family-friendly, 87
  Financial District & Downtown Crossing, 75–77
  Gloucester, 271
  with gyms, 182
  for last-minute planners, 68
  Marblehead, 257–258
  at and near the airport, 99–101
  outskirts and Brookline, 92–94
  Plymouth, 281–283
  Rockport, 276
  Salem, 263–264
  saving on, 68–69
  South Boston Waterfront (Seaport District), 80–81
  The South End, 83
  The Waterfront & Faneuil Hall Marketplace, 71–75
  what's new in, 1–2
Hotlines, 286
House of Blues, 237
The House of the Seven Gables (Salem), 261
Huntington Avenue, 59
Huntington Theatre Company, 228
Hynes Convention Center, accommodations, 85–92

Ice cream, 132
Ice skating and in-line skating, 182–184
Immigration and customs clearance, 32
Improv Asylum, 230
Independent Film Festival of Boston, 28

Independent Taxi Operators Association (ITOA), 38
Injeanius, 210
InLine Club of Boston, 184
Insight Vacations, 51
Institute of Contemporary Art, 143–144
Insurance, 286–288
  car-rental, 40–41
The International Ecotourism Society (TIES), 49
International Poster Gallery, 205
International Student Identity Card (ISIC), 48
International Student Travel Confederation (ISTC), 47–48
International Youth Travel Card (IYTC), 48
Internet access, 53–54, 288
Intrigue, 238
Ireland
  embassy and consulate, 285
  passports, 290
  visas, 292
Irish bars, 239
Isabella Stewart Gardner Museum, 144, 226, 238
Italian-American Feasts, 29
Itineraries, suggested, 60–66

Jacques, 240
Jamaica Plain, 170–171
James Hook & Co., 216
James Rego Square (Paul Revere Mall), 156
Jazz and blues, 232–234
JazzWeek, 232
Jean Therapy, 210
Jenney Pond (Plymouth), 279
Jeremiah Lee Mansion (Marblehead), 256–257
Jewelry, 215
Jillian's Boston, 241
Jogging, 184
John Adams Courthouse, 179
John F. Kennedy National Historic Site, 161
John F. Kennedy Park (Cambridge), 200
John F. Kennedy Presidential Library and Museum, 144–145, 171
John Harvard's Brew House (Cambridge), 237–238
John Joseph Moakley Federal Courthouse, 178
John Lewis, 215
Johnny Cupcakes, 210

Johnny D's Uptown Restaurant & Music Club, 231
Johnston Gate (Cambridge), 194
Joie de Vivre (Cambridge), 213
JP Licks Homemade Ice Cream, 171
    Cambridge, 132
Judson B. Coit Observatory at Boston University, 168

Kate spade, 209
Kendall Square Cinema (Cambridge), 242
Kendall Square Community Skating, 183
Kenmore Square, 59–60
Kennedy, John F., 150
    National Historic Site, 161
    Presidential Library and Museum, 144–145, 171
Kids
    accommodations, 87
    best activities for, 7–8
    information and resources, 47
    restaurants, 124
    shopping
        clothing, 211
        toys and games, 219, 252, 257
    theater, 228
Kiehl's, 218
King, Martin Luther, Jr., Birthday Celebration, 26
King Hooper Mansion (Marblehead), 257
Kings, 241
King's Chapel and Burying Ground, 152
King's Chapel Noon Hour Recitals, 227
Koo De Kir, 214

L. A. Burdick Chocolates (Cambridge), 199
Lacrosse, 185
Lafayette, Marquis de, 158
    House, 256
Lane, Fitz Henry, 270
La Perla, 209
Le Corbusier (Cambridge), 197
Legal aid, 288
Legal Sea Foods Fresh by Mail, 216
Legends Tour, 187
Le Grand David and His Own Spectacular Magic Company, 229

Lekker, 215
Lexington, 243–247
Lexington Historical Society, 245
Liberty Ride (Lexington and Concord), 246
Liberty Travel, 51
Lilac Sunday, 28
Lily's Apothecary (Plymouth), 281
LimoLiner, 35
Limousines, from the airport, 33
LinkPass, 37, 142
List Visual Arts Center (Cambridge), 168
Little Brewster Island, 177
Little Women (Alcott), 250–251
Lizard Lounge (Cambridge), 231
Lizzy's (Cambridge), 132
Lobster Tales (Plymouth), 280
Loeb Drama Center (Cambridge), 228
Logan International Airport, 32
    accommodations at and near, 99–101
    getting into town from, 32–34
Longfellow, Henry Wadsworth, 17, 155, 156, 244
Longfellow Bridge, 175
Longfellow National Historic Site (Cambridge), 164, 199
Long Wharf, 175
Longy School of Music (Cambridge), 226
Looney Tunes Records & Tapes, 217
Lost and found, 288
Louis Boston, 210
Louisburg Square, 169
Lush, 218
Lyric Stage, 228

McKim, Charles F., 159, 193, 279
Mail, 289
Main Street Antiques (Plymouth), 281
Make Way for Ducklings, 190
Malls and shopping centers, 215–217
Manchester-Boston Regional Airport, 31
Manchester Shuttle, 31
Mapparium, 160
Maps, 22, 289

Marathon, 187–188
Marathon, Boston, 28, 193
Marblehead, 254–258
Marblehead Arts Association & Gallery, 257
Markets, 217
Mary Baker Eddy Library, 160
Mascio-Ricci (Concord), 252
Massachusetts Audubon Society, 52
Massachusetts Audubon Society bird sanctuary (Marblehead), 257
Massachusetts Bay Lines, 178
    harbor tours, 176
Massachusetts Bay Transportation Authority (MBTA), 36–37
Massachusetts General Hospital, 45, 286
Massachusetts Golf Association, 181
Massachusetts Hall (Cambridge), 165, 194
Massachusetts Institute of Technology (MIT; Cambridge), 167–168, 228
Massachusetts Office of Travel and Tourism, 21
Massachusetts State House, 150
MassBike, 181
MassCap (Massachusetts Handicap), 187
Mather family, 169
Maupintour, 51
Mayflower II (Plymouth), 280
Mayflower (Plymouth), 277
MEDEX Assistance, 287
Medical conditions, 289
Medical insurance, 286–287
Medical requirements for entry, 24–25
MedjetAssist, 287
Memorial Church (Cambridge), 196
Memorial Drive, 181, 183–184
Memorial Hall (Cambridge), 197
Ménage Gallery (Gloucester), 270
Metro Cab, 38
The Middle East (Cambridge), 234
Midwest Airlines Vacations, 50
Minuteman Bikeway, 181
Minute Man National Historical Park, 244, 248–249
Minute Man National Historical Park (Lexington), 243

Minute Man statue (Lexington), 245, 249
MIT Coop (Cambridge), 207
MIT (Massachusetts Institute of Technology; Cambridge), 167–168
MIT Museum (Cambridge), 168
Modern Pastry, 113
Money and costs, 43–44
Monument Square (Concord), 252
Motif No. 1 (Rockport), 274
Mount Auburn Cemetery (Cambridge), 164, 166
Mount Auburn Hospital (Cambridge), 45, 286
Mount Vernon Street, 168–169
Movies, 241–242
    Boston in, 17–18
    tours, 180
Moxie, 218
Mr. Dooley's Boston Tavern, 239
Mugar Omni Theater, 147
Munroe Tavern (Lexington), 246
Muse's Window (Concord), 252
Museum-Goers' Month, 28
Museum of African American History, 160
Museum of Fine Arts Gift Shop, 213–214
Museum of Fine Arts (MFA), 145–146, 171, 238
Museum of Science, 146–147, 171
Museum of Useful Things (Cambridge), 213
Museums. *See also* Art museums
    best, 7
Music, 19
    classical, 224–226
    folk, 232
    jazz and blues, 232–234
    rock, 234
Music stores, 217
Mystery Train (Gloucester), 270
Mytown multicultural youth walking tours, 170

Nameless Coffeehouse, 232
Nanette Lepore, 209
Nashoba Brook Bakery (Concord), 252
National Heritage Museum (Lexington), 246

National Offshore One Design (NOOD) Regatta (Marblehead), 255
National Park Service Regional Visitor Center (Salem), 260
Natural History, Boston Museum of, 192
Natural History, Harvard Museum of (Cambridge), 165–167, 198
NCAA Women's Frozen Four, 27, 187
Ned's Groceria (Gloucester), 271–272
Neighborhoods. *See also specific neighborhoods*
    brief descriptions of, 55–60
    exploring, 168–171
Newbury Comics, 217
Newbury Street, 191, 209
New England Aquarium, 147–148, 171
    whale-watching trips, 178
New England Conservatory of Music, 226
The New England Holocaust Memorial, 155
New England Patriots, 186
New England Revolution, 185
New England Spring Flower Show, 27
Newspapers and magazines, 289–290
Newton Commonwealth Golf Course, 181–182
New Zealand
    customs regulations, 25
    embassy and consulate, 285
    passports, 290
    visas, 292
Nichols House Museum, 161
Nielsen Gallery, 205
Nightlife, 220–242
    bars, 235–240
    club and music scene, 229–234
    coffeehouses and tea salons, 240–241
    current listings, 220
    lectures and readings, 242
    performing arts, 220–229
    pool and bowling, 241
    suggested itineraries, 65
    tickets, 220
    what's new in, 3
Nini's Corner (Cambridge), 290
North Bridge Visitor Center (Concord), 249
Northeastern University, 186, 187

Northeastern University Bookstore, 207
The North End, 55, 58
    accommodations, 78–80
    exploring, 169
    restaurants, 107–114
North End Market Tours, 180
North of Boston Convention & Visitors Bureau, 254
The North Shore, 253–254
    beaches, 272
North Shore Arts Association (Gloucester), 269
North Station, 34
    accommodations, 78–80
The Nutcracker, 30–31

Oak Bar, 238
Oktoberfest (Cambridge), 30
Old Burying Ground (Cambridge), 199
Old City Hall, 152
Old Corner Bookstore Building, 152–153
Old Granary Burying Ground, 151
"Old Ironsides" (USS *Constitution*), 157–158
The Old Manse (Concord), 250
Old North Church, 28, 156
Old South Church, 227
Old South Meeting House, 153
Old State House Museum, 153–154
Old Town House (Marblehead), 256
Old Town (Marblehead), 254
Old Town Trolley Tours, 175
Old Yard (Cambridge), 194
Olmsted, Frederick Law, 163, 174
Oona's (Cambridge), 219
Opera Boston, 226
Opera House, 227
Orchard House (Concord), 250
Orpheum Theater, 224
Otis, James, 151
Otis House Museum, 162
Outdoor activities, 180–184
    best, 7
Outlet shopping, 211
Out of Town News (Cambridge), 194, 290

Package deals, 41, 50–51
Pain, Elizabeth, 152
Panificio, 190
Paper House (Rockport), 275

Paper Source, 207–208
Paradise (Cambridge), 240
Paradise Rock Club, 234
Parking, 41–42
Park Street Church, 151
Passports, 24, 290
Patriots Day, 28, 286
  Red Sox game on, 27
Paul Revere House, 28, 155, 172
Paul Revere Mall (James Rego Square), 156
Peabody Essex Museum, 259, 261–262
Peabody Museum of Archaeology & Ethnology (Cambridge), 167, 198
Pearl Art & Craft Supplies (Cambridge), 208
Penzeys, 212
Pepper Gallery, 205
The Perfect Storm (Junger), 17, 18, 266, 269
Performing arts, 220–229
  classical music, 224–226
  concert and performance series, 226
  dance, 227
  free and almost free concerts, 226–227
  theater, 227–229
  venues, 220–221, 224
Perfume and cosmetics, 218
Peter Pan, 36
Peter Pan Bonanza, 31
Petrol, 286
PGA Tour, 187
Pho Republique, 236
PhotoWalks, 180
Pickering Wharf (Salem), 263, 264
Picnic provisions, 126
Pierce/Hichborn House, 155
Pierre Lallement Bike Path, 181
Pilgrim Hall Museum (Plymouth), 280
Pilgrim's Progress (Plymouth), 281
The Place, 236
Planning your trip, 1, 21–54
  calendar of events, 26–32
  customs regulations, 25
  entry requirements, 24–25
  escorted general-interest tours, 51
  getting around, 36–42
  health concerns, 44–45
  Internet access, 53–54
  money and costs, 43–44
  package deals, 50–51

safety concerns, 45
seasons, 25–26
special-interest trips, 51–52
specialized travel resources, 45–48
sustainable tourism, 48
telephones, 52–53
traveling to Boston, 32–36
visitor information, 21–22
weather, 26
Plimoth Plantation (Plymouth), 30, 280–281
The Plough & Stars (Cambridge), 239
Plymouth, 277–283
Plymouth & Brockton, 36
Plymouth Rock, 278–279
Plymouth Rock Trolley, 278
Poison Control Center, 286
Police, 290
Porter Exchange (Cambridge), restaurants, 138
Porter Square Books (Cambridge), 206
The Prado, 156
Provincetown
  cruises to, 177
  ferries to, 177
Prudential Center, garage, 42
Prudential Center Skywalk Observatory, 146, 171
Prudential Information Center, 22
Public Garden, 163, 172, 189
  accommodations, 83–85
Pucker Gallery, 205
Puerto Rican Festival and Parade, 29
Puppet Showplace Theatre, 229
The Purple Shamrock, 236

Quincy Market, 142–143, 154
Quincy Market Colonnade, 216

Race Week (Marblehead), 255
Radcliffe Yard (Cambridge), 199
Radius, 236
Rainfall, average, 25
Ralph Waldo Emerson House (Concord), 251
Rape Crisis, 286
Real Deal Jazz Club & Cafe, 221, 232
Red Sox, 185–186
  Opening Day, 27

The Red Wagon, 211
Regattabar (Cambridge), 233
Restaurants, 102–138. *See also* Restaurant Index
  for, quick bites, 126
  afternoon tea, 125
  alfresco, 129
  the Back Bay, 123–128
  Beacon Hill, 118
  best, 5–6, 102–103
  for breakfast and Sunday brunch, 114
  Cambridge, 130–138
  Chinatown/Theater District, 118–121
  by cuisine, 104–106
  dim sum, 120
  Downtown Crossing, 117–118
  family-friendly, 124
  Faneuil Hall Marketplace & the Financial District, 114–117
  Gloucester, 271–273
  Kenmore Square to Brookline, 128–130
  late-night, 242
  Lexington, 247
  Marblehead, 258
  the North End, 107–114
  Plymouth, 283
  Rockport, 276–277
  Salem, 264
  the South End, 121–123
  steakhouses, 122
  The Waterfront, 106–107
  what's new in, 2
Restaurant Week, 116
Retire Beckett House (Salem), 261
Revere, Paul, 151
  equestrian statue of, 156
  House, 28, 155, 172
Richardson, H. H., 192, 196
Ringling Brothers and Barnum & Bailey Circus, 30
Road Scholar, 51–52
Robert Gould Shaw Memorial, 162
Robert Klein Gallery, 205
Rock music, 234
Rockport, 273–277
Rockport Art Association, 274
Rockport Chamber Music Festival, 274
Rocky Neck Art Colony (Gloucester), 269
Rowes Wharf Bar, 238
Rowes Wharf Water Transport, 33, 38

Rowing, 188
The Roxy, 231
Ryles Jazz Club (Cambridge), 233

Sacred Cod, 150
Sacred Heart Church, 155
Safety concerns, 45
Sail Boston 2009, 29
Sailing, 184
St. Patrick's Day Celebrations, 27
St. Stephen's, 156
Saint-Gaudens, Augustus, 150
Salem, 258–266
Salem Chamber of Commerce, 260
Salem Ferry, 260
Salem Haunted Happenings, 30
Salem Maritime Festival, 260
Salem Maritime National Historic Site, 262
Salem Trolley, 260
Salem Willows, 261
Salem Witch Museum, 262–263
Sales tax, 201
Salumeria Italiana, 212
Samaritans Suicide Prevention, 286
Samariteens, 286
Sanders Theatre (Cambridge), 197, 224
Savenor's Market (Cambridge), 126, 212
Schoenhof's Foreign Books (Cambridge), 207
School Vacation Week, 27
Science Center (Cambridge), 198
Scullers Jazz Club, 233
Seaport Express, 38
Seasons, 25–26
Semitic Museum (Cambridge), 198
Senior travel, 47
Sephora, 218
Sever Hall (Cambridge), 196, 197
Shake the Tree, 214
Shear Madness, 228
Shoes and boots, 218
Shopping, 201–219
    areas for, 201–202
    Concord, 252
    Gloucester, 270
    Lexington, 246–247
    Marblehead, 257
    Plymouth, 281

Rockport, 275–276
Salem, 263
    what's new in, 2–3
The Shops at Prudential Center, 216–217
Shubert Theatre, 227
Shubie's (Marblehead), 258
Sights and attractions, 139–180
    Cambridge, 162, 164–168
    the Freedom Trail, 148–159
    historic houses, 161–162
    for kids, 171–173
    money-saving options, 142
    neighborhoods, 168–171
    parks and gardens, 163–164
    top attractions, 139–148
    what's new in, 2
Silvertone Bar & Grill, 236–237
Simons IMAX Theatre, 148
Singing Beach (Manchester-by-the-Sea), 272
Sleeper-McCann House (Beauport; Gloucester), 270
Sleepy Hollow Cemetery (Concord), 251
Smoking, 290
    at hotels, 70
Soccer, 185
Society of Arts and Crafts, 207
Somerville Theater, 242
South Boston Waterfront (Seaport District), 58–59
    accommodations, 80–81
South Bridge Boathouse (Concord), 249
The South End, 170
    accommodations, 83
    restaurants, 121–123
South Station, 34, 36
Southwest Airlines, 31
Southwest Airlines Vacations, 50
SoWa Open Market, 217
Special events and festivals, 26–32
Spectacle Island, 183
Spectator sports, 184–188
Spike's Junkyard Dogs, 126
Sports Museum of New England, 171, 185
Spring Flower Show, New England, 27
Stage Fort Park (Gloucester), 269
Stata Center (Cambridge), 167–168
State House, 168
STA Travel, 48

Stellabella Toys (Cambridge), 219
Stereo Jack's, 217
Stir, 180
Stoughton Hall (Cambridge), 195
Street Performers Festival, 28–29
Stuart Street Playhouse, 228
Student travel, 47–48
Studio 73, 151
Subway, 37
    from the airport, 33
    wheelchair-accessible, 45
Suffolk Downs, 187
Suffolk University Bookstore, 207
Super Trolley Tours, 176
Sustainable tourism, 48–50
Swan Boats, 163, 172, 189
Swan Boats Return to the Public Garden, 28
Symphony Hall, 224
    tours of, 174
Syringe-administered medications, 289

T. F. Green Airport, 31
Tanglewood, 225
Tanner Rock Fountain (Cambridge), 198
Tauck World Discovery, 51
Taxes, 290–291
Taxis, 38
    from the airport, 33
    wheelchair-accessible, 46
TD Banknorth Garden, 185, 224
Tealuxe (Cambridge), 240
Tech Superpowers, 288
Telecharge, 220
Telegraph and telex services, 291
Telephones, 52–53
Television shows set in Boston, 18–19
Temperatures, average, 25
Tennis, 184
Tercentenary Theater (Cambridge), 196
Thanksgiving Celebration, 30
Theater, 227–229
    Gloucester, 269
Theater District
    accommodations, 81–83
    restaurants, 118–121
Therapy, 210
1369 Coffee House (Cambridge), 241
Thomas Pink, 210

Thoreau, Henry David, 248, 250, 251
Ticketmaster, 220
Time zones, 291
Tipping, 291
Toad (Cambridge), 234
Toilets, 291
Top of the Hub, 237
The Tortoise & Hare, 193
"Tory Row" (Cambridge), 164
Tours, 173–180. See also Walking tours
    biking, 179
    Liberty Ride (Lexington and Concord), 246
    orientation, 173–175
    Plymouth, 279–280
    specialty, 178–179
Town Taxi, 38
Toys and games, 219
Toy Shop of Concord (Concord), 252
Trader Joe's, 126, 212
Trafalgar Tours, 51
Train travel, to Boston, 34–35
Transportation, 36–42
    Concord, 248
    Lexington, 244
    Marblehead, 254–255
    Plymouth, 277–278
    Rockport, 273
    Salem, 259–260
    senior discounts, 47
Travel Assistance International, 287
Travel CUTS, 48
Traveler's checks, 44
Travelex Insurance Services, 288
Travel Guard International, 288
Traveling to Boston, 32
Travel insurance, 287–288
Travel Insured International, 288
TravelSafe, 288
Trident Booksellers & Café, 241
Trinity Church, 192
Trip cancellation insurance, 287–288
Trolleys, 37
Trolley tours, 175–176
T.T. the Bear's Place (Cambridge), 231–232
Tuck's Candy Factory (Rockport), 276
Tufts Medical Center, 45, 286
Turtle, 210–211
21st Amendment, 237
Twilight, 210

United Kingdom
    customs regulations, 25
    embassy and consulate, 285
    health insurance, 287
    passports, 290
    visas, 292
United Vacations, 50
University Hall (Cambridge), 195
Urban AdvenTours, 179
US Airways Vacations, 50
USIT, 48
USS Constitution cruises, 176
USS Constitution Museum, 158
USS Constitution "Old Ironsides," 157–158

Velvet Fly, 219
Vendome Memorial, 191
Vermont Transit, 31, 36
Via Matta, 237
Virgin Holidays, 50
Visas, 24, 292
Visitor information, 21–22
    Concord, 248
    Lexington, 244
    Marblehead, 255
    the North Shore and Cape Ann, 254
    Plymouth, 278
    Rockport, 274
    Salem, 260
Voice over Internet protocol (VoIP), 53
Volunteer and working trips, 52
Volvo Ocean Race 2008-2009, 28
Vose Galleries of Boston, 205
VSA Arts Massachusetts, 46

Wadsworth House (Cambridge), 194
Walden Pond State Reservation (Concord), 249
Walgreens, 285
Walking tours, 172–174
    Marblehead, 256
    with photography tips, 180
    Salem, 260
    self-guided, 189–200
        The Back Bay, 189–193
        Harvard Square (Cambridge), 193–200
Wally's Cafe, 233–234

Wang YMCA of Chinatown, 182
WardMaps.com (Cambridge), 214
Washington, George, 13, 153, 156, 164, 194, 198
    portrait of, 145
    statue of, 191
    equestrian statue, 190
Washington Street, 59
The Waterfront, 55
    accommodations, 71–75
    restaurants, 106–107
Water shuttles, 38–40
Water taxis, 38
    from the airport, 33
The Wayside (Concord), 251
Weather, 26
Websites, 22
West Concord shopping district, 252
West Elm, 215
The Western Front (Cambridge), 232
Western Union, 289, 291
Whale-watching, 172, 178
    Gloucester, 265
    Plymouth, 280
Wheelchair accessibility, 45–46
Whittard of Chelsea, 212
Widener Library (Cambridge), 165, 196
Wi-Fi access, 53–54, 288
    at Logan International Airport, 32
Wilbur Theater, 227–228
William J. Devine Golf Course, 182
Windsor Button, 208
Wine Festival, Boston, 26–27
Wingaersheek Beach (Gloucester), 272
Winter Island Park (Salem), 261
Winthrop, John, 152
Wish, 211
World Music, 226
Worldwide Assistance Services, 287
Wrentham Village Premium Outlets, 211

Yellow Cab (Cambridge), 38
Yin Yu Tang (Salem), 261

Zero Arrow Theatre, 228
Zoo, Franklin Park, 173
ZuZu (Cambridge), 234

ACCOMMODATIONS

Anthony's Town House, 94
Atlantis Oceanfront Motor Inn
  (Gloucester), 271
Best Western Bass Rocks Ocean
  Inn (Gloucester), 271
Best Western Boston/The Inn at
  Longwood Medical, 93
Best Western Cold Spring
  (Plymouth), 282
Best Western Hotel Tria
  (Cambridge), 98–99
Boston Harbor Hotel, 71, 74
Boston Marriott Copley Place,
  87–88
Boston Marriott Long Wharf, 74
Boston Park Plaza Hotel &
  Towers, 84–85
Brookline Courtyard by
  Marriott, 93
Bulfinch Hotel, 79
Captain's Bounty Motor Inn
  (Rockport), 276
Chandler Inn Hotel, 83
The Charles Hotel, 94
Charlesmark Hotel, 90
Coach House Inn (Salem), 263
Colonnade Hotel Boston, 85,
  87
Comfort Inn & Suites
  Boston/Airport, 100–101
Concord's Colonial Inn, 253
Copley Square Hotel, 85
Courtyard Boston Cambridge,
  97
Courtyard by Marriott Boston
  Copley Square, 88
Doubletree Guest Suites, 87,
  92–93
Doubletree Hotel Boston
  Downtown, 82–83
Eliot Hotel, 86
Embassy Suites Hotel Boston
  at Logan Airport, 100
The Fairmont Copley Plaza, 86
Fifteen Beacon, 78
Four Seasons Hotel, 83–84
Hampton Inn
  Boston/Cambridge, 98
Hampton Inn Boston Logan
  Airport, 100
Harbor Light Inn, 258
Harborside Inn, 75
Harvard Square Hotel
  (Cambridge), 99
Hawthorne Hotel (Salem),
  263–264
Hilton Boston Back Bay, 88–89

Hilton Boston Financial
  District, 75–76
Hilton Boston Logan Airport,
  100
Hilton Garden Inn (Plymouth),
  282
Holiday Inn Boston at Beacon
  Hill, 79
Holiday Inn Boston Brookline,
  87, 93
Holiday Inn Express Hotel &
  Suites (Cambridge), 99
Hostelling International-
  Boston, 91–92
Hostelling International-Boston
  at Fenway, 93–94
Hotel Commonwealth, 92
Hotel Marlowe, 87
Hotel 140, 90
Hyatt Harborside, 99–100
Hyatt Regency Boston Financial
  District, 76
Hyatt Regency Cambridge, 87
The Hyatt Regency Cambridge,
  97
The Inn at Harvard
  (Cambridge), 97
Inn on Cove Hill (Caleb
  Norwood, Jr., House;
  Rockport), 276
InterContinental Boston, 74
John Carver Inn & Spa
  (Plymouth), 282
The John Hancock Hotel &
  Conference Center, 90–91
Jurys Boston Hotel, 89
The Langham, Boston, 76
Le Méridien Cambridge, 97–98
The Lenox Hotel, 86–87
The Liberty Hotel, 78
Longwood Inn, 94
Mandarin Oriental, Boston, 85
Marriott Residence Inn Boston
  Harbor, 80
The MidTown Hotel, 91
Millennium Bostonian Hotel, 75
Newbury Guest House, 91
Nine Zero, 77
Omni Parker House, 77
Onyx Hotel, 79
Pilgrim Sands on Long Beach
  (Plymouth), 282–283
Radisson Hotel Boston, 82
Radisson Hotel Plymouth
  Harbor, 282
Renaissance Boston Waterfront
  Hotel, 81
The Ritz-Carlton, Boston
  Common, 81

Royal Sonesta Hotel, 87
Salem Inn, 264
Seaport Hotel, 81, 87
Sheraton Boston Hotel, 89
Sheraton Commander Hotel
  (Cambridge), 98
Taj Boston, 84
The Westin Boston Waterfront,
  80–81
The Westin Copley Place
  Boston, 89–90
YWCA Boston, Berkeley
  Residence, 83

RESTAURANTS

Abe & Louie's, 122
Alchemy Café and Bistro
  (Gloucester), 272–273
Artú, 111–112, 118
Aujourd'hui, 114, 125
Bangkok City, 127
Baraka Café (Cambridge), 136
Barking Crab, 107, 124
Bertucci's (Lexington), 124, 247
Billy Tse Restaurant, 112
The Blue Room (Cambridge),
  134
Bombay Club (Cambridge),
  133
Border Café (Cambridge), 133
Brasserie Jo, 127–128
The Bristol, 124–125
Buddha's Delight, 121
Café Fleuri, 114
Café Jaffa, 128
Cafe Mami (Cambridge), 138
Cafe Vanille, 190
Caffè dello Sport, 107
Caffe Pompei, 242
Caffè Vittoria, 107
Capital Grille, 122
Casablanca (Cambridge), 130,
  132
Casa Romero, 125–126
Centre Street Café, 114
Chacarero, 117
Charlie's Sandwich Shoppe,
  114
Chau Chow City, 120
Cheers, 190
China Pearl, 120
Così Sandwich Bar, 116, 117
Cupboard (Gloucester), 271
Daily Catch, 110
Dalí, 124
Dalí (Cambridge), 134–135
Darwin's Ltd. (Cambridge), 126

Davio's Northern Italian Steakhouse, 123
Dogwood Café, 171
Driftwood Restaurant (Marblehead), 258
Durgin-Park, 115–116, 124
East Coast Grill & Raw Bar (Cambridge), 135
The Elephant Walk, 128–129
Elephant Walk (Cambridge), 134
Empire Garden Restaurant, 120
Fajitas & 'Ritas, 117–118
Figs, 126
Finale, 129, 229
Fleming's Prime Steakhouse & Wine Bar, 118, 122
Franklin Cape Ann (Gloucester), 271
Galleria Umberto Rosticceria, 113
Gelateria, 107
Giacomo's Ristorante, 112
Ginza Japanese Restaurant, 119, 128, 242
Grand Chau Chow, 119–120
Great Harvest Bread Co. (Lexington), 247
The Greenery (Rockport), 277
Grill 23 & Bar, 122, 123–124
Grotto, 118
Halibut Point Restaurant (Gloucester), 273
Hamersley's Bistro, 121–122
Hei La Moon, 120
The Helmand (Cambridge), 136–137
Henrietta's Table (Cambridge), 132
Icarus, 122
Il Panino Express, 126
International House of Pancakes, 242
Intrigue, 114, 125
Ittyo (Cambridge), 138
Jacob Wirth Company, 120–121

Japonaise Bakery (Cambridge), 138
Jasper White's Summer Shack (Cambridge), 124, 135–136
Kotobukiya (Cambridge), 138
Langham, Boston, 125
La Summa, 112–113
La Voile, 126–127
Legal Sea Foods (the Waterfront), 106, 119, 130, 134
L'Espalier, 123
Les Zygomates, 115
Lobsta Land (Gloucester), 271
Lobster Hut (Plymouth), 283
Lobster Pool (Rockport), 277
Locke-Ober, 117
Lyceum Bar & Grill (Salem), 264–265
McCormick & Schmick's Seafood Restaurant, 114, 118
Maggiano's Little Italy, 118
Mamma Maria, 107, 110
Marco's (Cambridge), 129
Miel, 129
Mike's Pastry, 107, 169
Morton's of Chicago, 122
Mr. Bartley's Burger Cottage (Cambridge), 133–134
Nashoba Brook Bakery & Café (Concord), 253
Neptune Oyster, 110–111
News Restaurant & Lounge, 242
Novel, 128
Oak Room, 122
Oleana (Cambridge), 136
P. F. Chang's China Bistro, 118
Palm, 122
Paramount, 114
Peach Farm, 121
Peet's Coffee & Tea (Lexington), 247
Picco, 123
Piccola Venezia, 113
Pizzeria Regina, 114

Plimoth Plantation (Plymouth), 283
Portside Chowder House (Rockport), 277
Redbones (Cambridge), 124, 137
Red's Sandwich Shop (Salem), 264
Rialto (Cambridge), 132
Royal Sonesta Hotel's Gallery Café (Cambridge), 129
Run of the Mill Tavern (Plymouth), 283
Ruth's Chris Steak House, 122
Sail Loft (Cambridge), 129
Salem Beer Works, 266
Sam Diego's (Plymouth), 283
S&S Restaurant (Cambridge), 114, 138
Sapporo Ramen (Cambridge), 138
Sebastian's Map Room Café, 128
Sel de la Terre, 106–107
Shay's Pub & Wine Bar (Cambridge), 129
Smith & Wollensky, 122
Sorriso Trattoria, 115
South Street Diner, 242
Sugar Heaven, 128
Taj Boston Lounge, 125
Tampopo (Cambridge), 138
Tapéo, 124, 135
Taranta Cucina Meridionale, 110
Troquet, 119
Tu y Yo Mexican Fonda (Cambridge), 137
Upper Crust, 126
Upstairs on the Square (Cambridge), 125, 130
Victoria Station (Salem), 264
Volle Nolle, 126
Woodman's of Essex, 266
Ye Olde Union Oyster House, 115
Zaftigs Delicatessen, 129–130

A Guide for Every Type of Traveler

Frommer's Complete Guides

For those who value complete coverage, candid advice, and lots of choices in all price ranges.

Pauline Frommer's Guides

For those who want to experience a culture, meet locals, and save money along the way.

MTV Guides

For hip, youthful travelers who want a fresh perspective on today's hottest cities and destinations.

Day by Day Guides

For leisure or business travelers who want to organize their time to get the most out of a trip.

Frommer's With Kids Guides

For families traveling with children ages 2 to 14 seeking kid-friendly hotels, restaurants, and activities.

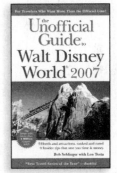

Unofficial Guides

For honeymooners, families, business travelers, and others who value no-nonsense, *Consumer Reports*–style advice.

For Dummies Travel Guides

For curious, independent travelers looking for a fun and easy way to plan a trip.

Visit Frommers.com

Now you know.

Explore over 3,500 destinations.

TOKYO 7766 miles

LONDON 3818 miles

TORONTO 4682 miles

SYDNEY 5087 miles

NEW YORK 4947 miles

LOS ANGELES 2556 miles

HONG KONG 5638 miles

Frommers.com makes it easy.

Find a destination. ✓ Book a trip. ✓ Get hot travel deals.
Buy a guidebook. ✓ Enter to win vacations. ✓ Listen to podcasts. ✓ Check ou
the latest travel news. ✓ Share trip photos and memories. ✓ And much more

Frommers.com

FROMMER'S® COMPLETE TRAVEL GUIDES

Alaska
Amalfi Coast
American Southwest
Amsterdam
Argentina
Arizona
Atlanta
Australia
Austria
Bahamas
Barcelona
Beijing
Belgium, Holland & Luxembourg
Belize
Bermuda
Boston
Brazil
British Columbia & the Canadian
  Rockies
Brussels & Bruges
Budapest & the Best of Hungary
Buenos Aires
Calgary
California
Canada
Cancún, Cozumel & the Yucatán
Cape Cod, Nantucket & Martha's
  Vineyard
Caribbean
Caribbean Ports of Call
Carolinas & Georgia
Chicago
Chile & Easter Island
China
Colorado
Costa Rica
Croatia
Cuba
Denmark
Denver, Boulder & Colorado Springs
Eastern Europe
Ecuador & the Galapagos Islands
Edinburgh & Glasgow
England
Europe
Europe by Rail

Florence, Tuscany & Umbria
Florida
France
Germany
Greece
Greek Islands
Guatemala
Hawaii
Hong Kong
Honolulu, Waikiki & Oahu
India
Ireland
Israel
Italy
Jamaica
Japan
Kauai
Las Vegas
London
Los Angeles
Los Cabos & Baja
Madrid
Maine Coast
Maryland & Delaware
Maui
Mexico
Montana & Wyoming
Montréal & Québec City
Morocco
Moscow & St. Petersburg
Munich & the Bavarian Alps
Nashville & Memphis
New England
Newfoundland & Labrador
New Mexico
New Orleans
New York City
New York State
New Zealand
Northern Italy
Norway
Nova Scotia, New Brunswick &
  Prince Edward Island
Oregon
Paris
Peru

Philadelphia & the Amish Country
Portugal
Prague & the Best of the Czech
  Republic
Provence & the Riviera
Puerto Rico
Rome
San Antonio & Austin
San Diego
San Francisco
Santa Fe, Taos & Albuquerque
Scandinavia
Scotland
Seattle
Seville, Granada & the Best of
  Andalusia
Shanghai
Sicily
Singapore & Malaysia
South Africa
South America
South Florida
South Korea
South Pacific
Southeast Asia
Spain
Sweden
Switzerland
Tahiti & French Polynesia
Texas
Thailand
Tokyo
Toronto
Turkey
USA
Utah
Vancouver & Victoria
Vermont, New Hampshire & Maine
Vienna & the Danube Valley
Vietnam
Virgin Islands
Virginia
Walt Disney World® & Orlando
Washington, D.C.
Washington State

FROMMER'S® DAY BY DAY GUIDES

Amsterdam
Barcelona
Beijing
Boston
Cancun & the Yucatan
Chicago
Florence & Tuscany

Hong Kong
Honolulu & Oahu
London
Maui
Montréal
Napa & Sonoma
New York City

Paris
Provence & the Riviera
Rome
San Francisco
Venice
Washington D.C.

PAULINE FROMMER'S GUIDES: SEE MORE. SPEND LESS.

Alaska
Hawaii
Italy

Las Vegas
London
New York City

Paris
Walt Disney World®
Washington D.C.

FROMMER'S® PORTABLE GUIDES

Acapulco, Ixtapa & Zihuatanejo
Amsterdam
Aruba, Bonaire & Curacao
Australia's Great Barrier Reef
Bahamas
Big Island of Hawaii
Boston
California Wine Country
Cancún
Cayman Islands
Charleston
Chicago
Dominican Republic

Florence
Las Vegas
Las Vegas for Non-Gamblers
London
Maui
Nantucket & Martha's Vineyard
New Orleans
New York City
Paris
Portland
Puerto Rico
Puerto Vallarta, Manzanillo &
    Guadalajara

Rio de Janeiro
San Diego
San Francisco
Savannah
St. Martin, Sint Maarten, Anguila &
    St. Bart's
Turks & Caicos
Vancouver
Venice
Virgin Islands
Washington, D.C.
Whistler

FROMMER'S® CRUISE GUIDES

Alaska Cruises & Ports of Call

Cruises & Ports of Call

European Cruises & Ports of Call

FROMMER'S® NATIONAL PARK GUIDES

Algonquin Provincial Park
Banff & Jasper
Grand Canyon

National Parks of the American West
Rocky Mountain
Yellowstone & Grand Teton

Yosemite and Sequoia & Kings
    Canyon
Zion & Bryce Canyon

FROMMER'S® WITH KIDS GUIDES

Chicago
Hawaii
Las Vegas
London

National Parks
New York City
San Francisco

Toronto
Walt Disney World® & Orlando
Washington, D.C.

FROMMER'S® PHRASEFINDER DICTIONARY GUIDES

Chinese
French

German
Italian

Japanese
Spanish

SUZY GERSHMAN'S BORN TO SHOP GUIDES

France
Hong Kong, Shanghai & Beijing
Italy

London
New York
Paris

San Francisco
Where to Buy the Best of Everything.

FROMMER'S® BEST-LOVED DRIVING TOURS

Britain
California
France
Germany

Ireland
Italy
New England
Northern Italy

Scotland
Spain
Tuscany & Umbria

THE UNOFFICIAL GUIDES®

Adventure Travel in Alaska
Beyond Disney
California with Kids
Central Italy
Chicago
Cruises
Disneyland®
England
Hawaii

Ireland
Las Vegas
London
Maui
Mexico's Best Beach Resorts
Mini Mickey
New Orleans
New York City
Paris

San Francisco
South Florida including Miami &
    the Keys
Walt Disney World®
Walt Disney World® for
    Grown-ups
Walt Disney World® with Kids
Washington, D.C.

SPECIAL-INTEREST TITLES

Athens Past & Present
Best Places to Raise Your Family
Cities Ranked & Rated
500 Places to Take Your Kids Before They Grow Up
Frommer's Best Day Trips from London
Frommer's Best RV & Tent Campgrounds in the U.S.A.

Frommer's Exploring America by RV
Frommer's NYC Free & Dirt Cheap
Frommer's Road Atlas Europe
Frommer's Road Atlas Ireland
Retirement Places Rated